Narrating the Pilgrimage to Mecca

Leiden Studies in Islam and Society

VOLUME 16

The titles published in this series are listed at *brill.com/lsis*

Narrating the Pilgrimage to Mecca

Historical and Contemporary Accounts

Edited by

Marjo Buitelaar
Richard van Leeuwen

TUTA SUB AEGIDE PALLAS · 1683 ·

BRILL

LEIDEN | BOSTON

Cover illustration: Young couple taking in the view of the Kaʿba (photograph published with consent of anonymized research participant project Buitelaar).

Library of Congress Cataloging-in-Publication Data

Names: Buitelaar, Marjo, editor. | Leeuwen, Richard van, editor.
Title: Narrating the pilgrimage to Mecca : historical and contemporary accounts / edited by Marjo Buitelaar, Richard van Leeuwen.
Description: Boston : Brill, 2023. | Series: Leiden studies in Islam and society, 2210-8920 ; 16 | Includes bibliographical references and index.
Identifiers: LCCN 2022052556 (print) | LCCN 2022052557 (ebook) | ISBN 9789004513167 (paperback) | ISBN 9789004513174 (ebook)
Subjects: LCSH: Muslim pilgrims and pilgrimages. | Muslim pilgrims and pilgrimages–Saudi Arabia–Mecca.
Classification: LCC BP187.3 .N268 2023 (print) | LCC BP187.3 (ebook) | DDC 297.3/5–dc23/eng/20221102
LC record available at https://lccn.loc.gov/2022052556
LC ebook record available at https://lccn.loc.gov/2022052557

Typeface for the Latin, Greek, and Cyrillic scripts: "Brill". See and download: brill.com/brill-typeface.

ISSN 2210-8920
ISBN 978-90-04-51316-7 (paperback)
ISBN 978-90-04-51317-4 (e-book)

This book is printed on acid-free paper and produced in a sustainable manner.

Contents

Acknowledgements

This volume is the synthesizing study of the research project 'More Magical than Disneyland: Modern Articulations of the Pilgrimage to Mecca'. We would therefore like to express our gratitude to all those involved in the realization of this book as well as those who facilitated the research project. First of all, we thank the Dutch Research Council NWO for their generous grant (350-25-150) which made this research possible and allowed us to organize the international conference 'Narrating the Hajj' in 2019. We are also delighted that thanks to subsequent NWO funding, we have been able to bring out this book with an Open Access License. We would like to thank the Faculty of Theology & Religious Studies of the University of Groningen and the Faculty of Humanities of Amsterdam University for facilitating the research project in numerous ways. In particular, for their indispensable help behind the scenes we would like to thank project controllers Doriena van der Horst-Smits at the UoG, and Saskia Plandsoen and Janneke Ravenek at the UoA. In addition, the faculty of Theology and Religious Studies of the University of Groningen was so kind as to host the international 'Narrating the Hajj' conference. To all participants in the conference; thank you for your presentations and lively discussions, which have contributed enormously to enhancing and integrating our knowledge and insights in historical and contemporary personal accounts of the pilgrimage to Mecca. We regret that we could not incorporate all papers in the volume. In addition to NWO and the Universities of Groningen and Amsterdam, we are equally grateful to the following institutions for facilitating our research: the Dutch Institute in Morocco (NIMAR), Dar al-Kutub in Cairo, the National Library in Tunis, the King Abd al-ʿAziz Al Saoud Library in Casablanca, the National Library in Rabat, and the National Library in Abu Dhabi.

Numerous people have contributed to the project in other ways. We would like to thank Kim Knibbe, Kocku von Stuckrad and Léon Buskens for their very productive feedback on the research proposal, and Jörn Thielmann for regularly sharing articles that might be of interest to the project. Léon has been a continuous support throughout the project, both as a dear friend and colleague, and also in his capacity as Director of the NIMAR, where several research team members were warmly welcomed and enjoyed using NIMAR facilities. It means a lot to us that on various occasions leading scholars in the study of pilgrimage to Mecca like Pnina Werbner, Robert Bianchi and Seán McLoughlin have provided us with the most valuable feedback. Similarly, the discussions within EASA's Pilnet have been invaluable for embedding the two ethnographic subprojects in the wider anthropological study of pilgrimage. In particular, we would like to thank Anne Fedele, Simon Coleman, John Eade and Mario Katić for their interest, support and valuable feedback at various stages of the research. It is a great honour that Simon accepted the invitation to write the epilogue to the book.

The researchers in subproject II and III have learned incredibly much from all research participants in Morocco and the Netherlands. If it were not for your commitment to sharing your experiences and knowledge about the pilgrimage to Mecca, much of the project's results would not have been realized. We thank you from the bottom of our hearts for your trust and will continue to treasure the stories you shared with us as precious gifts. We would like to express our gratitude also to Hanina Ajarai, Hanan Nhass and Mohamed Bouza for bringing us in touch with pilgrims who were willing to tell us about their pilgrimage experiences and for helping us refine the interview questions for the Dutch subproject. In addition, Hanina conducted invaluable interviews with elderly Moroccan-Dutch pilgrims, while Hanan has been of great help in knowledge dissemination about the project's results for a wider public through the online platform KIS. It was equally wonderful to work with Said el-Amraoui of Hadjinfo and Rixt Hulshoff Pol of the Tropenmuseum for two knowledge dissemination events at the Tropenmuseum. Thank you both so much. We are also most grateful to Dik Kootstra of the Groningen Scholierenacademie and Lilian Eggens of UptoUs for developing for us teaching kits on pilgrimage for high school and secondary vocational education students.

University policies on 'research-driven' education tend to focus on the added value of integrating our research projects in the courses we teach. We have found that vice versa, our research has benefited tremendously from the contributions of the students Lisa de Lang, Querien Mangel, and Gijs Wijers, who participated in the project for their MA thesis research. The discussions with them, as those with the student assistants Bas Sprenger de Rover, who interviewed managers at hajj travel agencies for us, and Lyset de Groot and Kjelda Glimmerveen, who not only meticulously transcribed the interviews for the Dutch subproject but also shared their reflections on the content of the interviews, were both very enjoyable and productive.

Last but not least, we would like to thank forrest kentwell and Iris Vartinian-van der Heide for text- and copy editing the manuscript, Pierke Bosschieter for creating an excellent index and the two anonymous reviewers for critically scrutinizing the manuscript and providing valuable feedback. Obviously, any errors that have remained in the text are there despite Iris' and forrest's professional help, and the editors are fully responsible for them.

Marjo Buitelaar and Richard van Leeuwen

Notes on Contributors

Kholoud Al-Ajarma
is a lecturer of the Globalised Muslim World at the University of Edinburgh, United Kingdom. She holds a PhD. in the fields of Anthropology and Religious Studies from the University of Groningen with primary focus on Islamic pilgrimage (Hajj) and its meaning in everyday life in Morocco. She also holds an MA in Peace and Conflict Studies (from Coventry University, England) and an MPhil in Anthropology and Development Studies (from the University of Bergen, Norway). Al-Ajarma has worked in the fields of Islam, gender, refugee rights, youth leadership, visual culture, water, and migration in several countries of the Mediterranean region.

Piotr Bachtin
is Humboldt Foundation Fellow at the University of Heidelberg.

Vladimir Bobrovnikov
is historian of (ex-)colonial borderlands in tsarist and Soviet Russia. His field of expertise is Islam in Russia, the Caucasus, and the history of Oriental Studies. He chairs Central Asian, Caucasus, and Volga-Ural studies in the Moscow Institute of Oriental studies, and teaches at the Higher School of Economics. He is the author of *Custom, Law and Violence among the North Caucasus Muslims* (2002, in Russian), *Voyage au pays des Avars* (2011), *Posters of the Soviet Orient, 1918–1940* (2013, in Russian), a chapter on Islam in the *Cambridge History of Russia* (Vol. II, 2009) and other research papers.

Marjo Buitelaar
is Professor of Contemporary Islam from an anthropological perspective at the Faculty of Theology & Religious Studies, University of Groningen. Her research interests concern Islam in everyday life and narrative identity construction in a post-migration context. She has conducted fieldwork in Morocco and the Netherlands. Her most recent co-edited books are *Hajj, Global Interactions through Pilgrimage* (2015, with Luitgard Mols); *Muslim Women's Pilgrimage to Mecca and Beyond. Reconfiguring gender, religion and mobility* (2020, with Manja Stephan-Emmrich & Viola Thimm); *Religion as Relation. Studying Religion in Context* (2021, with Peter Berger & Kim Knibbe).

Nadia Caidi
is a Professor at the Faculty of Information, University of Toronto, Canada. Her research focuses on human information behaviour and information policy.

Current research examines the emergent practices of young people's expressions of spiritual and religious identities online, specifically the contemporary manifestations of the pilgrimage tradition of Hajj, and how information in its multiple forms mediates and shapes the pilgrim's spiritual, physical, and informational journey. Her work has appeared in *The Oxford Handbook of Religious Space; Journeys: The International Journal of Travel and Travel Writing, and The International Journal of Information, Diversity, & Inclusion*. Her most recent co-edited book is *Humanizing LIS Education and Practice: Diversity by Design* (2021).

Simon Coleman
is Chancellor Jackman Professor and an anthropologist based at the Department for the Study of Religion, University of Toronto. He has published on both Pentecostalism and pilgrimage, and carried out fieldwork in Sweden, Nigeria and the United Kingdom. Recent books include *Pilgrimage and Political Economy: Translating the Sacred* (2018, co-edited with John Eade, Berghahn) and *Powers of Pilgrimage: Religion in a World of Motion* (2021, NYU Press).

Thomas Ecker
is a PhD candidate at the Institute for Iranian Studies in Bamberg, Germany. Since 2021 he has been working in the DFG funded research project: "Between Narration of Reality and Ego-document: Persian Pilgrimage Reports of the Qajar period" where he focuses on the hajj travelogues of Farhād Mirzā and his half-brother Ḥosām al-Salṭane, which are the subject of his PhD.

Zahir Janmohamed
is a visiting assistant professor of English at Bowdoin college. He received his MFA in fiction at the University of Michigan where he received awards in fiction, nonfiction, poetry, and playwriting. In 2019, the podcast he co-founded about food, race, gender, and class called Racist Sandwich was nominated for a James Beard Award. His articles have appeared in *The New York Times, Foreign Policy, Guernica, The Washington Post, The San Francisco Chronicle, Newsweek,* and many other publications. Prior to beginning his writing career, he worked at Amnesty International and in the US Congress.

Khadija Kadrouch-Outmany
holds a PhD in the field of Anthropology from Leiden University with a primary focus on funeral rituals of Muslim migrant communities in the Netherlands and Belgium. She holds an MA in Law and a BA in Religious Studies. Kadrouch-Outmany was a Postdoc researcher in the research project 'Modern Articula-

tions of Pilgrimage to Mecca'. She currently works as a qualitative researcher at The Netherlands Institute for Social Research (SCP).

Ammeke Kateman

worked as a postdoctoral researcher on Arabic Mecca travelogues in an age of Islamic reformism (1850–1945) within the research programme 'Modern Articulations of Pilgrimage to Mecca'. She holds a PhD in Humanities (Religious Studies) from the University of Amsterdam, and pursued her studies in Arabic and History at the same university. Her monograph *Muhammad Abduh and his Interlocutors: Conceptualizing Religion in a Globalizing World* appeared in 2019. She also published in *Die Welt des Islams*, *Qira'at* (KFCRIS), *Christian-Muslim Relations. A Bibliographical History—vol. 18, The Ottoman Empire (1800–1914)*, and *Philological Encounters*.

Richard van Leeuwen

(PhD 1992, University of Amsterdam) was senior lecturer in Islamic studies at the University of Amsterdam until his retirement in 2021. His main research fields are Middle Eastern history, Arabic literature, the history of orientalism, the hajj. His publications include *Notables and clergy in Mount Lebanon, 1736–1840* (Leiden 1994); *Waqfs and urban structures: the case of Ottoman Damascus* (Leiden: 1999); *The Arabian Nights encyclopedia*, 2 vols. (with U. Marzolph; Santa Barbara 2004); *Narratives of kingship in Eurasian empires 1300–1800* (Leiden etc. 2017); *The Thousand and one Nights in 20th century fiction* (Leiden etc. 2018; awarded with the Shaykh Zayed Book Award 2020). He also works as a translator of Arabic literature and was awarded the Sheikh Hamad Award for Literay Translation in 2021.

Yahya Nurgat

received his PhD in history at the University of Cambridge in 2022. His main interest lies in the religious and devotional landscape of the early modern Ottoman empire, as well as the history of Muslim devotion in general. Using guidebooks, pilgrimage narratives, and hajj-related objects and images, his dissertation ('Space, Ritual, and Religious Experience and the Ottoman hajj, c. 994/1586–1194/1780') tracks the impact of the hajj on the confessional, devotional, and spatial registers of Ottoman Islam. The dissertation also examines how the construction, interpretation, and experience of sacred space in Mecca and Medina evolved across the seventeenth and eighteenth centuries.

Jihan Safar
(PhD 2015 at Sciences Po) pursued her postdoctoral studies on marriage and fertility issues in three Gulf countries (Oman, Kuwait and Qatar). Since 2016, Safar is based at the IISMM-EHESS where, together with Leila Seurat, she has been working on the hajj and umra markets in France, producing two reports funded by the Bureau Central des Cultes (ministry of Interior).

Neda Saghaee
studied in the 'Comparative Studies of Religions and Mysticism' program and her master thesis concentrated on the studies of Islamic mysticism. Her PhD. thesis in Islamic studies at the University of Erfurt was entitled 'Muḥammad Nāṣir 'Andalīb's Sufi Path based on his Lament of the Nightingale: Revisiting Mystical Islam in Eighteenth Century India.' As far as her research interests are concerned, she is passionate about employing multidisciplinary methods to recognize the influence of mystical and theological discourses on all aspects of society, ranging from personal life to politics.

Leila Seurat
(PhD 2014 in political science at SciencesPo) has been working on Hamas' foreign policy. Her book, *Le Hamas et le monde* has recently been published in a revised version in English under the name *The Foreign Policy of Hamas. Ideology, decision Making and the Political Supremacy* (IB Tauris, Bloomsbury). Her postdoctoral research is dedicated to policing in Lebanon and policy transfer in the field of security. Since 2016, together with Jihan Safar Seurat has conducted with extensive research on the hajj and *'umra* markets in France, producing two reports funded by the Bureau Central des Cultes (ministry of Interior).

Miguel Ángel Vázquez
received his PhD in Spanish Literature at Indiana University, Bloomington in 2001. He is currently an Associate Professor of Spanish Language and Literature at Florida Atlantic University. He specializes in the clandestine literature of the last Muslims in Spain who, during the sixteenth century, produced a corpus of manuscripts written in Spanish but rendered with the Arabic alphabet. He is currently doing research on the Moriscos' mortuary rituals, specifically their 'Letters of the dead'.

Notes on Transcriptions of Arabic and Other Terms and Names

Harmonizing the transcription of names and terms from diverse languages within a single system is an impossible task. In the present work, articles are included which use written sources from Arabic, Persian, Ottoman Turkish, Tatar and Russian, and, moreover, interviews in Moroccan *dārija* and other North African dialects. To do justice to all the different conventions of transcription in these various languages, we have chosen to combine a number of different systems, complemented with some general considerations to enhance consistency to a certain extent. The rules can be summarized as follows:

1. Personal names, geographical names and terms which are commonly used in English retain their most common spellings (Jedda, Tehran, Khomeini, hajj, hadith). This also includes the name of the Prophet Muhammad.
2. Arabic personal names, geographical names and terms which are not part of common English are transcribed according to generally accepted conventions (Ḥusayn, *amīr al-ḥajj*, al-Ṣafā). This includes the name Muḥammad when it is not referring to the Prophet and occurs in written sources.
3. Persian names and terms are transliterated according to the conventions for Persian (Mo'ayyad al-Dowle), except when they refer to Arabic terms or persons; in that case, they are transcribed as Arabic names/terms (Hossein, but Ḥusayn if it refers to the grandson of the Prophet). In some cases two variants, Persian and Arabic, are given.
4. Ottoman Turkish, Tatar and Russian names and terms are spelled according to the respective conventions of these languages, except when they refer to Arabic terms or persons. In some cases two variants are given.
5. Arabic or Persian names within the European or American contexts are written according to the regular spelling in Latin letters (Khoja Ithna Asheri).
6. If quotations are given from Moroccan *dārija*, a phonetic rendering is given (*bled*), without diacritical marks.
7. In the articles referring to interviews, the names of the interviewees are given in phonetic spelling, without diacritical marks.

As can be seen above, in some cases, a name or term can be spelled in different ways, according to the category to which they belong in a specific situation. For instance, 'imam' refers to someone who leads prayer; '*imām*' refers to the honorific title of a religious scholar; '*Imām*' refers to the Shi'ite title for their religious leaders; 'Imām' is part of a name. The purpose of the preponderance of Arabic conventions of transcription is to enable an Index that is as consistent as possible. Of course, it should be acknowledged that there is no uniform, completely consistent and all-encompassing system of transcription for either of the languages involved, so the editors apologize in advance for any inconveniences caused by the decisions summarized above.

INTRODUCTION

Narrativizing a Sensational Journey: Pilgrimage to Mecca

Marjo Buitelaar

1 Reading Pilgrimage Accounts. A Preview

> I made my Umra 7 years ago and to this day the memories send shivers down my spine. It was magical; more magical than Disneyland!! Words alone can't explain the uplifting and exhilarating feeling rippling through myself! My favourite part was when we set foot inside the Haram [sacred Meccan space, MB] and my siblings and I were going to lay eyes on the Ka'ba [the cuboid building in the courtyard of the Grand Mosque in Mecca, MB] for the first time. We kept our eyes on the ground and only when we reached the courtyard did we look up. Wow. Gobsmacked. Amazing. I could only hear the birds singing and the general hum of people praying; I'd zoned out and no word in the entire dictionary will come close to describing how I felt. Pure, pure serenity ☺ The overall experience is very humbling. As I'm writing this, I'm smiling.

This is how a British Muslim summarized her experience of the *ʿumra*, the voluntary pilgrimage to Mecca. She did so on a website where pilgrims were invited to share their experiences for the exhibition 'Hajj: Journey to the heart of Islam' at the British Museum in 2012.[1] The quote is a particularly rich example that introduces the central theme of this book, which is how pilgrims to Mecca narrativize the pilgrimage—in other words, how they present their pilgrimage experiences in the form of a narrative.[2] Firstly, the comparison of Mecca with Disneyland in the quote is intriguing. It touches on the debate about the nature and scope of today's commodification of the hajj. Some Muslims might consider it sacrilege to openly compare the holy city of Mecca to a West-

1 The related page on the museum website, http://www.britishmuseum.org/whats_on/exhibitions/Hajj/Hajj_stories.aspx, which I accessed to download pilgrims' stories on 22 April 2013, is unfortunately no longer available.

2 To emphasize the patterning that occurs in pilgrimage storytelling, I use the verb 'narrativize' here rather than 'narrate', which I reserve for the act of telling a story.

ern commercial theme park. Others might say that commercialization—or 'McDonaldization', as the globalization of western commercial enterprises is often referred to (cf. Ritzer 1993)—is precisely what is jeopardizing the religious atmosphere in Mecca today, and is an issue that should be addressed. The Moroccan anthropologist Abdellah Hammoudi (2006) and Indian-American journalist Asra Nomani (2006), for example, are highly critical in their hajj memoires of the commercialization and consumerism that they observed in Mecca. However, several participants in my own research, particularly younger pilgrims, said that they had been happy to discover McDonald's and Kentucky Fried Chicken in Mecca. They felt that getting a taste of home while not having to worry whether the meat was halal and of good quality meant having the best of both worlds. It confirmed to them that one can be Muslim and modern at the same time. Indeed, the modernization projects implemented by the Saudi government to attract and accommodate an ever-increasing number of pilgrims and—equally importantly—to streamline pilgrims' movements in accordance with a strict Wahhābī interpretation of Islam is a hotly debated issue and a recurring theme in the accounts of contemporary pilgrims (cf. Larsson and Sorgenfrei 2021, 14–15; McLoughlin 2015, 55). These debates shed light on the ways in which globalization, mobility, and feelings of home and belonging are intertwined and reproduced in complex ways in both pilgrims' everyday activities and religious engagement.[3]

The description of the journey to Mecca as 'uplifting' suggests that the woman quoted did not intend the analogy with Disneyland as a criticism of Saudi's hajj management. Unfortunately, she does not elaborate on what triggered this comparison for her. An obvious parallel between Mecca and Disneyland is that stories that visitors have grown up with come to life in both places; one can literally come into contact with the characters of these stories or, as in the case of Mecca, with places where they have visited or lived. In terms of religion, it is not difficult to understand why Mecca was the 'more magical' place of the two for the woman quoted. Certainly, visiting Disneyland has been convincingly analysed as a kind of pilgrimage (Knight 2014, 24–43), and like (other) pilgrimage sites, represents specific conceptions about living a 'good life' (cf. King 1981). The primary motivation of most visitors to Disneyland, however, pertains less to specific ideals than the wish to enjoy themselves. Mecca, on the other hand, is for Muslims the most powerful, sacred symbol of purity, perfection and an exemplary Muslim way of life. Fulfilling the religious

3 Compare Germann Molz (2005), who discusses the meaning of McDonald's as a 'guilty pleasure' for round-the-world travellers.

obligation to perform the pilgrimage to Mecca is something that many Muslims yearn to do, a desire that is fuelled by the travel accounts of those who have made the journey. Like the British woman in the quote, most pilgrims describe stepping in the footsteps of key role models in Islamic historiography—such as the Prophets Muhammad, Ibrāhīm, Ismāʿīl and Ismāʿīl's mother Hājar—as an intense, emotional and 'uplifting' experience.[4]

Being 'gobsmacked' by experiences like seeing the Kaʿba with her own eyes is probably why this British pilgrim described her journey to Mecca as more magical than visiting Disneyland. Note how, in line with the informal term 'gobsmacked' to describe her feelings of being overwhelmed, she states that 'not a word in the entire dictionary' comes close to expressing how she felt. Nonetheless, when trying to convey her feelings, she describes her sensory experiences: memories of her first view of the Kaʿba, the hum of praying fellow pilgrims and the sound of birdsong still 'send shivers' down her spine, even though seven years have passed since she visited Mecca.

Interrelated with the theme of narrativization, a second key focus in this volume concerns how the performance of pilgrimage speaks to pilgrims through the senses and touches them emotionally. In this sense, the book ties in with a research project coordinated by Christian Lange, which studies how the senses have been conceptualized, and calibrated, in a variety of Muslim environments between 600 to 1900 CE.[5] In line with Lange's approach, we understand the sensory perceptions of pilgrims as not only a physical but also a cultural act: how they experience and understand sight, sound, smell, taste and touch during the pilgrimage journey varies for pilgrims from different historical, geographical, social and intellectual contexts.[6]

At the same time, however, stating—as the British pilgrim above does—that words cannot convey the pilgrimage experience is a common trope in accounts of the journey to Mecca written in very different historical and cultural contexts. Elaborate descriptions of sensory experiences belong in similar fashion to the tradition of storytelling about the journey, regardless of whether it concerns the hajj, the obligatory pilgrimage that all able Muslims should perform at least once in their lives, or the *ʿumra*, the voluntary and less elaborate pilgrimage to Mecca that can be undertaken at any time of the year outside the hajj season.[7] Variations on stories about starting to tremble, feeling one's scalp

---

4 Ibrāhīm, Ismāʿīl and Hājar are the Muslim Islamic versions of Abraham, Ishmael and Hagar in the Bible.

5 cf. Lange 2022a; 2022b; https://sensis.sites.uu.nl/.

6 https://sensis.sites.uu.nl/.

7 It should be noted that the rites that make up the *ʿumra* are also included in the hajj ritual.

tingle and one's eyes fill with tears when sighting the Kaʿba feature widely in both the historical and contemporary accounts of the pilgrimage to Mecca that are discussed in the following chapters.

Expressing the extraordinary experience of the journey to Mecca by comparing it to a visit to Disneyland is—as yet—rather unique and points to how the British woman's pilgrimage experience is embedded in her wider daily lifeworld. It would not surprise me, however, to learn that other pilgrims who have visited Disneyland draw similar parallels. In variation to comparing Mecca to Disneyland, two Dutch pilgrims who shared their pilgrimage stories with me referred to De Efteling, a Dutch theme park where one can physically enter the world of well-known fairy tales like Cinderella and Sleeping Beauty.[8] By using informal expressions like being 'gobsmacked' and 'zoned out', the woman quoted brings Mecca and Disneyland into the same lexical landscape, even though she gives priority to Mecca. The use of modern vocabulary illustrates that the narrator's everyday life is simultaneously informed by different cultural discourses. Although she does not state her age, the words she uses and the fact that she went to Mecca in the company of siblings suggest that she may still be young. It is not unlikely that her travelling with siblings may also relate to her gender. Whereas young male Muslims often go on *ʿumra* with male friends, unmarried women of the same age group generally perform the voluntary pilgrimage in the company of their father or a male sibling (cf. Saghi 2010). This is because Saudi pilgrimage regulations stipulate that female pilgrims under the age of 45 need to be accompanied by a *maḥram*, a male guardian, either in the person of their husband, or a male blood relative with whom marriage is prohibited (cf. Thimm 2021).[9] Furthermore, the quoted woman has apparently visited both Disneyland and Mecca, which points to a habit of travelling that bespeaks a consumerist lifestyle. This is confirmed by the fact that she performed the voluntary *ʿumra* rather than the mandatory hajj, which also suggests that she expected to have sufficient financial means to return to Mecca in the future to fulfil the religious obligation of hajj performance. The various factors contributing to the opportunities available to this female British Muslim to visit Mecca illustrate another analytical theme that runs through the various chapters of this volume: how age, gender, class, ethnicity and cultural

8 See https://www.efteling.com/nl/park/attracties/sprookjesbos/sprookjes, accessed 23 July 2021.

9 At the time of writing, it was not yet clear how the 2020 lifting of the prohibition in Saudi law on women travelling alone would translate into pilgrimage visas being issued for female pilgrims from outside Saudi Arabia after the Covid-19 pandemic.

embeddedness intersect to inform pilgrims' practices and experiences against the background of their everyday lives.

The woman's word choice and her comparison of Mecca and Disneyland also point to the importance of considering the specific audiences that are addressed in pilgrimage accounts. When uploading her narrative on the British Museum website during the 2012 hajj exhibition, the woman was apparently motivated to share her experiences with an anonymous and diverse general public. Except for mentioning the Kaʿba and the Ḥaram, as the sacred area of Mecca's Grand Mosque is called,[10] she avoids using words that have a specifically religious connotation. By expressing herself in mostly informal language instead, she casts her story in terms that both Muslim and non-Muslim visitors of the British Museum's website are familiar with. Comparing Mecca to Disneyland may have served a similar purpose of speaking to a wider audience. She takes as a point of departure a shared cultural practice, such as a visit to Disneyland, to convey to non-Muslims some of the meanings that a specifically Islamic practice has for her, thus claiming sameness and specificity at the same time.

These analytical comments on the opening quote give a foretaste of the issues addressed in this volume. The book sketches a detailed and diverse picture of how, in their stories, pilgrims draw on multiple cultural discourses and practices that shape their daily lifeworlds. Each chapter sheds light on the ways that being situated in a specific cultural context and moment in history informs the meanings that pilgrims attribute to their pilgrimage experiences. All chapters address the narrativization of the pilgrimage to Mecca as what the anthropologist Birgit Meyer has called a 'sensational form', that is, a ritual which speaks to the senses and emotionally moves people (Meyer 2016; 2012; 2011). Some, particularly the chapters that discuss historical pilgrimage accounts, do so by focusing more on how the storied experiences relate to the specific historical and cultural context of narrators and their intended audiences, while others place greater emphasis on scrutinizing the sensual and emotional trajectory of the pilgrimage.

The book contains both single-authored and jointly written chapters by the five members of the research project 'Modern Articulations of the Pilgrimage to Mecca' that will be introduced in the next section.[11] It also presents chapters

10 Sacred space in Mecca, the cradle of Islam, and Medina, the city where the Prophet Muhammad is buried, are often referred to together as the Ḥaramayn, the two sacred sites.

11 The research project was funded by the Dutch Research Council (NWO) (Research grant: 360-25-150). For a regularly updated overview of the project's entire output, see https://www.nwo.nl/en/projects/360-25-150.

written by participants of the 'Narrating the hajj' conference, which was organized at the University of Groningen in December 2019 to conclude the research phase of data production. These additional contributions have allowed us to expand on the historical and cultural contexts under scrutiny, and to include discussions of travelogues and stories in languages other than the Arabic or Dutch accounts that were studied in the research project.

The historical travelogues discussed in the book are all written by hajj pilgrims who travelled mainly over land and sea. For their own safety, most pilgrims from outside the Arabian Peninsula would join one of the annual hajj caravans for at least part of their journey until the 1920s. It is only with the introduction of air travel that the voluntary *ʿumra* pilgrimage has gained popularity among Muslims from outside the Arabian Peninsula. Pilgrims who can afford to make multiple journeys to Mecca may opt for the voluntary pilgrimage to gain a foretaste of the more important hajj variant, while others go on *ʿumra* to relive their hajj experience in a quieter season. The voluntary pilgrimage is also an attractive alternative for Muslims who are worried that the quota system may prohibit them from performing the hajj before they die, or who cannot afford a much more expensive hajj package tour. While we do consider how pilgrims' different motives for performing the mandatory or voluntary pilgrimage are reflected in their stories about their pilgrimage experiences, we do not systematically distinguish between hajj and *ʿumra* accounts in the book. One reason for this is that while the two forms differ in that only the hajj performance counts as fulfilling one's religious duty, conducting the rites of the *ʿumra* is also included in the hajj ritual, meaning that the experiences of hajj and *ʿumra* pilgrims overlap to some extent.[12] For most hajj and *ʿumra* pilgrims, seeing the Kaʿba with their own eyes and visiting the tomb of the Prophet Muhammad in Medina are the most emotional episodes of their journey and therefore predominate in their stories. 'Standing' at Mount ʿArafa is often, but not always, an additional highlight in the accounts of hajj pilgrims. The second reason why the distinction between hajj and *ʿumra* accounts is not systematically made in

---

12 Both *ʿumra* and hajj pilgrims enter the state of *iḥrām* (consecration), pronounce the *talbiya* invocation until they reach Mecca, perform the *ṭawāf* (the sevenfold circumambulation of the Kaʿba), drink water from the Zamzam Well and perform the *saʿy*, the 'running' between the hillocks of al-Ṣafā and al-Marwa. *ʿumra* pilgrims then cut their hair to mark the conclusion of the voluntary pilgrimage, while hajj pilgrims then move on to the tent camp in Minā. From there, they carry out the *wuqūf* ('standing' at the Mount ʿArafa to beg God forgiveness for one's sins), spend the night in the open air in Muzdalifa and collect pebbles in preparation of the *ramy* rite (pelting three pillars that represent the Devil), after which they end their *iḥrām*, make a sacrificial offer and cut their hair to mark the conclusion of the hajj.

the book is that many contemporary pilgrims whose stories are analysed have made multiple pilgrimages, and they discuss both the hajj and the *ʿumra* in their stories.

The book is divided into two parts. The first discusses historical textual accounts and the second consists of social scientific discussions of oral pilgrimage stories collected through ethnographic fieldwork and interviews with contemporary pilgrims. While the authors of the historical chapters take readers on the pilgrimage journey of one or several individual pilgrims whose written hajj accounts they discuss, the chapters on the pilgrimage experiences of contemporary pilgrims explore how specific dimensions of narrating the hajj in today's world feature in a larger body of interviews and informal conversations. The two parts are bridged by a chapter that combines the two approaches by focusing on the oral pilgrimage accounts of two young adult Dutch pilgrims who participated in the research project 'Modern articulations of pilgrimage to Mecca'. The next section presents the research project on which this volume is based. Subsequent sections will reflect on the narrativization of the pilgrimage to Mecca as a sensational form and discuss how this central theme is highlighted in the specific case studies discussed in this volume.

2 Modern Articulations of the Pilgrimage to Mecca

The question of how, in today's era of intensified globalization, Muslims' pilgrimage experiences are simultaneously informed by various cultural discourses is what prompted the two editors of this volume to design the research project on modern articulations of the pilgrimage to Mecca. Worldwide, an increasing number of Muslims educated in Western-style school systems have assimilated modern liberal values such as punctuality, bio-medical conceptions of hygiene, and self-enhancement (cf. Newcomb 2017; Hafez 2011; Deeb 2006; Starrett 1998). A much larger class of Muslims has been introduced to cosmopolitan lifestyles through the consumption of global media (cf. Graiouid 2011, 117–147; Sabry 2010).[13] As a result, new forms of religiosity have emerged in which implicit ideologies of individualism and self-realization through modern consumerism are rerouted towards religious consumption patterns (cf. Hoesterey 2016; Shirazi 2016; Deeb and Harb 2013; Schielke 2012; Pink 2009).

13 For a very informative documentary about the impact of soap operas on Muslim audiences, cf. 'Kismet: How soap operas changed the world', https://www.youtube.com/watch?v=NX8Un4nneXg, accessed 29 July 2021.

These developments have had an enormous impact on the pilgrimage to Mecca, which has been an impressive, distinctively Muslim form of global interaction from Islam's early history onwards (cf. Tagliacozzo and Toorawa 2016; al-Quāitī 2007; Peters 1994; Strattkötter 1991; Faroqhi 1990). Since the mid-nineteenth century, the pilgrimage has undergone two periods of unprecedented growth. The first relates to colonial infrastructure projects, such as the introduction of long-distance railways, oceangoing steamers and the opening of the Suez Canal in 1896. These made it possible for tens of thousands of Muslims from regions far beyond the Middle East to flock to Mecca and perform the annual pilgrimage (Kane 2015; Gelvin and Green 2014; Tagliacozzo 2013). The second spurt in hajj growth occurred following the introduction of civilian air travel in the 1960s (cf. Bianchi 2004). In the years just before the COVID-19 pandemic struck in 2020, two to three million pilgrims, 1.8 to 2 million of whom came from outside Saudi Arabia, performed the hajj each year, and of the 19 million annual *ʿumra* pilgrims, over seven million came from abroad.[14]

The explosive growth in the pilgrimage to Mecca has produced new categories of pilgrims and led to the routinization and commodification of pilgrimage (cf. Bianchi 2013; McLoughlin 2009a). In this respect, contemporary pilgrimage to Mecca reflects a broader trend of increased religious and heritage tourism (cf. Stausberg 2011; Timothy and Olsen 2006). Where the hajj differs from most other forms of pilgrimage or religious tourism is its compulsory nature for all Muslims who can afford the journey without risking an adverse impact on their own lives or those of their dependants. For most of Islam's history, this meant in effect that only a small number of privileged, mostly male, Muslims were able to fulfil their religious duty. Improved means of transportation and the global rise of new middle classes have now brought the pilgrimage to Mecca within reach of many more and different categories of people. In particular, the number of women who perform the pilgrimage has grown spectacularly, reaching nearly 48 % of the total number of pilgrims in 2019.[15]

To assess how these new forms of mobility have affected Muslims' conceptions of the desirability or necessity of performing the pilgrimage, it is import-

14 https://saudigazette.com.sa/article/592545, accessed 28 July 2021. Hajj attendance was severely restricted in 2020 and 2021 due to COVID-19: in 2020, only 6,000 Muslims of different nationalities residing in Saudi Arabia were allowed to participate, while in 2021 60,000 fully vaccinated Saudi residents were granted permission to perform the pilgrimage, cf. https://www.aljazeera.com/news/2020/10/4/pilgrims-return-to-mecca-as-saudi-eases-virus-restrictions, and https://www.aljazeera.com/news/2021/7/17/pilgrims-arrive-in-mecca-for-second-hajj-during-ongoing-pandemic, both accessed 30 July 2021.

15 https://www.statista.com/statistics/617824/saudi-arabia-foreign-hajj-pilgrims-by-gender/, accessed 7 September 2021.

ant to realize that 'mobility' is not merely a descriptive term. It also has a prescriptive dimension that either explicitly or implicitly conveys normative views on who is expected to be mobile, and in what ways and for what purposes. The rapidly increasing scope and density of flows of people, ideas and goods in today's globalized world influence people's desires to move as well as actual mobility practices. They also inform their conceptions and ideologies about the purposes and effects of mobility. Pertinent to understanding the pilgrimage to Mecca is the fact that a 'limit-form' representation of space and time, which became dominant with modernity in terms of bounded entities that one leaves behind as one moves from one place or phase to the next, is currently shifting towards a more 'flow-form' conception of movement, in which temporal and spatial boundaries are viewed as fluid and porous. Mobility no longer necessarily entails a clear-cut rupture or transition from one stage or territory to another but is often represented as a continual and gradual change, a moving back and forth between here and there, and between past, present, and future (Buitelaar, Stephan-Emmrich and Thimm 2021, 7; Mincke 2016, 16). In terms of life-course expectations, rather than conceiving of one's life as going through a limited number of transitions between fairly stable time-space constellations, 'being on the move' seems to have become a mode of living, particularly among younger generations.

Such lifestyle developments have significant implications for people's travel practices, including the pilgrimage to Mecca. Until a few decades ago, hajj performance was very much part of a 'limit-form' conception of mobility that poses clear spatial and temporal boundaries. Most Muslims tended to conceive of hajj performance as a once-in-a-lifetime event and a major rite of passage that marks a radical change in one's status and lifestyle. Those who could afford to make the journey did so mostly at an advanced age, postponing the 'ultimate' religious duty in preparation for taking leave of one's earthly existence. In addition, it was generally felt, in terms of piety, that one should be 'ready' to go on hajj and that one would be 'called' to Mecca when God thought it appropriate (cf. McLoughlin 2015, 47). Today, an increasing number of pilgrims do not expect to visit Mecca just once but anticipate making multiple journeys (cf. Buitelaar 2020). Another trend is that the number of young and female pilgrims has increased significantly (cf. Karić 2018, 60; Bianchi 2013, 34–35).

How conceptions of the self are informed by the fluidity and porosity of temporal and spatial boundaries that characterize increased mobility is highlighted by the fact that it has become less common, particularly among younger Muslims, to be addressed by vernacular variants of the term al-Ḥājj (for males) or al-Ḥājja (for females), the honorific title for people who have performed hajj. One reason for this is that these titles carry connotations of old age. Another is that many pilgrims no longer consider it possible or necessary to radically break with one's past after having been cleansed of all sins through hajj performance. They believe that one should strive to lead an ethical lifestyle both before and after hajj performance, and that nobody is perfect; lapses are likely to occur and can be repaired by going on hajj once more (Buitelaar 2018, 35).

These new trends in hajj practices are not self-evident to all believers. The apparent ease with which some perform hajj or *ʿumra* as if attending a seasonal festival is often criticized, for example by older Muslims who associate pilgrimage with exceptionality and taking leave of worldly affairs in preparation for 'meeting one's Creator' (McLoughlin 2009a, 138). Also, the common view that 'being called' to Mecca is 'in God's hands' may feed ambivalent feelings among people who observe more affluent Muslims making the coveted pilgrimage for what they suspect is a superficial longing for a touch of the sacred (cf. Al-Ajarma 2020; Haq and Jackson 2009).

Modern hajj practices, then, do not go uncontested. Such contestations often take the form of moral claims about 'pure religion' versus 'profanation of the sacred', whereby the latter is sometimes associated with 'Westernization'. The 9/11 attacks and subsequent events marked a new phase of popular discourse that suggests a supposed opposition between 'Islam' and 'Western civilization'. 'Muslims' are now pitted against 'Westerners' even more strongly than before. As a result, Muslim religiosity ties in ever more closely with identity politics. For many Muslims, particularly those living the West, this increases the significance of Mecca in their emotional geographies of belonging (cf. Kapinga 2021, 63).

The developments described above have affected the 'habitus' of contemporary Muslims: the embodied dispositions that form a matrix for perceptions, appreciations and actions (Bourdieu 1977). These dispositions shape people's 'sensibilities': the moral and aesthetic dimensions of their experiences and emotional lives (ibid.). Ideals of Muslim personhood and the *umma*, the global Muslim community, exist side by side with other 'grand schemes': powerful yet never fully attainable ideals that operate as models for a good life (Schielke 2015, 13). Therefore, in addition to pursuits that are based on a particular conception of the moral order in Islam, the imagination of Muslims is also inspired by other grand schemes that inform their daily lives on the basis of their specific location in various social constellations and power structures. They may be motivated, for example, by ideals about individual self-realization, romantic love, making money, or specific consumption patterns (cf. Schielke 2020; Gregg 2013; Bowen, Green and James 2008). Each of these ideals comes with its own normative discourse or, to borrow Samuli Schielke's terminology, with its own 'moral register' to frame or assess a situation. Each moral register has a specific style of argumentation and emotional tone. Moral reasoning is therefore an embodied practice that is highly performative, situational, and relational (Schielke 2015, 54; Zigon 2009).

The aim of the research project 'Modern articulations of the pilgrimage to Mecca' was to analyse how the multifaceted needs and desires that result from being informed by various discourses and how meanings and motivations related to different moral registers simultaneously feature in pilgrims' personal hajj accounts. To study the ways in which 'modern sensibilities' affect the choices and practices of contemporary pilgrims (cf. Mahmood 2009, 836), three sub-projects documented articulations of Meccan pilgrimage in the aforementioned two periods of far-reaching transformation: 1. Mecca travelogues at the time of late nineteenth- and early twentieth-century Islamic reform; 2. The meanings of the hajj in everyday life in Morocco; 3. Mecca and translocal senses of belonging among Dutch Muslims of Moroccan or Turkish descent.

The first sub-project, carried out by Ammeke Kateman and Richard van Leeuwen, studied Arabic travelogues written between 1850 and 1945. The specific focus was the impact of two important developments during that time on the pilgrimage to Mecca. One was the global public debate in which new intellectual networks emerged with novel views of religion and society and their interrelationship (cf. Jung 2011). This was especially important for the growth of Islamic reformism, which articulated modern views of Islam that were influenced by European concepts of religion, and focused on normative texts rather than on ritual practice. The formation of these networks was fostered by the spread of new media and the intensification of intercultural communication (cf. Bayly 2004; Hourani 1970). The second development was the impact of European colonial power on the hajj from the 1850s onwards, which enhanced travel facilities for Muslims and affected the logistics and organization of the pilgrimage as new regulations, means of transport and forms of supervision were established (cf. Green 2015; Slight 2014; Tagliacozzo 2014). Mecca's role as a centre of transnational networks was strengthened in this period, while Ottoman control of the Hijaz and the pilgrimage routes weakened (al-Quāitī 2007; Strattkötter 1991; Faroqhi 1990). The foundation of the Saudi kingdom resulted in new normative standards and organizational policies regarding the hajj (Chiffoleau 2013). Although pilgrimage remained the quintessential form of travel for most Muslims, it became linked to new lifestyles and perceptions of religion and society (cf. Gellens 1990; El Moudden 1990; also see Van Leeuwen's chapter 'Hajj narratives as a discursive tradition' in this volume).

The aim of the historical sub-project was to sketch the contours of the modernization process shaping present-day hajj practices as studied in the other two sub-projects. For one of these sub-projects, Kholoud Al-Ajarma conducted ethnographic research to study the socio-cultural embeddedness of the hajj in contemporary Moroccan society. She explored how the status of pilgrims and the meanings that people attribute to pilgrimage are negotiated in micro-practices. To this end, she conducted 18 months of multi-sited participant observation in Morocco to investigate in what ways Mecca and the hajj feature in the daily routines and social interactions of her interlocutors. In addition, she documented how the hajj operates in Morocco's national politics and how Saudi hajj management affects Moroccan pilgrims' experiences (cf. Al-Ajarma 2020).

For the third sub-project, Khadija Kadrouch-Outmany and the author of this chapter studied how the pilgrimage experiences of Dutch Muslims with Moroccan and Turkish backgrounds relate to their everyday life in the Netherlands. The focal points of analysis in this study concerned the significance of Mecca in pilgrims' translocal senses of belonging, and continuity and change in the practices and accounts of pilgrims of different generations. Especially for younger Dutch Muslims with migration backgrounds, feelings of belonging to the various communities with which they identify tend to be complex and ambivalent. Visiting the country of origin to stay in touch with one's 'roots' and relatives can be satisfying and frustrating at the same time, when experiences of exclusion as 'the Muslim other' in the Netherlands are replaced by feeling excluded as 'the rich European' in Morocco (cf. Stock 2017). In this context, envisaging Mecca as an imaginary spiritual homeland where being Muslim is the only identity that counts can have a strong appeal and an empowering effect on the descendants of Muslim migrants (cf. Buitelaar 2018; Toguslu 2017, 23; Werbner 2004, 455). To study how an imagined Mecca relates to one's experience of actually visiting the sacred city, Kadrouch-Outmany joined a group of pilgrims from the Netherlands for the hajj of 2016. Comparing their *in situ* 'embodied talk' (Bamberg 2011, 18) with the stories of pilgrims in retrospective interviews with Buitelaar allowed the researchers to study how personal narratives about the pilgrimage to Mecca 'mature' over time.

Until recently, little attention was paid to pilgrimage to Mecca in both Islamic studies and in the anthropology of pilgrimage. In the past few years, however, several interesting volumes have been published.[16] The present vol-

16 For an overview of historical publications, see Van Leeuwen's chapter 'Hajj narratives as a discursive tradition' in this volume. For an overview of anthropological publications on the pilgrimage to Mecca, see Buitelaar 2015. Since 2015, the following collective volumes with historical and/or anthropological contributions about Muslim pilgrimage have appeared: Buitelaar, Stephan-Emmrich and Thimm (2021); Rahimi and Eshaghi (2019); Flaskerud and Natvig (2018); Arjana (2017); and Ryad (2017).

ume stands out in two respects. Firstly, it focuses exclusively on personal accounts of the pilgrimage. Secondly, it combines both written and oral, and both historical and contemporary travel accounts. Moreover, all contributions study the connection between pilgrims' narratives about their experiences on the journey to Mecca and their everyday lives by applying the following two analytical lenses: narrativization of the pilgrimage and the hajj as a 'sensational form'.

3 Narrating the Pilgrimage to Mecca

Narratives do not simply give words to experiences, but experiences themselves are shaped by words, more specifically by the meanings they have acquired in the vocabularies of the discursive traditions available to narrators when interpreting their experiences (cf. Coleman and Elsner 2003, 8). With regard to hajj narratives, this means that such accounts are informed by the prevailing views on the pilgrimage to Mecca as expressed in stories about pilgrimage circulating within the specific Muslim community to which the narrator belongs.

As Van Leeuwen discusses more elaborately in chapter one, many episodes in the pilgrimage accounts discussed in this volume resonate with storylines from collectively shared stories about the hajj (cf. Chenganakkattil 2017). Descriptions of storms during a perilous sea journey, for example, feature in the historical hajj accounts discussed by Piotr Bachtin, Van Leeuwen, and Miguel Vázquez. Variations on 'yearning to quench the pain' caused by a 'burning desire' to see the Prophet Muhammad's grave, quoted by Kateman, occur in many travelogues discussed in the volume. Without exception, the enormous impact of sighting the Kaʿba for the first time occurs as a peak episode in both historical and contemporary travel accounts. Like variations on descriptions of feeling it 'pull like a magnet', which appear in the chapters by Yahya Nurgat and Buitelaar, the experience of being 'beyond words', which is mentioned in Al-Ajarma, and 'overwhelmed by emotion', as described in the chapters by Nadia Caidi and Van Leeuwen, are tropes that feature in numerous hajj accounts.

The hajj accounts discussed in this volume demonstrate that the heritage of hajj stories of those who have preceded them feeds the expectations of prospective pilgrims. These stories direct pilgrims' attention as they perform the pilgrimage and provide them with a vocabulary and already existing 'script' to interpret their own pilgrimage experiences. It is probably no coincidence that both the British author of the opening quote and a research participant in Caidi's contribution to this volume included observations about birds in their stories about the Kaʿba; the accounts of many of Buitelaar's interviewees similarly contain anecdotes about birds flying over the courtyard of the Grand Mosque in Mecca. Such parallels illustrate that storytelling is not a simple matter of creating personal meanings, but an intersubjective endeavour, involving a 'politics of experience' in which a multiplicity of private and public interests are at play (Jackson 2006, 11). Narrators and audiences are engaged in an ongoing negotiation of meanings. This is a first sense in which pilgrimage accounts are always co-authored and multi-voiced (cf. Zock 2013).

Particularly interesting in terms of the dialogical nature of storytelling are the contributions in this volume that discuss the pilgrimage accounts of Dutch and French Muslims with migration backgrounds. As well as being informed by the Islamic tradition as transmitted to them by their parents, the habitus and self-conceptions of Muslims who have grown up in Europe are also shaped by a modern liberal discourse and a culture of consumerism that dominate their daily lifeworlds. Their horizon is considerably wider than that of their parents, for whom visiting their country of origin and the pilgrimage to Mecca tend to be the only familiar travel options. As well as inheriting the habit of regular return visits to their family's country of origin, younger-generation Muslims have also had their personal longings shaped by growing up in a cultural context in which making a holiday trip to relax or explore hitherto unknown territory is almost considered a basic human need. As a consequence, they have expanded their views on desirable travel destinations. They also have high expectations regarding the efficiency and quality of transportation and accommodation. And, whereas their parents mostly have rural backgrounds and have enjoyed little or no formal education, most children of Muslim migrants have been raised in urban settings and educated in European educational systems.

As a result, like other modern-educated middle-class citizens both in Europe and elsewhere, they have incorporated particular norms about hygiene and punctuality, as well as liberal values such as individualism, gender equality, and self-enhancement. This comes to the fore in Buitelaar's chapter in the 'life lessons' that Asmae distilled from her pilgrimage experience about her rights as an individual to make her own choices. In the chapter by Buitelaar and Kadrouch-Outmany, the authors show that younger generations of pilgrims expect a high standard of travel accommodation and tend to be more vocal in their complaints about poor service than older pilgrims. Furthermore, the chapter by Jihan Safar and Leila Seurat demonstrates that the trend among Muslim couples in France to go to Mecca on their honeymoon is related to conceptions about romantic love and gender equality.

These case studies document how the descendants of migrants from North Africa and Turkey appropriate words, meanings, and storylines from conventional hajj accounts by intoning and placing them in relation to conceptual patterns and values they have incorporated from other discursive traditions, thus reshaping the meanings of these words and storylines as they use them in their own stories (cf. Shotter and Billig 1998, 24). This, then, is a second sense in which pilgrimage accounts are multi-voiced.

Based on the chapters in this volume that discuss the hajj accounts of young European pilgrims to Europe, I would argue that the descendants of Muslim migrants have become active co-authors of the prevailing 'grand narrative' of pilgrimage to Mecca in their Muslim community. More specifically, a comparison of the historical and contemporary hajj accounts sheds light on how these European Muslims contribute to the narrative's further development by inscribing their own understandings of the meanings of the pilgrimage into already existing representations such as presented by Van Leeuwen in chapter one. Since the hajj performance of young and female Muslims is a fairly recent development, this is both an act of 'emplacement', locating oneself in an existing 'grand narrative' about the hajj, and an act of 'emplotment', selecting events and putting them in a specific meaningful sequence (cf. Jackson 2006, 31). In this sense, Mecca can be seen as a 'palimpsest' in which individual pilgrims inscribe their own meanings on normative pilgrimage 'scripts'. Rather than adding completely new layers, however, this results in entangled meanings in which the past impinges on present meanings (cf. Kinnard 2014, 30; Smith 2008, 5).

The contributions to this volume also demonstrate that the freedom of narrators to improvise upon and add new dimensions to existing meanings is limited. Much as we can bend conventional meanings attributed to words in established views, if our stories are to be understood, they must be oriented towards the specific conceptual horizon of their recipients. In order to be recognized, the self-presentations of narrators depend on prevailing shared conceptions of, for example, a specific kind of personhood. In this sense, storytelling is always informed by the existential tension between 'being for oneself' and 'being for another' (Jackson 2006, 30). The freedom of narrators of pilgrimage accounts to shape their own stories is therefore far from absolute. It hinges on the specific constellation of power operations through which the articulation of certain imaginaries may be enabled or disabled (cf. Fricker 2007, 14; Ochs and Capps 1996, 32–35; Olson and Shopes 1991, 193). This is revealed in the chapter by Buitelaar and Kadrouch-Outmany in the differences between what could be said in public by whom during the hajj performance, and what topics were only shared in private conversations as pilgrims negotiated how to deal with setbacks. In the same chapter, the coercive impact that normative hajj storytelling can have on individual pilgrims is illustrated by a research participant's statement in a retrospective interview that she found the discourse of *ṣabr* (patience, endurance) 'suffocating' at times. The chapter also illustrates that as pilgrims tell and retell their experiences upon return, they are likely to edit their stories. Family and friends play an active role in the act of narration; their responses and questions help pilgrims to put their experience into a specific, shared context (Buitelaar 2020; also see McLouglin 2015, 54; Delaney 1990, 520).[17]

The social dimension of hajj storytelling is addressed specifically in Caidi's contribution, in which she documents how her interlocutors have archived their memories in the form of journals kept during the pilgrimage, photographs, and videoclips stored their phones, and, in the case of one pilgrim, paintings made after returning home. Caidi argues that these forms of curating memories serve three purposes. Firstly, they facilitate pilgrims' personal meaning-making process; as time goes by, cherishing their memories and keeping the experience alive help pilgrims to reflect on how they wish to anchor the transformative experience of the pilgrimage in their daily lives. In this sense, actively re-evoking hajj experiences by looking at mementos can be conceived of as an act of ethical self-formation (cf. Mahmood 2005). Caidi argues that pilgrims actively contribute to reinforcing a collective Muslim habitus by performing their position as Ḥājj or Ḥājja in their Muslim community. They do so by adopting an outwardly pious lifestyle and providing fellow Muslims with information about the steps and meaning of the hajj. In this sense, the active curating of memories is a ritual of community building as well as a means for pilgrims to acquire religious capital—the second and third purpose of curating memories that Caidi identifies. As illustrated by the anecdote that one of her interlocutors told her about the cousin who had reprimanded him for showing him a videotape he had made near the Kaʿba, pilgrims have to tread cautiously and reflect carefully on what to share with others; it can be a fine line between being appreciated for encouraging others to go on pilgrimage themselves and being accused of bragging about one's own accomplishments.

What events pilgrims select for their pilgrimage stories and how they narrativize them thus depends to a large extent on the intended audiences that they have in mind when putting their experiences into words. As Van Leeuwen argues in his contributions, it is the convention in hajj storytelling to represent the pilgrimage as the ultimate religious experience. To this end, narrators tend to present an idealized account of the hajj rites. To convince their

17 See also Frey (1998, 186), who noted a parallel tendency among pilgrims in her study of contemporary pilgrimage to Santiago de Compostela.

readers of the credibility and authenticity of their reports—and, I would add, to enhance the readers' identification with the protagonist—in chapter eight Van Leeuwen provides, alongside positive descriptions of religious activities, detailed examples of how narrators may add positively and negatively evaluated more personal anecdotes about the logistics of the journey, such as details about food, transport and accommodation.

In historical hajj accounts, sharing details about an arduous journey was also a way for narrators to demonstrate the extent to which they were willing to endure hardship to fulfil their religious duty to God. Today, the journey to Mecca is reduced to a few hours of comfortable air travel. In contemporary accounts, in addition to issues with Saudi hajj management, it is mostly the heat and basic facilities of the tent camp in Mina that feature as stressful experiences, although older generations of pilgrims tend to be more reluctant to share such stories than younger pilgrims.[18]

An extreme example of adapting the narration of one's hajj experiences to a specific audience is presented in Vázquez' chapter. The sixteenth-century anonymous Spanish author whose *coplas* or poem about the hajj Vázquez discusses, probably had good reason to memorialize the details of the pilgrimage in verse, and—except for the mention of a storm at sea—to present an idealized picture of the journey. All expressions of Islam were forbidden in Habsburg Spain at the time. Memorizing a poem was therefore safer than keeping a manuscript. Also, Vázquez argues that making a virtual pilgrimage by reciting the poem in a situation where the actual performance was beyond reach for Spanish Muslims was an act of defiance and a form of jihad.

In a similar vein, Neda Saghaee and Van Leeuwen argue in their chapter that while Sufi accounts of the pilgrimage to Mecca contain elaborate descriptions of participation in ecstatic rituals at the Sufi lodges visited on their way to Mecca, the audiences that the narrators addressed extend well beyond Sufi circles. They wrote their accounts with a didactic purpose of informing a wide audience of Muslims about the hajj and of feeding their readers' longing for the pilgrimage. The chapters about Spanish and Sufi pilgrims also illustrate how chronicling the pilgrimage can be a devotional act in itself. In this respect, narrating the hajj may go beyond linguistic representation and be part of the same religious experience it refers to.[19]

18 See Haq and Johnson (2009) and the chapter by Buitelaar and Kadrouch-Outmany in this volume.

19 See Popp-Baier (2021) and Bender (2007, 207) who describe similar merging of stories about devotional acts becoming a religious practice itself among Christian practictioners.

In contrast, the female-authored hajj narratives from Qajar Iran discussed in Bachtin's chapter were written for a very specific audience. The extensive criticism in these narratives of the comportment of Sunni Muslims indicates that these journals were clearly aimed at an audience of Shiʿi Muslims. Moreover, the travelogues contain passages about topics that were considered intimate and therefore only suitable for sharing among women. Scathing passages about fellow Shiʿi male travellers in the caravan on the journey to Mecca point similarly to an intended exclusively female audience.

In his contribution, Thomas Ecker discusses the impact of different intended audiences on how hajj accounts are written by comparing two travelogues whose authors were both members of the household of the Qajar dynasty that ruled Iran in the 1860s and 1870s. One author, Yaʿqub Mirzā, wrote for a circle of friends, sharing private jokes with them in the text and sometimes directly addressing them. The other, Farhād Mirzā, had recently been dismissed from a political post when he embarked on the pilgrimage to Mecca. Trusting that he might secure another position upon his return, his travelogue was written with publication in mind and contains many political details that might be useful for the court.

Political considerations also played a major role in how the Tajik journalist Fazliddin Muhammadiev addressed his intended audience in the novel discussed in Vladimir Brobovnikow's chapter. Muhammadiev based his novel on the diary he kept during his pilgrimage to Mecca in 1963. Rigorously adapting pre-Soviet conventions of hajj storytelling, the novel contains all the tropes that featured in Soviet travelogues at the time. Brobovnikow argues that the main purpose of this genre was to provide Soviet readers with a glimpse of the outside world and to convince them of the USSR's heroic role in world affairs.

The Internet and smartphone have had an enormous impact on the publics to which pilgrimage accounts can be communicated (cf. Karić 2018). Elsewhere, Al-Ajarma and Buitelaar (2021) compare the hajj blogs of pilgrims from Morocco and the Netherlands. They demonstrate how pilgrims from Morocco tend to use hajj blogs as a platform to present a different picture of the management of hajj logistics than the rosy sketches presented by government-linked national media in Muslim-majority countries. In Dutch hajj blogs, however, pilgrims tend to sketch a more positive picture to counter the dominant negative conceptions about Islam in Dutch society and to reach out to non-Muslim audiences by relating the pilgrimage to themes and values that transcend religion. At a more general level, pilgrims' self-representations on public platforms, such as the 'hajj selfies' on Facebook that Caidi and her colleagues studied (Caidi, Beazley and Marquez 2018), provide insights into how documenting one's experiences has become an integral part of the pilgrimage experience for pilgrims of the smartphone generation.[20]

Another implication of pilgrims' habitual use of the smartphone for hajj storytelling concerns the affordance the device offers to pilgrims to stay in touch with their dear ones at home throughout the journey. Until recently, a recurring storyline in pilgrimage accounts was the anxiety and grief that departing pilgrims feel upon saying farewell to their loved ones, only to find that once in Mecca, they are so absorbed by the sacred atmosphere that they miraculously forget everything and concentrate only on their acts of devotion. In his contribution, Nurgat presents a particularly telling example of the trope of forgetting everything related to home in the travelogue of the Ottoman pilgrim Yūsuf Nābī (1642–1712). After first describing in a general sense how approaching Mecca causes pilgrims to forget their wealth and loved ones and realize the priority of attaining God's forgiveness, Nābī then goes on to narrate how the 'natural order of the mind was completely disrupted' upon his first sight of the Kaʿba, and that his senses scattered in all directions. Illustrating the extent to which the smartphone has become part of the habitus of younger Muslims, Buitelaar and Al-Ajarma quote in their chapter a young Dutch pilgrim who flipped this storyline around by explaining that it was precisely because her smartphone allowed her to remain in contact with her children that she could fully concentrate on her acts of worship rather than worry about home.

Both Caidi's chapter and that of Buitelaar and Al-Ajarma also touch upon the sensorial dimensions of pilgrims' use of modern technology. The impact of modern technology on the pilgrimage experience takes centre stage in Zahir Janmohamed's auto-ethnographic contribution. On the basis of interviews with Shiʿi pilgrims from the US and his own personal experiences, Janmohamed discusses how modern technology has made it easier for Shiʿi pilgrims to say or listen to specific Shiʿi supplication prayers whilst in Mecca. The first time that Janmohamed went on *ʿumra*, his prayer book with Shiʿi invocations was confiscated at Jedda airport. Nowadays, however, Shiʿi Muslims can avoid both Saudi censorship and the frowning looks of Sunni pilgrims by listening to their favourite Shiʿi supplication prayers on their headphones. Janmohamed reports that it had moved him deeply to be able to listen to the Shiʿi invocations that he had grown up with when facing the Kaʿba during his most recent pilgrimage. As a result, the hajj now felt more like his own.

The sense of belonging evoked by listening to familiar supplication prayers illustrates the centrality of aesthetic forms in the making of religious subjects

20 See also the chapter by Caidi and that by Buitelaar and Al-Ajarma in this volume.

and communities. The next section will focus on what the hajj accounts discussed in this volume can tell us about how the pilgrimage to Mecca operates as an aesthetic form that speaks to pilgrims through their senses and moves them emotionally.

4 The Hajj as a Sensational Form

Like the British pilgrim in the opening quote, nearly all pilgrims report that words cannot (properly) convey the 'wow' that they experienced. When trying to articulate their feelings of awe, narrators of pilgrimage accounts tend to describe sensory experiences. In her chapter, Al-Ajarma documents the sensual lexicon of her interlocutors when they try to convey their ineffable experiences in terms of bodily responses. Ethnographic fieldwork enabled her to study the dialogical construction of hajj stories in a very direct way; she was witness to or a conversation partner in many oral exchanges between narrators of hajj stories and their audiences. Her observations reveal the performative quality of such exchanges: when narrators described how tears ran down their cheeks as they approached the Kaʿba, tears would flow again; when describing a paralyzing tingling in her legs as she stood in front of the Kaʿba, a female narrator first pinched her own leg and then that of the woman sitting next to her; when describing how her heart was burning with a desire to return to Mecca, another pilgrim beat her chest. Bodies convey feeling by immediate connection, one that enables what David Morgan (2010, 59) would call 'emotional contagion'. In other words, re-enacting how the emotional dimensions of their journey were mediated through bodily sensations allowed the narrators whom Al-Ajarma observed to relive their feelings, as well as to draw in their audiences and participate in the experience.

The preponderance of trembling bodies, palpitating hearts, and, most of all, tears flowing down cheeks reported in virtually all hajj accounts shows how the body actively shapes, colours, tunes, and performs pilgrims' religious orientation. Indeed, performing pilgrimage is a sensory experience *par excellence*; the whole body participates in its expression and production (cf. Jansen 2012, 6; Coleman and Eade 2004). As Vida Bajc argues, by speaking directly to the body, pilgrimage is 'a medium through which narrative imaginaries and places visited are conjoined to generate particular emotional awareness and evoke intensification of experience of being in that place' (Bajc 2007, 398).

To understand what engenders such an intense experience of the sacred, it is particularly helpful to adopt Meyer's approach to religion as a 'sensational form' when studying the pilgrimage to Mecca. Meyer argues that the sensation of 'awe' or immediacy of the sacred that religious practitioners may experience is not a prior quality of a sacred place or time, but a product of mediation (Meyer 2011, 23). Religious feelings are not just there, they are evoked by 'sensational forms':

> relatively fixed modes for invoking and organising access to the transcendental, offering structures of repetition to create and sustain links between believers in the context of particular religious regimes. These forms are transmitted and shared; they involve religious practitioners in particular practices of worship, and play a central role in modulating them as religious moral subjects and communities
>
> MEYER 2011, 30

Conceiving of the relationship between sensing subjects and their experiences of transcendency as mediated through sensational forms requires a focus on the material and sensory dimensions of religious mediation—that is, a focus on the aesthetics through which our sensory experience of the world and our knowledge of it is organized and 'tuned' in a way that yields a specific habitus (Meyer 2012, 165–167).

The pilgrimage to Mecca is a particularly powerful sensational form with a strong presence in the daily lifeworld of Muslims, regardless of whether they have performed the pilgrimage themselves. First of all, Mecca is an important point of bodily orientation in Muslims' lives; they are buried facing Mecca, and the *ṣalāt*, the five daily prayers, are likewise conducted facing Mecca. In societies with a Muslim-majority population, even those who do not practise the *ṣalāt* develop an awareness of their position in relation to Mecca as they go through their daily routines as a result of seeing Muslims pray, or being asked by someone who wishes to pray whether they happen to know the direction of Mecca.[21] In Moroccan-Arabic, Mecca as a point of orientation has even become

21 There are numerous aids to determine the direction of Mecca. In mosques, this is indicated by the *qibla*, the prayer-niche (see the photograph on page 117). In many hotel rooms in Muslim-majority countries, arrows on the ceiling or floor point to Mecca. In addition to information about the plane's height and speed, regardless of their destination, airlines like Royal Air Maroc include information about relative position to Mecca on the screens above passengers' seats. Travellers can also have recourse to a travel kit consisting of a compass and a table showing the number of degrees east or west of north that Mecca is situated from a particular region. Nowadays, these are mostly replaced by '*qibla* finder' apps that can be downloaded on a smartphone. For an account of the Kaʿba as the point of orientation in Islam's history, see O'Meara (2020).

proverbial; a person who gets confused or disoriented might express this by stating: '*tlift al-qibla*', literally: I got the direction of Mecca wrong.[22]

Mecca is also present in everyday life in material form, for example in the shape of souvenirs that pilgrims take home (cf. Flaskerud 2018, 47–50). Objects that are used in everyday devotional acts, like the prayer mats and prayer beads mentioned by the Turkish-Dutch pilgrim Enes in Buitelaar's chapter, are favourite souvenirs that connect their users to Mecca, while dates and sacred water from the Zamzam Well literally allow a taste of the sacred and the incorporation of its *baraka* or blessings. Perfume oil, jewellery, headscarves and dresses are other popular souvenirs that mediate Mecca through close bodily contact. For aspiring pilgrims, these tangible objects provide an imagined link with the sacred destination and evoke a longing for it. For those who have been on pilgrimage, they serve as 'touchstones of memory' (Morgan and Pritchard 2005, 41), which contain traces of the power of the original experience, thus helping to re-evoke the sacred journey in the imagination (cf. Mesaritou 2012, 107).[23]

As well as being mediated through souvenirs, Mecca is also conspicuously present in Muslim daily life in the form of images of the Kaʿba on wall tapestries, paintings, and photographs that many Muslims use to decorate their houses, shops and offices (cf. page 284 in this volume).[24] Representations of the Kaʿba are often paired with those of the Grand Mosque in Medina, where the

22 I'm grateful to Salma Bouchiba of the NIMAR (Dutch Institute in Morocco), who used this expression when we got lost in a lecture building at the University of Leiden at the time of writing this introductory chapter.

23 See also Coleman and Elsner (1995, 100), who describe the souvenirs that pilgrims take home as 'containers of the sacred', which serve to connect them to the site in the everyday context to which they have returned and to mark their identity as someone who has performed the pilgrimage. The authors argue that 'pilgrimage is as concerned with taking back some part of the charisma of a holy place as it is about actually going to the place.' While this probably holds true for most forms of voluntary pilgrimage, for hajj pilgrims taking part in a mandatory ritual, being able to fulfil their religious duty carries more weight. However, as the stories of the younger pilgrims interviewed by Buitelaar and Safar and Seurat illustrate, being able to tap into the power of the pilgrimage experience upon return to their daily lives is an important motivation for not postponing the hajj until they have reached old age, as previous generations tended to do.

24 See also McGregor (2010), who discusses material representations of the Kaʿba in nineteenth-century Egypt. Critiquing studies that approach the relationship between sacred sites and pilgrims' everyday lifeworlds in terms of a simple binary between centre and periphery, McGregor argues that the location of the Kaʿba and Mecca became 'scattered' by the distribution of pieces of *kiswa* cloth, the black, richly embroidered cover of the Kaʿba that is replaced annually, and of the *maḥmal*, the ceremonial palanquin that headed the pilgrim caravan from Egypt until the early twentieth century (McGregor 2010, 252).

Prophet Muhammad is buried.[25] Together, these images remind Muslims of the highlights of the much-coveted journey to Mecca.[26] Mecca also features widely in folktales and popular songs,[27] as well as entering people's homes in televised form, for example in an episode of the popular MBC animated children's series *Taysh ʿAyāl*, where an entire family goes on *ʿumra*.[28] More importantly, a popular channel for ambient watching is Makkah Live, which broadcasts 24/7 from the Grand Mosques in Mecca and Medina.[29]

As Seán McLoughlin (2009b, 288) has argued, Mecca's ubiquitous visual presence in people's daily lifeworlds at once demythologizes and re-mythologizes the hajj. Based on the findings of the hajj research project that this book builds on, I would argue that this is particularly the case for its representations on social media and in television broadcasts. Such 'live' images demythologize the pilgrimage to Mecca in the sense of leaving little to the imagination as to what the place actually looks like. At the same time, they re-mythologize the sacred city by making an enormous appeal to those who are routinely confronted with these images; its visual omnipresence in everyday life reinforces the idea that visiting Mecca is what Muslims should most desire, thus contributing to normative conceptions of Muslim subjectivity.[30] The reconfirmation by returning pilgrims that the experience is 'beyond words' further enhances Mecca's magical qualities in the imagination.

The fascination with the image of the Kaʿba obviously relates to the building's central role in Islam's sacred history. Firstly, it represents God's house on

25 See Witkam 2007, who discusses the tradition of illustrating copies of *Dalāʾil al-khayrāt*, a famous book with prayers and invocations to honour the Prophet Muhammad written by the fifteenth-century Moroccan Sufi and scholar al-Jazūlī, with painted images of Mecca and Medina.

26 Strictly speaking, visiting the Prophet's grave is not part of the pilgrimage, but virtually all tour operators include a stop in Medina in their package tours. Besides images of the most sacred sites of the Ḥaramayn, representations of the Dome of the Rock in Jerusalem, Islam's third most sacred city, also abound in Muslims' homes.

27 For songs and folktales in Morocco, see Al-Ajarma (2020). For the hajj in the Swedish-Muslim hip-hop scene, see Ackfeldt (2012). Rashid (2017) discusses the devotional songs of the US hip-hop group Native Deen, who sing about the desire to go on hajj in the song 'Labbayk'. Cf: https://www.youtube.com/watch?v=hnQZZFQ7ldk, accessed 9 July 2021.

28 See https://www.youtube.com/watch?v=EYVq9KsWE-c, accessed 6 August 2021.

29 See https://makkahlive.net/, accessed 6 August 2021.

30 Compare my conversation with an elderly Moroccan-Dutch woman who was preparing for her seventh visit to Mecca. Sitting in her living room and watching the channel 'Makkah Live' with her, I asked her why she wished to go to Mecca again. Communicating the incomprehensibility, or at least the inappropriateness in her view, of suggesting that a Muslim might not desire to go there whenever the opportunity arose, she responded with the rhetorical counter question: 'Why ever not?!' (Buitelaar 2020, 4).

earth. Secondly, shortly before he died, the Prophet Muhammad returned to Mecca in 632 CE, ten years after having left for Medina to escape persecution by its non-Muslim rulers, in order to perform his 'Farewell Pilgrimage' and restore the ritual to what Muslims consider its original Abrahamic form (cf. McMillan 2011, 19–20). The Prophet's triumphant return to Mecca marked the first step in Islam's worldwide expansion. Over time, the flow of pilgrims circumambulating the Kaʿba has come to symbolize the *umma*, the global Muslim community.

While the symbolic power of the Kaʿba in Muslim imagery largely explains why pilgrims are so often greatly moved when seeing the structure, I would argue that the enormous emotional impact that most pilgrims report when first seeing the Kaʿba is amplified by finally setting their eyes on a hitherto unattainable object whose image they have been familiar with from early childhood. The real-life encounter establishes what Britta Knudsen and Anne Marit Waade call 'performative authenticity': the thrill that travellers may experience as they authenticate the existence of a well-known place on the basis of a pre-existing sensuous and emotional relatedness to it (Knudsen and Waade 2010, 12–13). In this respect, the awe that seeing the Kaʿba evokes in pilgrims does not differ from the effect that particularly famous tourist destinations are known to have on visitors.[31] Indeed, travellers to such sites describe similar intense experiences of a 'loss of self', 'exhilaration', and 'transcendence' (cf. Whittaker 2012, 74–75).

Where seeing the Kaʿba with one's own eyes differs from, say, taking in the landscape at the Victoria Falls, is that these sites owe their authentication effects to different aesthetic forms (cf. Van den Port and Meyer 2018, 20). Pilgrims to Mecca are predisposed to interpreting the awe they experience when sighting the Kaʿba as a religious feeling. The ubiquitous visual presence of the Kaʿba in their everyday lives as a marker of a global Muslim identity, the stories about the significance of the various sites that make up the hajj in Islam's history, and the testimonies of pilgrims who preceded them, are all part of an Islamic aesthetics which maps the 'emotional itinerary' of the pilgrimage (Gade 2007, 38). In other words, pilgrims anticipate being moved to tears when they see the Kaʿba with their own eyes.

Indeed, pilgrims who do not live up to the expected emotions, for instance by not producing tears when seeing the Kaʿba, like Salma and Enes in the chapters by Al-Ajarma and Buitelaar respectively, tend to be surprised or disappointed, and some even worry that it might signal a lack of *ikhlāṣ*, or sincere devotion.

---

31 See Urry (2005, 78), who quotes Osborne (2000, 79) reporting hearing a visitor to the Victoria Falls state: 'Wow, that's so postcard'.

This points to the moral weight that is attached to being moved to tears. More generally, stories about being moved to tears or about disappointment when tears do not materialize illustrate that the experience and display of emotions are culturally mediated; in different cultural contexts, some emotions are actively cultivated, while others are neglected or suppressed (cf. Abu-Lughod and Lutz 1990, 11).

In Islam's emotional discourse, weeping is a praiseworthy emotion. It is mentioned in the Qur'an in verse 5: 83, for example, as the appropriate response to listening to God's word: 'when they listen to what has been sent down to the Messenger, you will see their eyes overflowing with tears because they recognize the Truth [in it]' (Abdel Haleem 2004).[32] Also, the Prophet Muhammad is documented as having regularly wept, a practice that was emulated by a group of early Sufis who went by the name of 'the Weepers' (Gade 2007, 40). In this emotional discourse, weeping is not an expression of pain or personal suffering, but a sign of awareness of God and being overwhelmed by his greatness and one's love for him (Mahmood 2005, 130–131).[33] As Anna Gade warns us, we should be cautious about tracing the emotions of 'ordinary' Muslims back to emotion theory in authoritative textual sources (Gade 2007, 42). The recurrent references to weeping in the pilgrimage accounts discussed in this volume demonstrate, however, that the conception of weeping as a highly valued ethical disposition has a long tradition in hajj storytelling.

Particularly interesting in terms of how narrators of hajj accounts narrate the emotional itinerary of the hajj is the chapter by Kateman, who maps how travelogues written in the early decades of the twentieth century reflect the great changes occurring at the time. Kateman found that the narrators of these accounts used the same conventional descriptions of sensory experiences as their predecessors, such as the heart skipping a beat and shedding copious tears, to describe how the rites and sacred sites affect them. She observed much more variation in their descriptions of emotional responses to new phenomena such as trains and steamships, quarantine measures imposed by European colonial powers and new rules of conduct introduced by the Saudi regime to impose its strict Wahhābī interpretation of Islam. Kateman's analysis thus

32 Note how in this Qur'anic verse, weeping is also connected to recognizing authenticity.

33 Pain and sorrow are not absent, however, from pious weeping: the burning desire to be reunited with God and the pain of separation can also provoke tears. In his hajj memoir Hammoudi, for example, mentions an inconsolable fellow pilgrim who wept copiously about being parted from the Prophet as their bus was leaving Medina (Hammoudi 2006, 124–127). Also, in Shi'a Islam, weeping is related to mourning over the martyrdom of Imām Ḥusayn, the grandson of the Prophet Muhammad who was murdered by the hand of the Umayyad caliph Yazīd (cf. Richard 1995, 32).

demonstrates that additional emotional styles related to other cultural discourses were introduced in the hajj accounts alongside emotional styles that are anchored in the Islamic tradition.

Several contributors to this volume point out that the strong religious feelings that narrators of hajj accounts report do not necessarily express their actual feelings, but should be understood as conventional tropes that their readers expect them to describe. Indeed, like any kind of self-narrative, travel biographies should not be read for factual information but for what the narrators wish to convey about the experiences they describe and the meanings they attribute to those experiences.

At the same time, discourses create real effects in people. Pilgrims are affected by the emotions that are communicated through hajj-related souvenirs, images, and stories. This comes to the fore particularly well, for example, in Hammoudi's observation that the hajj journey he was about to embark on out of academic interest turned into a personal quest as well: 'I had not foreseen the feelings that now I could no longer elude, for the more imminent and real my departure became, the more it seemed to authorize, even free up, certain words' (Hammoudi 2006, 5). Discursively mediated cultural understandings of feelings become part of pilgrims' habitus and inform their embodied experiences. Moreover, ritual performance can be deliberately applied as a 'bodily technique' to induce certain feelings (cf. Mahmood 2005). In fact, hajj storytelling probably owes much of its emotional vocabulary to the kind of Sufi treatises and personal accounts about the pilgrimage that Saghaee and Van Leeuwen discuss in this volume. The authors demonstrate that for Sufis, the salience of the physical journey to Mecca pertains first and foremost to its capacity to cultivate inner feelings that should bring the pilgrim closer to God. Like the British woman in the opening quote, many hajj tour guides tend to make use of this technique of inducing feelings through bodily acts: to increase the emotional impact on their clients of sighting the Kaʿba for the first time, they advise pilgrims to keep their eyes cast down until they are standing directly in front of it.[34]

This should obviously not be taken to mean that all pilgrims necessarily go through the same emotions. One reason for this is that the Islamic tradition is

34 Stimulating the emotional impact of first sightings has also been described for non-Muslim pilgrimage practices. Kaell (2014, 81) and Bajc (2007, 402), for example, describe similar instances in which tour guides direct the gaze of Christian pilgrims to Jerusalem for optimal effect. Also see Bender (2007, 210–212; 2003) for a discussion of the significance of vision and seeing in everyday religious experiences of American volunteers who identify as spiritual.

rich in emotional styles. While many pilgrims to Mecca hope to obtain blessings and be touched by the sacred in a direct, sensual way, those with more reformist inclinations may seek to strengthen their faith through detached contemplation (cf. Van Leeuwen 2015).[35] Still others, such as adherents to legalistic understandings of Islam, may be driven by an—at times even anguished—concern to carry out the rites correctly lest their performance be invalidated.[36] Furthermore, as the contributions by Bachtin, Ecker and Janmohamed to this volume illustrate, Shiʿi Muslims may not experience the same sense of belonging as Sunni pilgrims. For them, the hajj is connected to the martyrdom of the Prophet Muhammad's grandson, Imām Ḥusayn, at the hands of a Sunni Umayyad caliph who ruled Mecca at the time. They may therefore experience moments of intense grief or resentment (Fischer and Abedi 1990, 167). As Janmohamed's chapter illustrates, political tension, such as enmity between Saudi Arabia and the post-revolutionary Republic of Iran, may be reflected in hostile feelings between Sunni and Shiʿi Muslims from other countries. Indeed, like the narrators of the historical pilgrimage accounts discussed by Bachtin and Ecker, contemporary Norwegian Shiʿi pilgrims also report being afraid of Sunni harassment (Flaskerud 2018, 46).

The ways that pilgrims' sensibilities are shaped by class may also impact on their feelings. Both the historical and contemporary accounts discussed in this volume contain numerous examples of class-specific experiences. Nurgat, for example, mentions certain privileges that the pilgrims whose pilgrimage accounts he discusses enjoyed as members of the elite, such as entering the tomb of the Prophet Muhammad. The travel account of Farhād Mirzā discussed by Ecker similarly contains references to differential treatment, in his case being received by foreign state officials on his journey to Mecca. Other examples can be found in Kateman's chapter, where she describes how pilgrims' experiences in the quarantine camps were coloured by class, while in chapter eight Van Leeuwen refers to the poem of an ʿIbāḍī shaykh, who fiercely criticized the 'unhygienic behaviour' of pilgrims whom he classified as 'peasants'. Variation in emotional responses relating to the different sensibilities of

35 Compare Kaell (2014, 76–98) and Lock (2003), who describe, for different historical periods, similar variations in Christian pilgrims of different denominations who first set eyes on Jerusalem, some responding with outward emotional expressions, others stressing contemplative 'inner vision'.

36 See Hammoudi (2006, 47), who notes that some of his fellow pilgrims were anxious that they might make mistakes due to a lack of knowledge. See also Buitelaar (2020, 6), where younger pilgrims state that older pilgrims are preoccupied with 'ticking the boxes', whereas they themselves are more attuned to the spiritual experience.

pilgrims from lower-class rural backgrounds and those with middle-class lifestyles also emerges in the chapter by Buitelaar and Kadrouch-Outmany in relation to the sojourn of contemporary Dutch pilgrims in the Mina tent camp. The chapter by Buitelaar and Al-Ajarma discusses class differences in smartphone use between Moroccan and Dutch-Moroccan pilgrims.[37] More generally, being able to afford a five-star hotel room in the Mecca clock tower with a view of the Kaʿba and within the precinct of the sacred space of the Grand Mosque itself (cf. the photograph on page 340), creates a very different pilgrimage experience than having to sleep in the streets or in the Grand Mosque and beg for food.[38]

Gender similarly informs pilgrims' experiences. Women and men may differ, for example, in their emotional response to the genderedness of the Islamic role models whose stories are re-enacted in the hajj rites.[39] Also, while the basic rules for the hajj rites are the same for all pilgrims, some details differ for male and female pilgrims. In all such instances, the rules for male pilgrims allow for more outward expression. Most noticeable is the difference in dress code for pilgrims once they enter *iḥrām*, the state of consecration. The *iḥrām* clothes for men consist of two, unstitched pieces of white cloth, while women can wear any clothing provided that they hide their body contours and leave the face and hands exposed. The expression of women's liminal status is thus given less emphasis than men's. Also, all pilgrims utter the devotional *talbiya* prayer once they have pronounced their intention to enter the *iḥrām* state, and continue to repeat the invocation throughout the pilgrimage. Whereas men chant the *talbiya* out loud, women should murmur it softly to themselves. In a similar vein, for a specific part of the *saʿy*, the rite in which pilgrims walk back and forth seven times between the hillocks of al-Ṣafā and al-Marwa, men are advised to run, while women should continue at a walking pace.

---

37 See Al-Ajarma 2020 and Buitelaar 2020 for more examples in the contemporary era.

38 Formally, pilgrims who do not have a Saudi residence permit are only issued a hajj visa if they book a package tour from a recognized tour operator. Foreign Muslim migrant labourers with Saudi residence permits need to obtain an official permit to perform the hajj, but they can perform it individually or in self-organized groups. Some overstay their labour contract and residence permit in order to perform the hajj, putting them in an even more precarious situation. Lücking, for example, demonstrates that work and pilgrimage are closely intertwined in the views and practices of migrants to Mecca from the Indonesian island of Madura, for whom the waiting list for a hajj visa is 20 years. For some Madurese labourers, the *ʿumra* visa appears to have become a popular way of entering Saudi Arabia in order to work there and wait for the hajj season. Once they arrive in Saudi Arabia, they go into hiding and many of them work illegally while waiting (Lücking 2017, 261).

39 See Buitelaar (2021) for a discussion of how Asra Nomani aligns the meaning of the story of Hājar to her own experience as an abandoned single mother.

So far, Asra Nomani's hajj memoir is the only one I have come across that includes a critical remark on the Saudi laws prohibiting women from running during the *saʿy* (cf. Nomani 2006, 65). Many more female pilgrims, particularly younger ones, voice their discontent about being relegated to the rear of the courtyard of the Grand Mosque in Mecca during prayer time, from where they can only catch a glimpse of the Kaʿba (cf. Kadrouch-Outmany and Buitelaar 2021, 48–51). The restrictive measures for women at the *rawḍa*, the location in the Prophet's Mosque in Medina near his tomb, provoke even more female indignation (cf. Al-Ajarma 2020, 133–137; Janmohamed 2016, 220). Not only are the opening hours for women much shorter than for men, but female pilgrims—unlike pilgrims in the men's section—cannot see the shrine with the Prophet's tomb from the women's section, let alone touch it. An increasing number of women feel that this situation seriously hampers their spiritual experience.

Female pilgrims are prevented from setting their eyes on the Prophet's tomb for the same reason that women in most Muslim societies are prohibited from participating in funerals; it is feared that they might not control their feelings and start wailing (cf. Kadrouch-Outmany 2018). Like the rules that curb female pilgrims' bodily expressions whilst carrying out the hajj rites, the restrictive measures at the *rawḍa* lest they make a scene illustrate two things. First, feeling is as much a social practice as a subjective experience. Emotional discourses construct subjectivities and organize social relations (cf. White 2007). Second, emotional discourses are part and parcel of practices of inclusion and exclusion and other operations of power (cf. Irvine 1990). In this sense, emotions work as a form of capital (Ahmed 2004, 120).[40] I would therefore argue that prohibiting women from viewing the Prophet's tomb for fear of their emotional response is the result of a tradition of differently gendered valuations of pilgrims' emotionality, a tradition that is increasingly challenged by female pilgrims who feel that they should have the same access to the Prophet's tomb as male pilgrims.

The final factor that contributes to the different emotional responses of pilgrims concerns a key focus in all three sub-projects in the hajj research project on modern articulations of the pilgrimage to Mecca: the connection between the pilgrimage experience and pilgrims' everyday lives. Our findings show how the emotions that pilgrimage performance evokes in individual pilgrims tend to trigger further feelings that relate to people and issues that accompanied

40 Rather than speaking of concepts like 'emotional cultures' (Picard 2016) or 'emotive institutions' (White 2007), Ahmed uses the term 'affective economies' to emphasize that emotions have value and 'circulate' between people.

them to Mecca in their thoughts. Such personal feelings may surface unexpectedly, for example, if a pilgrim is suddenly engulfed by grief when saying supplication prayers for a deceased parent who never had the opportunity to perform the pilgrimage themselves. Similarly, being surrounded exclusively by fellow Muslims may trigger emotions relating to ambivalent senses of belonging in European pilgrims with migrant backgrounds, as discussed in the chapter by Buitelaar and the one by Safar and Seurat. It may prompt them to reconfigure their attachments to the country of their family's origin, their country of residence, and to Mecca as a spiritual homeland. Conversely, the encounter with Muslims who are very different from themselves, and performing the pilgrimage in a different environment than their familiar lifeworld, may make pilgrims reflect on how they have been shaped by the cultural context in which they live their daily lives.

Besides making sense of emotions that surface unexpectedly, pilgrims—in addition to wanting to fulfil their religious obligation—may be motivated to go on hajj with the explicit purpose of working on their emotions. They may hope that the experience will help them come to terms with a divorce, for example, or not being able to conceive, their own mortality or the death of a relative or friend. Alternatively, visiting Mecca may relate to a felt need to 'fuel up a bit', to quote one of Caidi's research participants, for example after suffering burnout,[41] or, like Enes in Buitelaar's chapter, to turn the page and start the next phase of life with a clean slate.

5 Concluding Reflections on Mecca as a Storied Place of Attachment

Without exception, the pilgrimage accounts discussed in this volume testify to the enormous significance of Mecca as a place of attachment for Muslims, which explains the tremendous increase of pilgrim numbers as the means of transportation have improved. At the same time, however, the much-coveted journey to Mecca remains beyond the reach of many. Therefore, besides its ubiquitous presence in the form of images of the Kaʿba, Mecca features, above all, as a 'storied' place in the lives of most Muslims.[42] By focusing on personal narrative accounts of the pilgrimage experience, this book enhances our

41 Note how the desire to 'refuel', 'recharge' or 'reboost', as several of the interlocutors in my own research have reported, resonates with the 'energy grammar' that Fedele (2018) discusses for contemporary pilgrims to Chartres and Vézelay.

42 Compare Smith (2008), who discusses several case studies of powerful places 'built' with words.

understanding of how emotional attachment to Mecca is both represented and (re)generated in storytelling. Combining chapters that discuss written historical travelogues with contributions that analyse oral contemporary accounts, the book sheds light on commonalities and specificities, and on continuity and change in the rich and multi-voiced tradition of hajj storytelling that Van Leeuwen discusses more extensively in chapter one.

The approach of this book to investigate the pilgrimage to Mecca as a living tradition by adopting the perspective of narrativization entails an inquiry into two paradoxical issues. The first pertains to the endeavour to study both continuity and change in the tradition of hajj storytelling. The pilgrimage derives much of its power from the fact that it is located in the place where Islam originated. Therefore, pilgrims tend to seek and cherish experiences of continuity and authenticity first and foremost. This makes researching how narrators have accommodated the enormous changes that have occurred since the mid-nineteenth century in their pilgrimage accounts all the more interesting. For this reason, from the outset, the aim of the historical sub-project of the research project on modern articulations of the pilgrimage to Mecca was to investigate, among other things, representations of the advent of modern technology in travelogues from the latter half of the nineteenth century and early decades of the twentieth century. The chapters addressing pilgrimage accounts from this period provide ample examples of pilgrims' variegated responses. Looking back, it is difficult to understand why the original research plan had a blind spot regarding the impact of a more recent technological innovation on pilgrimage practices: the introduction of social media. The desirability of including social media as a topic of investigation became evident as soon as the empirical phase of the project started. As the chapters in this book that address the use of social media demonstrate, its affordance to create co-presence between pilgrims and those they left behind has deeply influenced the mediation of the pilgrimage experience. Indeed, one could safely argue that the smartphone has become part of the repertoire through which Mecca's sacredness is experienced.

A second paradoxical element in the project's focus on the narrative mediation of the pilgrimage concerns the recurring statement in nearly all travel accounts that words cannot convey the powerful impact of performing the pilgrimage. The claim that the pilgrimage experience is beyond representation expresses the view that sensing Mecca's sacred power is ideally an unmediated experience that requires physical presence. The purpose of the book's focus on narrativization is not to invalidate such views, but to understand how narrators and their audiences come to interpret the pilgrimage experience in terms of an unmediated encounter with the sacred.[43]

---

43 Compare Meyer (2016, 8), who argues that the current trend in anthropology to retreat

The suggested lack of mediation is also reflected in the emphasis in pilgrimage accounts on the embodied emotions prompted by the physical encounter with the sacred place. Approaching the pilgrimage to Mecca from the perspective of narrativization elucidates how such 'emotions of encounter' are articulated at the interface between collectively shared storylines relating to an Islamic moral register and those connected to other grand schemes that inform pilgrims' everyday lives. Laila El-Sayed (2016, 3) speaks of 'emotions of encounter' to refer to the feelings triggered in travellers when meeting hitherto unknown people in unfamiliar lands. In my own use of the term here, it also encompasses feelings prompted by the experience of an encounter with the sacred. More specifically, I conceive of 'emotions of encounter' in terms of the feelings that result from the various ways in which different cultural discourses and moral registers conjoin in pilgrims' making sense of their encounters in Mecca. Such emotions of encounter encourage pilgrims to reflect on the connection between the meanings of the pilgrimage for them and significant events in their life. Various chapters in the book demonstrate how the narrators of pilgrimage accounts add their own voices to existing storylines and, conversely, re-align their life stories to these storylines.[44]

The analysis of pilgrims' narratives about the emotions of encounter in this book thus points to the salience of looking beyond the sacred sites themselves in order to trace the ways in which pilgrimage mediates between various realms of pilgrims' experiences.[45] Indeed, the book's focus on narrative mediation of the pilgrimage as a sensational form sheds light on how pilgrims make sense of their experiences by navigating storylines from a multiplicity of emotional discourses and grand schemes that inform their lives. Both the contributions that analyse historical pilgrimage travelogues and those that discuss contemporary accounts document how vocabularies belonging to different cultural discourses acquire novel meanings as pilgrims translate and reiterate them in new settings.[46] Moreover, the resulting picture indicates that moral registers

into a deep ontology-driven study of the specific ways of people's engagement with spirits, gods, and supernatural entities is ultimately unproductive. Instead, she proposes an approach to religion that not only explores a religious tradition or mode of being from within, but also offers a standpoint from which to say something about it.

44 See Picard (2016, 12) and Kaell (2014), who observed similar patterns in the storytelling of tourists and Christian pilgrims to Jerusalem respectively.

45 See Coleman (2021), who discusses numerous examples from other forms of pilgrimage to make a powerful argument about the need to reflect on how pilgrimage sites, journeys, rituals, stories, and metaphors are entangled with each other and with wider aspects of people's lives.

46 See also Bender (2003, 109), who makes a similar argument about the everyday religious experiences of American volunteers who identify as spiritual.

pertaining to different ideals in pilgrim stories do not necessarily operate separately or cause fragmentation. Ideals about Muslim personhood, social mobility, and romantic love, for example, may be mixed and merged in the specific moral lessons that pilgrims draw from their pilgrimage experiences.[47]

The contributions to the volume thus demonstrate that the narrators of pilgrimage accounts are active agents who appropriate the cultural discourses available to them in order to interpret and represent the pilgrimage in their accounts in ways that help them to make sense of their place in the world and to shape their relationships with others. In this sense, the meaning-making in pilgrimage accounts resonates with Thomas Tweed's understanding of religions as 'confluences of organic-cultural flows' (Tweed 2006, 54). As Tweed argues, by designating where we are from, identifying whom we are with, and prescribing how we move across space and time, religion is about 'crossing and dwelling', about making homes and crossing boundaries (Tweed 2006, 74–79). The meaning of Mecca as a strong point of orientation and place of attachment that comes to the fore in nearly all chapters in this book demonstrate that pilgrimage—and its narrativization—can be a very apt vehicle for such crossings and dwellings.

References

Abdel Haleem, Muhammad. 2004. *The Qur'an. A new translation*. Oxford and New York: Oxford University Press.

Abu-Lughod, Lila, and Catherine Lutz. 1990. 'Introduction: Emotion, discourse, and the politics of everyday life.' In *Language and the politics of emotion*, edited by Catherine Lutz and Lila Abu-Lughod, 1–23. Cambridge and New York: Cambridge University Press.

Ackfeldt, Anders. 2012, '"Imma march' toward Ka'ba": Islam in Swedish hip-hop', *Contemporary Islam* 6 (3): 283–296.

Ahmed, Sara. 2004. 'Affective economies.' *Social text* 22 (2): 117–139.

Al-Ajarma, Kholoud. 2020. 'Mecca in Morocco. Articulations of the Muslim pilgrimage (Hajj) in Moroccan everyday life.' Unpublished PhD thesis, University of Groningen.

47 For a particularly interesting historical example of mixing and merging different moral registers, see Petersen (2017, 97–101), who discusses three hajj travelogues written by Chinese Muslim scholars in the sixteenth and seventeenth centuries. The narrators of two of these hajj accounts translated important Islamic values into cardinal principles of the Confucian philosophical tradition.

Al-Ajarma, Kholoud, and Marjo Buitelaar. 2021. 'Social media representations of the pilgrimage to Mecca. Challenging Moroccan and Dutch mainstream media frames.' *Journal of Muslims in Europe* 10: 146–167. doi:10.1163/22117954-bja10027.

al-Quāitī, Sultan. 2007. *The Holy Cities, the pilgrimage and the world of Islam; a history: From the earliest traditions till 1925 (1344H)*. Louisville: Fons Vitae.

Arjana, Sophia. 2017. *Pilgrimage in Islam. Traditional and modern practices*. London: Oneworld Publications.

Bajc, Vida. 2007. 'Creating ritual through narrative, place and performance in evangelical Protestant pilgrimage in the Holy Land.' *Mobilities* 2 (3): 395–412.

Bamberg, Michael. 2011. 'Who am I? Narration and its contribution to self and identity.' *Theory & Psychology* 21 (1): 3–24.

Bayly, Christopher. 2004. *The birth of the modern world 1780–1914; Global connections and comparisons*. Malden: Blackwell.

Bender, Courtney. 2007. 'Touching the transcendent: Rethinking religious experience in the sociological study of religion.' In *Everyday religion. Observing modern religious lives*, edited by Nance Ammerman, 201–218. Oxford and New York: Oxford University Press.

Bender, Courtney. 2003. *Heaven's kitchen. Living religion at God's Love We Deliver*, Chicago and London: The University of Chicago Press.

Bianchi, Robert. 2013. *Islamic globalization. Pilgrimage, capitalism, democracy and diplomacy*. Singapore: World Scientific Publishing.

Bianchi, Robert. 2004. *Guests of God. Pilgrimage and politics in the Islamic world*. Oxford and New York: Oxford University Press.

Bourdieu, Pierre. 1977. *Outline of a theory of practice*. Cambridge: Cambridge University Press.

Bowen, Donna Lee, Alexia Green, and Christiaan James. 2008. 'Globalisation, mobile phones and forbidden romance in Morocco.' *The Journal of North African Studies* 13 (2): 227–241.

Buitelaar, Marjo. 2021. 'Stepping in the footsteps of Hajar to bring home the hajj; dialogical positioning in Asra Nomani's memoir *Standing Alone*.' In *Muslim women's pilgrimage to Mecca and beyond. Reconfiguring gender, religion and mobility*, edited by Marjo Buitelaar, Manja Stephan-Emmrich, and Viola Thimm, 180–199. London and New York: Routledge.

Buitelaar, Marjo. 2020. 'Rearticulating the conventions of hajj storytelling: Second generation Moroccan-Dutch female pilgrims' multi-voiced narratives about the pilgrimage to Mecca.' *Religions* 11 (7). doi:10.3390/rel11070373.

Buitelaar, Marjo. 2018. 'Moved by Mecca. The meanings of the hajj for present-day Dutch Muslims.' In *Muslim Pilgrimage in Europe*, edited by Ingvild Flaskerud and Richard Natvig, 29–42. London and New York: Routledge.

Buitelaar, Marjo. 2015. 'The hajj and the anthropological study of pilgrimage.' In *Hajj.*

Global interactions through pilgrimage, edited by Luitgard Mols and Marjo Buitelaar, 9–25. Leiden: Sidestone Press.

Buitelaar, Marjo, Manja Stephan-Emmrich and Viola Thimm. 2021. 'Introduction. Muslim pilgrimage through the lens of women's new mobilities.' In *Muslim women's pilgrimage to Mecca and beyond. Reconfiguring gender, religion and mobility*, edited by Marjo Buitelaar, Manja Stephan-Emmrich, and Viola Thimm, 1–18. London and New York: Routledge.

Buitelaar, Marjo, Manja Stephan-Emmrich and Viola Thimm. 2021. *Muslim women's pilgrimage to Mecca and beyond. Reconfiguring gender, religion and mobility*. London and New York: Routledge.

Caidi, Nadia, Susan Beazley, and Laia Marquez Colomer. 2018. 'Holy selfies: Performing pilgrimage in the age of social media.' *The International journal of information, diversity & inclusion* 2 (1/2): 8–31.

Chenganakkattil, Muhamed Riyaz. 2017. 'Unnaturalness of Hajj narratives: We-narrative and narrating performative collective subjectivity', *Performing Islam* 6(2): 155–171. doi: 10.1386/pi.6.2.155_1

Chiffoleau, Sylvia. 2013. *Le voyage à la Mecque. Un pèlerinage mondial en terre d'Islam*. Paris: Belin.

Coleman, Simon. forthcoming in 2021. *Powers of pilgrimage. Religion in a world of movement*. New York: New York University Press.

Coleman, Simon, and John Eade. 2004. 'Introduction: Re-framing pilgrimage.' In *Reframing pilgrimage: Cultures in motion*, edited by Simon Coleman and John Eade, 1–26. London: Routledge.

Coleman, Simon, and John Elsner. 2003. 'Pilgrim voices: Authoring Christian pilgrimage.' In *Pilgrim voices. Narrative and authorship in Christian pilgrimage*, edited by Simon Coleman and John Elsner, 1–16. New York and Oxford: Berghahn Books.

Coleman, Simon, and John Elsner. 1995. *Pilgrimage past and present in the world religions*. Cambridge, MA: Harvard University Press.

Deeb, Laura. 2006. *An enchanted modern. Gender and public piety in Shi'i Lebanon*. Princeton: Princeton University Press.

Deeb, Laura, and Mona Harb. 2013. *Leisurely Islam. Negotiating geography and morality in Shi'ite South Beirut*. Princeton and Oxford: Princeton University Press.

Delaney, Carol. 1990. 'The Hajj: Sacred and secular,' *American ethnologist* 17 (3): 513–530.

El Moudden, Aberrahmane. 1990. 'The ambivalence of *rihla*: Community integration and self-definition in Moroccan travel accounts, 1300–1800.' In *Muslim Travellers. Pilgrimage, migration, and the religious imagination*, edited by Dale Eickelman and James Piscatori, 69–84. London: Routledge.

El-Sayed, Laila Hashem Abdel-Rahman. 2016. 'Discourses on emotions: Communities, styles, and selves in early modern Mediterranean travel books: Three case studies.' PhD diss., University of Kent and Freie Universität Berlin.

Faroqhi, Suraiya. 1990. *Herrscher über Mekka; die Geschichte der Pilgerfahrt*. München: Artemis Verlag.

Fedele, Anna. 2018. 'Translating Catholic pilgrimage sites into energy grammar: Contested spiritual practices in Chartres and Vézelay.' In *Pilgrimage and political economy. Translating the sacred*, edited by Simon Coleman and John Eade, 112–135. New York and Oxford: Berghahn Books.

Fischer, Michael, and Mehdi Abedi. 1990. *Debating Muslims. Cultural dialogues in postmodernity and tradition*. Madison: The University of Wisconsin Press.

Flaskerud, Ingvild. 2018. 'Mediating pilgrimage. Pilgrimage remembered and desired in a Norwegian home community.' In *Muslim Pilgrimage in Europe*, edited by Ingvild Flaskerud and Richard Natvig, 58–69. London and New York: Routledge.

Flaskerud, Ingvild, and Richard Natvig, eds. 2018. *Muslim pilgrimage in Europe*. London and New York: Routledge.

Frey, Nancy. 1998. *Pilgrim stories. On and off the road to Santiago. Journeys along an ancient way in modern Spain*. Berkeley, Los Angeles and London: University of California Press.

Fricker, Miranda. 2007. *Epistemic injustice: Power and the ethics of knowing*. Oxford: Oxford University Press.

Gade, Anna. 2007. 'Islam.' In *The Oxford handbook of religion and emotion*, edited by John Corrigan, 35–50. Oxford: Oxford University Press.

Gellens, Sam. 1990. 'The search for knowledge in medieval Muslim societies: A comparative approach.' In *Muslim travellers. Pilgrimage, migration, and the religious imagination*, edited by Dale Eickelman and James Piscatori, 50–65. London: Routledge.

Gelvin, James, and Nile Green, eds. 2014. *Global Muslims in the age of steam and print*. Berkeley: University of California Press.

Germann Molz, Jennie. 2005. 'Guilty pleasures of the Golden Arches: Mapping McDonald's in narratives of round-the-world travel.' In *Emotional geographies*, edited by Joyce Davidson, Liz Bondi and Mick Smith, 63–76. Aldershot: Ashgate Publishing Limited.

Graiouid, Said. 2011. *Communication and everyday performance. Public space and the public sphere in Morocco*. Rabat: Publications of the Faculty of Letters and Human Sciences, Université Mohammed V.

Green, Nile. 2015. 'The hajj as its own undoing: Infrastructure and integration on the Muslim journey to Mecca.' *Past & present* 226 (1): 193–226.

Gregg, Gary. 2013. 'Religious voices and identity in the life-narratives of young adult Moroccans.' In *Religious voices in self-narratives. Making sense of life in times of transition*, edited by Marjo Buitelaar and Hetty Zock, 83–102. Berlin and Boston: De Gruyter.

Hafez, Sherine. 2011. *An Islam of her own. Reconsidering religion and secularism in women's Islamic movements*. New York: New York University Press.

Hammoudi, Abdullah. 2006. *A season in Mecca: Narrative of a pilgrimage*. Cambridge: Polity Press.

Haq, Farooq, and John Jackson. 2009. 'Spiritual journey to hajj: Australian and Pakistani experience and expectations.' *Journal of management, spirituality & religion* 6 (2): 141–156.

Hoesterey, James. 2016. *Rebranding Islam. Piety, prosperity, and a self-help guru*. Stanford, CA: Stanford University Press.

Hourani, Albert. 1970. *Arabic thought in the liberal age 1798–1939*. Oxford: Oxford University Press.

Irvine, Judith. 1990. 'Registering affect: Heteroglossia in the linguistic expression of emotion.' In *Language and the politics of emotion*, edited by Catherine Lutz and Lila Abu-Lughod, 126–161. Cambridge and New York: Cambridge University Press.

Jackson, Michael. 2006. *The politics of storytelling. Violence, transgression and intersubjectivity*. Copenhagen: Museum Tusculanum Press, University of Copenhagen.

Janmohamed, Shelina. 2016. *Generation M. Young Muslims changing the world*. London and New York: I.B. Tauris.

Jansen, Willy. 2012. 'Old routes, new journeys: Reshaping gender, nation and religion in European pilgrimage.' In *Gender, nation and religion in European pilgrimage*, edited by Willy Jansen and Catrien Notermans, 3–18. London and New York: Routledge.

Jung, Dietrich. 2011. *Orientalists, Islamists and the global public sphere; A genealogy of the modern essentialist image of Islam*. Sheffield: Equinox.

Kadrouch-Outmany, Khadija. 2018. 'Speaking of the dead: Changing funeral practices among Moroccan migrants in the Netherlands and Belgium.' In *Women and social change in North Africa: What counts as revolutionary?*, edited by Doris Gray and Nadia Sonneveld, 215–236. Cambridge: Cambridge University Press.

Kadrouch-Outmany, Khadija, and Marjo Buitelaar. 2021. 'Young Moroccan-Dutch women on hajj: Claiming female space.' In *Muslim women's pilgrimage to Mecca and beyond. Reconfiguring gender, religion and mobility*, edited by Marjo Buitelaar, Manja Stephan-Emmrich, and Viola Thimm, 36–55. London and New York: Routledge.

Kaell, Hillary. 2014. *Walking where Jesus walked: American Christians and Holy Land pilgrimage*. New York: New York University Press.

Kane, Eileen. 2015. *Russian Hajj. Empire and the pilgrimage to Mecca*. New York: Cornell University Press.

Kapinga, Laura. 2021. 'A place for religion. A geographical perspective on young Muslims' experiences, changing religious identities, and wellbeing.' Unpublished PhD thesis, University of Groningen.

Karić, Dženita. 2018. 'Online Bosniak hajj narratives.' In *Muslim pilgrimage in Europe*, edited by Ingvild Flaskerud and Richard Natvig, 58–69. London and New York: Routledge.

King, Margaret. 1981. 'Disneyland and Walt Disney world: Traditional values in futuristic form.' *The journal of popular culture* 15 (1): 116–140.

Kinnard, Jacob. 2014. *Places in motion. The fluid identities of temples, images, and pilgrims*. Oxford and New York: Oxford University Press.

Knight, Chere. 2014. *Power and paradise in Walt Disney's world*. Gainesville, FL: Florida University Press.

Knudsen, Britta Timm, and Anne Marit Waade. 2010. 'Performative authenticity in tourism and spatial experience: Rethinking the relations between travel, place and emotion.' In *Re-investing authenticity. Tourism, place and emotions*, edited by Britta Timm Knudsen and Anne Marit Waade, 1–21. Bristol, Buffalo and Toronto: Channel View Publications.

Lange, Christian 2022a. 'Introduction: The sensory history of the Islamic world', *The Senses and Society*, 17:1, 1–7, DOI: 10.1080/17458927.2021.2020603

Lange, Christian 2022b. 'Al-Jāḥiẓ on the senses: sensory moderation and Muslim synesthesia', *The Senses and Society*, 17:1, 22–36, DOI: 10.1080/17458927.2021.2020605

Larsson, Göran, and Simon Sorgenfrei. 2021. '"How is one supposed to sleep when the Kaʿba is over there?" Empirical data on Swedish Muslims performing the *Hajj*.' *Journal of Muslims in Europe* 10: 1–22. doi:10.1163/22117954-bja10036.

Lock, Charles. 2003. 'Bowing down to wood and stone: One way to be a pilgrim.' In *Pilgrim voices. Narrative and authorship in Christian pilgrimage*, edited by Simon Coleman and John Elsner, 110–132. New York and Oxford: Berghahn Books.

Lücking, Mirjam. 2017. 'Working in Mecca. How informal pilgrimage-migration from Madura, Indonesia, to Saudi Arabia challenges state sovereignty', *European Journal of East Asian Studies* 16(2):248–274.

Mahmood, Saba. 2009. 'Religious reason and secular affect: An incommensurable divide?'. *Critical inquiry* 35 (4): 836–862.

Mahmood, Saba. 2005. *The politics of piety. The Islamic revival and the feminist subject*. Princeton: Princeton University Press.

McGregor, Richard. 2010. 'Dressing the Kaʿba from Cairo. The aesthetics of pilgrimage to Mecca.' In *Religion and material culture. The matter of belief*, edited by David Morgan, 247–261. London and New York: Routledge.

McLoughlin, Seán. 2015. 'Pilgrimage, performativity, and British Muslims: Scripted and unscripted accounts of the hajj and umra.' In *Hajj. Global interactions through pilgrimage*, edited by Luitgard Mols and Marjo Buitelaar, 41–64. Leiden: Sidestone Press.

McLoughlin, Seán. 2009a. 'Holy places, contested spaces: British-Pakistani accounts of pilgrimage to Makkah and Madinah.' In *Muslims in Britain: Identities, places and landscapes*, edited by Richard Gale and Peter Hopkins, 132–149. Edinburgh: Edinburgh University Press.

McLoughlin, Seán. 2009b. 'Contesting Muslim pilgrimage: British-Pakistani identities, sacred journeys to Makkah and Madinah and the global postmodern.' In *Pakistani diasporas: Culture, conflict, and change*, edited by Virinder Kalra, 278–316. Karachi and Oxford: Oxford University Press.

McMillan, M.E. 2011. *The Meaning of Mecca. The politics of pilgrimage in early Islam.* London: Saqi Books

Mesaritou, Evgenia. 2012. 'Say a little hallo to Padre Pio: Production and consumption of space in the construction of the sacred at the shrine of Santa Maria delle Grazie.' In *Ordinary lives and grand schemes. An anthropology of everyday religion*, edited by Samuli Schielke and Liza Debevec, 98–112. New York and Oxford: Berghahn Books.

Meyer, Birgit. 2016. 'How to capture the 'wow': R.R. Marett's notion of awe and the study of religion', *Journal of the Royal Anthropological Institute* (*N.S.*) 22(1): 7–26.

Meyer, Birgit. 2012. 'Religious sensations. Media, aesthetics and the study of contemporary religion.' In *Religion, media and culture: A reader*, edited by Gordon Lynch and Jolyon Mitchell with Anna Strhan, 159–170. London: Routledge.

Meyer, Birgit. 2011. 'Mediation and immediacy: sensational forms, semiotic ideologies and the question of the medium.' *Social anthropology/Anthropologie Sociale* 19 (1): 23–39.

Mincke, Christophe. 2016. 'From mobility to its ideology: When mobility becomes an imperative.' In *The mobilities paradigm: Discourses and ideologies*, edited by Marcel Endres, Katharina Manderscheid, and Christophe Mincke, 11–33. Abingdon and New York: Routledge.

Morgan, David. 2010. 'Materiality, social analysis, and the study of religions.' In *Religion and material culture. The matter of belief*, edited by David Morgan, 55–74. London and New York: Routledge.

Morgan, Nigel, and Annette Pritchard. 2005. 'On souvenirs and metonymy. Narratives of memory, metaphor and materiality.' *Tourist studies* 5 (1): 29–53. doi:10.1177/1468797605062714.

Newcomb, Rachel. 2017. *Everyday life in global Morocco*. Bloomington: Indiana University Press.

Nomani, Asra. 2006. *Standing alone. An American woman's struggle for the soul of Islam.* New York: Harper Collins books.

Ochs, Elinor, and Lisa Capps. 1996. 'Narrating the Self.' *Annual review of anthropology* 25: 19–43.

Olson, Karen, and Lina Shopes. 1991. 'Crossing boundaries, building bridges: Doing oral history among working-class women and men.' In *Women's words: The feminist practice of oral history*, edited by Sherna Berger Gluck and Daphne Patai, 189–204. London: Routledge.

O'Meara, Simon. 2020. *The Kaʿba orientations: Readings in Islam's Ancient House*. Edinburgh: Edingburgh University Press.

Osborne, Peter. 2000. *Traveling light. Photography, travel and visual culture*. Manchester: Manchester University Press.

Peters, Francis. 1994. *The Hajj. The Muslim pilgrimage to Mecca and the Holy Places*. Princeton, NJ: Princeton University Press.

Petersen, Kristian. 2017. *Interpreting Islam in China: Pilgrimage, scripture, and language in the Han Kitab*. Oxford: Oxford University Press.

Picard, David 2016 [2012]. 'Tourism, awe and inner journeys.' In *Emotion in motion. Tourism, affect, and transformation*, edited by David Picard and Mike Robinson, 1–19. London and New York: Routledge.

Pink, Johanna. 2009. *Muslim societies in the age of mass consumption*. Cambridge: Cambridge Scholars Publishing.

Popp-Baier, Ulrike. 2021. 'Introduction: Religion, experience, and narrative.' *Religions* 12 (8): 639. doi:10.3390/rel12080639.

Rahimi, Babak, and Peyman Eshaghi. 2019. *Muslim pilgrimage in the modern world*. Chapel Hill: University of North Carolina Press.

Rashid, Hussein. 2017. 'Hajj. The pilgrimage.' In *The practice of Islam in America*, edited by Edward Curtis, 60–80. New York: New York University Press.

Richard, Yann. 1995. *Shi'ite Islam. Polity, ideology, and creed*. Oxford and Cambridge: Blackwell Publishers.

Ryad, Umar. 2017. *The hajj and Europe in the age of empire*. Leiden and Boston: Brill.

Ritzer, George. 1993. *The McDonaldization of society*. Thousand Oaks, CA: Pine Forge Press.

Sabry, Tarik. 2010. *Cultural encounters in the Arab World. On media, the modern and the everyday*. London: I.B. Tauris.

Saghi, Omar. 2010. *Paris—La Meque. Sociologie du pèlerinage*. Paris: Presses Universitaires de France.

Schielke, Samuli. 2020. *Migrant dreams. Egyptian workers in the Gulf States*. Cairo: American University of Cairo Press.

Schielke, Samuli. 2015. *Egypt in the future tense: Hope, frustration, and ambivalence before and after 2011*. Bloomington and Indianapolis: Indiana University Press.

Schielke, Samuli. 2012. 'Capitalist ethics and the spirit of Islamization in Egypt.' In *Ordinary lives and grand schemes. An anthropology of everyday religion*, edited by Samuli Schielke and Liza Debevec, 131–145. Oxford: Berghahn.

Shirazi, Faegheh. 2016. *Brand Islam. The marketing and commodification of piety*. Austin: University of Texas Press.

Shotter, John, and Michael Billig. 1998. 'A Bakhtinian psychology: From out of the heads of individuals and into the dialogues between them.' In *Bakhtin and the human sciences. No last words*, edited by Bell Michael Mayerfeld and Michael Gardiner, 13–33. London: Sage.

Slight, John. 2014. 'British imperial rule and the hajj.' In *Islam and the European Empires*, edited by David Motadel, 53–72. Oxford and New York: Oxford University Press.

Smith, Martyn. 2008. *Religion, culture and sacred space*. New York: Palgrave Macmillan.
Starrett, Gregory. 1998. *Putting Islam to work. Education, politics, and religious transformation in Egypt*. Berkeley: University of California Press.
Stausberg, Michael. 2011. *Religion and tourism. Crossroads, destinations and encounters*. London: Routledge.
Stock, Femke. 2017. *Home and migrant identity in dialogical life stories of Moroccan and Turkish Dutch*. Leiden and Boston: Brill.
Stratkötter, Rita. 1991. *Von Kairo nach Mekka; Sozial- und Wirtschaftsgeschichte der Pilgerfahrt nach den Berichten des Ibrâhîm Rif'at Bâsâ: Mir'ât al-Haramain*. Berlin: Klaus Schwarz Verlag.
Tagliacozzo, Eric. 2014. 'The Dutch empire and the hajj.' In *Islam and the European empires*, edited by David Motadel, 73–89. Oxford and New York: Oxford University Press.
Tagliacozzo, Eric. 2013. *The longest journey. Southeast Asians and the pilgrimage to Mecca*. Oxford and New York: Oxford University Press.
Tagliacozzo, Eric, and Shawkat Toorawa. 2016. *The Hajj. Pilgrimage in Islam*. Cambridge: Cambridge University Press.
Thimm, Viola. 2021. 'Under male supervision? Nationality, age and Islamic belief as basis for Muslim women's pilgrimage.' In *Muslim women's pilgrimage to Mecca and beyond. Reconfiguring gender, religion and mobility*, edited by Marjo Buitelaar, Manja Stephan-Emmrich, and Viola Thimm, 19–35. London and New York: Routledge.
Timothy, Dallan, and Daniel Olsen, eds. 2006. *Tourism, religion and spiritual journeys*. London: Routledge.
Toguslu, Erkan. 2017. 'The Meaning of Pilgrimage (Hajj): Re-shaping the pious identity of Belgian Turkish Muslims', *Islam and Christian-Muslim Relations*, 28(1): 19–32, DOI:10.1080/09596410.2017.1282721
Tweed, Thomas. 2006. *Crossing and Dwelling: A Theory of Religion*. Cambridge, MA: Harvard University Press.
Urry, John. 2005. 'The place of emotions within place.' In *Emotional geographies*, edited by Joyce Davidson, Liz Bondi, and Mick Smith, 77–83. Aldershot: Ashgate Publishing Limited.
van de Port, Mattijs, and Birgit Meyer. 2018. 'Introduction: Heritage dynamics politics of authentication, aesthetics of persuasion and the cultural production of the real.' In *Sense and essence. Heritage and the cultural production of the real*, edited by Birgit Meyer and Mattijs van de Port, 1–39. New York and Oxford: Berghahn Books.
van Leeuwen, Richard. 2015. 'Islamic reformism and pilgrimage: The hajj of Rashid Rida in 1916.' In *Hajj. Global interactions through pilgrimage*, edited by Luitgard Mols and Marjo Buitelaar, 83–93. Leiden: Sidestone Press.
Werbner, Pnina. 2004. 'The predicament of diaspora and millennial Islam: Reflections on September 11, 2001.' *Ethnicities* 4 (4): 119–133.

White, Geoffrey. 2007. 'Emotive Institutions.' In *A companion to psychological anthropology. Modernity and psychocultural change*, edited by Conerly Casey and Robert Edgerton, 241–254. Hoboken, NJ: John Wiley and Sons.

Whittaker, Elvi. 2012. 'Seeking the existential moment.' In *Emotion in motion. Tourism, affect and transformation*, edited by David Picard and Mike Robinson, 73–84. London and New York: Routledge.

Witkam, Jan Just. 2007, 'The battle of images: Mecca vs. Medina in the iconography of the manuscripts of al-Jazūlī's Dalā'il al-Khayrāt,' in *Theoretical Approaches to the Transmission and Edition of Oriental Manuscripts: Proceedings of a Symposium Held in Istanbul March 28–30, 2001*, edited by Judith Pfeiffer and Manfred Kropp, 67–82, 295– 300. Würzburg: Ergon Verlag.

Zigon, Jarrett. 2009. 'Within a range of possibilities: Morality and ethics in social life.' *Ethnos* 74 (2): 251–276.

Zock, Hetty. 2013. Religious voices in the dialogical self: Towards a conceptual-analytical framework on the basis of Hubert Hermans's Dialogical Self Theory. In *Religious voices in self-narratives. Making sense of life in times of transition*, edited by Marjo Buitelaar and Hetty Zock, 11–35. Berlin and Boston: De Gruyter.

PART 1

Historical Accounts

CHAPTER 1

Hajj Narratives as a Discursive Tradition

Richard van Leeuwen

The presupposition connecting the chapters in this volume is that both modern and pre-modern accounts of the hajj, transmitted in both written and oral form, should be seen as narratives that are governed by similar conventions.[1] Hajj accounts are—at least to a certain extent—structured and formally coherent; they are constructed in a situation of dialogue, with a presupposed audience, either readers or listeners; and, they are partly governed by social and discursive contexts, which influence the subjects highlighted by the narrator, including references to real circumstances and events, the framing of experiences, and the interpretation of the hajj as a meaningful, even symbolic, undertaking. The notion of narratives implies that experiences are by definition mediated by social conventions and by discursive traditions, which endows them with a coherent set of meanings. Of course, there are significant differences between written and orally transmitted narratives, for instance with regard to the availability of the account over time and the setting of the dialogic process involving diverse audiences. However, it can be argued that these differences are mainly related to the process of transmission and the media involved in them. Presumably, the conventions governing the process of narration and the discursive fields in which hajj accounts are embedded ensure a substantial overlap between early and modern accounts and between written and oral accounts.[2]

The suggestion that hajj accounts are part of a discursive field that is governed by conventions that partly define their form, content, and interpretation presupposes that both pre-modern and modern accounts are part of an identifiable and more or less coherent tradition. It also implies that this tradition of hajj accounts is not stagnant or based on imitation only. Instead, this volume suggests that the tradition is dynamic, able to adapt to new circumstances and outlooks, and able to incorporate influences that redefine its boundaries and

1 This chapter is based on an analysis of a large corpus of hajj travelogues from between the twelfth century and 1950, which is part of the project 'Modern articulations of the pilgrimage to Mecca' funded by NWO. A monograph about the same subject is in the course of preparation.

2 For a discussion of the cultural and narratological aspects of travelogues, see: Nünning, Nünning and Neumann 2010; and Gymnich, Nünning and Nünning 2008.

© RICHARD VAN LEEUWEN, 2023 | DOI:10.1163/9789004513174_003

conventions, including introducing new formats and mechanisms of transmission. With regard to hajj accounts, this dynamic element is secured by the component of the journey, which obliges the author to integrate references to a real environment and to a presumably authentic personal experience. Even if conventions are strong, the element of travel imposes a form of contingency upon the text, necessarily adding a referential strategy to the poetics of the tradition. This experiential component represents one of the key conventions of the tradition and is often the main incentive to talk or write about the hajj.

In this chapter, I briefly outline the main characteristics of the hajj account tradition as it developed over the course of several centuries. The chapter begins with the first examples from the twelfth to fourteenth centuries via the period of 'consolidation' in the seventeenth century and ends with the modern trends between 1850 and 1950. As the observations above indicate, it will be argued that both pre-modern and modern accounts can be seen as belonging to a single, dynamic, and coherent tradition, and that, as far as conveying the personal experience of the hajj is concerned, there is no essential rupture separating a 'traditional' category from a 'modern' category, nor written from oral accounts. All these forms are governed by a shared set of discursive and narrative conventions. These conventions can be analytically divided into two frameworks that help determine how the accounts are anchored and stabilized in a clearly distinguishable discursive tradition along with specific elements that allow for their flexibility and their links to a contingent and changing reality. In this chapter, I identify these two frameworks as references to religious discourse on the one hand, and the notion of the 'journey' as a mediated experience on the other hand.

1 The Religious Framework

One of the core obligations of Islam, the *ʿibādāt*, the practice and perception of the hajj, is rooted in the corpus of religious texts. These evidently include the Qurʾan, in which several verses can be found defining the hajj as a religious obligation, and a number of hadiths, which illustrate its practice by transmitting the acts and sayings of the Prophet with regard to the hajj and establishing these as binding examples. The references to the hajj in these authoritative sources situate the doctrine at the heart of the Islamic faith. The hajj is usually thought to be moulded after the example of the Prophet's 'farewell hajj', one year before his death, but a careful analysis of the relevant sources shows that it took some time before a consensus was reached about the proper procedures and the various rituals. It was only under the Umayyad Caliph ʿAbd al-Mālik (r.

646–705) that the form of the hajj as it is known today was established. From then on, the procedures remained remarkably stable, as it became connected to both the notion of orthodoxy and to the era of the Prophet as a source of piety and paradigms (Munt 2013).

The references to the Prophet and the early history of Islam inculcate the hajj with strong historical connotations. For pilgrims, a journey to the Holy Places of Mecca and Medina is first of all a visit to the places where the Prophet received his revelations, where his life unfolded, where his presence can still be felt, and where the great events of the early Muslim community occurred. This historical sensation is projected onto the Holy Places as a sacrosanct domain (Ḥaram), the buildings which embody Islamic history, and, of course, the Kaʿba, the symbolic centre of the Islamic universe, where God's proximity can be experienced. There is hardly any hajj account, pre-modern or modern that does not refer to this historical dimension emanating from the spatial setting of the pilgrimage. It is conceptualized in the notion of '*shawq*', or 'longing', that is, the desire to visit the 'House of God' and the grave of the Prophet. This desire is cultivated in a specific genre of texts (*tashwīq*) aiming to incite the believers to go on hajj, mainly consisting of compilations of Qurʾanic verses, hadiths, and religious-historical sources proving the merits (*faḍāʾil*) of the Holy Places (Munt 2014; Peters 1994a; 1994b; Casewit 1991).

A second field in which the religious significance of the hajj was anchored was the tradition of legal scholarship and the practice of juridical argumentation (*fiqh*) to uncover the requirements of the sharia, the God-given legal precepts. From an early age, all handbooks of legal rules contained a separate chapter on the hajj and many separate compendia were compiled summarizing the rituals and regulations (*manāsik*) of the pilgrimage. These compendia served as guides for (aspiring) pilgrims and were often kept at hand to be consulted during the rites, so as not to deviate from the proper procedures and render the pilgrimage invalid as a fulfilment of the religious obligation. The *manāsik* include the rules for both the obligatory hajj, which every Muslim should perform once in his life, if he is capable of doing so, and which takes place during fixed days on the Islamic calendar, and also for the *ʿumra*, the shortened pilgrimage, which is not obligatory and which can be performed throughout the year.

The main components of the pilgrimage treated in the *manāsik* manuals are, first, the conditions for embarking upon the journey, such as the ability of the pilgrim to travel without endangering his life and goods and without leaving his family in destitute circumstances; second, the types of hajj that can be performed: the *ʿumra* and hajj combined without interruption (*qirān*); the hajj without the *ʿumra* (but including the *ṭawāf* of arrival and the *saʿy*, see below) or preceding it (*ifrād*); the *ʿumra* and hajj with an interruption (*tamattuʿ*); third, the regulations concerning the actual rites of the hajj, including the taking on of the state of consecration (*iḥrām*) by declaring the intention (*niyya*) just before entering the *ḥaram* area, donning two unstitched garments (for men; for women the only rule is that their face may not be covered), and accepting the restrictions of the state of consecration; the circumambulation of the Kaʿba seven times (*ṭawāf*); running between al-Ṣafā and al-Marwa seven times (*saʿy*); the congregation, or 'standing', on the plain of ʿArafa on the ninth day of the month *dhū al-ḥijja*, which is the main collective ceremony of the hajj (*wuqūf* or *waqfa*); the stoning of three pillars representing the devil (*ramy*); the shaving of the head and ending the state of *iḥram*. Other recommended rites include the *ṭawāf al-ifāḍa* after the *wuqūf*, the sacrifice of animals (ʿĪd al-aḍḥā), and the farewell *ṭawāf* after which many pilgrims continue their journey to Medina to visit the tomb of Muhammad, which is called the *ziyāra* and is not officially part of the hajj.[3]

The doctrine and regulations of the hajj were developed by legal scholars over time within the four legal schools (*madhhab*s). A consensus formed about the main components, or 'pillars' (*arkān*), of the hajj, but differences remained regarding the assessment of other components, which are categorized by some scholars as 'mandatory' (*wājib*) and by others only 'custom' (*sunna*, in its general sense), while others state they are simply 'recommended' (*mandūb*). As can be expected, the *manāsik* are an integral part of the majority of hajj accounts. Sometimes complete compendia of the *manāsik* are inserted; sometimes the proper procedures are illustrated by the account of the narrator following the procedures; and, sometimes the regulations are discussed by the author with references to legal authorities. Sometimes authors refer to legal opinions, or *fatwā*, but in general, perhaps remarkably, *fatwā* collections contain very few issues relating to the hajj. Shiʿis have their own *manāsik*, which differ in the time-schedule and some devotional acts (Arjana 2017, 65ff.). Of course, the excursions into law inserted in hajj accounts are meant, first, to ascertain that the author's hajj is legally valid and accepted by God (*mabrūr*); second, as a guidance for future pilgrims; and, third, to represent, or construct, the religiosity and erudition of the author, reinforcing his credentials and reputation as a scholar and a pious believer. In modern hajj accounts, the legal component is often less prominent than before, but the framework of legal prescriptions is always referred to.

3 For recent general descriptions of the ceremonies, rules, and cultural aspects of the hajj, see: Buitelaar, Stephan-Emmrich and Thimm 2021; Arjana 2017; Tagliacozzo and Toorawa 2016; Mols and Buitelaar 2015; Porter and Saif 2013; Porter 2012; Peters 1994a; 1994b.

The rites of the hajj are not only discussed in the legal tradition, as a set of obligations, prescriptions, and conditions founded on the traditional methodologies and practices of Islamic jurisprudence. They are also considered as symbolic acts in the sense that they are based on specific 'wisdom' (*ḥikma*). This field of hajj discourse is connected with the domain of spirituality, and is explored most elaborately, but not exclusively, within Sufi thought. The hajj as an undertaking is generally symbolically imagined as a re-enactment of the believers death and journey to the hereafter. The pilgrims prepare themselves as if they are departing for their last journey; the *iḥrām* outfit of male pilgrims is usually compared to a shroud; and, the collective ceremony at ʿArafa is topically associated with the Last Judgement, when all believers together stand before God, but are individually responsible for their sins. After the completion of the obligatory rites, the pilgrims are cleansed of their sins 'as when their mother bore them,' according to a hadith (al-Ghazālī 2001, 116). Some of the rites have a plainer meaning, such as the *saʿy*, exhibiting the physical fitness of the Muslim community, while others have a mere allegorical meaning, such as the stoning of the pillars representing the devil, which, indirectly, symbolizes the purification of sins and the intention to denounce evil.[4]

Some ritual acts contain references to Mecca's legendary history. The *saʿy* and the drinking of water from the Zamzam well in the Grand Mosque, for instance, are associated with Hājar, who was banished to the desert by Ibrāhīm and feverously ran to and fro to find water for her son Ismāʿīl. The water is still associated with various magical attributes. Other acts contain mainly symbolic and spiritual connotations, such as the *ṭawāf* around the Kaʿba, which is imagined as the respectful approach to a royal palace, or the kissing of the Black Stone, which is not only a stone that descended from paradise, but also, symbolically represents the right hand of God—kissing it symbolizes the renewal of the covenant with God. In the Sufi tradition, these symbolic interpretations are developed as *ishāra* (allusive meaning; symbol), or *majāz* (metaphor), and are set in the general framework of a mystical cosmography or of trajectories on the Sufi path. In general, the significance of performing the rites is primarily to show total obedience to God (Peters 1994a; 1994b).

Both the pilgrimage's legal obligation and the long-felt desire for the Holy Places in the form of *shawq* are often mentioned in hajj travelogues as incentives to embark on the journey to the Hijaz. The notion of *shawq* introduces the emotional and experiential element into the very core of the hajj as a religious

4 For an overview of the 'meanings' of the hajj, see: al-Ghazālī 1983, 83–120; in the bibliography the Arabic texts and French and English translations are mentioned.

undertaking. It is a source of spirituality and the component that connects experience with the discursive referentiality of the accounts. It explains why, for instance, the Prophet's tomb in Medina is such a significant destination for pilgrims, although it is not officially part of the hajj obligations. It explains emotional responses at the first sight of the Kaʿba or the green dome of the Prophet's Mosque. It explains why travelogues often emphasize the physical hardships of the arduous journey to the Hijaz, or of the exhausting rituals in the blazing Arabian sun, or the illnesses and dangers to which the pilgrims are exposed during their journey. In this sense, it is associated with other tropes that indicate emotional and mental states during the hajj and that recur in hajj accounts, such as *khuḍūʿ* (humility), *khushūʿ* (humility), *rahba* (awe), and *ṣabr* (patience). In combination with legal precepts and awareness of the *ḥikma* of the rituals, this emotional spirituality connected the pilgrimage with everyday religiosity and determined its significance for the conduct and piety of the believers.

The spiritual connotations of the Holy Places and of specific sites fostered the incorporation of the hajj into wider patterns of pilgrimage and ritual practices. Pilgrimage to regional and local shrines of pious saints were part of everyday religiosity throughout the Muslim world. These visits (*ziyāra*) were a source of *baraka* (blessing) and an opportunity to ask the deceased saints for 'intercession' (*tawassul*) before God to obtain prosperity on earth and bliss in the hereafter (Arjana 2017, 5–16). These practices became widespread at the holy sites in the Hijaz as well, mainly because of the historical symbolism of the places and the belief that the Prophet was still alive in his grave. During the journey, pilgrims visited shrines and graves of pious saints, and in some places, such as the Dome of the Rock in Jerusalem and many saints' tombs in Africa and Asia, the hajj rites were enacted during the days of the hajj as a kind of pseudo-hajj to profit from its merits. These ideas and practices were condemned by some orthodox scholars, such as the reformer Ibn Taymiyya (1263), who restricted pilgrimage rites to the time and place of the hajj and rejected the notion of *tawassul* (Memon 1976).

The rich textual tradition which underlies the concept, doctrine, and practice of the hajj serves as a solid referential framework for hajj narratives. In virtually all travelogues, this religious framework is carefully and conscientiously constructed, in order to link them to the large and hierarchically organized tradition of religious discourse. The intention to go on hajj, including the various events and the spiritual experiences that are connected with specific Qurʾanic verses and hadiths, thereby defines the religious dimension of the text and the journey. During the journey, references to religious discourse may resurface from time to time in the form of quotations from the holy texts or from theological or historical sources, discussions of legal issues, the purchase of religious books, encounters with holy figures or scholars, visits to shrines and sacred places, summaries of the *manāsik*, etc. Often prayers or meditations are inserted, sometimes referring to the famous devotional work *Dalāʾil al-khayrāt*, by the Moroccan Sufi al-Jazūlī (1404–1465), which pilgrims were recommended to read during the pilgrimage. Evidently, the religious dimension of the narrative culminates in the actual hajj, both as a discursive element and as an experience. It is the hajj as a religious concept and an experience that structures the narrative as a 'signifier' and imbues all components with a religious value within specific cluster of meanings and symbols. It represents a stabilizing framework that determines the way in which the text should be interpreted and, to a certain extent, the main criterion to situate the hajj travelogue as a genre within the religious discursive tradition.

Still, the ways in which the religious framework is integrated in hajj narratives are diverse. Some authors emphasize specific aspects that are neglected by others. This diversity is strengthened by the secular components of the narratives, which are connected to the experiential impact of the journey through the perspective of individual authors. As we will see, the boundaries and coherence defined by the 'objective' framework of religious discourse are often subverted by the contingent influences of the actual journey.

2 Framing the Hajj as a Journey

Apart from any religious intentions, the hajj is a physical journey, with all the vicissitudes this implies. Within the Islamic textual tradition, the travelogue is categorized by the concept of *riḥla*, which is not precisely defined as a literary form, nor well-researched as a genre.[5] Here I will not attempt to present a generic definition of *riḥla*, but rather concentrate on the specific category of hajj accounts. This is partly justified by the consideration that most travelogues written by Muslims across time either were hajj accounts or at least contained a hajj episode. After all, the hajj was one of the few reasons the Prophet gave for travelling, next to education and the necessity to gain a livelihood. With its tendency to give extensive instructions with regard to the moral aspects of life, the Muslim tradition also produced an elaborate code of conduct for travel, covering the permitted reasons for travelling, auspicious days for departure, pious formulas, verses and prayers, luggage, and other practical matters, both for pilgrims and secular travellers. These instructions are often included in hajj

5 A study of the formal aspects of the hajj travelogue is al-Samaany 2000.

travelogues, not only to strengthen the religious layer in the text, but also as a way to contain the unpredictability of the journey by providing a detailed set of practical and moral instructions. Some of these are specifically related to the hajj and integrate the religious framework into the practical layer of the journey. After all, a journey, and especially a pilgrimage journey, is not a morally neutral, physical undertaking; it is also a journey through a 'sacred' landscape that contains and reveals the wonders of God's creation, and in which all kinds of religious references are hidden or exposed. It is the interaction between the vicissitudes of physical travel and the religious purport of the journey through which the experiential component of the narrative is negotiated, as an account of a personal experience embedded in a religious discourse of signification. The ultimate aim of the journey through space was to come closer to God in the spiritual sense (Eickelman and Piscatori 1990).

The tradition of travel literature in Islam is often traced back to the famous works of Ibn Jubayr (1145–1217) and Ibn Baṭṭūṭa (1304–1369). However, as has been remarked by others, these texts are perhaps too diverse to serve as the starting point for a definition of a coherent generic type. Whereas Ibn Jubayr's book is a straightforward hajj account, complemented with a brief journey to Syria and Iraq (Ibn Jubayr 2001; 1400/1980), Ibn Baṭṭūṭa's travelogue is best understood as a partial autobiography, which contains an important hajj episode, but which is concerned much more with the author's peregrinations through Asia (Ibn Baṭṭūṭa 1958–2000). Furthermore, whereas Ibn Jubayr's text is a well-balanced, well-structured, compact, and stylized narrative, Ibn Baṭṭūṭa's *Riḥla* is much more varied and filled with digressions, anecdotes, quotations, historical excursions, etc. (Netton 1996; 1993). From about the same period, we also have the less famous texts of al-ʿAbdarī (1289) and Ibn al-Ṣabāḥ (late fourteenth century). The former is a hajj travelogue from Morocco, which is less literary and more fragmentary than Ibn Jubayr's (al-ʿAbdarī 1968), while the latter, from Andalusia, is a more coherent account of an Ibn Baṭṭūṭa-like peregrination, although it is primarily a pilgrimage account (Ibn al-Ṣabāḥ 2008). Although these four texts certainly have many features in common, it is not evident that these are sufficient to categorize them as belonging to the same generic corpus, unless it is conceded that a certain measure of diversity is part of the definition. And to what extent can the hajj be seen as the element bringing coherence in the corpus?

If we look at the corpus of hajj travelogues in the pre-modern and early modern periods, roughly between the twelfth century and 1800, we find that diversity is an important and persistent quality of the texts, and further that it took some time before the corpus crystallized into a more or less coherent generic type. The diversity is, first of all, brought about by the intentions of each author. Ibn Baṭṭūṭa and Ibn al-Ṣabāḥ were primarily 'globetrotters', who were not irreligious, quite on the contrary, but whose intentions were first and foremost to explore the world and perhaps find a living elsewhere. Ibn Jubayr and al-ʿAbdarī, in contrast, were deliberately pursuing a religious aim—the pilgrimage. Apart from these two categories, there is another type of travelogue, also from the Maghrib, which can be characterized as 'literary' journeys, because, although their ultimate destination was Mecca, they were primarily focused on encounters with literati and scholars during the journey. An example is the travelogue by the Andalusian scholar al-Tujaybī, which dates back to the end of the thirteenth century (al-Tujaybī 1395/1975). These very diverse texts were connected by the 'event' and 'trope' of the hajj, but their intentions and formal structures as narratives are quite different. Still, together they exemplify the diverse elements that came to belong to the generic conventions of hajj travelogues, in all its diversity.

Apart from the intentions of the authors, most texts are also diverse with regard to their narrative strategies, structure, and form. The basic format of the travelogue is the journal, which is either divided temporally, from day to day, or spatially, from one town to the next. Al-ʿAbdarī, for instance, who travelled by caravan through North Africa, carefully registers the stages of his itinerary, the places where water can be found, the quality of the water, the kinds of landscapes, places to buy food, weather conditions, etc., as a guide for future pilgrims. In this way, several routes through the desert were documented, so pilgrims could prepare themselves for the difficult journey. The Syrian scholar, Sufi, and poet ʿAbd al-Ghanī al-Nābulusī's travelogue (1693) is systematically constructed as a day-to-day diary with a fixed formula opening the entry for each day. This structural layer of the text is a strong mechanism of referentiality, as a spatio-temporal framework that is directly related to the experience of the travellers and their interaction with their environment. This spatio-temporal structure is even more important because it is connected with the spatio-temporal schema of the hajj, which, of course, is situated in a very specific time and place (al-Nābulusī 1410/1989; Sirriyeh 1985).

The referential framework of the journey functions as a container for various kinds of inserted references to a vast reservoir of textual sources. I have already mentioned intertextual references to religious texts, legal handbooks, and theological and spiritual speculations, which link the narrative to the discursive environment of the religious tradition. As we have seen, sometimes complete compendia of *manāsik* were incorporated at a certain point into the spatio-temporal framework. Other inserted digressions, usually indicated as *fāʾida* (interesting note), *masʾala* (issue), *gharība* (strange anecdote), *laṭīfa* (nice anecdote), *faṣl* (chapter), etc., are concerned with all kinds of literary or scholarly curiosa, and are either comments or advice by the authors themselves or quotations or fragments taken from other works, such as histories, geographical handbooks, literature, biographical handbooks, other travelogues, etc. These intermezzos may be related to specific places where the author passes by, or to persons or events encountered on the way. Some authors make more use of this narrative strategy than others, but in general we can say that travelogues are, as a rule, constructed as collages of text fragments within the framework of the journal.

This strategy not only secures the narrative's integration into other discursive traditions, such as religion, history, and geography, but also characterizes it as 'literature', or *adab*, a term used to define literary refinement and erudition, which covers a wide range of texts and allows for a great internal diversity. By associating himself with this tradition, the author displays his piety, erudition, good taste, and literary versatility. Therefore, it is no coincidence that poetry is an important component in the corpus of hajj travelogues. There are many examples of hajj accounts in verse, particularly within the Persian and Turkish traditions, and, often, travelogues contain poetry either written by the author himself or quoted by him from other sources. The poems may not only prove the author's proficiency, but also illustrate his personal sentiments and meditations, as an aesthetic response to his environment. An interesting example of poetic interaction in a hajj travelogue is by al-Nābulusī, who often composed poems impromptu when he visited the graves of pious saints and recorded his emotional and intuitive epiphanic experiences (al-Nābulusī 1410/1989).

Whereas the inserted digressions usually refer to contingent discourses, the spatio-temporal framework firmly connects the narrative with the personal experiences of the author, which, after all, occur in a physical and material setting. This setting consists of physical and geographical conditions, but also of political circumstances, such as territorial boundaries, taxes, travel restrictions, oppression, warfare, rebellions, administrative measures, and general (in)security. Although references to political issues are often not systematic or elaborate, they are part of the referential framework of the journey, as a highly influential category of forces. Pilgrims needed permission to embark upon their journey or to pass through certain areas; they were often taxed and had to submit to specific administrative regulations; and, they were forced to make detours to avoid warfare, seditious regions, or aggressive nomad tribes. More generally, these circumstances represent an element of contingency and change in the corpus as a whole, since historical transformations leave their traces in the texts. Similarly, the encounter with different societies and peoples may evoke an anthropological interest resulting in observations of the customs of 'exotic' peoples, villages, and towns, which are often assessed based on religious knowledge and compliance.

Most of the references to history, geography, anthropology, or politics can be related to texts in some way or another and thereby contribute to the intertextual entanglement of the narrative. Other forms of referentiality are more exclusively related to the physical conditions of the journey, such as exhaustion, thirst, hunger, illness, accidents, heat, cold, rain, storm, fear, pain, anger, etc., and mishaps, such as being attacked and robbed by nomad tribes, brigands, and thieves. One pilgrim reports that even his clothes and the cooking pots on the fire were stolen by Bedouins on the way, while another complains about an ulcer in his foot. Travellers in a caravan through the desert are most always afraid of being attacked or of missing a water well, while travellers by sea are harassed by storms. These inconveniences are not restricted to the journey itself, but include the rites and experiences in Mecca. Many pilgrims become ill in the Holy Places and sometimes cholera causes the roads to be lined with corpses; pilgrims complain about crowdedness, particularly during both the *saʿy*, because the street is filled with sellers of vegetables, general goods, camels, and donkeys, and during the return from ʿArafa, when the pilgrims have to squeeze through a narrow passage where many fall from their camels and get killed; hygienic circumstances are insufficient and pilgrims complain about other pilgrims urinating at holy sites, cooking inside mosques, or using the graveyard as a place to graze their animals; the fighting around the Kaʿba to reach the Black Stone, resulting in casualties and endangering women, is generally condemned; and, theft and Bedouin attacks are rampant and cause casualties and property loss. In general, in most hajj narratives the experience of the rituals is euphoric, but the description is often combined with an unrestrained picture of their inconveniences, already in the earliest accounts.

Among the recurring structural components of the hajj travelogue, from an early stage onwards, is the practice of visiting scholars and literati on the way. This includes passing by specific religious sites, such as tombs of pious saints and scholars, prominent mosques, and religious institutions. We can already recognize this component in the account of al-ʿAbdarī (thirteenth century), who visits many scholars along the way to discuss religious issues, exchange texts, and report on colleagues. In general, these encounters resulted in *ijāza*s, or certificates attesting to the proficiency of a scholar in reciting and interpreting specific texts, thereby transmitting authority from one scholar to another. Some later travelogues by Maghribi authors, from the thirteenth century onwards, consist mainly of short biographies of scholars and literati with whom the authors communicated in various places during the journey, including examples of their poetry, prosopographic information, and references to their texts. It is not difficult to see that this practice, and the records which resulted from it, were conducive to the formation and preservation of scholarly and intellectual networks, in which texts circulated, forms of authority were constructed, and personal relationships were established. In al-ʿAbdarī's text we can see that these visits could result in personal friendships. In later travelogues, the encounters along the way and in the Hijaz remained a significant element, sometimes in the form of appendixes and lists along with the insertion of *ijāza* texts and their chains of transmission.

Among the inconveniences of the hajj was the inevitable intercourse with people of dubious religious credentials. Travelers through North Africa often complained about the lack of knowledge about the Qur'an or legal rules in certain villages, the impudent behaviour of women, or laxity in religious morality. Heterodoxy was even more abhorred, for instance when a caravan passed through ʿIbāḍī territory in Algeria and sometimes the hated and feared ʿIbāḍīs, an isolated heterodox sect, joined the travellers. In the Hijaz itself, it was the confrontation with Shiʿis that annoyed the Sunni majority of pilgrims. For Shiʿis, the pilgrimage to Najaf and Karbala, the holy sites in Iraq, were just as important as the hajj, and the two pilgrimages were usually combined (Arjana 2017, XXV). In Mecca, the Shiʿis, mostly Persians, were obliged to pay extraordinary taxes and were often harassed by Bedouins. They were despised because of their particular rituals and litanies, which were often more fraught with emotion than the Sunnis were accustomed to. Conversely, the Persians, who often spoke only rudimentary (or 'Qur'anic') Arabic, and who belonged to a privileged elite, looked down on the uncouth Bedouins and the unsophisticated conditions of the hajj. In this way, the hajj functioned as a touchstone of religious orthodoxy and normative behaviour and an occasion where differences in religious practice came to the surface. As a result of these encounters, in the early modern period Mecca and Medina became centres of religious debates and education, including the exchange of hadith scholarship and theological opinions, which subsequently influenced debates in the various parts of the Muslim world and strengthened a sense of orthodoxy and orthopraxis.

This brief outline suggests that it is possible to define a fairly consistent framework for identifying a coherent corpus that is governed by shared generic conventions. Hajj travelogues are internally fragmented texts with strong intertextual ramifications and organized primarily by spatio-temporal and religious frameworks; they are characterized by encounters, personal experiences, references to a combined physical and 'sacred' geography, and structured by the hajj as the main 'signifier'. It should be stressed that although this format is to a large extent shaped by narrative conventions and referentiality, hajj travelogues generally contain distinctly personal elements, both as experiences and as meditations. They can therefore be perceived as narratives in which personal forms of religiosity are constructed and conveyed by the author by combining the subjective, contingent experience of the journey with references to a solid, 'objective' framework of religious discourse, in order to negotiate a place in the broad spectrum of Muslim religiosity. Although tendencies to idealize the hajj experience can be perceived, the overall impression is that the corpus presents a genuine experience of the hajj, including its inconveniences and adversities. Significantly, over the course of time pilgrims began referring to their predecessors and incorporated often long excerpts from their accounts in their own travelogues, suggesting that the authors were conscious of being part of an ongoing tradition.

3 Periodization, Cultural Background, and Modernity

The overview presented above is mainly based on a textual approach to the hajj travelogue as a narrative form. However, as I have argued, the element of travel as a 'real', contingent experience implies that the texts are necessarily co-constructed by influences from outside the text and the historical setting in which they were conceived. We have seen that the paradigms I underscored were mainly derived from the Maghribi tradition (Andalusia and Morocco), which produced the earliest examples of hajj travelogues and which steadily developed into a coherent corpus over time (Māgāman 2014). This corpus came to maturation in the monumental work of Abdallāh al-ʿAyyāshī (1627–1679), which became a paradigm of hajj travel narratives and which contains all the elements that became part of the corpus during the previous centuries (al-ʿAyyāshī 2011). The question arises: To what extent do other traditions of hajj travelogues, from other parts of the Muslim world, fit in this paradigm, taking into their different cultural backgrounds and periodization into account?

In general, we can say that the hajj travelogues which emerged in Ottoman Syria, Persia, Central Asia, and the Indian subcontinent followed their own trajectories, which were influenced by the particular literary conventions and historical temporalities of those regions. Whereas the first Maghribi travelogues appeared from the twelfth century onwards, the Persian tradition, which included texts from Central Asia and the Indian subcontinent, dates back to the eleventh century with the hajj travelogue of Nāṣer-e Khosrow (1004–1088), a rather frugal but still personal diary, which was, however, not succeeded by other travel accounts until the mid-sixteenth century (Nasir-i Khusraw 2001). An important text within the Persian tradition was the *Futūḥ al-Ḥaramayn* by Muḥy al-Dīn al-Lārī (d. 1526), which is not a proper travelogue, but a description of the pilgrimage and the Holy Places, accompanied by drawings (Burak 2017; Milstein 2006). In the sixteenth to eighteenth centuries some interesting travel accounts were written in Persian, but the great upsurge came during Qajar rule in the nineteenth century (Kiyanrad 2020; al-Afsgar 2002; Daniel 2002; Hanaway 2002). The first travelogue in Urdu, from the Indian subcontinent, was written in the mid-nineteenth century, while the Ottoman-Turkish tradition evolved as an offshoot from the Persian tradition and was initially marked by rather factual itineraries and guidebooks. The poet Yūsuf Nābī (1642–1712) was among the first to write a personal hajj account in Ottoman Turkish in the early modern period (Çoşkun 2000; 1985). In Syria, travel literature as a literary genre began to flourish from the seventeenth century onwards and developed its own poetics. Its highlight was the aforementioned hajj travelogue written by al-Nābulusī, which gained a paradigmatic status similar to al-ʿAyyāshī's text (Elger 2003). Travelogues of pilgrims from West Africa, Malaysia, and the Indonesian archipelago were first written during the nineteenth century (al-Naqar 1972). The different temporalities of these traditions can be explained by historical circumstances, such as the combination of a sophisticated literary and scholarly culture in the pre-modern Maghrib combined with its distance from the Islamic core lands and the increased integration of the Muslim world after the emergence of the great early modern empires in the sixteenth century under the Ottoman, Safawid, and Mughal sultans.

It is beyond the scope of this chapter to discuss the peculiarities of the travelogues that were conceived within these diverse cultural and political environments. May it suffice to say that all these strands within the corpus of hajj travelogues show some remarkable similarities, such as the basic frameworks of religion and the journey along with an often-fragmented structure, enabling the author to include references and texts of various kinds. Some accounts are focused mainly on the practical component of the journey and the itinerary, as a guide for future pilgrims, while others reduce this part to a minimum, concentrating on the religious and spiritual aspects of the undertaking. The fascinating text written by the Mughal scholar and Sufi Shāh Walīallāh (1703–1762), for instance, uses the spiritual and historical symbolism of the Holy Places to report on his epiphanies and conversations with the Prophet. The aim is not only to use the connotations of the hajj to explain his spiritual philosophy, but also to present himself as an authority endorsed by the Prophet himself (Shāh Walīallāh 2007). However, this was not specific for Indian texts; another account from the Indian subcontinent, by Rafīʿ al-Dīn al-Murādābādī (1721–1788), who travelled to Mecca in 1786, shows a much more balanced composition of spiritual and practical components (al-Murādābādī 2004).

The different traditions seem to converge into a more or less coherent genre during the course of the seventeenth and eighteenth centuries, not only because of their shared referential frameworks, but also as a result of the increased interactions between the different cultural domains of the Muslim world during the advancing process of globalization. As a phenomenon transcending territorial boundaries, the hajj was particularly affected by the processes of globalization, which not only intensified encounters between Europe and the Muslim world, but also the communication and exchange between the various Muslim lands and empires. The hajj and the networks it maintained became a significant mechanism in the intricate political configurations that developed from the end of the fifteenth century onwards, and it can be argued that the hajj travelogue, as a genre practiced all over the Muslim world, was co-produced by processes of globalization, which provided the continuity between its early models and newly emerging trends.

It is my presupposition that no sharp rupture can be perceived in the development of the corpus of hajj between a 'traditional' and 'modern' period. Instead, I suggest that we should consider the changes that occurred as a development within a continuous and dynamic discursive field. The basic patterns of the hajj account, which I sketched above, remained in use during the nineteenth century and well into the twentieth century, even in its most conventional forms. Still, the circumstances in which these accounts were written underwent significant changes from the onset of the nineteenth century onwards, which also affected the form and content of hajj narratives. The invasion of Egypt by Napoleon, the rise of the alliance between the Saʿūd family and the Wahhābī reformers in the Arabian Peninsula, which resulted in their occupation of the Holy Places between 1805 and 1810, and the occupation of Algeria by the French in 1830, heralded a new era. European nations rapidly established their world-hegemony in the fields of politics, economy, and culture, and came to dominate most parts of the Muslim world in Africa and Asia through colonial rule. New routes for trade and travel were opened up, particularly after the introduction of steamships and railways, which made the need for caravans obsolete. The hajj, too, became increasingly supervised and organized by colonial governments, who attempted to control the rapidly increasing number of Muslim pilgrims from their domains (Green 2015; Gelvin and Green 2014).

The rise of European coloniality in Africa and Asia heralded the decline and eventual collapse of the Ottoman Empire during World War I, which brought the Middle East under European control and wiped away age-old administrative structures. Apart from the almost total control of travel routes by European maritime companies, the consequences for the hajj were twofold: first, due to the improved facilities for travel, the number of pilgrims rapidly increased during the nineteenth century; second, pilgrims became dependent on newly founded mechanisms of control, such as permissions for travelling, visas, transport tickets, passports, bank deposits, etc. An additional change during this time came about due to cholera epidemies in Mecca, which stemmed from the large growth of pilgrims. International conventions controlled by European powers imposed various sanitary regulations on the hajj, such as quarantines for pilgrims travelling to and from Mecca. The main facilities for quarantine were on the island Karamān near the Arabian coast, al-Ṭūr in Sinai, and Beirut, while temporary facilities were built in Yanbūʿ, on the Arabian coast, and Bombay. Obviously, these measures greatly affected the experience of pilgrims, who on the one hand profited from faster and cheaper modes of travel, but on the other hand had to suffer the restrictions imposed upon them by non-Muslims (Mishra 2011; Pearson 1996).[6]

The transformations during the nineteenth century were not confined to the practicalities of the hajj, but also involved the imposition of values, institutions, and administrative forms under European tutelage and the imposition of the European form of modernity in all fields of society. European domination was experienced as intruding and oppressive, and over the course of the nineteenth century throughout the Muslim world strategies were conceived to achieve a form of political and cultural emancipation, which aimed not only to restore the Muslims' past glory and sense of dignity, but also to cultivate new, modern vision of Muslim societies. A modern outlook on religion was thought to revitalize society and afford the Muslims their rightful place in the modern world. These strategies were directed at a re-orientation towards Muslim cultural heritage, the adoption of useful examples from European societies and culture, and the mobilization of modern ideologies of political emancipation, which could support the struggle against European colonial hegemony. These trends became particularly visible towards the end of the nineteenth and in the first half of the twentieth century, when colonial domination was experienced as a threat to cultural authenticity and the very survival of Islam more generally.

The nineteenth century programs of reform in the Muslim world, which were partly initiated before European colonial domination and partly by the subsequent colonial governments, had far-reaching consequences for Muslim social and cultural life. The traditional system of education was replaced by

6 For general historical studies of the colonial impact on the hajj, see: Chantre 2018; Chiffoleau 2015; Slight 2015; Tagliacozzo 2013; Papas et al. 2012.

new, secular curricula and institutions from which a new intellectual elite graduated well equipped to fill the new administrative positions. Printing presses were introduced all over the Muslim world, which produced new forms of communication through printed books and a wide array of periodicals, such as newspapers, popular-scientific journals, cultural and literary journals, translations, etc. These publications fostered intellectual exchanges between Europe and the Muslim world, but also between Muslim societies and contributed to the formation of what may be called a global public sphere in which social, cultural, and political matters were discussed (Jung 2011). Towards the end of the nineteenth century, these debates were dominated by a new class of intellectuals, who worked in the fields of culture and media or as officials and who developed a self-confident, modern outlook on life. They were nationalists and opposed European domination; they were deeply religious, but also modern and embraced a scientifically based, rational worldview (Ryzova 2014).

All these trends evidently affected the practice of the hajj, which, as an inherently transnational phenomenon in which religious, political, and cultural domains converged, was at the heart of the processes of globalization. Traces of these processes can be found in the corpus of hajj travelogues, not only in the practicalities of travel and the encounter with modern bureaucracies, but also in the perception of the hajj and the hajj narrative as a medium for expressing ideas, constructing identities, and stimulating debates. Moreover, whereas early modern accounts were usually compiled by religious scholars, the new facilities gave new social groups the opportunity to go on hajj and publish their experiences in books and journals. As a result, the impact of modernity is not only visible on the level of the journey, where mechanized transport replaced the camel caravans, but also in the style and structure of texts and authorial concerns. The formal aspects of the narrative were influenced by the rise of journalism, which required a simple style, a direct involvement of the reader in the events conveyed by the author, and a less fragmented structure. This new style preserved the conventional components by integrating them in a more coherent narrative, divided into thematic chapters.

As far as the perception of the hajj is concerned, the religious framework of the hajj, consisting of basic references to religious texts, the *manāsik*, and experiences of the physical and spiritual aspects of the rituals, remained mostly intact. Significantly, it became more common to philosophize about the hajj as compared to practices and rituals in other religions and to reflect upon the rituals from a modern, rational perspective. Sometimes, this resulted in thoughts about the cultural and political function of the hajj, as a symbol of Muslim unity, based on a shared past that was symbolized by the Holy Places, and as a potential framework for political debates and political activism.

Many pilgrim accounts complain about the oppressive and humiliating nature of European domination, which they directly experienced during their journey, and they present the hajj as an occasion to reconfirm their Muslim identity and dignity and to discuss resistance strategies. The travelogues increasingly reveal a confident self-image and cultural militancy that are constructed around shared connotations of the hajj. In this sense, the hajj travelogue was fully integrated in the debates about reform, modernity, and emancipation that took place throughout the Muslim world from the second half of the nineteenth century onwards, documenting the emergence of a modern Muslim worldview.

Perhaps the most paradigmatic hajj account of the nineteenth century is the monumental *al-Riḥla al-Ḥjāziyya* by the Tunisian writer, journalist, and politician Muḥammad al-Sanūsī (1851–1900). The text was written between 1883 and 1886 in three volumes, which contain his exile and journeys to Europe and Istanbul, his hajj in 1882, and his religious reflections, mainly focused on his adherence to various Sufi orders. A list of important contemporaries, with brief biographies, is added, most of whom al-Sanūsī met during his peregrinations. The account is structured according to the well-established conventions, combining a diary—covering the hajj and other journeys—, with all kinds of religious digressions and with poetry, indicating a clearly 'traditional' literary interest and taste. However, the text is permeated with reflections on modernity, politics, and transnational encounters, which are characteristic of the second half of the nineteenth century. The account shows the process of negotiation between conventional and modern elements and narrative strategies, which shows on the one hand the resilience of conventional forms, and on the other hand the capability of incorporating modern influences, in order to achieve the age-old aim of constructing an individual form of religiosity within a changing environment (al-Sanūsī 1396/1976).

The combination of religion and political activism cannot be separated from the growing influence of Wahhābism on reformist thought. In the first decades of the twentieth century, the coalition between the Saʿūd family and the Wahhābī scholars, dating back to the eighteenth century but defeated in the 1820s, was restored. ʿAbd al-ʿAzīz ibn Saʿūd embarked upon a renewed struggle against the Ottoman administrative structure of the Hijaz, represented by the age-old dynasty of Meccan Sharīfs and the Ottoman governors. During the First World War, when the Ottoman Empire collapsed, Sharīf Ḥusayn declared his independence, initially with British support, but he was defeated and expelled by ʿAbd al-ʿAzīz, who founded a new political entity that eventually became the kingdom of Saudi Arabia. ʿAbd al-ʿAzīz claimed to have founded an independent kingdom based on the sharia and Islamic values, and presented himself

FIGURE 1.1 Picture of the Mausoleum of Amir Hamza (c. 1907)
PHOTOGRAPHER: H.A. MIRZA & SONS [10R] (1/1), BRITISH LIBRARY: VISUAL ARTS, PHOTO 174/10, IN QATAR DIGITAL LIBRARY (DATE C. 1907) HTTPS://WWW.QDL.QA/ARCHIVE/81055/VDC_100023483748.0X00001F [ACCESSED 18 APRIL 2022].

as the guardian of the Holy Places in service of the Muslim community as a whole. This alleged universalism was contradicted both by the rather authoritarian regime that he installed and which consolidated his position as a local potentate (rather than an Islamic leader) and by the strict regulations introduced by the Wahhābī scholars who provided the regime with its ideological legitimacy (Mouline 2011; al-Rasheed 2002; Ochsenwald 1984).

The victory of Wahhābī reformism in the Hijaz had important consequences for the proceedings and the experience of the hajj. The strict regime succeeded in establishing more security for the pilgrims, who also profited from the abolition of certain taxes, the importation of automobiles, and the gradual improvement of health care and sanitary facilities. However, the Wahhābīs also demanded the destruction of several important historical sites in Mecca and Medina, such as the birth-house of the Prophet, the house of his wife Khadīja, several monumental graves of the Prophet's family and companions in the cemeteries of Mecca and Medina, and the mausoleum of Ḥamza, the hero of the battle of Uḥud in early Islamic history. According to the Wahhābī doctrines, referring to Ibn Taymiyya, the monuments were potential sites where humans were worshipped instead of God, and therefore were a source of *shirk* (polytheism). Moreover, the graves were places where the intercession of the deceased were sought and where prayers and ritual acts were common practice, which, according to the sharia, were prohibited as unlawful innovations (*bidʿa*). Guards were positioned at the sites to prevent pilgrims from entering or performing any kind of ritual act or displaying other kinds of devotion or veneration (Willis 2017).

In most hajj accounts after 1924, when the Saudi conquest of the Hijaz was completed, the victory of ʿAbd al-ʿAzīz is hailed as a felicitous event. The new state was the only significant independent Muslim polity, which combined religious conservatism and fundamentalism with a modern and optimistic view of the future, providing Muslims all over the world with a model of political emancipation. Still, the rigorous religious policy was criticized by most, not only because it clearly contradicted the beliefs and practices of mainstream Muslims, but also because it caused the destruction of an important part of the Muslims' historical legacy. In modern cultural and intellectual debates, historical awareness was one of the pillars of a modern self-image and cultural identity, which restored the place of Islam on the global scene. The monuments were seen as symbols commemorating the past glory of Islam and the unity of Muslims under the banner of the faith. The extremism of the Wahhābīs was mostly appreciated for its morality, gender segregation, prayer obligations, and use of corporeal punishment, but rejected as obscurantist in its intolerance towards divergent practices and opinions.

The modern corpus of hajj travelogues retains the basic structure of the conventional accounts, which were shaped by the interaction between a religious framework, referring to the discursive tradition of the hajj, and the framework of the journey as a physical undertaking. Still, the modern corpus emanates an increased globalized awareness, which links it to the historical transformations that occurred at the time and shows how authors were able to absorb new trends and influences. In the field of religion, the most important adaptations were the increasing influence of reformist thought, which, from the 1920s onwards, was dominated by the Wahhābī perspective, which, supported by the Saudis, succeeded in imposing a normative framework on the practice and concept of the hajj, and eventually, partly through the hajj, on Muslim thought and practice as a whole. A further change was the connection made between religion and politics as a counter-strategy against European dominance, which resulted in an emphasis on the secular function of the hajj and the Holy Places as a meeting place for Muslims and a potential occasion for mobilization. The function of the hajj as a mechanism for exchange and the preservation of networks changed as well: the new intellectuals were less interested in scholarship in the traditional sense, and instead preferred to visit fellow journalists and writers and the editorial offices of journals wherever they could. Political activists utilized the hajj to recruit members for their organizations and distribute pamphlets, exemplified by the Indian Salafist scholar al-Nadwī, who was a follower of al-Mawdūdī (al-Nadwī 1419/1999).

On the level of the journey, the basic form of the diary referring to a spatio-temporal setting remained, although obviously the temporal schemas changed as a result of new transport facilities, quarantine, political restrictions, etc. The practicalities of the journey were also adapted to the new circumstances: encounters with fellow pilgrims from other societies occurred on ships, in trains, and in the colonial, westernized capitals. Many pilgrims spent some time in European port towns, either voluntarily or as an inevitable stop over on their way to Mecca, and integrated their experiences into their account. Some expressed their disgust at the encroachments of non-believers into the religious prerogatives of Muslims, such as the hajj, but there were also pilgrims who praised the innovations introduced by modern technology. All these elements do not essentially differ from the conventions of the early modern hajj account, although references to history, geography, and politics become more prominent and acquired a new significance. They are not included to add information, but to incorporate a political vision into the construction of the author's self-image.

The possibilities offered by modern printing techniques strengthened specific aspects hajj account conventions. First, although providing instructions to future pilgrims had always been part of the conventions, the rise of printing technology enabled authors to develop new forms of guidebooks for pilgrims, in cheap, compact formats. During his hajj in 1916, the Egyptian reformist thinker and journalist Rashīd Riḍā distributed his brochure *Manāsik al-ḥajj* to fellow pilgrims on the boat to Jedda, while in the 1920s the Egyptian and Saudi governments together began publishing 'hajj guides', which contained not only instructions for the various rites, but also practical information about travel facilities, valuta, lodging, codes of conduct, formalities, etc. The booklets, which had the format of a tourist guide, also contained advertisements and photographs (Muẓhir 1348/1929).

A second development was the systematic insertion of photographs in hajj accounts, showing holy sites and the author in various outfits, before and after *iḥrām*. As we have seen, the tradition of adding illustrations to pilgrimage books goes back at least to the Persian example of al-Lārī in the first half of the sixteenth century. Another early example is a series of colour drawings dating from 1559 (Milstein 2001). It was particularly in the Persian tradition that illustrations of this kind, ranging from primitive images and plans of the holy sites to elaborate miniatures, were developed, mainly as a form of *tashwīq* (Marzolph 2014). In the Arabic tradition, the devotional work *Dalāʾil al-khayrāt* is famous for its images of the Holy Places, while sometimes rather primitive drawings and plans are found in nineteenth century travelogues, at times including images of steamships and trains. In the beginning of the twentieth century, it became common to add photographs to the text, which contributed to the construction of an author's modern self-image. It also became fashionable to send photographs as postcards during the hajj, which were for sale in Mecca (Murat Kargili 2014). Also during this time, an album with photographs of the Holy Places was printed in India as a modern form of *tashwīq*, that is, stimulating desire (Asani and Gavin 1998).

A remarkable development from the beginning of the twentieth century was the rapid emergence of an Egyptian corpus of travelogues, which had previously been conspicuously absent within the tradition. The sudden upsurge can be explained by noting that Egypt was, at that time, the core of political and cultural debates and that a group of intellectuals emerged who were inclined to adopt a modern lifestyle where religion played a prominent role. Moreover, after a period of conflicts, the Egyptian and Saudi governments took measures to stimulate the pilgrimage to Mecca by offering facilities, reducing prices, and issuing advertising campaigns. In the 1920s and 1930s, the Saudi king ʿAbd al-ʿAzīz invited Egyptian journalists and writers to come to the Hijaz and write about their experiences. This resulted in a diverse series of hajj accounts, ranging from ironic literary impressions and journalistic diaries to ideologically committed confessional texts. The apogee of this group of texts is *Fī manzil al-waḥy* ('In the house of revelation', 1939) by the writer, journalist, and politician Muḥammad Ḥusayn Haykal (1888–1956), who had some years before written an innovative biography of the Prophet. His text is a monumental achievement, which incorporates the tradition of the hajj account and moulds it into a modern narrative form (Gershoni 1994; Haykal 1952).

Another development which occurred in the first half of the 20th century, was the increase of hajj travelogues written by Muslims from Europe, both migrants who had settled in the European capitals and port towns, and converts for whom the pilgrimage was an essential stage in their trajectory of conversion. In the 19th century several European travellers visited Mecca and Medina during the hajj season, either disguised as a Muslim, or as converts to Islam. The most prominent example is John Lewis Burckhardt (1784–1817), the Swiss-British traveller, who participated in the hajj of 1814–1815, presumably as a converted Muslim, and who wrote a monumental anthropological work about his experiences (Burckhardt 1829/ 1993). Another interesting example is the account by the Hungarian orientalist and convert Gyula Germanus (1884–1979), who stayed in India and Egypt for some time to improve his knowledge of Islam, before proceeding to the Hijaz in 1935 to perform the hajj. His detailed travelogue is one of the landmarks of the tradition of hajj literature (Germanus s.d. [1938]). In some cases, the European pilgrims were converted in the colonies, for instance the artist Étienne Dinet (1861–1929), who lived in Algeria and travelled to Mecca in 1929, or Lady Evelyn Cobbold (1867–1963), who grew up in Muslim countries and performed the hajj in 1933 as a guest of the king, and as the first European woman (Dinet 1930; Cobbold 2009). The appearance of these travelogues marked the growing influence of globalization on the hajj, and represented a new strand in the tradition of hajj accounts, which, together with the accounts of modern European Muslims writing in European languages, straddled the traditions of European and Muslim travel literature. In the case of converts, the hajj accounts are often part of a biographical account in which the hajj was the component completing a trajectory of transition.[7]

One remark remains to be made before I proceed to the conclusion: The contribution of women to the tradition of hajj accounts is embarrassingly slight. Although we have evidence that women took part in the hajj from an early stage, accounts by women are hard to find (Fewkes 2021). In the corpus until 1950, it is only in the Persian tradition that we find travelogues written by women from the ruling elite, which provide interesting insights into the conditions of the hajj based on their personal experiences. The first of these accounts dates back to the late seventeenth century; other examples are from the late nineteenth century (Mahallati 2011; Alam and Subrahmanyam 2009, 24–44). Two well-known accounts were written by two Nawab Begums of Bhopal, in 1870 and 1913 (Jahan 2013; Sikandar 2007). In Arabic, no substantial hajj accounts by women seem to have survived in spite of the increased access for women to education and printed media from the mid-nineteenth century onwards.

4 Conclusion

This chapter is not intended as a kind of pre-history of the modern hajj, nor as a historical framework for contemporary practices and perceptions of the hajj. My argument is, rather, that contemporary narratives of the hajj, both oral and written, are part of a dynamic tradition whose conventions date back to its emergence and which retain its basic patterns while at the same time incorporate new trends, both in form and in content. These patterns are embedded

7 For more case studies, see Ryad 2017.

in a long and consistent discursive tradition. Evidently, contexts have changed and have affected hajj accounts in many ways, but since the genre was flexible and varied from the beginning, these influences could be absorbed without disrupting the basic patterns.

The references and concepts used by historical authors to construct their texts and convey their experiences, both as a form of self-representation and as a means to construct and display their religiosity, are to a large extent the same as those found in contemporary accounts by pilgrims, both written and oral. These narrators refer to basic conceptualizations and symbols of the hajj, shaped by the sharia, by longing (*shawq*), and by interpretations (*ḥikma*); they relate physical experiences (illness, crowds, etc.) and emotional responses (euphoria, annoyance, etc.); they see the hajj as a mechanism of encounter in various ways, reaffirming social and cultural connections; they allow social and political circumstances to co-create their experiences and their narratives; and, they have to deal with bureaucracies, authorities, organizers, and instructors who contribute to the hajj experience, either in a positive or in a negative manner. Conventional concepts, doctrines, and historical sensations provided by the hajj are used to renegotiate religious attitudes and accommodate them to new social contexts and sensitivities. The ultimate aim of these hajj narratives is to communicate a form of religiosity that is structured by the discursive connotations of the hajj through the authors personal experience of an extraordinary journey.

References

al-ʿAbdarī, al-Ḥīḥī, Abu ʿAbdallah Muḥammad ibn Muḥammad. 1968. *Riḥla al-ʿAbdarī al-Musammā al-Riḥla al-Maghribiyya*, edited by Muḥammad al-Fāsī. Al-Ribāṭ: Jāmi'a Muḥammad v.

al-ʿAyyāshī, ʿAbdallāh ibn Muḥammad. 2011. *Al-Riḥla al-ʿAyyāshiyya li-al-biqāʿ al-Ḥijāziyya al-musammā Mā' al-Mawā'id*, edited by Aḥmad Farīd al-Muzīdī. 2 vols. Bayrūt: Dār al-Kutub al-ʿIlmiyya.

al-Ghazālī, Abū Ḥāmid. 2014. *Le livre du voyage*, translated by Hassan Boutaleb. Paris: Dar Albouraq.

al-Ghazālī, Abū Ḥāmid. 2011. *The secrets of pilgrimage*, translated by Ibrahim Umar. Kuala Lumpur: Islamic Book Trust.

al-Ghazālī, Abū Ḥāmid. 1431/2010. *Inner dimensions of Islamic Worship*, translated by Muhtar Holland. Markfield: The Islamic Foundation.

al-Ghazālī, Abū Ḥāmid. 2001. *Les secrets du pèlerinage en islam avec un commentaire des cinq pilliers de l'islam*, translated by Maurice Gloton. Beyrouth: Al-Bouraq.

al-Ghazālī, Abū Ḥāmid. 1405/1985. *Asrār al-ḥajj*, edited by Mūrā Muḥammad ʿAli. Bayrūt: ʿAlam al-Kutub.

al-Ghazālī, Abū Ḥāmid. 1983. *Inner Dimensions of Islamic Worship*, translated by Muhtar Holland. Markfield: The Islamic Foundation.

al-Murādābādī, Rafīʿ al-Dīn. 2004. *Al-Riḥla al-al-Hindiyya ilā al-Jazīra al-ʿArabiyya*, translated by Samīr ʿAbd al-Ḥamīd Ibrāhīm. Al-Qāhira: al-Majlis al-Aʿlā li-al-Thaqāfa.

al-Nābulusī, ʿAbd al-Ghanī. 1410/1989. *Al-Ḥaqīqa wa-al-majāz fī riḥla bilād al-Shām wa-Miṣr wa-al-Ḥijāz*, edited by Riyāḍ al-Ḥamīd Murād. 3 vols. Al-Qāhira: Dār al-Maʿrifa.

al-Nadwī, Masʿūd ʿĀlim. 1419/1999. *Shuhūr fī diyār al-ʿArab*, translated by Samīr ʿAbd al-Ḥamīd Ibrāhīm. Al-Riyāḍ: Maktaba al-Mālik ʿAbd al-ʿAzīz al-ʿĀmma.

al-Naqar, ʿUmar. 1972. *The pilgrimage tradition in West Africa*. Khartoum: Khartoum University Press.

al-Rasheed, Madawi. 2002. *A history of Saudi Arabia*. Cambridge: Cambridge University Press.

al-Samaany, Nasser. 2000. 'Travel literature of Moroccan pilgrims during the 11th–12th/17th–18th centuries: Thematic and artistic study.' PhD diss., University of Leeds.

al-Sanūsī, Muḥammad. 1396/1976. *Al-Riḥla al-Hijāziyya*, edited by ʿAlī al-Shanūfī. 3 vols. Tūnis: al-Sharika al-Tūnisiyya li-al-Tawzīʿ.

al-Tujaybī al-Sabtī, al-Qāsim ibn Yūsuf. 1395/1975. *Mustafād al-riḥla wa-al-ightirāb*, edited by ʿAbd al-Ḥafīẓ Mansūr. Lībiyā-Tūnis: al-Dār al-ʿArabiyya li-al-Kitāb.

Afshar, Iraj. 2002. 'Persian travelogues: A description and bibliography.' In *Society and culture in Qajar Iran; studies in honor of Hafez Farmayan*, edited by Elton Daniel, 145–162. Costa Mesa: Mazda Publishers.

Alam, Muzaffar and Sanjay Subrahmanyam. 2009. *Indo-Persian travels in the age of discoveries 1400–1800*. Cambridge: Cambridge University Press.

Arjana, Sophia Rose. 2017. *Pilgrimage in Islam. Traditional and modern practices*. London: Oneworld Publications.

Asani, Ali and Carney Gavin. 1988. 'Through the lens of Mirza of Delphi. The Ḍebbas Album of early twentieth-century photographs of pilgrimage sites in Mecca and Medina.' *Muqarnas* 15: 178–199.

Buitelaar, Marjo, Manja Stephan-Emmrich and Viola Thimm. 2021. *Muslim women's pilgrimage to Mecca and beyond. Reconfiguring gender, religion and mobility*. London and New York: Routledge.

Burak, Guy. 2017. 'Between Istanbul and Gujarat: descriptions of Mecca in the sixteenth-century Indian Ocean.' *Muqarnas Online* 34 (1): 287–320.

Burckhardt, John Lewis. 1829/ 1993. *Travels in Arabia*. London: Darf Publishers.

Casewit, Daoud. 1991. 'Faḍā'il al-Madīnah. The unique distinctions of the Prophet's city.' *The Islamic Quarterly* XXXV (1): 5–22.

Chantre, Luc. 2018. *Pèlerinages d'empire. Une histoire Européenne du pèlereinage à la Mecque*. Paris: Éd. de la Sorbonne.

Chiffoleau, Sylvia. 2015. *Le voyage à la Mecque. Un pèlerinage mondial en terre d'islam.* Paris: Belin.

Cobbold, Lady Evelyn. 2009. *Pilgrimage to Mecca.* Introduction by William Facey and Miranda Taylor, notes by Ahmad S, Turkestani. London: Arabian Publishing.

Coşkun, Menderes. 2000. 'The most literary Ottoman pilgrimage narrative: Nabi's Tuhfetü; l—Haremeyn.' *Turcica* 32: 363–388.

Coşkun, Menderes. 1985. 'Ottoman attitudes towards writing about pilgrimage experience.' *Millî folklor* 95: 72–82.

Daniel, Elton, ed. 2002. *Society and culture in Qajar Iran; studies in honor of Hafez Farmayan.* Costa Mesa: Mazda Publishers.

Daniel, Elton, ed. 2002. 'The Hajj and Qajar travel literature.' In *Society and culture in Qajar Iran; studies in honor of Hafez Farmayan*, edited by Elton Daniel, 215–238. Costa Mesa: Mazda Publishers.

Dinet, Nacir ed Dine Étienne and Sliman ben Ibrahim Baâmer. 1930. *Le pèlerinage à la maison sacrée d'Allah.* Paris: Librairie Hachette

Eickelman, Dale, and James Piscatori, eds. 1990. *Muslim travellers: Pilgrimage, migration, and the religious migration.* Berkeley and Los Angeles: University of California Press.

Elger, Ralf. 2003. 'Arabic travelogues from the Mashrek 1700–1834. A preliminary survey of the genre's development.' In *Crossings and passages in genre and culture*, edited by Christian Szyska and Friederike Pannewick, 27–40. Wiesbaden: Reichert Verlag.

Fewkes, Jacqueline. 2021. 'Considering the silences: Understanding historical narratives of women's Indian Ocean mobility.' In *Muslim women's pilgrimage to Mecca and beyond; reconfiguring gender, religion, and mobility*, edited by Marjo Buitelaar, Manja Stephan-Emmerich, and Viola Thimm, 127–146. London and New York: Routledge.

Gelvin, James, and Nile Green, eds. 2014. *Global Muslims in the age of steam and print.* Berkeley: University of California Press.

Germanus, Julius. S.d. [1938]. *Allah akbar! Im Banne des Islams.* Trans. Hildegard von Ross. Berlin: Holle & Co. Verlag.

Gershoni, Israel. 1994. 'The reader—"Another production": the reception of Haykal's biography of Muhammad and the shift of Egyptian intellectuals to Islamic subjects in the 1930s.' *Poetics today* 15 (2): 241–277.

Green, Nile. 2015. 'The Hajj as its own undoing: infrastructure and integration on the Muslim journey to Mecca.' *Past and Present* (226): 193–226.

Gymnich, Marion, Ansgar Nünning, Vera Nünning, and Elisabeth Wåghäll Nivre, eds. 2008. *Points of arrival: Travels in time, space, and self. Zielpunkte: Unterwegs in Zeit, Raum und Selbst.* Tübingen: Francke Verlag.

Hanaway, William. 2002. 'Persian travel narratives: notes toward the definition of a nineteenth-century genre.' In *Society and culture in Qajar Iran; studies in honor of Hafez Farmayan*, edited by Elton Daniel, 249–268. Costa Mesa: Mazda Publishers.

Haykal, Muḥammad Ḥusayn. 1952. *Fī manzil al-waḥy*. Al-Qāhira: Maktaba al-Nahḍa al-Miṣriyya.

Ibn Baṭṭūṭa. 1958–2000. *The travels of Ibn Battuta*, translated by Hamilton A.R. Gibb, Charles F. Beckingham, 5 vols. Cambridge and London: Cambridge University Press and Hakluyt Society.

Ibn Baṭṭūṭa. 1853–1859. *Les voyages d'Ibn Battoutah*, edited and translated by Defrémery and Sanguinetti, 4 vols. Paris: Imprimerie Nationale.

Ibn Jubayr. 2001. *The travels of Ibn Jubayr*, translated by Roland Broadhurst. London: Goodword Books.

Ibn Jubayr. 1400/1980. *Riḥla Ibn Jubayr*. Bayrūt: Dār Ṣādir.

Ibn al-Ṣabāḥ, ʿAbd Allāh. 2008. *Ansāb al-akhbār wa-tadhkira al-akhyār; riḥla al-Mudajjin al-Ḥājj ʿAbd Allāh bin al-Ṣabāḥ (al-niṣf al-thānī min al-qarn al-thāmin al-Hijrī)*, edited by Muḥammad Binsharīfa. Al-Ribāṭ: Dār Abī Raqrāq.

Jahan Begum, Nawab Sultan. 2013. *The story of a pilgrimage to Hijaz*. Calcutta: Thacker, Spink.

Jung, Dietrich. 2011. *Orientalists, Islamists and the public sphere; A genealogy of the modern essentialist image of Islam*. Sheffield and Oakville: Equinox.

Kiyanrad, Sarah. 2020. 'No choice but to travel; Safavid travelogues written in Persian.' In *Islamische Selbstbilder. Festschrift für Suzanne Enderwitz*, edited by Sarah Kyanrad and Rebecca Sauer and Jan Scholz, 273–297. *Heidelberg: Heidelberg University Publishing*.

Māgāman, Muhammad. 2014. *al-Riḥlāt al-Maghribiyya (q XI–XII h/ XVII–XVIII m)*. Al-Ribāṭ: Kulliyya al-Ādāb wa-al-ʿUlūm al-Insāniyya.

Mahallati, Amineh. 2011. 'Women as pilgrims: Memoirs of Iranian women travellers to Mecca.' *Iranian Studies* 44 (6): 831–849.

Marzolph, Ulrich. 2014. 'From Mecca to Mashhad: The narrative of an illustrated Shi'i pilgrimage scroll from the Qajar period.' *Muqarnas* 31: 207–242.

Memon, Muhammad Umar. 1976. *Ibn Taimīya's struggle against popular religion with an annotated translation of his Kitāb iqtidāʾ aṣ-ṣirāṭ al-mustaqīm mukhālafat aṣḥāb al-jaḥīm*. The Hague and Paris: Mouton.

Milstein, Rachel. 2006. 'Futūḥ-i Ḥaramayn; Sixteenth-century illustrations of the hajj route.' In: *Mamluks and Ottomans: Studies in honour of Michael Winter*, edited by J. David Wasserstein and Ami Ayalon, 166–194. London and New York: Routledge.

Milstein, Rachel. 2001. 'Kitāb shawq-nāma—An illustrated tour of the Holy Arabia.' *JSAI* (2)5: 275–345.

Mishra, Saurabh. 2011. *The Haj from the Indian subcontinent 1860–1920. Pilgrimage, politics, and pestilence*. Oxford: Oxford University Press.

Mols, Luitgard, and Marjo Buitelaar. 2015. *Hajj: Global encounters through pilgrimage. Mededelingen van het Rijksmuseum voor Volkenkunde* (43). Leiden: Rijksmuseum voor Volkenkunde.

Mouline, Nabil. 2011. *Les clercs de l'islam. Autorité religieuse et pouvoir politique en Arabie Saoudite, XVIIIe–XXIe siècle*. Paris: Presses Universitaires de France.

Munt, Harry. 2014. *The Holy City of Medina. Sacred space in early Islamic Arabia*. Cambridge: Cambridge University Press.

Munt, Harry. 2013. 'The official announcement of an Umayyad caliph's successful pilgrimage to Mecca.' In *The hajj: collected essays*, edited by Venetia Porter and Liana Saif, 15–20. London: The British Museum and the Arts and Humanities Research Council.

Murat Kargili. 2014. *Hajj: The holy journey. The hajj route through postcards/Hac: kutsal yolculuk. Kartpostallari hac yolu*. Istanbul: Denizler Kitabevi.

Muẓhir, ʿAbd al-Wahhāb. 1348/1929. *Murshid al-ḥajj*. Al-Qāhira: Maktaba wa-Maṭbaʾa Khuḍayr.

Nasir-i Khusraw. 2001. *Nasir-i Khusraw's Book of Travels* (*safarnama*), translated by Wheeler M. Thackston. Costa Mesa: Mazda Publishers.

Netton, Ian Richard. 1996. *Seek knowledge; Thought and travel in the house of Islam*. Richmond: Curzon Press.

Netton, Ian Richard, ed. 1993. *Golden roads; Migration, pilgrimage and travel in medieval and modern Islam*. Richmond: Curzon Press.

Nünning, Vera, Ansgar Nünning, and Birgit Neumann. 2010. *Cultural ways of worldmaking. Media and narratives*. Göttingen: De Gruyter.

Ochsenwald, William. 1984. *Religion, society, and the state in Arabia. The Hijaz under Ottoman control*. Columbus: Ohio State University Press.

Papas, Alexandre, Thomas Welsford, and Thierry Zarcone. 2012. *Central Asian pilgrims; Hajj routes and pious visits between Central Asia and the Hijaz*. Berlin: Institut Français d'Études sur l'Asie Centrale, Klaus Schwarz Verlag.

Pearson, Michael. 1996. *Pilgrimage to Mecca. The Indian experience 1500–1800*. Princeton: Markus Wiener Publishers.

Peters, Francis Edward. 1994a. *Mecca; A literary history of the Muslim Holy Land*. Princeton: Princeton University Press.

Peters, Francis Edward. 1994b. *The Hajj; The Muslim pilgrimage to Mecca and the Holy Places*. Princeton: Princeton University Press.

Porter, Venetia. 2012. *Hajj; Journey to the heart of Islam*. London: The British Museum Press.

Porter, Venetia and Liana Saif, eds. 2013. *The hajj: Collected essays*. London: The British Museum, the Arts and Humanities Research Council.

Ryad, Umar. 2017. *The hajj and Europe in the age of empire*. Leiden and Boston: Brill.

Ryzova, Lucie. 2014. *The age of the efendiyya; Passages to modernity in national-colonial Egypt*. Oxford: Oxford university Press.

Shāh Walīallāh Dihlawī. 2007. *Fuyūḍ al-Ḥaramayn maʿa urdū tarjama saʿādat Kūnīn*, edited by Wākir Abd al-Jabār ʿĀbid al-Ghārī. Ḥaydarābād: Shāh Walī Allāh Akīdimī.

Sikandar Begum, Nawab. 2007. *A princess's pilgrimage. A pilgrimage to Mecca (1863–1864)*, edited by Siobhan Lambert-Hurley. Lercs: Kube Publishing.

Sirriyeh, Elizabeth. 1985. 'The mystical journeys of 'Abd al-Ghanī al-Nābulusī'. *Die Welt des Islams*. New Series 25 (1–2): 84–96.

Slight, John. 2015. *The British Empire and the hajj 1865–1956*. Cambridge and London: Harvard University Press.

Tagliacozzo, Eric. 2013. *The longest journey; Southeast Asians and the pilgrimage to Mecca*. Oxford: Oxford University Press.

Tagliacozzo, Eric, and Shawkat Toorawa, eds. 2016. *The Hajj; Pilgrimage in Islam*. New York: Cambridge University Press.

Vrolijk, Arnoud. forthcoming. *Early hajj photography*.

Willis, John. 2017. 'Governing the living and the dead: Mecca and the emergence of the Saudi bio-political state.' *American historical review*: 346–370.

CHAPTER 2

'Coplas del peregrino de Puey Monçón': A Sixteenth-Century Spanish Poem about the Hajj

Miguel Ángel Vázquez

1 Introduction

At the beginning of the sixteenth century, a Spanish Mudejar,[1] known as the 'Pilgrim of Puey Monçón', undertook the difficult journey from Spain to Mecca to perform the hajj. Upon his return to Spain, the details of his journey were memorialized in a poem, which narrates in 79 *coplas*[2] the author's travels: the journey by ship on the Mediterranean (including a storm that threatened the lives of the passengers); the stays in Tunisia and Egypt; the arduous trek over the desert from Egypt to Mecca; the holy places in and around Mecca; and the beginning of the return journey. The only version available to us of this poem is written in Aljamiado, a Hispano-Romance language of the sixteenth century rendered with the Arabic alphabet, instead of the Latin alphabet. In other words, the poem is written in a typically Spanish poetic form, but the text is written with the Arabic alphabet. It is also worth adding that this poem, even though it was written in Spanish, fits within the classical genre of *riḥla*: travelogues whose initial objective is to describe the journey to Mecca, but which often go beyond that to include descriptions of the places the pilgrims visited or the people they met as well as detailed accounts of the vicissitudes they experienced in their journey.

2 Aljamiado Literature

After the fall of the Muslim kingdom of Granada in 1492 and throughout the sixteenth century, Spain went through the process of constituting itself as a nation. The official discourse was one of homogeneity where purportedly all

1 Muslims who continued living in Christian-dominated territories after the Reconquista. Also, see page 76 in this chapter.

2 The traditional Spanish *copla* consists of a stanza of four verses, in this poem, however, the stanzas contain eight verses.

Spaniards spoke one language (Spanish), professed one religion (Catholicism), and were part of one culture. This entailed, under the threat of expulsion, the forced conversion of all Muslims into Catholic Christianity, and the obliteration of any expression of Muslim identity by means of royal edicts prohibiting an entire catalogue of habits and symbols considered Muslim. Those Muslims who decided to stay and convert came to be known as 'Moriscos'. The conversions, however, were, for the most part, not sincere but simply a way to remain on Spanish soil as the newly converted minority continued to practice Islam in secrecy. Aware of this, the Christian authorities intensified the persecution and inquisitorial trials of many Moriscos. Furthermore, Catholic Spaniards feared that Spanish Muslims might become a 'fifth column' and aid a Turkish invasion of Spain. This atmosphere consisting of constant tension and hostility toward the Moriscos culminated in 1609, with their expulsion from Spain. As exiles, the majority of Moriscos settled in North African countries (Morocco, Algiers, Tunisia), but not without leaving behind a silent testimony of their presence in Spain. The Moriscos participated in clandestine activities to preserve their culture. Throughout the sixteenth century, they produced a corpus of manuscripts written in Spanish that is written with the Arabic alphabet instead of the Latin alphabet. This is known as 'Aljamiado literature'. It contains everything a person would need to know about Islam based in the Morisco situation. Since the possession of such manuscripts was grounds for an inquisitorial accusation, the Moriscos hid them in false floors, walls or columns. This is why the manuscripts were able to survive until their discovery in the late nineteenth century. The mere presence of the Moriscos in the Iberian Peninsula during the Renaissance challenged the actuality of the aforementioned discourse of homogeneity. The canonical writers of the Golden Age never imagined that Spanish subjects would utter praise for Islam or fiery condemnations of Catholicism.

From the point of view of a Spanish reader, the first impression these manuscripts produce is that of something foreign: they are written, after all, with the letters of the Arabic alphabet. Nothing could be more alien to the canonical literature of Spain than this alphabet. Yet the reader is surprised by the fact that they are written in Castilian language dusted with Aragonese dialectal features, and some Arabic words. Not only does the alphabet force one to write—and to read—in the opposite direction than texts written with the Latin alphabet but, as Luce López-Baralt (one of the leading experts in the field) suggests, through these texts, Spain itself emerges as its own mirror image (López-Baralt 1995). One of the most striking examples of this mirror image is the appropriation of quintessentially Spanish poetic forms for Islamic poetic purposes. There are many examples of Aljamiado poetry from the Mudejar and Morisco periods written in traditional Spanish forms, such as the Cuaderna Vía, the Romance, the Silva, or the Octava Real, among others, that praise Allah, Muhammad, and Islam, as well as anti-Christian polemic poetry, and Islamic didactic poetry (Vázquez 2007). In the words of Gerard Wiegers:

> One might argue that from a formal point of view these Romance strophes and Islamic Spanish literature are different stages of the process in which Spanish became a literary language of Islam.
>
> WIEGERS 1994, 38

3 Background of the Poem

The poem 'Coplas del peregrino de Puey Monçón' can be found in a miscellaneous Aljamiado manuscript, which was edited in its entirety by Tarek Khedr in 2004, even though it had already been edited by Pano y Ruata in an unscholarly edition published in 1897.[3] It should be noted that the manuscript is somewhat deteriorated, and therefore, we are missing the title the author gave his poem. Also missing are verses from the first, third, fifth, and sixth stanzas, and it is possible that the last stanzas detailing the return to Spain were lost. The specific date or year when the pilgrimage was performed—or when the poem was written since we must not assume that both dates are the same—has been difficult to establish because there is very little internal evidence pointing towards a date. Attempting to ascertain to the best of our abilities the period in which the pilgrimage was undertaken is of key importance, since we would be dealing with very different situations depending on whether a Mudejar or a Morisco performed this hajj.

'Mudejar' and 'Morisco' both refer to Muslims living in Spain, but under different legal circumstances. 'Mudejar' (from Arabic: *mudajjan*, meaning 'tamed', 'domesticated', 'permitted to stay') was a term used to refer to Muslims who continued living in Christian-dominated territories after the Reconquista. Mudejars were free to practise Islam, and had to pay the crown a special tribute. In 1502, in the kingdom of Castille, and in 1526, in the kingdom of Aragon, Islam was outlawed, and Mudejars were forced to convert to Catholicism or face exile. Muslims who converted to Catholicism would be known thereafter as 'Moriscos'. Thus, during the Mudejar period it was not impossible for a Muslim to

3 The manuscript itself is a collection of shorter booklets of varying lengths and topics that were sewn together. The poem discussed here is section 61 of 89.

go on hajj; however, it was illegal for Muslims to go on pilgrimage to Mecca during the Morisco period (1502/1526–1609).[4] This means that performing the hajj as a Morisco would have implied a greater risk, and therefore a greater act of defiance to the Spanish authorities.

The first scholar to propose a date for the pilgrimage depicted in this poem was Pano y Ruata, who dated the actual pilgrimage to 1603 (Pano y Ruata 1897, 286–291), but his logic is not reliable, since he assumed several variables—such as, assuming the pilgrim spent about a month in Alexandria, even though the poem does not state so.[5] Following Pano y Ruata, Francisco Javier Sánchez Cantón (1956, 30), also used 1603 as the date the pilgrim went to Mecca. Epalza Ferrer on the other hand, based on a linguistic approach, suggested a much earlier date of 1505–1517 (Epalza Ferrer 1990, 56), placing the actual pilgrimage within the Mudejar period in Aragon.

When Khedr (2004, 14) published his edition of the manuscript where the poem is found, he did not propose an actual date for the poem, but simply quoted Montaner Frutos (1988) who, using codicological criteria such as watermarks, type of paper, and marginal notes, had suggested that the manuscript containing the poem was put together between 1579 and 1588 (Khedr 2010, 138). Even though he was not attempting to date the *coplas* in particular, his dating of the entire manuscript showed that the pilgrim could not have been on hajj in 1603. Later, both Khedr and Montaner Frutos (2010) appear to have echoed Epalza Ferrer's dating but without explaining why.[6]

It was not until 2018 that the dating issue was methodically taken up by Xavier Casassas Canals, who in his 'Tres *riḥlas* mudéjares' narrowed down the period of this hajj to between 1505 and 1509 (Casassas Canals 2018, 121–125).[7] Casassas Canals based his dating mainly on two clues provided by the poem. First, the pilgrim writes that he visited the al-Ghūrī mosque in Egypt which was built between 1503 and 1505, so the pilgrimage could not have taken place before that date. Second, the pilgrim states that he paid a tax to the *baile* of Valencia that would permit him to leave Spain for Mecca. This *baile* was the title given to an official tasked with dealing with issues pertaining to the Muslims. Once Islam was outlawed in Spain after 1525, the office of the *baile* was no

4 This period will be discussed in more detail in section 'Other hajj accounts from Spain: During the Morisco period' in this chapter.

5 Pano y Ruata (1897) also proposes 1571 as another possible date (291).

6 Montaner Frutos (2010) described the 'Coplas' as 'likely from the beginning of [the sixteenth, MV] century' (54); and Khedr (2010) states that the *coplas* 'include data that suggests it was composed in the Mudejar period, not the Morisco period' (222).

7 A year before he had anticipated this date in passing in his *De Ávila a la Meca*, but without any evidence.

longer needed (ibid., 121). Casassas Canals further narrowed the time window for this pilgrimage by taking into account detailed lists of Italian ships that set sail from Valencia to Tunis or Algiers (ibid., 123–124), and cross referenced these with those months that corresponded to the most likely dates in which any pilgrim would have left Spain to arrive in Mecca for the Muslim month of *dhū al-ḥijja* (ibid., 122–123).

Roza Candás, on his part, called attention to an article by Emilia Salvador, who cites a document from 1517 that registered two Mudejars from Puimonzón leaving for North Africa from the harbour of Valencia (Roza Candás 2018, 65). This detail is of note because it specifically names Puey Monçón as the pilgrims' place of origin, and also because in the poem the pilgrim talks about a travelling companion. Therefore, whether the date of the pilgrimage was between 1505–1509, or took place in 1517, there is strong evidence that the pilgrim was an Aragonese Mudejar—and not a Morisco—, since, as stated above, Islam was not outlawed in the kingdom of Aragon until 1526.

As for the identity of the poem's author, since this kind of literature is usually anonymous given the need of secrecy for any kind of Muslim endeavour in this period in Spain, we know nothing of him. The issue is complicated by the fact that we must not assume that the actual pilgrim was also the author of the poem. The pilgrim could have returned to Spain, told the story of his pilgrimage, and then someone else could have written the poem. In this sense, Roza Candás suggests that it was possible the poem was based on another written version of this pilgrimage originally written in prose (ibid., 66). In an attempt to ascribe authorship to the poem, both Ángel González Palencia (1928) and Juan Vernet (1972), perhaps influenced by Pano y Ruata's unlikely dating of the poem, gave authorship of this poem to Muḥammad Rabadán, one of the best Morisco poets of the late sixteenth century and early seventeenth century. However, neither González Palencia nor Vernet elaborate on the reasons why they reached that conclusion. In sum, the only thing that we can probably establish with some certainty about the poet is that he was a Mudejar who lived during the Aragonese Mudejar period in Pueyo Monçón—today known as Pueyo de Santa Cruz (Zúñiga López 1988–1989, 460)—, a small town north east of Zaragoza.

Before looking at the poem more closely, at the outset, it is important to remember that even though it depicts the journey of a Mudejar, it appears in a Morisco manuscript written in Aljamiado. Therefore, a question we must keep in mind as we follow the journey is: What made this and other hajj accounts—like that of ʿOmar Paṭōn[8]—worthwhile for the Moriscos to preserve in their

8 I follow here Roza Candás's rendering of the name (Roza Candás 2018).

Aljamiado manuscripts? In the context of Morisco Spain, the copying, writing, and owning of these manuscripts was dangerous since, if caught, the perpetrator faced an inquisitorial process. I hypothesize that, since the laws in Spain during this period made it so difficult for Moriscos to travel outside the Iberian Peninsula, these written logs of pilgrimages to Mecca might have allowed the Moriscos to travel to Mecca virtually, as it were.

4 Content of the Poem

Let me now turn to the content of this poetic *riḥla* and summarize the itinerary that the anonymous Mudejar followed. From his town of Puey Monçón he went to the port of Valencia where, after paying the *baile* the necessary fee to exit Spain, he paid for passage with a Venetian ship captain (*copla* 4). From there, he went to Tunis, where the ship, probably a merchant vessel, made several stops along different ports. The cities are not named in order in this part of the poem, but if we follow a West-East direction, we can easily reconstruct the order: Hammamet, Hergla, Sousse, Monastir, Mahdia, Sfax, Mahres, and Djerba (cc. 5–14). In Tunis, he is amazed by the size of the city and its riches; in Djerba, he admired the many fruit trees and 'delightful' sights:

Isla es muy deleytosa	It is a very delightful island
de muchos árboles fruytales	abundant in fruit trees
mançanos, priscos i peros	apple, peach, and pear
muchas viñas i figarales,	many vineyards and fig orchards
ay de muchas datileras	there are many date trees
qu-es una fruyta sabros[a],	which is a delicious fruit
isla es muy deleytosa,	a very delightful island
maguera toda arenales.	in spite of its sandy areas. (c. 14)[9]

But apparently not everything goes smoothly for the pilgrim, since he reports having spent three days without food before arriving in Sfax. Not receiving anything to eat out of charity, he and his companion were able to buy a lamb at a low price, which they cooked without water, sauce, or any spices (c. 11).

Continuing the voyage, on their way to Alexandria from Tunisia, close to the gulf of Sirte, a terrible storm threatened the ship. It must have been quite a

9 All quotes of the poem come from Khedr's 2004 edition.

frightening experience, since the poet dedicated nine *coplas* to describing the incident (cc. 15–21):

Partimos con alegría	We happily set sail
de Jerba los alḥiǧantes	from Djerba
con muchos de mercadantes	with many merchants
para ir en-Ališandría;	to go to Alexandria;
navegando nuesa vía	sailing on our way
por l-alta mar tenpestosa,	through the tempestuous sea
tomonos mala marina	a bad sea storm engulfed us
una muy terrible cosa.	it was a terrible affair. (c. 15)

As part of the efforts to save the ship, the captain ordered to 'empty the galleon' (c. 16), an order which the sailors frantically executed without regard for the contents of any of the boxes or packages they were throwing. As a result, the ship was saved, but most of the food provisions ended up at the bottom of the sea. They were able to make do with some cakes that the crew of the ship rationed until they arrived at an unnamed port in Monte Barca. Eighteen days later they finally arrived in Alexandria, where they continued on foot towards the city of Cairo. This city (cc. 25–33) amazed the pilgrim with its many inhabitants that 'cannot be counted' and its public lighting, which made the city look 'as clear when it is night, as when it is day' (c. 25). There, he visited the most important mosques: The mosque of Ibn Ṭūlūn, al-Azhar, and the mosque of Sultan al-Ghūrī. He also had the opportunity to visit the ruins of the ancient Heliopolis where he gazed with wonder at the obelisk:

todo de letras formado,	it is covered in letters
pareçe que oy enparten mano	far from human knowledge[10]
no las sabe leir moro	Muslims do not know how to read them
nin judío, ni cristiano.	neither Jews, nor Christians. (c. 33)

At Birka al-Ḥajj, a pond or water reservoir a few kilometers from Cairo that became a meeting spot for caravans embarking on the hajj (Zúñiga López 1988–1989, 462), the *amīr al-ḥajj* set up his tent for three days. The *amīr al-ḥajj*, or 'commander of the pilgrimage', was an office held by an individual appointed

10 The sense of this verse is not altogether clear, as Khedr points out. I follow his explanation in my translation.

by different Muslim empires from the seventh to the twentieth century. His duties included guiding the annual pilgrims' caravan from Egypt to Mecca, and protecting them against raids with soldiers and weapons. Travelling through the Sinai Peninsula, and into the Arabian Peninsula on his way to Mecca, the traveller reported seeing the tombs of ancient prophets[11] emanating light:

Deziros-é lo que ví,	I shall tell you what I saw,
por las tierras i collados,	along the lands and hills,
de las tierras que pasé,	about the territories I went through,
de los montes despoblados:	about the desolate hills:
ví aˡnnabīes enterrados	I saw buried prophets
llenos de gran resplandor,	full of great light,
que alabaron su Señor	who praised their Lord
fueron bienaventurados.	they were blessed. (c. 39)

Once in Mecca, the poem describes the ceremony where the Sharīf of Mecca, of the Sharīfian family ruling Mecca from the tenth to the twentieth century, receives the *amīr al-ḥajj* with great honours. In this ceremony *amīr al-ḥajj* gifts the Sharīf of Mecca a silk veil that adorns the Kaʿba, which was woven in Egypt (cc. 41–46). After this, there are other descriptions: the Grand Mosque and its impressive architecture, the Kaʿba with its Black Stone, the interior of the Kaʿba, and the Zamzam well as well as some of the rituals performed there, such as the prayers and walking seven times around the Kaʿba (cc. 47–59). The pilgrim also visited the tomb of Khadīja, the first wife of the Prophet Muhammad, as well as the houses of the Prophet's companions Abū Bakr and ʿAlī. Outside the city, he visited Muzdalifa, ʿArafa, Minā and the caves of al-Thawr, where the Prophet and Abū Bakr hid from the Quraysh on their way to Medina (cc. 60–66). Then, he travelled to Medina where he visited the tombs of the Prophet Muhammad, Abū Bakr, ʿUmar, and Fāṭima (cc. 68–70). There, he claimed to have seen the 'light of the Prophet/ that went as high as the heavens' (c. 73). On his way back through Tabūk and ʿAqaba, he lamented not having been able to visit Jerusalem, especially the Valley of Josaphat (where eschatological traditions say that Judgment Day will take place), and not having climbed Mount Sinai (cc. 75–78). Here, the poem abruptly ends, which leads scholars to believe that there were more stanzas that described his return from Egypt to Spain, and perhaps the reception he received from his community in Puey Monçón.

11 The pilgrim does not specify which prophets.

5 Other Hajj Accounts from Spain: Before the Morisco Period

This poem is a humble example of the *riḥla* genre, of which we have much finer and more ambitious specimens, such as Ibn Baṭṭūṭa's voyage and that of Ibn Jubayr. In the context of Spain in particular, this poem is not the only account of a hajj that started in Spain—the first accounts of which date back to the eighth century.[12] It is important to realize that Spain was at the periphery of the Islamic world at the time, which added extra considerations when it came to deciding whether or not to embark on the hajj. As an alternative to taking such a long and, by default, costly journey, many Muslims from Spain went on pilgrimages to local holy places within the peninsula as well as North Africa (Roza Candás 2018, 32–33). As far as those Mudejars who, in spite of all the difficulties, did go on pilgrimage to Mecca, I will highlight a few examples.

In a manuscript of possible Morisco origin copied at the end of the sixteenth century and edited by Epalza Ferrer in 1982–1983, there is an account of a Mudejar from Tortosa, in Catalonia, Aḥmad Ibn Fatḥ Ibn Abī al-Rabīʿ, who went on a pilgrimage in 1396. The route he followed is similar to that depicted in the sixteenth-century poem discussed above: he started in Tortosa, and sailed to Bijaya in Algiers and from there to Tunis, where he met with Muslim literati. In Tunis, he embarked on board a 'Christian ship' that took him to Alexandria. After that, he visited Cairo, and then, just like the Mudejar pilgrim, he joined other pilgrims who were going to Mecca at the aforementioned Birka al-Ḥajj (Epalza Ferrer 1982–1983, 26–27). Just like in the poem, this writer also described the ceremony where the Kaʿba's covering cloths are handed over.

We should also mention ʿOmar Paṭōn's *riḥla* from Ávila to Mecca between 1491 and 1495, whose pilgrimage account might have been important to Moriscos, since it appears in two Aljamiado manuscripts: one that was found in Teruel in 1988 and another that is part of the collection of the Escuelas Pías de Zaragoza.[13] From Ávila, Paṭōn and his travelling companion, Muḥammad Corral, travelled to a city in Catalonia (Zaragoza?), and from there, by river, they reached Tortosa, from where they sailed to Tunis. They spent a year there for reasons he does not explain; when they finally obtained access to a ship that was travelling to Beirut, but the ship was affected by an outbreak of a plague after a stop in Methoni (Greece). When the authorities at an unnamed port in

12 For a detailed account of pilgrimages performed from Spain before the Morisco period see Roza Candás (2018, 22–33). See also Epalza (1982–1983), and Sánchez Cantón (1956).

13 See the editions of Casassas Canals (2015), who edited only the manuscript found in Teruel; and Roza Candás (2018) who edited both.

the Aegean Sea prohibited the ship from docking, it was forced into the small port of Çesme (Turkey). Once he and his travelling companion were strong enough to continue, they travelled on camel back to Istanbul, then on horseback to Aleppo where they joined a caravan of pilgrims going to Mecca via Damascus. A year later they travelled to Jerusalem and Cairo. Then, fearful of the dangerous journey through the desert, they decided to go by boat on the Red Sea from the port of Sinai to the port of Jedda, and from there to Mecca. His return home starts again by boat through the Red Sea from Jedda to the port of Sinai. From there to Cairo, then Alexandria, and finally Malta. Of his return to his hometown we know nothing since the pages of the manuscript detailing this part of his trip are lost.

6 Other Hajj Accounts from Spain: During the Morisco Period

The above accounts of pilgrims from Spain performing the hajj come from a period when it was still legal, although not easy, for a Spanish Muslim to travel to Mecca and back. There is, for example, a document dated to November 12, 1491 that gives permission (*licencia*) to a *faqīh* from Ávila to travel outside Spain to perform the hajj (Casassas Canals 2015, 234). However, relatively soon after the fall of Granada, especially in 1502 after the Christian authorities quelled a two-year Mudejar revolt, the promises that Ferdinand and Isabella had made to preserve Muslim institutions in Spain were declared null and void. This begins of a policy of repression that a century later would culminate with the massive expulsion of the crypto-Muslims.

Thus, in 1511, the newly converted minority was forbidden from carrying weapons, owning books in Arabic, and even killing animals to produce halal meat. Also, in 1526, in Granada, an edict prohibits an entire list of activities considered Muslim, such as speaking or writing in Arabic, wearing Muslim garb, jewelry, or any kind of symbol that may identify the wearer as Muslim as well as circumcision, among other things (Vincent 1987, 83–99). As for the hajj, as Leonard Harvey states, 'during most of [the sixteenth century, MV] the legislation of the Spanish authorities did not leave Muslims free to travel to Muslim countries' (Harvey 1987, 14). Given that the Spanish Christian authorities made it so difficult for the Muslim minority to go on hajj, adding to other known difficulties such as high financial costs and the dangers of the long journey, the Moriscos would have been justified in not performing the pilgrimage. In spite of this, we must wonder: were the Moriscos so concerned about this pillar of Islam that they attempted it, in spite of the odds? Was our poem, and other written hajj accounts in Aljamiado, an inspiration for Moriscos to attempt the perilous journey to Mecca and back? Fortunately, we do have some documentation from the Moriscos themselves that allows us to attempt an answer to these questions.

One of the most important and interesting Morisco writers called himself the Mancebo de Arévalo (the Young Man of Arévalo). He is the author—or co-author—of at least three manuscripts, one of which is titled *Tafsira*. This is an extensive manuscript of over 450 folios written in Aljamiado, the text of which was edited in its entirety by María Teresa Narváez. It is of great importance to us, because throughout the text the Mancebo includes vignettes of the day-to-day lives of the Moriscos. The people he describes and to whom he talks were not famous characters and would have been forgotten to history had it not been for his *Tafsira*. Through this text we bear witness to a clandestine network of crypto-Muslim operations; it is precisely in what we may call the 'minutes' of a secret meeting of Moriscos in Zaragoza that the Mancebo de Arévalo discusses his hajj preparations, or '*romeağğe*' as he calls it, and how he received monetary help from his community:

> As my pilgrimage was already at hand, and all that was wanting was the arrival of the company from Ávila la Real, and since Don Manrique knew about the difficulties of my journey, he made up part of my need, and gave me ten Morisco *doblas*. The other scholars present all contributed in my favour. May Allah grant such merit as I may earn if Allah grant me grace to reach Mecca, exalted may it be.
>
> HARVEY 1987, 21

The Mancebo de Arévalo promised to write an account of his pilgrimage, and the nineteenth-century Arabist Pascual de Gayangos claimed to have seen a manuscript titled *Peregrinación del Mancebo de Arévalo*. However, it is not clear if this manuscript really existed or was lost (Harvey 1987, 20).[14] There is another manuscript by the Mancebo de Arévalo, his *Breve compendio de la santa ley y sunna*, that contains a brief indication of another Morisco's pilgrimage: the wise Morisca Nuzayta Calderán 'said (...) that the text at Mecca was inscribed on leaves whiter than silver inside a dome of marble with an iron grille to protect it' (ibid., 18–19).

14 Harvey, in fact, expresses doubts as to whether the Mancebo was ever able to go on hajj: 'Did he ever escape from Spain and make his *ḥajj*? I fear that the odds were against him, and the Inquisition may have picked him up before he ever put to sea. I would like to be proved wrong by finding one day that manuscript of his pilgrimage which Gayangos spoke of' (Harvey 1987, 21).

Two anonymous Morisco manuscripts provide further evidence of the Moriscos' concern about travelling to Muslim lands. Both manuscripts contain guides on how to leave and how to return to Spain safely and in secrecy (López-Baralt and Irizarry 1987). Manuscript 774 of the Bibliothèque nationale de France details an itinerary to be followed: starting from the northeast of Spain, the traveller would go on foot through the south of France to Italy, being careful not to set foot on the 'lands of the Emperor'.[15] Once in Italy, the traveller would go to Venice, where they could take a ship to the north of Africa or Turkey. This travel guide also gives the clandestine Moriscos 'warnings for the road', which constitute a fascinating view of practical considerations for Muslim travellers concerned with concealing their identity and goal, such as how much to pay for lodging or food or, when asked by the authorities why they are leaving Spain, that they should claim they are fleeing debts, and are going to hide in France. They are also advised as to whom it is safe to approach, although always keeping secret the final objective:

> [In Venice, those, MV] you will see wearing white head covers are Turkish, those you will see wearing yellow ones, are Jewish merchants of the Great Turk. To those you will ask everything you want, since they will guide you.
>
> LÓPEZ-BARALT AND IRIZARRY 1987, 561, translation by me, MV

The other clandestine text is found in manuscript T16 of the Biblioteca de la Real Academia de la Historia. It offers a very detailed itinerary (ninety towns or cities are mentioned) of a return to Spain from Venice via the north of Italy, traversing France and arriving in Spain through Catalonia (ibid., 580–582).

Aside from the Morisco sources themselves mentioned above, there is further evidence from non-Morisco sources pointing at Moriscos travelling to Muslim lands throughout the sixteenth century:

> (…) in 1561, the Spanish Ambassador in Venice insisted in his reports that many moors from Valencia and Aragon were travelling to the Levant, and this in spite of several edicts, like those published by the Zaragoza Tribunal, which prohibited Moriscos from leaving Aragon, and prohibited Christian from guiding them through the Pyrenees.
>
> ROZA CANDÁS 2018, 34–35, translation by me, MV

15 Likely a reference to Carlos V.

The fact that edicts prohibiting Morisco travel outside Spain had to be repeated suggests they were not being followed. Based on the above, it is safe to say that the need of the Moriscos to connect with their Muslim counterparts and to travel to Mecca was ever present and that some indeed attempted the dangerous journey to Mecca.

7 Back to the 'Coplas del peregrino Puey Monçón'

From the above, it is clear that in spite of the Spanish Christian inquisition and coercive conversion laws, the Muslim minority remained steadfast in their religious obligations, including the importance of performing the hajj. Aided by hundreds of texts of their own production written in Aljamiado, they devised ways to continue practicing Islam in secrecy. Furthermore, these texts aided in guiding their spiritual lives in a period in Spain's history when being caught with anything written with the Arabic alphabet was grounds for an inquisitorial trial. In this context, performing the hajj, with all the dangers the journey entailed, was a heroic act and, I would argue, a form of jihad. Kathryn Miller explores the concept of 'scholar's jihad' within the context of Aragonese Mudejar leadership. These Mudejars felt a sense of duty 'in remaining in Aragon, doing what it took to keep Islam alive among their unlearned brethren' (Miller 2008, 128–129) even against the insistent advice of North African and Granadan jurists who felt it was the duty of all Muslims living in Christian-dominated lands to emigrate to Islamdom. This sense of duty and disposition to fight the Christian authorities on a cultural and religious front continued well into the Morisco period at the hands of those literate crypto-Muslims, like the Mohammed Escribano family (López-Morillas 1984; 1983), who produced and distributed many Aljamiado manuscripts. As the story of the pilgrim of Puey Monçón shows, the next best thing for someone who cannot go on pilgrimage is to support someone elses' hajj. For example, in his *Tafsira*, as quoted above, the Mancebo de Arévalo related how his co-religionists came to his aid, gathering money to enable his pilgrimage to Mecca.

I wonder, in the case of the Mudejar author of the poem I have been following and contextualizing, whether the members of the small community of Muslims in Puey Monçón also pooled their resources together to enable his journey. We know that he made it safely back to Spain, because upon his return he either wrote an account of his trek himself or related it for someone to write. If we accept Roza Candás's theory of how the poem came into being, the unknown Mudejar's account of his pilgrimage was rendered into verses that made the narration easier to remember. The poem was then copied in Aljamiado, having in mind one audience: the Moriscos, who longed to practice their religion freely and without fear of persecution.

The fact that this poem was intended for an audience of persecuted Muslims, whose sense of identity hinged on proving that Islam was the one true religion, may explain some interesting omissions on the part of the poet with regards his pilgrimage. Aside from the storm at sea that threatens the ship in which he is travelling, the Morisco author of this poem makes no mention of the many dangers that pilgrims faced along their long trip to Mecca. There is documentation that thousands of pilgrims who started in Egypt died on their journey towards or returning from Mecca due to lack of water, drinking contaminated water from many of the wells found in the desert, or due to different illnesses that many of the pilgrims brought with them from their homelands (Casassas Canals 2015, 240; Zúñiga López 1988–1989, 468; Epalza Ferrer 1982–1983, 73). Let us also not forget the threat of Bedouin attacks, which explains one the *amīr al-ḥajj*'s duties: to provide protection to the pilgrims with armed soldiers. For the particular case of a Morisco attempting the hajj—if we can assume they went on pilgrimage—, there was also the language barrier issue once they found themselves in Arabic speaking countries (Casassas Canals 2015, 242), since, we must remember, the Moriscos had generally lost their knowledge of Arabic, which was limited to prayers and Muslim rituals. Once in Mecca, the traveller had to deal with the masses of pilgrims all of whom were trying to perform all the required rituals, which, inevitably, meant some mishaps as well as the inconvenience of losing one's travelling partner(s) in the middle of the tumultuous process (ibid., 247).

The anonymous author of this poem mentions nothing of the above, and the omissions may very well have been on purpose. I would suggest that the author explicitly left out these details to offer his audience an idealized hajj where light shone from the graves of prophets, where the light of the Prophet was so bright that it reached the sky, and where the city of Mecca itself bestowed its blessings upon him. However, if the author was idealizing the hajj for the sake of his readership, how are we to interpret the long passage describing the storm at sea mentioned above? The author dedicated nine *coplas* to this event, so it must have been somehow important. On the one hand, it is possible to accept the storm as a true account of what befell the pilgrim in his voyage to Mecca. But on the other hand, it is also possible that this episode responds to more generic conventions of hajj narrations that depict part of the journey by sea. In this regard, the poem could be part of a long tradition of literary hajj accounts that almost always include a section of the journey taken by sea that invariably described a perilous storm—'Omar Paṭōn's ship, for instance, was ravaged by the plague. This use of the storm might possibly be a metaphoric test of the pilgrim's faith and unyielding desire to reach Mecca.

The tenth-century author Ibn Abī al-Dunyā, from Baghdad, in his *Kitāb al-mawt* relates a story where, after death, the pious deeds of the believer, such as his prayers, his fasting, and his walking to the mosque on Fridays, surround his body to protect it from the torture of the grave (Ibn Abī al-Dunyā 1983, 46). This story suggests that in Islam the body of the believer itself, not just one's faith and morals, is key in the service of the religion. But in the context of the Mudejars, and especially in the case of the Moriscos, going on hajj was a particularly daunting task, not just because of the great distance the trip entailed, but also because the Spanish authorities made it so difficult for the Mudejars, and close to impossible for the Moriscos, to go on pilgrimage. In this context, reading narrations of the hajj afforded those Spanish Muslims who could not go to Mecca the possibility of being there vicariously. This poem is found in an Aljamiado manuscript most likely put together towards the end of the sixteenth century. The process of copying and producing these manuscripts implies the material selection to be included in any given volume. This was informed by what the copyist felt would be of interest and, especially, spiritually relevant to their readership. So, the fact that we find this poem in an Aljamiado manuscript (along with the other manuscripts containing the Aljamiado version of 'Omar Paṭōn's hajj and the manuscripts containing secret itineraries to leave and return stealthily to Spain) is evidence that the hajj was a central concern for the Moriscos. The poem itself, an emblem of their hybrid Spanish-Muslim identity, is an act of resistance against the Christian authorities, thus turning pen and paper into the weapons of their jihad.

References

Cassasas Canals, Xavier. 2018. 'Tres *riḥlas* mudéjares: El viaje de peregrinación a la Meca de los musulmanes castellano-aragoneses durante los siglos XIV–XVI.' In *Circulaciones Mudéjares y Moriscas. Redes de contacto y representaciones*, edited by Alice Kadri, Yolanda Moreno, and Ana Echevarría, 93–125. Madrid: Consejo Superior de Investigaciones Científicas.

Cassasas Canals, Xavier. 2015. 'La *riḥla* de Omar Patún: El viaje de peregrinación a la Meca de un musulmán de Ávila a finales del siglo XV (1491–1495).' *Espacio, Tiempo y Forma, Serie III, Historia Medieval* 28: 221–254.

Cassasas Canals, Xavier, Olatz Villanueva Zubizarreta, Serafin de Tapia Sánchez, Javier Jiménez Gadea, and Ana Echevarria Arsuaga. 2017. *De Ávila a la Meca. El relato de viaje de Omar Patún, 1491–1495*. Valladolid: Ediciones Universidad de Valladolid.

de Epalza Ferrer, Mikel. 1990. 'Le lexique religieux des Morisques et la littérature aljamiado-morisque.' In *Les Morisques et l'Inquisition*, edited by Louis Cardaillac. Paris: Publisud.

de Epalza Ferrer, Mikel. 1982–1983. 'Dos textos moriscos bilingües (arabe y castellano) de viajes a Oriente (1395 y 1407–1412).' *Hespéris Tamuda* 20–21 (1): 25–112.

de Pano y Ruata, Mariano. 1897. *Las coplas del peregrino de Puey Monçón, viaja a la Meca en el siglo XVI*. Zaragoza: Comas Hermanos.

González Palencia, Ángel. 1928. *Historia de la literatura árabigo española*. Barcelona: Labor.

Harvey, Leonard Patrick. 1987. 'The Moriscos and the hajj.' *Bulletin of the British society for Middle Eastern studies* 14 (1): 11–24.

Ibn Abī al-Dūnyā, Abū Bakr 'Abd Allāh ibn Muḥammad ibn 'Amr. 1983. *Kitāb al-mawt wa kitāb al-qubūr*, edited by Leah Kinberg. Hayfa: University of Hayfa.

Khedr, Tarek. 2010. 'Las Coplas del Alhichante de Puey Monçón.' *Memoria de los moriscos. Escritos y relatos de una diaspora cultural*. Madrid: Sociedad estatal de conmemoraciones culturales: 222.

Khedr, Tarek. 2004. *Códice aljamiado de varias materias. Manuscrito N.º XIII de la antigua Junta para Ampliación de Estudios*. Madrid: Instituto universitario seminario Menéndez Pidal/ Oviedo: Seminario de estudios Árabo-Románicos.

López-Baralt, Luce. 1995. '"Al revés de los cristianos": La España invertida de la literatura aljamido-morisca.' In *Culturas en la Edad de Oro*, edited by José María Díez Borque, 197–222. Madrid: Editorial del la Universidad Complutense de Madrid.

López-Baralt, Luce and Awilda Irizarri. 1987. 'Dos itinerarios secretos de los moriscos del siglo XVI. Los manuscritos aljamiados 774 de la Biblioteca Nacional de París y T-16 de la Real Academia de la Historia,' 547–582. *Homenaje a Álvaro Galmés de Fuentes*. Madrid: Gredos.

López-Morillas, Consuelo. 1984. 'Copistas y escribanos moriscos.' In *Actes du IIme symposium International du CIEM sur: Religion, identité et sources documentaires sur les Morisques Andalous* 2, edited by Abdeljelil Temimi, 71–78. Zaghouan: CIEM.

López-Morillas, Consuelo. 1983. 'Trilingual marginal notes (Arabic, Aljamiado and Spanish) in a Morisco manuscript from Toledo.' *Journal of the American oriental society* 103 (3): 496–504.

Mancebo de Arévalo. 2003. *Tratado* [*Tafsira*], edited by María Teresa Narváez Córdova. Madrid: Trotta.

Miller, Kathryn. 2008. *Guardians of Islam. Religious authority and Muslim communities of late medieval Spain*. New York: Columbia University Press.

Montaner Frutos, Alberto. 2010. 'La literatura aljamiada.' In *Memoria de los moriscos. Escritos y relatos de una diaspora cultura*, 45–55. Madrid: Sociedad estatal de conmemoraciones culturales.

Montaner Frutos, Alberto. 1988. 'El depósito de Almonacid y la producción de la literatura aljamiada (en torno al ms misceláneo XIII).' *Archivo de Filología Aragonesa* 41: 119–152.

Roza Candás, Pablo. 2018. *Memorial de ida i venida hasta Maka*. Oviedo: Universidad de Oviedo.

Sánchez Cantón, Francisco Javier. 1956. 'Viajeros españoles en oriente.' *Revista del Instituto Egipcio de Estudios Islámicos en Madrid* 4 (1–2): 1–45.

Vázquez, Miguel Ángel. 2007. 'Poesía morisca (o de cómo el español se convirtió en lengua literaria del islam).' *Hispanic review* 5 (3): 219–242.

Vernet, Juan. 1972. *Literatura árabe*. Barcelona: El acantilado.

Vincent, Bernard. 1987. *Minorías y marginados en la España del siglo XVI*. Granada: Excelentísima diputación provincial de Granada.

Wiegers, Gerard. 1994. *Islamic literature in Spanish and Aljamiado. Yça of Segovia (fl. 1450), His Antecedents and Successors*. Leiden: Brill.

Zúñiga López, Ramón. 1988–1989. 'Las coplas del alhichante de Puey Monçón. (Peregrinación a la Meca de un morisco aragonés a finales del siglo XVI).' *Miscelánea de Estudios Árabes y Hebraicos* 2: 449–479.

CHAPTER 3

Sufism and the Hajj: Symbolic Meanings and Transregional Networks; Two Examples from the 16th and 18th Centuries

Neda Saghaee and Richard van Leeuwen

Sufi literature on the hajj usually seeks to convey a symbolical interpretation of the pilgrimage to the Holy Land.[1] Sufi-minded authors, who are inspired by the spirituality of the hajj and the secrets of its rituals, tend to consider the hajj as a metaphorical journey from diversity (*kathra*) toward unity (*waḥda*), reflecting the trajectory of the Sufi disciple towards inner purification. Still, for Sufis as for regular pilgrims, the hajj contains an 'external', physical component, too, directed at the strengthening and preservation of spiritual bonds and networks along the way.

In this chapter explores the understandings of the external and corporal dimensions of the hajj among Sufi 'wayfarers' in the early modern period and discuss their interaction with Sufi networks before and after completing the pilgrimage as part of their spiritual trajectory. Adopting a social perspective we analyse the interrelationships between Sufi and non-Sufi pilgrims during their journey toward the Holy Land and during their residence in the two Holy Cities of Mecca and Medina. We examine the assumption that the pilgrimage expands the pilgrim's network and acts as a means to disseminate a Sufi worldview. The chapter is divided into three sections. The first section gives a brief overview of the early Sufis' thoughts concerning the issue of pilgrimage in Islam based on a select number of primary sources; the second section deals with the pilgrimage and its social aspects. Since Sufi written heritage contains rich primary accounts and mystic authors' opinions about socio-political circumstances, these can be used to ascertain what Sufi pilgrims faced during the hajj and how they responded. The third and final section narrows down the scope and offers a case study of two travel accounts. The first is a Persian travelogue entitled *Jādat al-ʿāshiqīn* ('The road of the passionate lovers'), a sample piece of Sufi literature that narrates the pilgrimage in 1549 of Kamāl al-Dīn Ḥusayn, who

1 The main part of this chapter was written by Neda Saghaee; the sections on al-Zabādī were added by Richard van Leeuwen.

DOI:10.1163/9789004513174_005

was the founder of the Ḥusaynī *ṭarīqa* from a Hamadānī branch of the Kubrāwiyya order in the sixteenth century (Khwarazmī 2011); the second is *Bulūgh al-marām bi-al-riḥla ilā Bayt Allāh al-ḥarām* ('Fulfilment of the desire for God's sacred House'), an account in Arabic by 'Abd al-Majīd al-Zabādī al-Murādī, a Moroccan Sufi, of his hajj in 1745 (al-Murādī n.d.).

1 The Hajj in Sufi Literature

Although Sufis recognize the Holy Cities of Mecca and Medina as the historical and spiritual centers of Islam, mystical approaches to pilgrimage reflect the dichotomy of spiritual understandings and religious/theological understandings of pilgrimage. From a mystical point of view, the observance of superficial aspects of the sharia only is rejected. In her work *Mystical dimensions of Islam*, Annemarie Schimmel (1975, 106) explains how in Sufi thought mystical training is the only way to obtain the hidden secret of the hajj and other rituals, such as prayer and fasting. The mystic's duty is to perceive the inner dimension of the pilgrimage as a means to gain nearness to God or the divine Beloved. Thus, the main issue is the relationship between humanity and divinity.

This dichotomy between the spiritual and material aspects of the hajj can be found in scattered narrations and anecdotes in hagiographies such as Farīd al-Dīn 'Aṭṭār's (d. 1220) *Tadhkira al-awliyā'* and 'Abd al-Raḥmān Jāmī's (*d. 1492*) *Nafaḥāt al-uns*. Other Sufi literature about prominent leading figures and Sufi masters are replete with attempts to demonstrate the personal influential and inner aspect of the hajj such as al-Hujwīrī's (d. 1077) *Kashf al-maḥjūb*, the works of Rūzbihān Baqlī (d. 1209), Jalāl al-Dīn Rūmī's (d. 1273) *Mathnawī*, Ibn al-'Arabī's (d. 1240) *al-Futūḥāt al-Makkiyya*, and Shāh Walīullāh's (d. 1763) *Fuyūḍ al-Ḥaramayn*.[2]

In *Kashf al-maḥjūb*, considered the earliest Sufi treatise in Islamic tradition, 'superficial', physical, aspects of the pilgrimage are perceived as a means to understand its deeper and inner meanings. Its author, al-Hujwīrī, expresses eleven veils between man and God in each chapter of his work and he deals with solutions to remove the obstacles he discusses. In his chapter on the hajj, he explains that whoever seeks the truth will find its signs in each step towards Mecca, since the pilgrim's aim is to obtain contemplation of God (*mushāhada*). The pilgrimage is:

2 Other titles include: al-Ḥakīm al-Tirmidhī (d. c. 905–910), *al-Ḥajj wa asrāruhu*; Abū Naṣr al-Sarrāj (d. 988), *al-Luma' fī al-taṣawwuf*; Abū Ṭālib al-Makkī (d. 996), *Qūt al-qulūb*.

> an act of mortification (*mujāhada*) for the sake of obtaining contemplation (*mushāhada*), and mortification does not become the direct cause of contemplation, but is only a means to it. Therefore, inasmuch as a means has no further effect on the reality of things, the true object of pilgrimage is not to visit the Kabah, but to obtain contemplation of God.
>
> AL-HUJWĪRĪ 2001, 429

With this in mind, the hajj is divided into the *ḥajj al-ghayba* (the 'absent' or 'hidden' pilgrimage) and the *ḥajj al-ḥuḍūr* (the 'present' or 'visible' pilgrimage). Regarding the first one, al-Hujwīrī states that whoever passes the stages of pilgrimage and is physically in Mecca but does not see God, is the similar to a person who stays confined to his home without any spiritual improvement. It must be mentioned that this distinction between the visible and inner aspects of the hajj has been expressed in different ways in Sufi literature. In comparison with al-Hujwīrī's words, 'Abd al-Qādir al-Jīlānī (d. 1166) categorized two types of pilgrimage which are 'the pilgrimage of the sharia and the pilgrimage of the *ṭarīqa*' (al-Jīlānī 1971, 45–46), showing that many Sufis considered the hajj first of all a religious duty, which could be seamlessly combined with its spiritual dimension.

According to al-Hujwīrī, to know the true value of the hajj we can refer to an anecdote by Bāyazīd Bisṭāmī (d. 874), known as *sulṭān al-ʿārifīn* ('king of the mystics'). Bistāmī says: 'On my first pilgrimage I saw only the house, the second time, I saw the house and its owner, and the third time I only saw its owner' (al-Hujwīrī 2001, 427). This passage is the best example of a critical Sufi point of view regarding superficial pilgrimage. Indeed, it turns attention toward the 'true' faith instead of visiting the stone building of the Kaʿba since the essence of the hajj performance is the remembrance of God in the heart. A purified heart, which belongs to the true mystic, is described as the true Kaʿba. Ibn al-ʿArabī considers, 'If the people go around the Kaʿba (*ṭawāf*), divine incoming thoughts (*khawāṭir ilāhiyya*) go around the mystic's heart' (Ibn al-ʿArabī n.d., 52). This idea is rooted in a hadith in which he Prophet says, 'The believer's heart is the throne of the Compassionate' (*qalb al-muʾmin ʿarsh al-Raḥmān*) (Majlisī n.d.).[3] Jalāl al-Dīn Rūmī expresses the idea most clearly in the following verse:

> O people who have gone on Hajj where are you, where are you?
> The Beloved is right here, come forth, come forth[4]

3 See Seyyed Hossein Nasr's translation in Nasr 2019.

4 Rūmī 2009, vol. 1:235. This verse is Seyyed Hossein Nasr's translation in Nasr 2019.

Thus, religious pretense as a worldly trend is rejected in the concept of the hajj because Sufi thought rejects worldly concerns and is more rooted in the ascetic tendency of early Sufis. The hajj is conceived as an allegory for an ascending esoteric journey (*safar*) toward the divine beloved that allows for the development of the soul in order to obtain submission to God and 'annihilation' of the self. The pilgrimage becomes a key metaphor for a movement from diversity (*kathra*) toward unity (*waḥda*), as pilgrims on the hajj must pass through different stages. Furthermore, the hajj is a metaphor for the return journey of man to God after death according to Dhū al-Nūn al-Miṣrī (d. 861):

> For [Dhū al-Nūn, NS], pilgrimage to Mecca is associated with the Muslim's journey to heaven after his death. To mention hajj as a divine call, Dhū al-Nūn put the performance of hajj to a complex undertaking along the course of a human soul to return to Divine origin. In short, Dhū al-Nūn formulated the mystical significances of hajj as sorts of vision of the spiritual states in the world to come (*mushāhadāt aḥwāl al-ākhira*). He put further the shared benefits of hajj, i.e. to increase certainty about the witness of Hereafter, about the existence of spirit, leisure (*rāḥa*), yearning to God, the need for intimacy within heart, tranquility to God, taking a lesson from the rituals, and to halt (*wuqūf*) on the mystical state of gnosis.
> SYARIFUDDIN 2017, 78[5]

While conducting the hajj, a visit to the Prophet's shrine is also valued, along with the Islamic concept of jihad. The Persian Sufi Abū Najīb Suhrawardī (d. 1168) narrated a hadith in which three groups are considered travellers of God: *ḥājjī*s (those who have completed the pilgrimage to Mecca), *ghāzī*s (warriors) and *ʿumra kunandihs* (those who undertake *ʿumra*) (Suhrawardī 1984, 28). In this way, introducing Sufi figures who fulfil all of the above-mentioned roles is very interesting particularly in Sufi biographies (*tadhkira*). For instance, Farīd al-Dīn ʿAṭṭār (d. 1220) in *Tadhkirat al-ʾawliyāʾ* introduced ʿAbd Allāh Mubārak as a great shaykh who performed the hajj in one year, participated in a jihad in another year and did business in the next year, and all Muslims benefited from his trade (Aṭṭār 2007, 184). This story shows how Sufis were engaged in both worldly and otherworldly matters.

A further point to be considered is how the difference between outward and inward aspects of the hajj indicates a distinction between two groups of

5 See the discussion in Sulamī 2001.

pilgrims: the elite (*khawāṣṣ*) and the common people (*ʿawāmm*) (Abrahamov 2018, 16). In many Sufi texts a distinction is made between the common believers, who have just to follow their obligations, and the privileged few who are able to develop mystical insights and reach inner purification. ʿAyn al-Quḍāt Hamadānī (d. 1131), for instance, believes that most pilgrims perform the 'visible' pilgrimage (*ḥajj-e ṣūrat*) while a minority performs the 'true' pilgrimage (*ḥajj-e ḥaqīqat*) (Hamadānī 1991, 57). Thus, only the minority perceives the profound meaning of the ritual. For the common believers, the ritual must be performed according to the rules to develop the soul and obtain nearness to God.

Because the long journey to Mecca was out of reach for most Sufis and filled with hardships and obstacles, Sufi poets liked to compare the journey to the path of lovers to obtain their beloved (Masud 2002, 13). Hence, Sufi literature benefited from the concept of divine love and described each stage of the hajj in subtle and poetic terms. From this perspective,

> the *iḥrām* is the expression of a clear contract with God through an obvious intention. Changing one's ordinary clothes before the *iḥrām* represents exorcizing bad traits and transgressions, and the *iḥrām* embodies a sign of the values of forbearance (*ṣabr*) and neediness (*faqr*). Running between al-Ṣafā and al-Marwa is a symbolic race with mysteries between the pure revelation of God's Majesty and His subtle Beauty.
>
> ABRAHAMOV 2018, 22

2 The Pilgrimage and Its Social Aspects

The social dimension of the hajj in terms of establishing and reconfirming Sufi networks and the social practices that pilgrims engage in, have been the topic of both general and more specific studies.[6] There are many associated questions such as: how can a Sufi pilgrimage be understood as a social activity? How can the hajj be perceived as a communal ritual in Sufism and not only

6 Many scholars try to disclose different aspects of the hajj. For instance, Coleman and Eade focused on the cultural, social and economic sides of pilgrimages in their work. See Coleman and Eade 2004, 6. They believe that 'pilgrims' own models of pilgrimage' are under the influence of common religious and cultural atmosphere in the society (ibid., 17). Pilgrimage can be seen as involving '(…) the institutionalization (or even domestication) of mobility in physical, metaphorical and/or ideological terms' (ibid.), cited in Valdinoci (2008, 207).

as a personal spiritual issue for individual salvation? To answer such questions, we have to look at the social practices in Sufi discourse which can be related to the hajj, such as the rituals in preparation to the journey toward the Holy Land; the rituals during the journey toward Mecca; and the sojourn in places where Sufis may meet leading figures, visit the tombs of great masters, and meeting masters in order to ask them to write amulets in order to pass through stages successfully.

The first point with regard to the social dimension of the hajj is the combining of the hajj with the concept of secular travel (*safar*) in many Sufi texts.[7] The relation between the hajj and the concept of travelling has been observed on two levels. From the outset, four allegorical and internal journeys (*al-asfār al-arbaʿa*)[8] which are analogous to the 'subjective' or 'inner' voyage (*seyr-e anfusi*), and the 'external' aspect of the hajj as an 'objective' voyage (*seyr-e āfāqi*) must be highlighted. For Sufis, the hajj has two sides to which ʿAbd al-Karīm al-Qushayrī (d. 1074) refers in his *al-Risāla al-Qushayriyya*:

> Know that travelling is in two divisions. The first way of travelling is by the body which transfers from one place to another place. The second way of travelling is by the heart, which turns from one attribute [of God, NS] to another. Thousands travel but few travel by the heart.
>
> AL-QUSHAYRĪ 2009, 488

Secondly, considering the concept of travel and the hajj together explains the undeniable physical interaction with non-Sufi pilgrims. Many masters collected the Sufi wayfarers and organized and managed caravans which can be seen as a significant social activity. Al-Ḥallāj's (d. 922) caravan can be referred to as an example, since he was accompanied by four hundred disciples during his

7 For the pre-modern context, travel accounts (Arabic: *riḥla*; Persian: *safarnāma*) routinely include the hajj, *ʿumra*, and *ziyāra* (the visitation of holy places) as part of the itinerary. Travel or journeying in the pursuit of knowledge (*riḥla fī ṭalab al-ʿilm*) is a central commandment in Islam, as in the hadith attributed to the Prophet Muhammad: 'Seek knowledge even in China.' Travel took on different forms, from travel in the pursuit of knowledge to performing the pilgrimage to Mecca and visiting holy sites. See Meri 2017. One of the pre-modern literatures is Ḥajj Sayyāḥ's travel account that is a mirror of religious and political circumstances of the time. See Lubis 2019, 63–87.

8 Four internal journeys (*al-asfār al-arbaʿa*) are: 'from creation to the Truth' (*min al-khalq ilā al-Ḥaqq*); 'in Truth with the Truth' (*fī al-Ḥaqq bi al-Ḥaqq*); 'from the Truth to creation with the Truth' (*min al-Ḥaqq ila al-khalq bi al-Ḥaqq*); 'with the Truth in creation' (*fī al-khalq bi al-Ḥaqq*). The discussion among mystics about these journeys can be traced in Ibn al-ʿArabī's *Risāla al-asfār ʿan natāʾij al-asfār* as well as ʿAfīf al-Dīn Tilmisānī's (d. 1291) commentary on the *Manāzil al-sāʾirīn* of Khwājah ʿAbd Allāh Anṣārī (d. 1088).

second pilgrimage (Aṭṭār 2007, 512).[9] Being a member of a Sufi master's caravan demonstrates strong affinities with the master's way of thinking and it gave fellow travelers a chance to observe rituals according to the leader's interpretation of Islam. In addition, travelling in a master's caravan protected fellow travelers from brigands and marauders and strengthened the sense of unity among the disciples.

Thirdly, debates on etiquette while on the journey and residence at home (*ādāb-e safar va ḥażar*), and on companionship and fellowship (*ādāb-e hamneshini va ṣoḥbat*), expose the social dimension of Sufi hajj rites. Many authors shared their thoughts on communication and interactions with others after a discussion about the hajj because the hajj developed strong bonds of friendship and companionship (Arabic: *ṣuḥba*, Persian: *ṣoḥbat*) with masters and other people. For instance, in his *al-Lumaʿ fī al-taṣawwuf*, Abū Naṣr al-Sarrāj writes a chapter immediately following one concerning the hajj, discussing 'etiquette of the paupers behavior with each other and the laws for the journey and residence at home' (*ādāb-e raftār-e fogharā bā ham va aḥkām-e safar va ḥażar*) then he talks about *hamneshini* and *ṣoḥbat*.[10] These topics are about the rules of ascetic practices, rules for sitting, sleeping, mystical dancing (*samāʿ*), as well as the disciple-master relationship.[11]

The fourth issue to understand Sufi concerns regarding social relationships in the broader cultural context is the etiquette that Sufi pilgrims must observe in the Holy Land. Residence in Mecca was very important for all 'wayfarers' and prominent masters because it extended their network widely and supported the spread of their mystical teachings. Being in the center of the Islamic world paved the way to not only interact with Sufi pilgrims but also with the rulers, leading scholars, religious leaders, well-known masters of the time, disciples, and common people. At this point, the narrated meetings in Sufi hagiographies (*tadhkiras*) can be mentioned. For instance, al-Fuḍayl ibn 'Iyāḍ (d. 803) met Abū Ḥanīfa (d. 767) in Mecca and they discussed various theolo-

---

9 See Aṭṭār 2017, 513 in which it is narrated four thousand people accompany him in his pilgrimage.

10 See al-Sarrāj 1914. It was believed that prophetic spirituality can only be conveyed chest to chest. See Renard 2009, s.v. 'companionship'.

11 Regarding *ādāb-e safar* and stories of mystical travel see Najm al-Dīn Kubrā's (d. 1220) *Ādāb al-ṣūfiyya* and Ṣayf al-Dīn Bākharzī's (d. 1269) *al-Taṣfiyya fī aḥwāl al-mutaṣawwifa* which are about the appropriate manner of personal conduct along the journey. In addition, fellow travelers, who are companions of a master in the hajj, could attain spiritual achievement through the mediatory role of their shaykh. They could obtain 'annihilation in the master' (*fanāʾ fī al-shaykh*) who himself had become annihilated in God (*fanāʾ fī Allāh*). Regarding the term *fanāʾ* see Renard 2009, s.v. 'annihilation'.

gical topics. Also, he was surrounded by many pupils who asked for his advice on the path (Aṭṭār 2007, 78) One of the famous mystics who benefited from al-Fuḍayl b. ʿIyāḍ's companionship was Ibrahīm Adham (d. c. 782) who met many other masters in Mecca such as Safyān al-Thawrī (d. 778), and Abū Yūsuf Ghasūlī (Jāmī 1996, 41). Moreover, travelling toward the Holy Land and staying in Mecca[12] for a long time were seen as attempts to revisit the Prophet's religiosity and imitate his morality. The aim was to increase one's faith and receive divine inspiration, seeking to obtain a clear vision at the most sacred site of Islam (Abrahamov 2018, 18). What is important in the present chapter is the social effect of the spiritual achievements that a stay in Mecca or a departure from the city offered. For instance, Shāh Walī Allāh, as he narrates in *Fuyūḍ al-Ḥaramayn*, a book about his spiritual experiences in the Holy Places in 1731, had a vision whilst in Mecca in which he could connect with the Prophet's spirituality and was appointed by him as the 'preserver of time' (*qā'im al-zamān*). What gave credibility and legitimacy to his authority were his physical presence in Mecca, his visiting the Kaʿba and establishing a spiritual relationship with the Prophet there. Consequently, he became an important and influential figure who led the Muslim community toward a revival of Islam in the eighteenth century (Rizvi 1983, vol. 2:253).

Fifthly, one of the mystical rituals is visiting the tombs of great masters (*ziyāra*) which is an inevitable duty to be performed before the hajj has even started. In thus paying reverence to deceased masters, who are called *'awliyā'* (friends of God, singular *walī*), the pilgrimage was blessed because wayfarers benefited from proximity to the holiness of the place in order to connect themselves to the religious authority of that *walī*, swearing allegiance to him and revisiting his teachings. It was an opportunity to perform collective rituals like *majles-e dhekr* (Arabic: *majlis al-dhikr*: a session for the recollection of God)

12 Although some Sufi pilgrims performed the hajj only once in their lifetime, many Sufis made pilgrimage to Mecca several times in order to be blessed by the effect of the hajj. Jāmī's work, *Nafaḥāt al-uns*, introduces many masters based on their performed pilgrimage. This sort of identification analyses the significance of pilgrimage for getting a reputation and gives criteria to assess their influential piety in ascetic Islamic lives. To illustrate Jami's method, some cases can be referred to: ʿAlī b. Muwaffaq al-Baghdādī who performed the hajj seventy-seven times (see Jāmī 1996, 83), Shaykh Aḥmad Naṣr went twenty times (ibid., 195), ʿAlī b. Shuʿayb al-Saqqā fifty-five times (ibid., 83) and Abū Shuʿayb Mughannaʿ Miṣrī, a disciple of Abū Sa ʿīd Kharrāz, seventy times (ibid., 64). The stay in Mecca was called *mujāwara* (literary means nearness) and some key figures who chose to be a *mujāwir* in Mecca can be referred here: Manṣūr al-Ḥallāj (d. 922), who stayed in Mecca for one year after his first pilgrimage (see Schimmel 1975, 66), al-Ghazālī (d. 1111), who chose a very ascetic life in Mecca, Abū Sa ʿīd Kharrāz (Jāmī 1996, 61), Abū ʿUthmān al-Maghribī (ibid., 70), and Abū ʿAmr al-Zujājī (ibid., 114).

and entrancing dances (*samā'*). What must be considered is that visiting the shrines was different from the pilgrimage to Mecca and its social consequence was also different since it was within reach for common people who lacked the financial means to travel to the Holy Land. Without the obligation to observe certain rituals and temporal limitations, *ziyāra* was more informal and was performed at several holy shrines in a broad geographic area which covered various local cultures. In comparison with the hajj, the etiquettes of *ziyāra* were not standardized. They were in compliance with local culture and varied from one *ṭarīqa* to another. It can be argued that the etiquettes of *ziyāra* were more flexible towards the culture and the different ways of thinking of visitors (Valdinoci 2008, 213).[13] In this way, *ziyāra* became an alternative for those who could not travel to the Holy Land,[14] not in the least since they would also encounter caravans of pilgrims at the shrines and at lodges. Pilgrims were considered to be intermediaries between God and the believers, and meeting them was a way to find spiritual release from concerns of everyday life and solutions for personal problems.[15]

Shrines functioned as communication centres between pilgrims and other travelers from different Muslim regions, bridges between far-flung religious places, which through the hajj were connected to the centre of Islam in Mecca. The result of such interaction must be considered as a means to unite disparate understandings of Islam which had educational and proselytizing consequences. However, *ziyāra* and the veneration of graves also caused clashes among Muslims, since it was labeled as an inadmissible innovation by strict adherents to the sharia because the practices of Sufis at shrines were marked by music, singing and dancing that evoked ecstasy. Therefore, the strict adherents of the sharia viewed the increasing popularity of *ziyāra*, that became more common than traveling to Mecca, as a danger for orthodox religiosity (Werbner 2013, 63).

The sixth point is also related to Sufi social institutions. Along with shrines, *madrasas* (religious schools) and Sufi hospices (*khānqāhs*) should be recog-

---

13 Regarding Sufi shrine pilgrimage, see Ernst 1994, 43–68.

14 The alternative pilgrimage has been named little hajj or the second hajj. For instance, performing pilgrimage three times to the shrine of Ahmet Yasawi, which was called 'the second Mecca' among the Kazakhs, was equal to a pilgrimage to Mecca (Ebadi 2016, 71).

15 For instance, shrines are very popular in India for a large number of people who call them *dargāh* and believe that these places are an 'interface between the human world and God.' See Bashir 2000, 302. Furthermore, Sufi orders value the practice of *ziyāra* since, for instance, Naqshbandīs in India believe that this practice grants spirituality to wayfarers. See Schimmel 1975, 175.

nized as active cultural and social centres.[16] They were places in which pilgrims stayed and rested. They provided the opportunity for travelers to become acquainted with local Sufi traditions since Sufi *khānqāh*s were full of disciples from different classes, ranging from common people to traders, notables, and soldiers. Sufi travelers and masters participated in rituals of the *khānqāh*s such as *dhikr*s, or they were asked to hold *majlis* gatherings based on their own methods. For example, Jāmī reports that Muḥammad b. al-Faẓl al-Balkhī (d. 931) held a *majlis* in a *khānqāh* in Nishapur on the way to Mecca (Jāmī 1996, 89). The opportunity to meet the masters gave travelling Sufis the chance to converse with them and to receive blessings and to be strengthened on the path of God. Therefore, the value of these places for the exchange of mystical experiences and knowledge is significant. The result of meeting other active Sufi orders significantly shaped the social performance of mystical worldviews since they shared their missions and ways of thought with each other. These meetings with the shaykhs and their vicegerents extended the circles of followers because they encouraged many disciples to join a specific *ṭarīqa* (Stauth and Schielke 2008).[17] For instance, after staying in Shihāb al-Dīn Suhrawardī's (d. c. 1234) *khānqāh* in Baghdad, Shaykh Bahāʾ al-Dīn Zakariyā Mūlatānī (d. 1262) was initiated in his *ṭarīqa* and became his disciple (Jāmī 1996, 319).

Finally, arguably the most important practice in Sufi tradition offering the means to gain spiritual benefits from social interactions was the practice of 'service' (Arabic: *khidma*, Persian: *khedmat*). It was believed that service to people (*khidma bi khalq*) is a devotional service to God (*khidma bi Allah*). A Sufi pilgrim who travels as a member of a caravan performs the *ziyāra* and stayed in a madrasa or a *khānqāh*, has the opportunity to perform *khidma* by providing a place of rest for others, offering sustenance, cleaning their shoes and clothes, and feeding their horses. In fact, repentance (*tawba*), purification from sins, and forbearance (*ṣabr*), are all inner changes, which lead the one serving to remove discriminations and help him to understand the notion of equality. Like an ethical act, the pilgrim performs *khidma* and has contact with others regardless of whether he is a master, disciple, rich, poor, male or female. Although this practice was not related only to the hajj pilgrimage, there are many anecdotes in Sufi literature about how great masters rendered *khidma* while traveling to Mecca. Jāmī demonstrates the significance of *khidma* by quoting a sentence from Abū al-Ḥusayn b. Jahẓam who

16 *Khānqāh*s were located near tombs of prominent spiritual figures and mosques.

17 Trimingham observes that in Indonesia, too, the pilgrimage was a means through which Sufism was spread (Trimingham 1971, 130).

believed visiting Sufi masters and serving them was an important duty on the path (Jāmī 1996, 185), with the ultimate aim to spread peace and harmony among Sufis and all members of the *umma* (Muslim community) who come together to complete their pilgrimage. This is illustrated by some verses by Rūmī:

> Ḥajj commands us to circumambulate the apparent Kaʿba
> —in order to soothe someone through it—
> [If] you do circumambulate barefoot the Kaʿba one thousand times,
> Ḥajj will not accept it if you hurt the feelings of someone.
>
> RŪMĪ 2009, vol. 2:1044

As is noted in Rūmī's poem, *khidma* is respect for others' rights because it suppresses pride and selfishness, fosters communication, and increases intimacy between wayfarers on the path of the hajj.

After focusing on different elements in the social lives of pilgrims, the remainder of the chapter scrutinizes two selected pieces of Sufi literature in order to provide a comparative understanding of similarities and differences between two groups of Sufis with various cultural backgrounds from two parts of the Islamic world.

3 Social Features of Kamāl al-Dīn Ḥusayn's Pilgrimage

Among several written Persian texts *Jādat al-ʿāshiqīn* ('The road of passionate lovers') can be mentioned in particular as illustrating the social aspects of the hajj (Khwarazmī 2011). *Jādat al-ʿāshiqīn* contains an account of the journey to Mecca in 1549 of Shaykh Kamāl al-Dīn Ḥusayn Khwarazmī (d. 1551), the founder of the Ḥusayniyya *ṭarīqa*, a branch of Kubrāwiyya.[18] The work was composed between 1561–1565 by Sharīf al-Dīn Ḥusayn Khwarazmī, who was Kamāl al-Dīn Ḥusayn's son and disciple. Along with *Miftāḥ al-ṭālibīn* written by Maḥmūd Ghajduwānī, it is the main source informing us about Kamāl al-

18 Muṭribī al-Samarqandī mentions that he was a disciple of Shaykh Ḥājjī Aḥmad Khabūshānī who was a pupil of Shaykh Shāh who was a disciple of Shaykh Rashīd who was a disciple of Amīr ʿAbdullāh Yazdash Ābādī who was a disciple of Amīr ʿAlī Hamadānī. Thus, his *ṭarīqa* traces back to ʿAlā al-Dawla Simnānī (d. 1336), a well-known Kubrāwī master, and from Najm al-Dīn Kubrā to Najīb Suhrawardī, Aḥmad Ghazālī. See Muṭribī al-Samarqandī, *Tadhkirat al-Shuʿarā* (1382 Sh./2003), 650–652, cited in Jaʿfariyān's Introduction of "Jādat al-ʿāshiqīn" (Khwarazmī 2011, 13).

Dīn Ḥusayn's teachings as a great master in Khwarazm, Bukhara and Damascus (Khwarazmī 2011, 12). The social and geographical area of *Jādat al-ʿāshiqīn*'s influence could be assessed since its audience were Kamāl al-Dīn Ḥusayn's disciples from Transoxiana, specifically Samarqand, Tashkent, Ḥiṣār, Khatlān and Badakhshān (Khwarazmī 2011, 14).[19] The work is organized in fifteen chapters, among which the ninth through the twelfth chapters are about the hajj and include a travelogue.

Analysing the text from the perspective of social practices shows that the author, Sharīf al-Dīn Ḥusayn, was personally engaged in the social affairs of Sufi pilgrims since he was appointed as a caravan leader by Kamāl al-Dīn Ḥusayn (Khwarazmī 2011, 18).[20] The members of the caravan were from different social classes and what united them was their being Kamāl al-Dīn Ḥusayn's followers. Moreover, the caravan had a multicultural composition since Kamāl al-Dīn Ḥusayn's disciples joined him from different areas, and many well-known Sufi and non-Sufi figures joined the caravan as the journey proceeded. Indeed, diverse levels of religiosity among fellow travelers is another social aspect of this caravan that provided Kamāl al-Dīn Ḥusayn with a chance to collect and guide a large number of wayfarers and initiate them to his *ṭarīqa* (Khwarazmī 2011, 50). Their journey toward the Holy Land started with the traditional visits to tombs in Samarqand and Bukhara such as the grave of Sayf al-Dīn Bākharzī (d. 1261), and two well-known Sufis of the Yasawiyya *ṭarīqa*, Ḥakīm Ātā (d. 1186) and Sayyid Ātā (lived in thirteenth and fourteenth centuries).[21] There were also gatherings in *khānqāh-e* Fatḥ-ābādi, which created a connection between their living master's teachings and his deceased mystic elders (Khwarazmī 2011, 28). Moreover, these meetings confirmed social relationships and the exchange of Khurāsānī, Turkistanī and particularly Kubrāwī ways of thinking. At the same time, they prepared pilgrims spiritually for the journey to Mecca and Medina (ibid., 19).[22]

The information contained in *Jādat al-ʿāshiqīn* about the Sunni predominance of Kamāl al-Dīn Ḥusayn's caravan allows us to analyse the religious tenor of their activities with regard to political conflicts between Shiʿi Safawids and Sunni Ottomans. It should be pointed out that the Safawids suppressed Sunnis and imposed their adherence to Shīʿī practices in Iran, encour-

19 Rashnu-zāda, *s.v.* 'Kamal al-Dīn Khwarazmī,' cited in Khwarazmī 2011, 14.

20 See also Khwarazmī's narration 34.

21 Aḥmad Yasawī (d. 1166), founder of Yasawiyya. See Khwarazmī 2011, 36. Sayyid Ātā was the founder of Ātā'iyya branch of Yasawiyya. See DeWeese 2011.

22 The members of the caravan were invited to join the caravan by their master's letters (Khwarazmī 2011, 33).

aging, for instance, an alternative pilgrimage to Karbala and the shrines of Shiʿi Imāms instead of Mecca (Bhardwaj 1998, 80). The caravan route went exclusively through Sunni territory and that demonstrates how interactions between Sunni Sufis legitimized Sunni rulers' power in the conflict between two communities of Islam. Among those rulers who visited Kamāl al-Dīn Ḥusayn, the name of the Shaybanid leader ʿUbaydullāh Khān Ghāzī, the ruler of Samarqand and Khwarazm, must be mentioned. He played a key role in the struggles with the Safawids (Khwarazmī 2011, 18). ʿUbaydullāh Khān Ghāzī, along with all his court and aristocrats, welcomed the shaykh and his caravan and solicited their spiritual blessing, so as to obtain the influence of a reputable leading master's support in their political operations.

The meeting, in 1549, between Kamāl al-Dīn Ḥusayn and the Ottoman Sultan Sulaymān (d. 1566), the most important political figure whom he met, can be understood in a similar way. When Kamāl al-Dīn Ḥusayn arrived in Istanbul with three hundred companions, he was welcomed by many notables (*sādāt*) and religious scholars (Khwarazmī 2011, 46). Kamāl al-Dīn Ḥusayn usually avoided visiting royal families and kings, and it was a tradition in the Ottoman Empire that the emperor did not visit persons outside his court, but after Sultan Sulaymān (r. 1520–1566) had sent his representatives to express his apologies and invite him to the court. He convinced Kamāl al-Dīn Ḥusayn and his disciples to accept his invitation for a meeting at the court by referring to a hadith of the Prophet expressing that he did not refuse any invitations (ibid., 48). The event coincided with the traditional public audience of the emperor wherein he saluted all people, from elites to paupers, but on that day the people were more excited by the presence of Kamāl al-Dīn Ḥusayn. In addition, a private meeting with the Ottoman emperor was arranged, who was impressed by Kamāl al-Dīn Ḥusayn and said: 'I had heard about many good men and I had met many [of them, NS]; But I have not seen and I have not heard [of someone, NS] like you' (ibid., 46–49).

The strong bond between the Ḥusayniyya *ṭarīqa* and the Ottomans was further developed after Bayazīd, the son of Sultan Sulaymān, joined Kamāl al-Dīn Ḥusayn's order. According to traditions in the Ottoman Empire, the prince had a private conversation with the shaykh, but after a while it was declared that all were invited to join the meeting because the prince had been initiated into the Ḥusayniyya (ibid., 53).

The next point regarding Kamāl al-Dīn Ḥusayn's pilgrimage is that it provided the opportunity to meet leading spiritual figures on the way to the Holy Land, for instance, Mīr Lājawardī, a master in the Khwājagān order (ibid., 59). These meetings with religious scholars and Sufis are important to comprehend his social activities. Among the pious men he met, the name should be mentioned of Dervish Bahrām, who devoted himself to the Ḥusayniyya *ṭarīqa*.[23] Kamāl al-Dīn Ḥusayn benefited from the interaction with masters and Sufis in *khānqāh*s as a way to expand networks in addition to exchanging spiritual practices. For instance, after visiting Rūmī's tomb in Konya, he and his disciples participated in a *majlis* according to the Mawlawiyya rules, namely, a mixture of reading the Qurʾan, remembrance of God (*dhikr*), prayer, commemorating earlier Sufis, reading passages from the *Mathnawī*, and music and dancing. The *majlis* was held for three days and Kamāl al-Dīn Ḥusayn and his companions experienced *wajd* or a state of ecstasy from *samāʿ* (ibid., 55). Additionally, Kamāl al-Dīn Ḥusayn's stays in *khānqāhs* and madrasas allowed him to connect with a large number of common people and novice Sufis from all classes and walks of life, some of whom could not carry out the pilgrimage. They participated in his sessions for the remembrance of God and he taught them the formulas of the *dhikr*.

The last point of interest from a social perspective is the building of a *khānqāh* for accommodating Ḥusaynī Sufis in Mecca which shows that Mecca was a center where various ways of thinking and cultural differences met (ibid., 23). For Kamāl al-Dīn Ḥusayn, new *khānqāh*s in different areas functioned as instruments for spreading his teachings and offered support to his adherents. After his pilgrimage, he settled in Damascus with the aim to represent the Ḥusayniyya as an active *ṭarīqa* in a city that was regarded a holy site among Sufis and was known for Ibn al-ʿArabī's grave and many shrines of other famous Sufis. He was buried in Damascus.[24]

Our discussion of Kamāl al-Dīn Ḥusayn's pilgrimage shows how the hajj served Sufi *ṭarīqa*s to build and uphold networks which connected often remote parts of the Muslim world with the center of the faith in the Hijaz. These networks not only facilitated the hajj journey for all kinds of pilgrims, but also supported the *ṭarīqa*s themselves, because they were able to strengthen their political significance, recruit new followers on the route and revitalize their spiritual activities through exchange with other *ṭarīqa*s and their infrastructural and symbolic connection with the Holy Places. In the next section we will

---

23 Dervish Bahrām was a sincere devotee to Sufi teachings who led an ascetic life. He became intoxicated under Kamāl al-Dīn Ḥusayn's influence. See Khwarazmī 2011, 35. Another example, when the shaykh and his caravan departed from Istanbul to Damascus, an ascetic called Muṣṭafā who had met many well-known masters but had not devoted himself to their spirituality, came to swear allegiance to Kamāl al-Dīn Ḥusain because he had finally found his true spiritual guide, or the perfect man, in the shaykh. See ibid., 50.

24 He built a *khānqāh* for Ḥusaynī Sufi in Aleppo before his death. See Khwarazmī 2011, 25.

explore how, in a somewhat later period, these mechanisms were relevant for a Sufi from the Maghrib, which, like Central Asia, was relatively far away from the central Muslim lands.

4 A Moroccan Sufi and His Journey to Mecca: ʿAbd al-Majīd al-Zabādī al-Murādī (1745)

In early modern Morocco, the boundaries between religious scholarship, Sufism and popular practices were not very strict. A respectable scholar would have at least some knowledge of the sciences of the 'invisible' (*ghayb*), while prominent Sufis would stress their adherence to the Mālikī school of legal orthodoxy. Whatever brotherhood they belonged to, when on pilgrimage to Mecca they would without explication combine the obligatory rites of the hajj with visits to graves of pious saints and fellow Sufis on the way. The element connecting the two was a fundamental spirituality and ethical consciousness, which could be expressed in various forms. This spirituality had a strong social component, which embedded Sufism in society in general and in regional and trans-regional Sufi networks more in particular. As a rule, before departing for the hajj, Sufis would make a tour around the lodges (*zāwiya*s) of their order in the region, thereby strengthening the bonds between the brothers and acquiring the permission and *baraka* from fellow-Sufis and spiritual masters. On the way, some would visit as many saintly graves as they could, while others would restrict their *ziyāra*s to the main figures and most convenient sanctuaries. The most important aim was the wish to strengthen the scholarly and spiritual networks in the different regions, both within the *ṭarīqa* and between different branches of scholarship and spiritual practice.

To illustrate how these aspects of spirituality and the hajj were combined by Sufi pilgrims in the Maghrib in the eighteenth century, we will here briefly discuss the interesting travelogue written by the scholar and Shādhilī Sufi ʿAbd al-Majīd al-Zabādī al-Murādī, usually called al-Zabādī, of his journey to Mecca in 1745. After explaining the 'rules for travelling' (*ādāb al-safar*), in the opening pages of his travelogue, and after stressing the necessity of 'patience' (*ṣabr*), since 'travelling is suffering' (al-Murādī n.d., 12), al-Zabādī proceeds to relate his trajectory from Fes to Tripoli, mentioning the various graves he visited on the way to obtain *baraka* from the pious saints who have 'knowledge of God' (*ʿārif bi-Allāh*),[25] and exchanging information about various Sufi practices, prayers

25 This refers to esoteric knowledge, as opposed to legal scholarship.

and litanies. Most of the saints are not well known and sometimes even the author cannot remember their names (ibid., 16–19, 21, 26, 29). The most significant visit is the one in Tripoli to the *zāwiya* of the great shaykh Sīdī Aḥmad al-Zarrūq al-Burnusī (d. 899), where al-Zabādī spends the night. Al-Burnusī, he explains, was one of the main shaykhs of the Shādhilī order, who wrote about the rules of the *ṭarīqa* which were still of fundamental importance in his day. Al-Zabādī adds a list of al-Burnusī's teachers and shaykhs (ibid., 42–44).

From Cairo, al-Zabādī travels to Mecca over land with the Egyptian caravan, on the way reading the famous *Burda* and *Hamziyya*, two poetic eulogies of the Prophet composed by al-Būṣīrī (1213–1294) (ibid., 26, 76). He dons the *iḥrām* costume in Juḥfa, near Rābigh, and buys adequate sandals, pronouncing the *talbiyya* and the *niyya*, or intention to perform the hajj. The first view of the Kaʿba is a highly emotional moment: his 'mind is bewildered', his heart 'reaches out to him', and 'peace descends on his soul'. This is, of course, a typical spiritual interpretation of the event, which is accompanied by references to Qurʾanic verses. Al-Zabādī kisses the Black Stone more than once, and not only with his mouth, because 'that would not be sufficient to heal the ailing pilgrim', again a spiritual allusion (ibid., 85). The sight of the Kaʿba fills him with humility (*khushūʿ* and *khuḍūʿ*), two topical terms for the emotions fitting the occasion. After completing the various obligatory rituals of the hajj and the *ʿumra*, he visits the many monuments related to the family of the Prophet and other historical figures. He does not refrain from mentioning the abuses and fighting among the pilgrims when the Kaʿba is opened for the public for one day. He adds that there is a separate day reserved for women (ibid., 105–106).

During his stay in Mecca, al-Zabādī meets several fellow-Sufis. He befriends a shaykh from Shinqīṭ (Mauretania) and a shaykh from Morocco who, in front of the Kaʿba, recites for him the great litany (*al-ḥizb al-kabīr*) of al-Shādhilī and asks for a written 'diploma' (*ijāza*), while al-Zabādī 'takes' from some members of the Nāṣirī order their particular prayer (*wird*) for which he acquires an *ijāza*. Another student, who had received a special hadith from him through a straight line of transmission from the Prophet (*al-musalsal bi al-awwaliyya*; the hadith 'al-Raḥma'), presents him with some frankincense in front of the Kaʿba, thereby endowing it with special *baraka*. In Medina, al-Zabādī prays in the *rawḍa* in the Prophet's Mosque, only one pillar separating him from the chamber of the Prophet's grave (*ḥujra*). He visits the cemetery al-Baqīʿ and the tomb of Ḥamza in Uḥud, the site of a famous battle in the early years of Islam. He also socializes with other pilgrims, attending *dhikr*s and *haḍra*s where the *Burda* and the *Ḥamziyya* are recited, two significant devotional texts in praise of the Prophet. His efforts to communicate with some Persians fail, because they are unable to understand him (ibid., 131, 142–143).

It is on his return journey to Morocco, and especially in Cairo, that al-Zabādī seriously delves into the Sufi-scenes. Here, he attends the *dhikr*s and *ḥalqa*s (prayer meetings) of the Rifāʿiyya order, which is known for its ecstatic rituals, to evoke a state of 'shared ecstacy' (*tawājud*) through singing, and a state of 'unconsciousness' (*ghaybūba*) through dancing, to such an extent that they are able to 'hold snakes, descend into blazing ovens and ride lions' (ibid., 172, 181). He also participates in a *ḥalqa* of the Khalwatiyya order, known for their strict rules and relentless discipline. Finally, al-Zabādī visits the tomb of the great Sufi master Aḥmad al-Badawī in Tanta, where he witnesses a *ḥaḍra* and learns the precise formulas that are uttered by the Sufis to attain a state of trance (ibid., 285).

Al-Zabādī's account of his encounters in Egypt shows that the various levels of religiosity are seamlessly combined in his spiritual practice. He visits not only the well-known Sufi orders, but also the graves of the great legal scholar al-Shāfiʿī, and the mausoleum of Sayyida Nafīsa, a descendant of the Prophet, which was a center of popular piety (ibid., 199–206). He visits a respected Azharī scholar of Mālikī law and hadith, next to a Sufi shaykh known for his knowledge of litanies, *dhikr*s, and chains of transmission of Sufi initiation, for instance, through handshakes, *ṣuḥba*, the transmission of *dhikr*s or the handing over of the *khirqa*, or Sufi robe (ibid., 247). He does not eschew meeting an eccentric shaykh who, during a teaching session, suddenly lets out a huge cry and falls down unconscious. People start shouting and weeping, while others faint or are struck dumb. When the shaykh regains consciousness, he begins to abuse the women present with obscene language, until finally he and his disciples retire to his room to have a frugal meal (ibid., 305–307).

After his return home, al-Zabādī will certainly have felt greatly enriched by his experiences while exploring the Sufi communities during his journey. He made full use of the hidden and less hidden opportunities which the sacred geography and its networks had to offer to strengthen and reshape his personal form of religiosity. He visited important and less important landmarks which were centres of local practices and spirituality, emphasizing that his journey was a spiritual trajectory, linking him to the rich heritage of Sufism, collecting *baraka* and *ijāza*s, and learning new ritual practices. His account also stresses the essential importance of legal scholarship, through his discussions with scholars and references to legal doctrines. This culminates in his discussion of the permissibility of smoking tobacco, which he explicitly rejects. Here, too, legal scholarship and Sufism converge, since not only legal arguments are referred to, but also a shaykh who says that anyone who has rendered himself impure by smoking, should not be allowed to recite the *Dalāʾil al-khayrāt*, the famous eulogy of the Prophet by the Moroccan Sufi Muḥammad al-Jazūlī (d. 1465), which was particularly popular among Sufis (ibid., 263).

However important these elements may be, the main significance of al-Zabādī's account lies in the way he explores and reveals how Sufi networks were interlinked in a kind of social substratum, which integrated not only forms of religiosity and piety, but also communities connected through ritual practices and common visions of religion. These networks were strengthened through encounters, visits and participation, but especially through the communication of texts, practices and chains of transmission, and the exchange of *ijāza*s, *baraka*, initiations, and shared ecstatic experiences. This reinforcement of Sufi networks is of course enhanced by the account itself, which not only reveals the existence of these networks, but also provides new information about practices, texts and people. It shows how in this phase of globalization, marked by intensified interaction between the different regions of the Muslim world, the practice of the hajj made possible the encounter and entanglement of different trends in Sufism, originating in Morocco, Egypt and Asia, such as the Khalwatiyya, Shādhiliyya, Naqshbandiyya, Rifāʿiyya, Badawiyya, Nāṣiriyya, Malāmatiyya, Qādiriyya and Aydarūsiyya, all referred to by al-Zabādī.[26]

A final interesting aspect of al-Zabādī's account is the way in which it emphasizes the physical and emotional dimensions of the hajj and spiritual practices, instead of focusing on the legal and ritual aspects only. Although his account of his stay in Mecca and the actual hajj is rather formal and framed in quotations, formulas to express his exaltation, we find remarks that betray his personal emotions. One remark epitomizes how for al-Zabādī experience and ritual prescriptions are integrated:

> *ʿUlāmā*ʾ and pious saints can be found in all places, but the Kaʿba is only here, so I preferred to stay in the Grand Mosque. Still, God will take care that the *baraka* of the saints will not pass by me.
>
> AL-MURĀDĪ n.d., 96

Clearly, al-Zabādī does not share the more common Sufi suspicion of the Kaʿba as a material site representing the Divine, which obscures true insight in His reality; he is confident that the various religious domains will converge in his person through God's grace.

26 al-Murādī n.d., 115, 116, 172, 174, 182, 183, 184, 236, 279, 285, 307, 309, 314.

5 Conclusion

Our discussion of two Sufi travelogues has shown that the main social achievement of the hajj among Sufis was communication which was helpful to spread the message of an individual *ṭarīqa* to other Muslims. The hajj served to distinguish the pious identity of Sufi leaders, who were considered elites in the spiritual sense, and who were separated from common pilgrims, who were adherents to juridical understandings of the pilgrimage or who initially focused on superficial, physical, aspects of religious laws. Although the aims of the hajj can be understood as an ascetic performance, involving the purification of the soul, the acquisition of higher knowledge, and the procurement of divine blessings, visitation to Islamic religious centres allows for the following: fellowship with shaykhs and their disciples, and being in contact with representatives of a *ṭarīqa* in a different part of the Islamic world. This all contributed to revisiting teachings and preserving Islamic spirituality.

Comparative analysis of the hajj accounts of Kamāl al-Dīn Ḥusayn and al-Zabādī's journeys shows, first, that the practices directed at social communication described by Kamal al-Dīn Ḥusayn in the sixteenth century, were common, too, among Moroccan Sufis of the eighteenth century. It seems that these practices had a clear and important function in stabilizing Sufi networks and preserving textual and ritual traditions. The visiting of graves and living fellow-Sufis, the exchange of information and texts, the confirmation of chains of initiation and teaching, the evocation of spiritual experiences through shared sessions, and the introduction to methods and practices from other Muslim lands all show how the basic strategies of the Sufi orders resisted historical transformations to a certain extent. They also show how the hajj was an essential mechanism to combine travelling with religious purposes as an integrated spiritual undertaking which represented a lifeline for the various Sufi communities. Finally, it shows how legal and spiritual components were combined in the concept and practice of the hajj, on the one hand by endowing it with a deep spiritual significance, which almost rendered the physical hajj redundant, or, on the other hand, by using the framework of legal obligations to construct specific forms of spirituality and religious experience. It seems that al-Zabādī effortlessly combines these different components of religiosity in his role as a devout pilgrim.

If we compare the two travelogues, it is remarkable how persistent the function of the hajj has been for the stabilization and vitality of Sufi networks throughout the Muslim world. It also shows how, ultimately, the Holy Places served as a center where these networks met. In Mecca and Medina, Moroccan Sufis encountered fellow Sufis from Asia and could observe each other's practices, although linguistic difficulties often prevented direct communication. Exchanges also took place during the journey, either fostering the spread of tariqas or enriching practices by new shared experiences. The two travelogues show that these functions were preserved and even further developed during the sixteenth to eighteenth centuries, a period which witnessed increasing interaction between the diverse parts of the Muslim world. This interaction is especially illustrated by Kamāl al-Dīn Ḥusayn's visit to the Ottoman Sultan, which established not only religious, but also political channels of communication.

References

Abrahamov, Binyamin. 2018. 'The Sufis' attitude toward the hajj (pilgrimage): The case of Ibn al-ʿArabī.' In *A Tribute to Hannah: Jubliee book in honor of Hannah Kasher*, edited by Avi Elqayam and Ariel Malachi, 7–43. Tel Aviv: IDRA publishing.

al-Hujwīrī, ʿAlī b. ʿUthmān al-Jullābī. 2001. *The Kashf al-Mahjūb*. Translated by Reynold Nicholson. Lahore: Zia ul-Quran.

al-Jīlanī, ʿAbd al-Qādir. 1971. *Sirr al-asrār wa maẓhar al-anwār fī mā yaḥtājū ilayhi al-abrār*. Edited by Aḥmad Farīd al-Mazīdī. Bayrūt: Dār al-Kutub al-ʿIlmiyya.

al-Murādīʿ, ʿAbd al-Majīd ibn ʿAlī al-Manālī al-Zabādī al-Ḥasanī al-Idrīsī Abū Muḥammad Faḍil. n.d. *Bulūgh al-marām bi-al-riḥla ilā Bayt Allāh al-ḥarām*. Edited by Muḥammad Zaynhum. al-Qāhira: al-Dār al-Thaqāfiyya li-al-Nashr.

al-Qushayrī, ʿAbd al-Karīm. 2009 [1388]. *Tarjume-ye risāle-ye Qushayriyya*. Translated by Ḥasan b. Aḥmad al-ʿUthmānī, edited by Badīʿ al-Zamān Foruzānfar. Tehrān: Enteshārāt-e ʿElmi va Farhangi.

al-Sarrāj, ʿAbd Allāh b. ʿAlī al-Ṭūsī. 1914. *al-Lumaʿ fī al-taṣawwuf*. Edited by Reynold Nicholson. London: Luzac & Co.

Aṭṭār, Farīd al-Dīn. 2007 [1386]. *Tadhkira al-awliyā'*. Edited by Moḥammad Esteʿlāmi. Tehrān: Zavvār.

Bashir, Shahzad. 2000. 'Enshrining divinity: The death and memorialization of Fazlallah Astarabadi in Hurufi thought.' The Muslim world 90: 302.

Bhardwaj, Surinder. 1998. 'Non-hajj pilgrimage in Islam: A neglected dimension of religious circulation.' *Journal of cultural geography* 17 (2): 69–87.

Coleman, Simon and John Eade, eds. 2004. *Reframing pilgrimage: Cultures in motion*. London: Routledge.

DeWeese, Dewin. 2011. s.v. 'Atā'īya order.' *Encyclopædia Iranica* vol. II, Fasc. 8, 904–905. New York: Encyclopædia of Iranica. https://iranicaonline.org/articles/ataiya-order-a-branch-of-the-yasaviya-sufi-brotherhood-especially-active-in-karazm-from-the-8th-14th-century.

Ebadi, Mehdi. 2016. 'Shrine pilgrimage (ziyārat) in Turco-Iranian cultural regions.' *International journal of religious tourism and pilgrimage* 4: 70–77.

Ernst, Carl. 1994. 'An Indo-Persian guide to Sufi shrine pilgrimage.' In *Manifestations of sainthood in Islam*, edited by Grace Smith and Carl Ernst, 43–68. Istanbul: The Isis Press.

Hamadānī, 'Ayn al-Quḍāt. 1991 [1370]. *Tamhīdāt*. Tehrān: Manuchehri.

Ibn al-ʿArabī, Muḥy al-Dīn. n.d. *al-Futūḥāt al-Makkiyya*. Bayrūt: Dār Ṣādir.

Jāmī, 'Abd al-Rahmān. 1996 [1375]. *Nafaḥāt al-uns min ḥaẓarāt al-Quds*. Edited by Maḥmud ʿĀbedi. Tehrān: Eṭṭelāʿāt.

Khwarazmī, Sharīf al-Dīn Ḥusayn. 2011 [1390]. 'Jādat al-ʿāshiqīn.' Edited by Rasul Jaʿfariyān. *Payām-e Bahārestān* 13: 11–88.

Lubis, Firuz-akhtar. 2019. 'Sufism and travel literature: Soul captivity in Hajj Sayyah's knowledge-seeking journey in Safarnāmah-yi Ḥājj Sayyāḥ bih Farang.' *Kemanusiaan: The Asian journal of humanities* 26: 63–87.

Majlisī, Mullā Muḥammad Bāqir. n.d. *Biḥār al-anwār*. Edited by Bāqir Maḥmūdī and 'Abd al-Zahrā 'Alawī. Bayrūt: Dār al-Turāth al-ʿArabī.

Masud, Muhammad Khalid. 2002. 'Sufi views of hajj: Understanding Islamic rituals.' *Sufi Illuminations* 3 (1): 1–13.

Meri, Yousef. 2017. 'Pilgrimage and religious travel.' *Islamic Studies*. https://doi.org/10.1093/OBO/9780195390155-0061, accessed July 22, 2021.

Nasr, Seyyed Hossein. 2019. 'Metaphysical significance of Makkah.' http://webcache.googleusercontent.com/search?q=cache:MVwWat8PEI8J:firstforum.org/DownloadSpecialReportDetail.13680.ashx+&cd=1&hl=en&ct=clnk&gl=de, accessed July 22, 2021.

Renard, John. 2009. *The A to Z of Sufism*. Toronto: The Scarecrow Press.

Rizvi, Athar Abbas. 1983. *History of Sufism in India*. New Delhi: Munshiram Manoharlal Publishers.

Rūmī. 2009 [1388]. *Ghazaliyāt-e Shams*. Edited by Moḥammad Reẓā Shafiʿi Kadkani. Tehrān: Sokhan.

Schimmel, Annemarie. 1975. *Mystical dimensions of Islam*. Chapel Hill: The University of North Carolina Press.

Stauth, Georg and Samuli Schielke. 2008. 'Dimensions of locality: Muslim saints, their place and space.' *Yearbook of the sociology of Islam* 8. Bielefeld: Transcript Verlag.

Suhrawardī, Abū Najīb 'Abd al-Qāhir. 1984 [1363]. *Ādāb al-murīdīn*. Translated by 'Omar Shirkāni, edited by Najib Māyel Heravi. Tehrān: Mowlā

Sulamī, Abū 'Abd al-Raḥmān Muḥammad b. al-Ḥusayn. 2001. *Ḥaqā'iq al-tafsīr: Tafsīr al-Qur'ān al-ʿazīz*. Edited by Sayyid 'Imrān. Bayrūt: Dār al-Kutub al-ʿIlmiyya.

Syarifuddin, Mohammed Anwar. 2017. 'The disseminated interpretations of hajj from Dhu al-Nun to al-Shibli and the problems of contemporary pilgrimage.' *Advances in social science, education and humanities research* (ASSEHR) 137: 77–83.

Trimingham, Spencer. 1971. *The Sufi orders in Islam*. Oxford: Clarendon Press.

Valdinoci, Mauro. 2008. 'Ritual journey and symbolic journey. Elements of pilgrimage to the Sufi saints' shrines in Hyderabad.' *Rivista di studi Sudasiatici* III: 201–232.

Werbner, Pnina. 2013. 'Reform Sufism in South Asia.' In *Islamic reform in South Asia*. Edited by Filippo Osella, 51–78. New York: Cambridge University Press.

CHAPTER 4

Religious Emotion and Embodied Piety in the Ottoman Turkish Hajj Accounts of Evliyā Çelebī (1611–c. 1683) and Yūsuf Nābī (1642–1712)

Yahya Nurgat

1 Introduction

After the defeat of the Mamluk Sultanate in 1516–1517, the duty of administrating the hajj passed into Ottoman hands. As a result, unprecedented numbers of Turkish-speaking pilgrims from the central lands of the empire (Rūmīs) began to undertake the pilgrimage by land and sea, seeking to fulfill the fifth and final pillar of Islam. A diverse range of evidence survives to this day as a testament to their peregrinations, from the khans and cisterns dotting the hajj road between Üsküdar and Medina (via Damascus) to the hajj guides produced by Rūmī scholars for their Turkish-speaking audience. While handwritten copies of these guides number in the thousands, comparatively (and perhaps surprisingly) few narrative hajj accounts in Ottoman Turkish survive from the first three centuries of Ottoman rule in the Hijaz. The accounts of Evliyā Çelebī (1611–c. 1683) and Yūsuf Nābī (1642–1712) stand as notable exceptions in this regard, providing an invaluable descriptive account of the hajj from the perspective of two Rūmī pilgrims who undertook the hajj just seven years apart from one another.

A self-styled 'wandering dervish and world traveller', Evliyā was born in 1611 and raised in Istanbul (Evliyā 2010, 146).[1] As the son of the imperial goldsmith Dervīş Meḥmed Ẓıllī Agha (d. 1648), Evliyā was apprenticed to the personal imām of Murād IV (r. 1623–1640), Evliyā Meḥmed Efendī, who tutored him in Qur'an recitation. He was also educated in a wide variety of arts and sciences at the Topkapı Palace School (*Enderūn*), where he graduated as a cavalryman (*sipāhī*) in 1638. Evliyā's real passion, though, was to be 'world traveller' (*seyyāḥ-ı ʿālem*), which he was able to pursue by means of his inherited wealth, high

1 For Evliyā's time in Medina, I cite the following, translated edition: Evliyā Çelebī. *Evliyā Çelebi in Medina*. For Evliyā's time in Mecca, translations are my own, based on volume nine of the Yapı Kredi Yayınları critical edition: Evliyā Çelebī. *Evliyā Çelebi Seyāḥatnāmesi*.

family status, and court connections. His travels across the breadth of the Ottoman Empire and beyond are recorded in his *Seyāḥatnāme* ('Book of Travels'), which covers ten volumes, and is 'a key text for all aspects of the Ottoman Empire at the time of its greatest extension in the seventeenth century' (Evliyā 2010, x). Evliyā's hajj journey is covered in the ninth volume, where he describes setting out from Istanbul in May 1671, and after taking an extremely circuitous route, arriving in Jerusalem in January of 1672. His next major stop was Damascus, from where he travelled to Medina and Mecca with the Syrian pilgrimage caravan. Finally, after completing the hajj in April 1672, Evliyā departed Mecca for Cairo with the Egyptian caravan.[2]

While Evliyā might be said to have grown up in the palace, Nābī was a relative latecomer.[3] He was born in 1642 in Ruhā (modern-day Şanlıurfa, south-eastern Anatolia) to a distinguished religious family claiming descent from the Prophet Muhammad. He arrived in Istanbul in 1665 at the age of twenty-three, one of many aspirant literary figures drawn to the Empire's capital city from the provinces (Woodhead 2011, 154). Through his literary ability, Nābī was able to gain the patronage of a close companion of Meḥmed IV (r. 1648–1687), the vizier Dāmād Muṣṭafa Paşa (d. 1685). Nābī initially served as the latter's secretary and thereafter as his steward (*kethüdā*). In 1678, after thirteen years in Istanbul, Nābī resolved to embark on the pilgrimage to Mecca. He set out in a small private caravan from Istanbul, passing through Konya, Urfa, Damascus, Jerusalem and Cairo, where he joined the Egyptian pilgrimage caravan. After returning from Mecca (via Medina and Damascus), Nābī composed an account of his journey for presentation to the Sultan, calling it *Tuḥfetü'l-Ḥaremeyn* ('The sanctuaries' gift'). He chose to do so in the elaborate, artistic Ottoman Turkish prose style known as *inşā*, and also incorporated occasional verses of poetry. While Evliyā's work appears to have remained unread until 1742, when it was brought from Cairo to Istanbul and copied, Nābī's *Tuḥfe* achieved more immediate popularity, a reflection of his prominence in the Ottoman literary landscape and his renown as a master of verse and prose. The *Tuḥfe*'s popularity endured into the eighteenth century, with most Turkish-speaking scribes, high officials, and littérateurs possessing a copy of the work (Shafir 2020, 20).[4]

---

2 The biographical information in this paragraph was taken from *Evliyā Çelebī. An Ottoman traveller*, x–xxiii and 292.

3 For Nābī, I rely on Menderes Coşkun's critical edition: *Nābī. Manzūm ve mensūr Osmanlı hac Seyāḥatnāmeleri*. Translations are my own unless quoted from Coşkun (1999). For an introduction to Nābī and his work see the introduction to Coşkun (1999) as well as Coşkun (2000).

4 The biographical information in this paragraph was taken from Coşkun 1999, 101–144 and Woodhead 2011, 143–158.

This chapter investigates the themes of religious emotion and embodied piety in the hajj narratives of Evliyā and Nābī. Together, these two lines of analysis provide a useful means of reconstructing the lived, embodied hajj experiences of two Rūmī pilgrims belonging to the same 'emotional community', defined by Barbara Rosenwein as 'largely the same as social communities,' and which could include families, neighbourhoods, institutions, and royal courts (Rosenwein 2010, 11). As Rosenwein explains, a researcher looking at an emotional community seeks above all to uncover their systems of feeling, the emotions that they value, devalue, or ignore, and the modes of emotional expression that they expect, encourage, tolerate, and deplore (ibid.). This is not to deny the bio-psychological aspects of emotions, but rather to also consider that emotions are socially constructed and historically situated discourses (Lutz and Abu-Lughod 1990, 7. Cited in El-Sayed 2016, 29). Probing religious emotion, meaning any emotion 'which refers to God or something else transcendent: thus joy in the Lord, fear of the Lord, awe before Being, reverence for Life, and so on,' (Roberts 2007, 493) is thus particularly beneficial as a means of understanding how Evliyā and Nābī's broadly shared cultures shaped their emotional discourse. At the same time, the chapter considers how emotion and belief are embodied and performed in the hajj narratives of Evliyā and Nābī. It does so in order to avoid perpetuating a false dichotomy between mind and body, one consequence of which is ignoring the embodied nature of ritual and religious belief and practice (Werbner and Basu 1998, 4). Sensational forms can be described as central to the making of religious subjectivities, which resonates strongly with Kenneth George's discussion of people as 'thinking and feeling subjects in the world, as well as being subject to the cultural and ideological formations that make up their world' (Meyer 2008, 129. See also George 2008, 175–176).

Undoubtedly then, any investigation of religious emotion and embodied piety is not without its challenges; analysing travel narratives of any kind entails the careful navigation of the author's 'community affiliation, religion, ideology, and other culture-specific discourses and practices such as Sufism, myths, folk traditions, natural and geographical phenomena, cultural scripts, social norms, and power relations' (El-Sayed 2016, 66). Therefore, as well as examining the emotional and bodily modes that dominate the hajj accounts of Evliyā and Nābī, this chapter also investigates how their historical and cultural context might have influenced their experiences and their writing. For example, it considers the impact of the aforementioned hajj guides, which reveal how their authors felt the hajj should be undertaken and are thus *prescriptive* in nature. The accounts of Evliyā and Nābī provide a more *descriptive* counterpoint, allowing us to examine how advice given by hajj guides might have influenced the lived experiences of pilgrims. As well as the impact of hajj guides and other texts (sacred and otherwise), the chapter also considers the impact of contemporary material and visual culture. Finally, the chapter considers the context of production of both hajj accounts, especially since travel writing is in many respects a communicative act and a social practice, in which the traveller's emphasis on specific emotions and emotional experiences is 'shaped by the travel book's context of production, the relation between the traveller's web of social networks and his intended audience' (El-Sayed 2016, 87).

2 The Hajj and Desire (*şevḳ*) in Early Modern Ottoman Culture

In his *Islam and the devotional object*, Richard McGregor describes how 'the hajj remained deeply grounded in the visual and material life of all Cairenes' (McGregor 2020, 20). The same can be said of Istanbul, a city which after 1517 joined Cairo and Damascus as points of assembly and departure for the hajj. Beginning in the 1640s, ceramic tiles depicting the Kaʿba and the sacred landscapes of Mecca and Medina were installed in mosques and other public settings (Maury 2013, 143–159). At least five such tiles were installed at different locations within the Topkapı Palace in the seventeenth century (see fig. 4.1 for an example). Popular prayer books like the *Dalāʾil al-khayrāt* ('Guides to the Blessings') and the *Enʿām-ı şerīf* also carried depictions of the Prophet's Mosque and his tomb in Medina, as well as the Kaʿba and the Grand Mosque in Mecca (Göloğlu 2018, 323–338; Roxburgh 2011, 33–41).[5] For members of the Ottoman elite like Evliyā and Nābī, it was not unusual to come into contact with fragments of cloth previously adorning the Kaʿba or the Prophet's burial chamber (*ḥujra*) (Tezcan 2017). Even pilgrims of more modest means could return home with vessels of sacred Zamzam water, and, according to Evliyā, water from the wells of Medina too (Evliyā 2012, 147–153). The effect of Zamzam water on aspiring pilgrims is perhaps best represented in a passage from the memoirs of the English slave Joseph Pitts (d. c. 1735), a resident of Ottoman Algiers in the late seventeenth century and who undertook the hajj with his master in c. 1685:

5 The *Dalāʾil* was a collection of prayers for the Prophet Muhammad by the Moroccan scholar Muḥammad Sulaymān al-Jazūlī (d. 1465). It enjoyed remarkable popularity especially between the sixteenth and nineteenth centuries across the Muslim world. For more, see Witkam 2007.

FIGURE 4.1
Multi-tile panel depicting the Kaʿba and the Grand Mosque. Located in the prayer-niche of the Mosque of the Black Eunuchs in Topkapı Palace, Istanbul. Dated 1666–1667
IMAGE: YAHYA NURGAT

> (…) many *Hagges* carry it home to their respective Countries, in little latten or tin Pots, and present it to their Friends, half a Spoonful, it may be, to each, who receive it in the hollow of their Hand with great Care and abundance of Thanks; sipping a little of it, and bestowing the rest on their Faces and naked Heads; at the same Time holding up their Hands, and desiring of God, that they also may be so happy and prosperous as to go on Pilgrimage to Mecca.
>
> PITTS 2012, 196

Pitts' description is a pertinent example of an artifact from the Holy Cities mediating remembrance and longing. Artifacts of this kind were ubiquitous in Ottoman society and certainly even more so in the elite surroundings that Evliyā and Nābī inhabited.

In their writing on the hajj, Evliyā and Nābī could draw on a broader Ottoman literary culture of celebrating the Holy Cities of Islam. Authors like Meḥmed el-Yemenī and Ebü'l-Fażl el-Sincārī composed Turkish-language works on the virtues (*feżā'il*; Arabic: *faḍā'il*) of Mecca, which were reproduced in both plain script and with elaborate calligraphy and illuminations (el-Yemenī 2017; el-Sincārī).[6] Authors could also compose history-topographies of the Holy Cities, like the Meccan qadi Quṭb al-Dīn al-Nahrawālī's (d. 1582) *al-I'lām bi-a'lām balad Allāh al-ḥarām* ('Reports on the luminaries of Mecca, the sacred land of God') (al-Nahrawālī, 1857). During the seventeenth century, his work was the most popular in the genre, and he paid particular attention to Ottoman patronage in the Ḥaramayn. Quṭb al-Dīn dedicated his work to Sultan Murad III, and at the behest of the vizier 'Ātiḳ Meḥmed Paşa, Bāḳī Maḥmūd 'Abdülbāḳī (d. 1600) produced a Turkish translation (Kātib Çelebī 1941, vol. 1:126). A similar type of patron-client relationship can be seen in the *Risāle-i Mekkiye*, a brief work in the format of a letter describing the *medrese* professor Fevrī's (d. 1571) pilgrimage journey of 1545–1546, with eulogies to its recipient and patron, the renowned biographer 'Āşık Çelebī (1520–1572). The *Risāle* was much like Nābī's work in that it features highly literary, elaborate prose interspersed with sections in verse. The similarities do not end there; as Menderes Coşkun explains, 'Fevri's main object in this letter was to give 'Āşık Çelebī a lit-

6 Since al-Sincāri's work is unpublished and exists only in manuscript form, I have not provided a date of publication. The same applies for Murād al-Bendī's *Delīlü'l-mütaḥayyirīn* and Sinān al-Rūmī's *Menāsik*. For manuscripts, I cite folios in place of pages from a printed edition. Al-Sincāri's date of death is not known, however his work features in a number of unpublished manuscripts from the early eighteenth century. For example, the manuscript cited here, from the Berlin State Library, was copied in 1709.

erary portrayal of his observations and experiences in the Hijaz,' as well as to sing the praises of his patron (Coşkun 2000, 95). Nābī sought to do the same for his own patron, the Sultan (and perhaps also Dāmād Muṣṭafa Paşa), to whom he presented his work, as well as for his wider audience. As for Evliyā, his section on the hajj differs from other parts of his travel writing in that he dedicates long passages to the *feżā'il* of the Ḥaramayn (the two Holy Sanctuaries of Mecca and Medina). He also mirrors contemporary guides by writing extensively on the proper way to execute the ritual of hajj and the *ziyāra* of the Prophet Muhammad. However, his detailed descriptions of landscapes, buildings and amenities, and his long passages describing his own experiences and interesting episodes that he witnessed, are a feature of all ten chapters of his *Seyāḥatnāme*.

While Nābī was a bureaucrat and poet at the Ottoman court, Evliyā was a seasoned traveller, for whom even a six-month break from his travels in Istanbul 'was like a prison' (Evliyā 2010, 293). Yet both hailed from environments that instilled them with a desire to see the Holy Cities and to undertake the hajj. Nābī was born and raised in Ruhā, held (especially in Ottoman culture) to be the birthplace of Prophet Ibrāhīm, who the Qur'an describes being given the responsibility of building the Ka'ba and announcing the hajj to mankind. Ruhā is also the site of the Balıklıgöl ('Fish Lake'), believed to be the place where Nimrod threw the Prophet Ibrāhīm into a fire with the flames miraculously turning into water and the logs transforming into fish. Having himself been born and raised in Ruhā, Nābī maintained a special connection to Ibrāhīm. This, in turn, contributed to his long-held desire to visit the Ḥaramayn: 'From my childhood onwards whenever I have heard the description of the sanctuaries I felt a strong desire to go there (...)' (Coşkun 1999, 174). Nābī's connection to Ibrāhīm's birthplace meant that he made sure to incorporate Ruhā into his hajj journey. Evliyā too maintained a connection to the hajj from childhood; his father was the chief goldsmith of the Sublime Porte and had installed the Spout of Mercy (*Mīzāb al-Raḥma*, known to Ottoman Rūmīs as *Altın oluk*, 'Golden spout') on the roof of the Ka'ba at the Sultan's behest (Evliyā 2010, 294). According to Evliyā, when his father returned to Istanbul, he 'uttered a benediction and prayed that I be vouchsafed pilgrimage to Mecca' (ibid.). Evliyā thus traced his desire for the hajj to his own familial ties, and held it to be his utmost ambition in relation to his great love of travelling.

From the textual and oral to the visual and material, a range of mediums stirred a sense of longing and desire in aspiring pilgrims. These mediums also shaped expectations and aspirations vis-à-vis the pilgrimage, thereby mediating the eventual hajj experience of pilgrims. As an account of the hajj, Nābī's *Tuḥfe* represents his own *mediated* hajj experience, but was itself a *mediating* force with the capacity to influence the conceptions and experiences of others. Thus, says Nābī, he composed his *Tuḥfe* as a source of renewed desire for those who had already undertaken the hajj (*vesīle-i şevḳ-i cedīd*), as well as to intensify the yearning of those who were still yet to do so (Nābī 2002, 163). To reiterate this idea, Nābī shares a verse of the Ottoman scholar and poet Zekerīyāzāde Yaḥyā Efendī (1552–1644): 'Have the lovers' eyes ever seen a light the like of the Kaʿba?/ The one who has seen it and the one who has not: both are desirers of its beauty' (ibid.). The verse demonstrates that the sense of yearning associated with aspirant pilgrims could apply as much to the hajj is as it did to those who had never laid eyes on the Kaʿba.

A popular verse attributed to the Ottoman poet Naḥīfī (d. 1738), and one which Evliyā quotes in his hajj account, states: 'God shows mercy to all who are granted the Kaʿba (*Kaʿbe naṣīb olsa*)/ For God invites those most beloved to Him to His House' (Evliyā 2005, 350). As Charlotte Maury points out, these verses emphasize the spiritual value of the hajj, framing the pilgrim as a personally invited pilgrim to the House of his Beloved as opposed to a traveller simply fulfilling a religious obligation (Maury 2013, 150). Interestingly, the verse features on at least two representations of the Grand Mosque on ceramic, underscoring the potential of these public depictions to stimulate viewers with a desire to visit the Kaʿba.[7] Nābī too frames the hajj as an invitation (*daʿvet*; Arabic: *daʿwa*) to God's own guesthouse (*ziyāfethāne*) (Nābī 2002, 160). In contrast, one who does not receive an invite is *bī-naṣīb* ('ill-fated' or 'unfortunate'). Would-be pilgrims thus desired to be one of these select invitees, and certainly did not want to be in the category of the *bī-naṣīb*. Nābī emphasizes that his own desire to visit the Ḥaramayn was of a different order, since it left him restless (*rāḥat-güdāz*) (ibid., 162). This served only to intensify his sense of gratefulness upon fulfilment of this desire; Nābī expresses 'a thousand thanks' (*hezār şükür*) to God that he was not deprived (*bī-naṣīb*) of the happiness of seeing the Kaʿba (ibid., 256).

The idea of longing for the hajj is brought to life by a unique ritual to be performed at ʿArafa, as recommended by Evliyā. Pilgrims were to form heaps out of stones, or something similar from the soil, each dedicated to a loved one that had been left behind at home. For each heap, one was to stand up,

7 One is in the holdings of the Benaki Museum (Benaki Museum, Athens. Inv 124) and the other in the Louvre, dating to c. 1675 (Musée du Louvre, Paris. Inv OA 3919/558). See Maury 2013, 150. Evliyā's quoted wording: *'Her kime Kaʿbe naṣīb olsa Hudā raḥmet eder/ Sevdiği kişiyi Ḥak hānesine daʿvet ider'* (Evliyā 2005, 350). The wording on the tiles is slightly different to that quoted by Evliyā: *'Her kime Kaʿbe naṣīb olsa Hudā raḥmet ider/ Her kişi sevdiğini hānesine daʿvet ider.'*

face the Kaʿba and say 'come, come, o so-and-so,' and thereafter invoke God, saying 'I invite so-and-so, O Lord, please accept.' Evliyā says that as a result, 'by the command of Allah, the person who you invited will certainly come to the Kaʿba in his lifetime' (Evliyā 2005, 355). This intriguing ritual emphasizes that one who had successfully reached ʿArafa felt privileged to have been invited there, and felt fortunate enough to share that invitation with others.[8] Nābī also emphasizes that to be present at ʿArafa is a blessing (*niʿmet*); on this day, one might pray for their own absolution but also thereafter pray for their friends and loved ones. Similarly, to be present on the day of ʿArafa is a happiness (*saʿādet*), which only increases because one might be able to pray for those who had requested prayers to be said on their behalf (Nābī 2002, 290).

The key metaphor used to communicate desire in Ottoman discourse, and which features heavily in the texts of both Evliyā and Nābī in relation to the hajj, is the idea of rubbing one's face (*yüz sürmek*) on the beloved object. The symbolism of rubbing one's face emerges perhaps most powerfully in Evliyā's account of his time in Medina, where he shares the wording of a calligraphic inscription close to the Bāb al-Salām ('The Gate of Peace') in the Prophet's Mosque:

> The custom of the Arabs is that if someone is a great prince,
> It is usual to let slaves go free at his graveside.
> You who are the pride of the world and prince of this world and the next,
> God forbid that he who rubs his face on your grave should not go free.
>
> EVLIYĀ 2012, 53

In some cases, face rubbing was intended literally, and encouraged, for example when clinging to the Multazam and kissing the Black Stone. At other sacred sites (*ziyāretgāhs*) too, rubbing was a means of attaining blessing (*baraka*), as in the case of the Station of the Messenger (*Maḳām Ḥażret-i Resūl*) located on the outskirts of Medina. Evliyā explains that in this location, 'the imprint of his [the Prophet Muhammad's, YN] exalted head remains on the floor,' leading pilgrims to 'rub their faces on this holy place' (Evliyā 2012, 27–28). However, in other cases, Evliyā wrote of wanting to rub his face on the *ḥujra*'s latticed enclosure while simultaneously asserting that touching and kissing the enclosure was

8 The practice is also mentioned by Murād Dervīş, a late seventeenth-century hajj guide author, who calls it a blameworthy innovation (*bidʿet*; Arabic: *bidʿa*). See Murād, fol. 31b–32a.

strictly discouraged (Evliyā 2012, 4).[9] In both cases, the phrase was intended to communicate the intense desire to visit the Holy Cities. Nābī uses it to describe a desire for the Ḥaramayn filling his imagination, saying: 'O Lord, when will I rub my face on the gates of Medina and Mecca? Sometimes Mecca and sometimes Medina, let me adopt both as my place of dwelling' (Nābī 2002, 254). The same idea of face rubbing is also used by him to describe the eventual fulfilment of this desire:

> A thousand thanks to God, who has not deprived me of seeing the sacred place, and of rubbing my forehead on the earth of the sacred territory before passing away from this world.
>
> COŞKUN 1999, 174

3 Entering Mecca: Emotion and Demeanour

In the accounts of both Evliyā and Nābī, yearning is a changing emotion and one which escalates especially when nearing each of the Holy Cities. Physical landmarks serve to increase the anticipation of pilgrims, who respond primarily by moderating their physical demeanour and conduct accordingly. For example, the process of entering Mecca is depicted by Nābī as a gradual one, in which pilgrims become ever more eager as they near the Holy City (Nābī 2002, 254–255). The sight of Mecca's gleaming mountains from afar endows pilgrims with renewed vigour in hurrying to the Kaʿba, despite having endured the rigours of the mostly desert road from Cairo. He describes pilgrims undergoing a collective rejuvenation, together hastening in the direction of the Noble Sanctuary (ibid., 254). Emphasizing the connection between seeing a physical landmark and physiological and emotional responses, Nābī says that pilgrims collectively fell to the ground at al-Tanʿīm (known to Rūmīs as 'Umre), where two milestones marked the boundary of the outer sanctuary (Ḥaram) area of Mecca, with some even proceeding barefoot (ibid., 255). Evliyā describes pilgrims descending their mounts at a later stage, when the minarets of the Sacred Mosque came into view from the Muʿallā cemetery on the city's outskirts. For Nābī, pilgrims were driven 'with desire' (*şevḳiyle*) to descend their mounts, whilst in Evliyā's account, pilgrims proceeded on foot out of veneration and respect (*taʿẓīmen ve teʾeddüben*) (Nābī 2002, 255; Evliyā 2005, 348).

9 'Might I roam the world? Might it be vouchsafed to me to reach the Holy Land, Cairo and Damascus, Mecca and Medina, and to rub my face at the Sacred Garden, the tomb of the Prophet, glory of the universe?' (Evliyā 2012, 4).

In Nābī's telling, desire gave way to ecstasy as pilgrims moved ever closer to realizing their long-held aspiration of worshipping at the Kaʿba. He emphasizes the intensity of desire at this stage by saying that the 'ecstasy of Divine love' (*cezbe-i maḥabbet-i Ilāhiyye*) caused pilgrims to forget their wealth and loved ones, with their priority instead to attain a portion of God's forgiveness (Nābī 2002, 256). Upon first sight of the Kaʿba, Nābī says that 'natural order of the mind was completed disrupted' (*şirāze-i şuʿūr bi'l-külliye güsiste olup*), with his senses scattered in all directions (ibid., 259). In the immediate vicinity of the Kaʿba, Nābī thus emphasizes bewilderment and astonishment as leading emotions. He reinforces this by saying that for a time, he simply stood by the Bāb al-Salām in bewilderment (ibid., 268). Indeed, he says that the Black Stone acted as a magnet drawing him towards the Kaʿba, without which he would not have found the strength to move from the Bāb al-Salām (ibid.).

Evliyā too describes being moved by the sight of the Kaʿba, yet his thankfulness upon reaching Mecca was of a different order; it stemmed more from a sense of relief than a fulfilment of anticipation, since the torrential rain faced by the caravan in Muzayrīb (a major place of assembly 26 hours from Damascus) had delayed the caravan by some days. Indeed, the Syrian *amīr al-ḥajj* Hüseyin Paşa sacrificed animals upon entering Mecca in gratitude for arriving two days before ʿArafa, for, as Evliyā explains, the pilgrims had otherwise given up hope of making the hajj that year (Evliyā 2005, 345). At the same time, Evliyā's entry into Mecca was somewhat overshadowed by Hüseyin Paşa's business with the rebellious Sharīf of Mecca. His narrative portrays an initial *ṭawāf* undertaken in haste in order that the issues with the Sharīf could immediately be resolved prior to the commencement of hajj. While Evliyā's association with the *amīr al-ḥajj* was generally of great benefit to him, it could also serve as a distraction to his performance of worship, as in the case of this initial *ṭawāf*.

Curiously in Evliyā's account, local, in-person guides (*delīl*s) are portrayed as essential mediators in maximizing the emotional benefits of hajj ritual. He advises that the first thing to do when entering Mecca's sacred precincts was to procure a *delīl* 'even if you are an *ʿālim* and [are able to, YN] perform *saʿy* and *ṭawāf* on the basis of reading hajj guidebooks.' This is, he explains, because it is:

> easier is go hand in hand with a *delīl* around the four sides of the Kaʿba, repeating whatever the *delīl* recites, thus completing *ṭawāf* and *saʿy* with pleasure and [eventually, YN] completing the hajj with freedom from worry.
>
> EVLIYĀ 2005, 350 and 351

Evliyā clearly felt that relying on *delīl*s would free pilgrims from concerns about where to go, what to recite, and whether they had missed any steps, all of which would lead to a more pleasurable pilgrimage. However, some Turkish guidebooks disagreed; Sinān el-Rūmī (d. 1592), author of the most popular Turkish hajj guide (up to the early nineteenth century), was the first to caution against following a *delīl* around the Kaʿba, arguing that this would take away from the necessary *huşūʿ* (Arabic: *khushūʿ*; inward and outward humility and attentiveness) required in *ṭawāf* (Sinān el-Rūmī, fols. 51b–52a). And writing in the same period as Evliyā, Murād ibn Dervīş (alive in 1690) was similarly critical of the practice, arguing that there was little benefit to parroting formulas in Arabic, the meanings of which Rūmī pilgrims were unlikely to understand, and that reciting supplications (*duʿāʾ*) aloud would disturb other pilgrims. Murad instead urged pilgrims to supplicate with whatever transmitted *duʿāʾ* they had already committed to memory, and to petition God in their own tongue for whatever they desired (Murād el-Bendī, fol. 44a).

Just as pilgrims are portrayed as entering the Holy City with a potent initial gaze at the Kaʿba, so too are they described as exiting while keeping their gaze locked upon this landmark until the last possible moment. This even meant walking backwards when exiting the Holy Sanctuary, so that one could see the Kaʿba as long as it was possible to be seen (Evliyā 2005, 409; Nābī 2002, 319). Nābī notes that his initial *ṭawāf* had been performed with great pleasure and speed whereas the farewell *ṭawāf* was performed with a sense of reluctance (Evliyā 2005, 367–368; Nābī 2002, 317). What prevented this sorrow from overcoming pilgrims was the consolation of being able to visit Medina. The thought of meeting the Prophet was a source of comfort (*tesliyet*) and of renewed desire (*şevḳ-i cedīd*) (Nābī 2002, 322). Pilgrims also had a sense of happiness having attained God's mercy through the hajj (ibid., 317). The sorrow of departure is represented by Nābī in the tears of pilgrims as they bid farewell to the Kaʿba, and might be contrasted with the tears that were shed upon first sight of the Kaʿba. The latter appear to have stemmed from a sense of being overwhelmed at both the sight of the Kaʿba and from the emotion of realizing a lifetime goal. These are described by Nābī as 'tears of happiness' (*sürūr*), in contrast to the 'tears of sadness' (*ḥüzün*) he shed while performing the farewell *ṭawāf* (ibid.).

4 ʿArafa: Sights, Sounds, and Emotional Benefits

The centrality of ʿArafa to the hajj is well-known; according to one hadith, the Prophet said that 'the hajj is ʿArafa' (*al-Ḥajj ʿArafa*) (al-Nasāʾī 1986, 5:256). Hajj guides emphasize that the day is one in which God is determined to forgive

His petitioning slaves 'who have come to Me dishevelled and dusty, from every faraway pass, longing for My mercy.'[10] While Nābī and Evliyā both emphasize this feature of 'Arafa, they also discuss its more varied emotional benefits. As mentioned above, yearning and desire are ever-present features of the hajj, and this is especially true of 'Arafa; Nābī reiterates that pilgrims on the day of 'Arafa itself were consumed with desire and hurried to the plain of 'Arafa, avoiding delay or wasting time with resting. This physical hastening conveys the urgency felt to maximize the limited time (noon to sunset) one had to worship and petition God (Nābī 2002, 279). Nābī associates the day of 'Arafa with visible forms of emotion, including bodies trembling and weeping with remorse (*nedāmet*), in the hope of attaining God's forgiveness (*ümīd-i gufrān*) (ibid., 285). He emphasizes this remorse as a collective emotion, though each pilgrim entreated God according to their own capacity (ibid., 287).

In Evliyā's telling, the eve of 'Arafa (the eighth of *dhū al-ḥijja*) was itself a sacred night, during which 'Arafa was lit up with thousands of candles. Evliyā calls the effect of this *nūr 'alā nūr*, thereby provoking a deliberate ambiguity between temporal and divine light (Evliyā 2005, 355). Throughout the early modern period, hajj pilgrims did not practice the sunna of staying the night at Minā prior to the Day of 'Arafa, and instead stayed the night at 'Arafa. Interestingly, Evliyā portrays Minā as more of a marketplace and a site of festivity. Indeed, Minā was known to most Rūmī pilgrims as a bazaar or marketplace ('Minā Pazarı'). This was in contrast to the night before 'Arafa, which Evliyā identifies firmly as one of worship: he says that some pilgrims busied themselves with undertaking *ziyāra* of nearby sacred sites, some worshipped privately in their tents, and some even went to 'Arafa in order to worship there (ibid., 355–356).

Both Evliyā and Nābī convey collective experiences by describing sounds; Nābī says that the clamour and outcry of pilgrims petitioning God on the night of Muzdalifa (on the ninth, following the Day of 'Arafa) reached the sky (Nābī 2002, 295). Evliyā described pilgrims similarly on the eve of 'Arafa; he says that the sound reached the heavens, as all the slaves of God busied themselves in worship in anticipation of the Day of Vigil (*wuqūf*) (Evliyā 2005, 355–356). Both writers also convey the visual spectacle of 'Arafa, primarily by comparing 'Arafa to 'Araṣāt, the latter being the plain on which humanity is to be gathered for the final judgment. This was especially so because of the sea of people (*ādem deryāsı*) in shroud-like white cloths, each of whom were focused

10 A hadith narrated by Ibn 'Umar (d. 693) in the *Muṣannaf* of al-San'ānī (d. 827), 5:15 (Hadith 8830).

on their own account with God and oblivious to their surroundings (ibid., 355). Nābī describes the *iḥrām* as a potential shroud when first wearing it: 'As long as I live this is my clothing, and if I die it is my shroud' (Nābī 2002, 253). At ʿArafa however, the *iḥrām* is framed more directly as a shroud (*kefen-i iḥrām*), since the day of ʿArafa resembles the Day of Reckoning (ibid., 286). Indeed, he says, the noise of ʿArafa was such that it surpassed the sounds that would be heard on Judgement Day (ibid.).

In Nābī's account, the main contrast between ʿArafa and ʿAraṣāt is that in the former pilgrims can find new life; he says that all pilgrims at ʿArafa were deceased, and it was through ʿArafa that they returned to life. Their hearts were now filled with happiness (*sürūr*) and tranquillity (*ḥużūr*) as they returned to Muzdalifa. This return (*ifāḍa*) is thus clearly associated with a sense of emotional cleansing and a new lease of spiritual life (ibid., 293). Similarly, the moment of removing the *iḥrām* is described by Nābī as 'the dead removing their shrouds from their bodies and taking the decree of life into their hands.' This rebirth is cemented in Nābī's telling by pilgrims donning their best clothes to celebrate the Feast of Immolation (Kurban Bayramı), and further emphasized by the wearing of perfume and the grooming of hair, all acts forbidden during *iḥrām* (ibid., 301).

As well as *sürūr* and *ḥużūr*, Nābī emphasizes his own sense of gratefulness to God for allowing him to experience the Day of ʿArafa (ibid., 292). The hajj is mentioned in the Qurʾan as 'a source of guidance for all people' (*hudā li-al-ʿālamīn*), and Nābī emphasizes his own lost state prior to his pilgrimage.[11] His gratefulness thus derives from the fact that God satisfied his desire to visit the Holy Cities and did not leave him in a lost state of yearning (ibid.). By saying that he witnessed rainfall at ʿArafa, Nābī further connects the place and time of ʿArafa to God's mercy. Rain itself is seen as a source of mercy and blessing, and Islamic tradition holds that supplication is more efficacious under rainfall. Interestingly, in Evliyā's account, rain is described as an annual occurrence, though it takes place at the end of the hajj, when God sends a great rainfall to cleanse Minā after thousands of animal sacrifices have been made there.

Evliyā is at his most effusive when describing ʿArafa, which he calls a mountain illuminated by the light of paradise due to it being beloved to God. Indeed, Evliyā says that the more one looks at the mountain, the more contentment and happiness (*ṣafā ve sürūr*) they will gain (Evliyā 2005, 354). Emphasizing its powers of absolution, Evliyā advises pilgrims that when departing ʿArafa, they should not look back, for this is where sins have been left behind. Indeed,

11 Verse 3:96. As translated in Abdel Haleem, *The Qurʾan*.

he says, some scholars say that the wisdom behind departing ʿArafa after sunset is that so no one becomes blind from seeing the sins, which by this point have taken the form of insects (*ḥaşerāt-ı zünūbu*) that slowly dissolve into the mountain (Evliyā 2005, 359). Evliyā also emphasizes the sacrality of Minā, connecting the remarkable sights, sounds, and smells found there to the hajj itself. For example, he says that trade at Minā is steeped in good-will; traders host patrons with rose water, fine perfume and incense, and invariably present them with a complimentary gift. This is because every person at Minā is thankful for having accomplished the hajj, and is thus consumed by love and happiness. Having shown diligence in their worship and having exerted themselves at ʿArafa and Muzdalifa, pilgrims thus spend the two days and two nights at Minā in enjoyment (*ẕevḳ*) and pleasure (*ṣafā*) (ibid., 366). For this reason, says Evliyā, even with the great crowds of people, no person complains to another about congestion (ibid., 364–365).

5 Ziyāra of the Prophet Muhammad: Visual Cues and Bodily Piety

Evliyā and Nābī's passages on their *ziyāra* of the Prophet Muhammad in Medina are among their most emotive. The accounts are also notable for their emphasis on bodily piety. In many ways, their entry into the Prophet's city appears to mirror the entrance into Mecca. Both narrators portray the trees and fortress walls of Medina as a powerful visual spectacle, which elicited significant shifts in the emotions and demeanour of the pilgrims. In response to their first sight of the Prophet's city, Evliyā suggests that pilgrims descended their mounts and offered their first greeting to the Prophet Muhammad. He narrates these events in the third person present simple tense, thereby suggesting that what he says is the normal behaviour for a pilgrim, which he himself practiced and which future pilgrims ought to follow as well. In other cases, he adopts the imperative form, such as when advising pilgrims not to neglect asking for the Prophet's intercession once Medina and the dome of the mosque come into view. Similarly, this suggests that Evliyā did so himself and strongly recommended others to do the same. Indeed, at the conclusion to his advice, he stresses that 'I carried out my visit to the Prophet (…) in this manner' (Evliyā 2012, 163).

Perhaps the most important visual step in the process of entering Medina was the dome of the Prophet's tomb. Nābī says that pilgrims began weeping as soon as it came in to view (Nābī 2002, 323–324), while Evliyā emphasizes that 'the gleam of the gilded pinnacle on the dome' rendered the plain of Medina 'light upon light' (*nūr ʿalā nūr*), thus dazzling the eye of the beholder (Evliyā

2012, 19). Here, Evliyā once again utilizes the Qurʾanic terminology from the well-known Verse of Light (Qurʾan 24:35), which possessed great currency in Ottoman culture and was often represented in images and calligraphy. He is clear that the dome, as an extension of the Prophet himself, was the source of light in this instance. Here too, Evliyā evokes the well-known name by which the city was (and continues to be) known, a name which both he and Nābī use in their respective accounts: 'the Illuminated City' (*Medine-i Münevvere*; Arabic: *al-Madīna al-Munawwara*). Evliyā further describes the moment when the dome of the Prophet comes into view as 'quite a marvel', since a change comes over not only the pilgrims but the animals too:

> The camels that were exhausted suddenly become strong again and grumble like thunder, the horses whinny and the mules and donkeys cry out (…) It is then impossible to hold the animals back, but they head toward Medina at great speed.
>
> EVLIYĀ 2012, 19–21

By extending the sense of anticipation to the animals, Evliyā conveys the great magnetism of the Prophet, which captivates man and beast alike.

By proceeding directly to the Prophet's tomb once inside the city walls of Medina, pilgrims demonstrated their reverence for him: It was improper to see to worldly affairs without first undertaking the *ziyāra*. For example, while Evliyā was outside the fortress walls of Medina, he spent time visiting other sacred sites associated with the Prophet and his companions. However, once he had entered the city's Egyptian Gate and was within its walls, Evliyā makes clear that he proceeded directly to the tomb of the Prophet without delay. Evliyā also narrates an even greater level of devotion on the part of some pilgrims, who apparently donned the pilgrim's garb even before entering Medina. Pilgrims would ordinarily enter *iḥrām* after exiting Medina at a place known as Biʾr-i ʿAli ("Ali's well', known also as Dhū al-Ḥulayfa). Yet, some 'lovers' chose to do so beforehand as 'a sign of separation from all that is worldly and as a form of turning to God' (ibid., 21). According to Evliyā, some pilgrims wanted to have this total sense of separation even while undertaking the *ziyāra* of the Prophet. Indeed, he himself was among these lovers, explaining that he visited a bathhouse in a suburb of Medina prior to his visit to the Prophet's tomb where he cleansed himself and emerged 'barefoot and bareheaded, free from all worldly attachments' (ibid., 29). The idea of being barefoot and bareheaded was an important one for Evliyā, as can be seen in his advice that one also visit the martyrs of Uḥud in this fashion; those who did otherwise would be 'committing an impropriety' (*bī-edeblik olmuş olur*) (ibid., 160–161). He went as far as to say that one should only visit Uḥud at dawn, since being barefoot and bareheaded would be impossible at any other time of the day (ibid., 159–161).

Nābī emphasizes his own reverent demeanour while walking within the Prophet's city, saying that he was like a 'lifeless shadow' rubbing his face on the ground of Medina (Nābī 2002, 327). This humble disposition only intensified once pilgrims entered the Prophet's Mosque. Evliyā emphasizes that while the 'lovers' (*ʿuşşāklar*) entered the Bāb al-Salām of the Prophet's Mosque and proceeded on foot, he in fact lay his 'sinful face on his precious ground and crawled in fish-like without using hands or feet' (Evliyā 2012, 29). Thus, Evliyā suggests that his love was even greater than the other 'lovers' of the Prophet, embodied not only by walking barefoot but also by lowering his entire body to the ground.

Significantly, both Nābī and Evliyā describe their *ziyāra*s as an experience that was as corporeal as it was an out-of-body one. Bodily conduct was clearly of great importance while standing in front of the Prophet's tomb; both writers describe expressing their respect and humility by placing their hands upon their chest and slightly bowing their bodies. Both also emphasize the need for appropriate manners and decorum (*edeb*; Arabic: *adab*). Along with this emphasis on the outer, Nābī and Evliyā describe experiencing significant inner transformations; Evliyā explains that he 'nearly fainted' when praying for the Prophet's intercession (Evliyā 2012, 31). Nābī says that he experienced a loss of senses (*şuʿūr güdāz ile*) as he made his way through the Bāb al-Salām (Nābī 2002, 333). Both writers thus convey a sense of being overwhelmed, which in turn conveys the intense sacrality of standing before the Prophet. In Nābī's case, it is a reaction quite similar to his first view of the Kaʿba. Evliyā certainly seems to attribute his reaction to the sheer momentousness of the situation, saying that once he came to himself, he chose this moment to complete a Qur'an recitation that he had previously left off at chapter 112 (thus two short chapters short of completion): 'I brought these noble recitations as presents worthy of the Prophet and, rubbing my face in the dust at his felicitous foot, begged for his intercession' (Evliyā 2012, 111). Here too, Evliyā deploys the vivid imagery of rubbing his face humbly at the Prophet's feet, thereby powerfully symbolizing his love and devotion.

Nābī's poetry while describing his *ziyāra* features extensive praise of the Prophet, his salutations (*ṣalavāt* and *selām*) placed upon him, and perhaps most importantly, his desire to be granted the Prophet's intercession (*şefāʿat*; Arabic: *shafāʿa*) with God (Nābī 2002, 333). Yet Nābī emphasizes that this was conditional on displaying the requisite *edeb* and on appropriately greeting and praising the Prophet. Nābī certainly felt that he had fulfilled these conditions, and thus described his great happiness at fulfilling his lifelong dream of rubbing his face at the intercessory threshold of the Prophet (ibid., 334). Another symbol of submission and humility was that, as a final act, pilgrims 'retired backwards according to etiquette' (*edeb üzere*) (Evliyā 2012, 30). And even after this initial *ziyāra*, Nābī emphasizes that he did not spend much time resting, and that all pilgrims expended maximum effort on continuously seeking the Prophet's intercession at his tomb (Nābī 2002, 341).

Pilgrims are described as departing the Prophet's city in the same way they entered it, gazing at the dome atop his tomb (Nābī 2002, 354). To convey his sadness (*hicrān*) on the day of departure, Nābī utilizes a powerful metaphor, saying that this heart was in as many pieces as the various gates of the Sacred Mosque of Medina (ibid., 349). This was also another juncture at which tears were shed profusely and where the pain of goodbye upon both mind and body was such that it could not be put it into words (*hāric-i ḳudret-i ḳalem-i ter-zebāndur*) (ibid., 349 and 354). Nābī describes his bodily demeanour as much like his final *ṭawāf* of the Kaʿba, which he says was performed slowly and reluctantly as opposed to his first one, performed with vigour and enthusiasm. He explains that he exited the Prophet's Mosque while sorrowfully and repeatedly throwing glances back at his tomb, and with his neck visibly bent over in sorrow, until finally he passed through the door (ibid., 354). While pilgrims travelling with the Cairene caravan visited Medina only once on their return journey, pilgrims travelling via Damascus did so twice. Yet, despite knowing that they would be able to return to Medina, Evliyā alludes to a similar level of sadness on the part of pilgrims departing Medina for Mecca, saying that they were all weeping as they entered *iḥrām* at Ali's Well (Evliyā 2012, 165).

Both Nābī and Evliyā deposited hand-written plaques at the Prophet's tomb prior to their departure, thereby forging a longer-lasting, material connection to the Prophet, and tempering the sorrow they felt at parting from him. Evliyā left two pieces of calligraphy in large letters, one which read, 'A *fātiḥa*[12] for the spirit of the world traveller Evliyā' (*seyyāḥ-ı ʿālem Evliyā rūḥiyçün el-fātiḥa*) and another reading: 'Intercession, o Muhammad, for Evliyā, year 1082' (*şefāʿat yā Muḥammed Evliyāʿya sene 1082*) (ibid., 57). Nābī copied a poem expressing his devotion to Muhammad onto a plaque and hung it facing Muhammad's grave (Nābī 2002, 341). Nābī himself wrote his 'sorrowful petition' (*ʿarż -ı ḥāl-i derd*) on paper in beautiful writing, which he hung in front of the Prophet's tomb. By describing his offering as an *ʿarż-ı ḥāl*, Nābī frames it as a petition offered to a sultan, much in the same way that his (and Evliyā's) physical demeanour

12 Al-Fātiḥa ('The opening') is the first chapter of the Qur'an, and is in the format of a brief liturgical invocation. In this context, it may denote a short supplication with or without the recitation of this chapter.

whilst undertaking the *ziyāra* echoed the way in which subjects were expected to behave before the Sultan (ibid.). The practice of composing these calligraphic plaques appears to have been a popular one; Evliyā explains many such plaques had been composed by scholars and placed above the iron railings of the Prophet's tomb. As well as his calligraphic offerings, Evliyā also set up a large crystal oil lamp in the Prophet's Mosque, of which he explains there were 7000 altogether. This was another lasting bond he formed with the Medinan sanctuary; not only would this enhance its light, it would also enable the various residents and visitors to Medina to 'read the Qur'an and engage in religious discussions until the morning prayer' (Evliyā 2012, 57).

As members of the Ottoman elite, Evliyā and Nābī could access experiences not ordinarily available to the average pilgrim. While the Kaʿba was opened to all on the tenth of *dhū al-ḥijja*, entering the *ḥujra* was a privilege reserved for nobles and dignitaries. Nābī was able to do so as an honorary member of the *ferrāşīn*, imperially appointed custodians of the Prophet's Mosque. As with his entry into the Kaʿba, Nābī's entry into the Prophet's tomb was undoubtedly an emotional highpoint, and one for which he thanked God profusely. To emphasize that it fulfilled a lifetime's wish, Nābī thanked God for not depriving him of this honour before his death (Nābī 2002, 342). Evliyā was also able to enter and clean the tomb of the Prophet as part of the entourage of Hüseyin Paşa. This was an experience in which Evliyā embodied his love through haptic engagement; he explains that he 'kissed the ground and prayed for the intercession of the Prophet.' Yet the experience was also one that he says was mentally disorientating: 'From pure love I was intoxicated and bewildered' (Evliyā 2012, 105). In this way his entrance into the tomb mirrored his first *ziyāra*, where an initial, highly bodily engagement was followed by a sense of overwhelming.

6 The *Seyāhatnāme* and *Tuḥfe* as Mediators of Pilgrimage Experience

Evliyā differs from Nābī in that he devotes entire sections of his account to explicating how to undertake the rituals of the hajj. In doing so, he mirrors hajj guidebooks of that period, which instructed pilgrims on correct ritual practices and also sought to shape their demeanour and emotional states during the execution of each ritual. The *edeb* of undertaking the *ziyāra* was important enough for Evliyā that he devoted a lengthy passage to explaining 'the form and manner of the visit (…) in detail' (Evliyā 2012, 30–31). His advice especially resembles that of Sinān el-Rūmī, whose guide Evliyā was acquainted with from at least his time in Bitlis in 1655–1656 (Evliyā 1990, 290) and from which he appears to have drawn heavily in this section. Yet much of the advice is also his own; for him, the *ziyāra* was an act of love, and thus descending one's horse or camel upon seeing the trees of Medina was something done by the 'sincere lover' (*ʿāşıḳ-i ṣādiḳ olan*) and was 'a matter of love' in itself (*ʿaşḳa dāʾir bir şeydir*) (Evliyā 2012, 19–20). He further advises that during the five-hour downhill stroll between the pilgrims' first view of the city and their eventual arrival, all should busy themselves with reciting 'the noble *ṣalavāt-i şerīf*' the simplest form of which is 'O God, bless Muhammad and his people!' Thus, even before stepping foot inside Medina, pilgrims would already be engaged in Prophetic devotion. Evliyā also advises his readers to follow him in first visiting a bathhouse to perform a major ablution and thereafter put on clean clothes and apply perfume. Pilgrims were then to 'enter into the Prophet's presence with solemnity and sincerity and avoid unseemly behaviour' (*ḥüzn-i ḳalb ile derūn-i dilden niyāzmend olarak vara, ammā bī-ebedlik etmeye*) (ibid., 88–89). It was not enough for pilgrims to have a submissive demeanour; by recommending an elaborate process of physical cleansing, Evliyā advocates for pilgrims to come before the Prophet in the right physical state too.

Significantly, Evliyā insists that pilgrims be accompanied by an in-person guide while undertaking the *ziyāra*, paralleling his advice for pilgrims in Mecca: 'You cannot do this without a guide (…) You should repeat everything the guide recites, standing in humility with both hands placed on your breast' (ibid., 89). For Evliyā, employing a guide would ensure that pilgrims stood in the correct place and recited the most efficacious formulas in a moment of great importance. These high stakes are driven home by Evliyā when he says: '(…) you are coming into the presence of the foundation of the world and the pride of mankind, whose intercession you must seek' (ibid.). For the cultivation of a proper emotional habitus, Evliyā gives his own advice; he recommends that pilgrims approach the Prophet's tomb 'bowed down and shedding tears', though a lack of emotional control was unacceptable even in this poignant moment; Evliyā warns that 'you should not grasp the railing or cry out' (ibid.). Thereafter one was to begin sending salutations and blessings on the Prophet before asking for his intercession with God. Here, Evliyā mirrors Sinān in saying, 'Just as one would come into an audience with the Sultan, so with a hundred times more respect should one enter into the presence of the Prophet' (ibid.). Framing the Prophet as a sultanic or kingly figure, albeit one deserving of 'a hundred times more respect' than a temporal ruler, emphasizes the solemn etiquette required of visitors to his tomb. The stakes were raised even higher by Evliyā's assertion that the Prophet 'is not dead, he has only exchanged one world for another.' One's respect and solemnity would be embodied by their proceeding 'slowly and deliberately' (ibid.). This contrasts with the greater speed with which one initially approaches and enters the city.

In some instances, Nābī's *Tuḥfe* too resembles contemporary hajj guides. Nābī himself might have engaged with such literature, implemented it in his own hajj and passed on his own advice for future pilgrims. He states that on the first day of the hajj (the day before ʿArafa), pilgrims must stand to attention and avoid excessive rest (Nābī 2002, 274–275). Comments such as these are designed to cultivate a particular habitus within the future pilgrims in his readership, as well as to convey the gravity of this time to the audience. On other occasions, Nābī communicated his personal emotions, or the collectively experienced emotions of his pilgrim group. This too would have indirectly shaped the experiences of future pilgrims, while his advices were a much more direct form of instruction.

Despite their associations with the Ottoman hierarchy, both Evliyā and Nābī were unafraid to communicate some of the more negative aspects of the hajj, perhaps in the hope of effecting change or to prepare pilgrims for the challenges they might face. For example, Evliyā criticizes the upkeep of the hajj road:

> If the rulers made an effort and kept good care of the road from Damascus to Medina, one could manage without camels and cover the stretch on horseback in comfort. May God grant ease!
>
> EVLIYĀ 2012, 19

Nābī mentions pickpockets operating at the fairs of Minā (Nābī 2002, 309) as well as severe overcrowding at the Black Stone and during entry to the Kaʿba. For the latter, he says many pilgrims were squeezed together as if in a vice, and alludes to loss of life as a result. Nābī describes staying back from the Kaʿba for fear of his own safety, instead looking on with longing (*ḥasret*) and hopelessness (*nā-ümīd*) (ibid., 305). At the same time, in Nābī's narrative, potentially negative situations are avoided, or more usually, turned into positive events. For example, when discussing the crowding and chaos usually associated with the return (*ifāḍa*) from ʿArafa to Muzdalifa, Nābī says that this was avoided as the Egyptians took over the reins of the Syrian *maḥmal* and vice versa, thus removing them from a potential competition (*müsābaḳat*) with one another (ibid., 293). And, as a sign of ultimate acceptance, Nābī does eventually enter the Kaʿba, suggesting that as a result of his sorrow he was beckoned into the Kaʿba by a voice calling 'enter inside, o so-and-so'. Here again, Nābī emphasizes above all his gratitude, saying that without God's acceptance of his prayers, he would not have been able to set foot inside the Kaʿba (ibid., 306).

7 Conclusion

This chapter has explored religious emotion and embodied piety in the hajj narratives of Evliyā Çelebī and Yūsuf Nābī, two Rūmī pilgrims belonging to broadly the same 'emotional community'. Both writers had long held associations with the hajj, whether through a father who had helped to furnish the Kaʿba or as a result of growing up in the city of Ibrāhīm. The hajj was deeply grounded and memorialized in Ottoman literary, visual, and material culture, all of which would have deepened these associations. Nābī's *Tuḥfe* and Evliyā's *Seyāḥatnāme* are firmly situated within this tradition; both are a celebration of the hajj and an articulation of what pilgrims ought to experience and achieve through the pilgrimage to Mecca. As self-narrative, both works are undoubtedly a 'communicative act' and a 'social practice', but this does not necessarily limit their utility in a historical examination of hajj practice. Instead, the manner in which the authors present themselves and their experiences (what might be called 'self-fashioning' (Reddy 2009)) reveals a great deal about the register of emotions and bodily interactions within which the hajj was imagined and realized in early modern Ottoman society. Evliyā's hajj account also maintains a noteworthy emphasis on pilgrim propriety, and seeks much more directly to shape the conduct of future pilgrims.

One of the few pre-modern Muslim thinkers to frame the hajj as a collection of emotional, mental, and physical stages was Abū Ḥāmid al-Ghazālī (d. 1111) in his magnum opus, the *Iḥyāʾ ʿulūm al-dīn* ('The tevival of the teligious sciences'). Al-Ghazālī talks of yearning (*shawq*) for the Kaʿba, of recalling the shroud (*kafn*) when donning the *iḥrām* garments, and of venerating the Kaʿba when first laying eyes upon it. Much of this is echoed in the hajj narratives of Evliyā and Nābī, although their work maintains its own historical and cultural specificities, or 'contemporaneity' (Brunner 2017, 270. Cited in Kateman 2020, 387). In other words, we might say that Evliyā and Nābī provide their own set of emotional, mental, and physical stages, framed as part of their own experiences and with the potential to both directly and indirectly mediate the expectations and experiences of future pilgrims. Their stages might be said to begin with yearning, longing, and desire (*şevḳ* and *ārzū*), followed by a sense of anticipation as pilgrims near the Holy Cities. A sight of the Kaʿba or the Prophet's tomb might provoke ecstasy (*cezbe*), a loss of senses, or a general bewilderment. The vigil at ʿArafa is characterized by repentance and remorse, and upon its conclusion, pilgrims feel a sense of happiness (*sürūr*) and tranquillity (*ḥużūr*). At the conclusion of the hajj and the *ziyāra*, the most prominent emotions are gratefulness and thankfulness (*şükür*).

In both accounts, these varied emotions could be embodied in equally varied ways and usually through interaction with the physical landscapes of the Ḥaramayn; a first visual clue of the Holy City is invariably followed by pilgrims quickening their pace with renewed vigour. A second, more pronounced clue is followed by pilgrims humbly proceeding on foot, perhaps even barefoot as a reflection of their love. Locking one's gaze is represented as a sign of devotion in the case of the Kaʿba and the *ḥujra*; pilgrims even walked backwards in order to keep their eyes on the beloved object as long as possible. Initial acts of worship are performed with greater speed: pilgrims eagerly enter cities and hasten to undertake the necessary rituals. In contrast, final acts of worship are performed slowly and reluctantly, signifying pain and sorrow. When departing sacred sites, tears might be shed as a marker of sorrow, though tears of a happier kind were also often shed when first encountering the landmarks of the Ḥaramayn. At ʿArafa especially, the donning of the pilgrim garb symbolizes temporary death, while the return to everyday clothes, as well as the practice of grooming and applying perfume, signifies the rebirth of pilgrims and their new lease of life. Especially at Medina, reverence is embodied by the placement of hands on one's chest and the slight bowing of one's body.

References

Abdel Haleem, Muhammed. 2005. *The Qur'an*. Oxford: Oxford University Press.

al-Nahrawālī, Quṭb Al-Dīn Muḥammad. 1857. 'al-Iʿlām bi-aʿlām balad Allāh al-ḥarām.' In *Die Chroniken der Stadt Mekka, Vol. 3: Geschichte der Stadt Mekka und ihres Tempels von Cutb ed-Dîn Muhammed ben Ahmed el-Nahrawâli*, edited by Ferdinand Wüstenfeld. Leipzig: F.A. Brockhaus.

al-Nasāʾī, Abū ʿAbd al-Raḥmān Aḥmad ibn Shuʿayb. 1986 [second edition]. In *Sunan al-Nasāʾī bi-sharḥ al-ḥāfiẓ Jalāl al-Dīn al-Suyūṭī wa-ḥāshiyat al-Imām al-Sindī*, edited by ʿAbd al-Fattāḥ Abū Ghudda. Ḥalab: Maktaba al-Maṭbūʿāt al-Islāmiyya. 9 vols.

al-Sanʿānī, ʿAbd al-Razzāq. 1983 [1970–1972]. *al-Muṣannaf*, edited by Ḥabīb al-Raḥmān al-Aʿẓamī. Bayrūt: al-Maktab al-Islāmī [Karachi: al-Majlis al-ʿIlmī]. 11 vols.

Brunner, Rainer. 2017. 'The pilgrim's tale as a means of self-promotion: Muḥammad Rashīd Riḍā's journey to the Ḥijāz (1916).' In *The piety of learning: Islamic studies in honor of Stefan Reichmuth*, edited by Michael Kemper and Ralf Elger, 27–91. Leiden: Brill.

Coşkun, Menderes. 2000. 'The most literary Ottoman pilgrimage narrative: Nābī's Tuhfetü'l-Haremeyn.' *Turcica* 32: 363–388.

Coşkun, Menderes. 'Ottoman pilgrimage narratives and Nābī's Tuhfetü'l-Haremeyn.' PhD diss., University of Durham.

el-Bendī el-Ḥanefī, Meḥmed Murād b. Dervīş b. ʿAlī. n.d. *Delīlü'l-mütaḥayyirīn fī edā' ḥacci'l-ḳādirīn ve'l-ʿācizīn*. Ankara Milli Kütüphane, Ms. Yz.A.6449. 100 ff.

el-Rūmī, Sinān. n.d. *Menāsik-i ḥacc*. Ankara University, Faculty of Divinity Library, Ms. 36615. 99 ff.

El-Sayed, Laila Hashem Abdel-Rahman. 2016. 'Discourses on emotions: Communities, styles, and selves in early modern Mediterranean travel books: Three case studies.' PhD diss., University of Kent and Freie Universität Berlin.

el-Sincārī, Ebü'l-Fażl. *Menāḳıb-i Mekke*. Staatsbibliothek zu Berlin, Ms. or. oct. 1602, fols 1a–14b.

el-Yemenī, Meḥmed. 2017. *Mekke Medine ve Kudüs'ün faziletleri*, edited by Gamze Beşenk. Istanbul: Büyüyenay.

Evliyā Çelebī. 2012. *Evliyā Çelebī in Medina: The relevant sections of the Seyāḥatnāme*, edited by Nurettin Gemici and translated by Robert Dankoff. Leiden: Brill.

Evliyā Çelebī. 2010. *An Ottoman traveller: Selections from the "Book of travels" of Evliyā Çelebī*, edited by Robert Dankoff and Sooyong Kim. London: Eland.

Evliyā Çelebī. 2005. *Evliyā Çelebi Seyāḥatnāmesi 9. kitap*. Edited by Robert Dankoff, Seyit Ali Kahraman, and Yücel Dağlı. Istanbul: Yapı Kredi Yayınları.

Evliyā Çelebī. 1990. *Evliyā Çelebi in Bitlis: The relevant sections of the Seyāhatnāme*, edited and translated by Robert Dankoff. Leiden: Brill.

George, Kenneth. 2008. 'Ethical pleasure, visual Dzikir, and artistic subjectivity in contemporary Indonesia.' *Material Religion* 4 (2): 172–192.

Göloğlu, Sabiha. 2018. 'Depicting the Islamic holy sites: Mecca, Medina, and Jerusalem in late Ottoman illustrated prayer books.' In *15th international congress of Turkish art. Proceedings*, edited by Michele Bernadini et al., 323–338. Ankara: Ministry of Culture and Tourism, Republic of Turkey.

Kātib Çelebī. 1941. *Kashf al-ẓunūn ʿan asāmi al-kutub wa-al-funūn*. Istanbul: Maarif Matbaası. 2 vols.

Kateman, Ammeke. 2020. 'Fashioning the materiality of the pilgrimage: The hajj travelogue of Muḥammad Labīb al-Batanūnī.' *Die Welt Des Islams* 60 (4): 384–407.

Lutz, Catherine, and Lila Abu-Lughod, eds. 1990. *Language and the politics of emotion, studies in emotion and social interaction*. Cambridge: Cambridge University Press.

Maury, Charlotte. 2013. 'Depictions of the Haramayn on Ottoman tiles: Content and context.' In *The Hajj: Collected essays*, edited by Liana Saif and Venetia Porter, 143–159. London: British Museum Press.

McGregor, Richard. 2020. *Islam and the devotional object: Seeing religion in Egypt and Syria*. New York: Cambridge University Press.

Meyer, Birgit. 2008. 'Media and the senses in the making of religious experience: An introduction.' *Material religion* 4 (2): 124–134.

Nābī. 2002. *Manzum ve mensur Osmanlı hac seyāhatnāmeleri ve Nābī'nin Tuhfetü'l-Harameyn'i*, edited by Menderes Coşkun. Ankara: T.C. Kültür Bakanlığı Yayınları.

Özel, Ahmet. 1989. 'Altın Oluk.' *Türk Diyanet Vakfı Islâm Ansiklopedisi*, volume 2. Istanbul: TDV Islâm ansiklopedisi Genel Müdürlüğü.

Pitts, Joseph. 2012 [1731]. *Encountering Islam. Joseph Pitts: An English slave in 17th-century Algiers and Mecca. A critical edition, with biographical introduction and notes, of Joseph Pitts of Exeter's A faithful account of the religion and manners of the Mahometans, 1731*, edited by Paul Auchterlonie. London: Arabian Publishing.

Reddy, William. 2009. 'Historical research on the Self and emotions.' *Emotion review* 1 (4): 302–315.

Roberts, Robert. 2007. 'Emotions research and religious experience.' In *The Oxford handbook of religion and emotion*, edited by John Corrigan, 490–506. Oxford: Oxford University Press.

Rosenwein, Barbara. 2010. 'Problems and methods in the history of emotions.' *Passions in context: Journal of the history and philosophy of the emotions* 1 (1): 1–32.

Roxburgh, David. 'Visualizing the sites and monuments of Islamic pilgrimage.' In *Architecture in Islamic arts: Treasures of the Aga Khan Museum*, edited by Margaret Graves and Benoît Junod, 33–41. Geneva: Aga Khan Trust for Culture, 2011.

Shafir, Nir. 2020. 'In an Ottoman Holy Land: The hajj and the road from Damascus, 1500–1800.' *History of religions* 60 (1): 1–36.

Tezcan, Hülya. 2017. Sacred covers of Islam's holy shrines. With samples from Topkapi Palace. Istanbul: Masa.

Werbner, Pnina, and Helene Basu. 1998. Embodying charisma modernity, locality, and performance of emotion in Sufi cults. London and New York: Routledge.

Witkam, Jan Just. 2007. 'The battle of the images: Mekka vs. Medina in the iconography of the manuscripts of al-Jazūlī's *Dalāʾil al-khayrāt*.' In *Theoretical approaches to the transmission and edition of oriental manuscripts, proceedings of a symposium held in Istanbul, March 28–30, 2001*, edited by Judith Pfeiffer and Manfred Kropp, 67–82. Beirut: Ergon Verlag.

Woodhead, Christine. 2011. 'Ottoman languages.' In *The Ottoman World*, edited by Christine Woodhead, 143–158. London: Routledge.

CHAPTER 5

Comparing Two Persian Hajj Travelogues: Yaʿqub Mirzā (1868) and Farhād Mirzā (1875/76)

Thomas Ecker

1 Introduction

At the turn of the nineteenth century, the Qajar dynasty had established themselves as rulers in Iran and over the following decade the country experienced a period of relative political stability and order, especially when compared to the preceding century. However, the new dynasty had to deal with the rise of imperial powers, which proved to be a potential danger to the territorial integrity of their domain. This situation led to the court and educated classes having an increasing interest in information about Europe and countries surrounding Iran, but also a growing need for the Qajar state to gather information about its own territories. Additionally, the establishment of commercial transportation in surrounding areas via steamship and railway incited greater numbers of Iranians travelling abroad. These developments resulted in a sharp increase in the number of Persian travelogues, whose overall number might be somewhere between 300 and 400 for the Qajar period (1797–1925).[1]

All these travelogues have a didactic intention and were written to inform their readers about the journey of the author and the places he travelled to. Most have stylistic similarities, suggesting a common genre of Persian travelogues. Travelogues about the hajj pilgrimage to Mecca of course share the same destination and travel purpose and many had similar itineraries. In this chapter, I will argue that a closer investigation reveals key differences that are contingent on the author and the audiences they wanted to address, as well as the social function of the text. For this reason, I will compare two hajj travelogues written by members of the Qajar household and show similarities

1 Travelogues have a long tradition in Persian literature, but only few are known from the early centuries, like the *Safarnāme* by Nāṣer-e Khosrow written in the eleventh century or the *Tuḥfa al-ʿIrāqayn* by Khāqāni Shervāni from the twelfth century. For the Safavid Era (1501–1722), a recent study lists 22 travelogues (Kiyanrad 2020). Morikawa (2001) listed 283 travelogues written in the Qajar era. Since then, a considerable number of travelogues have been published from this period.

and differences in the form and content of their narratives, pointing out that they address different audiences. While there is some overlap, the two texts occupied different social functions, which had an impact on each text's production. I will first introduce both authors and their travelogues and present some of the main features of the accounts, considering the main genre markers. I will then compare how both authors narrate their encounters with non-Islamic cultures and modern technology and evaluate the accounts of their sojourn in Mecca in Medina. I will end with a summary of my findings and some notes about how Persian hajj travelogues developed during the nineteenth century.

2 The Travelogue of Yaʿqub Mirzā

Yaʿqub Mirzā-ye Tabrizi, also known by his pen name Manṣur, was a minor prince of the Qajar dynasty. He travelled to Mecca as a member of the entourage of Moḥammad Ṭāher Mirzā, the son of the then governor of the Iranian province Azerbaijan, Ṭahmāsp Mirzā Mo'ayyad al-Dowle. Mo'ayyad al-Dowle himself was the son of Moḥammad ʿAli Mirzā Dowlatshāh, the oldest son of the second Qajar Shah Fatḥ ʿAlī Shāh (r. 1797–1834) whose descendants formed a branch of the Qajar dynasty. Since the author was a Qajar prince and associated with the family of Mo'ayyad al-Dawla, he may have been a part of this branch of the Qajar Family. Yaʿqub Mirzā travelled in the year 1868 from Tabriz in Iran via Erivan to Tiflis in Georgia. From there he went to the Black Sea, which he crossed with a steamer to Istanbul. After a short stay in the city he travelled to Beirut, again with a steamer, and from there by carriage to Damascus. In Syria he joined the official Ottoman hajj caravan travelling to Medina and finally Mecca. After completing the rites of the hajj, in nearby Jedda he boarded a steamer to Suez. Since the Suez Canal was not fully built yet, after five days in quarantine, he boarded a train to Ismailia and travelled to Cairo.[2] A few days later he took a Nile steamer to Alexandria and from there returned to Istanbul and via Tiflis to Tabriz, arriving there seven months and seven days after his departure.

Yaʿqub Mirzā mentions several times in his travelogue that he took notes during his journey, but the extant manuscript was produced seven years after his return to Iran for Moḥammad Ṭāher Mirzā (Tabrizi 2009, 38). At the end of the manuscript, there are notes from several readers which show that the text circulated for many years among acquaintances of the author (ibid., 296–298; 2010,

2 This quarantine station was near ʿUyūn Mūsā located in the Gulf of Suez (Tabrizi 2009, 247).

542). It transpires from these notes that they must have known him personally, because one reader mentions wanting to ask the author in person about the meaning of some words and another noted that he wanted the manuscript to be sent back to Yaʿqub Mirzā. We also learn that the author died in 1909 and that the text was part of the inheritance given to his son (Tabrizi 2009, 12).[3]

The main narrative of the journey is divided into chapters that open with the sentence '*goft: ey javān-e man*' (He said: Oh, my boy) and end with '*chun shab bar sar-e dast dar-āmad Manṣur lab az goftār foru bast*' (As the night fell on the wrist, Manṣur closed his lips and refrained from speaking). The second sentence is written in red colour in the manuscript and marks the chapter's end. Each chapter covers one stage of the journey.

These opening and closing sentences are addressed to a certain young man (*javān*) who tasked the author with writing the travelogue and whom he also met at the end of his journey (ibid., 294). Yaʿqub Mirzā writes:

> I address *javān* at the beginning of every stage because he was one of my friends in Tabriz. Record everything about the wonders of the travel stages and your experiences in written form, so that we may also be more or less informed about the state of affairs of foreign governments and land and sea.
>
> ibid., 37 [translation of all quotations from the two travelogues under discussion by me, TE]

Furthermore, the author assumes the readership to be a circle of his friends in Tabriz. He apologizes several times directly to them for his shortcomings as an author (ibid., 37, 229) and expresses on many occasions during his journey how he misses them and wishes they would be with him. He also alludes to inside jokes among his friends. For instance, when he was in Istanbul, he visited a theatre and watched women performing a dance. He describes their appearance in such a graphic way that the modern editor felt obliged to censor the word buttocks (*kun*) seven times in this description and replace the word with three dots. This censorship can be found throughout the modern edition. At the end of his description, he expresses the wish that some of his more impudent friends would have been with him, especially one friend called Jaʿfar Khān Mirzā. Here he was obviously mocking one of his friends, whose identity might well have been known to the readers (ibid., 112–113).

3 Today it is in possession of the Parliamentary Library of the Islamic Republic of Iran (item number 9908), and it was published in 2009 in a modern edition by Rasul Jaʿfariyān, who also included the text in his 2010 compilation of 50 Persian hajj travelogues.

True to his assignment, the main intent of the narrative is educational. For every stage of the journey Yaʿqub Mirzā describes the destination and the condition of the road. These descriptions encompass usually only a few sentences and characterize each stop in a general way, without providing too much detail. He tries to give his readers a clear account, focusing on the size of a city, village, or stopover, its inhabitants, and his general impressions. He shows interest in technological innovations and is especially impressed by Istanbul, depicting the Ottoman capital as an exceptionally large and densely populated city. In the Ottoman capital he describes his visits to touristic sights like the Hagia Sophia and to bathhouses, theatres, and other leisure activities. Enthusiastically, he notes in his journal that he could write day and night about Istanbul for the lifetime of the prophet Noah and it would still not be enough (ibid., 118). While travelling in the Caucasus on his way back to Iran, Yaʿqub Mirzā mentions that his perceptions have changed. He explains that on his outward journey he wrote much about the beauty of Tiflis, but now the city seems to him only like a village compared to Istanbul (ibid., 284).

The travelogue also contains twenty hand-drawn illustrations to further visualize his descriptions. These range from some dots and lines, for example when illustrating the marching order of the Hajj caravan (ibid., 165), to detailed, but still very simple and amateurish sketches of a steam powered crane (ibid., 97) or the layout of the Kaʿba and its immediate surroundings in Mecca (ibid., 229). He occasionally tries to provide direct advice to future travellers. While residing in the quarantine station next to Suez, he purchased a transit ticket from the station to Suez, only to find out that he was swindled, because no ticket was required. In his travelogue he gives an angry description of this experience, so that his friends would not make the same mistake (ibid., 249–250).

As specified in his assignment, the narration of his personal experiences is another important part of Yaʿqub Mirzā's travelogue. These go beyond mentioning the important events of the day. He also records many personal encounters, elements of his daily routine like making and drinking tea or smoking, and his everyday troubles during the journey. An example of the latter is a description of his first camel ride when travelling with the Damascus caravan. Because he had faced difficulties sitting in the camel litter, he attempted to ride on the back of the camel. He mounted it and tried to support himself by holding onto the camel's neck, but as it began to move, its neck moved as well, causing Yaʿqub Mirzā to fall to the ground. As this happened several times, he had to go back into the camel litter. If only his friends would have been there, to see him and laugh at him, he writes (ibid., 155–156).

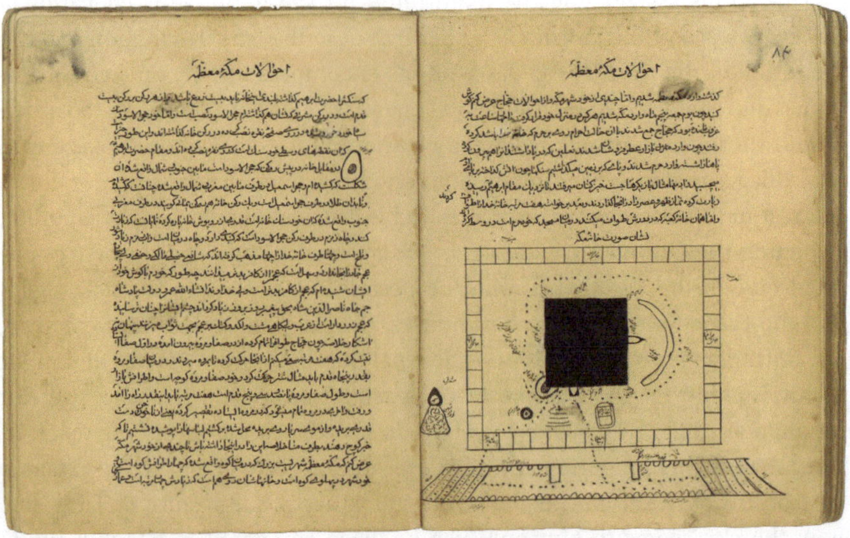

FIGURE 5.1 A drawing of the Kaʿba in Yaʿqub Mirzā's travelogue
PHOTOGRAPH OF MANUSCRIPT BY THE AUTHOR

In some passages Yaʿqub Mirzā offers a colourful description of his travel experiences. While travelling from Damascus to Medina, he describes his impressions of the moving hajj caravan.

> In the desert were so many lanterns that the desert became like the sky with shining stars. And in addition to the lanterns from every side was the sound of singing like talking nightingales, everyone singing a melody. Some of them were like garden's nightingales and some of them like crows on the winter's snow. And the voices belonged to the singers, inviting to the pilgrimage and emotionally stirred dervishes on the one hand and to the boastful Arabs, hurrying their camels, and Iranian travelers reciting poems like the sound of nightingales in the rose garden on the other hand. Everyone was talking in their own lovely voice that made the soul fly out of a man's body.
>
> TABRIZI 2009, 176

Yaʿqub Mirzā continues his description of this part of his journey by stating that he listened to them for hours, thinking about his friends, until he fell asleep.

A recurring theme in the travelogue of Yaʿqub Mirzā is his erotic interest in young men. While crossing the Caucasus on his journey to Mecca, he saw several youths he considered attractive. He narrates these encounters from his inner emotional perspective and relates how he was suddenly struck and emotionally 'altered' by their appearance: they were moon-faced and walked like partridges. Part of the narrative intrigue is his potential to be seduced by Christianity, as most of these young boys turn out to be Christians (ibid., 57). Later during his journey, he visited places with young male prostitutes in Istanbul he describes in detail his visit to a bathhouse where he made inquiries about sexual services, including what was charged for them (ibid., 116–117). While residing in Beirut, he describes the inhabitants of the city as proponents of 'boys' play', or *bachche-bāzi*.[4] He paints a picture of readily available and sexually attractive young boys. Near the place where he was accommodated, there was a school with fifteen young boys, whom he describes as attractive. Every day two or three were brought to his hotel, but because of the religious nature of his journey and the fasting month of Ramadan he declined their services. Describing his emotional distress, he compared himself to a cat who could not reach the meat with its mouth (ibid., 134). While staying in Damascus he uses several pages to report about his friendship with a young boy in a barber shop, also alluding to a sexual encounter (ibid., 146–150).

Ya'qub Mirzā's travel account is a personal narrative written for his friend group. The traditional elements of a travel report are present, such as descriptions of the places visited during the journey and the roads between them. These descriptions are complemented with many personal experiences, subjective impressions, and descriptions of the author's mental state during the journey. The main aim of Ya'qub Mirzā seems to have been to write an interesting and entertaining account for his friends about his pilgrimage to Mecca.

3 The Travelogue of Farhād Mirzā

Farhād Mirzā Mo'tamad al-Dowle was the fifteenth son of the former crown prince 'Abbās Mirzā and uncle of the ruling regent, Nāṣer al-Din Shāh (r. 1848–1896). For a long time Farhād Mirzā was a powerful figure in the Qajar administration and was appointed as governor to important provinces. He is known to have been in the possession of a large library and was a productive writer. In addition to his travelogue, he wrote religious treatises, poetry, and a loose translation of an English geographical work.[5]

4 Literal translation: 'boy play'. A term indicating the use of beardless young men for entertainment purposes, including prostitution.

5 For more information about Farhād Mirzā, see his article in the Encyclopaedia Iranica (Eslami 1999).

Farhād Mirzā undertook the pilgrimage in the years 1875 and 1876 after his dismissal at the court of Nāṣer al-Din Shāh in Tehran. During the first trip of Nāṣer al-Din Shāh to Europe in 1873, Farhād Mirzā had been appointed acting regent in Tehran. After the Shah's return to Iran, he prominently participated in a palace revolt against his Prime Minister Moshir al-Dowle Sepahsālār, who advocated to reform the Qajar administration and to introduce modern technology in Iran. Moshir al-Dowle was one of the driving forces behind the Reuters Concession in 1872, which entailed, among many other things, the construction of a railroad. At first the Prime Minister was dismissed and Farhād Mirzā sent back to his former post as governor of Kurdistan, but after several months he was replaced and called back to Tehran. There he was left without an assignment until he obtained permission to leave Tehran for the pilgrimage to Mecca. After his return he was once again assigned to a high post and appointed governor of Fars.[6]

His travelogue begins with his departure from Tehran to Anzali at the Caspian Sea. He boarded a steamer to Baku and travelled on to Tiflis by carriage. There he took the Transcaucasian Railway to Poti. By steamer he went to Batumi and travelled onward to Istanbul. After a short sojourn he again boarded a steamer to Alexandria and visited Cairo for a few days before proceeding to Suez. Because the steamer with which he was supposed to travel to Jedda was in a bad condition, he chose to disembark in Yanbūʿ, and he visited Medina before travelling to Mecca. Having completed the rites of the hajj, he embarked on a ship from nearby Jedda, which, after a stopover at a quarantine station, took him through the Suez Canal to Port Said.[7] A steamer brought him to Istanbul via several ports in the eastern Mediterranean. From there he travelled through the Caucasus back to Baku, Anzali, and arrived at Tehran seven months and 19 days after his departure. Farhād Mirzā was the head of a large travelling party starting with roughly twenty people, including his wife. During the course of the journey, more people temporarily joined his group.[8] Since he acted as a representative of the Qajar court, he was involved in several matters of foreign policy. Regarding his meeting with the viceroy of the Caucasus, for instance, he remarks that the latter complained to Farhād Mirzā about unlawful activity in the border region between Iran and Russia. Farhād Mirzā promised to report this to Nāṣer al-Din Shāh (Moʿtamad al-Dowle 1987a, 288–289).

6 About the palace revolt, see Bakhash 1978, 112–119.

7 The quarantine station was in al-Wajh, a city which is located halfway between Yanbu and the Sinai Peninsula.

8 In one case he was not even aware of their presence (Moʿtamad al-Dowle 1987a, 20, 131).

Farhād Mirzā dictated his travelogue to his scribe during his journey and a lithography was printed several months after his return to Tehran in January/February 1877 and again in November/December 1877 in Shiraz (ibid., 355, 359).[9] Even though he does not mention that he was specifically assigned to write the travelogue, already during his journey he expected it to be printed.[10] Additionally, Farhād Mirzā wrote several letters and telegrams on the way and when he arrived at Tehran he was interviewed by the Shah and submitted several additional reports to the council of ministers (ibid., 85, 331–333). His travelogue was meant as the official account for the broader public. According to its introduction the report was printed on the order of Nāṣer al-Din Shāh with the intent to reach a wide audience (ibid., 13).

The title *Hidāyat al-sabīl wa-kifāyat al-dalīl* ('Complete guide of the way') implied the educational intent of the text. Farhād Mirzā wrote an extensive survey of the route he travelled, and alongside his numerous descriptions of cities, buildings, and villages, he mentions and describes bridges, mountains, rivers, landscapes, and many other points of interest. He is especially attentive to geographical information, as he notes the distance between each travel stage and the itinerary of each day. In some cases, he recorded the degrees of longitude and latitude of a city, and he took great care to offer the correct pronunciation of travel stations, be they big cities or small villages. He carried scientific instruments with him and measured temperatures. In Tiflis he asked for a translation of a Russian geographical work about the origin of the river Kur, which he then summarizes in his travelogue (ibid., 59–60). In addition to his own observations, he adds information from other works, such as his own translation of an English geographical work (ibid., 121, 237). He also continuously refers to *Tuḥfa al-ʿIrāqayn* ('Gift of the two Iraqs'), a long poem depicting a pilgrimage to Mecca written by Khāqāni Shervāni in the twelfth century, and sometimes he compares Khāqāni's descriptions with his own impressions (ibid., 104). The travelogue also contains religious information, most notable is the entry of his last day in Medina, which includes a long treatise about the obligatory and desirable rites of the hajj and *ʿumra* (ibid., 160–187). After the main narrative of the journey a detailed map and description of the Prophet's Mosque in Medina are added, which he and his scribe produced while in the city (ibid., 334–338).[11]

9 Two modern editions of the text were published (Moʿtamad al-Dowle 1987a; 1987b), and the report was included in the third volume of the compilation of hajj travelogues published by Jaʿfariyān (Jaʿfariyān 2010).

10 In a letter to the Sublime Porte, Farhād Mirzā mentions that he will record his letters to them in his travel diary, which will be printed (Moʿtamad al-Dowle 1987a, 268).

11 With his inquiries about geographical information with scientific methods and the produ-

A large part of the travelogue is dedicated to his contacts with important political officials. In these sections his travelogue resembles reports written by diplomatic envoys. He relates in detail how he was treated by foreign officials, giving their names and his impressions of them. The importance Farhād Mirzā attributed to this aspect of his journey becomes clear during his stay in Ganja, a city in the Caucasus, where he was only received by the chief of police outside the city and escorted by him to his accommodation. After one hour the deputy of the city governor came to inquire about his well-being and asked if he wanted to meet the governor. Farhād Mirzā adamantly refused to see him, explaining that his rank was equivalent to the governor of Baku. He pointed out the differences in his reception, as he was received on his arrival at Baku at the harbour by the governor and nobles of the city in official costume. The governor accompanied him in the carriage to his accommodation, where a military band was playing for him. They sat together in his room for one hour with the head of the Cossacks and other military officers. He was visited daily by the governor, who later bade farewell to him at the outskirts of the city. Farhād Mirzā made it clear that his reception in Ganja had been inappropriate (ibid., 39–40). This unsatisfactory welcome remained an issue during the rest of his journey through Russian territory. While residing in Tiflis Farhād Mirzā met the deputy of the viceroy of the Caucasus. He explained to him that he would like to return to Iran via Tiflis, but only if he could avoid the city of Ganja. Afterwards Farhād Mirzā was assured by Fatḥʿ Ali Ākhundzāde, who acted as translator for the Russians during the conversation, that the deputy was aware of his complaints about the governor of Ganja and Ākhundzāde agreed with Farhād Mirzā's attitude (ibid., 57). During his return journey he took a detour to avoid passing through the city.

The detailed accounts of interactions with foreign state representatives, especially the ceremonial details attached to them, were meant to express the power relations between the Qajar state and its foreign counterparts. By narrating his official meetings, Farhād Mirzā ranked himself in the hierarchies of international diplomacy and showed the legitimacy the Qajar court enjoyed abroad.[12] According to Farhād Mirzā, his status was seen by the Ottomans as equivalent to a prince of a European royal house. During his first visit to Istanbul, he was received by the Ottoman Sultan on his last day in the city. The crown prince of Württemberg had visited the city two months earlier and had

cing of exact maps of holy sites, Farhād Mirzā was taking part in a contemporary 'culture of exploration', which was conveyed to Persian literary circles by translations of European geographical works and travelogues (Sohrabi 2012, 84).

12 For two other examples, see Sohrabi 2012, 40–44, 61–65.

also only been received on the day of his departure, which made Farhād Mirzā decide that he himself had been treated accordingly (ibid., 82, 112).

In his travelogue Farhād Mirzā reflects on his own political adversities and presents his version of events to a wider court audience. He attributes his dismissal not directly to his actions during his time as regent. Instead, he presents it as a conspiracy and a misunderstanding. According to Farhād Mirzā, after he was once again appointed as the governor of Kurdistan, he wrote a letter on another matter, which was intercepted by a hostile person. The letter was altered in a way that gave the impression that Farhād Mirzā supported attacks against the Shaykhīs in Tabriz, a heterodox sect of Shiʿi scholars with a strong presence in the city. The Shah then ordered his dismissal as governor for inciting violence between two Muslim sects. He even composed a long poem clarifying the matter, which he intended to read at the grave of Mary in Jerusalem, but in the end, he did not visit the city (ibid., 90–97).[13] Instead, at the grave of the Prophet Muhammad in Medina he cited another poem, defending his conduct as acting regent and highlighting his own piety (ibid., 153–155).

The travelogue of Farhād Mirzā was the official account of his journey, and it was printed for a wide audience at the court and beyond. Its aim was to educate readers about the hajj pilgrimage and the travel route to Mecca. It informed audiences about the journey of Farhād Mirzā in his capacity as a high representative of the Qajar state and provided him with the opportunity to present himself as an important public figure in a favourable light, including offering his perspective on current political issues.

4 The Genre of Persian Travel Literature and the Two Hajj Travelogues

In his survey of Persian travelogues, William Hanaway suggests that in the nineteenth century Persian travelogues 'form a discrete genre that can be identified by elements of inner and outer form' (Hanaway 2002, 265). The following elements that Hanaway articulates are present in both travelogues under discussion: they are written in prose, in the first person, and the subject matter is the actual travel experience of the author, relating actions of the author's daily routine, such as getting up and getting dressed. Furthermore,

13 His half-brother Ḥosām al-Salṭane would visit Jerusalem five years later after making the pilgrimage to Mecca. He brought the travelogue of Farhād Mirzā with him and recited the poem under the candlelight of Christian priests at the grave of Mary (Ḥosām al-Salṭane 2010, 234).

the travelogues have a didactic purpose and contain reconstructed dialogues. According to Hanaway the travel journey is presented in a dynamic manner, that is, the narrative of events continues chronologically with little reflection on the significance of the events for the travellers' life or his journey. Most Persian travelogues use an educated, but relatively simple literary style, with some occasional lapses in a more elevated style, and occasionally contained quotations of poetry by classical authors and poetry by the travel authors themselves. Hanaway explains that travelogues 'are all of an appropriate size, neither too short to convey the information intended nor so prolix as to be boring' (ibid.).

Yaʿqub Mirzā narrates his journey in simple, but sometimes obscene, prose. He presents poetry composed by himself and others in moderate amounts and only occasionally uses Arabic, for example to cite religious proverbs. This differs much from Farhād Mirzā's report. While in general his prose is written in a simple style, as is common in Persian travelogues, he very frequently incorporated poetry, quotations, and proverbs of varying lengths both in Arabic and Persian. In the compilation of Jaʿfariyān, the travelogues of Yaʿqub Mirzā and Farhād Mirzā amount to 291 and 467 pages respectively, which makes the latter the most extensive Persian travelogue to Mecca.

However, Hanaway's description of the genre of Persian travelogues is problematic, as it fails to consider that many Persian 'travelogues' are in fact a compilation of several texts—the actual travel narrative being only one of them.[14] In the case of Farhād Mirzā, if we also exclude the chapter about the obligatory rites of the hajj, his travel journal makes up around 80 % of the text. It is preceded by an introduction in an elevated style to the lithograph, which is customary in manuscripts produced by clerical scribes. His daily journal, which is interrupted several times by digressions, long poems, and quoted letters, is followed by a map of the Mosque of the Prophet Muhammad in Medina, which contains detailed descriptions. Then there is a chapter that provides the latitude and longitude of important cities that are not mentioned in the journal itself. Afterwards, there is an account written in high style by another scribe about events happening after the arrival of Farhād Mirzā in Shiraz. A scribe also added a poem containing 86 verses, eulogizing Farhād Mirzā and his journey as well as a chapter about desirable actions during the hajj in glosses. The last two chapters, which are most likely written by Farhād Mirzā himself, clarify some issues about the exact location of the corners of the Kaʿba and graves of Islamic martyrs in Medina, which are mentioned in the travel journal. Therefore, the

14 For a critical discussion about Persian Travelogues as genre, see Sohrabi 2012, 13–16 and for another example of a composite travelogue see Sohrabi 2012, 53–65.

'travelogue' of Farhād Mirzā is not simply a coherent travel account, but rather a compilation of texts written by different authors. The whole composition is coherent only in the sense that it fulfills common social functions: the education of the reader about the journey to Mecca as well as the pilgrimage itself and a positive presentation of Farhād Mirzā to a courtly audience.[15]

In the case of Ya'qub Mirzā, the main travel narrative is only preceded by an introduction, obviously added while producing the extant manuscript for Moḥammad Ṭāher Mirzā. He was required to comply with courtly conventions of manuscript writing, which is why the introduction contains a summary of the travel narrative followed by invocations of Muhammad, Imam Ali, the Shah, the crown prince residing in Tabriz, and the governor of Tabriz, all of which is written in a highly formal style. The introduction also reports that he was assigned to write the book and narrate the start of his journey. This is then followed by the main travel account.

Both texts belong to the same literary tradition of Persian travel writing, but considering the literary style and the composition of the manuscript the travelogue of Farhād Mirzā is a much more elaborate creation. This can be explained by his own literacy, the resources he had available, and the purpose of the text as an official publication by a high-ranking member of the court.

5 Comparing the Main Themes of Hajj Travelogues

Due to similar itineraries and the joint purpose of the hajj pilgrimage, several topics can be found in both hajj travelogues. In the following section I want to compare how these similarities are portrayed in both travelogues.

According to Nile Green, in the second half of the nineteenth century, as a result of its increasing integration into the infrastructure of steam travel 'the hajj was transformed from a ritual movement through a long-familiar Muslim memory space into a journey through a world governed by ideas, peoples and technologies of non-Muslim provenance' (Green 2015, 193). While travelling in the Russian Caucasus, Ya'qub Mirzā identified the area as a country dominated by non-believers who threatened the ritual purity of the pilgrim. He was disturbed that he could not distinguish between Muslim and non-Muslim traders

15 The modern editions differ from each other which parts are included. [Mo'tamad al-Dowle 1987a is complete, while Mo'tamad al-Dowle 1987b is missing the poem, the chapter about hajj rites and almost everything after the travel narrative. Ja'fariyān 2010 only omitted a late chapter about historical events, because it has no connection to the hajj of Farhād Mirzā.]

in the market or between Muslim and non-Muslim bathhouses. He explains that one might have taken a bath and imagine oneself to be clean, but still be ritually unclean. For him, the ritual impurity was unavoidable when travelling to Mecca via the Caucasus, and for this reason he did not recommend this itinerary (Tabrizi 2009, 95). One evening he stayed in an accommodation that served alcohol, and he saw Armenians and Europeans coming in, drinking, shouting, and making music. He could not sleep and explained that 'no-one going to Mecca should take this route. It is good for amusement but not to become a *ḥājjī*' (Tabrizi 2009, 74–75).

According to Hanaway, the two greatest challenges for Iranian travellers were storms at sea and the conduct of European women: 'This seems to represent the extremes to which Persians could be physically and morally challenged' (Hanaway 2002, 262). When Yaʿqub Mirzā travels from Istanbul to Beirut, he offers a vivid description of his experience during a storm. He paints the picture of a crowded ship with frightened passengers who are exposed to the forces of nature. Everyone looks at each other; they all fear drowning and are unable to talk. The sound of vomiting is heard from every direction, while rain, thunderbolts, and cold winds rock the ship. Water flows from the deck back into the sea like a river. When the lights of Beirut come into sight, people are relieved and embrace each other. When he finally sets foot on hard soil, Yaʿqub Mirzā feels like his mother has given birth to him anew (Tabrizi 2009, 129–131). Later on Yaʿqub Mirzā refers several times to this experience as very frightening, and when he arrives in the Caucasus on his return journey he prostrates a hundred times in prayer to thank God for having survived the sea journeys (ibid., 279).

In both travelogues European or Europeanized women are portrayed in a sexualized and potentially immoral manner. For Farhād Mirzā immoral European women are an expression of an invading European culture, which will eventually lead to the demise of the Islamic religion.[16] During the first evening dinner in the Iranian embassy in Istanbul, Farhād Mirzā was approached by the wife of an Austrian embassy member, who asked him for a dance. He refused. In his travelogue he then proceeds with a polemic about the revealing clothes and immoral conduct of European women. These manners will infect the people of the Ottoman Empire very soon and the Iranians a little bit later, Farhād Mirzā writes. When he sees a Jewish girl dancing, Farhād Mirzā remarks to a member of the Iranian embassy that this kind of dance is forbidden in the

16 On the topic of European women as a danger to Islamic culture in Qajar Iran, see also Tavakoli-Targhi 2002, 342–346.

Jewish religion, but it is explained to him, that this is 'civilization' and that soon every province will be 'civilized'. This, Farhād Mirzā saw as a great danger to the Islamic religion and customs. He writes that soon in all of Asia they—he probably means women—will walk in the streets and in the bazar without a veil. The children will learn how to speak French and learning how to read the Qur'an will be abandoned. If one has the wish to learn it, one will have to go to Mecca and Medina. On the next day he drives to his audience with the Sultan. While in the carriage the Master of Ceremonies of the Ottoman court explains to him that everything which is close to a railway becomes like Europe, and if in Iran a railroad is opened, Iran will over time become like Europe too (Moʿtamad al-Dowle 1987a, 79–80). Farhād's impression of Egypt is similar. While driving in a carriage, he sees several women wearing European clothes in the streets. He asks his guide who they are: The wives of some consul? His guide answers that these women are the daughters of an Egyptian official, and he tries to justify their conduct by saying that their country is 'free'. This earns him a strong rebuke by Farhād Mirzā who explains to him that in Islam there is no such freedom (ibid., 110–111).

Whereas Farhād Mirzā considered the sight of unveiled women in Istanbul and Cairo as a great danger to the Islamic religion, Yaʿqub Mirzā's attitude might best be described as voyeuristic. When he reflects on the European women he saw in Istanbul, he describes their clothing as revealing and showing their figure. He explains that this sight made him understand why poets compare the stature of women with a cypress, and he complains that one cannot see Iranian women as they hide themselves in a chador (Tabrizi 2009, 114). Like his description of young boys, his aesthetic perception is informed by metaphors of Persian poetry. However, while Yaʿqub Mirzā depicts himself interacting with boys, he does not report anything similar during his encounters with European women, whom he only looked at from afar.

For Farhād Mirzā another aspect of European culture were European dishes, which he contrasted with Islamic culture and food. When he is invited by the Ottoman Prime Minister, he asks him to refrain from serving alcoholic beverages and to not be served any European food. He later explains to the Prime Minister that there are some European dishes he likes, but one should not abandon one's own customs. There are also Europeans who eat food prepared by Muslims, but they do not eat it inside their homes. Therefore, the Muslims should not follow the Europeans by eating salad and soup in their homes every night (Moʿtamad al-Dowle 1987a, 260). Yaʿqub Mirzā makes a similar observation when eating dinner in the Iranian consulate in Cairo. Iranian food is served on a table in the European manner with a knife and fork. He starts to eat with them, but Yaʿqub Mirzā does not feel comfortable and says everyone should follow their own cultural customs. Subsequently, he and the other attendants put their forks down and start eating with their hands (Tabrizi 2009, 256–257).

Yaʿqub Mirzā is very enthusiastic about modern technology and progress and is aware of the 'backwardness' of Iran in this regard. While residing in Istanbul, he unsuccessfully tried to recruit a firemen trainer (ibid., 114–115). He also wanted to bring a windmill to Iran. On this occasion he says that the conditions in Iran made him sad, because of the examples of engineering he has seen during his journey (ibid., 122).

Farhād Mirzā's attitude is not that different, as he appreciates the usefulness of modern technology, and he obtained the plans for a windmill he had seen in Istanbul (Moʿtamad al-Dowle 1987a, 317). But he is critical regarding the building of railway in Iran. He states that he is not categorically against the construction of a railway, but he warns of negative consequences and argues for a self-financed modernization. Iran should not try to invite foreign capital but build railways slowly with her own money and not be dependent on foreign sponsors (ibid., 275). Farhād Mirzā's polemics against the railroad in Iran must be seen in relation to discussions about the Reuters Concession at court. He was politically opposed to a group of reformers, headed by Moshir al-Dowle and Malkom Khān, who had argued for foreign concessions and greater centralization of the Qajar state. Farhād Mirzā's position was on the other side, opposing not only administrative reform and the centralization of power in the hands of the Prime Minister, which ultimately aimed to weaken his position as governor, but also technological modernization, especially the building of a railroad. His arguments regarding the adoption of European manners in the Ottoman Empire and the construction of a railroad in Iran are part of a wider political argument he makes in his travelogue.

In both travelogues the daily events during their stays in Mecca and Medina are depicted in the same narrative style as the rest of the text. However, arriving in these cities, the first visit to the Kaʿba, and the hajj rites as well as visits to the tomb of Muhammad and the al-Baqīʿ-cemetery in Medina are emphasized in their travelogues and described in detail.

While arriving at Medina Farhād Mīrzā dismounts at the first sight of the dome of the Prophet's Mosque and prays. After his prayer he recites some verses of a poem. During a subsequent military reception with the governor of Medina, he mentions that one of his associates brought him a Qur'an, which must have fallen out of his pocket when prostrating outside of Medina (ibid., 138–139). A couple days later he visits the grave of the Prophet Muhammad to recite a poem, which he called the 'Maqāme Aḥmadiye' in praise of the Prophet. He explains it was just completed the night before and recites it standing close to the lattice of the grave. The attendant Arabs, who do not know Persian, listen and say in Arabic: 'He is reading a pilgrimage prayer in Persian,' indicating the pious impression he makes on bystanders. The poem itself is 52 verses long and quoted in full. It deals with stories of the Islamic prophets and Farhād's own spiritual biography. He then links the poem's recitation with his position as acting regent, deviating from his previous strategy to avoid ascribing his dismissal from his participation in the palace coup against Moshīr al-Dowle. Farhād Mirzā does not apologize for his actions, but rather defends his conduct as acting regent by highlighting his own piety and learning (ibid., 153–155). For Farhād Mirzā, the narrative of his pilgrimage and his sojourn in Medina was a way to portray himself as pious to a courtly audience. He does this with great symbolic gestures like performing the hajj rites or reciting a poem at the Prophet's grave in Medina, but also by mentioning passing details, such as the story of when his personal Qur'an falls out of his pocket. This is meant as a positive self-portrayal to legitimize his new role as governor of Fars, to which he was appointed immediately after his return to Tehran.

Ya'qub Mirzā was moved by the religious fervour of his fellow pilgrims. In the night before his arrival at Mecca, he reports his fellow travellers would stay awake, facing Mecca, praying, and reciting the Qur'an. 'From the sound of their recital, the human soul started to shiver in such a way that I cannot describe it,' he writes. About entering the city, he notes:

> At this time a state befell the pilgrims, how should I explain it, so that we went barefoot and bareheaded under the sun, exclaiming *labbayka labbayka* (I am at your service). I wished that one of my friends could look at our condition and cry or laugh about the state of the pilgrims.
>
> TABRIZI 2009, 228

After their arrival at Mecca, both authors go straight to the Ka'ba, perform the rituals of the *'umra* (short pilgrimage), and give elaborate, eye-witness accounts of the holy place and the surrounding mosque. Both depict their daily actions while performing the hajj rites. And while Farhād Mirzā sometimes expounds on a ritual in more detail, Ya'qub Mirzā mainly reproduces what his travel guide told him and reports some of his impressions along the way, the goal being in both cases to provide an eye-witness-account of the hajj rituals, to guide the reader through them, and to verify that the hajj was completed successfully and correctly by the author.

Apart from the hajj rites, both authors mention during their sojourn in Mecca and Medina the other rituals they performed, thereby reporting what additional religious rewards were obtained. Farhād Mīrzā mentions that he recited the entire Qur'an in the Grand Mosque surrounding the Ka'ba while being in Mecca and reported that circumambulations around the Kaʿba as well as recitations of suras of the Qurʾan were made by proxy for other members of the Qajar household. Farhād Mīrzā even presents a register to one of his associates, which contained a list of people to whom he had dedicated spiritual rewards during his stay (Moʿtamad al-Dowle 1987a, 213–214). Yaʿqub Mirzā reports about taking a brotherhood oath with one of his travel companions while visiting the Kaʿba and dedicated circumambulations to his friends and countrymen (Tabrizi 2009, 230–231, 236).

During their stay in Mecca and Medina, their affiliation as Shiʿi pilgrims in a majority Sunni pilgrimage is very prominent. Both accounts report about a disagreement between Iranian and non-Iranian pilgrims regarding the exact calendar date. At the time the calendar used in Iran deviated from the one in the Ottoman Empire by one day. This meant that Iranians started their hajj rites one day later than Sunni pilgrims. Yaʿqub Mirzā was at first confused and started his hajj with the Sunni majority until he learned from his countrymen about the dispute. He then followed the Iranian pilgrims and mentions positively how much less crowded Mecca was during their departure to Mina (ibid., 231). He also reports about the performance of Shiʿi mourning rituals at ʿArafa and Minā without being harassed by the Sunnis, who had already moved on (ibid., 232, 236). During the days of the hajj, Farhād Mirzā argued with the leaders of the hajj caravans over the issue, whom he accused of being wrong-headed. Still, the Iranian pilgrims, which he estimated to be 5000 individuals, followed his lead, and he reports that he convinced the highest judge of Medina (Moʿtamad al-Dowle 1987a, 201–202).

Anti-Sunni statements are scattered throughout the travelogue of Yaʿqub Mirzā. While residing in Istanbul, he listened to a lecture by a Sunni scholar in the Hagia Sophia. When he said, 'God made the earth in honour of five names,' meaning the Prophet Muhammad and the first four Islamic caliphs, Yaʿqub Mirzā became angry and left the building (Tabrizi 2009, 109). For Yaʿqub Mirzā, Damascus was first and foremost the place where the captives had been brought after the battle of Karbala.[17] During his stay he continuously alludes to this (ibid., 141–142). While in Medina and Mecca, Yaʿqub Mirzā reports about the mistreatment of Shiʿi pilgrims. Upon arrival in Medina with the hajj caravan, the inhabitants of the city throw stones at the Iranians in the caravan

17 The Battle of Karbala was fought between the followers of Ḥusayn, who is regarded as the third Imām by the Shiʿites, and soldiers loyal to the Umayyad caliph Muʿāwiya. After the Umayyad troops' victory, they stormed the encampment of Ḥusayn and imprisoned the women and children. They took them to the Umayyad capital of Damascus, presented them, and the severed head of Husayn to the victorious caliph.

(ibid., 210). He also reports a bloody encounter between a Shiʿi pilgrim and the guards of the al-Baqīʿ-cemetery, where several Imams are buried (ibid., 213). He explains that in Mecca the Iranians are considered worse than unbelievers. But this is a hundred times better than in Medina, as 'the inhabitants of Medina want to eat the Iranians alive, ripping their flesh off' (ibid., 229–230, 237).

On his way back to Iran, he was approached by a dervish in Nakhjavān, a city close to the border of Iran. He gave him some money in exchange for hearing the names of the Fourteen Infallibles in Shiʿi Islam.[18] This suddenly made him realize that he had not heard their names in months, and when reaching the city he finally felt safe (ibid., 293). In his accounts of this and other occasions, he uses obscene language to depict Sunnis, routinely calling them, among other names, *pedarsukhte*, a common term of abuse.[19] Many of these obscenities were censored in the modern edition.

The travelogue of Farhād Mirzā contains no anti-Sunni polemics. Instead, his experiences induced him to criticize the Ottoman Empire in its role as Custodian of the Holy Cities and the hajj. Farhād Mirzā does report about his conflicts with local Arabs. On his way from Yanbu to Medina, he criticizes his military escort as lazy and suspects them of thievery. He reports in detail an almost violent confrontation with Arab tribesmen who tried to collect additional fees from the passing pilgrims. During his stay in Mecca, Farhād Mirzā was robbed. His efforts to gain the support of local authorities were unsuccessful. In Mecca and Medina Farhād Mirzā had the opportunity to visit many places of religious significance and he explains their importance in early Islamic history and describes his impressions when visiting them. He also continuously suggests and openly states that the Arab and Ottoman authorities are unfamiliar with the details of Islamic history and neglect the holy sites in and around the Holy Cities. To give just the most noteworthy example, when he enters the interior of the Kaʿba on his last day in Mecca, he criticizes the Ottoman Sultans directly for neglecting the interior of the Kaʿba and the floors of the mosque (Moʿtamad al-Dowle 1987a, 216–217). After his return to Istanbul, he wrote letters to the Ottoman Sultan and the Sublime Porte, in which he highlighted the

18 In Twelver Shiʿa Islam the Prophet Muhammad, his daughter Fāṭima, and the twelve Imāms are considered to be infallible.

19 According to Steingass' Comprehensive Persian-English dictionary it refers to someone whose father is burning in hellfire, whereas ʿAlī Akbar Dehkhoda explains in his dictionary it refers to someone whose father was exhumed and burned after his death. According to Dekhoda this originated in a custom in ancient Egypt to exhume and burn the fathers of defaulting debtors.

responsibility of the Ottoman state to secure the roads, especially in the Hijaz. He complains to the Sultan that he had been robbed in Mecca and asks him for monetary compensation. Farhād Mirzā also makes several concrete suggestions on how to improve the holy sites around Mecca and Medina (ibid., 262–268). Farhād Mirzā did not have to limit himself to some angry remarks in his travelogue, like most other travellers. Instead, he is able to complain to the Ottoman Sultan himself. In his travelogue he did not report about the mistreatment of Iranian pilgrims, who were, after all, his personal responsibility as representative of Qajar Iran. Still, by making his case before the Sultan and reproducing his letters to the Ottoman authorities in his travelogue, Farhād Mirzā was able to present himself in a positive light and make the treatment of Iranian pilgrims a matter of foreign policy between Qajar Iran and the Ottoman Empire.

6 Conclusion

Qajar hajj travelogues were didactic texts with the main purpose of informing their readers and potential future travellers about the travelled route and the actual travel experience of the author. However, during the nineteenth century changes occurred regarding which kinds of didactic information were considered important for the readers of hajj travelogues. In earlier travelogues, like Keykāvus Mirzā and Moḥammad Vali Mirzā, who travelled in 1832 and 1847, there are long chapters with detailed instructions about traveling, especially caravan travel. This is due to the dangers and difficulties of travelling during this time, which required appropriate and serious preparation and planning. This gradually changed in the second half of the nineteenth century when travelling became easier and safer. Because of the progress in the means of commercial transportation more and more pilgrims travelled via Istanbul or Mumbai by steamship and railway. In their travelogues they recorded long descriptions of their impressions of foreign cultures, people, and modern technology encountered along the way, especially in the Caucasus, Istanbul, Egypt, and India. As the examples of Yaʿqub Mirzā and Farhād Mirzā indicate, these impressions were shaped by Iranian cultural and religious values and often showed astonishment and admiration for modern technology.

The dire situation of Iranian pilgrims on the Arabian Peninsula is a common theme throughout the nineteenth century and is present in virtually all Persian hajj travelogues. However, the actual experience in Mecca and Medina and its subsequent portrayal differed considerably depending on the social standing of the author.

There was also the emergence of a discourse about the journey to Mecca at the court of Nāṣer al-Din Shāh. During the 1870s and 1880s, the Qajar court tried to gather accurate information about its dominions and the rest of the world. The court commissioned local geographies and historical works, reports about journeys inside and outside of the country, and even sent a long questionnaire to provincial authorities in Iran (Gustafson 2016, 794–796). The travelogue of Farhād Mirzā complements these efforts and was an attempt to gather and compile a vast amount of information about the itinerary to Mecca and the pilgrimage. The discourse at court about travelling to Mecca went on afterwards and even became important for Iranian foreign policy. In 1879/80 (1296 AH)[20] Mirzā ʿAbd al-Ghaffār Najm al-Molk travelled to Mecca via Iraq and wrote a short report, which was printed in the official court gazette and highlighted the mistreatment of Iranian pilgrims in the Iraqi hajj caravan by the Āl Rashīd—the tribal leaders who had established themselves in the centre of the Arabian Peninsula after the decline of the first Wahhābī state and who had organized the caravan. He recommends a temporary prohibition of the route by the Qajar court (Najm al-Molk Monajjem-bāshi 2010, 831). This argument is also made in the travelogue of Mirzā ʿAbd al-Ḥoseyn Khān Afshār Orumi, a high-ranking officer in the Qajar army, who joined the Iraqi caravan to return from Mecca via Iraq in 1882/83 (1299 AH) (Orumi 2010, 631–632; 2007, 213). Farāhāni alludes to the text of Najm al-Molk in his travelogue when reporting during his journey in 1885/1886 (1302 AH) that there has been an effective ban of the route for two years. This has led to an improvement in behaviour by the organizers of the hajj caravan, who attempted to give a bribe to allow Iranian pilgrims to travel via this route. Farāhāni recommends ending the ban as guarantees for the safety of Iranian pilgrims will be made (Farāhāni 1990, 247).

Both Farhād Mirzā and Yaʿqub Mirzā address specific audiences, which they themselves identify in their texts. Therefore, I have emphasized in this chapter the relationships between the authors and their intended audiences to understand what kind of information is conveyed and how. Yaʿqub Mirzā mentions an assignment by a friend as the reason for writing his travelogue, and he addresses his group of friends throughout the text. This sets the stage for the travelogue, with which the author intends to give an entertaining but also informative account about the itinerary and his personal experiences and impressions. The style of his travelogue is simple, sometimes even obscene, and assumes a personal acquaintanceship between author and reader. Farhād Mirzā's text on the

20 The year in brackets is the Islamic calendar year in which the hajj rituals were performed by the author.

other hand is a voluminous lithograph, which was printed to reach a wide audience and intends to educate its readers about the itinerary and the pilgrimage to Mecca. But it also offers a detailed report about the author's interactions with important officials he met along the way to inform his readers about them and to narrate the legitimacy enjoyed by the Qajar court abroad. In addition, Farhād Mirzā also used this opportunity to address a wide audience at court to portray himself in a favourable light and supply his opinions on current issues. His report is a complex and elaborate literary creation to which considerable resources were dedicated.

In both texts the authors take the double capacity as storyteller and main protagonist. In his article about Persian hajj travelogues, Elton Daniel wrote that earlier hajj travelogues 'are like traditional guidebooks for pilgrims, with the narrator relegated to the background' (Daniel 2002, 224). He mentions the travelogue of Farāhāni as an example. Hajj travelogues later became more like 'personal diaries, concentrating on the author's individual experiences and sentiments' (ibid.). But with more hajj travelogues being published in recent years, it has become clear that Farāhāni is rather the exception than the rule. Farāhāni was a minor bureaucrat, who travelled to Mecca in 1885 and 1886, and presented a calligraphic manuscript of his report to the Shah in person (Farāhāni 1990, xxviii). He obviously considered his own personal experiences and everyday life during his pilgrimage of no relevance to his intended audience, the Shah. This resulted in an impersonal report, which in this regard is not exemplary for Qajar hajj travelogues. If we take Yaʿqub Mirzā and Farhād Mirzā as early examples, there appears to be no clear shift from an impersonal guidebook towards the recording of personal experiences and sentiments by the author. Rather, the latter has been a feature of Persian travelogues throughout the Qajar period. Still, they differ regarding what kinds of experiences and sentiments should be mentioned in the text. While Yaʿqub Mirzā reports to his friends about his longings for young moon-faced boys, Farhād Mirzā's situation as a public figure addressing a wide audience demands a more reserved attitude. It only gets personal when Farhād Mirzā wants to highlight his personal piety and the hardships he had to endure during his pilgrimage. Once again it is essential to consider the relationship between the author and the audience he addresses in his report.

References

Hajj Travelogues

Farhād Mirzā Moʿtamad al-Dowle. 1987a. *Safarnāme-ye Farhād Mirzā*, edited by Gholām-Reḍā Ṭabāṭabā'i. Tehrān: Sherkat-e Chāp va Enteshārāt-e ʿElmi.

Farhād Mirzā Moʿtamad al-Dowle. 1987b. *Safarnāme-ye Farhād Mirzā Moʿtamad al-Dowle*, edited by Esmāʿil Navvāb Ṣafā. Tehrān: Ketābforushi-ye Zavvār.

Jaʿfariyān, Rasul, ed. 2010. *Panjah safarnāme-ye ḥajj-e qājāri*. Tehrān: Nashr-e ʿElm. 8 vols.

Solṭān Morād Mirzā Hosām al-Salṭane. 2010. 'Safarnāme-ye Makke. Dalīl al-anām fī sabīl ziyāra Baīt Allāh al-Ḥarām wa-al-Quds al-Sharīf wa-Madīna al-Salām. 1297 q.', In Jaʿfariyān 2010 vol. 4, 7–332.

Mirzā ʿAbd al-Ḥoseyn Khān Afshār Orumi. 2010. 'Safarnāme-ye Makke-ye Moʿaẓẓame. 1299 q.' In Jaʿfariyān 2010 vol. 4, 437–688.

Mirzā ʿAbd al-Ḥoseyn Khān Afshār Orumi. 2007. *Safarnāme-ye Makke-ye Moʿaẓẓame. 1299–1300 q, 1261–1262 sh*, edited by Rasul Jaʿfariyān. Tehrān: Nashr-e ʿElm.

Mirzā ʿAbd al-Ghaffār Najm al-Molk Monajjem-bāshi. 2010. 'Safarnāme-ye Makke. 1296 q.' In Jaʿfariyān 2010 vol. 3, 803–831.

Mirzā Mohammed Ḥoseyn Farāhāni. 1990. *A Shi'ite pilgrimage to Mecca: 1885–1886. The Safarnâmeh of Mirzâ Moḥammad Ḥosayn Farâhâni*, edited, translated, and annotated by Hafez Farmayan and Elton Daniel. Austin: University of Texas Press.

Yaʿqub Mirzā-ye Tabrizi. 2010. 'Ḥajj-e Manṣur 1285 q.' In Jaʿfariyān 2010 vol. 2, 197–542.

Yaʿqub Mirzā-ye Tabrizi. 2009. *Safarnāme-ye ḥajj-e Manṣur 1285–1286 q*, edited by Rasul Jaʿfarīyān. Tehrān: Nashr-e ʿElm.

Secondary Literature

Bakhash, Shaul. 1978. *Iran: Monarchy, bureaucracy and reform under the Qajars: 1858–1896*. London: Ithaca Press.

Daniel, Elton. 2002. 'The hajj and Qajar travel literature.' In *Society and culture in Qajar Iran: Studies in honour of Hafez Farmayan*, edited by Elton Daniel, 215–237. Costa Mesa: Mazda Publishers.

Eslami, Kambiz. 1999. 'Farhād Mirzā Moʿtamad-al-Dawla.' Last modified December 15, 1999. http://www.iranicaonline.org/articles/farhad-mirza-motamad-al-dawla.

Green, Nile. 2015. 'The hajj as its own undoing: Infrastructure and integration on the Muslim journey to Mecca.' *Past & present* 226 (1): 193–226.

Gustafson, James. 2016. 'Geographical literature in nineteenth-century Iran. Regional identities and the construction of space.' *Journal of the economic and social history of the Orient* 59 (5): 793–827. https://doi.org/10.1163/15685209-12341414.

Hanaway, William. 2002. 'Persian travel narratives: Notes toward the definition of a nineteenth-century genre.' In *Society and culture in Qajar Iran: Studies in honour of Hafez Farmayan*, edited by Elton Daniel, 249–268. Costa Mesa: Mazda Publishers.

Kiyanrad, Sarah. 2020. 'No choice but to travel. Safavid travelogues written in Persian.' In *Islamische Selbstbilder. Festschrift für Susanne Enderwitz*, edited by Sarah Kiyanrad, Rebecca Sauer, and Jan Scholz, 273–297. Heidelberg: Heidelberg University Publishing. https://doi.org/10.17885/heiup.531.

Morikawa, Tomoko. 2001. 'Gajar-choki ryokoki shiryo kenkyu josetsu [Bibliographical Note on Safarnāme Materials in the Qajar Period].' *Seinan Ajia kenkyu* [*Bulletin of the society for Western and Southern Asiatic studies, Kyōto University*] 55: 44–68. (in Japanese).

Najmabadi, Afsaneh. 2005. *Women with mustaches and men without beards: Gender and sexual anxieties of Iranian modernity*. Berkeley and Los Angeles: University of California Press.

Sohrabi, Naghmeh. 2012. *Taken for wonder: Nineteenth-century travel accounts from Iran to Europe*. New York: Oxford University Press.

Tavakoli-Targhi, Mohamad. 2002. 'Eroticizing Europe.' In *Society and culture in Qajar Iran: Studies in honour of Hafez Farmayan*, edited by Elton Daniel, 311–346. Costa Mesa: Mazda Publishers.

CHAPTER 6

Othering and Being Othered: Religion, Ethnicity, and Gender in the Hajj Accounts by Iranian Shiʿi Women (1880–1901)

Piotr Bachtin

1 Introduction

In early modern Iranian society, where gender segregation was highly valued and strictly observed, women lived their lives concealed behind the walls of their houses (or, more precisely, the interior parts inaccessible to strangers, called *andarun*). When entering the public sphere, they would do so behind the 'portable wall' (Milani 1992, XII) of their hijabs. Significantly, among the traditional terms applied to women in Persian, one was *parde-neshin*, '(the one) sitting/living behind the curtain', and *ḍaʿife*, 'the weak one', both clear indications of the common image of women's nature and role in society. However, the personal narratives of the hajj written by Iranian women with high status before the 1900s, and successively published from the manuscripts during the last twenty-five years, challenge this vision and prove that Iranian women not only participated in the hajj before the recent era of technical revolution and globalization, but also actively contributed to the pre-modern travel/pilgrimage writing.

In Iran, travel writing gained particular popularity under the rule of Nāṣer al-Din Shāh (r. 1848–1896) from the Qajar dynasty (1794–1925), who himself wrote several travel accounts covering his trips in Iran and abroad. Travelogues were generally referred to as *safarnāme-hā*, 'travel books', although travel writers of that time would also use the term *ruznāme*, 'a diary', which modern Persian designates as 'a newspaper'.[1] In the late 1800s, travelogues became a prominent type of writing both among the members of the royal court in Tehran and the provincial aristocracy. Many of these accounts were commissioned by the shah or by people from his entourage, and they were treated '(…) as a means of information gathering and reporting on general conditions, both at home and abroad' (Farāhāni 1990, XXIV). William Hanaway, who attemp-

1 Throughout this chapter, I use the terms 'diary', 'journal', and 'travelogue' interchangeably.

ted to summarize the chief traits of the Qajar travel accounts, similarly points at the informative function of these texts, which would serve, as he put it, a 'didactic purpose' (Hanaway 2002, 265). This also applies to the subtype that is the focus here: hajj accounts (*safarnāme-hā-ye ḥajj* or *ḥajjnāme-hā*). Focusing on 'mundane' aspects of a pilgrimage journey, such as the state of the roads, the stations along the way, prices, security issues, etc., these pilgrimage diaries served as guidebooks for future pilgrims. They complemented the religious manuals called *manāsik al-ḥajj* that contained descriptions of the hajj rites, which people resorted to in cases of uncertainty.

Importantly, however, the female-authored hajj narratives from Qajar Iran seem to possess qualities that differ from those of guidebooks.[2] Apart from reporting on current events inside and outside the pilgrim caravans, Mehrmāh Khānom 'Eṣmat al-Salṭane, a high-born woman from Tabas, 'Āliye Khānom, and Sakine Solṭān Vaqār al-Dowle convey their thoughts and emotional states, and they often do so by using blunt language and resorting to irony and sarcasm. The difficult travel conditions, diseases affecting them and people around them, and finally death—an inseparable companion of pilgrims in those times—results in complaints that are apparently shared, as one would put it today, for auto-therapeutic purposes. In the preface to the travelogue by the woman from Tabas, Nāzilā Nāẓemi points out that:

> [p]erhaps it might be said that the writing of diaries (*ruznāme-nevisi-hā*) gave to the literate women from the court [and from the aristocracy, PB] an opportunity to express their hidden emotions and thoughts without shame and embarrassment.
>
> NĀẒEMI 2018, 11

Nāẓemi emphasizes the astonishing frankness of the female travel writers as well as noting the satirical tone present in their accounts (ibid.). In the foreword to the journal of 'Āliye Khānom, Raṣul Ja'fariyān shares a similar observation: he remarks that the writer 'has no self-censorship whatsoever' and regrets that she did not leave any other writings behind (Ja'fariyān 2007, 13).

The Qajar noblewomen performed a double act of transgression: first, by setting off for a journey, some of them 'alone', that is without a male relative acting as their 'guardian', which was 'against the social convention' (Nāẓemi 2018, 10). Second, keeping a diary as such might have been frowned upon by men. 'Āliye

2 Which is not to imply that the hajj accounts written by men did not possess such qualities.

Khānom therefore preferred to conceal her writing from her controlling travelling companion Vali Khān (Bachtin 2020, 15).

Leaving aside for the moment the question of the possible reasons why those women chose to write, it is worth emphasizing that it was while travelling abroad that they apparently discovered and, to a greater or lesser degree, exploited the transgressive potential of literary self-expression. Needless to say, the hajj, apart from possessing religious and spiritual meanings, was a long, tiring, and hazardous journey. Despite the limitations that the female pilgrims faced, particularly in terms of freedom of mobility within the entourage in which they travelled, they would inevitably face the new, the uncanny, and the dangerous.

My reading of the travelogues is inspired by the approach of Nasrin Rahimieh who in her book *Missing Persians: Discovering Voices in Iranian Cultural History* interprets some of the half-forgotten or unacknowledged pieces of Iranian life writing and social history as mirroring the 'identity trouble' of their authors. As Rahimieh observes, '(…) what remains constant, even in the least seemingly self-reflexive of these accounts, is the issue of identity, which at different moments of history finds varying designations and terms of reference' (Rahimieh 2001, 1). If we agree that the Self is defined in an encounter with its negative 'term of reference', the Other (understood as 'other than the Self'), to show the image of the Other that emerges from the hajj accounts by the Qajar noblewomen is also to reveal the way their selves were being (re)defined, negotiated, and (trans)formed outside a familiar environment. Since the otherness of the Other, albeit contingent and hence changeable, is significant in regard to the existing socio-cultural structure (Sarukkai 1997, 1406–1409), such reading may allow some conclusions to be drawn about the social perception of the Other in Qajar Iran, and consequently about the self-definition of Iranians in that time.

What I find particularly interesting in these travel accounts is that they were written by those who at the moment of performing the hajj might have been considered 'thrice Other' themselves: first, as the representatives of the Shiʿi religious minority in a predominantly Sunni land; second, as belonging to an ethnic and linguistic minority in what they would call 'Arabia' (*ʿArabestān*); and finally, as a gender minority, since in the nineteenth century most pilgrims were men. Their being Shiʿi had an effect on the course of their pilgrimage. As was usually the case with pilgrims from Iran, all women combined the hajj with sacred visits in today's Iraq to the mausoleums of imams, in Persian called *ʿatabāt-e ʿāliyāt*, 'the sublime thresholds', or just *ʿatabāt*, 'thresholds'. What is more, their texts are shot through with instances expressing fear of falling prey to the Sunnis driven by an anti-Shiʿi resentment. On the other hand, their descriptions of

Sunni Muslims are often marked by dislike and contempt, apparently derived from their conviction that the Sunnis were not the 'true' Muslims. Speaking of the second factor that shaped these women's pilgrimage experience, that is their ethnic and linguistic background, they would often express a sense of great pride on account of belonging to a more 'civilized' culture. It must be noted that the boundaries between ethnic and 'racial' features of the Other were blurred, and the diarists would comment either with disgust or with a certain fascination on physical traits of 'Arabs-"blacks"'. Finally, I discuss the various societal and personal implications of the diarist-pilgrims' gender. As some of them disclose, they were subject to limitations and control was exerted over them by their male relatives who accompanied them on the road. Importantly, however, some of their travelogues also inform us about different strategies of resistance and disobedience to men.

2 The Writers and Their Works

The oldest known personal account of the hajj written by an Iranian woman dates back to the end of the Safavid era (1501–1722). This extensive poem (*mathnawī*) of 1200 *bayts* (verses) was composed by a widow of Mirzā Khalil, a royal scribe who worked for the last shah of the Safavid dynasty, Solṭān Ḥoseyn (r. 1694–1722), in the then royal city of Isfahan (Babayan 2008, 240). Ḥājiyeh Hamdam Kafshgar Sichāni identifies the poet as Shahrbānu Beygom, based on an oral statement by Shahrbānu's supposed descendants who live in the city of Gaz in the neighbourhood of Isfahan (Kafshgar Sichāni 2007, *Dāl*; *He-Ṭā*). If this identification is correct, the account must have been written between 1694, the year of coronation of Solṭān Ḥoseyn, and 1707–1708 when Shahrbānu Beygom passed away.

Aside from this solitary example from the Safavid era, we currently know about four hajj accounts written by Iranian women between 1880 and 1901, that is, during the reign of two Qajar monarchs: Nāṣer al-Din Shāh and his son and successor Moẓaffar al-Din Shāh (r. 1896–1906). Although this number may appear small when compared to around sixty similar texts written by men in the Qajar period (Jaʿfariyān 2010; 2013), one must bear in mind various restrictions to which women were subject, both in terms of mobility and in terms of literary creation. Nevertheless, it may be assumed that more travelogues written by the Qajar women await unearthing and publication.

The author of the oldest narrative examined in this chapter is Mehrmāh Khānom ʿEṣmat al-Salṭane, daughter of Nāṣer al-Din Shāh's uncle, Farhād Mirzā (Jaʿfariyān 1996), whose 1875–1876 hajj narrative is discussed in this volume by

Thomas Ecker. Her journal covers a pilgrimage made in 1880–1881. ʿEṣmat al-Salṭane departed from Tehran on 24 *ramaḍān* 1297AH/31 August 1880. In what is present-day Iraq, she visited the *ʿatabāt-e ʿāliyāt* and headed south-west proceeding with a caravan to Mecca and Medina. From Medina she went to Jedda, where she boarded a ship to Bushehr, an Iranian port on the Persian Gulf. On the way back to Tehran, she passed through Shiraz, Isfahan, Kashan, and Qom and entered the capital on 9 *rajab* 1298AH/7 June 1881.

The second account was written between 1886–1887 and belongs to an anonymous woman from the city of Tabas in eastern Iran, who on her paternal side was a granddaughter of Fatḥ ʿAli Shāh (r. 1797–1834), the second Qajar king, and on her maternal side a granddaughter of Nāder Shāh (r. 1736–1747) from the Afsharid dynasty (Nāẓemi 2018). She began her pilgrimage on 21 *shaʿbān* 1303/25 May 1886. After having passed through the Iranian cities of Kashan and Qom, she crossed the Iranian-Ottoman border and made her first pilgrimage to the *ʿatabāt*. Then, she proceeded to Basra, took a ship to Bushehr and continued travelling the Arabian Sea around the Arabian Peninsula to reach Jedda, from where she went to Mecca and Medina. After the hajj, on her way back home, she visited the *ʿatabāt* for the second time. She entered Tabas after 11 *dhū al-ḥijja* 1304/31 August 1887.

The third travelogue was written between 1892 and 1894 by an aristocratic woman from Kerman. In the first edition prepared by the historian Raṣul Jaʿfariyān (Jaʿfariyān 2007), the author, whose identity back then was unknown, is tentatively called Ḥājiye Khānom ʿAlaviye Kermāni (Ḥājja ʿAlawiyya from Kerman). It was later discovered that it was the diary of ʿĀliye Khānom and the second edition of her travelogue was published under that name (Torābi 2018). Originally from Shiraz, she was a niece of the imam of the Friday mosque in Kerman and a wife of Āqā-ye Shāpur Khān, son of ʿAbbāsqoli Khān, and grandson of Ebrāhim Khān Ẓohir al-Dowle, governor of Kerman from 1803–1824 (Gozarestan, n.d.). ʿĀliye Khānom departed from Kerman, headed south to Bandar-e Abbas and went aboard a ship to Mumbai, in which city she spent ten days before boarding another ship to sail again to Jedda. On her way to the Arabian Peninsula, she stopped for the obligatory quarantine on the island of Kamaran, close to the Yemeni shore. In Jedda, she joined a caravan to Mecca. After the hajj and a pilgrimage to the Prophet's Mosque in Medina, ʿĀliye Khānom proceeded on the Iraqi route in the direction of the *ʿatabāt*. Upon arrival in Qom, she decided to travel to Tehran instead of returning to Kerman. In Tehran, where she spent about eighteen months before finally returning to Kerman, she acted as a 'society lady' (Khosravie 2013, 133–134), was a frequent guest at the royal harem of Nāṣer al-Din Shāh, participated in numerous betrothals and weddings, and engaged herself in matchmaking (Bachtin 2015).

The last account examined in this chapter belongs to Sakine Soltān Vaqār al-Dowle Esfahāni Kuchak, a widow of Nāṣer al-Din Shāh who performed the hajj in 1899–1901 (Jaʿfariyān and Kiyāni Haft Lang 2010). Vaqār al-Dowle departed from Tehran on 1 *rajab* 1317AH/5 November 1899 and passed through Qom in the direction of the *ʿatabāt*. After visiting the shrines of the imams, she proceeded with a caravan on the Syrian route to Aleppo and İskenderun, where she boarded a ship to Beirut. From there, she continued the trip on board ship through Port Said and the Suez Canal and arrived in Jedda from where she reached Mecca and Medina. On the way back from al-Ḥaramayn, she made a second pilgrimage to the *ʿatabāt*. In *jumādā al-ʾawwal* 1318AH/September 1900, she entered the Iranian city of Borujerd, where she joined her husband, Moʿtaṣem al-Molk, 'who was living there at the time on a government assignment' (Mahallati 2016, 846). She spent almost a year in Borujerd before returning to Tehran on 4 *dhū al-ḥijja* 1318AH/25 March 1901.[3]

3 'Bloody Sunnis' and 'Neat Shiʿi Boys'

During the hajj performance, and also during the pilgrimage journey to Mecca and back, adherents of different denominations of Islam share space and time. This diversity is mirrored in the following passage from the diary of ʿĀliye Khānom. After boarding the ship from Mumbai to Jedda, she described various reactions of pilgrims afraid of the sea voyage:

> Someone was throwing up, someone was like in lethargy (*bi-ḥāl*), another one was crying and someone else was praying. May God not grant the disbelievers [with such a fate, PB]. May God make all fulfil their obligation [to make the hajj, PB], but [may God let them travel, PB] on land. We were in that state for ten days. From evenings to morning you would hear '*Yā Allāh!*', '*Yā Muḥammad!*' and '*Yā ʿAlī!*' The Sunnis were calling for prayer. All of us were constantly reciting the *shahāda*. (…) From evening to morning you hear *Yā Allāh!* The Sunnis are calling for ill-time prayers. The dervishes from Herat, Kabul and India are saying '*Huwa, huwa*'. The Shiʿis are beating their chests. It's like the Day of Judgment (*Qiyāmat ast, methl-e ṣaḥrā-ye maḥshar*).
>
> JAʿFARIYĀN 2007, 57–58

3 For more information about these accounts, except the one by the woman from Tabas, see Bachtin 2020. On Sakine Solṭān Vaqār al-Dowle Eṣfahāni Kuchak and her pilgrimage diary, see Dusend 2013.

This seemingly 'anthropological' description quickly turns into a blunt and contemptuous remark when, after having pointed out that the Sunnis make up the vast majority on the ship (600–700 people) in comparison to the only twenty three Shiʿis, ʿĀliye Khānom uses the epithet *sonni-ye pedarsukhte* ('bloody Sunnis') and associates them with a lack of hygiene, dirt, and stench: 'All naked, bloody Sunnis, they don't perform the ablutions, the bastards smell so bad that you could suffocate' (ibid., 59). Such a remark not only dehumanizes the Sunnis who are described as disgusting, but also implicates that they are not 'real' Muslims. Although initially it seems that the diarist's aim might have been to present the fear of travelling by ship as a common experience that unifies the pilgrims, it rapidly turns out that, according to ʿĀliye Khānom, the difficult conditions at sea could not justify an overt violation of religious principles that was committed by the Sunni majority.[4]

Particular indignation toward Sunnis is elicited in the Shiʿi pilgrims when the inhabitants of Arabia organize the fireworks show on the night of *ʿashūrāʾ*. In the travelogue of Mirzā Moḥammad Ḥoseyn Farāhāni from 1885–1886 we find a possible explanation of this tradition. As stated by Farāhāni, the Meccans would feast on 10 *muḥarram* under the pretext that, according to the Qurʾan, on that day Noah's ark came to rest on Mount Judi near Mosul (Farāhāni 1990, 228). Interestingly, Farāhāni notes that under the reign of *sharīf* ʿAbdullah (r. 1858–1877) and Sharīf ʿAwn al-Rafīq (r. 1882–1905), since they '(…) were not hostile towards Shiʿism, this practice was abolished and stopped out of respect for the death of the Prince of Martyrs (Ḥusayn)' (ibid.). However, the observations of ʿĀliye Khānom, who also made the hajj during the reign of *sharīf* ʿAwn al-Rafīq, contradict Farāhāni's statement:

> On the day of *ʿāshūraʾ* they organized the feast, because it was Friday. Apparently, they feast on Thursday night and on Friday, and play on instruments because of a holiday for Muhammad and his companions.

---

4 This excerpt from ʿĀliyeh Khānom's account is one out of many in which she or other diarists complain about conditions preventing them not only from ensuring hygiene, but also the ritual purity attained through *ġusl*, *wużūʿ*, or *iḥrām* while travelling by ship. For example, while travelling by ship from Bandar-e Abbas to Mumbai, ʿĀliyeh Khānom laments about the dirt impeding her ability to properly perform quotidian religious rituals. Following the custom, she asks God to allow all her friends to make the hajj, but '(…) by land, not by ship, [where, PB] there is nothing left for a human being, no prayer (*namāz*), no worship (*ʿebādat*), no clean food. It's all dirt within dirt (*najes andar najes*)' (Jaʿfariyān 2007, 49). Also, Vaqār al-Dowle, who made her *iḥrām* on a ship before arriving in Jedda, laments about the dirt, hoping that God would accept the ritual performed in such conditions (Jaʿfariyān and Kiyāni Haft Lang 2010, 87, 89).

> On the night of *'āshūrā'*, on the 11th [of *muḥarram*, PB], the excellencies of Medina organized the fireworks show. They fired cannons and pistols and played on trumpets, drums and other instruments. I remembered what they did to the family of the Master of Martyrs in Karbala. I can't express what it did to me. When I heard those sounds, I wanted to kill myself. May God increase their torment and torture, for the sake of Muhammad and his companions.
>
> JAʿFARIYĀN 2007, 74

Unlike Farāhāni, 'Āliye Khānom spends *'āshūrā'* in Medina and provides a different explanation of the ways Sunnis celebrate it. Similar to Farāhāni, she notes that the feast itself, and especially the way the Sunnis celebrate it, is a deliberate, malicious slander against the Shiʿis and imam Ḥusayn in particular. The actual meaning of these celebrations notwithstanding, it is interesting to observe that even though she acknowledged that the reason for organizing the fireworks show and firing cannons is a religious holiday commemorating the Prophet, she suggested that the holiday is of lesser importance than *'āshūrā'*. This, in turn, might suggest that imam Ḥusayn is of greater importance than the Prophet. Quite ironically, she recalls Muhammad and his companions for a second time, wishing the Sunnis 'torment and torture'.

Such remarks are evidence of a profound resentment. One may look for the roots of the Shiʿi dislike for the Sunnis in the early history of Islam, or in the doctrinal differences. Yet while speaking of Iran, the political context is worth discussing as well. Iran became predominantly Shiʿi as late as in the 1500s, after the founder of the Safavid dynasty (1501–1736), shah Esmāʿil (r. 1501–1524), forcefully established Twelver Shiʿism as the state religion in 1501. This decision was at least partially driven by the desire to distinguish the Turkish-speaking Safavids from the Sunni Ottomans. Over the following centuries, Iran would remain in more or less intense conflict with its Sunni neighbour, on whose territory Mecca, as well as the Shiʿi *ʿatabāt* were located. Predictably, the political tensions would affect the lives of ordinary people, too. As many accounts of the hajj written in the Qajar period testify, the Shiʿi pilgrims travelling through the Arabian Peninsula might have been subjected to persecutions by the Ottoman authorities on the one hand, and to violence by local people on the other (Jaʿfariyān 2000, 54, 61–63).

In the account of 'Eṣmat al-Salṭane, the Sunnis are portrayed as menacing bandits who threaten the health and lives of innocent Shiʿis. This is how she relates an unpleasant event she witnessed on 6 *muḥarram* 1298AH/8 December 1880 in a small settlement between Mecca and Medina:

> (…) one person from among the [Iranian, PB] pilgrims went to the garden to convey the information about having been stripped of his belongings. A couple of gunmen followed him back in order to release the aforesaid one from the claws of pain, and then it turned out that if they had not come, the aforesaid man would have been killed. Imagine to what extent they must be hostile toward the Shiʿis, if they want to kill the poor men!
>
> JAʿFARIYĀN 1996, 79

Although ʿEṣmat al-Salṭane does not label the raiders as Sunni, she clearly explicates that the robbery and threat of murder were fuelled by a strong anti-Shiʿi resentment. In the case of the Shiʿis from Iran, many of whom did not know Arabic, ethnic and linguistic differences made them particularly vulnerable. However, the danger of robbery put all pilgrims at risk. As demonstrated by the case of Sikandar Begum—a Sunni ruler of the princely state of Bhopal in central India (r. 1844–1868), who is celebrated as the first Indian Muslim monarch in history to have made the hajj—it was rather the pilgrims' wealth that attracted raiders, not the branch of Islam to which they belonged. In a Persian-language abridgment of her pilgrimage narrative covering the hajj made in 1863–1864 and originally written Urdu, the *begum*, who initially planned to follow the same route as ʿEṣmat al-Salṭane, declares having abandoned the idea of going to Medina after the hajj 'because of the calamity of threatening Bedouins' (Ḥassanābādi 2009, 643).

Even though the woman from Tabas does not share overtly hostile views toward Sunnis, her observations perpetuate the stereotypical image of 'bad Sunnis' juxtaposed with 'good Shiʿis'. The following passage demonstrates that according to the author the 'inferiority' of being a Sunni might have been overcome by converting to Shiʿism:

> All people here [in Khān-e Khākestari, a caravanserai near Baghdad, PB] are Shiʿis. In the evening, a sentinel came to stand next to the women. Our people talked with him. I was listening. He said: 'I'm a cavalry commander (*yuz-bāshi savār*), from Istanbul, and I came to Baghdad with the pasha. I used to be his servant. The pasha died. I fell in love with a girl. She was a Sunni Arab, from Baqubah. I told her that if she wanted me to marry her, she must become a Shiʿi. She agreed. She became a Shiʿi and I married her. My parents were trying to make me come back to Istanbul, but I didn't agree. My heart was with the girl.' Apparently, she must be a good girl. He was a good young man, too. A neat Shiʿi.
>
> NĀẒEMI 2018, 53

Retelling her arrival in Medina, the noblewoman from Tabas expresses her excitement upon hearing the following words of a young Syrian adjutant: 'O Thou who forgive the guilt of sinners!' She remarks that she almost screamed of joy *despite the fact* that the boy was a Sunni (ibid., 91). It is interesting to note that these travelogue writers share strikingly similar comments when mentioning the 'disbelievers' (non-Muslims), as if they were as foreign to them as the Sunnis. This is how the same woman from Tabas empathizes with an old European woman ('They say she is 120 years old') she met in Bushehr, who was denied boarding a ship by the captain: 'They threw her out in such a way that in spite of her being a disbeliever it was really hard to watch' (ibid., 68). 'Āliye Khānom, in turn, shares conventional expressions such as, already quoted, 'May God not grant the disbelievers [with such a fate, PB]' (Jaʿfariyān 2007, 57–58) when she describes difficult situations and emotionally exhausting moments.

4 Who Is an 'Arab' and Who Is a 'Black'?

Grounded in a range of categories including ethnicity, language, and, broadly speaking, culture (or rather the alleged lack of it), the othering statements of the diarists demonstrate that they construed the Other not only as a non-Shiʿi or an anti-Shiʿi. Very often, the differences overlapped: the Arabs and Bedouins, both of whom are referred to with the term *ʿArab*, in addition to being predominantly Sunni, also belonged to another ethnic group and spoke a different language. On the whole, the diaries reveal the Arabophobic attitude of their authors that is summarized well in the words of Vaqār al-Dowle who left the following note during her stay in Port Said in March 1900:

> After waking up in the morning and having drunk some tea, Ḥājji Ḥoseyn and Ḥājji Gholāmʿali went to the city to buy something. My brother did not go. When they came back, they were complimenting [the city, PB] a lot. But no matter how much you praise these cities, you don't want to dwell there. I'm so tired with those Arabs (*bas ke az in ʿArab-hā badam āmade*) that I only repeat 'Oh, God! Oh, God!' so we will reach our destination and survive at sea, *in šāʾAllāh*.
>
> JAʿFARIYĀN AND KIYĀNI HAFT LANG 2010, 84

Elsewhere in her account, Vaqār al-Dowle depicts local people with epithets such as 'mice-/rat-eating Arab' (*ʿArab-e mush-khor*) (ibid., 38) or 'stinking Arab' (*ʿArab-e gandide*) (ibid., 104). Also, when her brother has to pay customs in

Jedda, she 'thanks God' that she does not have to 'wrangle' with *zabān nā-fahm-hā* (imbeciles, literally meaning 'not understanding the language') herself (ibid., 90). However, it is worth noting at this point that there were moments when the whole perspective changed and despised Arabs disappeared from Vaqār al-Dowle's sight. After completing the second series of pilgrimages to *'atabāt-e 'āliyāt*, she writes in her journal that she wants to return to Iran as soon as possible. It is not only the 'spoiled Arabs' that tire her (ibid., 130), she is also exhausted by 'the heat of Arabia' (ibid., 131). Yet right after arriving in Iran, she is close to 'dying of grief' at the sight of Iranian pilgrims heading toward 'the paradise': the *'atabāt* (ibid., 134). Soon after, she calls Karbala her *vaṭan* or 'homeland': 'I had Karbala as my home, and now I have moved away from my homeland' (ibid., 140). The narrative of Vaqār al-Dowle shows that space may be perceived differently depending on whether it is seen as belonging to sacred or mundane geography. It also points to the ambiguity of the notion of homeland in a pilgrim's experience, for sometimes it may refer to the 'earthly homeland', and at other times to the 'spiritual homeland'.

In 'Āliye Khānom's account, Arabs are described as stupid, clumsy, and dangerous. According to her report, at the moment they entered Mecca she and her companions were the only eleven pilgrims who had not performed the ritual ablution and entered the state of *iḥrām* yet. Therefore, they started to look for a donkey to take them to the *mīqāt* in Sa'diyya (Yalamlam) as soon as possible. Since they could not find a donkey, they finally hired a mule and went to Qarn al-Manāzil instead. During the trip, 'Āliye Khānom fell off the mule and injured her head. Expressing her distress that she could not perform a proper ablution in such a state ('Those who could, made ablution and became *muḥrim*. But my head is wounded, covered with blood; [anyway, PB] having apparently cleaned dirt (*nejāsat*), we became *muḥrim* in a mosque'; Ja'fariyān 2007, 67), she blamed the mule driver and repeatedly called him with no other epithet than that of 'a bloody Arab' (*'Arab-e pedarsukhte* thrice and *pedarsukhte 'Arab* once; ibid., 65–67).

'Āliye Khānom's narrative demonstrates as well that apart from being an object of derision and contempt, Arabs were also an object of fear. Writing about washing the corpse of her female travel companion who had died on the road from Mecca to Medina, she explained that this was done in great haste: 'Every hour they were saying: "Don't be long, because the Arab bandits (*'Arāb-e ḥarāmi*) will come and kill us!"' (ibid., 71). The diarist did not claim that the threat of falling prey to 'the Arab bandits' was due to the fact that she and her companions were Shi'is (as 'Eṣmat al-Salṭane did in the already quoted excerpt). The Qajar hajj journals demonstrate, however, that Iranian pilgrims tended to equate Arabs with Sunnis (and thus: with 'anti-Shi'i').

Imposing one category (ethnicity) on another (religion)—which may appear quite odd given the fact that Iranians would inevitably meet Shiʿi Arabs during the pilgrimage—can be observed in the travelogue of Mirzā Abdolḥoseyn Khān Afshār Orumi, who performed the hajj in 1299–1300 AH (1882–1883). Reporting on his pilgrimage made on the day of *ʿāshūrā'* to the Janna al-Baqīʿ cemetery in Medina, he wrote: '(…) I said the *ʿāshūrā'* prayer, but in secret, because if any Arab saw me and found out what I was reciting, nothing would stop him from killing me' (Afshār Orumi 2007, 172). The woman from Tabas, in turn, uses a religious-geographical category when describing her fear of the Turkish soldiers she and some other women had to confront after the obligatory quarantine in Jedda: 'We have no courage to step ahead, because these Sunnis and inhabitants of al-Hijaz mistreat Iranians (*ʿAjam*). They discriminate [them, PB] on religious grounds' (Nāẓemi 2018, 74). Afraid of the Ottoman soldiers, she apparently includes Turks in the class of 'inhabitants of al-Hijaz'. Her words prove that the self-identification of Iranians paralleled their understanding of the Sunni Other that they encountered during the pilgrimage: even if she does not declare it, it is evident that she equates *ʿAjam* with the Shiʿis, as she identifies Arabs and Turks with the Sunnis.

One more conspicuous feature complemented the image of Arabs: their 'black' (*siyāh*) skin. Within a domestic context inside Iran, the word *siyāh* would usually denote a black enslaved person. As noted by Behnaz A. Mirzai, it '(…) was the most commonly used term by which enslaved Africans were designated in nineteenth-century [Iranian, PB] manuscripts' (Mirzai 2017, 24). However, in the following derogatory remark made by ʿĀliye Khānom, 'blackness' is emphasized as a distinctive, negative feature of Arabs: 'All people here [in Qarn al-Manazil, PB] are black (*siyāh*) as coal, bloody Arabs' (Jaʿfariyān 2007, 67).

Still, the diarists would apply the same term *siyāh* with reference to people of African origin, too. ʿEṣmat al-Salṭane discloses that during the hajj journey she was accompanied by her *kaniz-e siyāh*, a black female servant (Jaʿfariyān 1996, 60). The noblewoman from Tabas also travelled with her Ethiopian servant (*kaniz-e ḥabashi*) whom she mentions by name: 'Dowlat, my Abyssinian servant who since the beginning is my right hand in housekeeping, is a good maid (…)' (Nāẓemi 2018, 33). It is interesting to note in the context of the hajj that black male servants were also called *ḥājji* and black female servants *ḥājiye* on account of being often brought to Iran from Mecca (Mirzai 2017, 24). Confirmation of this practice can be found in the journal of the woman from Tabas, who mentions having bought 'new female servants' (*kaniz-hā-ye now*) in Mecca (ibid., 88).

In contrast to Western racist discourse, in Qajar Iran 'blackness' was not perceived as a 'scientific' category. As the hajj accounts testify, dark-skinned people would not necessarily be described as 'black' in accordance with a racial or an ethnic key, but rather on the basis of an obvious physical difference. Still, as the quoted excerpts demonstrate, 'blackness' was more often emphasized as a negative feature rather than a positive one, and dark skin traditionally carried connotations of evil and sin. It should be noted that the term *ru-siyāh*, a possibly self-belittling epithet, quite often used by the diarists in the sense of a sinful person, in its basic, literal sense means a person with black face (*Farhang-e feshorde-ye Sokhan* 2011). Even Tāj al-Salṭane, a daughter of Nāṣer al-Din Shāh who in her famous, unfinished memoir from 1914 fervently disapproved of the terrible treatment of black slaves and servants by their owners and championed racial equality, did not fail to dwell on the perceived negative appearance of her black nanny:

> This dear nanny of mine, having also brought up my mother, had risen to the rank of 'Matron Nanny.' (…) She was very affectionate to me and very formal and serious with others. I had grown so accustomed to her presence that, *despite her fearsome looks and dreadful physique*, if she was parted from me for a day, I cried the entire time and nothing could console me.
>
> TAJ AL-SALTANA 1993, 114, emphasis added, PB

In Qajar Iran, black people usually ranked among the lowest social strata: as slaves and enslaved domestic servants. Bearing this in mind, it appears significant that the noblewomen despise and even animalize the *siyāhs* who are placed low on the social ladder and serve as menial workers. For example, 'Eṣmat al-Salṭane, who repeatedly complains about the slowness of the camel drivers, once calls them 'black dogs' (*sag-hā-ye siyāh-e jammāl*) (Ja'fariyān 1996, 79)[5] and Vaqār al-Dowle compares black people working in the port of Jedda to

---

5 It almost looks like complaining about camel drivers became some sort of tradition among the Iranian pilgrims: other *safarnāmes* from that time also show that camel drivers did not enjoy a good reputation. For instance, Farāhāni, describing the 'Flying Caravan', which circulated between Mecca and Medina (probably the same with which the Qajar ladies travelled), wrote: 'There is no method in the departure of this caravan. It sets out from Mecca going to Medina group by group from the twentieth of the month of Ẕi Ḥejjeh (*dhū al-ḥijja*) to the end of the month. There is no order or regularity in anything about this caravan. There is so much thievery both from within and without [the caravan, PB]. *Most of the camel drivers are thieves and robbers*. Along the way, if someone is lost, it is the responsibility of the camel driver. Because of this, few belongings of people are lost along the way. After an individual arrives at the lodgings, if he is a little careless, they steal his belongings at once. If 100,000 tomans [worth, PB] of the pilgrims' belongings are carried off one night, or fifty pilgrims are killed, or if [some, PB] of the thieves are

monkeys: 'All dockers (*balamchi-hā*) are black. The black slaves (*kākā-hā*) go up the ropes [hanging from the ship, PB] like monkeys to throw the luggage [from the ship, PB] into the boats' (Ja'fariyān and Kiyāni Haft Lang 2010, 89). On the other hand, the same Vaqār al-Dowle did not even mention that Khāzen-e Aqdas, Moẓaffar al-Din's confidant whom she visited before the pilgrimage to humbly ask for the shah's blessing, was a former black slave of her late royal husband. Elevated to an esteemed position at the royal court, she had, according to Vaqār al-Dowle, 'blessed eyes' and her mouth would utter 'blessed words' (ibid., 27–28). Hence, black skin was sometimes pejoratively emphasized and at other times glossed over in silence, depending on the social position and importance of a particular *siyāh*.

It should be noted that black skin might also have been conventionally aestheticized: when the woman from Tabas enters Mecca, she poetically contrasts the black skin of a *ḥaram* servant with the whiteness of his clothing: '(…) I saw that a person blacker than tar wearing clothes whiter than milk (*shakhṣi siyāh-tar az qir bā lebās-e sefid-tar az shir*) appeared' (Nāẓemi 2018, 81). In yet other situations, the mention of black skin may be considered either as a 'neutral description' or as an emphasis put on a significant, negative trait of the Other. Such interpretative ambivalence arises from the following account of a visit to the mausoleum of four imams in Medina, included in the journal of the woman from Tabas:

> A few black slaves (*gholām-e siyāh*) sit on top of the cupola [of the mausoleum, PB] and they take one *qerān* from each two people. If they don't take money once, [or rather, PB] if they don't take [it, PB] one thousand times, they won't let you come in. And the imams' *ḥaram* is in such a bad shape and poor state that a man's heart aches [seeing that, PB]. They [the imams, PB] have always been oppressed (*maẓlum*), and they still are.
>
> ibid., 92

Reporting on her arrival in Medina, the woman from Tabas mentions the local Shi'is (apparently members of the Nakhāwila community), among whom she and some other Iranian pilgrims stayed.[6] According to her description, those 'black-skinned' (*siyāh-jald*, equivalent to the modern *siyāh-pust*) people lived in 'an area of small houses' next to the cemetery of Janna al-Baqī' and were

killed, there is no redress or calling to account. Usually the pilgrims stay awake from nightfall to morning, with weapons in hand, saying "Keep away, keep away!"' (Farāhāni 1990, 248, emphasis added, PB).

6 For more information about the Nakhāwila community, see Ende 1997.

believed to be descendants of former slaves (ibid., 91). The Shiʿis of Medina combined the features of 'us' and 'them': they were the diarist's co-religionists, yet they also possessed qualities of the Other, because of their appearance and low social status.

5 'In Fact, I Am Not a Human Being': Women and Men

The narratives demonstrate that the Imāmī Shiʿi women, who in theory were able to perform the pilgrimage on their own (Sayeed 2016, 68), usually were, in fact, dependent on the consent of their spouse, father, or another close male relative in the cases of unmarried or fatherless women. It is significant that Vaqār al-Dowle expresses gratitude to her husband for 'not objecting' to her performing the hajj without him:

> May God grant long life and good health to Moʿtasem al-Molk—may his good fortune endure forever—for not having objected to my journey but for having allowed instead, *in shāʾAllāh*, my hajj to be accepted by the Almighty and for having released me from this obligation [of performing the hajj, PB].
>
> JAʿFARIYĀN AND KIYĀNI HAFT LANG 2010, 114

In turn, in an introductory part of her travelogue, the woman from Tabas describes how she finally convinced her more-than-thirty-years-older husband to let her perform the hajj on her own. Although she expresses respect for him and emphasizes that he was guided by concern and fear for her health and life, and not by a desire to control her, at some point she shares the following remark:

> (…) because of this sudden travel of mine they are [he is, PB] very affected and pensive, and for the sake of us they seemingly never oppose, but in fact, I am not a human being.
>
> NĀẒEMI 2018, 28–29

This statement, that is not elaborated upon, not only indicates the subordination of the Qajar women to men, but above all: their awareness of this subordination, which at least some of them perceived as dehumanizing, as the 'in fact, I am not a human being' indicates. Whereas the words of the woman from Tabas are particularly suggestive, similar comments testifying to the subordination of women to men can be found in the other diaries as well. It is interesting to note that both ʿĀliye Khānom and Vaqār al-Dowle use their travel journals as a space where they can complain about their freedoms (*ekhtiyār*) being limited by men (Bachtin 2020, 21–22). For instance, when the latter wants to go to Damascus in order to visit the mausoleum of Zaynab,[7] her brother decides to proceed through Beirut. Vaqār al-Dowle then bitterly concludes: 'Whoever a woman would be, men will [always, PB] get it all their own way' (Jaʿfariyān and Kiyāni Haft Lang 2010, 83).

Importantly, apart from complaining, the female writers use irony and derision as ways of communicating their critical views about men. Sarcastic comments directed toward men are recurrent in the account of ʿĀliye Khānom and also present in Vaqār al-Dowle's travel journal (Bachtin 2020). For example, in the Tehrani part of ʿĀliye Khānom's diary, written after the hajj, she mocks a male tailor who was supposed to teach her and some courtly women how to use a sewing machine by calling him 'a jealous lazy-bones' who would not be able to teach them anything worthwhile (Jaʿfariyān 2007, 177). Such remarks show that women—themselves othered by men in the patriarchal Qajar society—would treat men as objects of othering, too.

The one diarist who actively fought to regain her *ekhtiyār* or freedom was ʿĀliye Khānom. On the way back to Iran she left her male custodian, Vali Khān, and took one of her female fellow travellers, a young woman called Fāṭeme under her wing (ibid., 89). Judging by the journal entry recorded after the split with Vali Khān, the decision to continue her journey without a male custodian must have entailed a veritable feeling of liberation in her:

> Since the day that I left the service of Khān, thanks God, I have seen all kinds of places and eaten all kinds of food. *Al-ḥamdu li-Allāh*, finally I am at ease!
>
> ibid., 93

The first reference to Fāṭeme appears in the opening part of the travelogue (ibid., 40). The fact that ʿĀliye Khānom refers to her by name may mean that she was significantly younger. While not explicitly stated, it must be assumed that Fāṭeme was a temporary wife (*ṣighe*) of Vali Khān, who got rid of her in Najaf and left her to her fate as soon as it turned out that she had become pregnant by him. Subsequently, ʿĀliye Khānom abandoned Vali Khān and then, together with Fāṭeme, both women joined a spouse of a certain Ḥājji Kalāntar (ibid., 89).

---

7 Sayyida Zaynab is the daughter of ʿAlī and Fātimah and granddaughter of the Prophet Muhammad.

Was ʿĀliye Khānom's choice to separate from Vali Khān partially driven by his cruel treatment of the pregnant woman? It seems likely, although she did not share any details explaining her decision. Albeit in different ways and to varying degrees, both ʿĀliye Khānom and Fāṭeme were subject to Vali Khān's oppression, and we have reasons to interpret ʿĀliye Khānom's move as an act of solidarity in the face of open injustice and violence that Khān directed at women of his entourage. But her act of solidarity was, as she disclosed, a religious act of merit, too. Her decision to take care of the pregnant and ill woman seems to be, at least in part, dictated by her desire to achieve a spiritual reward in this life or in the hereafter. Yet her bitter remarks reveal that she apparently came to regret her decision: complaining about Fāṭeme's 'uselessness' (*bi-maṣrafi*), she demonstrates how the sacred intertwined with the profane:

> So now, when I have decided to perform *thawāb* [a religious act of merit, PB], there's no one to say: 'Woman! What's your business here? Vali Khān kicked her out, is it your business to take her along?' Again, I do everything out of love for God, but she doesn't do anything. It's winter, it's cold, there is a journey of two months ahead and I don't spend anything, [there is, PB] no one to borrow money from and I don't have [enough, PB] money. I'm woebegone and don't know what to do. If I were alone with a servant girl, it would be easier.
>
> ibid., 97

Sylvia Chiffoleau observes that the return journeys from Mecca were usually very difficult, which was caused by, among other things, fatigue and dwindling supplies (Chiffoleau 2015, 42). In the case of ʿĀliye Khānom, both tiredness and expenses increased because of Fāṭeme's presence, and this was constantly troubling her mind on the road back to Iran. In her journal, she complained not only about the lack of money, but also about feeling overwhelmed by embarrassment (Jaʿfariyān 2007, 97). At some point, she became embittered by Fāṭeme's 'uselessness' and ungratefulness to such an extent that she became carried away by anger and renounced performing any meritorious acts in the future:

> Even if I would have to eat shit a thousand times, I won't do *thawāb*. I have to take care of myself. And then I'm supposed to take care of Fāṭeme too. Anytime, with no desire. *I vowed not to do thawāb in this world anymore.*
>
> ibid., 101, emphasis added, PB

ʿĀliye Khānom's diary informs us that she helped at least one more young woman in a difficult situation. After the hajj, during her long sojourn in the capital, she was regularly engaged as a stylist of brides (Bachtin 2015, 998–999) and became a sought-after matchmaker. Precisely on account of being *ḥājji khānom*, her intervention was believed to give blessing (*baraka*) and provide happiness and prosperity in marriage (Jaʿfariyān 2007, 127). She matched, among others, ʿAbdolvāheb Mirzā, one of the servants of her host, Ḥeshmat al-Salṭane, with an orphan girl whose name is not mentioned in the journal (it was a temporary marriage, but the writer did not specify the contract details). As was often the case, the bride and groom did not meet before the wedding. The day after the ceremony, ʿAbdolvāheb Mirzā demanded a divorce on account of the unattractive looks of his newlywed wife. Then, ʿĀliye Khānom asked Ḥeshmat al-Salṭane to intervene, arguing that the ugliness of the girl was not a sufficient reason to divorce her, and that her fate was, at least, uncertain:

> Poor orphan with no father! I went to His Lordship [Ḥeshmat al-Salṭane, PB] and told him: 'There is nothing we can do now. It is impossible to divorce her for this reason!'
>
> ibid., 146

Eventually, thanks to her intervention, ʿAbdolvāheb Mirzā changed his mind about divorcing the girl (ibid.).

The participation in the hajj is an important factor elevating one's social position and those who have made a pilgrimage to Mecca enjoy a special respect in their communities. According to the traditional view, however, such a change of social status applies mostly to men, since women, rather than being associated with the social and the cultural, are perceived to be closer to nature.[8] Yet the case of ʿĀliye Khānom shows that in Qajar Iran the participation in the hajj could have social implications for women, too. To become a bride stylist and

---

8 For example, Carol Delaney, who juxtaposed the contemporary hajj experiences of Turkish immigrants in Belgium with those of Turks living in Anatolia, argued that '[f]or a woman hajji there are no outward signs of changed status; whatever the rewards, they are invisible and internal. A woman who has made the hajj may be an object of curiosity, envy, and admiration to her friends, but her journey does not confer any new privileges. It does not indicate arrival at a new stage of life, since stages in woman's lives are defined rather by bio-sexual events of the female body: menstruation, defloration, childbirth, and menopause. After her journey she returns to the same life and resumes all her domestic tasks' (Delaney 1990, 520). Obviously, Delaney's observations concerned a different place and time, but they may be considered to stem from a specific view on roles and functions of women in Muslim societies, both in the past and now.

to be thought of as a carrier of *baraka* was an important distinction on both religious and social levels. Even if embedded in a patriarchal framework, ʿĀliye Khānom's actions served to provide the girl with no *maḥram* relative with financial stability, at least temporarily. Her journal demonstrates that she was able to use her high social status as well as the esteem she enjoyed as *ḥājji khānom* to advocate for less privileged, younger women.

6 Conclusions

The female selves emerging from the pilgrimage accounts by ʿEṣmat al-Salṭane, the woman from Tabas, ʿĀliye Khānom, and Vaqār al-Dowle appear to function in a paradoxical, contradictory dynamic of othering the Other (a Sunni, an Arab, a 'black') and being othered by others (men). Importantly, however, what the narratives of the woman from Tabas, Vaqār al-Dowle, and ʿĀliye Khānom demonstrate is that the women writers approached Iranian men as objects of othering, too. The fact that they often wrote unfavourably about men from their own environment indicates that their travel journals were intended, chiefly or exclusively, for a female readership. Vaqār al-Dowle explicitly states that she wrote her account for the female readers of her class and was asked to do it by a high-born woman connected to the royal court (Bachtin 2020, 12–14, 19, 24). As it was observed by Safaneh Mohaghegh Neyshabouri, one must bear in mind that the gender of the authors and their envisioned, mostly female readerships shaped both the language and the contents of their journals:

> They did not write in the veiled language that the women who wrote for the press used, nor did they write employing quite the same unveiled language that they used in their private female circles. They did, however, use a language that was unembellished, and if their subject of description was not related to the royals, fairly unveiled. In most cases it seems that the author is expecting a relatively narrow readership, of mostly like-minded women, although there are obvious cases of writing that seems to anticipate that male companions and either the Shah himself or people close to him (such as his wives) will read the travelogue.
>
> MOHAGHEGH NEYSHABOURI 2020, 134

The narrative of ʿĀliye Khānom proves that some women would attempt to abandon the circle of oppressive socio-cultural norms. It must be emphasized that, paradoxically, ʿĀliye Khānom's comparatively lower status of a non-royal provincial aristocrat made her less entangled in the network of dependencies that hampered the other female authors. One could also wonder whether her act of defiance against the patriarchal order (embodied by Vali Khān) was somehow triggered by the liminal, and thus possibly transformative, nature of the pilgrimage. Whereas it is impossible to answer this question, what can be ascertained is that the hajj journey, apart from being an object of description, provided ʿĀliye Khānom and other women writers with an opportunity to write about themselves and problematize their relationships with men.

The female-authored travelogues from the Qajar era clearly show that their relationships with the representatives of the opposite gender were of salient importance for them. Symptomatically, in the contemporaneous male-authored texts, co-travelling women, with rare exceptions, are glossed over in silence. Even if accompanied by their wives, male travellers usually did not mention female travelling companions in their diaries. Mentioning women would be considered either irrelevant or, perhaps even more importantly, breaking the taboo, since wives belonged to the private sphere. Traditionally, they might have been overtly identified with *ʿawra*, 'the most private part of the body (…)' (Sprachman 1995, IX).

When it comes to the image of the hajj, the narratives discussed here are not coloured by a romantic vision of the pilgrimage, supposed to obliterate differences of any kind among believers who peacefully gather in the House of God. These travelogues rather show that, despite the egalitarian idea of unity among all Muslims, differences prevailed. They reveal that their writers' subjectivity was chiefly defined by religious difference (Muslims versus non-Muslims, and even more importantly: Shiʿis versus Sunnis), ethnic difference (Iranians versus non-Iranians, mostly Arabs), 'racial' difference ('white' Iranians versus 'blacks'), and finally linguistic difference (Persian speakers versus those not speaking Persian). Apparently, for the female pilgrims the journey outside of the home country rarely was a stimulus to redefine their subjectivity. On the contrary, the Qajar women's attachment to their religious affiliation and place of origin seems to have undergone reinforcement through contact with the Other.

References

Afshār Orumi, Mirzā ʿAbdolḥoseyn Khān. 2007. *Safarnāme-ye Makke-ye moʿaẓẓame: 1299–1300q (1261–1262sh)*. Tehrān: Nashr-e ʿElm.

Babayan, Kathryn. 2008. '"In spirit we ate each other's sorrow": Female companionship in seventeenth-century Safavi Iran.' In *Islamicate sexualities: Translations across temporal geographies of desire*, edited by Kathryn Babayan and Afsaneh Najmabadi, 239–274. Cambridge, MA and London: Harvard University Press.

Bachtin, Piotr. 2020. 'Women's writing in action: On female-authored hajj narratives in Qajar Iran.' *Iranian studies* 54: 1–2, 67–93. https://doi.org/10.1080/00210862.2020.1724506.

Bachtin, Piotr. 2015. 'The royal harem of Naser al-Din Shah Qajar (r. 1848–1896): The literary portrayal of women's lives by Taj al-Saltana and anonymous "Lady from Kerman".' *Middle Eastern studies* 51 (6): 986–1009.

Chiffoleau, Sylvia. 2015. *Le voyage à La Mecque. Un pèlerinage mondial en terre d'Islam.* Paris: Éditions Belin.

Delaney, Carol. 1990. 'The "hajj": sacred and secular.' *American ethnologist* 17 (3): 513–530.

Dusend, Sarah. 2013. 'Pilgern nach Mekka—zur Reisewirklichkeit einer qajarischen Prinzessin und den Funktionen ihres Pilgerberichtes Rūznāme-ye safar-e ʿatabāt va-Mekkeh.' In *Venturing beyond borders—Reflections on genre, function and boundaries in Middle Eastern travel writing*, edited by Bekim Agai, Olcay Aky, and Caspar Hillebrand, 75–118. Würzburg: Ergon Verlag.

Ende, Werner. 1997. 'The Nakhāwila, a Shiʿite community in Medina past and present.' *Die Welt des Islams* 37 (3): 263–348.

Farāhāni, Moḥammad Ḥoseyn. 1990. *A Shiʿite pilgrimage to Mecca: 1885–1886. The Safarnâmeh of Mirzâ Mohammad Ḥosayn Farāhāni.* London: Saqi Books.

Farhang-e feshorde-ye Sokhan. 2011. Tehrān: Sokhan, s.v. 'Ru-siyāh'.

Gozarestan. n.d. 'Zan-e kermāni ke ketāb-e "Ruznāme-ye safar-e ḥajj" rā nevesht ke bud?' Accessed June 8, 2020. https://www.gozarestan.ir/show.php?id=1878.

Hanaway, William. 2002. 'Persian travel narratives: Notes toward the definition of a nineteenth-century genre.' In *Society and culture in Qajar Iran: Studies in honor of Hafez Farmayan*, edited by Elton Daniel, 249–268. Costa Mesa, CA: Mazda Publishers.

Ḥassanābādi, Akram, ed. 2009. 'Gozāresh-e safar-e ḥajj-e bānu-ye hendi Shāh Jahān Beygom [!] dar sāl-e 1280 qamari.' *Payām-e Bahārestān* 3: 641–654.

Jaʿfariyān, Raṣul, ed. 2013. *Chahārdah safarnāme-ye ḥajj-e qājāri-ye digar.* Tehrān: Nashr-e ʿElm.

Jaʿfariyān, Raṣul, ed. 2010. *Panjāh safarnāme-ye ḥajj-e qājāri.* Tehrān: Nashr-e ʿElm.

Jaʿfariyān, Raṣul, ed. 2007. *Ruznāme-ye safar-e ḥajj, ʿatabāt-e ʿāliyāt, va darbār-e Nāṣeri 1309–1312 q/1271–1273 sh.* Qom: Nashr-e Movarrekh.

Jaʿfariyān, Raṣul, ed. 2000. 'Ḥajj-gozāri-ye Irāniyān dar dowre-ye Qājār (1).' *Miqāt-e Ḥajj* 32: 53–84.

Jaʿfariyān, Raṣul, ed. 1996. 'Safarnāme-ye Makke-ye dokhtar-e Farhād Mirzā.' *Miqāt-e ḥajj* 17: 57–117.

Jaʿfariyān, Rasul, and Kiyānush Kiyāni Haft Lang, eds. 2010. *Ruznāme-ye safar-e ʿatabāt va Makke 1317q/1279sh.* Tehrān: Enteshārāt-e ʿElm.

Kafshgar Sichāni, Ḥājiye Hamdam, ed. 2007. *Safar-e sabz. Khāṭerāt-e manẓum-e yek ḥajj.* Eṣfahān: Enteshārāt-e Puyān-Mehr.

Khosravie, Jasmin. 2013. 'Iranian women on the road—The case of Ṣadīqe Doulatābādī in Europe, 1923–1927.' In *Venturing beyond borders—Reflections on genre, function and boundaries in Middle Eastern travel writing*, edited by Bekim Agai, Olcay Aky, and Caspar Hillebrand, 131–156. Würzburg: Ergon Verlag.

Mahallati, Amineh. 2016. 'Women as pilgrims: Memoirs of Iranian women travelers to Mecca.' *Iranian studies* 44: 831–849.

Milani, Farzaneh. 1992. *Veils and words: The emerging voices of Iranian women writers*. Syracuse and New York: Syracuse University Press.

Mirzai, Behnaz. 2017. *A history of slavery and emancipation in Iran, 1800–1929*. Austin: University of Texas Press.

Mohaghegh Neyshabouri, Safaneh. 2020. 'Resistance and encroachment in everyday life: A feminist epistemological study of Qajar era Iranian women's travel journals'. PhD diss., University of Alberta.

Nāzemī, Nāzilā, ed. 2018. *Se ruz be ākhar-e daryā: safarnāme-ye shāhzāde khānom-e qājāri*. Tehrān: Aṭrāf.

Rahimieh, Nasrin. 2001. *Missing Persians: Discovering voices in Iranian cultural history*. Syracuse and New York: Syracuse University Press.

Sarukkai, Sundar. 1997. 'The "Other" in anthropology and philosophy.' *Economic and political weekly* 32 (24): 1406–1409.

Sayeed, Asma. 2016. 'Women and the hajj.' In *The hajj: Pilgrimage in Islam*, edited by Eric Tagliacozzo and Shawkat Toorawa, 65–84. New York: Cambridge University Press.

Sikandar Begum. 1870. *A pilgrimage to Mecca by the Nawab Sikandar Begum of Bhopal, G.C.S.I.* London: Wm. H. Allen & Co.

Sprachman, Paul. 1995. *Suppressed Persian: An anthology of forbidden literature*. Costa Mesa, CA: Mazda Publishers.

Taj al-Saltana. 1993. *Crowning Anguish: Memoirs of a Persian princess from the harem to modernity, 1884–1914*. Washington, DC: Mage Publishers.

Torābi, Zohre, ed. 2018. *Chādor kardim raftim tamāshā: safarnāme-ye 'Āliye Khānom Shirāzi*. Tehran: Aṭrāf.

CHAPTER 7

Experiencing the Hajj in an Age of Change: Tuning the Emotions in Several Hajj Accounts of Pilgrims Travelling from Morocco and Egypt in the First Half of the Twentieth Century

Ammeke Kateman

The second half of the nineteenth century and the first half of the twentieth century were times of remarkable change around the world, also for Muslims (Gelvin and Green 2014). Revolutionary innovations in terms of steam, print, and empire had an effect on the hajj, the annual Islamic pilgrimage to Mecca and its surroundings (Chiffoleau 2015). Steamships and trains increasingly replaced the Egyptian and Syrian caravans, transporting larger numbers of pilgrims to Mecca from more remote locations such as South and South-East Asia and Morocco in a safer, cheaper, and faster way. Colonial empires such as Britain, France, and the Netherlands monitored, regulated, and, at times, prohibited the hajj journey for their Muslim subjects. International conferences imposed a period of quarantine on all pilgrims returning from the Arabian Peninsula. The publication and distribution of narrative and visual representations of the hajj in travelogues, guides, and photos were part of a global circulation of images and ideas, facilitated by cheap print technologies. These and other global processes and discourses inevitably also had an impact on the region of the Hijaz as well as on the regimes of governance there—first that of the Sharīfs under the Ottomans and subsequently that of the new Saūdi rulers from the mid-1920s onwards.

Amidst these locally impacting global processes, Arab pilgrims travelled to Mecca in order to perform the hajj, which they often recorded in travelogues, as many of their predecessors had done. This chapter draws on a small set of these travelogues that were written in Arabic by pilgrims travelling through or from Egypt in the first four decades of the twentieth century in order to analyse their experience of the hajj. More specifically, I am interested in how these pilgrims assessed some of the great changes of their time, especially the obligation of quarantine for returning hajj pilgrims and the governance of the Hijaz by ʿAbd al-ʿAzīz Āl Saʿūd (or Ibn Saʿūd). I also try to gauge their feelings about these changes—however elusive emotions might be to an historian.

DOI:10.1163/9789004513174_009

The travelogues referred to in this chapter comprise a set of travel accounts that circulated in manuscript-form in the anti-colonial and revivalist context of a Moroccan Sufi order in Fes at the turn of the century. These texts describe the 1904 hajj journey of shaykh Muḥammad ibn ʿAbd al-Kabīr al-Kattānī, the leader of the Kattānī order at that time, and his party, as well as the journey of his cousin, hadith-scholar and biographer Muḥammad ibn Jaʿfar al-Kattānī and his son Muḥammad al-Zamzamī al-Kattānī (al-ʿAmrānī 2010; al-Kattānī 2005).[1] The chapter also draws upon several texts originating in Cairo and dating to the first half of the twentieth century. These texts are highly diverse, ranging from a travelogue by the conservative journal editor Aḥmad ʿAlī al-Shādhilī published in 1904 (al-Shādhilī 1322 AH); an account from the modernist travel writer Muḥammad Labīb al-Batanūnī, who was part of the Egyptian ruler's hajj entourage in 1909 (al-Batanūnī n.d.); an account of poet and translator ʿAbd al-ʿAzīz Ṣabrī from 1923 (Ṣabrī 1342 AH); a travelogue written by the wealthy retiree Muṣṭafā Muḥammad al-Rāʿī in 1931 (al-Rāʿī n.d.), published by the ʿAzamiyya order (a reformist Sufi order established in the second decade of the twentieth century); a text by the journalist Muḥy al-Dīn Riḍā (nephew of Islamic reformer Rashīd Riḍā) in 1935 (Riḍā 1353 AH/1935); and one by the legal official Ibrāhīm Muḥammad Ḥabīb in 1938 (Ḥabīb 2014).

This chapter explores the diversity of hajj experiences articulated by pilgrims who encountered the new contexts of steam transportation, quarantine and Saudi governance. To be sure, many more travelogues were written in Arabic during this period (as well as in other languages)—as had been written before and would be written later—and studying these might reveal more variation of the hajj experience in relation to these changes. This chapter ends with a reflection on this variety, and relates it to the role the genre of hajj travelogues might play in preparing pilgrims for particular emotional states and ways of interpreting their experiences of the hajj.

1 Elusive Experiences and Emotions

Pilgrimage—leaving one's familiar and familial environment behind in order to make a long-awaited journey to a place filled with meaning—is likely to

---

1 The two groups of the Kattānī family did not travel together, but occasionally met during their journey (in Medina) (al-ʿAmrānī 2010, 223; al-Kattānī 2005, 153). The travelogue written by the son, Muḥammad al-Zamzamī al-Kattānī, seems not to have been published independently. Large parts are quoted in footnotes in the published edition of his father's travel text, however. For this chapter, I relied on these citations.

constitute a very special experience that typically arouses intense feelings (on emotions and travelling, see Robinson and Picard 2016; El-Sayed 2016). Feelings and emotions have often been acknowledged as a central mode for believing, accessing, and practicing Islam, which includes performing the pilgrimage to Mecca (Bauer 2017; Gade 2007).[2] Despite this, scholars of the hajj have largely overlooked the experiential and emotional dimension of the hajj and the ways these experiences and emotions have been shaped and articulated.

Barbara Metcalf's 1990 chapter on South Asian accounts of the hajj makes clear that modern hajj travelogues are particularly rich sources for studying individual religious experiences and 'changing patterns of religious sensibilities' in a world of great transition (Metcalf 1990). Similarly, in his 2015-article 'The hajj as its own undoing: Infrastructure and integration on the Muslim journey to Mecca,' Nile Green discusses a corpus of modern South Asian hajj travelogues to argue how industrial travel radically transformed the experiences of and writings about the hajj journey for these Muslim authors—from a journey through a Muslim world to an itinerary through 'a world governed by ideas, peoples and technologies of non-Muslim provenance' (Green 2015, 193). Building on Metcalf and Green, this chapter considers two formative changes in the early modern international contexts and in the Hijaz by turning to Arabic hajj travelogues from that era in order to gain insights into how the changes discussed above impacted the experiences and emotions of pilgrims.

It is not always easy to distil pilgrims' experiences from hajj travelogues. This is particularly the case for discerning emotions, as Sylvia Chiffoleau and John Slight acknowledge somewhat regretfully in their histories of the hajj in colonial times (Chiffoleau 2015, 16; Slight 2015, 247). Evidently, it is impossible for historians to retrieve emotions themselves, since they can only study the mediated articulation of an emotional experience (Matt 2014, 43). So, when analysing pilgrims' experiences and emotions, this chapter has to carefully draw on narrative descriptions of feelings (anger, sadness, disappointment) and expressions that suggest an emotional experience (such as crying or laughing). In addition, it is also difficult to extract the experiential dimension, because the accounts discussed here do not always overtly display a great degree of emotionality and introspection. Dwight Reynold's analysis of pre-modern Arabic autobiographies and their particular ways of being introspective and self-

2 For the interior prerequisites of the hajj, for example, one might think of Abū Ḥāmid al-Ghazālī (1058–1111) and his discussion of the importance of the right intention (*niyya*). For a discussion of these ideas in relation to the entering of the state of *iḥrām*, see Peters (1994, 114–116).

interpreting is helpful in this respect.[3] Reynolds refers to common practices—quoting poems, describing dreams, relating the emotional state of others, or describing certain actions (such as visiting a saint's tomb to wish for success)—as alternative means to represent a writer's emotional state (Reynolds 2001, 87–99). Reynolds' analysis suggests historians ought to be attentive to alternative and subtle markers that signal an emotional response to something. Similarly, Barbara Rosenwein recommends historians to not only pay attention to overt emotions to things 'assessed as valuable or harmful (for it is about such things that people express emotions)' (Rosenwein 2010, 11), but also to 'read the silences' (ibid., 17). In order to distil the experiential dimension from the travelogues selected here, this chapter focuses on descriptions and expressions of emotions, explicit in-text markers—such as the sudden and typically modern use of (several) exclamation marks for something scary, repulsive, angering, shocking, or wonderful—as well as instances when emotions were *not* expressed.

The articulation of emotions in the travelogues I discuss cannot be seen in isolation. Centuries of hajj travelogues and other textual and visual forms of hajj representation had prepared the authors for what to feel or how to express these feelings during their journey and their sojourn in Mecca. In turn, these travelogues reiterated and re-shaped what pilgrims experience and feel while on hajj. Following Birgit Meyer's analysis of religions' 'making of awe', these travelogues can thus be seen as one medium amongst other religious media that 'tune the senses and induce specific sensations, thereby rendering the divine sense-able, and triggering particular religious experiences' (cf. Meyer 2016; Meyer 2008, 129). In addition, while the hajj travelogues studied here were part of a chain of hajj narrations that prepare the pilgrims towards what to think and feel, they also had to respond to the highly variable context of the first half of the twentieth century. This chapter's conclusion will further examine this interplay of change and continuity in the genre of hajj travelogues.

2 Journeying through a New World

Within the Hijaz region, most pilgrims continued to travel in caravans until the 1940s, whether by camel, donkey, or on foot—and only incidentally by car from the 1930s onwards. By then, the journey towards the Hijaz had changed

3 I thank El-Sayed for pointing me to Reynolds' and others' work on autobiography in her dissertation (El-Sayed 2016, 54).

radically with the introduction of the steam ship and train. Indeed, in the course of the 1880s, the official Egyptian *maḥmal* caravan abandoned the land route for steam trains (from Cairo to Suez) and boats (across the Red Sea to Jedda). Moroccan Muslims also used this route through Egypt, after British or French commercial shipping companies had taken them across the Mediterranean to reach Alexandria, docking at several ports along the way (Chiffoleau 2015).

For the narrators of the hajj travelogues studied here, travelling from Morocco and Egypt, this journey by steam ship and train presented a new reality that invariably invited commentary. Very frequently, the narrators describe in their travelogues the facilities, itineraries (stopping at several ports across the Mediterranean), and the remarkable speed of the new transportation they boarded—sometimes for the first time in their life (al-Kattānī 2005, 118, 322). At times, these descriptions seem to radiate a sense of pride—sometimes bordering on bragging—for example in the case of the Egyptian pilgrim al-Rāʿī, travelling in 1931, who never missed an opportunity to mention the luxury in which he and his wife travelled, commenting on the various ships, trains, and cars they experienced. He also included a photograph of himself in his travel outfit with accessories (al-Rāʿī n.d., 13–23, 29–39, 158–159 (photo), 212–218).

Even though pilgrims often appreciated the new ease with which they could travel to Mecca, they also considered these new travel conditions quite challenging. The Moroccan pilgrims Muḥammad ibn Jaʿfar al-Kattānī, his son Muḥammad al-Zamzamī al-Kattānī, and ʿAbd al-Salām ibn Muḥammad al-Muʿṭī al-ʿAmrānī, all connected to the Kattānīya order in Fes and travelling between 1903–1904, pay specific attention in their travelogues to whether the steam journey was compatible with Islam. For example, they worried if it was permitted to travel on ships to Mecca that were owned by British commercial businesses and staffed with British crew. Furthermore, they wondered if they would able to perform their religious duties, such as praying and fasting, on board (al-ʿAmrānī 2010, 147, 150; al-Kattānī 2005, 118, 119 n.1, 145–147, 327). They treaded carefully when mooring at European ports, such as Marseille, Naples, and Malta, trying to avoid imitating unlawful Christian European customs (*tashabbuh*) and sometimes simply refusing to disembark because of the unbelief (*kufr*) there (al-ʿAmrānī 2010, 152; al-Kattānī 2005, 121). At the same time, for Muḥammad ibn Jaʿfar al-Kattānī, the new possibilities for going on hajj with steam transportation renewed the obligation of the hajj for Moroccan pilgrims, who had been considered exempt from this obligation by some Islamic scholars because they concluded that Moroccans lacked the possibilities to travel that far, and because Moroccans had to prioritise jihad due to their frontier position (al-Kattānī 2005, 107; see Hendrickson 2016).

One of the most salient features of the challenges that came with these changes in transportation was the necessity for pilgrims to undergo a period of quarantine in special facilities. This quarantine was implemented in order to detect and separate those carrying infectious diseases and thus prevent diseases from spreading further towards Europe (see Huber 2016; Chiffoleau 2015; Slight 2015; Low 2008; Roff 1982) The cholera pandemic of 1865 had made many European colonial powers acutely aware of the risk of contagious diseases spreading from India to Europe through Mecca during the hajj season.[4] Initiated by France, an international conference in Constantinople in 1866 imposed a period of quarantine for pilgrims, targeting pilgrims travelling by sea from India (on the island of Kamaran) and Egypt (near the village of al-Ṭūr on the Sinai Peninsula). These quarantine camps were first placed under Ottoman control and were later governed by Egyptian and British authorities (as Egypt was a de facto protectorate of the British Empire since the mid-1880s). Furthermore, these camps were mainly staffed by medical personnel of European origin. The obligation of quarantine considerably slowed down the newly steam-powered pilgrims en route to and from Mecca, until the quarantine obligations were gradually relieved for hajj pilgrims in the middle of the twentieth century—first on the route to and from India in the 1930s and then, yet only in the 1950s, on the route to and from Egypt (Chiffoleau 2015, 199; Slight 2015, 250).

Several travelogues studied in this chapter elaborately discuss the quarantine facilities in al-Ṭūr (as the pilgrims studied here came through the Egyptian route).[5] For the Moroccan Sufi hadith-scholar Muḥammad ibn Jaʿfar al-Kattānī, his fourteen-day stop at the quarantine station at al-Ṭūr in 1904 was quite disturbing. In his introduction, he announces that he wanted to avoid it at first by residing in Medina for a longer time—a more common strategy for affluent pilgrims (al-Kattānī 2005, 107; see also Chiffoleau 2015, 196). Furthermore, he includes an Islamic legal verdict (*ḥukm*) on the quarantining of hajj pilgrims in his travelogue, in which he considers the establishment of quarantine not permissible for several reasons. First, al-Kattānī writes that it is unlawful that Christians and Jews govern these quarantine facilities, as this elevates 'people of false religions' over Muslims. In addition, he states that quarantine is not in the

4 Incidentally, Mecca was not only seen as a hotbed for diseases like cholera, but also for the spread of potentially subversive, anti-colonial and pan-Islamic ideas. See Chantre 2013.

5 Some of the travelogues indicate other quarantine-stations frequented by the pilgrims travelling to North Africa: in Beirut (for Muḥammad ibn Jaʿfar al-Kattānī and his party), Marseille (also for Muḥammad ibn Jaʿfar al-Kattānī) and Algiers (for al-ʿAmrānī in the entourage of Muḥammad ibn ʿAbd al-Kabīr al-Kattānī).

pilgrims' best interests, since he considers these sanitary measures useless as is indicated by the many flies and foul smells in the quarantine camp. Instead, al-Kattānī writes that quarantine is a plot of the Christians to hinder the ritual of the hajj and weaken the power it has over Muslims. He finds the quarantining practices particularly harmful to Muslims, mentioning that pilgrims are scolded and scowled at, cursed, abused, and insulted. In addition, they have to take off their clothes and are made to wait for a long time (al-Kattānī 2005, 231–233).

Al-Kattānī's evaluation does not include reflections on his personal experiences and emotional states. Yet, his strongly worded assessment of the absolute impermissibility of quarantine for Muslim pilgrims and his use of multiple exclamation marks accompanying his description of Muslims being scolded and insulted seem to signal that it was a humiliating and also an anger-invoking experience for him personally. Historians, relying on other travelogues and eyewitness accounts, similarly describe al-Ṭūr as ill-facilitated, chaotic, depressing, and humiliating, for example because of the indiscriminate mixing of sexes and classes—especially in the first decades of the camp (Chiffoleau 2015, 193–197; Stratkötter 1991, 103).

In that same year, others coming from the same Sufi circles in Morocco did not detail the experience of quarantine in equally negative terms. The Moroccan jurist ʿAbd al-Salām ibn Muḥammad al-Muʿṭī al-ʿAmrānī, travelling in the entourage of al-Kattānī's aforementioned cousin, the shaykh of the Kattānīya, in that same year, writes that the quarantine regime was not 'too heavy on the pilgrims' since, he explains, there was no major outbreak of diseases in that year (1903–1904). This brief statement is the only words he devotes to this experience (al-ʿAmrānī 2010, 281, 283 n.1).

The descriptions and evaluations by others are actually very positive and seem to aim at stirring up their readers' pride in these technological and medical advancements, marking them as signs of the high level of Muslim progress and civilisation. The Egyptian Muḥammad Labīb al-Batanūnī, travelling in the entourage of Egypt's ruler ʿAbbās II Ḥilmī in 1909 as an official travel writer, reported about the good organization of the quarantine facilities at al-Ṭūr—such as their abundance of medical and technological means, including neatly separating those diagnosed with different diseases.[6] He states that this quarantine facility under Egyptian care is the best quarantine in the world, which does not come as a surprise given his function in the entourage of the Egyptian

6 I am not completely sure al-Batanūnī travelled to al-Ṭūr himself, as the khedive and his following seem to have taken the northern land route and then the boat to Alexandria from Haifa. This route took pilgrims along the quarantine facility of Tabūk.

ruler. While he acknowledges that there are some difficulties with the quarantine, he considers these inevitable and sees no reason to abandon the efforts (al-Batanūnī n.d., 358).

Two decades after al-Batanūnī, the Egyptian businessman and retired government official Muṣṭafā Muḥammad al-Rāʿī was equally impressed with the quarantine facilities. Al-Rāʿī describes the delight he took in seeing al-Ṭūr for the first time: the clean and well-functioning hygienic facilities, the private accommodation he stayed in with his wife, the 'lenient and brotherly' personnel, and the smoothness of even the smallest details in the overall organization (al-Rāʿī n.d., 219–224).

Even so, being held in these facilities was not an easy experience for al-Rāʿī or for others, and many were ambivalent about it.[7] Al-Rāʿī expresses joy when he is told he could leave this 'prison', for example, because, he writes, freedom is man's natural right and he misses his loved ones at home (ibid., 225).[8] In addition, it seems clear from his descriptions that he was uncomfortable with the mixing of social-economic classes. He describes himself as playing 'the role of hero' (*dawr al-baṭal*) in this 'story of equality' (*riwāya al-musāwāh*) for taking a disinfecting salt shower together with others of his company, even though the quality and cleanliness of his clothes gave his high status away. He hastens to add that his wife did not shower together with the other women, but instead waited in the changing room (ibid., 222).

Even though he found the experience in some respects clearly uncomfortable, he boasts that he endured the period of quarantine patiently and even heroically—unlike some of the other pilgrims who protested against the waiting period. He complains that these pilgrims were protesting merely for the love of protesting and the joy of hearing oneself only, reminding his readers that courage actually consists of patience (*ṣabr*) and self-control (ibid., 224). In this way, al-Rāʿī's travelogue provides insight into the virtue of a non-display of emotions for hajj pilgrims. While he notes that feelings of discomfort and anger are justified, he conveys the importance of regulating and suppressing these

---

7 Also consider the somewhat ambiguous impression the account of Ibrāhīm Rifʿāt Pasha—commander of the Egyptian hajj delegation in the early twentieth century—gives with regard to al-Ṭūr. In his analysis of the photos in the travelogue of Ibrāhīm Rifʿāt Pasha, Stephen Sheehi argues that his photos present an orderly and progress-filled image of the quarantine facilities, matching the discourses of science and order of the Arabic progressivist and modernist Nahḍa elite of that time (Sheehi 2016, 175–192). Yet, according to Rita Stratkötter, Ibrāhīm Rifʿāt Pasha—commander of the Egyptian hajj delegation in the early twentieth century—lists numerous complaints in his travelogue in the first year he commanded the hajj, even though he sees improvement in the following years (Stratkötter 1991, 103).

8 cf. a pilgrim's account similarly likening quarantine to a prison, referred to in Slight 2015, 250.

emotions. In addition, al-Rāʿī's call for patience and his sharp rejection of the overt anger of his fellow pilgrims are a reminder that pilgrims can also employ emotions and the control over emotions as modern markers of difference in their narratives, distinguishing composed Muslims like themselves from their passion-driven counterparts (cf. Pernau 2014).[9]

For many (but not all) pilgrims travelling through al-Ṭūr at the beginning of the twentieth century, quarantine seems at least worthy of (elaborate) commentary—albeit in a large variety of ways. One explanation for the differences in quarantine experiences are the varying political loyalties of each narrator. During this time, the 'steam geography and demography' (see Green 2015) and the quarantining facilities represented multiple levels of colonial and Egyptian politics. It seems not particularly surprising that an Egyptian official, such as travel writer Muḥammad Labīb al-Batanūnī, wrote a strongly positive and proud evaluation about the Egyptian governance of the camp in Tor. Vice versa, Muḥammad bin Jaʿfar al-Kattānī's sharply negative assessment of al-Ṭūr as 'a conspiracy of the Christians' (al-Kattānī 2005, 233) fits well with his own anti-colonialist ideas and those of his cousin Muḥammad ʿAbd al-Kabīr (shaykh of the Fes-based Kattānīya order at that time) (see Bazzaz 2008; 2010; Munson 1993).

One might also think of the way pilgrims' experiences in al-Ṭūr were coloured by the privileges (such as private rooms) pilgrims such as al-Batanūnī and al-Rāʿī enjoyed, related to their official status as well as their wealth. Another explanation would refer to the pilgrims' varying participation in discourses of health, technology, and science. Al-Batanūnī's praise for the organization of the camp in al-Ṭūr fits in well with his well-ordered and factual travelogue that radiates a positivist belief in science and orderliness, while al-Kattānī's disbelief in the benefits of quarantine matches his own trust in medical treatments he deems Islamic and his aversion to customs or knowledge he considers European (al-Kattānī 2005, 285, 313–314).

Pilgrims' experiences in quarantine camps were thus coloured by their political loyalties, class status, and particular situatedness in global discourses on health and science. But the international-colonial imposition of quarantine was not the only change that affected pilgrims' hajj experiences in several ways

9 One might also think of Duncan Black Macdonald's scholarly description of the emotional aspect of the hajj, with overt racist and sexualised overtones, marking the distance between Muslims (and others) and Protestants (like himself): 'These [the pilgrimage to Mecca and the many imitation pilgrimages [sic] all over the Muslim lands, AK] are the scenes of orgasms of ecstatic emotion comparable in many ways to those at negro camp-meetings.' (Macdonald 1909, 215–216).

at that time. The next section addresses regime changes within the Hijaz and how these changes impacted the hajj experience.

3 The Hijaz Experience Reformed

Between 1924 and the beginning of 1926, ʿAbd al-ʿAzīz Āl Saʿūd (or Ibn Saʿūd) conquered Mecca and the rest of the Hijaz region in addition to already being sultan and later king of the Najd region. His conquest of the Hijaz ended Ottoman rule of Mecca, replacing Sharīf Ḥusayn al-Hāshimī (r. 1916–1924) and his son ʿAlī (r. 1924–1925), thereby ending the Sharīfian dynasty that had ruled the Hijaz for centuries. Protecting and propagating a Wahhābī interpretation of Islam, Ibn Saʿūd's hajj governance entailed a reform of hajj procedures and experiences. Under his rule, pilgrims were prohibited from performing rituals or customs that committees of Wahhābī jurists considered incompatible with the doctrine of *tawḥīd* (asserting that God is one and unique). This meant that pilgrims were corrected if their utterances and ritual movements during the hajj deviated from the Wahhābī opinions of that time. Saʿūdi soldiers redirected the pilgrims as well as newly trained hajj guides (*muṭawwif*s), who for ages had been employed by pilgrims upon their arrival in the Hijaz in order to help pilgrims navigate practical and ritual matters. The pilgrims' behaviour was also regulated beyond the rituals, prohibiting swearing, making music (also as part of the *maḥmal* celebration), smoking, or wearing perfume in public. In addition, many historical structures, domes, and tombs of companions or family of the Prophet Muhammad (Cf. figure 7.1 below) were demolished in 1926 by the Wahhābī militia. This was done in order to prevent pilgrims from touching tombs, venerating the buried, or asking for their intercession. Soldiers and *muṭawwif*s were also instructed to correct these types of veneration, which were considered to be a form of *shirk* (polytheism) or *bidʿa* (unlawful innovation)—even though some soldiers were more lenient or more amenable to bribes than others. The implementation of these reforms varied in degree. They were strongest in the 1920s and were slowly loosened in the 1930s when Ibn Saʿūd subdued an insurrection started by the particularly puritan Wahhābī militia and felt the need to attract more pilgrims in order to provide a greater income to the kingdom after the global financial crisis of 1929 (Willis 2017, 358–368; Al-Sarhan 2016; Chiffoleau 2015, 316–322; Slight 2015).

The demolition of the Hijaz's historical landscape was not entirely novel in its history. The Egyptian travel writer Muḥammad Labīb al-Batanūnī describes the destruction of domes and tombs during the first Saʿūdi conquest at the beginning of the nineteenth century in addition to late-nineteenth-century

FIGURE 7.1 Majmunah's Grave (c. 1886–1889)
PHOTOGRAPHER: AL-SAYYID ʿABD AL-GHAFFĀR [9R-B] (1/1), BRITISH LIBRARY: VISUAL ARTS, X463/10, IN QATAR DIGITAL LIBRARY HTTPS://WWW.QDL.QA/ARCHIVE/81055/VDC_100023510750.0X000026 [ACCESSED 18 APRIL 2022].

*sharīf*s' emulating the Wahhābī zeal, destroying several tombs and domes (Al-Batanūnī n.d., 81, 146, 148). He does not comment on any of these measures in his travelogue, although he labels the Wahhābī creed one of 'great excess' and considers Eve's grave—which was also nearly destroyed—in Jedda a legitimate place to visit (ibid., 78–79, 146).

In spite of these historical precedents, the 'Wahhābization' of the hajj and its landscape from the mid-1920s onwards drastically changed the hajj experience for many pilgrims. Visiting holy places (*ziyāra*) was a common feature especially for Egyptian and North African pilgrims (as well as others) travelling to and within the Hijaz. Pilgrims visited shrines, tombs, and mosques as well as other sites connected to Islam's sacred history in order to collect blessings (sg. *baraka*) and ask for the intercession of saints as well as family and companions of the Prophet Muhammad (al-ʿAmrānī 2010; al-Kattānī 2005).

Travelling in 1931, the Egyptian pilgrim Muṣṭafā Muḥammad al-Rāʿī mentions on several occasions in his account that his *muṭawwif* or the deputy of his *muṭawwif* was constantly with him and his party, but did not guide them to Islamic 'sacred antiquities' or 'holy places', like the birthplace of ʿAlī. Some of these places he found closed, such as the house of al-Arqam where the earliest community of Muslims had convened. Alternatively, Saʿūdi soldiers blocked the entrance to the cave of Ḥirāʾ, where the Prophet is considered to have received his first revelations, and they prohibited pilgrims from touching the fence around the tomb of the Prophet in Medina, telling them it was merely green copper from Istanbul and that the man in the grave had fulfilled his duty and then died (al-Rāʿī n.d., 67–68, 99, 122, 169–170). Al-Rāʿī also describes how the house of Khadīja—the first wife of Muhammad and the first Muslim—as well as the graves in the graveyard of al-Baqīʿ in Medina were completely levelled to the ground (ibid., 68).

Al-Rāʿī seems surprised as well as deeply upset about these new circumstances. In the passage on the house of Khadīja, he calls upon God and asks in disbelief: 'The house of *sayyida* Khadīja, daughter of Khuwaylid, is erased without a trace?' In various wordings he repeats that this was the very house from which God's message spread (ibid., 68). This type of repetition might be another indication of his shock and distress. On another occasion, he writes that he was deeply moved after finally having located the house of al-Arqam, one of the companions of the Prophet Muhammad, in a small alley, only to find it closed. He perceives its closure as a ban on being blessed, because it prevents him from rubbing its doorsteps with his hands and its ground with his forehead (ibid., 99). Similarly, reminiscing about what happened to him at the cave of Ḥirāʾ (or rather, what did *not* happen there due to the presence of soldiers), he writes that he strongly wished to have rubbed his cheek at the place where the Prophet's footsteps once were (ibid., 124).

This type of yearning (in vain) seems to build on existing emotional patterns in Arabic hajj travelogues, because yearning for the hajj and especially for being close to the Prophet in the City of Light (al-Madīna al-Munawwara) and being in proximity to his tomb is a common theme in many older hajj travelogues (Al-Samaany 2000, 84–87, 138).[10] For example, Muḥammad al-Zamzamī al-Kattānī, son of the aforementioned Moroccan Sufi scholar Muḥammad ibn Jaʿfar al-Kattānī, describes in his hajj travelogue from 1903–1904 that he and his party went to the mosque straight away upon arriving in Medina to quench the pain of their passions and their burning desire to meet the Prophet (al-Kattānī 2005, 191, n.1; cf. Slight 2015, 251–252). Similarly, the Egyptian travel writer Muḥammad Labīb al-Batanūnī writes about his pilgrimage in 1909 how

10 Yearning in vain as well as crying is also what John Slight and John Willis describe for particularly Indian, Sufi and Shīʿite pilgrims travelling to Mecca in the wake of its Wahhābization (Willis 2017, 359–362, 363–364; Slight 2015, 236, 251–252). cf. Peters on Eldon Rutter's observations in the Hijaz in 1925 (Peters 1994, 358–359).

he and his travel companions stretched their necks at the first sight of the minarets of Medina, filling the heart, body, and soul with joy, pleasure, and excitement (al-Batanūnī n.d., 300). For centuries, pilgrims had been able to satisfy this type of yearning. Because of Ibn Saʿūd's Wahhābī governance of the Hijaz in the mid-1920s and 1930 and his prohibitions on certain practices, the desire of pilgrims who wished to touch the Prophet's grave (as well as visit other sacred sites) remained at least partly unfulfilled.

In addition to lamenting this new situation, al-Rāʿī seeks to defend the banned practices and pleads for the preservation of the closed or demolished sites. He argues that Islamic antiquities and graves should be adorned with precious stones and that impressive buildings should be erected around them. This would remind the pilgrims of their great past and make them emulate the Prophet Muhammad and his companions—similar to the way Europeans erect grand memorials for their heroes (al-Rāʿī n.d., 71). In this way, al-Rāʿī writes, these antiquities would instil Muslims with zeal and lead to future progress and civilisation. According to him, such a reverence for Islamic antiquities is not a matter of unlawful worship. These structures are not erected and revered for the purpose of worship, but as lawful 'markers of civilization'. Given this symbolic and commemorative function, al-Rāʿī also writes that touching and rubbing these antiquities or graves is not strictly necessary, because there are sufficient blessings emulating from the great men and women being commemorated (ibid., 68–72). Yet, he also explicitly states that he does not see *kufr* or hypocrisy in this practice, and he expresses a desire to do so himself on occasions. Similarly, in response to the soldiers preventing him and others from touching the grave of the Prophet, he writes that no Egyptian would think that the Prophet or saints are divine, yet their body is still full of *baraka* (ibid., 68–72, 99, 121–123, 170; cf. Slight 2015, 247). Moreover, in a final call to the Saʿūdi government, he asks it not to deviate too far from the religious opinions of the masses and to heed the preservation of Islamic antiquities (al-Rāʿī n.d., 156).

Besides triggering feelings of shock and unfulfilled yearning, Ibn Saʿūd's governance also invoked a sense of contentment at the level of progress as well as a sense of safety for many pilgrims travelling in the late 1920s and 1930s—even though there was the risk of heavy physical punishment for transgressing the new religious rules.[11] For example, al-Rāʿī was very pleased that people who were late for morning prayer were punished under the new Saʿūdi regime. Al-

11 Colonial authorities reported a similarly positive evaluation of Ibn Saʿūd's reign in the Hijaz by colonial authorities. The British, for example, extensively praised the improvement in justice, physical safety and health, although they also worried about the Wahhābī

Rāʿī considers this harsh, but also just. It is in the public interest, he writes, as prayer prevents crime (referring to a Qurʾanic text) and also kills bacteria (because of the required ritual cleansing beforehand). With admiration, he writes that there is no theft even when owners abandon their shops at the time of prayer (ibid., 75–76). Similarly, al-Rāʿī is very pleased with the improved traffic safety in Medina as compared to an earlier visit (ibid., 202). He calls upon Muslims from all over the world to support the development of Mecca even further, for example by funding newly paved streets (ibid., 155, cf. ibid., 111, 113, 118, 156).

Al-Rāʿī thus combines two types of sentiments in his travelogue. His ambivalent appreciation of the Saʿūdi regime and its reforms seems to fit a branch of modernist Sufism he might have been sympathetic to. The press that published his travelogue was connected to the ʿAzamiyya, a Sufi order established in 1915 by Muḥammad Māḍī Abū al-ʿAzāʾim, who became very critical of both Wahhābism and Salafism in the course of the twentieth century. Similar to al-Rāʿī in this travelogue, this order combined an appreciation of modern reform with a renewal of (popular) Sufi practices, for example by introducing discourses of rationality, order, and discipline into Egyptian celebrations at the *mawlid*s for saints (Schielke 2006, 132–133; see also Luizard 1991, 31).

Al-Rāʿī was not the only pilgrim who positively reported on Ibn Saʿūd's orderly governance of the Hijaz. Several other Arab pilgrims, such as journalist Muḥyi al-Dīn Riḍā in 1935 and legal officer Ibrāhīm Muḥammad Ḥabīb in 1938, were similarly content with the progress, revival (*nahḍa*), and reforms (*iṣlāḥ*) made by the renewer (*mujaddid*) Ibn Saʿūd and other government officials in the realms of public health, justice, organization (*niẓām*), physical safety, and morality. Some of this praise went hand in hand with a defence of Ibn Saʿūd's religious reforms (Ḥabīb 2014, 21–22; Riḍā 1353 AH/1935, 33–34, 43–61, 92–95). Ibn Saʿūd himself also actively sought to portray his government as one furthering safety and progress. He invited pilgrims to see for themselves and report back positively in their hajj accounts (Slight 2015, 232–237).

This assessment of progress and successful reforms presented a break from the way the governance of the Hijaz was often evaluated at the end of the nineteenth and beginning of the twentieth century. Many pre-Saʿūdi reform-minded Arabic travelogues complained that the Hijaz under the *sharīf*s was in great need of reform. For example, Muḥammad Labīb al-Batanūnī laments

religious interventions in Mecca and Medina as well as the harsh punishments (Chiffoleau 2015, 316–321; Slight 2015, 228–243).

the inadequate schools, libraries and hospitals in 1909 and is disgusted by the unsanitary practices of his fellow pilgrims (al-Batanūnī n.d., 132–140; see also Kateman 2020).[12]

In particular, several pilgrims at the end of the nineteenth and beginning of the twentieth century report that they deeply feared the hardship and danger of the journey in the interior of the Arabian Peninsula—especially the attacks made by Bedouin tribes along the strenuous route to Medina (al-ʿAmrānī 2010, 187; al-Kattānī 2005, 189–191, n.2; cf. Peters 1994, 281–282, 298–300). For the conservative journalist Aḥmad ʿAlī al-Shādhilī in 1904, the lack of physical safety in the Sharīf-governed Hijaz was actually the main reason to write his travelogue, according to his introduction (al-Shādhilī 1322 AH, 2–5). The Moroccan pilgrim Muḥammad al-Zamzamī al-Kattānī, who travelled with his father Muḥammad ibn Jaʿfar al-Kattānī in 1903–1904 and whose diary notes are quoted in the published edition of his father's travelogue, also reports the great fear he felt on his way to Medina. He relates how one of the Moroccan pilgrims was accused of killing a local camel driver. The camel driver's tribe then came to the Moroccan pilgrims' camp demanding compensation from his father who represented the group of Moroccans. Even though al-Kattānī and his group denied any involvement, they were left to choose between handing over the murderer, paying blood money, or all be considered free game on their way to Medina. In the end they paid, but felt great fear that these 'ferocious barbarians' (*al-wuḥūsh al-ḍārīya*) would not keep their word (al-Kattānī 2005, 189–191, n.2).

It is clear that Muḥammad al-Zamzamī al-Kattānī found this emotional moment worth describing in quite some detail. His father, however, did not say a word about this undoubtedly scary experience in his account. On the contrary, Muḥammad bin Jaʿfar al-Kattānī praised the conditions of the road, the sufficient amount of food, the honest governance of the hajj, and the lack of diseases in 1903–1904, considering them *karāmāt* (miracles, favours) from God (al-Kattānī 2005, 186–187). Similarly positive, the Egyptian poet and translator ʿAbd al-ʿAzīz Ṣabrī actually lauded the developments in public health and science (which he called a *nahḍa*, or 'renaissance') in his travelogue dedicated to Sharīf Ḥusayn in 1923–1924 (Ṣabrī 1342 AH, 193–215). Perhaps coloured by an allegiance to the Sharīf or a desire to emphasise the blessed nature of the experience, the sanitary conditions and safety under the administration of the Sharīf were not articulated negatively in these hajj travelogues.

---

12 One might also think of the visual 'staging' of the backwardness of the Meccan nobility (as an anti-image of his own progressiveness) by the Egyptian hajj-commander Ibrāhīm Rifʿāt Pasha in his photos, as analysed by Stephen Sheehi 2016, 177–179.

4 Conclusion. Tuning the Emotions: Change and Continuity

This chapter explored Arabic pilgrims' hajj experiences and emotions in the first half of the twentieth century, linking these to central events of that time that had a transformative effect on the hajj and its journey. These changes did not have a uniform or univocal effect on pilgrims' experiences and emotions. Some experienced the quarantine as humiliating and upsetting, especially because it was being governed by non-Muslims. Others saw it as a symbol of order and hygiene, something that at times invoked pride while at other moments patience was prescribed—even if it was not easy. Pilgrims often appreciated the safety and ease of the steam journey, but the new means of travelling also presented pilgrims with new challenges. Similarly, the reforms Ibn Saʿūd introduced were met with feelings of shock and sadness, but also of contentment and safety—sometimes at the same time.

Nevertheless, this chapter does not go as far as Nile Green, who, in his article 'The hajj as its own undoing' concludes that:

> the *hajj*'s integration into the new geography of steam rendered it, paradoxically but axiomatically, a journey among infidels. Far from placing the Ka'ba at the centre of a ritualized universe, through the spaces of industrial transport the *hajj* introduced hundreds of thousands of ordinary pilgrims to a world system in which Islam and Muslims were evidently marginal.
>
> GREEN 2015, 224

For Muḥammad bin Jaʿfar al-Kattānī, as we have seen, the new possibilities for going on hajj by way of steam transportation actually renewed the obligation of the hajj for Moroccan pilgrims.

The hajj experience in an age of steam was not completely renewed, however. In many of the travelogues analysed for this chapter, the pilgrims also relate their reflections and feelings in a similar manner to earlier travelogues, for example their stories about the experience of standing at the plain of ʿArafa or seeing Medina or the Kaʿba for the first time. The Egyptian travel writer al-Batanūnī describes his encounter with the Kaʿba in a particularly sensorial and emotional passage:

> The whole assembly stood there in the greatest reverence before this highest majesty and most powerful inspirer of awe before which the greatest souls become so little as to be almost nothing. And if we had not been witness of the movements of the body during the salat and the rais-

> ing of the hands during the prayers, and the murmuring of the expressions of humility and if we had not heard the beatings of the hearts before the immeasurable grandeur we would have thought ourselves transferred to another life. And truly we were at that hour in another world: we were in the house of God and in God's immediate presence, and with us were only the lowered head and the humble tongue and the voices raised in prayer and weeping eyes and the fearful heart and pure thoughts of intercession.
>
> AL-BATANŪNĪ n.d., 103, in the translation of Wensinck 1993, 588[13]

In fairly similar terms, but much less elaborately, the Moroccan jurist al-ʿAmrānī, travelling in 1904 in the entourage of his Sufi shaykh, reports feelings of humility and insignificance and a sense of submission at the sight of the Kaʿba. He also describes how people started crying and uttering prayers of supplication (al-ʿAmrānī 2010, 228).

Centuries of hajj travelogues and other textual and visual forms of hajj representations had prepared pilgrims such as al-Batanūnī and al-ʿAmrānī for what to feel and how to express these feelings when encountering these much-anticipated parts of the hajj ritual. In turn, these travelogues repeat what to experience and feel. These travelogues might be considered part of a tradition in which the pilgrims' senses are tuned: they are prepared for feeling specific emotions and sensations (at times also by *not* displaying certain types of emotions that did not fit this emotional regime), as conceptualized in Birgit Meyer's analysis of religions' 'making of awe'.

In addition to informing prospective pilgrims what to think and feel when going on hajj, these travelogues also specifically prepared readers for what to expect of the hajj in the new world of the first half of the twentieth century. These new contexts required new ways of tuning the pilgrims' emotions and senses, as there was no century-old tradition of travelogues and other media in place to shape the pilgrims' experiences in a similar way as there were to prepare pilgrims for certain emotions and thoughts when standing at the plain of ʿArafa or seeing Medina or the Kaʿba for the first time. This might be part of the reason why the assessments and feelings experienced with regard to international and domestic politics and the effects thereof defy uniformity. New contexts invite a new round of tuning the emotions, with various and sometimes ambiguous results—this observation probably applies not only to modern times.

13 See also al-Batanūnī n.d., 176 for a fascinating description of pilgrims in fearful awe.

As much as new contexts had an impact on aspects of the journey and the pilgrim's stay in Mecca and Medina (including ritual aspects, such as the visitation of the Prophet's grave), centuries-old modes of experiencing may have also impacted the experience of these new contexts. For example, al-Rāʿī articulated the age-old trope of yearning in a slightly new way under Ibn Saʿūd's rule. He expressed a great desire to visit the Prophet's grave—as well as other graves and sites connected to figures and events in Islam's sacred history. But where this type of yearning used to be quenched during the hajj journey, al-Rāʿī's desire could not be fulfilled under the new regime, or at least not completely, which only intensified and elongated his desire. Similarly, al-Rāʿī's use of the term *ṣabr* (patience) when calling Muslims to endure quarantine patiently and heroically may indicate a continuation and re-application of older Islamic emotional rules to new contexts (also see Buitelaar and Kadrouch-Outmany in this volume). His travelogue is an example of how some pilgrims articulated their experience of the new through existing tunes in their travelogues, for which they had been prepared over and over, in travelogues, stories, and other hajj accounts. It was one of the ways in which Arabic pilgrims travelling from and through Egypt experienced new contexts of the hajj in the first half of the twentieth century.

References

al-ʿAmrānī, ʿAbd al-Salām ibn Muḥammad al-Muʿṭī. 2010. *al-Luʾluʾa al-fāshīya fī al-riḥla al-ḥijāzīya. Wa hiya waqāʾiʿ riḥla ḥajj al-imām Abī al-Fayḍ Muḥammad bin ʿAbd al-Kabīr al-Kattānī ʿām 1321 hijrīyya*, edited by Nūr al-Hudā ʿAbd al-Raḥmān al-Kattānī. al-Dār al-Bayḍāʾ and Bayrūt: Markaz al-Turāth al-Thaqāfī and Dār ibn Ḥazm.

al-Batanūnī, Muḥammad Labīb. n.d. [1911]. *al-Riḥla al-Ḥijāziyya*. al-Qāhira: Maktaba al-Thaqāfa al-Dīniyya.

al-Kattānī, Muḥammad ibn Jaʿfar. 2005. *al-Riḥla al-sāmīya ilā al-Iskandarīya wa-Miṣr wa-al-Ḥijāz wa-al-bilād al-Shāmīya*, edited by Muḥammad Ḥamza ibn ʿAlī al-Kattānī and Muḥammad bin ʿAzzūz. al-Dār al-Bayḍā and Bayrūt: Markaz al-Turāth al-Thaqāfī al-Maghribī and Dār ibn Ḥazm.

al-Rāʿī, Muṣṭafā Muḥammad. n.d. [1932] *Fī al-mamlaka al-rūḥiyya li-al-ʿālam al-islāmī: riḥla ilā al-arḍ al-muqaddasa ʿām 1349 hijriyya/1931 mīlādiyya*. al-Qāhira: Maṭbaʿa al-Madīna al-Munawwara.

Al-Samaany, Nasser. 2000. 'Travel literature of Moroccan pilgrims during the 11–12th/17–18th centuries: Thematic and artistic study.' PhD diss., University of Leeds.

Al-Sarhan, Saud. 2016. 'The Saudis as managers of the hajj.' In *The Hajj. Pilgrimage in*

Islam, edited by Eric Tagliacozzo and Shawkat Toorawa, 196–212. New York: Cambridge University Press.

al-Shādhilī, Aḥmad ʿAlī. 1322 AH [1904]. *al-Riḥla al-wahbiyya ilā al-aqṭār al-Ḥijāziyya*. al-Qāhira: Maṭbaʿa al-Islām.

Bauer, Karen. 2017. 'Emotion in the Qurʾan: An overview.' *Journal of Qurʾanic studies* 19 (2): 1–30.

Bazzaz, Sahar. 2010. *Forgotten saints: History, power, and politics in the making of modern Morocco*. Cambridge, MA: Harvard University Press.

Bazzaz, Sahar. 2008. 'Reading reform beyond the state.' *The Journal of North African studies* 13 (1) 1–13.

Chantre, Luc. 2013. 'Entre pandémie et panislamisme: L'imaginaire colonial du pèlerinage à La Mecque (1866–1914).' *Archives de sciences sociales des religions* (163): 163–190.

Chiffoleau, Sylvia. 2015. *Le Voyage à La Mecque*. Paris: Belin.

El-Sayed, Laila Hashem Abdel-Rahman. 2016. 'Discourses on emotions: Communities, styles, and selves in early modern Mediterranean travel books: Three case studies.' PhD diss., University of Kent and Freie Universität Berlin. https://kar.kent.ac.uk/56635/, accessed October 20, 2020.

Gade, Anna. 2007. 'Islam.' In *The Oxford handbook of religion and emotion*, edited by John Corrigan, 35–50. Oxford: Oxford University Press.

Gelvin, James, and Nile Green, eds. 2014. *Global Muslims in the age of steam and print*. Berkeley: University of California Press.

Green, Nile. 2015. 'The hajj as its own undoing: Infrastructure and integration on the Muslim journey to Mecca.' *Past & present* 226 (1): 193–226.

Ḥabīb, Ibrāhīm Muḥammad. 2014. *Riḥla fī al-arḍ al-muqaddasa (bayna Miṣr wa-l-Ḥijāz) 1356 Hijrīyya /1938 Mīlādīya*, edited by Fāʾiz al-Ruwaylī. Bayrūt: al-Dār al-ʿArabiyya li-al-Mawsūʿāt.

Hendrickson, Jocelyn. 2016. 'Prohibiting the pilgrimage: Pilgrimage and fiction in Mālikī Fatwās.' *Islamic law and society* 23: 161–238.

Huber, Valeska. 2016. 'International bodies: The pilgrimage to Mecca and international health regulations.' In *The hajj. Pilgrimage in Islam*, edited by Eric Tagliacozzo and Shawkat Toorawa, 175–195. New York: Cambridge University Press.

Kateman, Ammeke. 2020. 'Fashioning the materiality of the pilgrimage: The hajj travelogue of Muḥammad Labīb al-Batanūnī.' *Die Welt Des Islams* 60 (4): 384–407.

Low, Michael. 2008. 'Empire and the hajj: Pilgrims, plagues, and pan-Islam under British surveillance, 1865–1908.' *International journal of Middle East studies* 40 (2): 269–290.

Luizard, Pierre-Jean. 1991. 'Le rôle des confréries soufies dans le système politique égyptien.' *Monde arabe* (131): 26–53.

Macdonald, Duncan Black. 1909. *The religious attitude and life in Islam*. Chicago: University of Chicago press.

Matt, Susan. 2014. 'Recovering the invisible. Methods for the historical study of the emotions.' In *Doing emotions history*, edited by Susan Matt and Peter Stearns, 41–54. Urbana: University of Illinois Press.

Metcalf, Barbara. 1990. 'The pilgrimage remembered: South Asian accounts of the hajj.' In *Muslim travellers: Pilgrimage, migration and the religious imagination*, edited by Dale Eickelman and James Piscatori, 85–109. London: Routledge.

Meyer, Birgit. 2016. 'How to capture the 'wow': R.R. Marett's notion of awe and the study of religion.' *Journal of the royal anthropological institute* (*N.S.*) 22 (1): 7–26.

Meyer, Birgit. 2008. 'Media and the senses in the making of religious experience: An introduction.' *Material religion* 4 (2): 124–134.

Munson jr., Henry. 1993. *Religion and power in Morocco*. New Haven: Yale University Press.

Pernau, Margrit. 2014. 'Civility and barbarism: Emotions as criteria of difference.' In *Emotional lexicons: Continuity and change in the vocabulary of feeling 1700–2000*, edited by Ute Frevert, 230–259. Oxford: Oxford University Press.

Peters, Francis Edward. 1994. *The hajj: The Muslim pilgrimage to Mecca and the holy places*. Princeton: Princeton University Press.

Reynolds, Dwight, ed. 2001. *Interpreting the self: Autobiography in the Arabic literary tradition*. Berkeley: University of California Press.

Riḍā, Muḥyi al-Dīn. 1353 AH/1935. *Riḥlatī ilā al-ḥijāz*. Miṣr: Maṭbaʿa al-Manār.

Robinson, Mike, and David Picard. 2016 [2012]. *Emotion in motion: Tourism, affect and transformation*. London and New York: Routledge.

Roff, William. 1982. 'Sanitation and security. The imperial powers and the nineteenth century hajj.' *Arabian studies* 4: 143–160.

Rosenwein, Barbara. 2010. 'Problems and methods in the history of emotions.' *Passions in context: Journal of the history and philosophy of the emotions* 1 (1). https://www.passionsincontext.de/index.php/?id=557, accessed October, 19 2020.

Ṣabrī, ʿAbd al-ʿAzīz. 1342 AH [1923]. *Tidhkār al-Ḥijāz; khaṭarāt wa-mushāhadāt fī al-ḥajj*. al-Qāhira: al-Maṭbaʿa al-Salafīya.

Schielke, Samuli. 2006. 'On snacks and saints: When discourses of rationality and order enter the Egyptian Mawlid.' *Archives de sciences sociales des religions* 51 (135): 117–140. https://doi.org/10.2307/30122873.

Sheehi, Stephen. 2016. *The Arab imago: A social history of portrait photography, 1860–1910*. Princeton: Princeton University Press.

Slight, John. 2015. *The British Empire and the hajj: 1865–1956*. Cambridge, MA: Harvard University Press.

Stratkötter, Rita. 1991. *Von Kairo nach Mekka: Sozial- und Wirtschaftsgeschichte der Pilgerfahrt nach den Berichten des Ibrāhīm Rifʿat Bāšā: Mirʾāt al-Ḥaramain*. Berlin: Schwarz.

Wensinck, Arent Jan. 1993 [1913–1938]. 'Kaʿba.' In *E.J. Brill's First Encyclopaedia of Islam*,

1913–1936, edited by Martijn Theodoor Houtsma, Arent Jan Wensinck, Thomas Walker Arnold, Willi Heffening, and Évariste Lévi-Provençal, 4:584–592. Leiden: Brill.

Willis, John. 2017. 'Governing the living and the dead: Mecca and the emergence of the Saudi biopolitical state.' *The American historical review* 122 (2): 346–370.

CHAPTER 8

Inconveniences of the Hajj: The Arduous Journey of a Moroccan Shaykh in 1929

Richard van Leeuwen

Since for Muslims the hajj is probably the most momentous religious experience of their lives, not only because it is often a unique life-event, but also because no other ritual will bring them closer to God and the Muslim community, one would expect narratives relating this experience to be highly stylized and idealized. It is first of all an exalting experience, confirming membership within a community and a tradition, and the environment would expect reports to reflect the sacredness and exaltation of the event overwhelming the pilgrim. The strength of emotions, the aesthetic qualities of the site, and the physical awareness of spirituality should result in an account that is inspired and moulded, through its form and its content, to express and evoke emotions and an aesthetic response in audiences, and most of all, such stories should convey a sense of common jubilation celebrating the shared faith of the narrator and their audiences.

The conventions of written hajj accounts reflects the desire to represent the pilgrimage as the ultimate religious experience. Still, it is remarkable that during the gradual development of this tradition pilgrims have never shunned from mentioning negative aspects of their journey, referring to both the difficulties encountered on the way and the inconveniences experienced in the Holy Land itself. Although idealized accounts existed, the tradition as a whole is certainly not shaped only by the wish to conform the narrative to some ideal model, editing away experiences that would spoil the positive qualities either of the form or the content. Most accounts from the twelfth century until the present day contain a prominent personal element that situates them in a specific spatio-temporal frame and relates them to specific personal experiences, thereby stressing their authenticity and credibility. Apparently, for most pilgrims, it was more important to share a sense of personal involvement than to present an objectified idea of a common practice.

It should be kept in mind that the conveying of experiences, especially emotions, in writing is always subject to forms of mediation derived from generic and narrative conventions. These conventions may predispose readers to expect certain emotions described in specific ways after the model of predecessors' texts or aesthetic rules. It can be argued that mediation through objectification by editing, stylizing, copying, quoting, changing registers or genres, is much more relevant for positive experiences than for negative ones. After all, acknowledging that one does not feel elated by the first view of the Kaʿba would really spoil the account and even throw doubt on the sincerity of the pilgrim's faith. The room to transgress genre conventions is very small: Muslim audiences have come to expect that travelogues echo previous responses of trustworthy predecessors, possibly through quotations or by mimicking their idealized representation. There is no such requirement in the case of complaints or negative experiences, because there is no convention to be followed; negative experiences are by definition individual and are much more difficult to relate to a common sense of spiritual bliss. Although they are inevitably mediated by the narrative medium, they are potentially a more authentic reflection of an individual experience, deconstructing the idealized image and contributing to a sense of realism.

The extent of strategies applied by authors to idealize their account can be related to differences in form. An account composed in verse is more likely to contain standard tropes, images, and expressions than, for instance, day-to-day journals. Highly stylized poetic accounts are found more often in Persian and Turkish traditions, subjecting content to form and avoiding realistic, subjective elements (Alam and Subrahmanyam 2007, 24 ff.; Coşkun 1999). However, poetic form does not preclude negative elements. An interesting example is a long poem by al-Muṣʿabī, an ʿIbāḍī shaykh from the Algerian desert, who went on hajj in 1781, and who adds a few lines in prose to complain about the treatment he underwent by the governor of Cairo—clearly an 'unpoetic' event—, but does not refrain from spending five verses of his poem to fiercely criticize the unhygienic behaviour of some pilgrims ('peasants'), who even urinate inside the Grand Mosque—clearly an 'unpoetic' element, too (al-Muṣ ʿabī 2006, 62, 74, 79, 84). This irritation would probably have been experienced by the audience (listeners?) as a breach of generic conventions much more than the readers of the pilgrim's diary of the Moroccan scholar al-ʿAbdarī, who travelled to Mecca in 1289, and who complains about the fighting among pilgrims to reach the Black Stone, even hurting women; pilgrims cooking inside mosques, charring the walls and casting away garbage; and pilgrims letting their donkeys graze in historical graveyards (al-ʿAbdarī 1968, 175–177).

The negative experiences related by al-ʿAbdarī and al-Muṣʿabī affect the spiritual experience and the impression they convey to their audience, by apparently integrating a genuine feeling of irritation. Although this does not endorse an image of sacredness, nor an idealized image of the hajj, it can be argued that it was meant as a strategy to convey a positive individual attitude. The authors perhaps wanted to show that they upheld certain standards of propriety and cleanliness, which attests to a level of civilization that is suited for the elevated events they are experiencing and that cannot be affected by trivial, worldly circumstances. Inconveniences and annoyances may also enhance the spiritual merits of the pilgrimage, as in the case of the Moroccan Ibn Ṭayyib al-Sharqī (hajj in 1727), who at ʿArafa was robbed of his tent, his donkey, his money, his clothes, and his shoes. He had to return to Mecca barefooted, but still remarked that God should be thanked in both good fortune and adversity (al-Sharqī 2014, 384–385). Apparently, negative elements can add a level to the account which enriches the experience it conveys and thus become a conscious narrative strategy.

In this chapter, I will discuss a hajj account by a Moroccan pilgrim from 1929, which appears to disclose the vicissitudes and inconveniences of the hajj in a remarkably authentic way. The text has the form of a diary and has no literary pretensions; it seems to be an honest, detailed journal of the pilgrim experience meant to convey an authentic, unadorned picture of the journey, not written by an important or self-important scholar or official, but by an unpretentious Sufi shaykh from the Rif, interested in telling his story rather than adapting his report to a preconceived image. Sīdī Muḥammad al-Tawzānī al-Miḍārī, known as Sīdī al-Ḥājj Muḥammad (1883–1943), had studied in the Qarawiyyīn mosque in Fes and acted as a religious scholar in Nador and Hoceima in the Moroccan Rif, which was governed by the Spanish at the time (al-Miḍārī 1997, 3). The text was probably not written to reach a wide audience, but intended for his family and a small circle fellow-Sufis, since it does not seem to have been widely distributed at the time and only a single copy of the manuscript has been preserved.

1 The Political Context

Before we proceed with a discussion of Muḥammad's text, it is convenient to briefly outline the political situation at the time of his journey. In 1929, Morocco was administratively divided among two colonial powers. The French had established a mandate administration in most parts of Morocco in 1912, while the Spanish controlled the northern parts—the Rif and the towns of Melilla, Ceuta, and Tangier.[1] Colonial rule had important consequences for the annual undertaking of the hajj. First, the traditional overland route through North

1 For the historical circumstances in Morocco, see Pennell 2003.

Africa and the Sahara to the Hijaz was now completely under the domination of the Western colonial powers: Spain, France, Italy and Great Britain. Second, the colonial administration implemented a system of regulations, including passports, visa, permissions, and health regulations by which they gradually took control of pilgrimage traffic. During World War I, they initially prevented pilgrims from travelling to Mecca, as they were unable to guarantee their safety. In 1916, however, after Sharīf Ḥusayn of the Hijaz had revolted against the Ottoman government, the French and British authorities (later followed by the Spanish and Italians) organized a much-advertised hajj expedition for a selected group of pilgrims on a sumptuous ship and surrounded by French and British protocols, in order to express their support for the Arabian leader and Muslims more generally. It was surely the only occasion in history that the 'Marseillaise' and 'God save the king' were played during the *wuqūf* at ʿArafa (Tresse 1937, 62).

Another consequence of the colonial administration of North Africa and the transformations it incurred was the rapid deployment of new systems of transportation, through the construction of railroads and the introduction of steamships, automobiles, and buses. Already over the course of the nineteenth century, steam traffic in the Mediterranean had made the annual caravans through the desert virtually obsolete, especially after the opening of the Suez Canal in 1869. Obviously, travel by ship from Casablanca or Tangier was more comfortable than jolting on camels and it greatly reduced the duration of the journey, but it was also rather expensive. That is probably the reason why our traveller preferred to travel by land to Tunis and take a 'very old' ship from there (al-Miḍārī 1997, 42). The background of colonial rule is conveyed by descriptions of French visa requirements, the border at Oujda, and the presence of the French and English soldiers in the ports of Oran and Port Said respectively (ibid., 22–23, 43, 121).

In the meantime, the situation in the Hijaz was changing rapidly.[2] During World War I, Sharīf Ḥusayn declared his independence from the Ottoman Empire in 1916, and in the aftermath of the revolt he became entangled in a struggle for power with his local rival ʿAbd al-ʿAzīz ibn al-Saʿūd. The latter declared himself king of Najd and in 1924 succeeded in defeating Ḥusayn and establishing his own rule in the Hijaz. This change in government set in motion a process of reform and modernization that greatly affected the practical and religious aspects of the hajj. Motorized transport was extended, health

2 For a concise survey of developments on the Arabian Peninsula in this period, see al-Rasheed 2002.

conditions were gradually improved, levies were abolished, and the danger of Bedouin raids was neutralized. Apart from these measures, the actual rites of the hajj and associated practices, such as *ziyāra* or visitation to the grave tomb of the Prophet Muhammad and other important early role models in Islamic history were subjected to a new, strict regime, inspired by the doctrines of the eighteenth-century reformer Muḥammad ibn ʿAbd al-Wahhāb.[3] The conspicuous monuments of sacred history, especially the tombs of the Prophet's family, were razed to the ground and certain expressions of piety at graves and monuments, such as touching and weeping, were discouraged or forbidden. For Moroccan pilgrims, with their tradition of Sufism and the veneration of saints, these reforms were often difficult to accept.

These circumstances, relating to a process of far-reaching transformation and the spread of modernity, were not merely a diffuse background of Sīdī Muḥammad's pilgrimage; they decisively shaped the experience of the journey, since they affected both the logistic and the religious components of the hajj.

2 The Journey

In 1929 the time of the great caravans from the Maghreb to Cairo through the North African desert was past, and the trajectory of Sīdī Muḥammad's journey shows how modern means of transport began to be organized. The group of travellers consisted of seven pilgrims, Maymūn, ʿAbd al-Razzāq, Muḥammad, Aḥmad, ʿĪsā, Muhannad, and the narrator, Sīdi Muḥammad (here not yet called al-Hājj) (ibid., 16, 24, 28, 104). Maymūn and Sīdī Muḥammad belonged to the followers of the Sufi Shaykh Ibrahīm al-Būdālī who was popular in the region and who founded a branch of the Darqawiyya-Shādhiliyya order in Mascara, Algeria. As was customary at the time, the days before departure are spent buying provisions for the journey and food for the many gatherings held to say farewell to the pilgrims. In Midar, the imam of the village and the disciples of the village shaykh accompany the group in the rain to the *zāwiya* (Sufi lodge), which is filled with 'brothers and sisters'. They travel first by taxi to Nador, where they meet with other Sufis from the region and then by taxi to Melilla to buy provisions and later to Zaïo and Oujda at the Algerian border to say goodbye to Sufi friends and to arrange visas from the Spanish and French authorities. They

3 For the history of the Wahhābī movement, see Mouline 2011; the best and most concise discussion of the reform measures after the takeover of ʿAbd al-ʿAziz ibn Saʿud can be found in Willis 2017.

try in vain to find out the departure schedule of the trains, so they decide to travel to Oran by car and bus instead (ibid., 18–22).

From Oran the group travels by train to Mascara to visit the *zāwiya* of the son of the famous Sufi master (*quṭb*),[4] Shaykh al-Būdālī. However, when they call the *zāwiya* by telephone, they are informed that the shaykh is not present, because he went to visit his sick son. They then decide to continue their journey to Saida, hoping to meet the shaykh there. They negotiate with the train conductor so as not to pay an extra fare. However, in Saida, the *zāwiya* appears to be deserted, so they spend the night in a hammam (a public bath). Afterwards, on horses and mules, through rain and mud, they ascend a mountain to a remote *zāwiya* of the Būdāliyya order in Takhmirt, where they wash their clothes that are stained by the smoke of the train. Here they meet with their shaykh, the son of Ibrahim al-Būdālī, whom Sīdī Muḥammad has previously met during a *khalwa* (or meditative seclusion of sixty days). Subsequently, they journey to Mascara to visit the *zāwiya* and the mausoleum of Shaykh al-Būdālī. The leader of the Sufi community there, 'the great ecstatic knower of God Sufi Muḥammad al-Qadarī' (*al-faqīr al-majdhūb* and *al-ʿārif bi-Allāh*), a disciple of Shaykh al-Būdālī, assigns roles to each of the travellers: Maymūn will have the authority to take decisions; ʿĪsā and Jalūl[5] have to be silent; ʿAbd al-Razzāq is responsible for the finances; Aḥmad will be the tea-server; Sīdī Muḥammad will be the imam, and the other two will be 'donkeys' carrying the luggage (ibid., 28). The group returns to Oran by bus, which is so crowded that people sit on the roof, and take the train to Tunis via Algiers. The narrator complains about the train to Algiers, which is full of mice and shakes so heavily that they are unable to boil water for tea. After a 39-hour train ride, they arrive in Tunis, where they stay in a hotel owned by the captain of the ship, who will take them to Jedda, together with a group of fellow-pilgrims (ibid., 34–39).

The extensive regional tour as a preparation for the actual journey to Mecca was a long-standing tradition in Morocco. It shows especially how the hajj was connected with the networks of Sufi communities in the region; and was taken as an opportunity to strengthen social and religious bonds between them. An element of authority was involved, too, since the pilgrims had to receive both the permission for their journey from their shaykh and the blessing of other brothers. Moreover, the visiting of sacred places, such as *zāwiya*s and saints' tombs, was an integrate part of the journey, affirming its sacred nature. This religious preoccupation is maintained throughout the journey. In Tunis, the

4 *Quṭb* literally means 'pole' and is an honorific title for a Sufi master with great spiritual authority.

5 Jalūl is not mentioned in the remainder of the account.

travellers take the time to delve into the religious institutions as well, visiting scholars, schools and libraries, and a graveyard where 3,066 holy men lie buried. They inspect the teaching methods of the Zaytūna *madrasa*, the salary of professors, and the subjects that were taught, as compared to Fes. They remark that both the pupils and the teachers shave their heads and indulge in smoking, saying that this habit costs no more than 11/2 francs a day. This clearly frustrates the author, who is against permitting the use of tobacco (ibid., 34–39).

From Tunis they board a 'very old' ship, praying and pronouncing the appropriate formulae—Qur'anic verses and hadiths before sailing—for safety and protection. Nevertheless, they become seasick on the journey and the boat is also forced to stop for repairs. After crossing the Suez Canal, they don the *iḥrām* clothes at the level of the *mīqāt* of Rābigh, saying the *niyya* (the formula is cited in the text), and putting on sandals that have been officially approved by the qadi of Tunis as complying with the prescriptions for the outfit of pilgrims. Arriving in Jedda, Sīdī Muḥammad is relieved that the sea journey has passed reasonably well, apart from seasickness, a storm, and the mattress of a woman that had caught fire and had to be thrown overboard, but which ended up on a lower deck. In Jedda they are met by their *muṭawwif* (pilgrims' guide), who takes care of the customs formalities and their lodgings. They purchase provisions and visit the nearby grave of Eve, which is partly destroyed by the Wahhābī authorities, who especially frown upon the veneration of this particular grave, since its historical credentials are thin. The grave used to be a fixed component of the 'touristic', non-obligatory part of the pilgrims' journey, but they are sent away by a guard (ibid., 42–54).

3 Mecca

Until this point, Muḥammad's travelogue is straightforward and focused on practicalities, giving little space to religious formalities or even religious framing in the form of hadiths, prayers, or Qur'anic verses. Still, the text is steeped in religious connotations, which are clearly an integrated part of the narrative. Conventional references to religion are the reciting of the obligatory Sufi litanies and prayers (*ḥizb* and *wird*) each morning (ibid., 26, 105, 122); the prayers, formulae, and hadiths for protection when embarking on a sea journey; and the ceremony of entering the state of *iḥrām* (ibid., 44, 45). In the *zāwiyas* in Morocco and in Mascara, and even on the ship from Tunis, the group attends Sufi ceremonies with entrancing music and dancing (*ḥaḍra; samāʿ*; and *ʿammāra*, an ecstatic ritual continuing the whole night), according to the rites of the Būdāliyya and Raḥmāniyya orders ('only shaking the head') (ibid., 26,

28, 46). They visit the graves of Shaykh al-Būdālī in Mascara, and a place of seclusion (*khalwa*) of the great master Abū al-Ḥasan al-Shādhilī (1196–1258), the founder of the Shādhiliyya order, and the mausoleum of his wife and son (ibid., 37). When the group arrives in Mecca, to emphasize the solemnity of the undertaking, they decide that the fine for speaking trivialities, set by Maymūn at ½ *riyāl*, will be increased to 1 *riyāl* (ibid., 25, 48). There are also references to the juridical aspects of the hajj. During his meetings with other shaykhs on the way, in Algeria and Tunis, the *manāsik al-ḥajj* (the rules for the rituals) are discussed in debating sessions (*mudhākira*). The narrator especially mentions the *Mukhtaṣar* by al-Khalīl, a compendium of Mālikī law that was extremely popular in North and West Africa from the fourteenth century until the present day, and is referred to by many pilgrims. He also mentions the well-known scholars al-Nawawī and Ibn ʿĀshir (ibid., 49). Later on the boat they receive lessons in the rules for the rituals of the hajj, and the *muṭawwif*, too, helps them abide by the rules. He explains to them, that, since they are from the Rif, their *iḥrām* is for the *ḥajj al-ifrād*, that is, a hajj detached from the *ʿumra*, according to Mālikī law, instead of a combined, uninterrupted sequence of ritual acts (ibid., 68). At a certain point, Sīdī Muḥammad feels sufficiently confident to insert a summary of the rules for the hajj. Still, in spite of these preparations, they meet inconvenience from the Saudi authorities, who not only prevent them from visiting the tomb of Eve and entering the cave of the Prophet, but also forbid them to climb Mount ʿArafa at the day of the *wuqūf*, since this is not part of the orthodox ritual (ibid., 662). Sīdī Muḥammad observes that the authorities have also abolished the tradition that four imams, one from each of the legal schools, led the prayer in the Grand Mosque; now only the Ḥanbalī imam is allowed to lead the prayer (ibid., 48).

Of course, these religious references in the text concern only either everyday routine or preparations for the actual religious experience of the hajj. Not surprisingly, the account of the ceremonies in Mecca is the most formalized part of the text. Here poems are added besides prayers, hadiths, and descriptions of the Grand Mosque, which conform to the conventions of hajj accounts. The prayers are supplemented with summaries of the lives of Fāṭima, the daughter of the Prophet Muhammad, and others, as well as lists of the Prophet's sons and spouses (ibid., 89–94). The ceremonies are mentioned without much personal flavour, except the repeated remarks that the group is very tired. They kiss the Black Stone and avoid the crowd as much as possible. After the obligatory ritual acts, they buy camping gear and rent camels to proceed to Minā, where, according to the *muṭawwif*, 2,000 pilgrims die of illness every day. Here the hardships really begin. It starts raining and thundering and many pilgrims faint because of the heat or illness. At ʿArafa and Minā the crowds are enormous and the group falls apart, only reuniting by coincidence the following evening. In spite of the hectic circumstances, our narrator falls asleep on his camel, and bumps against the hump of the camel, losing two teeth. They are exhausted and only succeed to perform the stoning of the devil (*jamra*) with great effort, seated on their camels, which are beaten by soldiers (ibid., 60–71).

To add to the hardships, they inadvertently drink a sweet, yellow liquid, which immediately makes them sick, forcing them to postpone certain rites, such as the *ṭawāf al-ifāḍa* (the circumambulation of the Kaʿba after ʿArafa). They drink large quantities of Zamzam water, known for its healing qualities ('only for true believers, not for hypocrites') (ibid., 65), because they cannot stand normal water, and eat only *ḥarīra*, a rich Moroccan chickpea-tomato soup, and sometimes made with pumpkin, onion, and oil. The narrator is unable to chew bread, because of his missing teeth, but fortunately he is still able to drink tea with the others. The inconveniences do not stop here. The group fails to arrange for a bus to take them to Jedda, and from there to Medina, and therefore they haves to split up. One of Muḥammad's companions—now called al-Ḥājj Muhannad,—decides to travel to Medina on foot. Our narrator has to share a car with some Arabs, which is fortunate, he observes, because they are much more patient, pious and polite than their Berber brothers, who are irascible and have no patience (*ṣabr*), especially in this extreme crowdedness. They arrive in Jedda sick and tired, with hardly any water even for the ailing Aḥmad (ibid., 71–72).

Although transport by automobile, which emerged in the Hijaz in the 1920s, was in principle more comfortable than on camel back, it still had its particular inconveniences. Cars tended to get stuck in the sand or to break down somewhere in the middle of the desert, and the tracks were bumpy and dusty. Although the car carrying al-Ḥājj Muḥammad was checked by a (Christian) mechanic, it still breaks down on the way and the passengers have to wait for hours in the blazing sun to have it repaired. The driver is described as a scoundrel who asks for a *baqshīsh*, and as an 'enemy of God', since he does not perform his prayers and smokes tobacco. Moreover, he drives too closely behind the car preceding them, so that the sand blows into their faces. Because they are feverish and coughing, they wind shawls around their faces, so they are unable to see the road or the landscapes surrounding them. When they protest, the driver, who wears protective goggles, just makes jokes and laughs at them, which infuriates Maymūn, who shouts: 'You will be held accountable before God and His Prophet!' (ibid., 78). Soon afterwards, the car breaks down unexpectedly. At some points the car stops for unknown reasons and they have to wait while the driver exchanges pleasantries with his colleagues. Just as suddenly they depart again, the chauffeur driving so fast that they fear to be thrown out of the car. During all these tribulations, the Arabs remain calm, polite, and full of respect until they arrive in Medina (ibid., 76–78).

At the gate of Medina, they have to wait a whole day before the others arrive; their car has also broken down on the way. The guide (*murshid*) advises them to rent a car to enter the town, because they are too weak to walk, but they insist on going by foot, because this is the place where the Prophet has put his feet (ibid., 83).

The part of al-Ḥājj Muḥammad's journal about the group's stay in Medina is, like the Meccan episode, dominated by references to religion, rules, and prayers for the occasion of the visit to the Prophet's grave. This account was been written later, in Tunis, because, as the author states, in Medina he was too ill to write. Unfortunately, he adds, he failed to copy the Qur'anic verses written on the walls in the Prophet's Mosque, which he had forgotten by then. In the Medinan part, first a eulogy is given for Mālik ibn Anas, the great legal scholar and founder of the law school that is predominant in Morocco, and whose tomb is located in Medina. According to our narrator, Mālik had visions of the Prophet every night; he knew 100,000 hadiths; he was the most distinguished scholar in Medina in his time and mufti of the Ḥaramayn; of all human beings, he was the most beloved by God and most cognizant of the Qur'an during his lifetime (ibid., 83).

Apart from visiting the tomb of Mālik, the highlight of the group's stay in Medina is, of course, the visit (*ziyāra*) to the Prophet's Mosque and his grave. Here, the pilgrims are again confronted with the strictness of the new Wahhābī authorities. After they have been sent away from the grave of Eve in Jedda and the cave of the Prophet near Mecca, which, according to the new doctrines, were potential sites of unlawful veneration and polytheism (*shirk*), they are now prevented by guards from touching the grille of the Prophet's tomb. Still, they are allowed to visit the graves of the family of the Prophet in al-Baqīʿ, the cemetery, and the tomb of the martyr Ḥamza at Uḥud. Due to the oppressive heat and general illness, the group is unable to visit other sites. Al-Ḥājj Muḥammad supplements his account with prayers and formulae dedicated to the many religious and historical figures buried in Medina, including the Prophet, cited from well-known religious and historical texts (ibid., 83–99).

FIGURE 8.1 Picture of the Sanctuary of Medina the Radiant (c. 1907)
PHOTOGRAPHER: H.A. MIRZA & SONS [4R] (1/1), BRITISH LIBRARY: VISUAL ARTS, PHOTO 174/4, IN *QATAR DIGITAL LIBRARY* HTTPS://WWW.QDL.QA/ARCHIVE/81055/VDC_100023483748.0X000013 [ACCESSED 18 APRIL 2022].

4 Practical Concerns: Food

Among the remarkable features of the travelogue summarized above, is its strong emphasis on the material aspects of the hajj and how it combines the physical and spiritual aspects of the undertaking. A clear sign and solid anchoring of this materiality in the narrative is the author's preoccupation with food, to such an extent that a discussion of the text would not be complete without referring to it. At several occasions, Sīdī Muḥammad carefully registers the victuals purchased by the group, either as provisions for the journey or to be consumed by the group on the way or with brothers in the *zāwiya*s. In Melilla, before their departure, the group buys butteroil, olive oil, and dried couscous, and enjoys a dinner of meat and green beans (ibid., 19–21). In Oran a brother of the ʿAlīwa order serves them a meal of string beans and fish (ibid., 21, 23). In Saida, during their meeting with members of the Būdāliyya order, they are treated on *muḥammiṣa*, a pasta with chickpeas and vegetables, with bread and meat, two tagines with meat, and couscous with meat, a 'vegetable dish they call "salad" with vinegar,' and, finally, *lisān burtaqāl* (ibid., 24–25). They are also served skewers with meat. Later they have a more frugal breakfast made up of bread, butteroil, and tea. Also on the way, they regularly consume a simple meal consisting of butteroil, olives and bread (ibid., 21).

For the journey, the first commodity purchased in Oujda is tea (because 'in the east there is no good tea available'), which is later supplemented with butteroil, olives, couscous, flour, and spices (ibid., 30, 105, 107). They carry with them a primus enabling them to boil water in less than ten minutes, apparently to be used in the train (ibid., 31). Since later they have to collect wood to make a fire for boiling water, the primus was apparently dispensed of on the way (maybe because of a lack of petroleum). On the boat they have difficulty eating because of their seasickness. Food is available, but rather expensive, so when they halt in Port Said they buy and prepare Egyptian cucumbers with meat (ibid., 43). After arriving in Jedda, they buy a stock of victuals consisting especially of sugar and tea, although they have brought tea from Oujda and Oran in tins (ibid., 48–57). The narrator remarks that they drink tea three times a day and usually have one or two guests at every meal (ibid., 49). Their breakfast consists of honey, butter, and eggs mixed with jerked meat (ibid., 122). In Mecca they eat bread with honey, bread and beans, and fava beans with tomatoes. However, everything changes when they become ill after drinking lemonade: al-Ḥājj Muḥammad only consumes tea, Zamzam water, *ḥarīra* soup, and sometimes pumpkin with onion and olive oil. Again, he does not take bread, because he is unable to chew it, probably because of his missing teeth.

In Medina al-Ḥājj Muḥammad buys baked liver with bread and two thermos water containers (ibid., 103). On the way back they seem to be feeling somewhat better, because they buy meat and rice, and fried fish (ibid., 105). They still have tea left from Oujda and Oran. In Rābigh, on the return journey, some of them are unable to take in food and only chew a piece of melon, while the others feast on fried fish. In Jedda, they are reunited with Muhannad, who had gone to Medina on foot, and who is so exhausted and ill that he is unable to eat anything (ibid., 71, 77, 106). They prepare sour *ḥarīra* boiled in the morning, like they did in Mecca when they were ill. Fortunately, Maymūn, who is ill, has spices, which they use to have in the *zāwiya*. For themselves, they prepare meat with spaghetti with or without milk and a bit too many lentils, which causes some inconvenience, along with another dish consisting of meat with bread. Other pilgrims gave them some uncooked, crushed seeds (ibid., 77, 106–107). Al-Ḥājj Muḥammad declares that he enjoyed the tea and meat the most. They drink green tea with sugar and mint in Mecca, Medina, and Jedda, apart from the tea they brought from Morocco, because they do not like the black Medinan tea, and they eat watermelon, of which he remarks: in 'our dialect' *dallāḥ*, one during the day and one in the evening, instead of water (ibid., 107). On the boat they buy potatoes, bread, and onions in Port Said along with two sheep from the captain to make a 'delicious' meal consisting of roasted mutton, boiled potatoes, brain, and eggs (ibid., 110–120). Remarkably, when al-Ḥājj Muḥammad has returned to Midar, he is served a welcome meal at home, which is mentioned without any specifications (ibid., 121–124).

Al-Ḥājj Muḥammad's careful registering of the culinary events of their journey not only suggests that he was a gourmand, enjoying good food and drink, but also that the hajj was basically experienced as a primarily physical journey. The connection between consumption and illness is the basic substratum of almost all the rites and acts performed in the Holy Places, next to other physical inconveniences such as fatigue, dust, accidents, transport, heat, etc. Some of the less crucial components of the hajj have to be omitted or postponed as a result of indispositions partly caused by the consumption of water. Conversely, although it is not made explicit, Zamzam water is at least psychologically adopted as a cure. They even drink it instead of food, as is recommended in popular lore. On the other hand, exhaustion is not taken as an excuse to diminish the physical-religious experience, symbolized by their entering Medina on foot. At other times, they are forced to arrange for transport, for instance a donkey to relieve the poor, sick Maymūn, or camels for the *jamra* (ibid., 95).

Some interesting observations can be made by examining at the narrator's remarks about food. First, it is remarkable that the group takes only minimal provisions for the journey. Tea seems to be the most important commodity that has to be brought from Morocco, since the quality of other teas cannot be relied upon in the Hijaz. Even on the way back, they still have a stack of Moroccan tea. Apparently, the group did not visit many coffeehouses along the pilgrimage routes in the Hijaz; in fact, there is no mention of coffee. Second, the pilgrims clearly preferred to prepare Moroccan dishes as much as possible, according to familiar recipes and with familiar ingredients (and names). Third, the fact that al-Ḥājj Muḥammad elaborates particularly on the more copious meals indicates that there was a pattern of eating quite simple meals of bread, butteroil, and olives. Meat and fish were purchased when they were not too expensive. Fourth, this shows that foodstuffs were mainly bought at the local markets where and when they were available. Finally, meals were preferably shared with others, either with brothers in Morocco or fellow pilgrims. Meals are portrayed as enhancing the narrator's sense of community and the intensity of the common spiritual experience.

5 The Return Journey

After saying farewell to the Prophet, the resilient pilgrims, with the title al-Ḥājj added to their names, prepare for the return journey from Medina to Jedda. Unfortunately, when they want to buy bread it appears that there is no bread left on the market, because previous travellers have bought it all. But to their relief, the obnoxious driver has been fired by the transport company and is replaced by a pious and polite chauffeur who does not smoke. On the way they are reunited with other pilgrims, and they meet two pilgrims from the Rif who have journeyed to Mecca on foot in about eight months, almost all the way from Morocco through Libya—under Italian administration—and Egypt—under British administration. The boat journey to Tunis is bearable, except for seasickness and vomiting; references to the days of quarantine and disinfection in al-Ṭūr, in Sinai, are unfortunately lacking from the journal. In Tunis, al-Ḥājj Muḥammad cannot leave the hotel because of his illness, but he is able to continue his journey by boat to Oran and from there by bus to Oujda (the 'French' border) and by car to Berkane, where he is met by a group of members from the local orders of Aḥmad 'Alīwa, Muḥammad al-Ḥabarī, and Shaykh al-Būdālī (ibid., 103–122).

In Nador, our pilgrim is awaited by a large crowd on the square in front of the *zāwiya* where carpets are spread out. When the car arrives, he is taken aside by his brother, who, seeing how exhausted, dusty and emaciated he is, gives him a new *jallāba*, two shirts, a vest, shoes, and a turban, which he immediately puts on before appearing before the crowd. Horse races are held and the district official arrives to greet him with two soldiers, a Spanish captain, and a tribal chief. After the festivities, he is taken to his home in Midar where dinner is served, which, remarkably, is not specified (ibid., 123–124). In a supplement to the text, a list is added of gifts that people had requested him to bring them from the Holy Places: a rosary from Mecca, some sand from the Ḥaramayn, and a razor blade sharpener, probably one that had been used for the shaving incident in Minā (ibid., 125, 128).

6 Conclusion

Although it is clear that the account of al-Ḥājj Muḥammad was written as part of a long tradition of Moroccan pilgrimage accounts, it is a unique text in several respects. It is not unique in the sense of consciously distancing itself from the tradition, but rather because it shows a particular balance between conventional and personal components. As has been observed above, the tradition of

Muslim pilgrimage accounts allows for a certain degree of individual observations and impressions, and in that sense the text is no anomaly. What is different is an impression of directness and authenticity that seems to prevail over strategies of mediation and deliberate efforts by the author to construct a specific virtuous self-image. This may be the result either of a conscious attempt by the author to write a text that is different from other texts; it may also be the result of a changing intellectual climate, allowing for a more diverse field of discursive expression; or it may be that the text represents a kind of narrative that has always existed within the tradition but has largely remained out of sight.

At a superficial level, the text seems to conform neatly to the generic requirements. It begins with an account of the customary tour around the region to visit befriended *zāwiyas* and brotherhoods, to strengthen spiritual bonds and social networks, and to lay a solid spiritual foundation for the momentous undertaking through a kind of 'permission' to depart with the blessing of the saintly milieu. It proceeds to give an account of the journey, with its inconveniences and problems along with observing unfamiliar places, focusing on networks of scholars and religious and educational institutions. In the Holy Places, the focus shifts to the religious discursive framework of pilgrimage, referring to doctrines, law, prayer, rituals, acts of piety, etc., elevating the text to a more ceremonial and formal level. These structural features leave no doubt that the author situates his text within a specific genre, but at the same time he seems rather to add to its diversity than to its coherence.

What distinguishes this text from others is that, first, it has no formal and stylistic pretensions; second, that it focuses in much more detail on the practicalities of the journey, not so as to give guidelines for future pilgrims, but to convey the way they are experienced by the author; and, third, that there is a systematic emphasis on the physical and material aspects of the journey, as an experience in an often-hostile environment. These aspects of the text make it a distinctly individual narrative, a personal account. The perspective is personal to such an extent, that observations from a more distant perspective are scarce. There are no or very few remarks about the colonial authorities or the modern means of transport; there are only implicit complaints about the strict regime for pilgrims imposed by the new Saudi rulers; there are no comments related to the rapidly evolving environment of modernity, which required new visions of the hajj as a journey and as a religious obligation and practice.

The directness and suggestion of authenticity of the account can be compared to a similar diary that was written by a pilgrim from India also in 1929 (Alawi 2009). This account is also composed as a detailed diary, reporting on food and the illnesses of the author, but is still more consciously stylized to give a specific representation of the author, mainly by complaining about the restrictive measures of the Saudi government. It is a text aimed at a form of self-constitution vis-à-vis a specific audience by contrasting Indian practices with Wahhābī rules. This conscious effort to constitute the self seems to be lacking in al-Ḥājj Muḥammad's text; even if he touches upon subjects of law or spirituality, his intention seems to be to enhance the sense of piety, humility, and submission that the text exudes rather than constructing an image of a proficient, modern scholar, or a knowledgeable literate, or a specifically Moroccan Muslim, or an esoterically inclined Sufi. It seems that the author inserts himself into the tradition of the hajj in a self-evident way, without overly clashing with the forces of modernity, because the tradition transcends these specific circumstances represented by modern means of transport, colonial occupation, or Wahhābī reforms. The harshness of the caravan route has just been replaced by new, modern inconveniences.

If the text was not written as a conscious effort of self-constitution by the author, nor as a guide for future pilgrims, then why was it written? Was it perhaps an unconscious product of the mingling of traditional and modern styles? Could a text such as this never have been written in the early modern period? Or would it just have remained hidden beneath a layer of more sophisticated texts? Questions such as these can only be answered when more texts of this kind are found, published, and examined, which is, in my opinion, a truly enviable task. Still, analysing texts can only to a certain extent provide answers to questions about the intention of authors, since these are dependent on social, rather than discursive, contexts. For whom were these texts written and in which contexts were they read? In the case of al-Ḥājj Muḥammad's text we can be fairly sure that it was not distributed beyond a limited circle of close friends and family, and perhaps even as a personal diary to commemorate a momentous experience. This would explain the intimate tone of the journal and its lack of sophistication.

References

al-ʿAbdarī, Abū ʿAbdallāh Muḥammad. 1968. *Riḥla al-ʿAbdarī*, edited by Muḥammad al-Fāsī. al-Ribāṭ: Jāmiʿa Muḥammad v.

al-Miḍārī, Sīdī Muḥammad al-Tawzānī. 1997. *al-Riḥla*, edited by ʿAbdallāh ʿĀsim, al-Ribāṭ.

al-Muṣʿabī, Ibrahīm b. Baḥmān b. Abī Muḥammad b. ʿAbdallāh b. ʿAbd al-ʿAzīz al-Thamīnī al-Yasajinī. 2006. *Riḥla al-Muṣʿabī*, edited by Y. b. Buhān Ḥājj Amḥammad. al-ʿAṭf/ Ghardāya: Mondial Print Service.

al-Rasheed, Madawi. 2002. *A history of Saudi Arabia*. Cambridge: Cambridge University Press.

al-Sharqī, Abū ʿAbdallāh Muḥammad ibn al-Ṭayyib al-Sharqī al-Fāsī. 2014. *al-Riḥla al-Ḥijāziyya*, edited by Nūr al-Dīn Shawbad. Bayrūt/Abū Ẓabī: al-Muʾassasa al-ʿArabiyya li-al-Dirāsāt wa-al-Nashr/Dār al-Suwaydī li-al-Nashr wa-al-Tawzīʿ.

Alam, Muzaffar and Sanjay Subrahmanyam. 2007. *Indo-Persian travels in the age of discoveries 1400–1800*. Cambridge: Cambridge University Press.

Alawi, Amir Ahmad. 2009. *Journey to the Holy Land: A pilgrim's diary*, translated by Mushirul Hasan and Rakhshanda Jalil. Oxford: Oxford University Press.

Coşkun, Menderes. 1990. 'Ottoman pilgrimage narratives and Nābī's Tuhfetü'l-Haremeyn.' Doctoral thesis, Durham University.

Mouline, Nabil. 2011. *Les clercs de l'Islam: Autorité religieuse et pouvoir politique en Arabie Saoudite, XVIIIe–XXIe siècle*. Paris: Presses Universitaires de France.

Pennell, C.P. 2003. *Morocco: From empire to independence*. Oxford: Oneworld Publications.

Tresse, René. 1937. *Le pèlerinage Syrien aux villes saintes de l'islam*. Paris: Chaumette.

Willis, John. 2017. 'Governing the living and the dead: Mecca and the emergence of the Saudi biopolitical state.' *The American historical review* 122 (2): 346–370.

CHAPTER 9

From Moscow to Mecca: Entangled Soviet Narratives of Pilgrimage in the Unlikely 1965 *ḥajjnāme* of Fazliddin Muhammadiev

Vladimir Bobrovnikov

Muslims from Central Asia remained enthusiastic travellers and passionate readers of travel accounts before and after the Russian conquest in the nineteenth century. Every year from early pre-modern times they visited the sacred sites of Islam in 'noble Mecca and radiant Medina' (the Ḥaramayn). Literate Muslim elites shared their hajj and *ʿumra* experience in letters, diaries, and pious travelogues known as *ḥajjnāme*, *siyāḥatnāme*, or *riḥla*. Numerous travelogues were printed by them in the late nineteenth and early twentieth centuries in Arabic, Persian, and Turkic languages. Some of these narrative sources have been meticulously studied (Can 2020; Green 2015; 2013; Papas, Welsford and Zarcone 2012; etc.) and even translated into European languages (Chokri 2018; Ibrahim 2004; Marjani 2003). The abundance of traditional religious travelogue genres disappeared by the beginning of the 1930s when all the religious pilgrimages, which had been performed abroad and within Russia, were prohibited.

Hajj was resumed on the wave of relative liberalization of the Soviet policy toward Islam in 1944–1945 with a longer policy change in 1953–1991, but the traditional genre of *ḥajjnāme* disappeared already in the early Soviet times. Of course, Soviets *ḥājjī*s were less literate in terms of Islamic written tradition. Furthermore, during the Soviet era there were few pilgrimages and the number of pilgrims in a group never exceeded 21 (Akhmadullin 2016, 136–138, 182–189, 194–197, 201). Most of them never recorded their impressions. At the same time, the head of every pilgrim group was charged with submitting an official report (*otchet*) for 'administrative use' only. The State Archive of the Russian Federation (GARF) still keeps dozens of these documents (see Babakhanov 1963, 1–24; Babakhan 1945, 14–20). The Central Asian mufti Ziyauddin-khan Babakhanov, who composed numerous reports of this sort, was also a prolific author and published a book on contemporary Soviet Muslims (Babakhanov 1981). Sometimes writers, journalists and scientists (mostly medical doctors) took part in the pilgrimage. For instance, in 1974 the Tajik politician, journalist, scholar, and director of the academic Institute of Oriental studies Bobojan

DOI:10.1163/9789004513174_011

Gafurov visited Saudi Arabia and performed *ʿumra* (Akhmadullin 2014, 7). However, neither Gafurov nor the others published accounts of their hajj journey.

There is one intriguing exception to this rule. In April–May 1963 the young Tajik journalist Fazliddin Muhammadiev from Dushanbe made a journey with a group of Soviet pilgrims from Tajikistan to Moscow, then to Khartoum and Jedda, and eventually to Mecca and back. During the trip he kept a diary, which he turned into a novel under the title *Dar on dunye* (*In the other world*) and published it first in Tajik in 1965. Later it was translated into multiple languages, including Russian. It was the only hajj account (Borshchagovskiy 1976, 8) to be published in the Soviet Union. To date nobody has examined it as primary source of the late Soviet pilgrim's experience, although many post-Soviet philologists referred to the novel in their studies of the Tajik language (Khomidova 2018; Grassi 2017; Murodov 2009; Bozorov 2002; Tursunov 1999 etc.). Recently, Moscow-based historian Viacheslav Akhmadullin used it to clarify some details about the still poorly-known factual history of Soviet Islamic policy (Akhmadullin 2016; 2020).

However, historians have overlooked the important cultural dimension of late Soviet religiosity as it was reflected in *Dar on dunye*. Using archival sources, contemporary responses, and memoir accounts, in this chapter I discuss the insights that a discourse analysis of the text provides with regard to hajj narratives in the Soviet Union during the Cold War.[1] The research was guided by the following set of questions: How far does the novel reflect the writer's personal experience of performing the hajj ritual? Is Muhammadiev's fictional diary reliable enough to evaluate late Soviet religiosity as a whole? What written and oral evidence did the author base his account on? Did the novel contain any religious blasphemy? What role, in this respect, did translation play from Tajik into Russian and other languages? How did readers respond to the publication of the novel?

1 The first draft version of the chapter was written when the author worked at the Netherlands Institute for Advanced Studies in the Humanities and Social Sciences (NIAS) in Amsterdam. For feedback on earlier drafts and comments offered in conversation or in writing, I am grateful to editors of this volume as well as to Sergei Abashin, Vyacheslav Asadullin, Artemy Kalinovsky, Michael Kemper, Alexander Knysh, Shawkat and Aziz Niyazi, and Nikolay Ssorin-Chaykov.

FIGURE 9.1 Bookcover of the 1970 Russian translation of Muhammadiev's *Travel to the Other World* by Irfon Publishers in Dushande
PHOTOGRAPH BY THE AUTHOR

1 The Author and His Journey

Fazliddin Muhammadiev was born in Samarkand in 1928 into a Tajik bookbinder's family. In 1947 he started a career as news reporter with *Tojikistoni surkh* ('Red Tajikistan') in Stalinabad (today Dushanbe) before being sent to the Higher Komsomol School in Moscow, where he studied from 1949 to 1951. In the year of his graduation, Muhammadiev joined the Communist Party. After that he wrote for a number of Tajik periodicals, and he acted as executive secretary of *Jovononi Tojikiston* ('Youth of Tajikistan') (1951–1954), editor of *Gazetai muallimon* ('Teachers' Newspaper') (1954), and section editor for a number of other publications, including *Tojikiston Sovyeti* ('Soviet Tajikistan') and the satirical journal *Horpushtak* ('Hedgehog') (1956–1957). He returned to Moscow at the end of the decade to attend advanced courses at the prestigious Gorky Literary Institute, graduating in 1962 (Muhammadiev 1978, 8rev, 11, 11rev, 12).

From then on, he seems to have primarily earned his living as a writer, although he continued to sit on various boards, including that of Tajik Film studio (1965–1966), the publisher Irfon (1967–1968), and the Tajik Soviet Encyclopedia (1969–1973) (Muhammadiev 2012, 158; Muhammadiev 1968b, 29). In March 1963, he reported an impressive income of 276 roubles 50 kopecks per month, while the average Soviet wage was then 85 roubles 40 kopecks (Akhmadullin 2016, 203; Vyezdnoe delo 1963, 20; cf. Alaev 2020; Panarin 2020). Muhammadiev was a member of the Soviet Union of Writers and had a short tenure as the secretary of the board in its Tajikistan branch, from 1978–1981 (Muhammadiev 1968b, 14). From that point on he appears to have focused exclusively on writing (Vyezdnoe delo 1963, 15), but five years later his life was cut short: Muhammadiev was stabbed in an altercation with street thugs in June 1986 and died on October 6 the same year.

By the time Muhammadiev took part in the hajj, he had been publishing fiction for a decade and had achieved some recognition in the Soviet Union (Niyazi 2020; Makarov 1965, 15; Tursunzade 1964, 1). His early pieces trended toward the satirical or didactic side, particularly contrasting 'old' and 'new' types of people; in this sense, he was working with familiar master narratives established in the Stalin era (see Clark 2000). It seems that Soviet authorities were hoping to gain more propaganda value from the 1963 hajj than they had from previous ones. From 1956, hajj delegations began to include party members and, increasingly, members of the intelligentsia: high school teachers, journalists, and writers, as well as doctors. Muhammadiev's companions included the Bashkir journalist and writer Zulfar Khismatullin, who worked for the satirical and anti-religious journal Henek ('Pitchforks') in Ufa, two doctors, a lecturer from an agricultural college in Ufa, and a teacher and student from the Mir-i ʿArab madrasa in Bukhara. Of the eighteen pilgrims, four were members of the Communist Party, including Muhammadiev himself (Materialy o palomnichestve 1963, I:168, 185, III:60). At the time of the hajj, Muhammadiev was not known outside the USSR. Authors like Mirzo Tursunzade, a classic of Soviet Tajik fiction, were too well-known as Soviet officials and high-ranking communists to pass as pious Soviet pilgrims when applying for a Saudi visa.

2 Journey to the Other World

The hajj pilgrimage narrated by Muhammadiev is reflective of a more general openness of the USSR to the world under Khrushchev's rule (Kalinovsky 2013, 192, 202–204). To bring into the socialist block Muslim-majority countries in the Third World from the middle of 1950s, the Soviet Union began to court foreign tourists, cultural delegations, and students—particularly from post-colonial 'Third World' nations. It also became possible for separate Soviet citizens to travel and even work abroad, although the majority of ordinary people including Muslim believers had no hope of seeing the world outside the socialist bloc. Soviet travellers were encouraged to write about their experiences, and their accounts referred to in Tajik as *safarnāme* were often published (Bozorov 2002, 66–96). In the 1950s two popular all-Union book series were created for this purpose. The 'Geografizdat' publishers in Moscow issued *Puteshestviia. Prikliucheniia. Fantastika* ('Travels. Adventures. Science Fiction'). The orientalist branch of the Moscow-based 'Nauka' publishers set up by Gafurov in 1959 initiated another series devoted to the 'Countries and Peoples of the East' ('*Strany i narody Vostoka*'). Like the novel of Muhammadiev, one of its books was entitled 'Reportage "From the Other world"' (Riffaud 1961). This was an account of a French female reporter who blamed the colonial regime in Algeria of crimes against humanity.

Real and fictional travelogues became the preferred genre for young, teenage Soviets. They allowed Soviet readers to feel like real travellers in the wider world, and they provided them with an awareness of world affairs and the USSR's role on the right side of history. Very few Soviet readers could expect to ever visit North Africa and almost none had a chance of ever seeing the two Holy Cities (al-Ḥaramayn) in Saudi Arabia. As a rule, Soviet travelogues of the 1950s–1980s followed similar arcs: they described the suffering of the country under colonialism that the writer had visited and its struggle for freedom, supplementing facts from Soviet publications with some eyewitness accounts. Often, the author pointed to the new nation's yearning for friendship with the Soviet Union and Moscow's willingness to extend a helping hand. Sometimes the writers expressed their nostalgia for home. All these tropes are presented in *Dar on dunye*.

Following the conventions of the *safarnāme* (Baruzdin 1989, 365), the narrator of Muhammadiev's novel—his alter ego Qurbon Majidov—sees much that is strange, even wild, but is convinced that Soviet propaganda is essentially correct and tries to assure the reader of this belief: life in post-colonial Sudan and Saudi Arabia is shaped by the realities of American neo-imperialism. At the same time, the novel is a satire of western propaganda about religious oppression in the USSR: its destruction of historical and cultural monuments, the religious elite (*'ulamā'*), wife-sharing,[2] poverty of everyday life, and the persecution of believers.

It is not accidental that Muhammadiev makes his alter ego in the novel a doctor: his profession hints at the author's identity, class perspective, and nationality. '*Ba gumoni shumo man kistam*? *Man dukhturi soveti hastam*! *Soveti, fahmided*?' ('Whom do you take me for? I am a Soviet doctor! I am Soviet [emphasis added by the author, VB], really!'), confesses Qurbon at the beginning of the story (Muhammadiev 1965, no. 3: 47). According to the plot, he works in a hospital in the capital of Tajikistan, often visits Moscow, but like the majority of Soviet nationals he never travelled abroad. In the journey to the Other world, medicine embodies Soviet modernity for him. As a doctor, Majidov is particularly perturbed by the lack of hygiene, for example the hajj bans on cutting one's fingernails or hair, on shaving, or on using soap or toothpaste during the pilgrimage—all highlighting the distance between modernity and what he considers anachronistic medieval fanaticism of religious injunctions. But he can also highlight how the USSR has helped its own citizens and humanity more broadly by training doctors, building modern comfortable hospitals, advancing medical science, and making its benefits widely available.

The narrative about the 'foreign Orient' as the 'Other world' (*on dunye*) is not central to the novel, but to a significant extent it determines the intended reading of the novel. Along these lines, the Soviet critic Alexander Borshchagovskiy compared Muhammadiev to the Georgian painter Niko Pirosmani (Borshchagovskiy 1976, 5), as an artist who does not like half-tones. The narrator constantly compares 'our country, homeland' with 'foreign land[s]' like Afghanistan and Saudi Arabia. This dichotomy reflects Cold War ideological orientations and their orientalist backdrop (Fort 2019, 44, 63–64, 198–199). Typical for classical colonial orientalism is the comparison of the Muslim East and the Christian West; here, however, the dichotomy is between the foreign Orient and Soviet Central Asia. The former is full of disease, pollution, dirt, poverty, and is under the heel of 'shameless American imperialism' (Muhammadiev 1970, 241). The latter is a country of industrial cities, science, doctors, hospitals, space exploration, Yuri Gagarin, and the dog-cosmonaut Layka, familiar even to the pious Muslims whom the narrator meets abroad (ibid., 16, 19, 44, 145, 261). When we hear about industrial sites being built in Sudan, Somalia, or Egypt, it

2 'Wife sharing' was a Western stereotype of the Cold War period, suggesting that communists in the USSR shared their wives.

is because these countries are receiving the fraternal assistance of the Soviet Union (ibid., 64).

The particularities of post-war Soviet orientalist approaches to the foreign Orient are most clearly presented in the narrator's ruminations on seeing a crowd of pilgrims making the ritual circumambulation of the Kaʿba (*ṭawāf*), hurried along by soldiers wielding whips:

> I couldn't help thinking 'Asia ... Asia ... Once you were the cradle of human culture. Wasn't the first written language, pencil and paper, the first lines of poetry and the first architectural drawing a result of your sons' mental efforts? Was not the first surgery scalpel, the first book about health a result of your children's wisdom? Why did you give yourself over to evil spells and sorcery? Who needs your deep sleep, in which you've been for so many centuries? Truly, the time of sleep has passed into eternity. The light of a new day has shown upon half the world, and yet, land of mine, your children still come here in search of sleep, and asking for soporifics ...'
>
> MUHAMMADIEV 1965, no. 4: 89

The title of the novel contains a pun that is lost in the Russian translation. In Tajik, *dunyo* can mean 'World' in a general sense. This word of Arabic origin entered the Persian and Tajik languages also in the sense of 'wicked mortal life' opposed to eternal celestial bliss in paradise known as *akhirat*. Believers who are able to resist its temptations will escape the tortures of hell and enter paradise (Tritton 1991, 626; Lane 1968, 922). Theoretically, every pilgrim should reject all the habits of mortal life when in the Ḥaramayn. The narrator claims that this obligation is impossible in the capitalist countries of the Third world visited by Soviet pilgrims. In Mecca he feels himself thrown from the twentieth century into the 'hellish sufferings of the middle ages,' which he associates with practices such as veiling, marrying off underage brides, the punishment of a hungry man who has stolen 10 rials worth of food by chopping off his hand, the presence of domestic slavery, and the spread of epidemiological diseases (Muhammadiev 1970, 91, 124, 131, 143–144, 180, 217, 234–235, 246, 255).

It is noteworthy that similar complaints appeared in the late nineteenth century in many hajj diaries written in Arabic, Turkish, Tatar, Persian, and Urdu.[3] Although Muhammadiev could not read them, because he did not know these oriental languages (Muhammadiev 1978, 2; Vyezdnoe delo 1963, 15) and

3 As the Indian pilgrim Sikandar Begum commented as early as 1864, 'the city of Mecca is wild

these writings were unavailable in libraries in Dushanbe, upon his return to the Soviet Union he probably compared his observations of Saudi Arabia with similar critical notes of Russian-speaking tsarist agents in the Hijaz, including Shakirzian Ishaev from Samarkand, Dmitry Sokolov, and Mikhail Nikolsky (cf. Nikolsky 1911, no. 4: 274–276; Sokolov 1902, 637–647; Ishaev 1896, no. 11: 21–24, 34).

It is unlikely, however, that Muhammadiev shared demands of some pre-Soviet *ḥājjīs* for religious reform (Green 2015, 208, 209). Rather, the narrator of *Dar on dunye* dreams of his Soviet homeland. The further the narrator gets away from the USSR the more he feels that he is interacting with a land and people stuck in the past. But these daydreams are not solely about the 'big homeland', the USSR, but also the narrator's home republic, Tajikistan. The narrator imagines himself conversing with his good friend Iskandar, a fellow radiologist doctor and man of science, with whom he always finds an understanding. The squalid, petty life of Tajik émigrés in Mecca who fled from Central Asia during the collectivization is contrasted in his mind with great modern factories, mines, theatres, hospitals, schools, and institutes in his homeland, kolkhoz markets like that in Leninabad, and huge palaces of culture including the magnificent building constructed in the kolkhoz 'Moscow' (today Arbob Cultural Palace in Hujand) (Muhammadiev 1970, 37–38, 134). He thinks about the meaning and importance of Soviet patriotism:

> What man in his right mind would renounce his homeland?! If you have no more homeland, what do you have left?! As one folk song says, 'He who has lost his homeland is a slave in a foreign land!'
>
> MUHAMMADIEV 1970, 41, 139

3 A Guide to the Holy Cities of Islam

While many of the above tropes are common to other Soviet travel writings about the post-colonial 'Third World', Muhammadiev's novel is unique in its

and melancholy looking and (…) has a dreary, repulsive aspect'; its air was bad owing to 'the stupidity and carelessness of the inhabitants, who allow accumulations of dirt to taint and vitiate it'; and 'the majority of the people are miserly, violent-tempered, hardhearted and covetous' (Sikandar Begum 2007, 129, 131, 132). The Tatar pilgrim 'Abd al-Rashid Ibrahim, who approached Mecca from Tara in Siberia through Singapore and Bombay in 1909, was stricken by the bad administration of the city. He noted that too many pilgrims were admitted for its size; its officials could not cope; there were no toilets for the many thousands of pilgrims; and everywhere its streets and public places were filled with excrement (Ibrahim 2004, 238–243).

description of the rites of the great pilgrimage (*ḥajj akbar*) and the ironic commentaries made about the stories behind these rites from the hagiographic lives of the prophets (*qiṣaṣ al-anbiyāʾ*). These two elements represent the most important interlocking narratives of *Dar on dunye* and together comprise the greater part of the novel. The narrator devotes most of his attention to the road from Jedda to Mecca, Medina, al-Ṭāʾif, and back, starting from the journey of the Soviet pilgrims into the state of *iḥrām* before their departure from Khartoum (ch. 6). If it were not for the ironic commentary that accompanies Muhammadiev's descriptions of the hajj stages (*manzils*), the novel could be read as the kind of devout *ḥajjnāme* popular among pilgrims from Central Asia and the Volga-Ural region up to the beginning of the twentieth century.[4] But writings of Muhammadiev's pre-Soviet predecessors focus primarily on the believer's thoughts and impressions on the way to the Ḥaramayn and back as illustrated by the diary of the famous Tatar scholar Shihab al-Din Marjani (1818–1889), who performed his hajj in 1880. In the centre of Marjani's work are the books he read during the journey, different rituals among pilgrims he encountered on the way to Mecca and back, as well as accounts of his discussions with Arab and Ottoman scholars (Marjani 2003, 185–186, 190–194; cf. Can 2020, 37).

Muhammadiev, by contrast, concentrates on providing substantial details on the *ṭawāf* (ch. 10, 11, 16), the ritual running (*saʿy*) between the hills of al-Ṣafa and al-Marwa (ch. 10–11), the standing at the foot of mount ʿArafa, or *wuqūf* (ch. 12), the stoning of Satan with pebbles from Minā (ch. 13–14), the sacrifice (ch. 14), and the exit from *iḥrām* (ch. 14–15). He lists all of the prohibitions affecting pilgrims who have donned the *iḥrām* (Muhammadiev 1970, 75–76), discusses the norms of behaviour for pilgrims while on the territory of the Ḥaramayn in Saudi Arabia, and writes out in Cyrillic the entire *talbiya* prayer, also providing a Russian translation. Muhammadiev also describes the exterior of the Kaʿba, the Grand Mosque, the Mosque of the Prophet in Medina, the valley of ʿArafa, the pillars of Satan, the opulent beauty of the summer residences of the Saudi elite in al-Ṭāʾif, and other important sites on the path of the pilgrims. In this respect his narrative is closer to that of Russian travellers and imperial officials in the Hijaz (Nikolsky 1911, no. 4: 256–292, no. 5: 603–638; Sokolov 1902, 616–649; Ishaev 1896, no. 11: 60–81, no. 12: 43–83). If authors of pre-Soviet hajj accounts happened to write about these duties, rites, and stages of the hajj, which would have been known to all practicing Muslim believers, they often asked readers to excuse them for their trivial descriptions (Chokri 2018, 63–64).

4 In the Russian North Caucasus, this genre did not circulate widely.

In this respect, it is interesting to take a closer look at the lexicon Muhammadiev refers to when recording his own hajj experience. In the late nineteenth and early twentieth centuries, Marjani and other pilgrims introduced in their travel notes a new European vocabulary for steamships and trains: distances are measured mostly in *kilomitars*; stages, or *manzils*, of yore, are mentioned only in the Ḥaramayn. They use neologisms for rail transportation and sea travel, including new words for train (*rel-ghari*), station (*estashan*), train compartments (*kabin*), the railway itself (*rah-e ahan*), *aghbut* (literally 'fire ship'), and *kishti-ye bukhar* (a calque for 'steamship') (Marjani 2003, 184–189, 192; see also Green 2015, 224–226; Metcalf 1990, 85–86). Contrary to these prior hajj accounts, Muhammadiev's novel is saturated with old-fashioned oriental loanwords and phrases. There are numerous oriental terms of Arabic origin in it—in both the Tajik original and especially in the Russian translation. Some pages contain long lists of such words and even whole Muslim prayers and pious formulations of the hajj rites in Arabic are recorded in Cyrillic. Here is a characteristic passage of such linguistic usage that appears at the very beginning of the novel:

> Traveling inside the IL-18 [aircraft, VB], we are going on the hajj. There is eighteen of us. Seventeen are clerics—mullahs, imams, *mudarris*es, *khaṭīb*s, *mutawallī*s and others. I am the eighteenth member of the group, your humble servant, doctor therapist, as the saying goes, 'a victim (*shahīd*) of the science among the dead men.'
>
> Every year on the Qurban Bayram festival (sacrificial feast) a group of Muslims visits (*ziyorat-i/ziyāra*) Mecca and Medina in order to redress their sins and get *thawāb* (religious merit) in the Prophet's homeland. Pilgrims are usually accompanied by a doctor who takes care of their health, but this time, like a roofer who repairs others' roofs but whose own roof is leaking. The physician fell ill, and I was privileged to accompany our prominent Muslims to the land of the Prophet for him.
>
> MUHAMMADIEV 1965, no. 3: 43

Considering that few Soviet Muslims had been on the hajj or *ʿumra* since the late 1920s, and that religious education was heavily circumscribed from the 1930s, Muhammadiev's account provided a unique source of information for readers interested in rites of Islamic pilgrimage. The usage of numerous words of Arabic origin in Cyrillic letters most likely attracted Muslim readers to his novel. In the 1960s being unable to go abroad, some pious Muslims relegated the performance of hajj to rare Soviet pilgrims who had already been to Mecca, according to the tradition of *ḥajj-badal* (Babakhanov 1963, 24). Even more people wished to feel for themselves the real *ḥājjīs* and to use their imagination to pass through all the stages of the great pilgrimage. At the same time, Muhammadiev 'orientalized' his record of the hajj. Laymen among his readers surely encountered difficulties when reading the Arabic terms. Those who did not belong to the limited, specialized audience of practicing Muslim clergy and academic experts in Islam would have required the glossary that was attached in some Russian editions of the book. Most of the Oriental words, names, and expressions in the 1970 Russian edition were footnoted. Their total number exceeds 165! Almost every page is accompanied by one or more footnotes.

4 Satire of the Clergy or Religious Blasphemy?

Muhammadiev draws a distinct line between Qurbon Majidov and the other pilgrims. The first and the last chapters of the novel are even called '17+1' and '1+17' (Muhammadiev 1965, no. 3: 43, no. 6: 65). It is by accident that Qurbon went on the pilgrimage, so he is more an observer (and comments sarcastically) than a participant. Muslim pilgrims are portrayed in a caustic, orientalist manner. They are all older clergymen (*sviaschennosluzhiteli*) preoccupied with religious precepts. They speak Arabic a bit but do not know Russian fluently, shave their heads, have beards, and wear turbans and dressing gowns (*chalmy i khalaty*). Their clothes, habits, and views date back to pre-Soviet colonial Central Asia but look anachronistic in the twentieth century (Mukhammadiev 1970, 9, 14, 20). The narrator blames them for exploiting religious superstition of ignorant believers and for being ignorant themselves. According to his pessimist conclusion, 'people also need servants of religion, alas, not for today and tomorrow's urgent matters but for the respect for relics of the past' (Muhammadiev 1965, no. 4: 71).

Much of the orientalist, anti-religious narrative of the novel belongs to Muhammadiev personally and to the milieu in which his early career as a writer took shape, including his work as editor of the satirical journal *Horpushtak* ('Hedgehog') in Dushanbe from 1956–1957. During the Thaw years, in 1955–1964, journalists were encouraged to probe the failings of Soviet institutions, as long as they did not challenge the Soviet order as such. This meant satirizing both the 'internal' opponents, such as bureaucrats, as well as alleged slackers (*tuneiadtsy*), sectarians, religious bigots, and others. These satirical tools are used against the pilgrims in the novel who are 'far from being exemplary Soviet people' (Mukhammadiev 1970, 40, 140). For example, there is Mullah Urok-aka, always smoking other people's cigarettes, and the pompous and round-bellied Mahsum Abdirazikdzhan-aka. Out of the seventeen pilgrims, only twelve are mentioned by name, and even fewer receive something like an individual portrait. The rest appear as wordless and comic fat old men in turbans, something underlined in the illustrations by the Soviet Jewish artist Sergei Vishnepolsky, which accompanied the most popular Russian edition (ibid., 2, 6–7, 13, 16, 20–21, 82–83, 92, 95, 102–103, 166, 177, 185, 199). As already noted, not everyone is subject to the same level of satire: Qori-aka and Isrofil both get a sympathetic portrait, but the upshot is that in both cases the narrator laments that these smart and talented individuals did not do something more useful with their lives.

The narrator laughs at the dogmatism and superstition he finds among believers. In Khartoum, Allanazar-qori confuses Fahrenheit and Celsius and tries to convince the others that the temperature had reached 102 degrees—that is, above the boiling point (ibid., 52–53).

Qurbon is similarly perturbed that his companions seem to believe that turnips originated from black rocks:

> all these pundits never doubted that turnips came into being from miracles performed by Goody Fatima; that rice came from a tooth of the Prophet which fell out; that wheat had been brought to earth from the seventh heaven by hazrat Adam; that mice came out of the nostril of a pig, and the cat from the mouth a tiger, when the latter happened to sneeze while on hazrat Noah's Ark …
>
> ibid., 141–142

Even the educated Qori-aka believes that birds avoid flying over the Kaʿba and therefore respect the Almighty Allah, even as the pilgrims see birds flying directly over it (ibid., 126–127). The superstitions of his companions mystify the narrator and cause him discomfort; their behaviour belongs to the 'Other' world, which belongs to the past but has somehow made its way into the present.

Friends and colleagues who knew him personally insisted that Muhammadiev did not attack religion, but only superstition and bigotry (Niyazi 2020; Kuhzod 2009, 7; Tursunov 1999, 86; Baruzdin 1989, 365). Of course, this was also the official Soviet position towards religion. Nevertheless, Muhammadiev's descriptions and commentary of episodes from the lives of the prophets and Muhammed's companions suggest a satire that goes to the very foundations of the faith. This includes his description of the Prophet Ibrahim, who in the Islamic tradition has (re-)built the Kaʿba (Muhammadiev 1970, 108–109, 169–171), and Muhammad himself, who made it the main holy site of Islam (ibid., 55, 114–115, 225–226, 230). Retelling in a sarcastic manner some controversial episodes from the Prophet's biography mentioned in the *sīra* (biography of the Prophet Muhammad) and *qiṣaṣ al-anbiyā'* (tales of the prophets) by the Khwarazmi poet Naṣr al-Dīn Rabghūzī (1309–1310), Muhammadiev presents the Prophets Ibrāhīm and Muhammad as old and lustful men, and the latter also as a cuckold. He does not spare 'Ā'isha, the Prophet's favourite wife, accusing her of having an affair (ibid., 226–228); he even pokes fun at the angel Jibrīl for helping the prophets (ibid., 84–85, 203–204). He explains the tradition of donning *iḥrām* as a primitive pagan ritual (ibid., 76), and he states repeatedly that the water from the Zamzam source is polluted (ibid., 106–107, 111).

It is noteworthy that the blasphemous connotation of the *Journey to the Other world* was accentuated in the Russian translation by Iurii Smirnov. The styles of the Tajik original as well as the early Uzbek version that appeared in Tashkent in 1968 were different from the other translations that addressed mostly non-Muslim readers. Despite all the late Stalinist attacks against Iranian and Arabic terms and other national minority languages in the 1930s, there was no distinction between sacred and secular vocabulary in literary Tajik and Uzbek languages in the 1960s. Many abstract notions, even those expressing the Soviet realities and ideas, were borrowed from Iranian and Arabic. Correspondingly, any blasphemous play on religious words was less sensitive for pious Muslim readers of the Tajik (and Uzbek) versions of the novel. As the Tajik hajj lexicon retained mostly authentic Islamic terms of Arabic origin, readers of the novel from Central Asia would not be offended by ambiguous jokes and word play based on the Orthodox Christian synonyms used in the Russian translation.

The novel's offensive connotations towards believers may have been strengthened by anonymous, atheistically-minded experts in Islamic and religious studies from different centres in Dushanbe, Tashkent, and Moscow, who seemed to consult Muhammadiev when they worked together to edit the Russian translation of the book. Sources do not mention their names. However, the style of footnotes and spelling of Oriental terms in the 1970 Russian edition (Mukhammadiev 1970, 5, 10, 12, 48, 55, 74, 105, 114, 125, 137, 167, 170), some misprints which occurred in it (ibid., 14, 87, 98, 213, 222), as well as memories of Muhammadiev's close friends (Niyazi 2020; cf. Kemper 2009, 93–133) allow us to suggest that Muhammadiev edited the manuscript in Moscow with the help of Lucian Klimovich, who chaired the department of Literary Translation at the Gorky Literature Institute and specialized in atheistic criticism of Islam, as well as other academic Orientalists, including specialists in Iranian and Arabic studies from the academic Institute of Asia's Peoples (Prozorov 2020). Its director Gafurov, whom Muhammadiev mentioned in passing in the novel (Muhammadiev 1970, 134), might have asked them to help the writer.

In the most popular edition, which was published in 1970 and was issued in 100,000 copies, the effect of the Russian translation (that appears to be a collaboration with Muhammadiev himself doing a word-for-word translation and Smirnov then making the text more literary) was emphasized by the cartoons of Vishnepolsky. Through them readers saw vivid street scenes and caricature portraits: Mullah Urok-aka smoking the narrator's cigarettes; Mahsum 'the Chewer' contemplating his white American underpants; a group of old clergymen staring at the water-skiing Sudanese girl in a skimpy swimsuit; the mob of sweaty angry pilgrims in *iḥrām* clothes circumambulating the Kaʿba; four veiled wives following their salafi husband in a single-file line; the narrator's bare heels sticking out of a pilgrims' tent on the slope of 'Arafa; a half-naked pilgrim clothed in *iḥrām* drinking Coca-Cola; another skinny pilgrim riding on his sacrificial sheep over the bridge Ṣīrāṭ in the Afterlife; a pilgrim-mullah carrying a bunch of illegally imported goods; two pilgrims beating each other in the valley of Minā; the emigrant Sufi master Ishan Ahmad seducing an old man's wife; the American guy placing his legs on the table, cowboy style, and many other genre pictures (Muhammadiev 1970, 12, 50, 69, 81–82, 198–199, 131, 136, 164, 167, 178, 180, 238). The cartoonist readily mocks different people but avoids picturing heroes and events of Islamic sacred history. Not one of his 49 cartoons contains any apparent anti-religious references.

5 Audiences and Responses

We do not know how the general public responded to the novel when it first appeared in *Sadoi sharq* in 1965. Sources are silent on this matter. Ironically, the only known vocal opponent of the novel was Sharif Kaiumovich Shirinbaev (1908–1982), the head of the Council for Religious Affairs for the Uzbek Soviet Socialist Republic, a Committee for State Security colonel and party member, and, like Muhammadiev, originally from Samarkand. In the summer of 1966, he intervened to stop the first Russian edition from appearing in *Zvezda vostoka*, a Russian-language literary journal published in Tashkent. Shirinbaev then wrote to Vladimir Kuroedov, the head of the all-Soviet Council of Religious Affairs, asking him to stop further editions of the novel (Shirinbaev 1966, 195). According to a close friend of Muhammadiev, the author then appealed to Ziyauddin-khan Babakhanov, the head of SADUM (Ecclesiastical Board of Central Asia and Kazakhstan Muslims), and with the latter's support he had the novel published as a book in Tajik in 1966 and in the spring of 1967 in Russian in *Zvezda vostoka* (Kuhzod 2009, 7).

Shirinbaev had a number of complaints about the novel. He accused the writer of revealing a state secret by publishing extracts from instructions to Soviet pilgrims and other documents for 'administrative use' only (Shirinbaev 1966, 199; cf. Perechen' svedenii 1976, 89–90, 95, 98). But most of Shirinbaev's criticism concerned the novel's treatment of Islamic rituals. According to Shirinbaev, the novel's militant atheism was too outdated and would not help anti-religious activists within the USSR. Abroad, it could actually be used for anti-Soviet propaganda, since it suggested that the USSR sent atheists on the hajj, something that would make future pilgrimages more difficult (Shirinbaev 1966, 199, 198). Shirinbaev then cited a number of passages which he found particularly insulting to believers, including the narrator's behaviour (which clearly violated hajj norms) and attitude towards Islamic dogma: the idea of heaven and hell, Judgement day, his disrespectful descriptions of the hajj, his drinking of cognac on the way to Mecca, and so on (ibid., 196–198; cf. Muhammadiev 1970, 24, 36–37, 102–103, 106–107).

Muhammadiev prevailed in his conflict with Shirinbaev, but was forced by Glavlit censors to accept some cuts and changes in most editions both in 1966–1969 and again in the 1973 edition. In all I found 35 changes, all of them relatively minor. These included jokes about the Saudi flag (ibid., 130), removed presumably to avoid offending Riyadh. They also concerned the comments about instructions to pilgrims, the description of customs procedures in Moscow, the comment that pilgrims were instructed to move around as a group while they were abroad (ibid., 11, 13–14, 22, 178), as well as an allusion to Stalin's 'personality cult' (ibid., 45). The remaining deletions were mostly those requested by Shirinbaev, such as removing the mockery of Soviet mullahs and references to their habit of picking their noses in public (ibid., 40, 58–59, 193), depictions of behaviour unbecoming of Soviet citizens, as well as certain observations of the hajj itself, including the Saudi soldiers whipping pilgrims during *ṭawāf*, the Zamzam well as a source of infection (ibid., 103, 106–107, 111), the illnesses of Soviet pilgrims at ʿArafa (ibid., 153), and unhygienic conditions in Minā after the end of Qurban-Bayram (ibid., 184). Otherwise, the novel maintained its structure, style, and most of the episodes and meditations of the narrator.

The first full Russian translation under the extended title *Journey to the Other world: Tale of the Great Hajj* appeared in *Druzhba narodov* in 1967 (Muhammadiev 1967). The journal, published by the USSR Union of Writers, showcased work from writers across the USSR, along with criticism and debates about Soviet literature. In 1966 Sergei Baruzdin, as a new editor, decided that rather than publishing what was best for each republic, *Druzhba narodov* would try to select the best pieces for the whole Soviet Union. Whatever the literary merits of Muhammadiev's work, an account of the hajj would have been a first for readers of the journal. If Soviet authorities hoped to use the novel as a demonstration of Soviet *respect* for religion, *Druzhba narodov* was the natural place to introduce the novel to the wider reading public.

From that point on the novel went through a number of editions, throughout the USSR and eventually abroad. The *Journey to the Other world* became a Soviet best seller. In 1966 the Dushanbe publisher Irfon released the novel in book form with additional printings in 1968, 1980, and 1989. In 1968 the Uzbek translation was released in Tashkent (Muhammadiev 1968a) in 15,000 copies. The Russian version served as the source of further translations into Armenian, Ukrainian, Estonian and Latvian (1982), Turkmen (1992), Hungarian (1978), Czech (1979), German, Romanian and Bulgarian (1980), and even Arabic. All in all, the book saw 32 editions with a total print run of over 1 million copies.

Muhammadiev's recognition as a classic of contemporary fiction began in Tajikistan after his premature death. From the mid-1980s his novels and short stories became the subject of numerous literary reviews and dissertations. Some Russian literary sources have suggested that Muhammadiev was killed because he refused the title of '*ḥājjī*' after returning from the trip (Borshchagovskiy 1986). There does not seem to be any support for this claim, and it is especially unlikely considering that he was stabbed by drug addicted youths more than twenty years after the novel was first published. However, it should be noted that the article appeared just as Mikhail Gorbachev was promoting an anti-corruption drive and replacing elites around the USSR. More generally, the central Soviet press began publishing sensationalist articles on corruption, child labor, and other issues in Central Asia. At the moment, it is more likely that the reception of *Dar on dunye* by Soviet Muslims was more favourable than is usually thought of.

6 Conclusion

The novel under study is a complex and hybrid text in which diverse genres and narratives are intertwined. First, it can be read as a travel account of the fictional narrator, doctor Qurbon Majidov. He compares what he sees in the 'Other world' to realities at home. This procedure closely resembles late Soviet travel accounts that became popular in the post-war decades and were referred to in Tajik as *safarnāme* (Grassi 2017). The second narrative is a guidebook through which the author presents a description of the hajj ritual; it is as much an eyewitness description as an information bulletin explaining the meanings of the various rites. Here the author imitates, completes, and criticizes the genre of traditional pre-Soviet *ḥajjnāme*. The third narrative contains an ironic retelling of and sometimes even blasphemous commentary on the pious stories of Ibrāhīm, Muhammad, and some other prophets from Islamic sacred history, styled after modern European and Soviet atheist writings.

Dar on dunye shows well the outcome of the gradual transformation of the traditional travelogue genre of *ḥajjnāme* into a secularist sort of late Soviet version of the *safarnāme*. Fazliddin Muhammadiev did not follow basic conventions of his Muslim predecessors but rather parodied their pious hajj accounts. The plot of his novel is built on his own personal experience and a very individual reading of the pilgrimage rites. But, at the same time, within the text one can distinguish multiple factual and fictional sources, along with multiple written and oral sources, of different historical periods and cultural backgrounds. The novelist presented to readers competing narratives about the hajj he recorded from high-ranking officials of regional Muslim directorates, state bureaucrats, ordinary believers, and even academic scholars and literary translators.

Despite its fictional character *Dar on dunye* sheds light on the ambiguous development of the late Islamic discourse in relation to the Soviet Islamic policy in the Cold War period. On the one hand, the Soviet Union maintained its commitment to atheism and restricted freedom of worship. On the other hand, it proclaimed the right to religious freedom and touted this commitment in relations with the outside world. This became particularly important for the USSR in the late 1950s, when it began to support post-colonial states and liberation movements in Asia, Africa, and the Middle East, including Muslim-majority countries like Indonesia, Egypt, and Syria. In this respect, pilgrims going to Mecca every year after the death of Stalin were also cultural intermediaries (Kirasirova 2011, 107–109) and agents in Soviet public diplomacy, particularly if they were Central Asians visiting countries where the USSR was trying to establish a foothold.

The domestic Islam policy of the Soviet state was still based on a hypothetic assessment that religion was practiced only by elderly believers. The persistence of belief and ritual was explained as a 'survival of the past'. We should not assume that Soviet readers would have focused on the anti-religious aspects of the novel. Denunciations of religion had largely become a routinized discourse by the 1960s. Almost nobody took it seriously. What would have been completely new to Soviet readers, whether Muslim or not, were the descriptions of the hajj rites, which, for all of the author's satire, are also highly detailed. The author's direct, journalistic style, which he uses to try to show the 'true' nature of the capitalist world and religion, also makes it possible for a Soviet reader to imagine what it would be like to go on such a journey, although only a handful of them would ever have such an opportunity.

References

Akhmadullin, Vyacheslav. 2020. 'Gosudarstvenno-musul'manskie otnosheniia v SSSR v 1944–1965 gg. [The relationship between the state and Muslims in the USSR in 1944–1965].' Habilitation diss., Moscow State University.

Akhmadullin, Vyacheslav. 2016. *Deiatel'nost' sovetskogo gosudarstva i dukhovnykh upravlenii musul'man po organizatsii palomnichestva (1944–1965): analiz istoricheskogo opyta i znachenie dlia sovremennosti* [Activities of the Soviet state and Muslim Religious Directorates to manage the pilgrimage in 1944–1965: Analysis of its historical experience and legacy for nowadays]. Moscow: Islamskaia kniga.

Akhmadullin, Vyacheslav. 2014. 'Deiatel'nost' sovetskogo gosudarstva po organizatsii khadzha sovetskikh musul'man [Activities of the Soviet state to manage the hajj journey of the Soviet Muslims].' *Khadzh sovetskikh musulman* no. 5: 1–9.

Alaev, Leonid. 2020. 'Average wages and cost of living of Soviet researchers in he Academy of sciences in Moscow in the first half of the 1960s.' Interview by Vladimir Bobrovnikov. Moscow, March 5, 2020. Audio, 25:14.

Babakhan, mufti Ishan Abdulmajidkhanov. 1945. 'Otchet glavy Dukhovnogo upravleniia musul'man Srednei Azii "Moia poezdka v Mekku" [Report of the Chairman of the Muslim Religious Directorate of Central Asia "My trip to Mecca"].' In the State Archive of the Russian Federation (GARF). f. r-6991, op. 3, d. 45, ll. 14–20. Available in English translation at https://islamperspectives.org/rpi/items/show/16267.

Babakhanov, Ziyauddin-khan. 1981. *Muslimū-l-Ittihād al-Sūfyati* [Muslims of the Soviet Union]. Tashkent: Muslim Religious Directorate of Central Asia and Kazakhstan.

Babakhanov, Ziyauddin-khan. 1963. 'Otchet o poezdke gruppy musul'man Sovetskogo Soiuza na palomnichestvo v Mekku (Saudovskaia Araviia) v 1963 godu 26 aprelia—16 maia [Report on travel of the group of the Soviet Union Muslims on the pilgrimage to Mecca (Saudi Arabia) on April 26—May 16, 1963].' In GARF, f. r-6991, op. 3, d. 1451, ll. 1–24.

Baruzdin, Sergei. 1989. 'Nepokhozhii na drugikh. Slovo o Fazliddine Mukhammadieve [Unlike the others. Some words about Fazliddin Muhammadiev].' In *Fazliddin Muhammadiev, Uglovaia palata: Roman, povest'* [The corner room: Novel and story], 363–366. Moscow: Sovetskii pisatel.

Borshchagovskiy, Alexander. 1986. 'Prestuplenie na ulitse Sharaf [The crime on Sharaf street].' *Literaturnaia gazeta* no. 12, December 10.

Borshchagovskiy, Alexander. 1976. 'Obrazy meniaiushchegosia mira [Images of the changing World].' In *Fazliddin Muhammadiev, Povesti i rasskazy* [Novels and short stories], 3–10. Moscow: Khudozhestvennaia literatura.

Bozorov, Nuriddin. 2002. 'Zhanr safar-nama v sovremennoi tadzhikskoi literature (na materiale zhurnala "Sadoi Sharq") [The genre of *safarnāme* in contemporary Tajik fiction on the materials of the journal *Sadoi sharq*],' PhD diss., Rudaki Institute of Language and Literature.

Can, Lâle. 2020. *Spiritual subjects: Central Asian pilgrims and the Ottoman hajj at the end of empire*. Stanford: Stanford University Press.

Chokri, 'Ali. 2018. 'Dastan ḥajjnāme [Notes of the hajj journey].' In *Khadzh musul'manskikh narodov Rossii: istoriia i sovremennost'. Khrestomatiia* [Hajj of the Russia's Muslim peoples. A Reader], edited by Zilia Khabibullina, 63–91. Ufa: Izdatelstvo Bashkirskogo gosudarstvennogo pedagogicheskogo universiteta.

Clark, Katerina. 2000. *The Soviet novel: History as ritual*. Bloomington: Indiana University Press.

Fort, Cristopher. 2019. 'Inhabiting socialist realism: Soviet literature from the edge of empire,' PhD diss., University of Michigan.

Grassi, Evelin. 2017. 'From Bukhara to Dushanbe: Outlining the evolution of Soviet Tajik fiction.' *Iranian Studies* 50 (5): 691–704.

Green, Nile. 2015. 'The hajj as its own undoing: Infrastructure and integration on the Muslim journey to Mecca.' *Past & Present* 226 (1): 193–226.

Green, Nile. 2013. 'The rail Hajjis: The Trans-Siberian railway and the long way to Mecca.' In *Hajj: Collected Essays*, edited by Venetia Porter and Liana Saif, 100–107. London: British Museum.

Ibrahim, Abdürecchid. 2004. *Un Tatar au Japon. Voyage en Asie 1908–1910*. Translation, introduction and notes by François Géorgeon and Işık Tamdoğan-Abel. Paris: Actes Sud.

Ishaev, Shakirzyan. 1896. 'Mekka—sviashchennyi gorod musul'man [Mecca is a holy city of Muslims].' *Sredneaziatskii vestnik* no. 11: 21–81, no. 12: 43–83.

Kalinovsky, Artemy. 2013. 'Not some British colony in Africa: The politics of decolonization and modernization in Soviet Central Asia, 1955–1964.' *Ab imperio* no. 2: 191–222.

Kemper, Michael. 2009. 'Ljucian Klimovič. Der ideologische Bluthund der sowjetischen Islamkunde und Zentralasienliteratur [Lucian Klimovich as ideological bloodhound of the Soviet Islamic studies and Central Asian literature].' *Asiatische Studien* 63 (1): 93–133.

Khomidova, Manzura. 2018. 'Osobennosti izobrazheniia i evolutsiia vospriiatiia v proizvedeniiakh Fazliddina Mukhammadieva [Particularities of artistic representations and evolution of sensibility in the works of Fazliddin Muhammadiev],' PhD diss., B. Gafurov Khujand State University.

Kirasirova, Masha. 2011. '"Sons of Muslims" in Moscow: Soviet Central Asian mediators to the Foreign East, 1955–1962.' *Ab imperio* no. 4: 106–131.

Kuhzod, Urun. 2009. 'Kuda smotrela tsenzura? [What the censors looked at?].' *SMI i pravo* 37: 4–7.

Lane, Edward. 1968. *An Arabic-English lexicon* vol. 3. Beirut: Librairie du Liban.

Makarov, Aleksander. 1965. 'O velikom khadzhe: Predislovie [About the great hajj: Preface].' *Druzhba narodov* no. 3: 15–16.

Marjani, Shihab al-Din. 2003. 'Rihlat al-Marjani [Marjani's journey].' In *Ocherki Marjani o vostochnykh narodakh* [*Marjani's essays of Eastern peoples*], edited by Aydar Yuzeev, 184–194. Kazan: Tatarskoe knizhnoe izdatel'stvo.

'Materialy o palomnichestve musul'man SSSR v Mekku (perepiska, vyezdnye dela) [Materials on the pilgrimage of the USSR Muslims to Mecca (correspondence and personnel files on travel abroad)].' February 15—April 26, 1963, vol. I–III. In GARF, f. r-6991, op. 3, d. 1449, ll. 1–202, d. 1450, ll. 1–220.

Metcalf, Barbara. 1990. 'The pilgrimage remembered: South Asian accounts of the hajj.' In *Muslim travellers: Pilgrimage, migration and the religious imagination*, edited by Dale Eickelman and James Piscatori, 85–109. London: Routledge.

Muhammadiev, Fazliddin. 2012. In *Entsiklopediia kino Tadzhikistana* [*Encyclopedia of Tajikistan's cinema*], edited by Galina El'baum and Saadullo Rahimov, 158. Dushanbe: ER-graf.

Muhammadiev, Fazliddin. 1978. 'Lichnoe delo [F.A. Muhammadiev's personnel file].' In the Russian State Archive of Literature and Art (RGALI), 08.07.1978, f. 631, op. 39, d. 4015, ll. 1–23.

Muhammadiev, Fazliddin. 1970. *Puteshestvie na tot svet ili povest' o velikom khadzhzhe* [Journey to the Other world or a tale of the great hajj]. Dushanbe: Irfon.

Muhammadiev, Fazliddin. 1968a. *U Duneda. Eki hazh qissasi: povest'* [In the Other world or a tale of the hajj]. Toshkent: Badiiy adabnashr.

Muhammadiev, Fazliddin. 1968b. In *Kratkaia literaturnaia entsiklopediia* [Abridged literary encyclopedia], edited by Alexey Alexandrovich Surkov, 5: 29.

Muhammadiev, Fazliddin. 1967. 'Puteshestvie na tot svet ili povest' o velikom khadzhzhe [Journey to the Other world or a tale of the great hajj].' *Druzhba narodov* nos. 3–4.

Muhammadiev, Fazliddin. 1965. 'Dar on dunye. Qissai hajji akbar [In the Other world. A tale of the great hajj].' *Sadoi Sharq* nos. 3–6.

Murodov, Murod. 2009. 'Publitsisticheskaia satira v tadzhikskoi periodicheskoi pechati (problemy istorii, teorii i praktiki) [Journalistic satire in the Tajic periodicals: problems of history, theory, and practice].' Habilitation diss., Tajik National University.

Nikolsky, Mikhail. 1911. 'Palomnichestvo musul'man v Mekku [The pilgrimage of Muslims to Mecca].' *Istoricheskii vesnik* no. 4: 256–292, no. 5: 603–638.

Niyazi, Shawkat. 2020. 'Life and works of the Tajik novelist Fazliddin Muhammadiev.' Interview by Vladimir Bobrovnikov. Peredelkino, Moscow, January 10, 2020. Audio, 04:11:53.

Panarin, Sergei. 2020. 'Average wages and cost of living in Moscow, Leningrad, and Soviet Central Asia in the first half of the 1960s.' Interview by Vladimir Bobrovnikov. Moscow, March 5, 2020. Audio, 45:13.

Papas, Alexandre, Thomas Welsford and Thierry Zarcone, ed. 2012. *Central Asian pilgrims: Hajj routes and pious visits between Central Asia and Hijaz*. Berlin: Klaus Schwarz.

Perechen' svedenii, zapreshennykh k opublikovaniiu v otkrytoi pechati, peredachakh po radio i televideniiu [List of data that are prohibited to be published in press, radio and television broadcasting]. 1976. Moscow: Glavlit SSSR.

Prozorov, Stanislav. 2020. 'Islamic studies and orientologists in Dushanbe in the first half of the 1960s.' Interview by Vladimir Bobrovnikov. St. Petersburg, May 29, 2020. Audio, 55:10.

RGASPI (*Russian State Archive of Modern History*), f. 5, op. 35, d. 225.

Riffaud, Madeleine. 1961. Reportazh 's togo sveta' (Alzhirskie deti v ogne voiny) [Reportage 'From the Other World' (Algerian children in the fire of the war)], translated from French. Moscow: Nauka; Strany i narody Vostoka.

'SDRK (Sovet po delam religioznykh kul'tov pri Sovete ministrov SSSR [Council for the Affairs of Religious Cults at the Council of Ministers of the USSR)].' In GARF, f. r-6991, op. 3.

Shirinbaev, Sharaf. 1966. 'Zamechaniia po proizvedeniiu tadzhikskogo pisatelia Fazliddina Mukhammadieva "Puteshestvie na tot svet ili povest' o velikom khadzhzhe" [Comments on the work of the Tajik writer Fazliddin Muhammadiev *Journey to the Other world or a tale of the Great Hajj*]'. In GARF, 23.08.[19]66, f. r-6991, op. 6, d. 51, ll. 196–200.

Sikandar Begum, Nawab. 2007. *A Princess's pilgrimage: Nawab Sikandar Begum's 'A Pilgrimage to Mecca'*, edited by Siobhan Lambert-Hurley. Delhi: Oxford University Press.

Sokolov, Dmitry. 1902. 'Poezdka v gorod Dzheddu [Journey to the city of Jedda].' *Istoricheskii vesnik* 5: 616–649.

Tritton, Arthur Stanley. 1991. 'Dunyā.' In *The Encyclopaedia of Islam*, edited by Bernard Lewis, Charles Pellat, and Joseph Schacht, 626. Leiden: E.J. Brill.

Tursunov, Faezjon M. 1999. 'Leksiko-semanticheskii analiz poslovits i pogovorok v tadzhikskom i russkom iazykakh (na materiale proizvedenii Fazliddina Mukhammadieva) [Lexical-semantic analysis of proverbs and sayings in the Tajik and Russian languages after he works of Fazliddin Muhammadiev],' PhD diss., Rudaki Institute of Language and Literature.

Tursunzade, Mirzo. 1964. 'Molodost' tysiachiletnei literatury.' *Literaturnaia gazeta*, no. 47. November 28.

'Vyezdnoe delo Mukhammadieva F. [F. Muhammadiev's personal file of travel abroad].' 1963. GARF, f. r-6991, op. 3, d. 1450, ll. 11–22.

PART 2

Contemporary Accounts

CHAPTER 10

Coming of Age in Mecca: Pilgrimage in the Life Stories of Two Young Adult Dutch Pilgrims

Marjo Buitelaar

1 Introduction[1]

In this chapter I explore how the meanings that individual pilgrims attribute to their experiences during the pilgrimage to Mecca are connected to their life stories. To this end, I analyse the pilgrimage accounts of two young adult pilgrims from the Netherlands. Late adolescents and young adults are a particularly interesting age-group to focus on for an analysis along these lines.[2] One reason for this is that performing the pilgrimage to Mecca is a recent phenomenon for Muslims of this age-group. Moreover, emergent adulthood is a crucial life-phase for finding one's own place in society. During this phase, individuals face developmental tasks and transitions in their life that tend to have a long-lasting impact on their sense of self, their social relations, and their personal value system (cf. Kunnen 2019; Crocetti 2018; Erikson 1968). The aspirations of young adults in designing their own life and the opportunities that they are offered tend to be strongly gendered. Therefore, I will focus on how age and gender intersect in the ways the two young pilgrims whose accounts I discuss here attribute meanings to their pilgrimage experiences.

This chapter thus creates a bridge between the historical contributions in the first part of the book and the contributions that analyse contemporary hajj practices and stories from a social scientific perspective in the second part. While the historical chapters take readers along on the pilgrimage journey of one or a few individual pilgrims whose written hajj accounts are discussed, the chapters on the pilgrimage experiences of contemporary pilgrims tend to

1 For their inspiring comments on an earlier draft of this chapter, I am most grateful to Willy Jansen and Simon Coleman, two brilliant anthropologists who feature prominently as role models in my own academic biography. Thank you Willy for your presence in my life story since the beginning of my studies, and Simon for entering it in the last decade of my life in academia.

2 In development psychology research, adolescence usually refers to youth between 15 and 27 years old. My focus here is on youth between 20 and 30 years old, a life stage that I will refer as emergent adulthood.

explore how various modalities of a specific theme feature in a larger body of interviews.[3] In this chapter, the two approaches are combined by zooming in on the oral pilgrimage accounts of two young adult pilgrims who participated in my research project on the salience of the hajj in the personal lives of Dutch Muslims of Moroccan or Turkish parentage.

Particularly informative for the ways in which the meanings of pilgrimage are embedded in pilgrims' biographies is the question of what motivates them to embark on the pilgrimage to Mecca at a certain point in their life, or, considering the growing trend of multiple visits, at specific moments in their life. For Muslims living in Europe, whether or when to fulfil one's religious duty of performing the hajj has become a pertinent question. The present quota-system that was implemented to regulate the annual influx of pilgrims hampers the hajj ambitions of many Muslims in Muslim majority countries, but,due to covid-19, has only begun to affect those who live in European countries like the Netherlands since 2022.[4] Also, most Muslims in Europe enjoy a standard of living that allows them to put aside money for the journey to Mecca.[5] As a result, the number of pilgrims to Mecca from the Netherlands and other West-European countries has increased enormously over the past decade (McLoughlin 2013; also see Safar and Seurat elsewhere in this volume). Living in a cultural context where going on a holiday is virtually considered a basic need, and where families with migrant backgrounds habitually visit their country of origin, deciding where to spend one's annual leave has become a considerable moral issue for European Muslims who have not yet fulfilled their religious duty of hajj performance. Such decisions may be informed by both individual motives and peer pressure. This makes it all the more informative to learn how the decision to make the journey to Mecca relates to what pilgrims consider key events in their lives.

How Dutch pilgrims of Turkish and Moroccan descent link their pilgrimage experiences to their wider aspirations in life was one of the topics I investig-

---

3 Much has been written on the issue of authority, representation, and audience in approaches to the study of written and oral self-narratives that may account for this difference. See e.g., Berger Gluck and Patai (1991) and Geiger (1990).

4 The quotas for diasporic Muslim minorities in Europe and other nations like Singapore, South Africa and the U.S. correspond to their countries' total populations (Bianchi 2004, 53).

5 It must be noted that when living in a predominantly non-Muslim environment it can be a challenge to obtain an employer's permission to take leave to go on pilgrimage when the hajj season falls outside the regular holiday seasons in the Netherlands. Also, in line with Saudi hajj regulations, women under the age of 45 face the hurdle of needing a *maḥram*, a male chaperone to accompany them on the journey, although it is unclear how changes in the Saudi law that allows women to travel alone will affect hajj regulations after the measures related to the COVID-19 will be fully lifted.

ated as part of the larger hajj research project which was the point of departure for this volume. In this project, a team of researchers from the University of Groningen and the University of Amsterdam studied how narrations about religiosity, social identifications, and self-identity in pilgrimage accounts reflect the ways in which the habitus of pilgrims, that is, the embodied dispositions that form a matrix for perceptions, appreciations, and actions of narrators is informed by various cultural discourses simultaneously (cf. the introduction to this volume). For my own subproject on the meaning of the pilgrimage to Mecca in the lives of Muslims of Turkish or Moroccan descent in the Netherlands, a total of 77 pilgrims were interviewed, 52 of whom were from Moroccan descent, and 25 of Turkish descent.[6]

To study the relationship between pilgrims' life stories and the meanings they attribute to the hajj, in the first part of each interview, I asked my interlocutors to sketch their 'life-line' by demarcating on a sheet of paper different phases of their lives so far and marking occasions that either positively or negatively stood out for them. The 'life-line' served as a point of entry to discuss key events, significant others, achievements, and challenges in their lives. This open, biographical part of the interview was concluded by inviting the interviewees to reflect on their religious upbringing and personal religious development. Asking for childhood recollections about people who had gone on pilgrimage to Mecca created a bridge to the second, slightly more structured part of the interview, which concentrated on the interviewee's own pilgrimage experiences, either in the form of the *ʿumra*, the voluntary pilgrimage to Mecca, or the hajj, the mandatory pilgrimage.

The pilgrimage to Mecca is a popular conversation topic among Muslims (cf. Al-Ajarma 2020), and most pilgrims gladly share stories about their experiences in Mecca with family and friends. As Khadija Kadrouch-Outmany and I argue elsewhere in this volume, by telling and retelling their stories pilgrims

---

6 All research participants were recruited through 'snowballing': initial contacts in existing personal networks, mosques, and community centres serving as starting points to approach subsequent interviewees. The majority of research participants were in their mid-thirties to late-fifties, all of whom grew up in the Netherlands. Ten Moroccan participants belong to the older generation of economic migrants that came to the Netherlands in the 1960s and 1970s. Most interviews with pilgrims who grew up in the Netherlands were conducted in Dutch by the author, 8 were conducted by Kadrouch-Outmany, while a research assistant conducted interviews with 10 older pilgrims of various Moroccan backgrounds in Tamazight or *dārija* (Moroccan-Arabic). In addition, two students in religious studies each conducted 10 interviews with Dutch based pilgrims for their MA research traineeship and MA thesis, about half of whom were from Turkish or Moroccan parentage (cf. Wijers 2019; de Lang 2017). All interviews were audio-taped and fully transcribed.

present themselves as moral agents. Dan McAdams' theory on narrative identity construction that informed the interview design I used is particularly apt to study such self-representations in storytelling (cf. McAdams 1993). McAdams conceives of identity as 'personal myths' or stories that people tell themselves and others to explain how they have become the person they are at the time of narration. Besides the narrators themselves—who act as main character of such stories—a small selection of significant others tend to feature as positive or negative role models in their life stories. As people's circumstances change, so do their stories about the self and about the role models that populate their stories. McAdams argues that the motor behind the 'plots' in self-narratives is finding a satisfactory balance between agency, the capacity to act upon the world, and 'communion', being embedded in meaningful relationships.[7] Having conducted his research in mostly in white middle class American settings, McAdams conceives of agency as personal autonomy and individual achievements. He therefore focuses on the potential contradictory nature of agency and communion. As I have argued elsewhere, however, developing and maintaining meaningful personal relationships also takes much agency (Buitelaar 2016). Furthermore, not only can meaningful relationships constitute a powerful source of agency, but agency may also be experienced communally rather than referring exclusively to an individual capacity. In relation to the pilgrimage to Mecca, for example, this comes to the fore in the intensifying effect it has on experiencing the sacred for those who circumambulate the Kaʿba to be absorbed by the flow of thousands of other pilgrims who perform this rite simultaneously.[8] Slightly adapting McAdams' approach to agency, then, I use the term here to refer to the capacity to make well-informed biographical choices in order to lead a morally 'good life'. Besides the competence to formulate and pursue life plans, in my understanding of the term, agency also includes coping strategies: one's response to challenges and threats that may jeopardize one's life plans (cf. Skinner and Edge 2002).

---

7 Although related to it through the shared concept of 'agency', McAdams' theory about agency and communion should not be confused with the agency/structure debate in the social sciences, which concerns the issue to what extent social structure defines the scope and nature of the power that individuals possess to act as agents, for example to change that structure, cf. Giddens (1984) and Bourdieu (1977).

8 Cf. the part of a sermon that Werbner (2003, 109) quotes of a Muslim scholar from the reformist Deobandi tradition, who reminded his congregation of the power of simultaneous presence of millions of pilgrims in Mecca as follows: 'When one person asks blessings alone from his God, he shall get the blessing. But if many people ask for blessing all together, they will get manifold blessings. The bigger the congregation is when they ask for blessings, the more blessings Allah will give them.'

What people consider a satisfactory balance between agency and communion can vary between different individuals, depending on their temperament, their life experiences, and on how specific modalities of agency and communion are valued for different categories of people in the cultural contexts they participate in, not in the least on the basis of their age and gender.[9] According to McAdams, so-called 'nuclear episodes', that is narrations concerning key events in the life of the narrator, are particularly informative about challenges to and shifts in the balance between agency and communion.

Since it is relatively easy for Muslims in the Netherlands to go on hajj, it is particularly interesting to learn whether the motivation of my interlocutors to perform hajj at a certain moment in their lives was related to such 'nuclear episodes' in their life stories, and if so, how performing the pilgrimage has affected their sense of agency and of communion. Dividing the interview into a biographical part and a part focusing on the interviewee's pilgrimage experiences worked very well in most cases; many interlocutors enjoyed looking back on their lives when filling in the life-line.[10] How people sketched their life-line provided much information about the significance of their pilgrimage experience for their lives. While some did not mark the journey to Mecca on their

9 This then, is how the balance between agency and communion relates to the agency/structure debate.

10 An exception to this were interlocutors over the age of sixty, consisting of Moroccan women and men who had come to the Netherlands as (the spouse of) economic migrants. They tended to find this part of the interview difficult or appeared to feel somewhat uncomfortable about it. A possible explanation for this might be that in the Moroccan cultural context where they were raised, they were less encouraged to reflect on their personal life story than on stories relating to their family and tribal belongings. Indeed, life stories are never purely private constructions, but are informed by specific cultural conceptions and discourses about personhood (cf. Roberts 2002, 118; Widdershoven 1993, 15). Also, most of the older research participants were illiterate and felt uncomfortable drawing a life-line on paper, so that the interviewer did this for them. Another reason for the slight discomfort could be that overall, these older pilgrims were quite happy to talk about the hajj, but could not imagine why their life story might be interesting in relation to their pilgrimage experience. Their life-line stories mostly consisted of listing events like their marriage, migration, birth of children, etc. In comparison with younger interlocutors—who grew up in the Netherlands—they were more concerned with providing 'correct' information about the hajj, and less eager to contemplate the more personal meanings of their own experiences. At the end of the interview, for example, several female interlocutors asked the interviewer if they had answered her questions correctly. This resonates with my fieldwork experiences in Morocco between 1987 and 1991 when I conducted research concerning practices and meanings of Ramadan, the fasting month. Women would often direct me to their husbands; attending the Friday mosque sermon and the possession of 'correct' knowledge of religion was clearly considered the domain of men at the time (Buitelaar 1993).

life-line and only began describing it when asked in the second part of the interview, others presented their hajj or *ʿumra* journey as a crucial episode of personal transformation or development.

In what follows, I summarize the pilgrimage stories of Enes and Asmae, who both belong to the youngest age-group of interviewees between 20 and 30 years old.[11] I decided to select the interviews with Enes and Asmae for several reasons. First of all, both produced particularly rich pilgrimage accounts. Secondly, while their stories contain many parallels, crucial divergences can also be noted, especially in terms of their genderedness. Drawing a comparison between their hajj accounts therefore provides a glimpse of the shared challenges young adult Dutch Muslims may face in realizing their goals in life as well as shedding light on the gendered dimensions of pilgrimage practices and the meanings attributed to them.[12] After presenting Enes' and Asmae's pilgrimage stories, in a subsequent section I shall compare them by reflecting on how age and gender intersect in the ways each narrator relates their pilgrimage experiences to specific modalities of agency and communion that they strive for in their lives.

2 Enes: Ending Naughty Days[13]

Enes was one of the interviewees who began filling in his life-line by marking the year he went on pilgrimage to Mecca: 2012, three years before the interview

11 To protect the interviewees' privacy, their names and other non-essential personal details such as city of birth/residence that might expose their identity have been changed.

12 While aiming to discuss the interviews of research participants with different ethnic backgrounds also played a role in opting for Enes, who is of Turkish descent, and Asmae, who has Moroccan roots, in practice the cultural differences in their stories did not stand out enough to include them as a focal point in my analysis here. In fact, I was struck by the commonalities in their stories in this respect. The fact that both Enes and Asmae are Sunni Muslims may account for this to some extent, but does not fully explain the overlap of cultural traditions in their stories. Another explanation might be that we are presently witnessing a process of convergence between the practices and stories of Dutch pilgrims of different backgrounds. As the material produced in the interviews for this research does not allow me to draw clear conclusions in this direction, the issue would be interesting to explore in follow-up research. Also, the stories of Enes and Asmae should not be taken to represent those of larger categories of Dutch Muslims. In fact, many more Turkish Muslims are brought up in more conservative families than Enes, and having a mixed marriage, as Asmae does, is as yet rather atypical.

13 The interview with Enes was conducted and transcribed by my former student Lisa de Lang. While she quoted the interview with Enes in her MA thesis, the selection of quotes and the analysis of the interview for this chapter is mine.

took place. At the time of the interview, he was 25 years old and engaged to be married. Enes and his only sibling (a younger brother) belong to the second generation in his family that grew up in the Netherlands; his paternal grandfather migrated to the Netherlands from Turkey in the 1960s. Enes received his diploma in management studies a few months prior to the interview, and had recently been offered a job in the company where he had done an internship. He hoped that his new position would allow him to buy a house and get married in the near future. Enes did not have to be asked about his upbringing. Within the first few minutes of the interview, he described his parents as 'very liberal' Muslims who have always given him much freedom to explore:

> I've always been free to do as I like. In line with our religion, my parents taught me that I am responsible for my own deeds; no imam or fellow Muslim can provide forgiveness: one has one's own responsibility towards God.

Although his mother has recently begun to observe the *ṣalāt*, during most of his life, Enes' parents seldomly engaged in religious practices. Unlike many other Turkish-Dutch children, for example, Enes was not send to a weekend Qur'an school. As a result, until his teenage years, he knew little about Islam. His father taught him what Enes calls the Islamic 'basics' of what it means to be a good person, like not lying, stealing, or hurting others. Enes marks his teens as the phase where he began to develop a general interest in religion. Wondering 'why should Islam be the truth?', as he put it in the interview, he looked up information about Islam and Christianity on the Internet and in booklets. He taught himself how to pray and began to attend the Friday service at the local mosque every now and then.

Enes marked the year that he turned sixteen as the conclusion of a phase that he characterized as having led a 'normal' life as a disciplined and successful student. Next came what he calls his 'discovery phase': he began to drink and smoke pot, joined his friends to house parties, and engaged in what he calls 'naughty things'.[14] Not surprisingly, his study results deteriorated and, after a while, so did his physical condition. Realizing that 'this is not me, I must stop,' as of 2010 he struggled to get back to 'normal' life. He joined a soccer club, thinking: 'playing soccer calms you down: you come home exhausted, so you don't have the energy to go out again.' Also, soccer training provided him with an

14 He did not elaborate on the latter other than stating that he was grateful for having managed to stay out of the hands of the police.

alibi not to join his friends if they asked him to go out. Although he felt better for a while, in the long run the soccer strategy did not work and he relapsed into 'naughtiness'.

Enes' 'naughty phase' lasted for five years. All this time, together with a friend he continued to visit the mosque occasionally. And then, in 2012, he happened to attend the Friday mosque service when an announcement was made that would change his life:

> There was this announcement about an *ʿumra* trip they were organizing, and for youths under 25 it was subsidized: just 700 euros rather than 2000, so that's super cheap! I decided that I would go on the spot. The announcement was made two days after I had attended a birthday party of a friend where I had gotten very drunk. Meaning that there were *exactly* 40 days between the party and our departure to Saudi Arabia, which I remember very well as it was King's Day [italics added to indicate the emphasis, MB].[15] (...) They say it takes 40 days for alcohol to leave the body (...) and I was very lucky because our flight was delayed one day, so that there were *exactly* 40 days between my last drink and our departure for the *ʿumra*.

Enes explained that the moment he heard the mosque announcement, he realized this would be his best chance to stop his bad habits:

> I knew that if I'd go there, I wouldn't touch alcohol any more, no more pot or pills either. Also, I figured: once I've been to Mecca, my friends won't try to persuade me to go out again, you know, they will respect me for my religiosity. So I realized: this will save me.

As young male Muslims tend to do more often, Enes and his friend decided to go on pilgrimage together. The *ʿumra* journey that they signed up for was organized by two Turkish mosque organizations with Dutch branches: Diyanet, the Turkish state mosque organization, and *Milli Görüş*, together assembling 300 pilgrims with Turkish backgrounds from all over the Netherlands for this specific *ʿumra* journey. The information supplied by the organizers pertained predominantly to the logistics of the journey and descriptions of how the various rites should be carried out. Enes watched a DVD about the pilgrimage,

15 King's Day or *'Koningsdag'* is a Dutch national holiday with festivities in all Dutch cities and villages to celebrate the birthday of King Willem Alexander.

but otherwise he took to heart his grandfather's advice not to seek too much information on the meanings of the hajj, but to just 'let it happen':

> My grandfather is the only person in our family who has been on hajj. I was still a child at the time. Besides the ring he gave me upon his return, what I remember is what he'd say when someone asked him about the hajj: 'You cannot describe it, you can only feel it.' (…) When I told him that I was going on *ʿumra*, he said: 'Just go. You will see what I mean when I told you that it cannot described. Just feel it.' And so I decided to let myself be surprised.

Before Enes left for Mecca, his mother organized a barbecue party that many family members attended:

> We call that *helalleşmek* in Turkish, you ask everyone: 'Forgive me if something between us has happened' and then you kiss each other. (…) Everybody gave me some money and they said things like: 'I'm so happy for you.' (…) It was a great day, my whole family was there, we had lots of fun. (…) Not any different than the parties we organize before going on holiday to Turkey, mind you, just a nice family gathering. Great fun as always.

The first stop on the *ʿumra* journey was Medina, where the pilgrims visited the grave of the Prophet Muhammad. For nearly all pilgrims, 'greeting' the Prophet is an intense emotional moment. Rather than elaborating on what it meant to him to visit the Prophet's grave, however, Enes stressed how impressed he had been by how modern and proper the town was:

> I was like: 'Wow!' Medina is such a luxurious city, no beggars or anything. Our hotel was only a ten minutes' walk from the mosque, and the entire mosque area was super clean. The marble floor is so clean you can eat from it, that was so beautiful! (…) So I thought: the Kaʿba and Mecca can't be more beautiful than this, this must be it, this must be the peak moment.

Enes deftly plays with raising expectations in his narrative here:[16] after stating that he had assumed seeing Mecca could not impress him more in the last

---

16 Enes may be born story teller who spontaneously used this narrative technique in the interview. However, considering the coherence and flow of his account, which resonates

FIGURE 10.1 Courtyard of the Prophet's mosque in Medina
PHOTOGRAPH: ANONYMIZED RESEARCH PARTICIPANT IN BUITELAAR'S RESEARCH

sentence of the quote above, the enormous impact his first sighting of the Kaʿba had on him during stands out all the more. Indeed, he relates how his initial encounter with the Kaʿba exceeded his wildest expectations:

> That's where I fell in love [*verliefd werd* in Dutch, MB], I can't express the feelings I felt then. My friends and I have visited many places, like Spain and Denmark, and that was all great and nice too, but this ..., this was falling in love, there's no other way of putting it. (...) When I started to circle the Kaʿba, I felt it pulling me towards it like a magnet. Whenever I was near the Kaʿba during those five days we spent in Mecca, I never felt tired or sleepy. I wanted to stay close to it, so during our entire stay, I think I only

---

with the narrative structure of a conversion story according to which a previous, bad way of life is left behind to embrace a much better lifestyle (cf. Sandage and Moe 2013), it is likely that he has told the story more often.

> slept in the hotel a few hours. For the rest, I'd sleep a bit in the courtyard of the Grand Mosque, but mostly I'd be sitting there looking around.

Enes is quite unique to use the phrase 'falling in love' to describe his emotions upon seeing the Kaʿba for the first time. Similar to its English equivalent, the Dutch '*verliefd worden*' has connotations with romantic love. As such, however, being overwhelmed by emotions and feeling a strong love for God is a recurring topic in both oral and written hajj accounts (also see the contributions by Al-Ajarma, Kateman, and Nurgat elsewhere in this volume). Most pilgrims are moved to tears by the experience, and Enes had expected the same to happen to him. Tour leaders often try to maximize emotional effects on pilgrims during their first sighting of the Kaʿba by suggesting they keep their eyes closed or heads down and let themselves be guided by someone who has been there before until standing in front of the Kaʿba. This also happened to Enes. A fellow pilgrim offered to lead the way so that Enes could keep his eyes shut until reaching the Kaʿba. To his disappointment, however, no tears started to flow:

> When I got there and opened my eyes, I saw that it was so beautiful and I saw all these people crying, and I thought: 'Wow, this is pure love, how come I don't cry?' (…) I longed to cry too; it is a sign of sincere love. But no tears appeared! That is, not when we started out circling the Kaʿba. But during each round I managed to get closer to it, so the second, third, fourth, fifth, sixth … [Enes takes his time to draw seven, increasingly smaller circles with his finger on the table to illustrate the circling, MB] and then, during the seventh time round, I could actually touch the Kaʿba and I pressed my faced into the black cover. That's the moment I started crying!

During the hajj, when millions of pilgrims have gathered in Mecca to perform the *ṭawāf* at the same time, it takes much determination and elbowing to get to the Kaʿba and touch it. Many of my interlocutors commented critically on the selfishness of pilgrims they had seen push others out of the way. In their view, this goes against the spirit of the hajj, which, besides worshipping God, is also about celebrating unity and solidarity among all Muslims. The chance to touch the Kaʿba without having to take recourse to drastic measures is much greater during the *ʿumra*, not only because there are fewer pilgrims then, but also because *ʿumra* pilgrims tend to spend several days if not weeks in Mecca and are able to do the *ṭawāf* numerous times. This was also the case for Enes, who was even lucky enough to be able to kiss *al-ḥajar al-aswad*, the Black Stone set into the eastern corner of the Kaʿba:

> One of the most special moments I experienced was at the Black Stone. The Prophet kissed it, which means that everyone wants to kiss it too. I myself managed to kiss it, and when I did, I saw something there that made me realize 'Wow!' … I guess what I saw then has made the biggest impression on me of all I've seen in Mecca.
> [Interviewer]: What was it you saw?
> One isn't supposed to tell …

Note again the trope in Enes' storytelling of the ineffability of certain experiences. Enes was quite happy, however, to repeat several times how much it had moved him to touch what to Muslims is God's house on earth and to be able to spend ample time in its proximity. Wanting to share that feeling with his loved ones at home, he saw to it that some of the souvenirs he bought for his friends and relatives, like himself, had been in direct contact with the Kaʿba:

> I did not feel like shopping much, but there are lots of shops right outside the Grand Mosque so that's where I went a few times to buy some stuff. I filled one rucksack with souvenirs for family members and close friends that I rubbed against the Kaʿba so that I when I'd give them something I could say: 'This has been in touch with the Kaʿba.' I also rubbed some strings of prayer beads against the black cover, as well as some prayer mats. I like the idea that saying your prayers on that mat you can visualize its having been in contact with the Kaʿba.

When asked if rubbing his souvenirs against the black cover of the Kaʿba was a way to transmit God's *baraka*, blessings, Enes laughed a bit before stating that 'No, no, no; it's just a nice idea.'[17] Interestingly, while denying the power of the Kaʿba to transmit *baraka*, shortly afterwards he did refer to Zamzam water as having extraordinary properties. Like virtually all pilgrims, besides souvenirs he also brought home a five-liter-bottle of Zamzam water:

> Unfortunately, I put it in my suitcase and then the lid burst, so that by the time I got home, there was only about one liter left. Never mind, I was able to give everyone who came to the house to welcome me home a small cup to drink. (…) Zamzam water is very special, you know: it digests com-

17 Cf. Bursi 2022 who discusses different historical views on whether touching the Kaʿba is laudable or should be avoided.

> pletely in your intestines, so that you don't produce urine. You can drink as much as you like, but you don't have to go to the toilet.
> [Interviewer]: What makes Zamzam water so special?
> Oh, I don't know exactly, it's got something to do with Safa and Marwa, it welled up from under Ismael's foot.

Telling about Zamzam water reminded Enes of how pilgrims sitting in the courtyard of the Grand Mosque shared drinks and food with complete strangers:

> There is so much positivity there. It shows on everybody's faces; everybody is merry. It is just so awesome that you're given the opportunity to be there, you realize that is something that you all share, so people greet each other, shake hands, rub perfume oil on your hands, it's all pure love: 'Here you are, brother, sister,' 'Have a piece of cake,' that kind of thing, you know. (...) You're all there with the same goal; 'I want to make a fresh start.' That makes you feel like you're being born again. I really felt like: 'Wow, this is it, grab your chance.' It's very difficult to describe, actually, just like my granddad had predicted.

Enes then took his smartphone out of his pocket to show the interviewer some photographs. Almost echoing his grandfather, he stated that while they do give an impression, they cannot possibly convey what it feels like when you are actually there:

> It's like watching a soccer match on television. That can be cool, but only when you're actually there in the stadium, that's where you really feel the atmosphere.

After his return home, having experienced God's love and the emotional power of collective worshipping inspired Enes to become a more active member in the local Turkish mosque in the town where he lives. Shortly before the interview he had even joined the mosque board, and he now applies the management skills that he acquired during his studies to the benefit of the local Muslim community. Having reiterated several times throughout the interview the love he felt in Mecca, as he summed up his pilgrimage experience towards the end of the interview Enes mentioned his love one more time:

> This [Mecca, MB] is the place where I fell in love, and it has been my salvation, really. I did not have great expectations; it was more like an excuse

> to turn away from my previous life. But I really fell in love, I could feel it in my whole heart. (…) The way I was pulled towards the Kaʿba, that was really magical.
> [Interviewer]: Do you feel as if it has changed you in any way?
> I think what changed is that I have become more balanced. As in: no more doing my prayers one day and then skip them the next. In terms of my expectations for the future: those haven't really changed. I still want to settle down into married life and raise a family. The standard story, so to speak. But my self-image has changed in the sense of having found a calm. (…) I've grown up, become more mature, more focused on my future. So, going on *ʿumra* has helped me climb that wall and step into a new chapter.

3 Asmae: Mapping One's Own Path in Life

Asmae was 30 years old and had been married for a year when we met in July 2019, three weeks before she and her husband would go on hajj. We met for a second interview five months after the couple's return. Like one of her two older sisters and two younger brothers, Asmae was born in Amsterdam to a Moroccan family that had come to the Netherlands in the early 1980s. Her oldest brother and sister were born before the family's migration. Asmae's husband is of Pakistani parentage and, like herself, was born in the Netherlands. I conducted the biographical part of the interview during our first appointment. Asmae began to draw her life-line by demarcating her educational trajectory from elementary school to university. Subsequently, she added marks for her discovery of a Sufi approach to Islam through the Muslim student association she joined during her studies, and her marriage in 2018. Only later in the interview she mentioned having been on *ʿumra* three times. Realizing my specific research interest in the pilgrimage to Mecca when mentioning one of those trips, she went back to the sheet of paper with her life-line to add marks for each of these journeys.

Two girls who were Asmae's close childhood companions are still her best friends. Making an exception for these friendships, Asmae describes the years before she went to university to study pedagogical sciences as a life-phase when she felt lonely and unhappy within her family:

> There are quite some years between my sisters and me, and my younger brothers more or less kept me at a distance because I was a girl. So in hindsight, I was the odd one out in my family. I could not go to my parents if

> I needed advice—they wouldn't know how to help me anyhow—but I wasn't close enough to my older siblings to turn to them.

Looking back, Asmae realizes that her parents could not help her because of their poor education and rural Moroccan background. They felt insecure in the Netherlands and held on strongly to the Moroccan culture they had grown up with, particularly in how they raised their children. Until recently, Asmae had a tense relationship with her mother because of what she characterizes her mother's 'traditional Moroccan views' on gender roles:

> Boys and girls were treated very differently in my family. (…) In my parents' view, men should have freedom. They belong to the outside world, so to speak, whereas we [women, MB] belong to the inside world. My sisters and I were supposed to do lots of domestic chores, but my brothers were exempted and free to do as they liked. At the same time, like them, we went to school and had to do homework. So we always had more tasks. My mum insisted we should learn how to cook. To her, that's how you invest in a good marriage.

The restrictions Asmae experienced and her parents' expectation that she marry a Moroccan man are the main topics in her stories about her teen years. Thanks to the mediation of one of her sisters, she was allowed to go to university, which marked the beginning of a happier phase in her life. She joined a Muslim student association that introduced her to a very different kind of Islam than what she views as the 'culturally inflected religiosity' of her poorly educated parents. The student association invited highly learned speakers like the British convert Abdul Hakim Murad, a neo-traditionalist Islamic scholar with Sufi inclinations (cf. Sedgwick 2020). It is particularly the Sufi approach that speaks to Asmae: its emphasis on the love of and for God; of having what Asmae calls 'a short line' between oneself and God, that is, a close, personal relationship of trust.[18] As an example she mentioned the opportunity to go on hajj: 'I see that as a personal gift that God grants me. It is as though He says: "There you are, my girl, it's yours" you know. He's doing me favour.' The conception of God that she developed as a university student differs much from how her parents raised her:

---

18 Asmae used the term '*liefde*' here, that is, love in a more general sense than the '*verliefdheid*', or having fallen in love, which Enes spoke about. See a similar emphasis on the love of God in Pnina Werbner's extensive quotation of a Sufi Muslim who shared his Sufi interpretations of the pilgrimage to Mecca with her (Werbner 2003, 105).

> The God I grew up with was always condemning and punishing: good or bad, right or wrong, He was judging all the time. But I definitely got rid of that image.

What also appealed to Asmae was the relaxed socializing between male and female members within the student association, many of whom were of Pakistani parentage. She found that Pakistani males 'act normal' around women, unlike Moroccan men who, in her experience, are brought up to believe that they are princes and superior to women. It is through the religious networks she participated in during her studies that Asmae met her husband. Since her parents had rejected several previous suitors of non-Moroccan parentage who had asked for the hand of one of their daughters, she was convinced that they would forbid her to marry the Pakistani-Dutch friend she had fallen in love with. Indeed, after she stated her wish to marry him, a long, conflictual period ensued. Eventually, however, her parents consented to the marriage.

In her narrations about the student association and how her participation in it marked a major turning point in her life, Asmae mentioned in passing that she had had a most wonderful time when she went on *ʿumra* with some lecturers and a group of friends from the student association. She stated that this visit to Mecca was quite different from the time she had been there with her brother and sister-in-law shortly after having begun her studies, even though her first visit had been very special precisely because it was her first time in Mecca. It was only then that she realized that she had not yet marked her *ʿumra* trips on her life-line and hastened to remedy the omission. In response to my subsequent question what had motivated her first visit to Mecca, Asmae 'avowed' that the decision had been taken light-heartedly; she had simply wanted to go on a vacation. Once in Mecca she had realized that it was a very 'different holiday' than other travel destinations:

> Obviously, my parents would not allow their daughters to travel unaccompanied, so whenever one of my brothers would go on holiday, I'd ask if I could join him. Usually they'd go with other guys, meaning that joining them wasn't an option, but this time, my oldest brother had just gotten married and he wanted to visit Mecca with his wife. So my sister and I asked if we could join them, and it was no problem. Actually, it was, of course, his duty to take along two sisters who need a *maḥram* when they want to go to Mecca [laughs, MB]. But any way, he didn't mind, and my sister-in-law actually liked the idea; considering that so much is gender-segregated there [in Saudi Arabia, MB], she liked having female company.

> So that's how it started, but once I was there I thought: 'Wow, I never want to go on a different holiday [than Mecca, MB].'
> [Interviewer]: Can you remember what made you think that?
> First of all, it's how you feel when you're there: the only thing that occupies your mind is worshipping God, concentrating on your faith, there is nothing else to distract you. (…) Being in *iḥrām* strips you from all irrelevant things in life. It's like a home coming. (…) And then, of course, what makes it different from any other trip abroad is its historical significance: if you realize that Ibrāhīm built the Kaʿba—well, actually the history goes all the way back to Adam, peace be upon him. (…) All those prophets and *aṣ-ṣaḥāba*, the companions of the Prophet Muhammad that are buried there. They died as *shahid*, martyrs, but they are still alive in their graves. So, you feel that kind of spirit all around you there. I had made sure to read a lot about the history of those places, and having that knowledge when you see them makes it very special.

Like Enes and many other pilgrims, the first time Asmae entered the courtyard of the Grand Mosque in Mecca, she refrained from looking up until she was standing in front of the Kaʿba:

> I was nervous and preoccupied with deciding which *duʿā* (supplication) I'd do first when I'd get there. Because the first wish you pray for will be fulfilled instantly. So it didn't sink in immediately. But I do remember being very impressed standing there, thinking: here's that building that I know so well from television, and now I am here myself. That was very surreal. I remember finding it slightly smaller than I had imagined, but, to be honest, I can't recall if that was the first time or maybe during my second *ʿumra*. What I do clearly remember is thinking: 'Here is where my journey begins.' Both literally: my *ʿumra*, but also my journey into Islam.

The second time Asmae visited Mecca was quite different. Being there with friends from her student association added greatly to the joy of the experience. This time her youngest brother joined her as a *maḥram*:

> Rather than my asking 'Can I join you', this time it was 'Would you like to come along?' I have more power over my younger brother [laughs, MB], but that wasn't the point really: I explained how important it was to me to go there with this group of friends and that I needed him to accompany me as a *maḥram*. He understood and was happy to come along.

What also differed from Asmae's first *ʿumra* was that their tour leader informed them about the deeper layers of meaning in the hajj rites, for example about the angels that circle the *bayt al-maʿmūr*, God's House in heaven directly above the Kaʿba, at the same time as pilgrims circumambulate the latter. This added to a multi-layered sense of unity that Asmae experienced:

> I was very conscious of the fact that we were there as pilgrims from many different nationalities, all saying supplication prayers, everybody worshipping God. That sense of unity meant a lot to me. As did the connection to God, and with the hereafter, because of those angels circling the *bayt al-maʿmūr*. (…) When you are there, it is all so much within reach, as though … as though your life on earth no longer matters, as though you live in the hereafter.

Tears flowed down Asmae's cheeks as she was telling me this. When asked what touched her so deeply, she explained feeling a kind of 'homesickness': a strong longing for Mecca and the wish to get back in touch with that feeling of connectedness she experienced there:

> It's like: I belong to God, and He sent me to earth to learn how to grapple with life and to think of Him. But I'm not that good at it, I struggle. So then He brings me back—either on *ʿumra* or on hajj—to give me a boost. To stimulate me, or to bring me calm, peace of mind.

Asmae's yearning for Mecca explains why she has been on *ʿumra* three times already—the third time in the company of yet another brother and sister-in-law. During the interview prior to her hajj journey, I asked her why for her upcoming visit to Mecca she and her husband had decided to perform the hajj. Considering her strong longing for Mecca, her answer surprised me:

> Once it is an option, it becomes a duty. We have the money: 'check'. I have a *maḥram*, that's another 'check'. (…) We discussed it when we got married: shall we go on a honeymoon or on hajj? We decided it makes more sense to get the hajj out of the way before buying a house or spending money on holidaying. So: duty first, and after that we can start enjoying ourselves. Mind you, going on hajj is also very enjoyable, of course. But we thought we'd do it before getting a mortgage.[19] It's as down to earth as that, I'm afraid.

---

19 Because of Dutch tax regulations, it is not only complex, but also very expensive to get an

Indeed, when I met Asmae for the second interview five months after her return from the hajj, she and her husband had recently returned from a holiday in Malaysia:

> When we just came back from the hajj, we said: 'Great, that's done, now we can go on holiday and do whatever we like.' But looking back … I mean, Malaysia is nice and beautiful and all that, but it is nothing compared to an experience like the hajj, which gives me such a wonderful feeling, much better than going on a vacation. So I guess I would like to go again, either for the hajj or the *ʿumra*.

For several reasons, performing the hajj felt very different to Asmae than her previous *ʿumra* journeys:

> First of all, some parts are really tough, you suffer ['*het is afzien*' in Dutch, MB]. Also, because it is an obligation it carries more weight. My husband and I had this ongoing conversation: Why would God ask this of us? What is the purpose of it all? Furthermore, doing the pilgrimage together with my husband obviously made it very different from my *ʿumra* experiences.

What stands out most for Asmae are the 'life-lessons' that performing the hajj together with her husband taught her. She has written them in bullet points in the notebook on her smartphone so that she can look at them whenever she feels she needs their support. The first lesson concerned the realization that she should let go of being such a perfectionist; it is okay to do her *ibādāt*, the acts of worship, in a more relaxed and 'one step at a time' manner. This she learned from conversations with her husband in Medina, where their group stayed the first days of their package tour. Initially, Asmae was inclined to spend as much time as possible to say *duʿā* or supplication prayers in the courtyard of the Grand Mosque where the Prophet Muhammad is buried. Her husband, however, told her to take it easy; just the *ṣalāt*, the obligatory five daily prayers and some additional *duʿā* prayers would do according to him. For the rest, he told her, it was alright to enjoy themselves:

> We decided to first and foremost enjoy ourselves in Medina, and make sure that we'd be fit for the hajj later on. We'd go to the mosque for the

---

Islamic mortgage in the Netherlands, that is, one that does not include paying rent, which is forbidden according to Islamic law.

> *ṣalāt* but didn't do not much else. (…) We didn't join the excursions or anything. We just indulged in the luxury of the hotel. (…) We had, after all, deliberately opted for a five-star package tour with a room to ourselves rather than having to share with others. So we savoured every moment of being together. Not surprisingly, of course, being newlyweds.

When the actual hajj ritual in Mecca started, the couple similarly tried to stay together as much as possible. Asmae abhorred the gender-segregated tents in Minā. Being surrounded by noise and dirt, she could hardly sleep. Therefore, on the day of the first *ramy* or pelting rite at the *jamarāt*, the pillars representing the devil, she and her husband decided to carry out the rite early, so that they would have some time together back in the tent camp when the group would leave for the pelting:

> That tent is so very small, I really don't want to be in it when the group is there, I get very claustrophobic. So we thought we'd stay behind and have a tent to ourselves and chill for a bit. That's not allowed, of course, but we did it anyhow [laughs, MB], and since we hadn't slept well the previous night, we fell asleep. (…) But then we overslept and missed the bus that would take the group to Muzdalifa. The tour guide later told us that he had kept phoning us, but apparently we had put our phones on silent. So the bus had left. When we woke and found that the whole tent camp was almost deserted I panicked: how on earth were we going to get there? But my husband saw some groups that were still waiting for their bus and were were allowed to join one of them. (…) When we finally found our group in Muzdalifa the tour guide was furious! Some people sniggered but others looked annoyed.

Asmae interpreted the fact that all ended well as a sign that God had not disapproved of what the couple had done. She also felt encouraged by the independent stance her husband had taken to confront the group and make his own plans:

> I realized how well we communicate … and how easily other people can disturb that. (…) I must admit that I often felt guilty towards the group. (…) I mean, we operated mostly independently whereas they were all busy sharing food and taking care of each other. But sorry: I did not choose you; I don't feel like bonding with you, I prefer operating independently from others.

While, like Enes, Asmae was captured by the visualization of the *umma* in Mecca, the above quotation indicates that it is particularly the idea of the community of Muslims in the abstract that speaks to her. She is happy that—contrary to the Netherlands—in Mecca she does not stand out. Simply being among other Muslims instils her with a sense of belonging. In practice, however, she finds that having to engage with fellow pilgrims often hampers her own decision making and her freedom of movement. Extrapolating her courage to not succumb to the social pressure of the group of fellow pilgrims she travelled with, she decided then and there that she is entitled to follow her own path and make her own choices in life:

> The hajj triggered that: I realized I was growing into myself. I didn't feel at home among Moroccans, I didn't feel at home in my family, and I did not feel at home among my colleagues at work. But I do feel very much at home with my husband. (…) And if there is one place where I do feel I belong, it's in Islam; I belong to God.

Once more, tears welled up in Asmae's eyes when she narrated this 'life-lesson' that the hajj had taught her. As it turned out, despite the empowering realization that she is entitled to follow her own path, and despite feeling nurtured by the fact that her sense of belonging as a Muslim matters more to her than her belonging to an ethnic group or a specific family, it has been very difficult for her to face the complexities of everyday life since her return to Netherlands:

> I have been feeling very down since we came back. I guess it is the contrast between feeling very much at home there, and not feeling at home here. Not having to worry about anything else than doing the rites, in comparison with everything you have to do here. Since our return home, it somehow bothers me all the more that I feel the odd one out at work, for example.
> [Interviewer]: What makes you feel the odd one out?
> … Why is it fine for my colleague to say 'I'm having a break for a fag', whereas I can't say: 'I'm having a break for my prayers'? Small details like that show that I still hide myself … I so much want to come out, but somehow I just don't dare. (…) But if there is one thing that I learned from the hajj, it is that it's alright how I am. So I will go for it, even if it means going against the mainstream. (…) Being Muslim is such a primal feeling.

Asmae feeling very much 'at home' during the hajj and homesick after her return to the Netherlands should not be mistaken as meaning that she would actually like to live in Mecca. Like most interviewees, she is very critical of the Saudi regime and in general does not like the ways foreigners and women are treated in Saudi Arabia. Rather, the pilgrimage to Mecca symbolizes and reinforces her sense of belonging to Islam. At the same time, she is struggling how to reconcile this sense of communion with fellow Muslims with her wish to act as an individual who makes her own decisions rather than adapting to the expectations and demands of others.

The open, biographical interview design that was used in this research allowed narrators to select the stories and highlight elements of their pilgrimage experiences that they themselves deemed important.[20] As a consequence of the open interview format, the topics different interviewees address can vary significantly. A recurring theme in Asmae's stories, for example, is how she relates her pilgrimage experiences to her various senses of belonging and not-belonging. While Enes also addressed his sense of belonging to the *umma* or community of Muslims, unlike Asmae's stories, his narrations do not contain any references to a potential tension he experienced between acting as an individual on the one hand and as a member of the *umma* on the other hand. I would argue that one factor contributing to this difference in Enes' and Asmae's stories concerns the gendered dimensions of their experiences. In the next section I will reflect on how age and gender intersect in the ways Enes and Asmae

---

20 The open, biographical approach is frequently used, particularly in feminist research, with the aim to 'give voice' to subaltern groups in society. Besides the unfortunate word choice—the subaltern have voices, it is a platform they need—the ideal of letting interlocutors speak for themselves can obviously not be fully realized; as Dan Goodley et al. (2004, 167) argue, by compiling story fragments 'researchers are always pulling strings'. The ideal to let research participants speak for themselves would require presenting the near integral transcript of our interlocutors' stories, as, for example, Ozlem Ezer (2019) does in her impressive example of collaborative storytelling in her book *Syrian Women Refugees* in which she presents the personal accounts of Syrian refugees. While for the purpose of this chapter Enes and Asmae were invited to tell the stories they themselves found important, eventually it was I who selected episodes from the interview transcripts that, in my view, represent best how each of them narrated their pilgrimage experiences and attributed meaning to them. Another reason why 'giving voice' can at best only be partial is that storytelling is always dialogical; the stories that interviewees share are attuned to the research topic they agreed to be interviewed about. Also, in this particular research project, many interviewees were motivated to participate to contribute to sketching a different picture of Islam than the often-negative representations found in public discourse (also see Al-Ajarma and Buitelaar 2021). Indeed, storytelling is a process in which narrator and audience are engaged in an ongoing negotiation of meanings. In this sense, the pilgrims who participated in the research are not the sole author of their stories; their hajj accounts are necessarily co-authored and multi-voiced (Buitelaar 2021; cf. Zock 2013).

interpret their pilgrimage experiences in relation to the kinds of agency and communion they strive for in their wider lives.

4 Enes' and Asmae's Stories Compared

A first point to note when comparing the pilgrimage accounts of Enes and Asmae, is the wider social context in which they are embedded; their familiarity with holiday trips, and their having been able to visit Mecca when the occasion arose, illustrate that both research participants belong to a generation of modern middle class citizens with consumerist lifestyles and desires. Asmae has visited Mecca four times already, while Enes expects to go back for the hajj in the near future. Although older Muslims in the Netherlands also engage in repetitive pilgrimage, as was mentioned in the introduction to this chapter, multiple hajj performance differs significantly from patterns that can be discerned in Muslim majority countries like Morocco and Turkey, where the pilgrimage to Mecca very much continues to be a 'once-in-a-lifetime journey' that remains beyond the reach of many Muslims. Also, for most people from Muslim majority countries who are able to realize their wish to visit Mecca, it often takes a life time of saving money to do so, meaning that the pilgrimage tends to be postponed until old age (cf. Al-Ajarma 2020). For this reason, the honorific title of al-Ḥājj(i) or al-Ḥājja that is used to address people who have conducted the pilgrimage, have connotations with old age and are therefore avoided by and not used for young pilgrims like Enes and Asmae.[21] When young pilgrims are addressed by the title, it is often done flippantly.

The new trend among Muslims in the West to visit Mecca in emergent adulthood and to perform repetitive pilgrimage comes with shifts in the meanings of the pilgrimage and new ways of narrativizing the experience. For elderly Muslims, going on hajj is an important step in taking leave of life on earth and preparing to meet one's Creator. Undertaking the journey is motivated first and foremost by the wish to settle one's debts with God and beg forgiveness for one's sins before dying (cf. Buitelaar 2020; Haq and Jackson 2009; McLoughlin 2009, 138; also see Buitelaar and Kadrouch-Outmany, and Safar and Seurat elsewhere in this volume). The *helalleşmek* party that Enes' parents organized for their son echoes the notion of preparing to take leave of one's earthly life. Rather than emphasizing the dimensions of seeking forgiveness and bidding farewell

21 Strictly speaking, the honorific title al-Ḥājj or al-Ḥājja only applies to a person who has conducted the hajj. In practice, however, in many Muslim communities any pilgrim who has been to Mecca tends to be addressed by the title.

from one's dear ones that characterized such farewell ceremonies in the past, however, for Enes the party was 'just a nice family gathering' similar to the ones his family organizes before going on holiday to Turkey.

While Enes and Asmae both mention the mandatory nature of the hajj, the main argument in this chapter is that instead of viewing pilgrimage as a fitting conclusion of one's life trajectory, for many young pilgrims like Enes and Asmae visiting Mecca serves the purpose of preparing them for adult life first and foremost. Indeed, the two pilgrimage accounts discussed here are very much coming of age stories. Enes and Asmae explicitly interpret their pilgrimage experience in terms of overcoming previous biographical hindrances and repositioning themselves as active agents in their social networks and in Dutch society more widely.

In particular, in line with the main developmental tasks that characterize emergent adulthood, their accounts illustrate a reconsideration of agency and communion and a focus on activities that aim to shift the balance between the two. Feeling he had not handled the freedom his parents had allowed him in his teenage years well, in terms of agency Enes is seeking to find more discipline in his life, so that he can start his own career. In terms of communion, besides wishing to start a family, what stands out in his account is how his experience of being 'reborn' by performing the *'umra* is mediated through his mimetic relationship with his grandfather. Being the only member of the family who has performed the hajj, Enes' paternal grandfather features prominently in his account. Enes has developed a strong identification with his grandfather on the basis of their shared pilgrimage experience. Furthermore, the communion with fellow pilgrims Enes experienced in Mecca motivated him to become more active in the local mosque community in his Dutch hometown. In his position as member of the mosque board, he is able to apply and develop his professional management skills. His new engagement with Islam that resulted from his pilgrimage thus involves both agency and communion.

Asmae is likewise seeking a new balance between agency and communion. In terms of agency, she interprets her pilgrimage experiences as a crucial step in her journey toward a more liberal Islam that allows her to make her own choices and distance herself from the demands and restrictive environment of her family. In terms of communion, she moves away in the stories about her subsequent pilgrimage journeys from her family towards her friends and eventually her husband. Similar to what can be observed in Enes' stories, different modalities of agency and communion intertwine and mutually reinforce each other in her narrations; as her relationships with significant others in her life change, Asmae's sense of agency increases. Interestingly, her sense of empowerment is very much linked to the relationship with her husband; she relies heavily on his orchestration and interpretation of the couple's hajj performance. This comes to the fore, for example, in the frequent use of the plural 'we' that appears in the narrations about her fourth pilgrimage journey. By telling her that she can take a more relaxed stance, it is her husband who provides legitimacy to the liberal Islamic approach that speaks to Asmae.

Besides interpreting their pilgrimage experiences in terms of equipping them for adult life, what also transpires in Enes' and Asmae's stories is a view on the pilgrimage to Mecca as something to be enjoyed rather than purely an act of atonement or obedience in preparation to death. In this respect, Asmae is most explicit in presenting the pilgrimage as a 'present' given to her by God, which she understands both as a spiritual 'boost' and a time-out from the complexities of everyday life.

For my analysis here, two points in the narrations of Enes and Asmae stand out in particular. First of all, conceiving of their pilgrimage experiences as a sign that God approves of them and intervenes to help them reinforces their future-oriented views on the significance of the pilgrimage in their earthly lives. Both Enes and Asmae discuss their experiences predominantly in terms of self-realization and personal growth. Enes summarizes the significance of the *'umra* for him in terms of 'step into a new chapter', cleansing the soul and body and seeking forgiveness from God for his previous 'naughty life'. The pilgrimage experience offered him a 'calm' that enabled him to settle down. Asmae describes her pilgrimage experiences as 'growing into myself' and discovering what she really wants for her life.

Secondly, in keeping with an emphasis on personal growth, both Enes and Asmae speak of God in terms of a loving and nurturing power. For Enes, this is more or less in line with how he was raised. His parents taught him to approach Islam as a guideline to learn how to be a 'good' person, similar to alternative sources that non-Muslims may draw from. Also, rather than threatening him with a relentless God as a way to control him, his parents allowed their son to experiment with different lifestyles and emphasized his responsibility for his own deeds. Asmae's parents, to the contrary, presented their daughter with the image of a punishing God. The Muslim student association that she joined in her university years, however, allowed her to develop a more personal relationship with God. Subsequently, her husband taught her that it is okay to be ritually relaxed. Eventually, being introduced to a new perspective that emphasizes one's personal relationship with God, Asmae's hajj experience marked the culmination of her religious journey into her realization that 'it's alright how I am'.

As I have discussed more elaborately elsewhere, the conception of God as a loving entity and an interpretation of the pilgrimage to Mecca in terms of its contribution to self-realization can be discerned more generally among the children of Muslim migrants who grew up in the Netherlands (Buitelaar 2020; Beekers 2015, 145). This stance strongly resonates with a modern conception of personhood in terms of an 'authentic self'. The idea of an 'authentic self' implies an understanding of life according to which each individual should realize their own way of life through self-exploration and self-expression rather than 'surrendering to conformity with a model imposed from the outside, by society, or the previous generation, or religious or political authority' (Taylor 2002, 83).[22]

Looking through the lens of modern subjectivity in terms of an 'authentic self', the pilgrimage accounts of Enes and Asmae appear to have much in common. The stories of both research participants illustrate how the polysemous Islamic tradition intertwines with other globalized social imaginaries to construct modern Muslim personhood (cf. Jung 2016). Although his grandfather features prominently as a role model in his pilgrimage stories, Enes reiterated that he had found his way to God independently. By underscoring his personal agency and the voluntary character of his religious development, he emphasized his personal motivation to conduct the pilgrimage and his strong commitment to worshipping God. Similarly, a notion of free choice underlies Asmae's view that rather than having to conform with the model of Islam imposed on her by her parents, she is entitled to follow her own path and become the kind of Muslim she wants to be. In this sense, both Enes's and Asmae's stances are in line with modern conceptions of Muslim subjectivity according to which 'submitting to God', as the literal translation of the word Islam indicates, is considered to be more authentic and sincere if it is done voluntarily (Jouili 2015, 37; Fadil 2008; Mahmood 2005).

At the same time, resonating with a general conception among Muslims that pilgrims are 'called by God' (cf. Al-Ajarma 2020), both Enes and Asmae interpret having been able to visit Mecca as a direct sign or intervention by God. Enes interpreted the fact that he happened to be present in the mosque when the call for a next *'umra* trip was announced as a sign that God was helping him to get back on the straight path. Likewise, Asmae conceives of each visit to Mecca as an opportunity granted to her by God with a purpose. Likewise, she presents the fact that she and her husband managed to catch a lift to Muzdalifa after disregarding the rule of gender-segregation and falling asleep

22 Although the discourse of the 'authentic self' suggests a liberation from conventional social constraints, it also dovetails with the demands of today's global neoliberal political economy by carrying with it the normative imperative to take full responsibility for one's own life and wellbeing.

together in a tent in Minā as a sign from God that he did not disapprove of their behaviour and that it is alright to go their own way rather than adapt to the group.

Asmae's narrations about operating independently from fellow pilgrims not only points to how her interpretations of the pilgrimage experience are informed by her desire for specific modalities of agency and communion related to her specific phase in life, but also sheds light on the import of gender in her experiences. Her stories diverge significantly from Enes' account in terms of references to gendered dimensions of the pilgrimage. The presence of fellow pilgrims in Enes' and Asmae's narratives is a case in point. While Asmae's account contain several references to her fellow travellers, they are conspicuously absent in Enes' stories; he only mentions chance encounters with pilgrims from other countries that he very much enjoyed. I would argue that Enes' feeling free to do and go as he pleases, such as spending most of his time near the Kaʿba rather than returning to the hotel to sleep, points to the genderedness of his experiences. As a male pilgrim he does not need a *maḥram* as Asmae did on her pilgrimage trips. Also, as I describe in my contribution with Khadija Kadrouch-Outmany elsewhere in this volume, several women who participated in my research reported that female women are expected to adapt to their fellow pilgrims in the group far more than male pilgrims are.

Indeed, when looking through the lens of gender, in certain respects Asmae's narrative is the mirror image of Enes' pilgrimage account. The red thread that runs through Asmae's stories concerns the empowering effect the hajj has on her efforts to liberate herself from social conventions, more specifically to break free from a restrictive parental milieu characterized by gender discrimination. By contrast, Enes felt empowered by the pilgrimage in the sense of its helping him to develop the willpower to withstand the enticement of an excess of freedom and to adopt a more disciplined life. Although he did not address gender in his stories—or perhaps precisely because he did not problematize it—his account is equally gendered as Asmae's. He volunteered the information about his liberal upbringing early in the interview, and mentioned it again several times as the interview progressed. Considering that his father is not principled about abstaining from alcohol and that his mother has only recently started to perform the *ṣalāt*, it is likely that, indeed, the freedom Enes enjoyed as he grew up is due to the more liberal religious style of his parents. Since Enes's only sibling is also male, it would be difficult for him to answer the question to what extent his gender played a role in the freedom of movement and space for exploration that his parents allowed him. What can be established is that not relating their freedom of movement to gender occurred more generally among male interviewees.[23] The majority of female interlocutors, to the contrary, addressed gender restrictions frequently, both in the stories about their upbringing and in stories about their pilgrimage experiences, such as the need to be accompanied by a *maḥram* (also see Al-Ajarma 2021; Thimm 2021; Buitelaar and Kadrouch-Outmany elsewhere in this volume).

I would argue that Enes' struggle to curb his freedom, and Asmae's fight to expand hers, not only shaped how each interpreted their pilgrimage experience, but also informed their religious trajectories more widely. The contrasting motives that characterize their accounts can be linked, for example, to the emphasis on sensing the divine in Enes' pilgrimage stories and the focus on life lessons in Asmae's narrations. Although both Enes and Asmae longed to be touched by the pilgrimage and much appreciated its overall spiritual ambience, Asmae was more strongly oriented towards the historical and deeper meanings of the pilgrimage rites and sites than Enes. Similarly, she also reflected much on the life lessons they had in store for her. This is directly related to her search for a spiritual home where she can feel more truly herself than in what she experiences as the restrictive religious atmosphere in her parental home and an exclusivist environment at work.

In comparison to Asmae, Enes clearly represents a less reflexive religious style. Following the advice of his grandfather, he had deliberately not looked up much information about the pilgrimage to Mecca beforehand but focused on letting himself be overwhelmed by the experience. The significance of the ritual for him pertained predominantly to its potential to provide him a transformational experience that would help him make a new start. As I read his pilgrimage account, contrary to Asmae, he was not in search for religious knowledge, let alone for new, liberating interpretations of the pilgrimage ritual. For him what counted first and foremost was the powerful effect of the *ʿumra* and the sojourn in Mecca on his body and mind. He hoped that experiencing this power might fortify him and help him adopt a more disciplined life style.

To conclude, reading the pilgrimage accounts of Enes and Asmae through the lenses of age and gender sheds light on both commonalities and differences. The comparison of their stories indicate that the commonalities relate mostly to their positions as modern, middle class Dutch Muslims in emergent adulthood, while the differences pertain to their gendered experiences both in their daily lives in the Netherlands and during the pilgrimage to Mecca. Moreover,

---

23 Male interviewees often did mention restrictions in their freedom of movement during childhood by having had to attend mosque lessons at times that their non-Muslim friends were free to play or do sports.

by zooming in on the life stories of Enes and Asmae, I hope to have demonstrated that embedding pilgrimage accounts within the wider context of the narrators' biographies enhances our understanding of how the significance of the pilgrimage to Mecca to individual pilgrims relates to life-cycle transitions and their relationships at home.[24] While the more thematic approach that this chapter shares with the chapters to follow provides insights in how their specific positionality informs the ways contemporary pilgrims appropriate their Islamic heritage to make it meaningful in their daily lifeworlds, the 'travel biography' approach that this chapter shares with the discussion of historical accounts in the preceding chapters draws attention to how what pilgrims identify as key events in their personal lives also contributes to the experience and meanings of the pilgrimage to Mecca.

References

Al-Ajarma, Kholoud, 2021. 'Power in Moroccan women's narratives on the hajj.' In *Muslim women's pilgrimage to Mecca and beyond. Reconfiguring gender, religion and mobility*, edited by Marjo Buitelaar, Manja Stephan-Emmrich, and Viola Thimm, 56–74. London and New York: Routledge.

Al-Ajarma, Kholoud, 2020. 'Mecca in Morocco. Articulations of the Muslim pilgrimage (Hajj) in Moroccan everyday life.' Unpublished PhD thesis, University of Groningen.

Al-Ajarma, Kholoud, and Marjo Buitelaar. 2021. 'Representations of the hajj on social media. Challenging Moroccan and Dutch mainstream media frames.' *Journal of Muslims in Europe* 10, 2 (June): 146–147. https://doi:10.1163/22117954-bja10027.

Beekers, Daan. 2015. 'Precarious piety. Pursuits of faith among young Muslims and Christians in the Netherlands.' Unpublished PhD diss., Vrije Universiteit Amsterdam.

Berger Gluck, Sherna, and Daphne Patai, eds. 1991. *Women's words. The feminist practice of oral history*. New York and London: Routledge.

Bianchi, Robert. 2004. *Guests of God. Pilgrimage and politics in the Islamic world*. Oxford and New York: Oxford University Press.

Bourdieu, Pierre. 1977. *Outline of a theory of practice*. Cambridge: Cambridge University Press.

24 cf. Hillary Kaell (2014, 13) who demonstrates in a most convincing way how the American Christian pilgrims to the Holy Land she studied are motivated by 'the belief that flying far away will help them meet the responsibilities and deepen the identities they inhabit at home.'

Buitelaar, Marjo. 2021. 'Stepping in the footsteps of Hajar to bring home the hajj; dialogical positioning in Asra Nomani's memoir *Standing Alone*.' In *Muslim women's pilgrimage to Mecca and beyond. Reconfiguring gender, religion and mobility*, edited by Marjo Buitelaar, Manja Stephan-Emmrich, and Viola Thimm, 180–199. London and New York: Routledge.

Buitelaar, Marjo. 2020. 'Rearticulating the conventions of hajj storytelling: Second generation Moroccan-Dutch female pilgrims' multi-voiced narratives about the pilgrimage to Mecca.' *Religions* 11 (7): 373. https://doi.org/10.3390/rel11070373.

Buitelaar, Marjo. 2016. 'The implications of having drunk the water of the Netherlands. Narrations on agency and communion in the life story of a Moroccan-Dutch woman.' In *Moroccan feminisms: New perspectives*, edited by Moha Ennaji, Fatima Sadiqi, and Karen Vintges, 221–243. Trenton, NJ: The Red Sea Press.

Buitelaar, Marjo. 1993. *Fasting and feasting in Morocco. Women's participation in Ramadan*. Oxford: Berg.

Bursi, Adam. 2022. '"You were not commanded to stroke it, but to pray nearby it": debating touch within early Islamic pilgrimage.' *The Senses and Society*, 17(1): 8–21.

Crocetti, Elisabetta. 2018. 'Identity dynamics in adolescence: Processes, antecedents, and consequences.' *European journal of developmental psychology* 15 (1): 11–23. https://doi.org/10.1080/17405629.2017.1405578.

de Lang, Lisa. 2017. 'Je probeert een ander mens te zijn. Een studie naar de beleving van de bedevaart naar Mekka in termen van religiositeit en identiteit onder Nederlandse moslims van Turkse en Marokkaanse afkomst.' Unpublished MA thesis, University of Groningen.

Erikson, Erik. 1968. *Identity, youth and crisis*. London: Faber & Faber.

Ezer, Ozlem. 2019. *Syrian women refugees. Personal accounts of transition*. Jefferson, NC: McFarland & Company.

Fadil, Nadia. 2008. 'Submitting to God, submitting to the Self. Secular and religious trajectories of second generation Maghrebi in Belgium.' Unpublished PhD thesis, Leuven University.

Geiger, Susan. 1990. 'What's so feminist about women's oral history?' *Journal of women's history* 2 (1): 169–182. https://doi.org/10.1353/jowh.2010.0273.

Giddens, Anthony. 1984. *The constitution of society*. Cambridge: Polity Press.

Goodley, Dan, Rebecca Lawthom, Peter Clough, and Michelle Moore. 2004. *Researching life stories. Method, theory and analyses in a biographical age*. London and New York: Routledge & Falmer.

Haq, Farooq, and John Jackson. 2009. 'Spiritual journey to hajj: Australian and Pakistani experience and expectations.' *Journal of management, spirituality & religion* 6 (2): 141–156.

Jouili, Jeanette. 2015. *Pious practice and secular constraints. Women in the Islamic revival in Europe*. Stanford, CA: Stanford University Press.

Jung, Dietrich. 2016. 'Modernity, Islamic traditions, and the good life: An outline of the modern Muslim subjectivities project.' *Review of Middle East Studies* 50 (1): 18–27.

Kaell, Hillary. 2014. *Walking where Jesus walked: American Christians and Holy Land pilgrimage*. New York: New York University Press.

Kunnen, Saskia. 2019. 'Identity development from a dynamic systems perspective.' In *Psychosocial development in adolescence. Insights from the Dynamic Systems Approach*, edited by Saskia Kunnen, Naomi de Ruiter, Bertus Jeronimus, and Mandy van der Gaag, 146–159. London: Routledge.

Mahmood, Saba. 2005. *Politics of piety. The Islamic revival and the feminist subject*. Princeton and Oxford: Princeton University Press.

McAdams, Dan. 1993. *The stories we live by. Personal myths and the making of the self*. New York: The Guilford Press.

McLoughlin, Seán. 2013. 'Organizing Hajj-going from contemporary Britain. A changing industry, pilgrim markets and the politics of recognition.' In *The Hajj. Collected essays*, edited by Venetia Porter and Liana Saif, 241–252. London: British Museum.

McLoughlin, Seán. 2009. 'Holy places, contested spaces: British Pakistani accounts of pilgrimage to Makkah and Madinah.' In *Muslims in Britain: Race, place and identities*, edited by Richard Hopkins and Richard Gale, 132–149. Edinburgh: Edinburgh University Press.

Roberts, Brian. 2002. *Biographical research*. Buckingham and Philadelphia: Open University Press.

Sandage, Steven, and Shane Moe. 2013. 'Spiritual experience: Conversion and transformation.' In *APA handbook of psychology, religion and spirituality vol. 1: Context, theory and research*, edited by Kenneth Pargament, Julie Exline, and James Jones, 402–422. Washington DC: American Psychological Association.

Sedgwick, Mark. 2020. 'The modernity of neo-traditionalist Islam.' In *Muslim subjectivities in global modernity: Islamic traditions and the construction of modern Muslim identities*, edited by Dietrich Jung and Kristine Sinclair, 121–146. Leiden: Brill.

Skinner, Ellen, and Kathleen Edge. 2002. 'Parenting, motivation, and the development of children's coping.' In *Agency, motivation, and the life course*, edited by Lisa Crockett, 77–143. Lincoln: University of Nebraska Press.

Taylor, Charles. 2002. *Varieties of religion today. William James revisited*. Cambridge and London: Harvard University Press.

Thimm, Viola. 2021. 'Under male supervision? Nationality, age and Islamic belief as basis for Muslim women's pilgrimage.' In *Muslim women's pilgrimage to Mecca and beyond. Reconfiguring gender, religion and mobility*, edited by Marjo Buitelaar, Manja Stephan-Emmrich, and Viola Thimm, 19–35. London and New York: Routledge.

Werbner, Pnina. 2003. *Pilgrims of love. The anthropology of a global Sufi cult*. London: Hurst & Company.

Widdershoven, Guy. 1993. 'The story of life. Hermeneutic perspectives on the relationship between narrative and life history.' In *The narrative study of lives vol. 1*, edited by Ruthellen Josselson and Amia Lieblich, 1–20. London: Sage Publications.

Wijers, Gijs. 2019. 'Jong en Nederlands in Mekka. Een onderzoek naar de betekenissen van de bedevaart voor jonge, Nederlandse moslimmannen.' Unpublished MA thesis, University of Amsterdam.

Zock, Hetty. 2013. 'Religious voices in the dialogical self: Towards a conceptual-analytical framework on the basis of Hubert Hermans's Dialogical Self Theory.' In *Religious voices in self-narratives. Making sense of life in times of transition*, edited by Marjo Buitelaar and Hetty Zock, 11–35. Berlin: De Gruyter.

CHAPTER 11

'Beyond Words': Moroccan Pilgrims' Narrations about Their Ineffable Hajj Experiences through Stories about the Senses

Kholoud Al-Ajarma

1 Introduction

A group of female tailors from Fes gathered in Hanan's workshop to help design and prepare traditional Moroccan dresses, *qafṭāns*, and *ṭaqshiṭas*.[1] Hanan performed the hajj in 2006 and has been to *ʿumra* several times. When I asked Hanan about her experience in Mecca, her first reaction was a sigh followed by a few seconds of silence. She then told me that if I wanted to learn about the experience of being in Mecca, I should go to visit it myself because—as she saw it—that was the only way one would understand the importance of the journey and the feelings she experienced. In her words: 'The pilgrimage was an unforgettable experience,' and 'a chance in a lifetime to experience a place that is better than any other place.' When Hanan's neighbour, Amina, joined us, I learned that she too had been on hajj. Hanan suggested that Amina too should tell me about her journey to Mecca. Amina's response to the suggestion was this comment: 'What is there to say? That experience cannot be described with words!'

Many Moroccan pilgrims I talked to during my research on the socio-cultural embeddedness of the hajj—the pilgrimage to Mecca—in present-day Moroccan society used similar words and images to Hanan and Amina.[2] In their narratives, my interlocutors often insisted that many events and moments of their pilgrimage experience were 'beyond words' and that one 'has to person-

1 *Qafṭān* in Morocco is commonly used to mean a one-piece dress worn exclusively by women, both as an everyday outfit and haute-couture attire—depending on the material. *Taqshiṭa* (a loanword from Tamazight) is a two-piece version of the *qafṭān* that is worn with a large belt, primarily on formal occasions.

2 The narratives discussed in this chapter are based on data collected during my 18-month ethnographic study of Muslim pilgrimage in Morocco between the summer of 2015 and winter of 2017. For a discussion of this fieldwork, see Al-Ajarma and Buitelaar (forthcoming 2023).

© KHOLOUD AL-AJARMA, 2023 | DOI:10.1163/9789004513174_013

ally experience the journey to understand it.' Despite the insistence that the hajj pilgrimage defies verbal expression, my interlocutors often used readily understandable sensory terminology as means to convey this ineffable experience. Through this sensory lexical field, they sought to recount details of the holy sites they visited, the people that they encountered, the food that they ate, and the prayers they recited or heard. Over time, I came to understand that the realm of sensory experience offered an avenue for sharing experiences that the pilgrims perceived as extraordinary by using language with which everyone could connect. Therefore, the senses became a point of entry to the powerful emotions and awe that were encountered during hajj.

In this chapter, I reflect on the emphasis placed on sensory experiences in the stories of Moroccan pilgrims as a way to express emotional responses to significant moments and encounters during the hajj. I examine the pilgrimage experience through Birgit Meyer's concept of a 'sensational form', which helps to highlight the ways in which pilgrims express and interpret different moment of their hajj journey (cf. Meyer 2006). I also identify and discuss the dimensions of the pilgrimage that inspire the assertion by pilgrims that their experience is indeed 'beyond words'. I argue that by referring to their five senses as a medium of expression, pilgrims aim to present their religious and spiritual connectedness to the holy sites they visited during their pilgrimage, their piety in performing the ritual, and the authenticity of their experience. At the personal level, I argue that the use of senses when describing the pilgrimage allows individual pilgrims to memorialize sacred time and space upon return by narrating their embodied experiences of hajj. At the group level, sharing the hajj experience stimulates feelings and emotions for both those who have previously been to hajj and those who have not.

2 Pilgrimage as a Sensory Experience

Since the 1980s, several scholars have advocated a research perspective that takes into account the role of senses and emotions in understanding how social worlds are shaped (de Witte 2011; Meyer 2009; 2006; Howes 2003;1991; Feld 1991; 1982; Stoller 1989). Anthropological writings on the senses initially tended to explore specific sensory domains, such as sound, taste, smell, or touch (cf. Feld 1991; Stoller 1989) and critiqued the predominantly visual focus of much anthropology. Anthropologists focus not simply on individuals' sensory experience, but also on the attribution of meaning to those physical experiences, including the capacity of the sensory to affect deep, abstract feelings and emotions. Addressing the role of sensory experiences in the formation of religious subjectivities and communities, Birgit Meyer explains that sensational forms make possible a sensory involvement with, and access to, the transcendental:

> Sensational forms (…) are relatively fixed, authorized modes of invoking, and organizing access to the transcendental, thereby creating and sustaining links between religious practitioners in the context of particular religious organizations. Sensational forms are transmitted and shared, they involve religious practitioners in particular practices of worship and play a central role in forming religious subjects. (…) The notion of 'sensational forms' can also be applied to the ways in which material religious objects—such as images, books, or buildings—address and involve beholders.
>
> MEYER 2006, 9

In their ability to make the transcendental accessible, Meyer argues, sensational forms play a key role in constructing religious subjects and communities; the ways the transcendental is experienced and invoked in the here and now underpins individual and collective identities (ibid.).

My research findings confirm that sensory experiences—as described by pilgrims—can be awe-inspiring and appear to be beyond comprehension (cf. Meyer 2015). Pilgrims tended to speak about their religious or spiritual experience by describing its effect on their bodies. For example, one pilgrim spoke about her hair standing up when she saw the Kaʿba and feeling shivers on her skin when she visited the Prophet's Mosque. I would argue that my interlocutors often described the pilgrimage as an emotionally powerful experience exactly because of its strong impact on the senses. Meyer further describes the role of sensational forms in the construction of religious subjectivities and communities with the term 'aesthetic formation'. According to Meyer, aesthetic dimensions of religion are central in generating shared sensory experiences. These shared experiences are not to be seen as mere expressions of a community's beliefs and identity, as in Benedict Anderson's notion of the 'imagined community' (Anderson 1983), but they are also actively involved in an ongoing process of constructing or making religious subjectivities and communities:

> 'Aesthetic formation' captures very well the formative impact of a shared aesthetics through which subjects are shaped by tuning their senses, inducing experiences, molding their bodies, and making sense (…).
>
> MEYER 2009, 7

Bodily responses as well as emotions evoked during the pilgrimage, however, do not exist separately from socio-culturally inflected collectively shared meanings attributed to the pilgrimage experiences (Al-Ajarma 2020). Marjo Buitelaar (2015) points out the importance of understanding specific instances of hajj performances within their wider historical and cultural contexts, thus testifying that the hajj is a living tradition in Islam. While sensory experiences provide a framework for emotions, I shall argue that socio-cultural discourses and expectations about emotions attached to a specific experience also shape that sensory experience in an interactive manner (cf. Davies 2011; Schielke 2010, 10). By looking at the sensory dimension of the pilgrimage experience, I highlight 'the lived and emergent nature of the senses' as well as 'the cultural embeddedness of sensory experience' (Porcello et al. 2010, 53). Following Davidson and Milligan who argue that 'most immediate and intimately *felt* geography is the body' (Davidson and Milligan 2004, 523, italics in the original text), I discuss how pilgrims use the five bodily senses in their recollections of the pilgrimage experience.

3 Sight: 'You Have to See to Understand'

In his discussion of the early Muslim intellectual al-Jāhiz (d. 255AH/869CE), Christian Lange demonstrates that common views that link the primacy bestowed on the eye over the other sense organs to the European enlightenment and theorize that Oriental societies privilege nonvisual senses do not stand the test of evidence (Lange 2022a, 1; 2022b). Similar to the importance that al-Jāhiz accorded to the eye, sight was the most dominant sensory experience described by my interlocutors. They spoke about their first encounters on hajj, starting with their arrival in Mecca, its lights, buildings, and mosques, moving to the sight experience of significant places like the Grand Mosque of Mecca, the Kaʿba, the hills of al-Ṣafā and al-Marwa, ʿArafa, and the Prophet's Mosque and his tomb. Pilgrims also described the people they encountered by commenting on the diversity of their appearances along with the numbers they noted in crowds and at gatherings in Mecca, Minā, ʿArafa, and Medina. Despite the great diversity of narratives, narrations about seeing the Kaʿba for the first time were accorded greatest significance by most pilgrims. In a conversation with Yusra, a pilgrim from Rabat who performed the hajj with her husband in 2014, she recollected her arrival in Mecca as follows:

> I took a nap on the bus taking us from the airport to Mecca; when I woke up my husband said that we just entered the city ... I looked out of the

> window and screamed to my husband: 'Where is the Kaʿba; I cannot see it!' I thought that I would see the Kaʿba first thing when entering Mecca. My husband said: 'Be patient … be patient … We will see it when we go to the Grand Mosque.'

Yusra described seeing the Kaʿba as a moment that she had longed for. She was only satisfied when she was finally able to stand in front the Kaʿba and physically see it. Amina and Hanan, the two women from Fes mentioned in the introduction, described their first sight of the Kaʿba as an unforgettable moment that brought them both to tears. Many pilgrims described that seeing the Kaʿba invoked a range of other bodily sensations, including shivering, cold skin, or instant feelings of strength. For example, Ruqayya, a pilgrim from Fes, described her experience as follows:

> My legs could not carry me anymore; my whole body refused to move. I was like a stone … I sat down, my head on the shoulder of my sister-in-law. It was as if something was going on under my skin. Then I felt something pinching my skin … It was like I was struck by energy that I could not tell where it comes from. Then I stood, I felt I was strong, and I circled the Kaʿba in full strength.

The physical impact of seeing the Kaʿba on Ruqayya was so immense that her habitual leg pain when walking vanished. When Ruqayya described how she had felt her skin being pinched, she pinched my leg to convey the bodily sensation to me. Like Ruqayya, many of my interlocutors described sudden strength, disappearance of physical pain, and seeing flashes of colours, all of which were the result of one sensory experience—the sight of the Kaʿba—that stimulated other physical responses. Yusra, for example, told me:

> As I was performing *ṭawāf* around the Kaʿba someone stepped on my foot … I only knew about it later when I went to the hotel and found that my foot was swollen in red and blue … I did not sense it when I was performing *ṭawāf*.

Many pilgrims described the Kaʿba as a place embedded within, and possessing, a powerful force, probably due to the religious significance of the site. Therefore, many pilgrims talked about being 'overwhelmed with emotion' upon seeing the Kaʿba, being 'moved to tears', 'unable to hear people' around them, or 'frozen in the moment'. The sight of the Kaʿba when standing in front of it for the first time is arguably a 'totemic' image, the apex of the pilgrimage journey, and therefore often mentioned in hajj narratives (Al-Ajarma 2020). By using the term 'totemic', I seek to convey a spiritual relationship that pilgrims assume with the Kaʿba.[3] A totemic object is a physical one that has acquired symbolic representation and even spiritual qualities and connotations. A totem becomes a focal point for the entire group to recognize its core significance and consequently venerate it. It seemed to me that this was what the Kaʿba represented for many pilgrims.

When pilgrims spoke about seeing a significant place like the Kaʿba, they often pointed out the spiritual rewards of their experience. Sami, an old pilgrim I met in Casablanca, told me about the importance of looking at the Kaʿba, referring to God's reciprocal gaze on humanity:

> God, Almighty, looks each night upon the people of earth. The first He sees are the people of the Ḥaram … He forgives those He sees circumambulating, those He sees praying, and those standing in front of the Kaʿba.[4]

Sami mentioned a hadith of the Prophet Muhammad according to which God sends 120 blessings to descend on the Kaʿba and those around it every day: 60 blessings for those who do *ṭawāf*, 40 for those who pray, and 20 blessings for those who look at the Kaʿba.[5] The mere sight of the Kaʿba, then, is believed to be a central element for Muslims receiving blessings. Arguably, the religious texts through which pilgrims learn about holy sites are brought to life for them when they perform the pilgrimage and may precondition, or at least influence, the construction of their experience. Such prior knowledge of the religious importance of Kaʿba may also contribute to personal reflections that pilgrims sometimes share, as was the case with Yusra:

---

3 Spirituality in this chapter is understood as the feeling of personal connectedness with God which includes reflection or thinking about the self that would bring one closer to God (cf. Ahmad and Khan 2016).

4 Sami's narrative resonates with a paragraph by al-Ghazālī: '… the following is found in the tradition: "Verily God Most High looks upon the people of the earth each night. The first of those upon whom He looks are the people of the Sanctuary (Ḥaram), and the first of the people of the Sanctuary upon whom He looks are the people in the Sacred Mosque (al-Masjid al-Ḥarām). Those whom He sees performing the circumambulation He forgives; those whom He sees praying He forgives; and those whom He sees standing with their faces toward the Kaʿba He forgives"' (1853, vol. 1. 307); see also Campo (1991).

5 A reference to this hadith can be found in *al-Muʿjam al-Awsaṭ*, a hadith collection book of Ṭabarānī (1995, vol. 4, 381). Also, al-Azraqī in *Kitāb Akhbār Makka* ['Book of Reports about Mecca'] stated that 'Whoever looks at the Kaʿba with faith and belief, his sins will drop as leaves drop from a tree' (1964, vol. 2, 9).

> I cannot describe how I felt when I saw the Kaʿba … There were so many emotions all over me at once … Then I thought: 'I feel all this in front of the Kaʿba which is only a building; how then will I feel when I meet God on Judgment Day?'

The importance of the visual experience is often reflected in the souvenirs and artifacts, depicting key sites that Moroccans bring from Mecca and Medina or, less frequently, purchase locally for their own use or to share with relatives and friends. Images of the Kaʿba or the Grand Mosque of Mecca were displayed in almost every house that I visited in Morocco. In the house of a pilgrim I visited in Fes, for example, there was a large wall hanging, approximately 100 inches (254 centimeters) in width, depicting the Kaʿba and pilgrims circumambulating it. Framed pictures of the Grand Mosque of Mecca or the Prophet's Mosque in Medina, or both, were hung in people's places of work, bus stations, restaurants, and sweetshops in the market. These photographs captured both the strength of the personal experience and the shared community experience. Pilgrims not only shared gifts and souvenirs, but also their experiences, stories, and memories with family members and friends, insisting on the significance of what they saw and experienced. Many pilgrims echoed the words of Hanan who told me:

> Had I not known that I have been to those holy places and saw them in my own eyes, I would have thought it was a dream … You have to see with your own eyes to understand (…).

To underscore the importance of seeing the Kaʿba, I will close this section with a tale told to me by Lubna, a woman from Mohammedia; the story had circulated via Facebook, possibly changing in the process, but it nevertheless illustrates the point I wish to convey here. In the story, a woman goes on hajj but fails to see the Kaʿba. She panics and cries. People around her point at the Kaʿba but she insists she cannot see it. When she later asks a scholar, he tells her that she must have committed a grave sin. The woman confesses that she was involved in black magic to harm others. The moral of the story, as explained by Lubna, is that the woman was punished by God for her immoral deeds by precluding her from seeing the Kaʿba at the very moment all pilgrims aspire to see it.

I interpret the story as reflecting the central religious significance of the Kaʿba, not just the desire to see it but, importantly, as a symbol of merit, in a spiritual sense. To see it is a sign from God, who sees and knows all, that a pilgrim is accepted. This significance might be a reminder of the metaphor of God looking at the pilgrims even as they look at the Kaʿba. For some pilgrims, the act of seeing the Kaʿba validates their sense of worthiness and perhaps even

FIGURE 11.1 Living room in a Moroccan house with wall painting of the Kaʿba
PHOTOGRAPH TAKEN BY AL-AJARMA IN FES, AUGUST 4, 2015

spiritual success, invoking a feeling that God is aware of everyone's conduct. The failure of the sinner in the story to see the Kaʿba reasserts the moral imperative to live a worthy life, which will enable spiritual inclusion in the apex of the faith—seeing the Kaʿba.

4 Soundscapes: 'One Goes to Hajj when Hearing God Call'

Vocal practices are an important element for performing pilgrimage rites. One of the first soundscapes pilgrims are immersed within, and talk about later, is the *talbiya*, the prayer invoked by pilgrims as an expression of their determination to perform the hajj. Pilgrims participate in this sound creation process once dressed in their *iḥrām* and continue to repeat it until they reach Mecca:

Here I am at Your service, O Lord,	*Labbayka Allāhumma labbayk;*
Here I am; You have no partners.	*Labbayka lā sharīka laka, Labbayk;*

Yours alone is all praise;	*Inna al-ḥamda,*
and all bounty;	*Wa al-niʿmata;*
Yours alone is the sovereignty.	*Laka wa-l-mulk;*
You have no partners.	*Lā sharīka lak.*

Regardless of their different languages and backgrounds, all pilgrims take part in creating this soundscape and collectively preparing themselves for the pilgrimage. In the words of Mousa, a pilgrim from Fes:

> When pilgrims start the *talbiya*, they all chant together 'Here I am'. Every pilgrim would say this as an answer to the call of the Almighty, Who, in the Qur'an commands Prophet Ibrāhīm in *sūra* 'al-Ḥajj': 'And proclaim unto mankind the pilgrimage.' Whenever I hear *talbiya*, I remember my pilgrimage (…).[6]

For Mousa, participating in the *talbiya* and hearing other pilgrims chant it was an aural memento of the hajj, recalling moments of being immersed within his pilgrimage experience. Mousa accounted for his ability to perform the hajj as being his answer to God's call, that of Prophet Ibrāhīm, and later Muhammad (Al-Ajarma 2020). According to Jamal, a pilgrim from Casablanca, no one can go to Mecca or perform the pilgrimage unless they hear God's call. 'When you hear the call, you should go to Mecca and perform the pilgrimage,' Jamal pointed to his ear as he told me these words, indicating the sense of hearing.

Another sound was also significant for my interlocutors: the *adhān* or call for prayer that Muslims hear five times a day during their pilgrimage. Although my interlocutors are familiar with the call for prayer in their daily lives in Morocco, hearing it in Mecca implies another layer of significance. As Mousa put it: the *adhān* 'unifies all pilgrims in one heart in sacred moments at a sacred place.' In addition to the daily prayers, many pilgrims pointed out the particular significance of the call for the *janāza* (funeral) prayer.[7] For the duration of the hajj, this prayer takes place five times a day after every mandatory prayer. For several of my interlocutors, the *janāza* prayer was a constant reminder of death, that

6 The full verse from the Qur'an reads as follows: 'Proclaim the Pilgrimage to all people. They will come to you on foot and on every kind of swift mount, emerging from every deep mountain pass' (Qur'an 22:27). According to Ibn Kathīr, Ibrāhīm said to God: '"But my voice cannot reach all peoples." God responded: "You make the call, and We will deliver the invitation to all"' (Ibn Kathīr 1986 vol. 3, 216–217).

7 The *janāza* prayer is part of the funeral ritual in Islam (cf. Kadrouch-Outmany 2016).

life is short, and that one should be more pious in their actions and deeds. In the words of Mousa:

> We prayed *janāza* after every prayer; after *fajr, ẓuhr, ʿaṣr, maghrib,* and *ʿishāʾ* ... The call for *janāza* prayer every time it reminded me of death and of Judgment Day ... I felt that it was a call to remember human weakness and to be thankful for the life God has given me ... Then, I thanked God and I made *duʿāʾ* prayers asking God for mercy and forgiveness (...).

The significance of supplication or *duʿāʾ* prayers mentioned by Mousa was also highlighted by other pilgrims. Some of my interlocutors said that they performed their supplication prayers individually and others in groups, repeating *duʿāʾ* prayers after a hajj guide, from their phones, or by reading small booklets that they carried from Morocco or purchased in Mecca.

Pilgrims did not only share experiences of actual aural patterns, but also spoke of auditory experiences that were beyond the natural. For example, in a women's gathering in Fes, Ruqayya told a group of female relatives that during her pilgrimage she had encountered the following inexplicable experience:

> I was performing my *ṭawāf* around the Kaʿba when I heard someone calling ... Amina ... Amina ... That's the name of my daughter! I looked around trying to identify where the sound might be coming from. But everyone was performing their *ṭawāf* ... Could it have been my imagination? Was it a divine call? I did not know what that meant!

Upon asking a religious scholar in Mecca about her experience, Ruqayya learned that this might be a *karāma*, an expression that means an extraordinary favour from God.[8] She was told that the meaning of her experience was that good fortune awaits her daughter. For Ruqayya, what she heard was a spiritual message that would stir her thoughts for a time afterwards. Two years later, Ruqayya's daughter Amina, indeed, performed hajj with her father, being the youngest in the family to do so; something that Ruqayya related back to her own seemingly extraordinary auditory experience in Mecca.

8 *Karāma* (pl. *karāmāt*) refers to the extraordinary favor given by God towards a human, often worked by Muslim mystics and saints (cf. Gardet 2012).

5 Smell: 'The Mosque Smelled like Musk'

Out of the five senses, Moroccan pilgrims mentioned smell least of all. Although it was never in great detail, the discussion about smell was limited to three subjects: the cleanliness of mosques and their scents, the smell caused by unhygienic conditions in Minā, and perfumes or incense experienced in Mecca and Medina and then brought home as gifts. Several pilgrims commented on the cleaning process that takes place at the Grand Mosque of Mecca where throughout the day they saw large groups of workers cleaning the entrances to the mosque along with its bridges, minarets, and columns. Pilgrims told me that rosewater was used to scent the passages and hallways of the mosque. *Bukhūr* or incense was burnt to scent the mosque between sunset and evening prayer, while the mosque's officials scented the Kaʿba's *kiswa* and Black Stone five times a day (cf. Bursi 2020).[9] According to Mousa:

> Despite the large number of pilgrims coming and leaving the mosque, you would only smell perfumes … The Grand Mosque is frequently cleaned and washed with Zamzam water … When you sit there and just breath in and out or when you perform prayers; you can enjoy it … It smelled like musk (…).

Thus, when talking about the Grand Mosque of Mecca, my interlocutors only mentioned the good smells that they remembered when speaking about their pilgrimage experience. Smell, Margaret Kenna argues, is a strong mediator between sensual perception and the transcendent realm (Kenna 2005, 62–63). Indeed, this is recognized in the wide use of incense at holy sites and in religious ceremonies, arguably enhancing the sensory perceptions of the worshippers (cf. Howes 1991).

Unlike the overwhelmingly positive responses by pilgrims regarding the cleanliness of the Grand Mosque and its positive smells, only a few pilgrims complained about their experience in Minā, which was mainly caused by the unhygienic conditions in the tent camp. In 2015, one of my interlocutors shared with me a video recording of Moroccan pilgrims at Minā who complained about the piles of trash built up near their tents. There is of course a difference between the immediate registering of dissatisfaction whilst on the pilgrimage and the act of narrating the hajj when it is over (cf. Buitelaar and Kadrouch-

9 *Bukhūr* is a blend of natural ingredients, mainly woodchips, which is used as perfume or incense.

Outmany elsewhere in this volume). In the narratives of hajj memories, pilgrims may emphasize the positive memories over the negative ones for a range of psychological and religious reasons (cf. Al-Ajarma 2020). I would argue that the narratives of pilgrims regarding their experiences may also be related to a hegemonic collective discourse in which it is mostly positive connotations that are ascribed to the pilgrimage (cf. Buitelaar 2020). It can similarly be related to the idea that pilgrims should exert *ṣabr*, patience, and tolerate slight discomforts or negative experiences during the pilgrimage and should refuse to be distracted from the main focus (cf. Buitelaar and Kadrouch-Outmany elsewhere in this volume). On the other hand, some pilgrims related that they had anticipated the hygiene standards in the Minā tent camp to be lower than in the hotels of Mecca. Furthermore, pilgrims' social backgrounds can be a factor in differential experiences of matters such as cleanliness and hygiene issues (ibid.).[10]

My interlocutors also talked about bringing scents as gifts from Mecca, including scented bricks, *bukhūr*, mixed with musk or agarwood, *ʿūd*, as well as perfumes made from musk, ambergris, and Aquilaria.[11] These gifts are often given to family members and friends, signifying the social aspect of sharing the experience of hajj with those at home. Hassan, for example, told me that he brought scented perfumes for his relatives and some for his own personal use. The smell, he insisted, reminded him of his time in Mecca. In his words:

> I was introduced to the scent of *ʿūd* in the Grand Mosque of Mecca where it is regularly used … I liked the smell very much … I then recognized it in many other mosques that I visited in Mecca and Medina. It is a fragrance that does not vanish easily … I bought some for myself and some perfumes for my siblings as gifts to take home (…).

On multiple occasions, I smelled *ʿūd* and *bukhūr* in Moroccan houses. It was sometimes burned to remove the smell of cooked food, but more often simply to enjoy the calming scent. For pilgrims, these scents sometimes reignited and catalyzed connections and memories formed during the pilgrimage, enabling the experience to be accessed from the recesses of memory more fully.

---

10 Also see Aourid (2019) and Hammoudi (2006).

11 *ʿūd* is the Arabic name for agarwood/aloeswood soaked in fragrant oils and mixed with other natural ingredients (resin, ambergris, musk, sandalwood, essential oils, and others).

6 Touch: 'When You Touch It, You Absorb the *baraka*'

In a recent article, Adam Bursi, highlights the disputed role of touching holy spaces during pilgrimage between those who associated it with pagan and idolatrous practices and those who encouraged this practice (Bursi 2022). During my reseach in Morocco, many of my interlocutors told me about the importance of reaching the Kaʿba, touching it, and, if possible, kissing the Black Stone, despite the fact that physical contact with the Kaʿba is not mandatory. Here is how Hanan related her experience:

> When we were in Morocco, I wished that I would at least see the Kaʿba and circumambulate it even if I was the furthest from it. But when we made it to the Kaʿba at night, it was crowded but not to a suffocating extent; so, I made my way through the crowd and I could reach the Kaʿba. I touched it with my hands … It was like absorbing the *baraka* at that holy site.

In addition to the Kaʿba, pilgrims also spoke about touching other places of importance in Mecca and Medina, such as the areas in and around *al-rawḍa al-nabawiya* in the Prophet's Mosque in Medina. *Al-rawḍa al-nabawiya* (also known as *riyāḍ al-janna* or *rawḍa* for short) has great significance among pilgrims. Following a famous hadith narrated by Prophet Muhammad, 'That which is between my house and my pulpit is a garden from the gardens of Paradise' (Muslim 1983, book 15, hadith 572), many Muslims consider the *rawḍa* as a highly significant place that they wish to visit and in which they strive to perform prayers. The *rawḍa* is also where the Prophet is buried (together with Abū Bakr and Umar, the first and second caliphs). I was also told by Moroccan pilgrims that supplications uttered in the *rawḍa* are never rejected.

Despite the importance of the *rawḍa*, entrance into this space is limited. This is especially the case for female pilgrims who are allowed only into a small section of the *rawḍa* for shorter periods of time than those designated for men (cf. Kadrouch-Outmany and Buitelaar 2021). Female pilgrims are also prohibited from physically reaching the tomb of the Prophet. During my participant observation of the *ʿumra* in Medina, I joined a group of female pilgrims to visit the *rawḍa* at the time assigned to women (cf. Al-Ajarma 2020). Once at the *rawḍa*, however, each woman barely had time to pray two *rakʿa*s of ritual prayer (often less than five minutes) before being obliged to withdraw by female guards. Feeling the urgency of being allowed to spend only a very short time at the *rawḍa*, I noticed that the expressions of these women often become very intense. Many women cried as they raised their hands in prayer and others rubbed their hands on the carpets or spread them on the walls surrounding the place. Some women gathered around the marble pillars to touch them with their hands and kiss them. Using the tip of their index finger, I saw some women writing the outline of their names on the pillars before female guards noticed and physically forced them to leave. The gender privilege of men, the time limitations of women's visits, and the guards' control seemed to hinder a spiritually satisfying experience (Al-Ajarma 2020). It seemed to me that female pilgrims—using the sense of touch—were compensating for other limitations, including their inability to reach the tomb of the Prophet, as they are neither permitted to see nor touch it (cf. Al-Ajarma 2021).

For many of my interlocutors, the sense of touch seemed to be connected with the religious importance of the sites they visited, and they often described it as one of the many channels for deriving divine blessings or *baraka*. *Baraka* is believed to be found within physical objects, places, and people, which/whom are chosen by God (cf. Buitelaar 1993; Eickelman 1976). In Morocco *baraka* is often used to express an understanding of divine blessing, which could be obtained in many ways including the performance of pilgrimage itself and also other actions like visiting mosques, shrines, and even tombs of religious figures. In the eyes of many people, by obtaining the *baraka* through pilgrimage or *ziyāra*—and specifically mediated by the sense of touch—they transfer the efficacious power that they attribute to the divine into themselves. For many pilgrims, touching sacred places and objects becomes a tangible memory of blessing that they refer to when they narrate aspects of their pilgrimage experience. According to some, particularly traditionally inclined pilgrims, the *baraka* could even be transferred to others through touching the souvenirs and objects that the pilgrims brought home (cf. Buitelaar 2020; Al-Ajarma 2018).

When I joined my interlocutors to welcome their loved ones returning from the hajj in Morocco, I witnessed numerous encounters where returning pilgrims were welcomed with flowers, dates, milk, hugs, and kisses. What struck me most was how some members in the crowd would touch the hands, arms, or clothes of pilgrims and then rub their hands against their own face and arms, as if absorbing the *baraka* from returning pilgrims by touch transferal. This assumption was confirmed when I asked some of my interlocutors about these encounters. I was told by Sarah, a young woman from Mohammedia, that returning pilgrims possess *baraka*, having successfully completed the pilgrimage and visited Mecca and Medina. Remembering her father's return from hajj, Sarah, told me:

> One of our family friends likes my father very much. When he returned from hajj, she visited us and kept holding his arm. He was shy and told her

> to stop but the woman did not. The woman said that she wanted to have *baraka* because my father had visited the Prophet and the holy places in Mecca and Medina.

This connection between touch and *baraka* seemed to be accepted by a considerable number of my interlocutors as a channel of accessing blessings. This came to the fore particularly when discussing the taste and power of Zamzam water, which I discuss next.

7 Taste: 'One Could Taste Communities and Cultures'

The main experience that my interlocutors talked about in relation to taste was that of Zamzam water.[12] My interlocutors spoke about how they consumed large quantities of Zamzam water, especially after their *ṭawāf* around the Kaʿba and throughout their stay in Mecca and Medina.[13] They often discussed the taste of Zamzam water; some saying that it is distinctively different from tap or mineral water and others commenting on its ability to quench both thirst and hunger. On various occasions, my interlocutors described Zamzam water to me as 'pure and colourless' and 'odorless', or stated that 'it has an authentic taste', 'it is mildly salty' or 'clean'. Here is how Ruqayya, a pilgrim from Fes, put it:

> In the Qur'an, God stated: 'We made every living thing from water.'[14] Zamzam is not just any water; it is the most sacred and miraculous water … It has [blessings, KAA]; just think of how long it has existed, and it still satisfies millions of people … The Prophet said: 'Zamzam water is for what one intends to drink it for.'[15] So, when you drink it, you should make a prayer (…).

12 Zamzam water comes from the Zamzam well, which is located within the Grand Mosque of Mecca and is believed to be a miraculously granted source of water from God to Hājar, wife of Ibrāhīm and mother of Ishmael (cf. Chabbi 2012).

13 For example, in 2018 pilgrims consumed eight and a half million liters of water outside the pilgrimage season alone, according to a Saudi newspaper (cf. https://english.alarabiya.net/News/gulf/2018/08/16/Hajj-pilgrims-consume-8-mln-liters-of-Zamzam-water; Accessed 20 August 2018).

14 Referring to Qur'an 21:30.

15 Referring to a saying by Prophet Muhammad: 'The water of Zamzam is for whatever it is drunk for' (Ibn Mājah 1999, vol. 4, book 25, hadith 3062).

Like Ruqayya, many pilgrims emphasized the taste and consumption of Zamzam water in relation to its sacred character. Believing that 'Zamzam water is what one intends it to be drunk for', pilgrims assume that when one drinks it they will be healed through God; when one drinks it to quench their thirst, God is quenching it. In this sense, the water of Zamzam is seen as something transformative, possessing mystical and unique qualities, including *baraka*. According to my interlocutors, the *baraka* of Zamzam water is capable of being transmitted to those who did not personally visit Mecca for the pilgrimage. Consequently, those who visit Mecca carry back quantities of water for relatives and friends in Morocco. In a way, Zamzam water is considered a doorway to the realm of sacredness and spiritual experiences beyond the sensory.

Pilgrims also discussed the taste of types of food they consumed during the pilgrimage. Since the meals that are distributed during the hajj are mostly provided as part of their travel package, comments on the food were limited to expressing a liking or disliking of its quality and quantity. During the voluntary *ʿumra* pilgrimage, nonetheless, pilgrims have more time to explore food options as most meals need to be prepared by the pilgrims themselves or bought locally (depending on the package provided through travel agencies). Pilgrims performing *ʿumra* in *ramaḍān* were specifically vocal about their experience as they often shared breaking their fast at the Grand Mosque of Mecca (or in Medina) with other pilgrims in groups. For example, Hassan, a pilgrim from Safi, often expressed how much he had enjoyed spending *ramaḍān* in Mecca. In addition to the spiritual dimension of the experience, he explicitly appreciated sharing food with other pilgrims and tasting their dishes. He told me about the dishes he shared with Muslims from Egypt, Palestine, Malaysia, Bangladesh, and Turkey. Every sunset in the month of *ramaḍān* (as he spent all 30 days in Mecca), he would sit with a new group of people, place his food next to theirs, and enjoy conversations while everyone broke their fast. He relished both the food and the interactions, and, in a way, he was, literally, tasting the global Muslim community:

> At sunset, people would first break their fast with dates and water; something small to sustain us until we pray. After prayer, we had big meals … Each group of people prepared and brought their traditional food; Moroccans would bring *ḥarīra* [traditional Moroccan lentil, chickpea and tomato soup, KAA], bread and mint tea; Turkish pilgrims would bring rice cooked with meat or chicken … Excellent foods that people shared together … A friend of mine and I made sure to join different groups and share their food; not for the sake of eating but to taste their food and learn about their traditions … I tried dried fish that was brought

> from Niger, beef stew prepared by Sudanese pilgrims, and chicken and rice prepared by Indian and Pakistani pilgrims.

Hassan embraced the diversity of food traditions that he described in much detail. In my estimation, of greater significance were the conversations that took place in these gatherings and the concept that tasting of different foods was, metaphorically, a way to experience diverse Muslim cultures and traditions. Hassan described the foods he tasted in a social sense, as an activity that has a social and cultural value. He was not only satisfying his hunger but also nourishing his curiosity about other Muslims. He expressed much satisfaction in these encounters and fondly remembered fellow pilgrims with whom he shared more than meals.

8 Reflections on Pilgrim's Stories: Senses, Feelings, and Expectations

The discussion of pilgrims' stories about sensing Mecca illustrates that, although most Moroccan pilgrims insisted that their experience could not be described with words, the vocabulary of the senses was always present in what they shared about their pilgrimage. The senses were channels to remember, to imaginatively recreate and connect with the pilgrimage, and to connect with the Holy Places. In pilgrims' passionate accounts about their encounters in Mecca and Medina, nevertheless, I noticed a recurrent pattern—such as crying when seeing the Kaʿba for the first time. These encounters led me to question to what extent descriptions of sensory experiences during hajj were pre-determined by culturally transmitted narratives or influenced by the experience of individual pilgrims. To illustrate the reasoning behind my query, I share one of numerous conversations in which pilgrimage experiences were discussed. This conversation took place between Salma, a young woman from Rabat who performed *ʿumra*, and her mother, who performed the hajj a few years earlier:

> Salma: I remember all the moments of my *ʿumra* trip; I cannot wait to go again …
> Mother: You should try to go in *ramaḍān* … After my hajj, I went for *ʿumra* three times; my favourite was in *ramaḍān* … But I always like to go to Mecca … No doubt … [Salma's mother laughed when she made the comment about her constant desire to go to *ʿumra*, KAA]. *ʿUmra* in *ramaḍān* might be difficult as you would be fasting; but you can break the fast with Zamzam water and dates and join communal prayers … I remember

> how people cried while the imam made *duʿā'* during *tarāwīḥ* prayers[16] .... My thoughts and soul were concentrating on ritual away from daily life here ...
> Salma: Yes, I also forgot about everything I left behind [in Morocco, KAA] I also cried, *ḍarūrī* [for sure, KAA] ... I cried when I visited the *rawḍa* in the Prophet's Mosque; I was less than three meters away from the Prophet and I felt his presence although I could not see his tomb ... But I did not cry when I saw the Kaʿba; I was surprised that I did not since many people do ...
> Mother: I cried when I saw the Kaʿba ... I told you before ...
> Salma: Yes, I remember ... But I was mainly excited and in a happy mood. I could not wait to see the Kaʿba ... It was larger than I had imagined and different from seeing it on TV.
> [Both women laugh at Salma's comment about the size of Kaʿba compared with footage that she had seen before her *ʿumra* trip, KAA].
> Salma: When I was at al-Ṣafā and al-Marwa; I remembered my mother told me that a part of the original rocks of the hill were there ... It was not in my head but my mother told me to try to touch it to see what it felt like in the past ...
> Mother: Now there is a barrier between pilgrims and those rocks because people in the past would climb them to make prayers and would not come down ...
> Salma: Yes, many changes have been made to the place ... But I think it makes one have less feelings because I really would have wanted to live the things as they used to be in the past (...).

The conversation in which Salma and her mother shared memories of time spent in Mecca and Medina carried on for three hours. Salma compared her own experience with that of her mother, especially when reflecting on emotional moments. Like other pilgrims, Salma went to the Grand Mosque of Mecca to perform *ʿumra* and to Medina to pray at the Mosque of the Prophet. She also followed her mother's recommendation and touched the rocks of the hills of al-Ṣafā and al-Marwa. The link between Salma's desire and her mother's instruction to try to touch the rocks seemed to have exercised a deep influence on Salma, structuring her expectations. Salma's personal surprise that she did not cry when she saw the Kaʿba, for example, reflects an expectation of how

16 *Tarāwīḥ* literally 'rest and relaxation' refers to additional ritual prayers performed by Muslims at night after the *ʿishā'* prayer during the month of *ramaḍān*.

one ought to react, created arguably by the narratives of others including her mother. Furthermore, the use of expressions like 'for sure' and 'without doubt' to point out being moved by the experience in a way suggests no other, less positive response was possible. When sharing experiences, mediated via the senses, Salma and her mother (and my interlocutors in general) were engaging in a cultural act that may condition people's expectations of what physical and emotional reactions they might expect to experience during the pilgrimage (cf. Buitelaar 2020). Both those who have performed the hajj and prospective pilgrims may thus—consciously or unconsciously—anticipate certain sensations and emotions related to the various rites during the pilgrimage. This is unsurprising as the pilgrimage experience itself assumes such magnitude of importance for pilgrims that the narrations of that experience are laden with significance for them and for others.

My intention here is definitely not to question the authenticity of the sensory experiences of individual pilgrims nor the meanings they relate to those experiences, but rather to reflect on these aspects in relation to the lexical label, 'beyond words', as a description that pilgrims often attributed to their pilgrimage. Since their feelings were 'beyond words', pilgrims attempted to narrate their experiences through the five senses, using these medium to explain their reportedly ineffable experiences at religious sites. It seemed to me that when pilgrims described their experiences through the senses, they were engaging in acts of memory that fixed the experience both in their own minds and in the minds of those who listened. Sometimes these narratives stimulated expressions of longing towards the Holy Places among listeners. One example of how these feelings were expressed is the story of al-Ḥājja Zahra, a woman in her seventies, who performed the hajj in the 1990s and wished to visit Mecca again. Her husband, however, did not approve of her wish. In a women's gathering at her house, following a conversation about a cousin's visit to Mecca for *ʿumra*, I heard Zahra whisper to a younger cousin: 'I miss those places, I want to see the Kaʿba again, and to visit the Prophet … I feel … It is like there is fire burning in my chest; right here [hitting her chest, KAA].' As Zahra's eyes filled with tears, I could not tell if the feeling of fire in her chest was one of sadness that she could not visit Mecca again, of anger at her controlling husband who does not take her along with him when he goes to Mecca every year, or of longing to visit the Holy Places one more time. She could not voice the exact feelings she had but was clearly using references to her physical body and her senses to metaphorically to express her longing, dramatizing her message further with sighs and a heart-broken tone.

In narrating the pilgrimage experience through references to the senses, pilgrims give voice to what they initially described to be 'beyond words'. Being overwhelmed by the sight of the Kaʿba, crying, and forgetting bodily pains, are some examples of emotions mediated by the senses. The ability to share what one saw, heard, touched, smelled, and tasted during the pilgrimage with others at home also stirs emotions in the listeners, such as their own happiness when they performed the pilgrimage or a longing to visit the Holy Places (again). After all, the ineffable is given form and made accessible via the senses.

References

Ahmad, Mahjabeen, and Shamsul Khan. 2016. 'A model of spirituality for ageing Muslims.' *Journal of Religion and Health* 55: 830–843.

Al-Ajarma, Kholoud. 2021. 'Power in Moroccan women's narratives on the hajj.' In *Muslim women's pilgrimage to Mecca and beyond. Reconfiguring gender, religion and mobility*, edited by Marjo Buitelaar, Manja Stephan-Emmrich, and Viola Thimm, 56–74. London and New York: Routledge.

Al-Ajarma, Kholoud. 2020. 'Mecca in Morocco. Articulations of the Muslim pilgrimage (Hajj) in Moroccan everyday life.' Unpublished PhD thesis, University of Groningen.

Al-Ajarma, Kholoud. 2018. 'Cadeaus, souvenirs en verhalen van Palestijnse pelgrims naar Mekka.' *Zemzem. Tijdschrift over het Midden-Oosten, Noord-Afrika en Islam* 14, no. 1: 62–71.

Al-Ajarma, Kholoud, and Marjo Buitelaar. Forthcoming in 2023. 'Studying Mecca elsewhere: Exploring the meanings of the hajj for Muslims in Morocco and the Netherlands.' In *Approaching pilgrimage: Methodological issues involved in researching routes, sites and practices*, edited by Mario Katić and John Eade, London and New York: Routledge.

al-Azraqī, Muḥammad ibn ʿAbd Allāh. 1964. *Kitāb akhbār Makka* ['Reports about Mecca']. B'einit: Khayats.

al-Ghazali, Abū Ḥāmid. 1853. *Iḥyāʾ ʿulūm al-dīn* ['The Revival of the Religious Sciences']. Vol. 2, Book 8. Cairo: s.n.

Anderson, Benedict. 1983. *Imagined communities. Reflections on the origin and spread of nationalism*. London: Verso.

Aourid, Hassan. 2019. *Riwāʾu Makka* ['The waves of Mecca']. Beirut: al-Markaz al-Thakafi.

Buitelaar, Marjo. 2020. 'Rearticulating the conventions of hajj storytelling: Second generation Moroccan-Dutch female pilgrims' multi-voiced narratives about the pilgrimage to Mecca.' *Religions* 11, no. 7: 373. https://doi.org/10.3390/rel11070373.

Buitelaar, Marjo. 2015. 'The hajj and the anthropological study of pilgrimage.' In *Hajj: Global interactions through pilgrimage*, edited by Luitgard Mols and Marjo Buitelaar. Leiden: Rijksmuseum voor Volkenkunde Leiden.

Buitelaar, Marjo. 1993. *Fasting and feasting in Morocco. Women's participation in Ramadan*. Oxford: Berg.

Bursi, Adam. 2022. '"You were not commanded to stroke it, but to pray nearby it": debating touch within early Islamic pilgrimage.' *The Senses and Society*, 17:1, 8–21.

Bursi, Adam. 2020. 'Scents of space: Early Islamic pilgrimage, perfume, and paradise.' *Arabica* 67, no. 2–3: 200–234.

Chabbi, Jacqueline. 2012. 'Zamzam.' In *Encyclopaedia of Islam, second edition*, edited by Peri Bearman, Thierry Bianquis, Clifford Bosworth, Emeri van Donzel, and Wolfhart Heinrichs. Leiden: Brill Online. http://dx.doi.org/10.1163/1573-3912_islam_SIM_8112.

Campo, Juan. 1991. 'The Mecca pilgrimage in the formation of Islam in modern Egypt.' In *Sacred places and profane spaces*, edited by Jamie Scott and Paul Simpson-Housley, 145–161. New York: Greenwood Press.

Davies, Stephen. 2011. 'Infectious music: Music-listener emotional contagion.' In *Empathy: Philosophical and psychological perspectives*, edited by Amy Coplan and Peter Goldie, 134–148. Oxford: Oxford University Press.

Davidson, Joyce, and Christine Milligan. 2004. 'Embodying emotion, sensing space: Introducing emotional geographies.' *Social and cultural geography* 5, no. 4: 523–532.

de Witte, Marleen. 2011. 'Touched by the spirit: Converting the senses in a Ghanaian charismatic church.' *Ethnos* 76, no. 4: 489–509.

Eickelman, Dale. 1976. *Moroccan Islam: Tradition and society in a pilgrimage center*. Austin: University of Texas Press.

Feld, Steven. 1991. 'Sound as a symbolic system: The Kaluli drum.' In *Varieties of sensory experience: A sourcebook in the anthropology of the senses*, edited by David Howes, 79–99. Toronto: University of Toronto Press.

Feld, Steven. 1982. *Sound and sentiment: Birds, weeping, poetics and song in Kaluli expression*. Philadelphia: University of Pennsylvania.

Gardet, Louis. 2012. 'Karāma.' In *Encyclopaedia of Islam, second edition*, edited by Peri Bearman, Thierry Bianquis, Clifford Bosworth, Emeri van Donzel, and Wolfhart Heinrichs. Leiden: Brill. http://dx.doi.org/10.1163/1573-3912_islam_COM_0445.

Hammoudi, Abdellah. 2006. *A season in Mecca. Narrative of a pilgrimage*. New York: Hill and Wang.

Howes, David. 2003. *Sensual relations: Engaging the senses in culture and social theory*. Ann Arbor: University of Michigan Press.

Howes, David. 1991. *The varieties of sensory experience: A sourcebook in the anthropology of the senses*. Toronto: University of Toronto Press.

Ibn Kathīr, Ismāʿīl. 1986. *Tafsīr Ibn Kathīr* ['Ibn Kathīr's Interpretations of the Qur'an']. Beirut: Dār al-Fikr.

Ibn Mājah, Muhammad. 1999. *Sunan Ibn Mājah*. Makka: Maktaba Nizār Muṣṭafa al-Bāz.

Kadrouch-Outmany, Khadija. 2016. 'Religion at the cemetery Islamic burials in the Netherlands and Belgium.' *Contemporary Islam: Dynamics of Muslim life* 10 (1): 87–105.

Kadrouch-Outmany, Khadija, and Marjo Buitelaar. 2021. 'Young Moroccan-Dutch women on hajj. Claiming female space.' In *Muslim women's pilgrimage to Mecca and beyond. Reconfiguring gender, religion and mobility*, edited by Marjo Buitelaar, Manja Stephan-Emmrich, and Viola Thimm, 36–55. London and New York: Routledge.

Kenna, Margaret. 2005. 'Why Does Incense Smell Religious? Greek Orthodoxy and the Anthropology of Smell.' *Journal of Mediterranean studies* 15, no. 1: 51–70.

Lange, Christian 2022a. 'Introduction: The sensory history of the Islamic world', *The Senses and Society*, 17:1, 1–7, DOI: 10.1080/17458927.2021.2020603

Lange, Christian 2022b. 'Al-Jāḥiẓ on the senses: sensory moderation and Muslim synesthesia', *The Senses and Society*, 17:1, 22–36, DOI: 10.1080/17458927.2021.2020605

Meyer, Birgit. 2009. *Aesthetic formations: Media, religion, and the senses*. New York: Palgrave Macmillan.

Meyer, Birgit. 2006. 'Religious sensations: Why media, aesthetics, and power matter in the study of contemporary religion.' Inaugural Lecture, Vrije Universiteit Amsterdam. http://www.fsw.vu.nl/nl/Images/Oratietekst%20Birgit%20Meyer_tcm30-36764.pdf.

Muslim, Ibn al-Ḥajjāj. 1983. *Ṣaḥīh Muslim*, edited by Muḥammad Fu'ād 'Abd al-Bāqī. Bayrūt: Dār al-Fikr.

Porcello, Thomas, Louise Meintjes, Ana Maria Ochoa, and David Samuels. 2010. 'The recognition of the sensory world.' *Annual review of anthropology* 39: 51–66.

Schielke, Samuli. 2010. 'Second thoughts on the anthropology of Islam.' *ZMO Working Papers*. https://nbn-resolving.org/urn:nbn:de:0168-ssoar-322336; Accessed 26 May 2018.

Stoller, Paul. 1989. *The taste of ethnographic things: The senses in anthropology*. Philadelphia: University of Pennsylvania Press.

Ṭabarānī, Sulaymān Ibn Ahmad. 1995. *Al-Mu'jam al-awsaṭ* ['Intermediate dictionary']. Cairo: Dār al-Ḥaramayn Publishing House.

CHAPTER 12

Newlyweds and Other Young French Muslims Traveling to Mecca: Desires, Motivations and Senses of Belonging

Jihan Safar and Leila Seurat

In France, the hajj has recently become the object of particular attention. The number of departures has doubled from 10,000 to 20,000 pilgrims between 2010 and 2012, standing at around 17,000 pilgrims per year since this date.[1] Alongside this enormous increase of pilgrims, other sociological developments can also be observed: the number of pilgrims with French citizenship has increased, including sub-categories of converts and young pilgrims. In 2014, pilgrims with French citizenship outnumbered foreign residents for the first time. Until recently, most Muslims postponed concluding their religious duties by performing the fifth pillar (hajj) at an advanced age. Today, younger generations choose to visit Mecca in early adulthood, and thus hajj performance often marks a turning point in their religious trajectories. The number of women has also steadily increased in the last decades; women presently make up around 50% of the total number of French pilgrims.[2] Parallel to the feminization of hajj, more and more couples perform the sacred journey, particularly within the first years of marriage. Most of the time, however, they do not travel as a couple but either accompany widowed mothers or invite their parents to join them. Finally, the journey is no longer considered a once-in-lifetime event; pilgrims returning regularly to Mecca either to perform repetitive hajj pilgrimages or to undertake the ʿ*umra*—the small pilgrimage—is a growing trend.

By analysing the hajj and the ʿ*umra* practices of young French pilgrims, this chapter aims to shed light on developments in the religiosity and sociality of

1 These numbers (until the year 2014) were given to us by a representative from the French Ministry of Foreign Affairs. After 2014, the official statistics on the number of pilgrims from France are difficult to gather. The data we could gather from the hajj organizers and from the Saudi consul in Paris reveal however important gaps between the two sources in terms of the number of pilgrims.

2 On their website, the travel organizer PartirenOmra indicates for example that in 2018, 80% of its pilgrims were younger than 40 years old, while the number of males equalled the number of females. Also, 80% of the pilgrims travelled with their family; and out of them 50% were couples.

today's young French Muslims. In particular, we seek to understand in what ways the pilgrimage to Mecca contributes to the empowerment of these young pilgrims. What motivates young Muslims to perform the pilgrimage? Why do they choose to visit Mecca so regularly? In addition to religious motivations, several factors will be examined in an attempt to explain a pilgrim's desire to visit the holy sites around Mecca—where the hajj and *ʿumra* are performed—and Medina, where the grave of the Prophet Muhammad is located. We argue that the current context of social and political discrimination in France is central for understanding any pilgrim's desires and motivations. Another key factor is generational, migratory narratives. In this regard, to understand the motivations of pilgrims to visit Mecca in addition to the circumstances in France as the home country of young pilgrims, the country of origin of their parents must also be taken into account.

Two erroneous views continue to inform debates about Muslims in the French public sphere. The first view claims that leading a religious life is a way to compensate for the precarious existence of people living at the margins of modernity. This can be dispelled by considering the high cost of a hajj package in France, which on average costs around 6000 euros per pilgrim, and the rising number of hajj participants from France with migration backgrounds. Together, these statistics indicate that today's French Muslims with migrant backgrounds are fully integrated into the consumer society (Göle 2015). French pilgrims are, however, diverse in terms of their income bracket, varying from those who are unemployed to engineers and doctors.[3] This diversity confirms the emergence of a Muslim middle class and the presence of religious lifestyles in the marketing sphere (Haenni 2005).

The second misconception is to interpret the intensification of religious practices as a decline in non-religious senses of belonging, such as language or nationality. In France, as elsewhere in European countries, migrants who visit their country of origin or participate in the pilgrimage to Mecca are often viewed by non-Muslim fellow citizens as withdrawing from the national community. Indeed, an idea in the dominant French discourse is that Muslim citizens with migration backgrounds are more loyal to their 'home' countries Algeria, Tunisia or Morocco than to France. This chapter aims at demystifying such misconceptions. Furthermore, this chapter participates in anthropological literature in recent years that has begun to analyse the effects of globalization on national and religious belonging, which includes examining public

3 Young pilgrims often contribute to the payment of their parents' pilgrimage, also illustrating their middle class positions.

controversies considering the loyalties of Muslims with migration. According to some scholars, migration and the resulting transnational senses of belonging destabilize the nation-state and notions of national identity (Cordero-Guzman, Smith and Grosfoguel 2001; Giddens 1991). For others, the increasing permeability of borders reinforces national and local identifications (Fourchard 2005; Hervieu-Léger 2001). Pilgrimage to Mecca clearly questions the assumption according to which the construction of national identities depends on strong and permanent geographical roots. We argue that the hajj and the *ʿumra* are actually part of larger patterns of movement. Besides the fulfillment of one's religious obligations, they also allow pilgrims to reconnect with their familial heritage, thus creating a link between Islam's holiest sites, their country of residence, and their country of origin.

Having operated in the margins of academic research for a long time, the study of 'Islam de France' in the late 1990s has resulted in a large body of literature focusing either on the involvement of state institutions in the religious sphere or on notions such as 'integration', 'islamophobia' or 'radicalization'. Despite its richness, there is a gap in this literature; it tends to not take into consideration the impact of globalization on the religious sphere. Sometimes perceived as a sign of an emotional attachment to the country of origin and other times as the adherence to the Wahhābī model, we propose to study the pilgrimage to Mecca in a wider social context in order to better understand French Muslims' practices in their articulations with the observed forms of globalization.

The first part of this chapter will show how performing the hajj at a young age enables pilgrims to represent themselves as messengers of the 'true Islam' freed from what they conceive of as the 'superstitions' inherited by their parents' generation. Also, visiting Mecca is part of a desire to re-appropriate their Islamic patrimony and to revalorize their cultural and religious heritage in response to perceived or experienced forms of discrimination.

The second part will more specifically investigate the recent phenomenon of young couples performing the hajj and the meanings that these journeys have for them. A recent phenomenon among French Muslim communities is for brides to demand a package tour to Mecca as a dower (*mahr*). Compared to older generations, today's trend to travel to Mecca as a couple points to a stance of gender equality in terms of sharing religious obligations and financial responsibilities.

The third part will underline the importance of analysing the hajj and *ʿumra* as part of other forms of travel, including to the country of origin. If, on the one hand, young pilgrims disapprove of some of their parents' religious practices, which in their eyes are based on religious ignorance, on the other hand, Mecca appears to be a place where young Muslims reinitiate their parents into—what to them is—the 'true Islam'. Mecca is also a place that paradoxically allows for a reconnection with the country of origin. Indeed, after visiting the Holy Cities, pilgrims often initiate return trips to their country of origin, whether labeled or not in religious terms (*hijra*). It also appears that pilgrims mentally link Mecca to parental stories about past migration trajectories.

This chapter is based on a joint study on the hajj market in France that the authors carried out by between 2016 and 2019, during which they collected over 150 interviews with various stakeholders in the hajj business. Most interviews were with officials, guides, and hajj organizers, but their customers, that is, pilgrims, have also been interviewed. Our empirical data thus focuses on both the discourses of hajj tour leaders along with the stories of female and male pilgrims. The results of this study are also the outcome of a postdoctoral research conducted by Leila Seurat[4] and of additional semi-structured interviews conducted by Jihan Safar on the dower (*mahr*) issue during the pilgrimage.

In this chapter, the term 'French Muslims' is used, because the majority of young pilgrims carry a double nationality. Our research participants were mostly young Muslims with migration backgrounds but also included converts. In addition to discourse analysis of the pilgrimage stories of our interlocutors, in order to grasp their subjectivities, we also paid attention to the biographies of individual pilgrims.

1 Grasping a Cultural and an Islamic Patrimony beyond the Beliefs Inherited from the *bled* (country of origin)

The trend among European young Muslims to perform the pilgrimage to Mecca at an early age reflects the individualization of religiosity. A large number of sociologists have demonstrated that religion has not disappeared among Muslims but is rather relocated, provoking an individualization of practices and beliefs. They argue that globalization has transformed the religious expressions and the relation between religion and citizenship. Marjo Buitelaar has shown how, in the case of Dutch Muslims, being embedded 'in Islamic discourses of ethical self-formation', the hajj experience is also 'merged with a modern liberal discourse on self-identity' (Buitelaar 2018). Therefore, the motivations of young French Muslims should be first and foremost understood

4 European University Institute Florence 2017–2018.

as a desire to distinguish themselves from the religious styles of their parents and develop their own religiosity.

For a majority of our interlocutors, the decision to undertake the hajj is related to the wish to fulfill the religious obligation for all Muslims, regardless gender, who are financially and physically able to perform it.[5] Their 'correct' understanding of Islam makes them conceive of the hajj as an obligation to be performed as soon as possible. The fact that their parents did not perform the hajj during their youth but believed that it was better to postpone it until old age is seen as a misconception of religion, as, for example, Soraya, a 35 years Algerian Berber woman, who arrived in France in 2004, and works as an accountant, stated:

> We need to undertake the hajj as soon as possible because the older you get, the more difficult it is. It's a *farḍ* (obligation). Our parents used to do it as part of tradition, but we don't follow traditions. The real Islam has nothing to do with the traditions inherited by our parents.

This description shows that younger generations perceive a break between themselves and older generations with regard to Islamic practices. Younger generations present themselves as Muslims who know best how to believe and practice. Jaouad, a young Franco-Tunisian born in France in 1988, stated:

> My parents say to me: 'Wait until you retire for the hajj'; but I have the physical and material abilities to go, so why shouldn't I go? Parents are full of misconceptions they brought with them from the days in the *bled* [place of origin, usually implied to be a rural area, authors]. They often came back from Tunisia with a hand of Fāṭima to hang on the wall.

Several reasons were given by pilgrims to explain their motivations to perform the hajj. Many informants referred to the benefits of having accomplished the pilgrimage, such as the expiation of sins, while others referred to their fear of death. For them, death can announce itself any time. For this reason, it is preferable to perform the compulsory pilgrimage as soon as possible. Besides these

5 The obligation to perform the hajj concerns both men and women. A husband does not have the right to refuse the pilgrimage of his wife because it is an obligation (*farḍ*) for all Muslims. While a wife must ask her husband's permission to go on hajj, his approval is not stipulated for the obligatory pilgrimage. However, if the hajj is supererogatory, a husband can refuse that his wife travels to Mecca.

explanations, it is also important to situate the hajj and the *ʿumra* in the social and political context of the home country—in this case study, France.

One of the main motivations our interlocutors mentioned for performing the pilgrimage is to acquire more knowledge about Islam. The decision to go to Mecca generally builds up by attending Arabic or Qurʾanic courses in schools, mosques, or through eLearning. In particular, the close relationship between the teacher and their students amplifies the desire to travel with a religious teacher rather than with a classical hajj travel agency. During the pilgrimage, the teacher becomes a religious guide. The majority of preachers, such Abdelmoneim Boussenna and Rachid Eljay, recruit their 'pilgrim-clients' via their Facebook pages. Zeid, a 32 years Moroccan, and a bank employee who performed his hajj in 2019, explained: 'I have chosen a guide and not a travel agency. My guide is an imam; he is not famous but I trust his ethics.' Wahid, 33 years, a Franco-Tunisian working in IT, and a future pilgrim, argues similarly: 'I will choose a guide and not an agency because the guide cares for his pilgrims.'

All of our interviews revealed the importance of the specific religious teacher or guide. Marwan Muhammad, the president of the non profit organization 'La plateforme des Musulmans', also stresses the need to follow a good guide:

> The pilgrim goes on hajj in order to end up with a 'white page', to erase his past and live a better life. He needs the religious security to smooth his *manāsik* (hajj rites).

Also, in our interviews, pilgrims avowed being worried about not knowing enough about Islam. In such circumstances, the presence of a guide they trust appears decisive. However, Abir, a Franco-Moroccan born in France, was very disappointed by the guide during her last *ʿumra*:

> We hardly saw the guide! They only organized one meeting at the airport in Paris, that was all. We had no courses, no conferences. They pretended to be busy with the organization.

Historically, the hajj was never organized around the figure of a religious teacher as a guide. The phenomenon of popular religious guides appears to be quite recent. And their success as a guide for these pilgrimages is not related to any specific certificate (*ijāza*) in Islamic scholarship. It seems that their rising popularity is more the result of the dynamics of social networks. These religious leaders have their anchoring in French society and derive their popularity from their ability to speak to younger generations. This phenomenon reflects the sociological change of pilgrim's profiles: they are much younger, they desire to learn about the history and meaning of rites, and they seek a personal spiritual experience rather than acting out rites as a sign of obedience only (cf. Buitelaar 2020).

During the pilgrimage, the guide answers all kinds of questions related to the rites that make up the hajj, the kind and number of ablutions required, and the nature and appropriate moments for specific supplication prayers (*du'ā*) and supererogatory prayers (*nawāfil*). The guide also helps non-Arabic speakers to memorize the different supplications. If, in theory, any logistic guide is supposed to be able to answer these questions, in practice, the presence of a spiritual guide reassures the pilgrim: their journey will be organized around conferences (*durūs*) where talks take place before entering the state of *iḥrām* or consecration. Such lectures are also held in the tents in Minā and at ʿArafa during the hajj, while for *ʿumra*, the preacher gives his talks in hotels and other venues and has more time to provide conferences (*durūs*) or initiate pilgrims to the appropriate Arabic formulas and prayers.

An example of how pilgrims learn more about Islamic history is the battle of Uḥud, a well-known battle between the followers of the Prophet Muhammad and the army of the Quraysh who ruled Mecca, which took place in 625 CE. Most hajj and *ʿumra* package tours include an excursion to the site where the battle took place at the mountain of Uḥud, which is located a few kilometers outside Medina. This site is particularly suitable for powerful narratives. During the battle of Uḥud, Ḥamza, the uncle of the Prophet Muhammad, died and the Prophet himself almost lost his life. The story about the battle of Uḥud functions as a narrative to teach lessons about military strategy, faith, and kinship. The story also includes the theme of female devotion through an articulation about the role of Nusayba in the battle, who is known as the first female Muslim warrior: while her initial mission was to bring water to the fighters and take care of the wounded, she took up the sword to protect the Prophet. A large number of our young interlocutors told us that they had named their daughter Nusayba in memory of this female role model in the battle of Uḥud.[6] Actually, most of the hajj packages offer a stay in Medina before or after the stay in Mecca, proposing visits to the first mosque (al Quba mosque) and to the Uḥud mountain where the guide tells the story of the battle.

We would argue that the desire of young pilgrims to acquire knowledge through their hajj performance is also a desire to gain recognition and has to be understood in the context of lived and experienced discrimination in France. In

6 This name has become fashionable among the French Muslims.

our interviews, a large number of pilgrims complained that the kind of knowledge that is taught at the republican schools they attended acted to other them. Thus, the desire for Islamic knowledge needs to be interpreted as an alternative path of knowledge acquisition, allowing young Muslims to valorize themselves by appropriating a patrimony they perceive as their own. It struck us that particularly women are active in this search for specific knowledge to reconcile religious commitment with living in a stigmatizing environment. As we will discuss in more detail in the next section, acquiring religious capital is, for most younger female pilgrims, a way of regaining their own sense of dignity and femininity. In the words of Nabil Ennasri, president of al-Shāṭibī institute:

> Our community is very fragmented, with generational and ideological cleavages. We have also noticed a gender shift in our association: twenty years ago, the public of the conferences was exclusively male, and today, we have 80% women.

The quest for knowledge does not necessarily pertain to the acquisition of formal theological knowledge, but should rather be seen as part of what anthropologists refer to as the 'do-it-yourself kit' of modern religious individualism.

Besides guiding pilgrims and teaching them about Islam's history on their journey to Mecca, outside the pilgrimage season many spiritual guides act as marriage brokers and advisers. Identifying and addressing a 'marriage crisis' in the Muslim community, coming to the fore in serious marital conflicts, and helping a considerable percentage of singles and divorcees, these guides surf on the so-called 'couple crisis' by proposing ways to 'succeed in marriage'. The case of Nader Abou Anas, a preacher who regularly organizes hajj and *ʿumra* trips, is emblematic. *MyNisf* (literally: My half) is the new matrimonial website promoted by Abou Anas that offers ways for couples to meet in a modern context legitimized by the presence of imams. There are also charismatic imams such as, Ismael Mounir and Hassan Bounemcha ('Uncle Hassan') who organize marriage lectures. All three of these speakers are active during the pilgrimage season and even more particularly so during *ʿumra* trips, giving lectures at the Association Entraide at Aubervilliers.[7] Suhail, a 33 years Franco-Tunisian, a divorcee who is in search of a husband and who performed the hajj with her parents, often visits the Association Entraide, which has a *Pole marriage*

7 https://www.entraide92.com/entraide-mariage/, accessed November 21, 2020.

or marriage platform where people meet in a halal (lawful) way. The marriage platform allows pilgrimage guides to expand their audience and, indirectly, to recruit new pilgrims. In the following section, we will zoom in on the nexus between marriage and hajj with reference to the motivations and desires of pilgrims.

2 Hajj, Marriage and Female Empowerment

'What comes first, the hajj or marriage?'; 'Which is more important, to go on hajj once one has amassed the money, or use it to get married?' The dilemma of choosing between hajj and marriage is at the heart of many of the narratives of young Muslims and points to a reinterpretation of the hajj obligation. The dilemma of prioritizing the hajj over marriage was almost non-existent for older generations of Muslims, who tend to view the hajj as a religious duty to be performed at an advanced age after many years of marriage (cf. Buitelaar 2020).

Another generational change is how married couples go on hajj. For the older generation, it is common for men to perform their first pilgrimage in the company of male friends or relatives, while the women usually only perform their hajj once their children have reached adulthood and have left the parental home. If their husbands cannot join them, older women generally travel with another member of the family, such as a son, a daughter and/or son-in-law. Alternatively, they travel with a group of women on a trip organized by a local mosque. Sabiha, a Franco-Moroccan who arrived in France in 1980, for example, was 65 years old in 2018 when she went on hajj with a friend and her husband's friend. She explained: 'My husband went on hajj alone; that was a long time ago.' Sabiha then performed the *'umra* in 2019 with six of her friends.

Young couples, on the contrary, prefer to undertake their first hajj in each other's company and often do so shortly after their wedding, before starting a family. This has been also observed among young Moroccan-Dutch women (cf. Kadrouch-Outmany and Buitelaar 2021). One of our interlocutors, who herself travelled to Mecca a year after she married, pointed out the difference between herself and Muslims of an older generation by stating: 'My parents-in-law went on hajj the year of my marriage … once their son was finally married!' The male privilege of men who perform the pilgrimage before their wives that can be observed among older generations, is thus disappearing among younger couples. Salima, a young Malinese pilgrim who visited several countries with her husband, explains her mother's attitude towards the couple's journey:

> My father went on hajj in 2011, while my mother went recently with ten Malinese women from her association. Even my aunts went alone to Mecca without their husbands. My uncles too, they went alone. I find it very bizarre not to travel as a couple! My mother says she was not ready to go with my father in 2011. She also says she doesn't want to keep the apartment empty or leave her children alone. They have this particular fear, but I don't understand why! I told her: 'Would you at least go for a *ʿumra* with my father?' She answered negatively, saying she won't leave her children and grandchildren alone.

But even when older couples do travel together to Mecca, the significance of this sacred journey for them in some respects differs from the meanings that young couples at the beginning of their marital life attach to hajj performance. For the elderly, a feeling of 'entering the last stage of life' remains dominant. Abas, a pensioner who went on hajj in 2016 together with his wife, explains this logic:

> I saved money for two years to pay for this journey thanks to my retirement pension. I had to accomplish the hajj once in my life. From now on, I can die quietly any time.

In an interview with us, an imam from Trappes pointed to another new trend he noticed: 'Couples now also perform *ʿumra* with their children. Before, it was myself myself (*nafsi nafsi*).' Indeed, different from prior generations, this younger, French Muslim generation not only make repeated *ʿumra* trips, but they also choose to bring their children to see Mecca. In this way, pilgrimage becomes a family trip.

The decision of new married couples to perform the hajj together is often informed by a combination of motivations. The first relates to the idea that it will confirm and strengthen their marriage bond. This motivation is related to the Islamic heritage. A large majority of pilgrims believe that Adam and Eve 'met' again in ʿArafa after a long separation, beginning with their expulsion from Paradise. To honor this reunion, at ʿArafa—derived from the Arabic root 'to know, to meet'—Muslims perform the most important rite of the hajj: the *wuqūf* or 'standing' between midday and sunset to contemplate their life and beg God for forgiveness for their sins. While couples spend much time during the hajj in sex-segregated groups, like Adam and Even they are reunited in ʿArafa. At this particular moment, the pilgrims reconstruct Islamic themes that older generations are often not aware of (Saghi 2010). Designated by *Jabal al Raḥma*, (or Mountain of Mercy), ʿArafa is also considered as a place of forgive-

FIGURE 12.1 Young couple taking in the view of the Kaʿba (photograph published with consent of anonymized research participant project Buitelaar)

ness.[8] In this regard, ʿArafa is marked as a key site of signification for young, married couples.

Another motivation we discerned is related to socio-demographic factors in the French context. Currently, there is a high and rising divorce rate among Muslims.[9] One reason for couples to go to Mecca early on in their marriage is to conduct supplication prayers (*du'ās*), for preserving and bringing *baraka* or

8 It is also the place where the Prophet delivered the Farewell Sermon.

9 Data on divorce rates among French Muslims are not available, but many imams commu-

blessings to their union. In the case of conjugal conflicts, the hajj can have a healing effect. However, as our interlocutor Zeid, 31 years, a Franco-Tunisian pilgrim married in 2017, stated, this effect is not automatic:

> People think problems will disappear if a couple goes on hajj! It's a superstition. Going on hajj is a good intention when couples face problems, but if the basis is not solid, problems will restart!

In a same vein, Saliha, head of 'Muslim Trotter', a halal travel designer, stated:

> Going on hajj as a couple is not a pledge for marriage! But for me, the fact that my husband had already performed his hajj before our marriage was a strong incentive for choosing him as a husband.

Amina, 32 years, Franco-Berber Algerian born in France, who went on hajj in 2017, explained in our first interview with her that her marriage had become more harmonious after she and her husband had been on hajj, including that she felt a stronger religious bond: 'We pray together every day, in addition to supererogatory prayers, we perform *dhikr*, Qur'anic recitation … My husband has a beautiful voice.' Unfortunately, however, apparently the beneficial effects of joint hajj performance did not last long; during our second interview in 2019, Amina announced her desire to separate.

Amina is not the only person we spoke to for whom the hajj eventually did not result in an improved relationship with their partner. Sometimes it can even lead to conjugal conflicts upon return, particularly in regard to the issue of veiling. While some women desire to wear a veil after their hajj, their husband might not be in favour, some fearing the severe consequences it might have on employment and mobility in French public space.[10]

Nevertheless, many young couples value performing the hajj early in their marriage. This may be particularly the case in ethnically mixed marriages, especially when family members of the couple disapprove of these unions. As Rabih, an interviewed pilgrim of 39 years old, Franco-Algerian born in France

---

nicate about the divorce problem. On Facebook, Nader Abou Anas mentions that in France, about one marriage out of two ends in divorce according to the INSEE statistics, representing 130,000 divorces per year, adding: 'Unfortunately, the Muslim community is no exception to this rule. In view of the information we receive as leaders of the association, we believe (even if nothing is official) that the number is much higher.'

10 This is mainly the result of discriminatory measures felt by the Muslim community in France, in particular since the veil affair in 2004, followed by other 'Muslim affairs' such as the burkini one (see Scott 2018; 2009).

explained, going on hajj may facilitate family approval: 'We observe more and more mixing between Algerians and Africans. Some families are still racist ... They go on hajj to bless their marriage, taking Bilal as an example.'[11]

Besides wishing to strengthen one's marriage bond, atoning for sins is another explanation that couples give. A person may, for example, seek forgiveness for sexual relations before marriage, visiting nightclubs, alcohol and drug consumption, etc. Men and women see hajj performance as a good incentive to start a chaste life. This is particularly the case for converts, for whom Islamic regulations are new. Hajj performance is considered as cleansing the soul and a 'reset' that allows one to start a new life. Conducting the hajj also creates an image of a 'good Muslim spouse', facilitated today by selfies, snapchats, or videos distributed by the couple to family and friends. The couple's image in Mecca appears symbolically as strong as a wedding picture. Other couples go to Mecca just after marriage to simply get their religious obligations out of the way, as an imam explained: 'They want to finish and perform their obligation rapidly. They want to respect their duties, even if the person is not ready in his mind.' Furthermore, one could say that going on hajj has also become 'fashionable'. Some of our interlocutors pointed to the social mimicry and social status increase that comes with the hajj:

> The hajj was not scheduled. It's more that once married, the idea crossed my mind; and more specifically when my sister-in-law returned from hajj. I then asked myself if I was financially capable of paying a hajj.

Going to Mecca as a couple also has a pragmatic aspect for women in need of a *maḥram*, a male 'guardian' that all women under the age of 45 must have according to Saudi hajj regulations. A husband is the most obvious companion for women. One guide even stated: 'There are cases where women marry just to perform a pilgrimage!' For Suhail, a 33-year-old divorcee, Franco-Tunisian with two children, the option of remarrying would be an ideal solution to perform her pilgrimage. 'I would love to find a husband who accepts to go for a *ʿumra* with me every year.' As part of the *Vision 2030* in October 2019, the Saudi authorities took a radical measure to cancel the *maḥram* law for the *ʿumra*, allowing women of all ages to travel without a *maḥram*.[12] With this new law, we expect

11 Bilal was a black man who became Islam's first muezzin, that is, a person who performs the call for prayers, mostly from a minaret.

12 In addition to that, new tourist visas have been issued for citizens of 49 countries, among them France.

to see a growing number of single and divorced women travelling in groups in Mecca in the coming years.

A last motivation that deserves mention is for couples who have difficulties to conceive a child to perform the hajj to make invocations for pregnancy. This practice is also quite new: older women tended to be more 'fatalist' in terms of their fertility. Lamia, 35 years, Franco-Algerian born in France, explains:

> Three friends of mine went to hajj with their husbands after more than five years of marriage. They were trying to have children, and went to Mecca to make *du'ā*. Thanks to God, all of them had a baby after their hajj! Difficulties in having babies can be related to changes in the climate, stress and work of women. The generation of our mothers generation was fatalist, and such a practice was not observed.

All of these factors are part of a larger trend in the last decades: a generational shift in how pilgrimage performance is signified, particularly among young married couples who today share the sacred travel experience. The re-interpretation of the hajj obligation by women is another generational change with women's desires to share economic responsibilities and to participate in the payment of their own hajj and also of their parent's hajj.

2.1 *Employed Women and Sharing Responsibilities*

According to Bianchi (2015, 33), women's empowerment and their role 'in making the hajj a distinctly family affair reflects their wider importance in the workforce, in managing businesses, and in owning property'. In France, women financing their own hajj is one of the most noticeable changes in the hajj market with women re-appropriating the compulsory pilgrimage to Mecca in egalitarian terms.[13] As one of our female interlocutors stated: 'All my friends went to hajj after marriage, we don't have any excuses when we have money' (compare Asmae in Buitelaar's chapter 10 in this volume). Again, this view is relatively new, particularly among young women. Many older women with a professional life only undertake the hajj after retirement rather than at the beginning of their professional life. 'A large number of women in their late fifties work in care jobs, namely as nannies; they constitute the majority of my pilgrims,' declared the director of a travel agency. Halima's story serves as an example: she is a 67-year-old Franco-Moroccan widow who travelled to Mecca in 2018 with a group

13 According to Islamic law, a man is not obliged to pay for his wife's hajj; and if he does pay, he gains *ḥasanāt* (good deeds) and *ajr* (religious merit one earns by performing *ḥasanāt*).

of women from her mosque. She paid the 5,400 euros for the package tour by drawing from her own pension and that of her deceased husband. Differently, young, pious Muslims start planning their hajj as soon as they enter the labour market. Alia, 29 years, Franco-Moroccan born in France, for example, is a mother of two children, who paid for her hajj after getting her first job:

> I was a married medical student for eight years before getting a job at the hospital two years ago; I then decided to perform the hajj with my husband who waited until I had finished my studies. Hajj is an obligation, plus I started working. When I was a student, it was difficult to plan a hajj because of my exams and my schedule, although I could perform a *ʿumra*. Today, the hajj comes first. I paid my hajj from my own salary, and my husband did the same for his hajj.

In addition, employed women often finance the hajj of their parents. For some, being offered a hajj by others is not quite the same as having saved money oneself. They consider the religious merit one is rewarded by God to be higher for a person who paid for their own hajj journey. Ismail Mounir, a famous guide, for example declared:

> My brothers and sisters, we all paid for the hajj of my mother. But of course, the benefits for a person who saved money all his life are higher than for a person who was offered a hajj.

The status of the employed female pilgrim is a recent phenomenon, showing that young French Muslims are today part of a middle class society. This status reveals also a generational change that has occurred in the new family logistics of the hajj organization.

2.2 *Complex Family Logistics*

When both spouses are employed, they must organize their vacation time from work together for the pilgrimage. Going to Mecca for a short period of time—usually around fifteen days—is much more feasible today compared to the 1990s when pilgrims used to travel from France by bus. Short-term package tours that include air travel is particularly popular amongst women, because it is more adaptive to familial and professional obligations. In general, young couples prefer to perform the hajj before having a child. This is because the biggest hurdle for some hajj participants is organizing childcare.[14] 'It's more

14 For couples with children, much planning and organization of family affairs precedes the

practical for couples to go on hajj when they don't have babies! They are also psychologically more ready,' explained Rabih, a pilgrim of 39 years, Franco-Algerian born in France himself father of five children. Newly-wed women are actually encouraged by female organizers, such as bloggers or women working for hajj travel companies, to perform the hajj before motherhood. Female organizers thus play an active role in modifying women's agency with regard to their hajj decision. When the hajj market was still dominated by male actors, such support for female pilgrims was quite absent. The director of the travel agency Muslim Trotter stated:

> Having postponed the hajj for years before performing it is the main regret of women who get pregnant. That's the reason why I recommend them to perform the hajj when they are young and before having children. They will otherwise always feel a big frustration, will fantasize about the journey, and return disappointed from their hajj.

Women bloggers also play a role in stimulating women's personal growth by recommending couples not to stick together during the hajj, and instead choose physical and spiritual detachment; 'hajj is an individual experience with God, and a collective experience with peers' is what Linda from the travel organizer PartirenOmra stated, adding that women must try to see their husbands not simply as husbands but rather as 'creatures of God': 'Nothing must distract us from performing the hajj. We are not the wife or the husband of someone, but the servant of God.' In her view, sharing a room with other women rather than with one's husband is a sacrifice for God, and it builds relations with other sisters.[15]

In addition to professional, familial, and organizational dimensions of planning one's hajj, bank loans are another major hindrance for couples wishing to accomplish their pilgrimage. According to Islamic law, a bank loan is not tolerated, nor is it permissible to borrow money to finance one's hajj. For this reason, those who plan to go on hajj strive to settle their debts before performing the pilgrimage to Mecca. Our interlocutors Jean, a French converted and Abir, a Franco-Moroccan born in France, for example, endeavoured to pay off their mortgage before organizing their hajj journey in 2017: 'We paid off our

---

trip to Mecca. Generally, children stay with their grandmothers or aunts who live in France or are invited to come over to France for this purpose. Other couples go to the country of origin to drop children at their family's place.

15 https://www.partir-en-omra.com/category/chroniques-linda-hajj-2018/, accessed November 21, 2020.

credit in five years thanks to the help of our parents.' This, and other testimonies, shows that French married couples are re-investigating and re-interpreting performing the hajj obligation in more egalitarian terms. Other generational changes on the nexus between hajj and marriage in the French context have been observed in regards of the dower (*mahr*) practice.

3 *Mahr* and Pilgrimage

Performing the hajj as a couple either as a honeymoon or a year after marriage has emerged among Muslims in France around the 2010s (Saghi 2010). Moreover, brides are asking to receive their dower (*mahr*)[16] in the form of a pilgrimage package tour. Regarding this trend, a young member of Milli Görüs, a Turkish confederation that organizes the hajj, stated the following:

> It is logical to perform the hajj as a couple. First of all, I want my wife to get rid of her sins. Second, I consider the hajj her best dower. The hajj is emotional; it's romantic to be in Mecca for a wedding night.

A wife can also help her husband finance his hajj thanks to her dower. A father of four children explained:

> My wife decided, by herself, to sell her *mahr* which consisted of jewelry, so that I can accomplish my hajj. At the time of our marriage, I had a better salary.

In comparison to older generations, where the *mahr* was an important asset safeguarding the wife's financial security should the marriage break up, brides today often ask for a 'symbolic' *mahr* in the form of a pilgrimage.

Women's employment and growing religiosity are thus transforming both the matrimonial and the pilgrimage market. The *mahr* has become less important to Muslim women in France, in part due to their changing economic capacities. Since women can obtain well-paying occupations far more easily, they are less reliant on their husbands and on their *mahr* for financial security, as a woman working for a hajj travel agency declares:

16 According to Islamic law, the groom is obliged to pay a *mahr* to his future wife.

> Young Muslims are into *dīn* (religion). My two friends asked the hajj as a dower. Women work today, they can buy whatever they want. That's why they ask for a hajj (…) Women work and don't need a set of gold like in the past. They have everything; they don't know any more what to ask as a dower!

This shift in the meaning of the *mahr* is part of the islamization process that can be witnessed in France. Indeed, the *mahr* is considered by young Muslims to be part of their 'distinctive identity' in western societies where Muslims constitute a minority. 'It's very French to go on hajj when a woman asks for it as a dower, because it brings more piety,' confirmed Ismail Mounir. It should be noted that despite its 'symbolic' value, the *mahr* remains costly, particularly because hajj packages cost more than 6,500 euro. Husbands use both religious and economic arguments as reasons for offering the hajj as a *mahr*, explaining that 'it is shared with God'; 'it is a communion with God'; 'a man cannot refuse such a demand because it is a religious duty'; and also that it is not a 'waste of money'. In this manner, women 'buy' conjugal happiness and accumulate *ḥasanāt* (religious merit) for the afterlife.

It must be noted, however, that some of the men interviewed were surprised to hear about the hajj being offered to women as a *mahr*. In our first interview, Wahid, 33 years, Franco-Tunisian working in IT, who married in 2018, mocked the idea: 'The link between *mahr* and hajj is nonsense! Let a woman find a husband before thinking about this. The real problem is celibacy, not the hajj as a dower.' In our second interview with Wahid, he was a bit embarrassed:

> After our interview, I spoke to my wife about the idea of giving the hajj as a *mahr*, which I found very weird. But, I was very much surprised to discover that my wife herself had thought about having the hajj for her *mahr*! She had apparently hesitated between jewels and hajj and finally chose the jewels. She never mentioned the idea of hajj!

Wahid then explained his 'relief' regarding his wife's decision:

> If she had asked for the hajj, it would have been hard, because the *mahr* is usually given to women to help them rebound in case of divorce. So, for me, the *mahr* is associated with divorce; and linking hajj with divorce is a sad idea.

Despite the attractiveness of the hajj and *'umra* for newly-weds, it appears that couples also consider more 'extraordinary' travels, which, like the pilgrimage to

Mecca, may also be asked as a dower. 'Muslim tourism to holiday destinations is becoming a trend because it offers more intimacy for couples than *'umra* or the hajj', explains Saliha, head of Muslim Trotter. For Saliha, this trend is explained by the market transformation:

> In 2015, it was a trend to go for a *'umra*. But the prices for other destinations have decreased due to numerous offers in the market, that's why people desire more extraordinary travel destinations today. Performing a *'umra* has become accessible to all and at any time; this was not the case for couples before 2010.

Finally, when compared to the older generations, the wish to share religious duties and financial responsibilities is stronger among young pilgrims who tend to frame their marriage—and thus travelling to Mecca—more in terms of gender equality. Undertaking religious travels with parents or children also illustrates the middle class affordances of both male and female young French Muslim's, which places this study within the realm of global religious tourism.

4 Reconnecting with the Familial Cultural Heritage and Country of Origin

4.1 *The Hajj and the 'umra Embedded in Other Forms of Movement: When Mecca Meets the* bled

In today's globalized world, traveling is becoming more and more accessible for an increasing number of people; many pilgrims point to this accessibility, a reason that allows them to perform the hajj at a younger age. Layla, a Franco-Algerian with a PhD in Islamic studies who arrived in France in 2003, declared:

> When traveling, I often noticed pilgrims at the airport and felt very guilty about not going to hajj. How can I continue to travel so much while ignoring Mecca? It wasn't possible anymore.

Indeed, the pilgrimage to Mecca is one of many other forms of travel and movements that may or may not be described as religious travel. Understanding the motivation of pilgrims to visit Mecca lead us to consider the pilgrimage alongside others forms of travel, particularly for those who wish to travel as an 'ethical Muslim'. The French term '*Islam compatible*' defines touristic tours that match the basic precepts of Islamic ethics, such as staying in Muslim-friendly halal hotels. In this regard, travel agencies like Terre de Culture, Les Clés du

Savoir, or Havre de Savoir offer tours to Bosnia under the guidance of famous preachers such as Mohamed Bajrafil or Hassan Iquiouissen.

Travelling must also be understood as an exploration of one's migratory heritage. In the first part of this chapter, we described how the pilgrimage practices of younger French Muslims reveal a breaking point with traditional familial practices. However, a critique on popular forms of religiosity does not necessarily imply a willingness to distance oneself from family ties. Rather to the contrary: in the stories of our interlocutors, Mecca appears as a place for intergenerational encounters that help older generations to familiarize themselves with new religious practices. A large number of younger pilgrims perform the hajj together with their parents. Alternatively, many who have performed the pilgrimage before their parents often choose to return to Mecca with their parents at a later time. This is notably the case when these parents have resettled in their homeland in North African countries like Algeria, Tunisia, and Morocco, where access to the hajj is severely restricted due to the Saudi visa policy for Muslim majority countries, according to which only a very small percentage of applicants can obtain a visa. The countries mentioned above have organized the distribution of visas through a lottery system. For this reason, many young Muslims with French residence permits decide to bring parents who live in North Africa to France in order to realize their dream and religious obligation of performing hajj.

Apart from being a place for family reunion and bonding, Mecca is also a place where some pilgrims forge plans for future projects of returning 'to the *bled*', meaning to rediscover the country of their ancestors. Some see this kind of return as a religious obligation to leave a country where Islam does not rule, emulating the so-called Hijra or migration of the Prophet Muhammad from Mecca to Medina. Others decide to make a short trip to their parents' country of origin. The hajj tour guide Sami of PartirenOmra is a good example; he took up the idea of organizing other forms of travelling while he was in Mecca. Thanks to his solid group of followers, he now offers a selection of travel tours, such as trekking in the Algerian desert. To a large extent, his customers consist of pilgrims he first accompanied to Mecca. Similarly, Nabil Ennasri, president of Al Shatibi Institute, organizes what he calls 'Remembrance trips'. Ennasri emphasizes the importance for young Muslims to discover their heritage:

> We have organized five trips this year; to Andalusia, Malaysia, Uzbekistan and Jordan, all with the objective of discovering new cultures that are of spiritual interest, as well as building a perfect cohesion amongst our groups' members. Next year, we are heading for Fes and maybe to other North African cities for a trip that immerses one into the Arabic language.

> Our parents are at the end of their lives we need to get close to our primary identity to educate our children and future children.

The way our interlocutors link Mecca and the country of origin sheds light on their identifications and confirms the analytical relevance of notions such as 'transnational social space' (Pries 1999) or 'circulatory territories' (Tarrius 2001) to underline the diversity of spaces in which senses of belonging that people may experience in today's context of globalization (Sassen 2001).

4.2 *Hajj, ʿumra and the Interiorization of Past Familial Migratory Memories*

To understand these religious travels, we considered different temporalities and spatialities not only pertaining to the geographical locations themselves, but also to the narratives in which they feature. Our research data indicate that pilgrims' attachment to Mecca tends to reactivate painful familial memories. Without suggesting that all pilgrims clearly link the pilgrimage to Mecca to a parental country of origin, the analysis of pilgrims' discourses and practices enable us to shed light on a complex relationship with a migratory memory.

Amina's trajectory shows how this memory can be activated around the pilgrimage project. As a young Moroccan-French woman who arrived in France in 1992 at the age of three, Amina performed her hajj in 2016 together with her husband. During our interview, she detailed the journeys the couple has undertaken over the past years, recalling, amongst others, their numerous *ʿumra* trips. While living in the Parisian suburb of Creteil, Amina went as far as the North of France to book her pilgrimage trip to Mecca from the association Havre de Savoir, which regularly recruits spiritual guides for the pilgrimage who are affiliated to the Muslim Brotherhood, an initiative that might appear strange. Amina studies at the IESH (Institut Européen des Sciences Humaines), a private institute offering courses in the Arabic language, Islamic science, and Qurʾanic studies, which is connected to the Union des Organisations Islamiques de France (close to the Muslim Brotherhood) (Godard 2015). During our interview, Amina largely referred to Ḥasan al-Bannā, the founder of the Muslim Brotherhood, or to Ahmad Jabala, the president of the IESH. But, rather than ideological motives, the reason that Amina travelled to the north to book her pilgrimage with Havre de Savoir was related to the familial history and her wish to insert herself into her family narrative about that past. She explained that coming from Morocco, Le Havre is the city where her father had settled after a brief stay in Corsica. His trajectory—Corsica, Le Havre, and finally the Paris suburbs—is the classical trajectory of hundreds of Moroccan recruits in the French army after the Second World War. Departing for the hajj from Le Havre represents, for Amina, both a religious trip to Mecca and a return trip through her family's migration memory, as it has been narrated to her throughout her childhood. This mental connection illustrates the importance of taking into account the interiorization of past familial trajectories in the shifting identifications of the pilgrims.

5 Conclusion

In this chapter, we have analysed the motivations of French pilgrims to Mecca at the crossroads of several dynamics: the individualization of religiosity, an increase of mobility, multiple identifications and their relation to migration and colonial history.

The narratives that our interlocutors shared with us about their longing for Mecca point to a form of religiosity that is far removed from the popular Islam transmitted to them by their parents. In particular, our research demonstrates how young pilgrims who live in a context where they are often confronted with discrimination try to re-appropriate their Islamic heritage in new ways, illustrated, amongst others, by the emergence of the figure of the spiritual guide that we described. The stories about the hajj and *ʿumra* experiences of our interlocutors and the meanings they attribute to pilgrimage to Mecca also point to a trend away from more patriarchal views and practices towards a more gender egalitarian view on sharing religious and financial dimensions of undertaking the hajj. This comes to the fore particularly in the practice of young couples who now mostly perform the hajj together with their spouse to strengthen the marriage bond, rather than waiting until old age or the husband preceding his wife while she takes care of the children and the house.

The hajj and *ʿumra* are also embedded in other forms of travel and movement: the ease to travel in the contemporary world contributes to explaining why young French Muslims choose to perform the pilgrimage at an early age. While the pilgrimage practices of young French Muslims are part of trends such as the individualization of belief and a break with the kind of popular Islam transmitted to them by their parents, the hajj and *ʿumra* are also occasions for family reunion and reconnections with a family heritage. It is no coincidence that return journeys to the *bled* often originate in Mecca. In fact, the relation of young French Muslims with their country of origin remains complex. The pilgrimage to Mecca contributes to a plural and complex spatial and temporal redefinition of identities. Far from testifying to supposedly unchanging identities of French Muslims, the pilgrimages offer young French Muslims various senses of belonging and different ways to revalorize themselves and their history. This can help them to reappraise or at least clarify their place in the French society.

References

Bianchi, Robert. 2015. 'Islamic globalization and its role in China's future.' *Journal of Middle Eastern and Islamic studies (in Asia)* 9 (3): 29–48.

Buitelaar, Marjo. 2020. 'Rearticulating the conventions of hajj storytelling: Second generation Moroccan-Dutch female pilgrims' multi-voiced narratives about the pilgrimage to Mecca.' *Religions* 11 (7). doi:10.3390/rel11070373.

Buitelaar, Marjo. 2018. 'Moved by Mecca. The meanings of the hajj for present-day Dutch Muslims.' In *Muslim Pilgrimage in Europe*, edited by Ingvild Flaskerud and Richard Natvig, 29–42. London and New York: Routledge.

Cordero-Guzman, Hector, Robert Smith, and Ramon Grosfoguel, eds. 2001. *Migration, transnationalization and race in a changing New York*. Philadelphia: Temple University Press.

Fourchard, Laurent, André Mary, and René Otayek, eds. 2005. *Entreprises religieuses transnationales en Afrique de l'Ouest*. Paris: Karthala.

Godard, Bernard. 2015. 'L'Imamat en France: Magistère religieux et formation.' *Revue des Deux mondes*, 85–93.

Giddens, Anthony. 1991. *The consequences of modernity*. Stanford: Stanford University Press.

Haenni, Patrick. 2005. *L'Islam de marché*. Paris: Le Seuil.

Hervieu-Léger, Danièle. 2001. 'Crise de l'universel et planétarisation culturelle: Les paradoxes de la "mondialisation religieuse".' In *La globalisation du religieux*, edited by Jean-Pierre Bastian, François Champion, and Kathy Rousselet. Paris: L'Harmattan.

Göle, Nilüfer. 2015. *Musulmans au quotidien. Une enquête Européenne sur les controverses autour de l'Islam*. Paris: La Découverte.

Kadrouch-Outmany, Khadija, and Marjo Buitelaar. 2021. 'Young Moroccan-Dutch women on hajj: Claiming female space.' In *Muslim women's pilgrimage to Mecca and beyond. Reconfiguring gender, religion and mobility*, edited by Marjo Buitelaar, Manja Stephan-Emmrich, and Viola Thimm, 36–55. London and New York: Routledge.

Pries, Ludger. 1999. *Migration and transnational social spaces*. Aldershot: Ashgate.

Saghi, Omar. 2010. *Paris-La Mecque. Sociologie du pèlerinage*. Paris: Presses Universitaires de France.

Sassen, Saskia. 2001. 'Cracked casings: Towards an analytics for studying transnational processes.' In *New transnational social spaces: International migration and transna-*

tional companies in the early twenty-first century, edited by Ludger Pries, 187–209. London and New York: Routledge.
Scott, Joan. 2018. *La religion de la laicité*. Paris: Editions Flammarion.
Scott, Joan. 2009. *The politics of the veil*. Princeton: Princeton University Press.
Tarrius, Alain. 2001. 'Au-delà des États-nations, des sociétés de migrants.' *Revue Européenne des migrations internationales* 17 (2): 37–61.

CHAPTER 13

Patience and Pilgrimage: Dutch Hajj Pilgrims' Emergent and Maturing Stories about the Virtue of *ṣabr*

Marjo Buitelaar and Khadija Kadrouch-Outmany

> Bring along two suitcases on your hajj journey: a small one with your clothes and daily necessities, and a big one filled with *ṣabr* (patience). That's all you really need: *ṣabr*.[1]

∵

1 Introduction: Hajj Morality and Pilgrims' Wider Moral Universe[2]

In preparation for her fieldtrip to Mecca as part of their joint research within the wider hajj project on which this book is based, the second author of this chapter and her husband booked their hajj package with Celebrity Hajj, a popular travel agency among pilgrims of Moroccan-Dutch descent who grew up in the Netherlands.[3] Celebrity Hajj has an attractive website that clearly targets younger pilgrims, for example by giving a discount to recently married couples. As the name suggests, Celebrity Hajj operates in the higher segment of the Dutch hajj customer market. It offers luxurious hajj packages and provides its customers with 'cool' promotional gifts such as Dutch design water bottles (Dopper) displaying the logo of the agency, and key chains with the agency's logo and the text 'I ♥ Mecca' on it. Each page of the agency's website features

1 This was the advice of the imam of a Dutch mosque to one of our interlocutors who was preparing to go on hajj.

2 We would like to thank Léon Buskens and Kim Knibbe for their *ṣabr* to read a previous draft of this chapter and provide us with the most valuable feedback.

3 In line with Saudi hajj regulations that female pilgrims under the age of 45 must be accompanied by a *maḥram*, a male companion, Kadrouch-Outmany's husband joined her on the hajj journey. The couple also brought their two-year-old son, who helped his mum to quickly build rapport with other pilgrims by being quite adorable.

the slogan: 'Nothing beats the carefree fulfilment of your Islamic duty. We are confident that our care will offer you satisfaction.'[4]

One of the services provided by Celebrity Hajj is a preparatory meeting in which pilgrims are informed about the time table of their sojourn in Saudi Arabia and the proper way to carry out the hajj rites. There, in his opening speech for the hajj of 2016 that Kadrouch-Outmany attended, after thanking his audience for having chosen Celebrity Hajj, the first thing the tour leader told his listeners was that the journey they were about to embark on was not an ordinary trip, but a journey to the sacred city of Mecca, for which Allah had invited every single one of them. Having replied to this invitation with the *niyya*—the intention to fulfil one's hajj duty—the pilgrims were now expected to prepare themselves for the most important journey of their life. The tour leader explained that besides formulating the *niyya*, what pilgrims would need most was *ṣabr*. Huge amounts of *ṣabr*, that is: patience or endurance. The journey could only succeed if they would exercise *ṣabr* from the moment they departed from Schiphol airport until their return back home. The second point the presenter stressed was that the pilgrims should take to heart that they would be travelling as a group; they should realize that they constituted a community and that the tour leader would be their *amīr* or 'commander'. In former days, the leader of caravans on their way to Mecca was called *amīr al-ḥajj*, 'commander of the pilgrimage' (Peters 1994, 167–168). For pilgrims with Moroccan backgrounds, the word *amīr* has a second connotation, referring to the title held by the Moroccan king: 'Commander of the faithful'.

To underscore the relevance of his statement, the presenter quoted a well-known hadith, a saying attributed to the Prophet Muhammad: 'Whosoever obeys me, obeys Allah; and he who disobeys me, disobeys Allah; and whosoever obeys the Amir, in fact, obeys me; and he who disobeys the Amir, in fact, disobeys me.' In variation to the slogan on the Celebrity Hajj website, the tour leader then concluded his welcoming speech by saying: 'You just take care of your *'ibāda* (religious obligation) and we will take care of all organizational aspects (…). We are your servants.'

The emphasis on the hajj as a test of one's *ṣabr* is a recurring topic in preparatory classes for prospective pilgrims. It also features in numerous booklets and websites on the hajj that pilgrims can consult before departure. On the website page where he discusses the 'Basics of the hajj', the Dutch spiritual care

4 In Dutch: *'Er gaat niets boven het zorgeloos vervullen van uw islamitische plicht. Wij zijn er van overtuigd dat onze aanwezigheid u tevreden zal stellen.'* https://celebrityhajj.nl/, accessed August 2, 2020.

giver Mohamed Ben Ayad, for example, mentions *ṣabr* as one of the dimensions of hajj morality: 'During the hajj pilgrims train themselves in patience, forgiveness, charity and supporting the weak.'[5] The advice given by an imam in the epigraph—to bring a big suitcase full of *ṣabr* when embarking on the pilgrimage—has become a trope in hajj storytelling; variations of the story frequently occur in narratives in which our interlocutors look back on their pilgrimage experiences.

Although *ṣabr* is a highly valued Islamic virtue, it is also surrounded by ambivalence: views vary as to whether exercising patience is a stance of passive endurance, as those with secular orientations often claim in their critique, or if it concerns a virtuous disposition that must be actively cultivated. Also, should exerting *ṣabr* be one's default mode of behaviour, or do only certain circumstances demand it? Moreover, cultural conceptions on the appropriateness of exerting *ṣabr* are closely related to power structures and may vary for different categories of people. A connected issue is whether one has the right to request others to exert *ṣabr*, or if it should be an entirely voluntary practice.

In this chapter, we will address the ambivalence surrounding the invocation of *ṣabr* during the hajj in pilgrims' practical moral reasoning. The welcoming speech of the Celebrity Hajj tour leader summarized above sketches the contours of the kind of ambivalences surrounding the concept of *ṣabr* that pilgrims are confronted with during their sojourn in Mecca and Medina. It should come as no surprise that he foregrounded the religious character of the package tour that his customers had booked in the speech. Note, however, that through the claim concerning the necessity of exercising *ṣabr* from the moment of departure until the return home, the mutual responsibilities between the Celebrity Hajj tour leader and his customers are also couched in religious terms. The suggestion by conduit of a saying attributed to the Prophet Muhammad that obeying the travel agent's tour leaders would amount to obeying God, firmly consolidates this religious framing. In his final words, however, the presenter switches back to the discourse of another moral register he referred to in the first sentence of his opening speech; that of the responsible entrepreneur whose moral obligation it is to serve his customers. Here, he addresses his audience not as pilgrims, but as consumers of his services.

The simultaneous appeal on two different moral registers confronts pilgrims with a recurrent ethical dilemma: are hardship and setbacks part of the overall hajj experience, and should they, as devout pilgrims, therefore respond to

5 Translated by the authors. cf. http://www.benayad.nl/vrijdagpreken/de-essenties-van-de-hadj/, accessed July 22, 2020. For other examples, see: https://www.umrah-en-hajj.nl/tips and http://www.haremeynvakfi.com/wat-kan-je-meenemen.html, accessed July 31, 2020.

them by exerting *ṣabr*? Or are they, as customers, entitled to complain if their expectations were not met and demand that the services they had paid for be delivered? Although on the surface this might seem a simple matter of appraising religious and non-religious considerations, in practice the religious and non-religious are not always easy to disentangle.

In what follows, we examine how pilgrims assess and negotiate the appropriateness of exerting *ṣabr* during the hajj. To this end, we analyse the dialogues between various personal and collective moral voices in pilgrims' situational moral reasoning. Our focus is on pilgrims in their thirties to fifties of Moroccan or Turkish descent who grew up in the Netherlands. We focus on this category for two, interrelated reasons. First, the hajj has only become popular among Dutch Muslims in this age-group over the past decade. Second, because the overall integration of Muslims of this generation in Dutch social domains is more thorough than that of their migrant parents, they also find themselves in situations where their Muslimness is interrogated more often, stimulating reflection on their religious heritage (cf. Göle 2017; Jouili 2015). To a considerable extent, exploring the meanings of the hajj in their own life therefore accounts for the increasing popularity of the pilgrimage to Mecca among Dutch Muslims of Moroccan and Turkish descent. Since we are particularly interested in the relationship between experience, meaning making, and narration, a discussion of data produced through Kadrouch-Outmany's participant observation during the hajj of 2016 will be supplemented by analytical description of data generated through interviews with pilgrims who reflected on their pilgrimage several months or years after the experience. Comparison between the two data sets allows us to explore how stories about ethical dilemmas pilgrims are confronted with as the hajj journey unfolds develop over time once pilgrims have returned home.

Furthermore, the sacred journey to Mecca offers a particularly interesting case study for investigating *ṣabr* as a moral practice: visiting Islam's holiest city and stepping in the footsteps of the Prophet Muhammad attune pilgrims to the highest of religious values. As the journey approaches, many prospective pilgrims prepare themselves mentally by paying more attention to being patient and forgiving, thus striving to develop the right mind-set to perform their hajj correctly (cf. Caidi 2020, 49). During the hajj journey itself, pilgrims tend to monitor their comportment vigilantly lest their performance of the ritual should be invalidated. This self-reflexive stance is stimulated by the behavioural regulations concerning the state of *iḥrām* or consecration during the hajj, such as the prohibition to have sex, use perfumed toiletries, cut one's nails and hair, or kill living creatures. Furthermore, the hajj not only puts one's *ṣabr* to the test, but many pilgrims also conceive of it as a disciplinary practice through which to fortify their disposition to exert *ṣabr*. In this respect, the hajj can operate as a 'pressure cooker for personal development' as one our interlocutors put it; it is a journey full of moral lessons to benefit from upon return to everyday life.

But just as the merits of the moral lessons of the hajj are supposed to spill over in everyday life, vice versa, everyday life concerns also permeate the hajj experience. They do so in at least two respects. First of all, although ideally pilgrims spend as much time as possible on devotional acts during the hajj journey, more mundane daily necessities must also be attended to. Friends and relatives expect to receive souvenirs, so shopping is also on the to-do list of many pilgrims, as is sightseeing. Secondly, as illustrated by shopping and sightseeing activities, the dispositions of pilgrims are not only shaped by the Islamic tradition; other cultural traditions inform their daily lifeworlds as well. Ideals of Muslim personhood and the *umma*, the global Muslim community, thus exist side by side with other 'grand schemes': powerful yet never fully attainable ideals that operate as models for a good life (Schielke 2015, 13). Therefore, in addition to motivations that are based on a particular conception of the moral order of Islam, on the basis of their personal locations in various social networks and power structures, the various pursuits of pilgrims are also inspired by other grand schemes in their daily lives. They may be motivated, for example, by specific ideals about self-realization, romantic love, making money, or consumption. Each of these ideals comes with its own normative discourse or, borrowing Samuli Schielke's terms, a 'moral register' to frame or assess a situation. Each moral register houses a specific style of argumentation and a specific emotional tone. Schielke uses the term normative or moral 'registers' rather than 'discourses' or 'traditions' to highlight the performative, situational, and dialogic character of norms (Schielke 2015, 54). We follow his approach here.

Various moral registers thus simultaneously shape the 'sensibilities' of pilgrims, that is, the moral and aesthetic dimensions of their experiences and emotional lives. These sensibilities tend to vary for different categories of pilgrims. For instance, for most Muslims who came to the Netherlands in the 1960s and 1970s from Turkey or Morocco as economic migrants, pilgrimage to Mecca is the only alternative journey besides visiting their country of origin. The horizon of their offspring, however, is much wider. Besides being accustomed to the travel practices of their parents, their personal longings have also been shaped by growing up in a country where making a holiday trip to 'chill' or explore hitherto unknown territory is almost considered a basic human need. As a result, their consumer wishes concerning desirable travel destinations have expanded, as have their expectations concerning the efficiency and quality of transportation, accommodation, and time-management whilst traveling. Also, whereas their parents generally come from rural backgrounds and enjoyed little or no formal education, having predominantly grown up in Dutch cities, the participants in our research are mostly modern-educated middle-class urbanites. As a result, incorporated norms about hygiene and punctuality as well as liberal values like individualism, gender equality, and self-enhancement inform their expectations concerning the conditions of the hajj (cf. Kadrouch-Outmany and Buitelaar 2021; Buitelaar 2020).

Although different 'grand schemes' and moral registers may be related to different domains in life, by zooming in on instances during the hajj of 2016 that gave rise to ethical dilemmas concerning the appropriateness of the moral practice of *ṣabr*, in what follows we will demonstrate that while practical moral reasoning is mostly situational, it is not necessarily compartmentalized. Rather, as the conversations among pilgrims concerning the appropriateness of invoking *ṣabr* we discuss here indicate, moral registers may be mixed and merged. Besides discussing the negotiation of the appropriateness of invoking *ṣabr* as a first objective in this chapter, our second objective is to shed light on the ongoing narrative construction of morality. We do so by comparing what we propose to call 'emergent' and 'maturing' stories. Emergent stories pertain to the performative, situational and dialogic character of on-site moral reasoning of pilgrims as they try to make sense of their experiences as the events of the hajj unfold. We understand maturing stories to be the telling and retelling of narratives in which individual pilgrims retrospectively reflect on the moral lessons of the hajj several months or years after they have returned home. More specifically, we study these 'maturing' stories in the versions that are produced in interviews with pilgrims who were willing to participate in our research project.

The chapter is organized as follows. In the coming section, we will reflect on the research methods used within this study—such as participant observation during the hajj along with interviews with pilgrims reflecting on their hajj experiences—and the implications of these different methods with regard to the nature of the different data sets thus produced. In the subsequent section, we will discuss the moral practice of *ṣabr* and the anthropological study of moral registers on a conceptual level. In the remainder of the chapter, we will discuss negotiations and deliberations over the appropriateness of invoking *ṣabr* during the hajj in emergent and maturing stories about hajj morality.

2 Studying Emergent and Maturing Hajj Stories

Stories about the hajj and the actual experience of the pilgrimage are mutually constitutive. Narratives do not merely give words to experiences, but experiences themselves are shaped by words, more specifically by the meanings these words have acquired in the vocabularies of the discursive traditions available to narrators as they interpret their experiences (cf. Buitelaar 2020; Coleman and Elsner 2003). On the basis of both personal and collectively shared stories about the hajj, prospective pilgrims learn what kind of experiences and accompanying feelings to expect whilst in Mecca. The frequent occurrence in the interviews of variations to the story about bringing a suitcase full of *ṣabr*, for example, taught us that this trope prepares prospective pilgrims for hardship and their patience to be tested during the hajj. Since the habitus of pilgrims is informed by several 'grand schemes' however, the moral register of Islam is not the only discourse that shapes their experiences and provides them with words to give meaning to these experiences. Comparing pilgrims' 'emergent' stories as the events of the hajj unfold with their 'maturing' stories that have had time to develop in the telling and retelling over time after the return home sheds light on the impact of being informed by different 'grand schemes' simultaneously on the specific interplay between experience, storytelling, and meaning making. To this end, we draw on two different sets of empirical data. For the discussion of 'emergent' stories, we analyse the data produced through participant observation conducted by Kadrouch-Outmany, who joined a group of pilgrims from the Netherlands on their journey to Mecca for the hajj of 2016.[6] For the more 'mature' stories, we draw on data produced through interviews conducted with Dutch pilgrims of Moroccan and Turkish backgrounds.[7]

6 The group that Kadrouch-Outmany travelled with consisted of 220 pilgrims, 80% of whom were younger than 45 years old. The number of male and female pilgrims were more or less equal. There were many young couples in the group, quite a few of whom in the company of parents, in-laws and/or siblings. In this sense, as is often the case for pilgrims from the Netherlands, the hajj was very much a 'family affair'. In this particular group, the large majority of pilgrims consisted of Moroccan-Dutch citizens. In addition, there were some Dutch converts and Dutch speaking pilgrims with Surinamese, Pakistani, Palestinian, Iranian, Iraqi, Afghani, Turkish backgrounds.

7 The participants were recruited through 'snowballing', initial contacts in existing personal networks, mosques, and community centres serving as starting points to approach subsequent interviewees. A total of 77 interviews were conducted for the hajj research as a whole, 52 of whom were pilgrims of Moroccan backgrounds, 25 of Turkish descent. The majority of research participants were in their mid-thirties to late-fifties, all of whom grew up in the Netherlands. Ten Moroccan participants belong to the older generation of economic migrants that came to the Netherlands in the 1960s and 1970s. The bulk of the interviews with pilgrims who

Obviously not all experiences during the pilgrimage to Mecca find their ways into hajj stories; in their recollections most pilgrims focus predominantly on the highlights of their journey (cf. Delaney 1999, 520). As pilgrims are overwhelmed by a plethora of intense emotional impressions, they may not remember the more mundane dimensions equally vividly or deem them too insignificant to recollect. Also, in order to cherish the memories of the pilgrimage as a rewarding journey, pilgrims may decide that negative experiences are best forgotten or reframed in terms of important moral lessons both for themselves and their audiences (cf. Kaell 2014, 168). It therefore takes significant narrative work to process hajj experiences into stories. Chit-chatting with fellow pilgrims on the airplane back to the Netherlands, Kadrouch-Outmany noted, for example, that the homeward bound pilgrims already started to actively engage in such narrative work by exchanging experiences of highly valued moments of the journey and downplaying the moments of friction. The general conventions of hajj storytelling that they are familiar with help pilgrims to process their various experiences into more or less coherent narratives. Thus, they align their stories, at least to some extent, to one or more already existing, 'grand narratives' about the hajj that they are familiar with (Buitelaar 2020). In line with Martyn Smith's argument concerning the collective stories about sacred places, such 'grand narratives' tend to have a highly idealising character (cf. Smith 2008, 26).

Joining a group of pilgrims during the hajj journey and enduring challenges and hardship with them offered Kadrouch-Outmany a unique opportunity study the 'embodied talk' (Bamberg 2011, 17) in conversations about the fragmented, complex, and sometimes contradictory emotions and experiences that pilgrims go through as the events of the hajj unfold.[8] In other words, participant observation allowed her to observe how pilgrims draw on the various moral registers available to them to assess and negotiate the appropriateness of exercising *ṣabr* when confronted with difficulties and setbacks. In this respect, the nature of the data produced by Kadrouch-Outmany through participant observant as events unfolded differs significantly from the data produced in

---

grew up in the Netherlands was conducted in Dutch by Buitelaar, while a research assistant conducted interviews with 10 older pilgrims of Moroccan backgrounds in Tamazight or *dārija* (Moroccan-Arabic). In addition, two students in religious studies each conducted 10 interviews with Dutch based pilgrims for their MA research traineeship and MA thesis, about half of whom from Turkish or Moroccan parentage (cf. Wijers 2019; de Lang 2017). All interviews were audio-taped and fully transcribed.

8 Kadrouch-Outmany has reflected on participating in the hajj as an insider's outsider in Kadrouch-Outmany 2018.

interviews with pilgrims who looked back on their hajj experiences, the bulk of which were conducted by Buitelaar.

However, the two data sets also overlap. Regardless whether pilgrims discuss their experiences as events unfold or reflect on them afterwards, an important factor that informs how these experiences are narrated concerns the more public or private character of the setting in which the narration occurs. As we will argue later in the chapter, in the overall ambiance of heightened religiosity during the hajj, arguments framed in terms of an Islamic moral register are more likely to gain group support and are more difficult to refute than arguments pertaining to other moral registers, such as the desire for comfort or privacy. Religious arguments are more in line with the normative character of the 'grand narrative' of the hajj that pilgrims are familiar with, and they are therefore more easily expressed in public. Social control may induce pilgrims to be hesitant to forward non-religious arguments in the presence of a wider audience and more inclined to share those in more private conversations. In other words, group dynamics play an important role in how pilgrims express their appreciation of disappointments and challenges. In this sense, Kadrouch-Outmany's conversations with individual pilgrims when not being overheard by others and the recollections interviewees shared with Buitelaar in the private setting of an interview have more in common than performative instances of moral reasoning in public places.

Overall, however, the different temporalities and spatialities involved in the narrations of pilgrims whilst still on hajj and those narrated several months or even years afterwards have a significant impact on the stories produced, as we will demonstrate later in this chapter. In the holy cities of Mecca and Medina and in the tent camp in Minā, the pilgrims are in the company of Muslims only.[9] The post-pilgrimage interviews were all conducted in the Netherlands, where the majority of the population is non-Muslim. This is also true for Buitelaar, who by implication belongs to a category of Dutch citizens whom her interlocutors consider likely to have one-sided preconceptions about Islam. In most cases Buitelaar's long-term research in Morocco and knowledge of Islam proved to be helpful in developing rapport. However, the interview being set in an everyday context where Muslims are routinely questioned about their religious stance by non-Muslim fellow citizens must have informed how her presence mediated an imagined non-Muslim audience to her interlocutors.[10]

9 The pilgrims in the group that Kadrouch-Outmany joined knew that she performed the hajj both for research purposes and to fulfil her own religious duty.

10 For the effect of a dominant Islamophobic discourse in the Netherlands on self-presentations of Dutch Muslims, also see Al-Ajarma and Buitelaar (2021).

It is therefore likely that some of the feelings and views that pilgrims shared with Kadrouch-Outmany during the hajj journey would not have been equally shared with Buitelaar, lest certain stories might feed negative conceptions about Islam among non-Muslims. The opposite, however, also holds true: several interviewees indicated that one reason for agreeing to the interview with Buitelaar was that it appealed to them to anonymously share with an outsider feelings and views that they were (as yet) hesitant to express within their Muslim networks, fearing disapproval. Besides being able to 'unburden one's heart' as one woman put it, a felt need to start exploring how to add new story lines to the kind of one-sided, positive hajj stories that pilgrims of their parents' generation tend to share was another motivation explicitly expressed by some interlocutors (also see Buitelaar 2020). Being able to do so anonymously to someone who does not belong to one's social network made it easier to begin such storytelling. Voicing (presumed) dissonant views concerning the moral practice of *ṣabr* in specific situations was a case in point.

Considering that ethnographic data on the pilgrimage to Mecca are rare,[11] and, moreover, since we are particularly interested in the dialogues between voices representing different moral registers simultaneously as pilgrims negotiate the appropriateness of exerting *ṣabr* or the legitimacy of critique and protest, in what follows the focus will predominantly be on Kadrouch-Outmany's fieldnotes, which will be compared to the hajj stories produced in the interviews. Before we turn to our research data, we first zoom in on views on the concept of *ṣabr* in the Islamic tradition and anthropological insights concerning the moral discourse and practice of *ṣabr* among contemporary Muslims.

3 The Moral Practice of ṣabr

In colloquial Arabic, *ṣabr* is often used to simply mean 'patience'. In *dārija*, the Moroccan dialect, for example, *ṣabar wahed dqiqa* means 'hang on for a minute'. Beyond the prosaic, *ṣabr* is a highly valued Islamic virtue. It is beyond this study to investigate to what extent our interlocutors are familiar with the ethical debates about *ṣabr* in authoritative texts in the Islamic tradition. We briefly mention them here to indicate that the conception of *ṣabr* as a highly valued Islamic virtue resonates with a long discursive tradition. Al-Ṣabūr is

11 To our knowledge, Saghi (2010) is the only ethnography, while the auto-ethnographic account of Hammoudi (2006) also offers very valuable information. Also see Al-Ajarma (2020) for ethnographic analysis of the *ʿumra*, the voluntary pilgrimage to Mecca.

one of the 99 attributes or divine names of God, for instance (Schimmel 1975, 177) and another name for the fasting month of Ramadan is *shahr al-ṣabr*, the month of patience (Buitelaar 1993, 129). Derivations from the root *ṣ-b-r* occur frequently in the Qur'an and hadith. The Prophet Muhammad is told to be patient like the prophets before him, in Qur'an 38:16 and 46:34, for example, and a reward is promised to those who are patient in Qur'an 33:113, 28:54; and 25:75 (Wensinck 2012). Another example is a well-known story from the hadith that concerns an epileptic woman who asked the Prophet Muhammad to pray to God to heal her. In response, he stated that if she refrained from her request and exercised *ṣabr*, paradise would be her part (ibid.). Muslim scholars have often emphasised the connection between *ṣabr* and *shukr*, gratitude. In his *Iḥyā ʿulūm al-dīn*, the Muslim scholar Abū Ḥāmid al-Ghazālī (d. 1111 CE), for example, stated that 'belief consists of two halves: the one *ṣabr* and the other *shukr*' (ibid.). In classical Sufi thought, *shukr* and *ṣabr* similarly occur in combination; *ṣabr* in its more basic sense relating to patience and on the highest level to renunciation. Some stern, quietist mystics even went so far as to consider perfect resignation and silent patience in times of affliction to be more suitable than prayer; however, this view is not generally shared (Schimmel 1975, 124–126).

In the anthropological study of Islam, the discussion of Islamic virtues like *ṣabr* has come to receive considerable attention recently. This is related to the 'ethical turn' that characterizes much research since the early twenty-first century. Saba Mahmood's seminal study *Politics of Piety* has been very influential in this respect. Following Talal Asad's argument that in the Islamic discourse the notions suffering and endurance should not be mistaken as synonymous with passivity but instead as creating space for moral action (Asad 2003, 89–91), Mahmood argues that for the women in the Egyptian revivalist movement she studied, *ṣabr* is a moral practice and a virtue that must be actively cultivated. Rather than aiming to fortify one's ability to confront suffering, Mahmood's interlocutors emphasized that the primary purpose of *ṣabr* should be to bear and live hardship appropriately (Mahmood 2005, 172). The pursuit of ṣabr as a moral practice to cultivate a mode of being as a *ṣābir* or *ṣābira* (one who practises *ṣabr*) is likewise discussed in research on ethical self-fashioning among Belgian, French, and German Muslim women with Moroccan and Turkish backgrounds who attend religious classes and workshops organized by Islamic revival circles (Groeninck 2017, 177–182; Jouili 2015, 185–186).

In all these studies, the research participants closely connect *ṣabr* to *tawakkul*, reliance on God's will. As Sherine Hamdy shows, many terminally-ill dialysis patients in Egypt prefer to accept God's will than pursue kidney transplantation. Hamdy argues that such a stance should not be seen as merely a 'comfort mechanism' nor does this disposition of submission to God's will negate human agency.[12] The patients she talked with actively consider the options for different treatments and take responsibility for their own choices, trusting that whatever the outcome, it will be God's will. Like the authors mentioned above, Hamdy argues that exerting *ṣabr* is a mode that must be actively cultivated through work on the self. She points out that in their pursuit of the ethical disposition of *ṣabr*, the patients she studied drew on Islamic notions of faith in the face of suffering as redemptive of past sins (Hamdy 2009, 189).

Several studies point to gendered conceptions of the moral practice of *ṣabr*. For instance, the Moroccan women among whom Buitelaar conducted research with in the late 1980s held that women are better at fasting during Ramadan, as they have more patience than men (Buitelaar 1993, 129–131). To explain women's greater capacity to exert *ṣabr*, Buitelaar's interlocutors referred to the practice of gender segregation. As a result of the specific gendered division of space, women's freedom of movement was more restricted than that of men. 'When men have worries, they just go out and seek distraction from it. But as women we stay at home and have to come to terms with the situation,' one woman stated. Davis (1983, v) and Dwyer (1978, 153–154) similarly found that in the 1970s and 1980s Moroccan women lauded *ṣabr* as a specifically female quality.

Illustrating that an unequal division of space is not the sole cause but part of a wider power structure in which women are expected to have *ṣabr*, the virtue of *ṣabr* continues to have connotations with a virtuous female stance of modesty even though today women's freedom of movement has increased in the Middle East and mixed gender public spaces have become more common. Schielke, for example, notes that Egyptian women feel less at ease to openly express dissatisfaction, whereas men are encouraged to vent discontent (Schielke 2015, 33).[13] In a similar vein, in her study among middle-aged migrant Pakistani women in the UK, Kaveri Qureshi found that *ṣabr* is closely related

12 Also see Sardar (2011, 275), who interprets the contemporary relevance of the Qur'anic discussion of *ṣabr* as follows: 'The function of patience is to persevere, against all odds, as one seeks to change what is, into what ought to be.'

13 Also see Ghannam (2013, 140), who writes that 'the display of certain emotions such as rage and anger are expected and accepted of Egyptian men, but other emotions, especially sadness and sorrow are expected to be kept under control.' This also holds true for the Moroccan settings that the authors of this chapter are more familiar with. Also, while individuals are ideally also expected to keep their emotions under control under all circumstances, it is more acceptable for Moroccan women to express sorrow than for men, but less so to show anger and discontent.

to female subjectivity while '*ṣabar*'[14] is a nickname used to denote an effeminate man who is walked over by others (Qureshi 2013). Besides a disposition that must be actively cultivated, the people Qureshi studied also consider *ṣabr* as a capacity granted by God (Qureshi 2013, 127). She demonstrates that as a specific feminine quality, *ṣabr* allows women to inhabit a high moral ground, as they associate exerting *ṣabr* both with the capacity to do so as a sign of being blessed by God and earning religious merit. Moreover, she argues that cultivating *ṣabr* cannot be reduced to a discourse of submission to God, as Mahmood suggests, and is better understood as women's creative appropriation of *ṣabr* for their own intentions.[15]

Particularly relevant for our argument here is that besides discussing *ṣabr* in an Islamic ethical framework of cultivating pious dispositions, Qureshi also looks at the dynamics of *ṣabr* in social relations. The women she studied do not only hope for recognition from God for displaying *ṣabr*, but also seek acknowledgement from others. By closely scrutinizing the situations in which her interlocutors invoke *ṣabr* in their family circles, Qureshi demonstrates that middle-aged women often enact a patient endurance of their heavy domestic burden in ways that make family members feel that their mother's self-sacrifice requires some kind of reciprocation from them (Qureshi 2013, 130). Qureshi concludes that there is too much emphasis in the ethnography of Muslim societies on how everyday interactions are placed within an Islamic moral frame and not enough on how this moral frame derives its significance through the 'flow of sociality' in which individuals participate (Qureshi 2013, 133).

In line with the approach Qureshi proposes, in the next section we will discuss how pilgrims negotiate the appropriateness of exercising *ṣabr* by focusing predominantly on the flow of sociality during the hajj. Contrary to the everyday situations studied by Qureshi, the interactions between pilgrims in our study take place in an extraordinary time and space constellation that characterizes the pilgrimage to Mecca. In this context, the virtue of *ṣabr* gains particular significance. Despite the atmosphere of heightened religiosity, however, pilgrims clearly cannot always live up to the ideal of *ṣabr* and sometimes lose their temper or are driven by non-religious desires. By zooming in on instances of 'failure' to live up to Islamic ideals, we follow Kloos and Beekers who propose to focus on people's 'experiences of moral instability, fragmentation or ambivalence on the one hand and their attempts to achieve a level of moral coherence groun-

14 *ṣabbār* in Modern Standard Arabic.

15 Also see Menin (2020), who similarly points to the intentionality in the ways a revivalist Islam inspired Moroccan woman shapes her relationship with God by taking a stance of having one's own responsibility to work towards God's will.

ded in religion on the other' (Kloos and Beekers 2018, 12). We do so by first exploring how stories emerge as pilgrims draw on an Islamic frame of reference as well as other moral registers in their deliberations about the appropriateness of invoking *ṣabr* in specific settings. In the subsequent section, we examine more matured narratives in which pilgrims retrospectively volunteered reflections on instances where their *ṣabr* was challenged during the hajj in interviews several months and sometimes years after their return home.

4 Emergent Stories: Contested Invocations of ṣabr during the Hajj Performance

In what follows, we will first zoom in on instances where the issue of *ṣabr* came up in relation to issues that any traveler expects their travel agency to organize adequately regardless the purpose of their travel: transport, food, and accommodation. Subsequently, we will briefly turn to two topics that were discussed much less explicitly on a group level, but came up recurrently in more private conversations during the hajj journey and in interviews with a wider group of pilgrims who looked back on their experiences: gender equality and the longing for privacy.

4.1 *Transport*

While similar instances would follow suit, the first transport incident that tested the patience of the group of pilgrims Kadrouch-Outmany travelled with occurred just one day after the group had arrived in Mecca. It concerned the bus transport between the hotel in Aziziya, a suburb of Mecca, to the city centre where the pilgrims would perform the *ʿumra*, the first rites of the hajj that are carried out within the confines of the Grand Mosque of Mecca.[16] If, on the way to the Grand Mosque someone noted that the buses were old and shabby, elated with the prospect of performing their first hajj rites, nobody remarked on it. Things were different on the way back. Performing the *ʿumra* is a very intense experience both spiritually and physically. Immersing oneself in the flow of thousands of pilgrims circling the Kaʿba is described by most pilgrims as overwhelming. It is also very demanding, particularly for pilgrims who are not accustomed to Mecca's hot climate. While tour leaders try

16 The *ʿumra* consists of performing the *ṭawāf*, the sevenfold circumambulation of the Kaʿba, drinking Zamzam water and performance of the *saʿy*, the 'running' between the hillocks of al-Ṣafā and al-Marwa. While the *ʿumra* is part of the hajj ritual, on its own it can also be performed throughout the year as a voluntary pilgrimage.

to keep their own flock of pilgrims together, one can easily fall behind, and one runs the risk of stumbling as bolder pilgrims push to try to get closer to the Kaʿba.

Therefore, most pilgrims were exhausted after having done the *ʿumra* and longed to go back to the hotel for a shower. The buses, however, were late and the sun's heat added to the day's discomforts. After a while, people started sighing and complaining about the heat. Eventually, one man addressed the tour leader: 'It's annoying how you keep us waiting. I knew things wouldn't all go smoothly, but this is absurd.' The tour leader explained that in Mecca transport was organized by Saudi companies and that Celebrity Hajj had no say in what buses would be sent and when exactly they would arrive. Once one pilgrim had stood up to voice his discontent, other people also felt free to share their annoyance among themselves: 'What is all this waiting about? We were promised our bus would be ready to collect us!'; 'I expect to be picked up and dropped off on time, that's all I ask'; 'It's steaming hot, why are we standing in the burning sun?'. The arrival of the bus did not stifle the complaints: 'What a rickety vehicle'; 'I have to fold my legs, is this what they call a celebrity hajj?'. All this time, elderly pilgrims mostly kept silent or reminded their fellow pilgrims of the virtue of *ṣabr*.

4.2 *Food*

In the evening following the bus incident, another dispute occurred in the hotel dining hall. The previous night, having arrived late after a long journey from the Netherlands, the hungry and exhausted pilgrims had arrived to a dinner buffet consisting only of left over plain spaghetti. The next evening, the group went down to the restaurant early to make sure to have had dinner before the *ʿishāʾ* prayer, only to find that more than one hundred people were already standing in queue and that food was not yet being served. After waiting for more than half an hour, a pilgrim in his mid-forties lost his temper and began to complain loudly. Some fellow pilgrims tried to calm him by saying '*yā* al-Ḥājj, show some patience (*taṣbar*)'. Others reminded him about his state of *iḥrām* by starting to chant the *talbiya*, the devotional prayer recited by pilgrims upon entering a state of consecration.[17]

The man could not be placated, however, and furiously called for a 'strike': 'We should not accept this behaviour from the organization and we should go

17 Compare Kaell (2014, 92) who describes a similar response among Christian pilgrims to the Holy Land when confronted with a situation they felt uncomfortable with. Kaell argues that song is a particular strong tool that may be used by pilgrims to 'counteract' the unsatisfying character of a place.

out to find our own food.' To those who had found seats, he shouted: 'It is almost *'ishā'* now. What are you all doing still sitting here?' About twenty people joined him on his way out. Of those who remained, several complained that it was, indeed, a shame that they would be late for the *'ishā'* prayer, while mostly elderly women just kept silent, sighed, or said to no one in particular: '*Eywah* (well), what can we do? We must exert *ṣabr*.' The next day, with the entire group as his audience, the still annoyed man addressed the tour leader. He pointed out that being an entrepreneur himself he knew unprofessional behaviour when he saw it:

> We won't have *ṣabr* for this! Seeing to it that there is enough food and that it is served on time is your responsibility as a travel organization and has nothing to do with me being on hajj.

4.3 *Accommodation*

After concluding the hajj rites that are carried out in Mecca itself, pilgrims move to the tent camp in Minā, some five kilometres outside Mecca. From there, they perform several other rites, the most important of which the *wuqūf*, the 'standing' at 'Arafa. Once this rite is carried out, properly speaking, one's hajj is completed, even though several other rites follow, one of which the *ramy*, the 'stoning of the Devil'.

FIGURE 13.1 A tent for female pilgrims in Minā
PHOTOGRAPH BY KADROUCH-OUTMANY

During the preparatory meeting organized by Celebrity Hajj, prospective pilgrims had been informed that the facilities in Minā would be very basic. Regardless of whether one books a premium package offering a private double room in the hotel in Mecca, as most couples in the age-group between thirty and fifty do, or a cheaper arrangement where one shares a hotel room with four to six fellow pilgrims of the same gender, in the tent camp in Minā all pilgrims sleep in gender-segregated tents accommodating up to 100 fellow pilgrims. Most older pilgrims with migration backgrounds had been used to sleeping on thin mattresses on the ground in close proximity to others in Morocco or Turkey, and appeared to handle the discomfort without much difficulty. Pilgrims who grew up in the Netherlands, however, tend to conceive of the days in the tent camp as the biggest trial of the hajj, only surpassed by the ordeal of the compulsory night spent in the open air in Muzdalifa to collect pebbles for the *ramy*. Arguing that standing in queue for more than an hour just to use the toilet hampered performing prayers on time and carrying out other devotional practices such as reading the Qurʾan or saying *duʿās*, supplication prayers, a small group of younger women in Kadrouch-Outmany's group protested against the poor sanitary facilities by confiscating three toilets from the men's block, which had twice as many toilets as the women's block.[18] Otherwise, although in face-to-face conversations women might complain about the lack of comfort and privacy, overall they accepted the hardship as inevitable and as a test of one's *ṣabr*.

Besides the rewards that all pilgrims hope will await them in the hereafter for having exerted *ṣabr*, customers of Celebrity Hajj can also expect an earthly reward; after completing the stoning rite, for the last five days in the Mecca area before travelling on to Medina, the programme promised accommodation in a five star hotel in the Makkah Clock Tower adjacent to the Grand Mosque in Mecca. However, on the planned return date to Mecca just before the group assembled to leave for performance of the *ramy*, the organization announced that, unfortunately, the hotel in the clock tower was not ready to receive them yet, so that for the coming night the pilgrims would be taken back to the much simpler hotel in Aziziya. And furthermore, all those who wished to attend the Friday sermon in the Grand Mosque the next day would have to organize their own transport.

Not surprisingly, the by now exhausted pilgrims were utterly disappointed. Some protested that it was very difficult to find a taxi from Aziziya to the Grand Mosque in time for the Friday service. One man angrily shouted at the tour

18 cf. Kadrouch-Outmany and Buitelaar (2021), in which we describe this incident in more detail.

FIGURE 13.2 Pilgrim praying from her hotel room in the Clock Tower
PHOTOGRAPH BY ANONYMIZED RESEARCH PARTICIPANT PROJECT BUITELAAR

leader: 'This is outrageous! You promised us the clock tower as of Thursday, was that all a lie?!' Another male pilgrim tried to calm him: 'We should have *ṣabr*, this too is part of hajj. The organization is doing the best they can!' A third man remarked bitterly: 'It's all about money: the less days we spent in the clock tower, the more profit they [the travel agency, MB] make.' This time, also a female pilgrim spoke up: 'You keep talking about *ṣabr*, but this is just unfair! The organization has to come up with a workable solution.' She then turned to the women around her. Referring to her own professional experience as the owner of a taxi company that caters for weddings and other luxurious events, she sneered: 'To be fobbed off with *ṣabr* all the time, as if I don't know how these things work.' Another woman added: 'Rather than talk about *ṣabr*, as a company they should abide by the Islamic principles of honesty and transparency.'

Eventually, on their way back from the *ramy* to collect their baggage, the pilgrims received a message on the group WhatsApp that the hotel in the Clock Tower would be ready to receive them that night after all. Through the same medium, the man who had earlier defended the organization suggested that his fellow pilgrims ought to express gratitude and offer apologies for the accusations that had circulated in the group. He received a few supportive messages, but the one that voiced the overall feeling was clearly opposed: 'I'm relieved, yes. But thankful? No need!'

4.4 *Gender Equality and Privacy*

As the above case studies illustrate, the appropriateness of exercising *ṣabr* concerning issues that were directly related to the logistics of the journey were frequently discussed among pilgrims as a group. At least among female pilgrims—in whose circles Kadrouch-Outmany spent most of her time—in more private conversations, two additional topics were shared concerning mixed feelings about discontent on the one hand and willingness to exert *ṣabr* and be grateful on the other: gender discrimination and lack of privacy. Women's indignation about the unequal distribution of toilet blocks in the tent camp in Minā was already mentioned. Other instances of gender discrimination in which women questioned the need to exert *ṣabr* concerned the way female pilgrims are relegated to the rear of the courtyard of the Grand Mosque in Mecca during prayer time, where they cannot see much of the Kaʿba, and the specific restrictions for women at the *rawḍa*, the location in the Mosque of the Prophet Muhammad in Medina that is close to the Prophet's tomb and considered to be a part of the gardens of Paradise.[19] Adding insult to injury, in one of his lectures during

19 We discuss women's claims to more female space at several hajj sites in more detail in

an excursion after the hajj was completed, the imam whom the travel agency had hired reprimanded some female pilgrims whose husbands had remained in the hotel to care for their children for their 'un-Islamic' selfish behaviour. When the women concerned—including Kadrouch-Outmany—told their husbands about the incident, the latter confronted the tour leaders in a private conversation.

Another issue that, for obvious reasons, pilgrims only shared in private conversations with those whom they felt close to, concerned the difficulty to muster enough *ṣabr* to cope with the lack of privacy during the hajj journey. This tended to be communicated mostly in indirect terms, as in the relieved 'me-time again at last!' that a befriended female pilgrim whispered to Kadrouch-Outmany when the announcement was made that the group would go to the hotel in the clock tower after all.

4.5 *Comparing Instances of Practical Moral Reasoning*

Several points stand out when comparing the instances where the appropriateness of exerting *ṣabr* was discussed. First of all, the issues discussed at a group level mostly concerned negotiations over hajj morality on the one hand and ethical entrepreneurship on the other. We take the fact that the negotiations took place in the presence of the entire group to suggest that the actors involved considered both lines of moral reasoning valid to frame the problem and gain support from their fellow pilgrims. Indeed, in most situations, some members in the audience tried to placate angered pilgrims or expressed their agreement to those around them. This was different in the dispute that arose when the group was informed that their stay in the Clock Tower hotel would be delayed. The pilgrim who accused the travel agent of cheating its customers and save money was corrected by others. The woman who supported him did so by integrating the moral register about ethical entrepreneurship into an Islamic one by emphasizing that honesty and transparency are key Islamic principles. Another pilgrim who had defended the tour leader when the accusation was made went further: when it turned out that the hotel would welcome the group after all, he asked the accuser on the group's WhatsApp to apologize to the travel agent. Drawing on different registers of moral reasoning, then, was accepted as long as this did not contravene Islamic moral principles by falsely accusing someone.

Kadrouch-Outmany and Buitelaar (2021). Note that visiting the Prophet's Mosque in Medina is not part of the hajj ritual itself. Since it is recommended to pay one's respect to the Prophet when undertaking the pilgrimage, most travel agencies include a visit to Medina in their packages.

Moreover, the disputes over the appropriateness of *ṣabr* illustrate that drawing on different moral registers does not necessarily imply that pilgrims are always torn between different desires or that they experience fragmentation. While we set out to analyse the assessment of the appropriateness of *ṣabr* as an entry to study how pilgrims distinguish between mundane and religious dimensions of their hajj experience, our findings indicate that in fact these dimensions are closely interrelated for them: problems with mundane issues concerning food and accommodation arrangements hampered pilgrims' engagement in devotional practices. Voicing discontent about poor services rather than glossing them over as an exercise in the moral practice of *ṣabr* was therefore also religiously motivated. This fits in with a current, hegemonic religious discourse among Muslims, according to which piety should inform all dimensions of one's life and devotional acts should be part of one's daily routine.

This is not to suggest that pilgrims are motivated by religious considerations only. The discontent about transport, food, and accommodation also points to modern, middle-class sensibilities concerning punctuality and a certain level of luxury. Our findings indicate, however, that in the atmosphere of heightened religiosity during the hajj, pilgrims are more hesitant to publicly voice feelings of discomfort about issues that do not hinder their devotional practices, lest fellow pilgrims should question their piety. Instead, such feelings are shared mostly in more private conversations. The hesitance to express one's desire for more personal autonomy or indignation about gender discrimination turns out to be even stronger. Perhaps this is because gender equality and individualism are highly contested values among Muslims of different religious inclinations and walks of life. Besides being the effect of peer pressure, not addressing such loaded subjects at a group level is probably motivated by the wish to preserve the harmony of the group and respect the overall atmosphere of celebrating Muslim unity.[20] As we will see in the next section, these topics came to the fore during the subsequent interviews.

A last point that stands out in the negotiations about the appropriateness of exerting *ṣabr* at a group level concerns differences in gender and age. In line with the picture that emerges from the ethnographic literature on *ṣabr* regarding the genderedness of the moral practice of *ṣabr*, men were more vocal in expressing discontent at a group level than women. Similarly, pilgrims under sixty tended to be more assertive than those of the older generation. Both

20 Also see Kaell (2014, 58) and Dahlberg (1991, 39) who point to a similar tacit understanding among pilgrims to Jerusalem and Lourdes respectively, to avoid quarreling and downplay internal differences between pilgrims of one's own group.

observations were confirmed in an interview with an experienced hajj tour leader.[21] Asked whether he perceives differences between different categories of pilgrims, he took a moment to think and then very carefully chose his words: 'Men ..., how can I explain? Well, you know, the problem with men is that they want to show that they are the boss.' Resonating the observations of Samuli Schielke and Farha Ghannam among Egyptian men, the tour leader's formulation in terms of the performative dimension of men's complaining suggests that speaking up rather than exerting *ṣabr* is, amongst other things, related to the enactment of masculinity (Schielke 2015, 33; Ghannam 2013, 165).[22] The assertiveness of pilgrims who grew up in the Netherlands was likewise confirmed in the interview with the travel agent:

> Younger pilgrims tend to be very, very critical. They expect the buses to arrive exactly on time. (...) They complain about the quality of a three-star hotel ... It is really a problem.

Similarly, Farooq Haq and John Jackson (2009) report that the consumer expectations of younger Pakistani-Australian pilgrims are much higher than those of older generations and pilgrims from Pakistan. The former also tend to be considerably more assertive and critical than the latter, most of whom adopt a stance of humble acceptance of all setbacks they find on their path.

Having discussed the situational, performative, and dialogic dimensions of practical moral reasoning in instances during the hajj which gave rise to ethical dilemmas concerning the appropriateness of exerting *ṣabr* so far, in the next section we will turn to how the interplay of voices representing different moral registers comes to the fore in stories about the moral practice of *ṣabr* once pilgrims have returned home and reflect on their hajj experiences several months or years later.

5 Maturing Stories about Hajj Morality

Processing the countless fragments of positive and sometimes negative experiences of the hajj into stories involves much narrative work for pilgrims. Carol Delaney, for instance, notes in her article about the hajj as an interpretive

---

21 Not affiliated with Celebrity Hajj.

22 Also see Saghi (2010, 211), who describes another example of enacted masculinity during the hajj in the form of (tacit) male competition concerning the number of *ʿumra* sequences one can perform in one day's time.

framework for Turkish villagers and migrants, that the accounts that Turkish pilgrims who had just returned from Mecca told their relatives and friends consisted mostly of impressionistic fragments. In time, these fragments were put together to form a coherent story that conformed more closely to widely shared expectations (Delaney 1990, 520).

A comparison between the sometimes heated *in situ* discussions about the moral practice of *ṣabr* with retrospective stories about occasions where one's *ṣabr* was tested in the interviews, likewise illustrate the observation by Simon Coleman and John Elsner that: 'Retelling is thus an important part in the return, allowing one to reinterpret the experiences and simultaneously "create oneself as pilgrim"' (Coleman and Elsner 2003, 5).[23] First of all, while many narratives contained references to indignation about Saudi hajj management and the treatment of pilgrims, critical recollections about fellow pilgrims feature much less often in the hajj stories produced in the interviews. The stories that do occur pertain to more mundane situations, such as losing one's temper with someone who takes too much time in the shower or instances in which one's *ṣabr* was tested during the hajj rites, such as getting pushed by pilgrims who set their mind on touching the Kaʿba no matter how much elbowing it takes. Our interlocutors tended to tell such stories in a general way, rather than describing a particular scene involving particular persons. Furthermore, narrators usually present themselves as a witness to the scene. Mostly, these stories bespeak ambivalence about the fact that 'people will be people' as several interviewees put it: a realistic avowal that no one can live up to their ideals all of the time, mixed with a disapproval of comportment that blatantly contravenes the morality of the hajj. In other words, this kind of narration first and foremost serves the purpose of conveying a moral lesson that the narrator learned during the hajj. That such stories are told in general terms rather than providing particulars can probably be explained by the fact that being forgiving and not talking badly about other people are part of the same lessons about sound moral behaviour that the narrator wishes to convey.

Similarly, in stories about challenges that the narrators themselves grappled with, the focus is predominantly—but not exclusively—on how the sacred atmosphere of the hajj helped to fortify their capacity to exert *ṣabr*, thus contributing to their spiritual development. Not surprisingly, the tent camp in

23 Also see Robinson (2016, 44), who describes how tourists tend to re-invent their experiences in post-trip narratives: 'In retrospect we almost joyously describe our fear or disgust directed to a situation. We struggle for descriptive precision, we conflate different feelings, elongate the moments in which we felt angry and sad, and exaggerate the intensity of affect.'

Minā and the night in the open air in Muzdalifa feature most often in stories about one's *ṣabr* being tested. A woman in her mid-forties, for example, explained that she had experienced the nights in Minā and Muzdalifa as the biggest trial of the hajj, but that things had become easier once she realized how it all boiled down to a lesson in humility:

> First you are in a hotel bed [in Mecca, MB]. Next you only have a thin and small matrass [in Minā, MB], and then you find yourself on the bare ground [in Muzdalifa, MB]. Before you know, you will be under the ground. So, it is a process you go through, a lesson about humility and life's transient nature.

This excerpt shows that one of the lessons heavily emphasized in interviews about a person's *ṣabr* being tested during the hajj concerns an increase of gratitude to God for the blessings in one's life.[24] Illustrating that various identifications intersect in pilgrims' sensibilities, it was often in relation to a perceived lack of comfort that pilgrims who grew up in the Netherlands positioned themselves specifically as Dutch Muslims. They did so, for instance, by pointing out their privileged position in comparison to pilgrims from poorer countries. Talking about the lack of comfort in the Minā tent camp, a man in his early thirties, for example, stated: 'It's not that bad. It's just that we're terribly spoiled, used as we are to a life in luxury.' In a similar vein, a considerable number of narrators compared themselves to pilgrims of their parents' generation, whose backgrounds lie mostly in poor, rural areas in Morocco and Turkey. Several female pilgrims, for example, explained that they had found it more difficult to deal with the lack of comfort and privacy in the tent in Minā than female pilgrims of their mother's age-group. Resonating Qureshi's descriptions of middle-aged Pakistani women in the United Kingdom who reminded their family members of the *ṣabr* they had exerted and the sacrifices they had made for them, a woman in her mid-forties quoted her mother, who had told her: 'Your generation is so spoiled. If only you knew how tough things were on us at your age.' After a pause, the interviewee added: 'She has a point, actually. We do have less patience than our parents.'

In line with conventional hajj storytelling, an Islamic moral register is obviously dominant in the hajj stories produced during the interviews. However, as was often the case in the negotiations over the appropriateness of exerting

24 Obviously, variations occur. For a particularly strong account about being bewildered by the circumstances in Muzdalifa, see Buitelaar (2020, 11).

ṣabr in the group that Kadrouch-Outmany accompanied, the hajj stories shared in the interviews also contain voices that point to other moral registers that inform the desires and sensibilities of our interlocutors. Stories about needing all the *ṣabr* one can muster to spend several nights in a gender-segregated tent with a hundred other pilgrims, for instance, illustrate the impact of grand schemes like individualism and romantic love in the lives of female pilgrims who grew up in the Netherlands. While pilgrims of the generation of their mothers are accustomed to spending much time in the company of other women, younger women are not only used to more 'me-time' as the earlier quoted pilgrim called it, but they are also more strongly oriented towards sharing time and experiences with their husbands.[25] As Jihan Safar and Leila Seurat argue elsewhere in this volume, a recent trend for Muslim couples is to perform the hajj as a honeymoon or shortly after their wedding as a way of bonding and thanking God and asking him to bless the marriage.[26] Travel agencies like Celebrity Hajj play into this trend by offering newly married couples a discount.

Also, as coming to the fore in the story of Asmae discussed by Buitelaar elsewhere in this volume, several younger pilgrims mentioned the burden of having to operate in a group, albeit rarely formulated as explicitly as by Asmae. Rather, interviewees would state that next time, they would try to distance themselves more from the group and make sure to chart their own path. Although coincidence cannot be excluded, pressure to take care of fellow pilgrims was only mentioned by female pilgrims, thus pointing to the genderedness of felt or expected responsibilities.[27] Concluding several stories about gender discrimination, a female pilgrim stated that it was not fair how female pilgrims were treated in the group by critiquing the emphasis on *ṣabr*:

> Of course, we must all be accommodating and exert *ṣabr*, but some people are expected to have more *ṣabr* than others, and it just isn't fair. As the Moroccan proverb goes: *as-ṣabr keydabbar*. Meaning as much as: patience can turn against you and suffocate you.

---

25 Also see Buitelaar's discussion of Asmae's hajj account elsewhere in this volume.

26 Also see Kadrouch-Outmany and Buitelaar (2021).

27 This is not to deny that sons who act as *maḥram* for their widowed mothers and not seldom a considerable group of other female relatives take on huge responsibilities to take care of their female relatives. On the other hand, some older women told us how, after the stay in the Minā tent camp, relieved they were to be back in a hotel where they could put their family members' laundry in the washing machine rather than washing clothes by hand.

Several female pilgrims mentioned that an additional factor contributing to the feeling of having one's patience tested to the limit in the Minā tent camp was the intense socializing among (mostly) older women. Apparently, this seriously hampered the younger women's personal wishes to dedicate their time to devotional activities like reading the Qur'an and performing supplication prayers. The frustration that comes to the fore in such stories illustrates that the desire of younger pilgrims for more time and space for themselves is not simply the result of modern sensibilities concerning autonomy, gender equality, or the desire to operate as a couple. Equally important is that these younger women have developed a religious style that differs from the religiosity of pilgrims of the older generation. For older pilgrims, gratefulness for having been 'called by God' to perform the hajj dominates; they tend to be strongly motivated to humbly accept all discomfort as a way to expiate for sin and earn more *ajr*, religious merit (cf. Buitelaar 2020). While the forgiveness of sins is also important to younger pilgrims, they tend to conceive the hajj predominantly as a project of self-reflection and spiritual growth. Although in the stories that pilgrims told us we recognize the argument that Mahmood (2005) makes concerning the exercise *ṣabr* as part of the cultivation of a pious self, the examples discussed here demonstrate that in certain situations pilgrims experience patiently accepting circumstances rather than trying to change them as a hindrance.

6 Conclusion: Piety and Middle-Class Consumerism

In this chapter, we have mapped how the advice given to prospective pilgrims to take along lots of *ṣabr* on their journey to Mecca translates into the assessment of pilgrims and negotiations between pilgrims over the appropriateness of exerting *ṣabr* as events during the hajj unfold, and, secondly, how references to *ṣabr* feature in the stories of pilgrims who reflect on their hajj several months to years after their return home. To explore how the desires and sensibilities of pilgrims relate to various models of a good life, we focused on invocations of the Islamic virtue of *ṣabr* to study the interplay between different 'grand schemes' in the practical moral reasoning of Dutch pilgrims with Moroccan and Turkish backgrounds as they try to make sense of their hajj experiences.

Comparison of 'emergent' stories as the events of the hajj unfold to more 'matured' stories that pilgrims narrate about their hajj experiences once they have returned home, indicates that an Islamic moral register gains more prominence as stories mature, while voices speaking from other moral registers, such as that of ethical entrepreneurship and the related grand scheme of consumerism, become less vocal. Illustrating the dialogical and situational nature of practical moral reasoning, in the more matured stories that were shared within a Dutch interview setting, voices representing the moral registers of gender equality and individualism that had remained more or less silent in public negotiations over appropriate moral assessment of the pilgrims experiences as they were in Mecca had become more vocal.

In the context of the heightened religious hajj atmosphere, it is not surprising that an Islamic moral register predominates in the dialogues and stories we presented. This does not mean, however, that the moral practice of *ṣabr* took precedence in all situations where pilgrims were confronted with ethical dilemmas due to tensions between religious desires and needs based on other grand schemes like consumerism, gender equality, and self-realization in terms of personal autonomy.

Moreover, while Schielke tends to focus on fragmentation and contradictions that people experience on the basis of being informed by various grand schemes, our findings indicate that moral registers pertaining to different ideals do not necessarily operate separately, but can also be mixed and merged in the practical moral reasoning of individuals. Our initial expectation that analysing situations where pilgrims considered it appropriate or not to exert *ṣabr* would point to distinctions they make between mundane and religious dimensions of the hajj journey was therefore based on a wrong assumption. Pilgrims voiced their discontent about seemingly mundane problems concerning food, transport, and accommodation first and foremost in terms of how these issues hampered their devotional practices. Similarly, younger female pilgrims who claimed gender equality and time and space for themselves equally explained their annoyance in terms of how gender discrimination contravenes the overall spirit of Islam and a desire for pious self-cultivation.

Within the exceptional, sacred time-space constellation of the hajj, religious arguments obviously carry more legitimacy to express discontent about the logistics of the hajj than, for instance, stating that one wants more comfort or 'me-time'. In that sense, looking at what arguments (predominantly male) pilgrims voiced on a group level and which considerations (predominantly younger female) pilgrims shared in a more private setting is informative of the limitations of creatively mixing and merging of moral registers in the context where hajj morality reigns. The pattern that we discerned in arguments valuing ethical entrepreneurship and the virtue of exerting *ṣabr* were presented at a group level, while complaints about gender discrimination, lack of comfort, and lack of privacy mostly were expressed in private conservations points to the performative, situational, and dialogical nature of practical moral reasoning.

This should not be interpreted as indicating that religious arguments are foregrounded for mere strategic reasons of receiving recognition. Giving precedence to religious motivations is very much in line with pilgrims' overall motivation to perform the hajj. In addition to fulfilling their religious duty and asking forgiveness for past sins, the Dutch pilgrims in the age-group focused on here felt that hajj performance is a deliberate, embodied exercise to develop virtuous dispositions (cf. Buitelaar 2020). We would argue that framing one's feelings as much as possible in terms of a religious moral register is therefore best explained as a self-disciplining act.

Exactly because Mecca symbolizes perfection and pilgrimage counts as the ultimate devotional act, the hajj is posited above and outside the imperfections of everyday life where its sacredness can be evoked to seek guidance and strength. This comes to the fore specifically in the hajj stories of pilgrims who have resumed the routines of everyday life after their return from Mecca. In those more matured stories, fragmented experiences and ambivalent feelings have been processed into more coherent narratives in which the moral lessons of the hajj are foregrounded. Failures to live up to one's own high ideals, for example by acknowledging feelings of extreme discomfort or even despair in the tent camp in Minā or the night in the open air in Muzdalifa, tend to be turned into important moral lessons on 'working on oneself'.

At the same time, in addition to the ideal of the *umma*, grand schemes like gender equality and individualism have regained prominence in the quotidian lifeworlds of pilgrims. Also, the audiences they address in the stories produced in the interviews are more diverse than their audience in Mecca. As a result, reflections on the appropriateness of exerting *ṣabr* in the face of gender discrimination or pressure to adapt to the group rather than seek one's own path likewise prove to be more prominent in the hajj stories, thus illustrating once more that moral reasoning is a dialogical and situational practice.

References

Al-Ajarma, Kholoud. 2020. 'Mecca in Morocco. Articulations of the Muslim pilgrimage (Hajj) in Moroccan everyday life.' Unpublished PhD thesis, University of Groningen.

Al-Ajarma, Kholoud, and Marjo Buitelaar. 2021. 'Social media representations of the pilgrimage to Mecca. Challenging Moroccan and Dutch mainstream media frames.' *Journal of Muslims in Europe* 10: 146–167. doi:10.1163/22117954-bja10027

Asad, Talal. 2003. *Formations of the secular: Christianity, Islam, modernity*. Stanford, CA: Stanford University Press.

Bamberg, Michael. 2011. 'Who am I? Narration and its contribution to self and identity.' *Theory & psychology* 21 (1): 3–24.

Buitelaar, Marjo. 2020. 'Rearticulating the conventions of hajj storytelling: Second generation Moroccan-Dutch female pilgrims' multi-voiced narratives about the pilgrimage to Mecca.' *Religions* 11 (7): 373. https://doi.org/10.3390/rel11070373.

Buitelaar, Marjo. 1993. *Fasting and feasting in Morocco. Women's participation in Ramadan*. Oxford: Berg.

Caidi, Nadia. 2020. '"I was not willing to risk my hajj." Information coping strategies of hajj pilgrims.' *Journeys* 21 (1): 41–62.

Coleman, Simon, and John Elsner. 2003. 'Pilgrim voices: Authoring Christian pilgrimage.' In *Pilgrim voices. Narrative and authorship in Christian pilgrimage*, edited by Simon Coleman and John Elsner, 1–16. New York and Oxford: Berghahn Books.

Dahlberg, Andrea. 1991. 'The body as a principle of holism: Three pilgrimages to Lourdes.' In *Contesting the sacred: The anthropology of Christian culture*, edited by John Eade and Michael Sallnow, 30–50. London: Routledge.

Davis, Susan. 1983. *Patience and power. Women's lives in a Moroccan village*. Cambridge, MA: Schenkman Publishing Company.

Delaney, Carol. 1990. 'The hajj: Sacred and secular.' *American ethnologist* 17 (3): 513–530.

de Lang, Lisa. 2017. 'Je probeert een ander mens te zijn. Een studie naar de beleving van de bedevaart naar Mekka in termen van religiositeit en identiteit onder Nederlandse moslims van Turkse en Marokkaanse afkomst.' Unpublished MA thesis, University of Groningen.

Dwyer, Daisy Hilse. 1978. *Images and self-images. Male and female in Morocco*. New York: Columbia University Press.

Ghannam, Farha. 2013. *Live and die like a man. Gender dynamics in urban Egypt*. Stanford, CA: Standford University Press.

Göle, Nilüfer. 2017. *The daily lives of Muslims. Islam and public confrontation in contemporary Europe*. London: Zed Books.

Groeninck, Mieke. 2017. 'Reforming the self, unveiling the world. Islamic religious knowledge transmission for women in Brussels' mosques and institutes from a Moroccan background.' Unpublished PhD thesis, KU Leuven.

Hamdy, Sherine. 2009. 'Islam, fatalism, and medical intervention: Lessons from Egypt on the cultivation of forbearance (sabr) and reliance on God (tawakkul)'. *Anthropological quarterly* 82 (1): 173–196.

Hammoudi, Abdellah. 2006. *A season in Mecca. Narrative of a pilgrimage*. New York: Hill and Wang.

Haq, Farooq, and John Jackson. 2009. 'Spiritual journey to hajj: Australian and Pakistani experience and expectations.' *Journal of management, spirituality & religion* 6 (2): 141–156.

Jouili, Jeanette. 2015. *Pious practice and secular constraints. Women in the Islamic revival in Europe*. Stanford: Stanford University Press.

Kadrouch-Outmany, Khadija. 2018. 'Antropoloog in Mekka. Onderzoek doen binnen je eigen gemeenschap.' *Zemzem. Tijdschrift over het Midden-Oosten, Noord-Afrika en Islam* no. 1: 124–131.

Kadrouch-Outmany, Khadija, and Marjo Buitelaar. 2021. 'Young Moroccan-Dutch women on hajj. Claiming female space.' In *Muslim women's pilgrimage to Mecca and beyond. Reconfiguring gender, religion and mobility*, edited by Marjo Buitelaar, Manja Stephan-Emmrich, and Viola Thimm, 36–55. London and New York: Routledge.

Kaell, Hillary. 2014. *Walking where Jesus walked: American Christians and Holy Land pilgrimage*. New York: New York University Press.

Kloos, David, and Daan Beekers. 2018. 'Introduction. The productive potential of moral failure in lived Islam and Christianity.' In *Straying from the straight path: How senses of failure invigorate lived religion*, edited by Daan Beekers and David Kloos, 1–19. New York and Oxford: Berghahn Books.

Mahmood, Saba. 2005. *Politics of piety: The Islamic revival and the feminist subject*. Princeton, NJ: Princeton University Press.

Menin, Laura. 2020. '"Destiny is written by God": Islamic predestination, responsibility, and transcendence in Central Morocco.' *Journal of the royal anthropological institute* (*N.S.*) 26: 515–532.

Peters, Francis. 1994. *The Hajj. The Muslim pilgrimage to Mecca and the Holy Places*. Princeton, NJ: Princeton University Press.

Qureshi, Kaveri. 2013. '*Sabar*: Body politics among middle-aged migrant Pakistani women.' *Journal of the royal anthropological institute* (*N.S.*) 19: 120–137.

Robinson, Mike. 2016. 'The emotional tourist.' In *Emotion in motion: Tourism, affect, and transformation*, edited by Mike Robinson and David Picard, 21–46. London and New York: Routledge.

Saghi, Omar. 2010. *Paris-La Mecque. Sociologie du pèlerinage*. Paris: Presses Universitaires de France.

Sardar, Ziauddun. 2011. *Reading the Qur'an: The contemporary relevance of the sacred text of Islam*. Oxford: Oxford University Press.

Schielke, Samuli. 2015. *Egypt in the future tense: Hope, frustration, and ambivalence before and after 2011*. Bloomington and Indianapolis: Indiana University Press.

Schimmel, Annemarie. 1975. *Mystical dimensions of Islam*. Chapel Hill, NC: University of North Carolina Press.

Smith, Martyn. 2008. *Religion, culture and sacred space*. New York: Palgrave Macmillan.

Wensinck, Arent Jan. 2012. 'Ṣabr.' In *Encyclopedia of Islam* (*second edition*), edited by Peri Bearman, Thierry Bianquis, Clifford Bosworth, Emeri van Donzel, and Wolfhart Heinrichs. Leiden: Brill. https://dx.doi.org/10.1163/1573-3912_islam_SIM_6379.

Wijers, Gijs. 2019. 'Jong en Nederlands in Mekka. Een onderzoek naar de betekenissen van de bedevaart voor jonge, Nederlandse moslimmannen.' Unpublished MA thesis, University of Amsterdam.

CHAPTER 14

Crowded Outlets: A North American Khoja Shiʿi Ithna Asheri Pilgrim's Auto-ethnographic Memoir

Zahir Janmohamed

1 Introduction

Years ago, on my second hajj in 2011, I was pulled aside at the Jedda airport and 'randomly' selected for additional screening. My travel companion was an Indian filmmaker named Parvez Sharma who at the time was working on a film about being a gay Muslim in Mecca (Sharma 2015). Upon watching security guards escort me aside, he began to panic. I had spent the previous decade doing human rights work in Washington DC, first at Amnesty International and later in the US Congress, and he worried that my writing on Saudi Arabia might get us both in trouble.[1] But I felt anxious for another reason: I am a Shiʿi Muslim and in my possession—albeit in digital form—were traditional Shiʿi supplications like *Ziyāra Ḥusayn* and *Duʿāʾ Kumayl* that during my previous trips to Mecca were confiscated by Saudi authorities because they told me these texts are *bidʿa*, or heretical.

I grabbed my suitcase and followed the Saudi guard to a small room. He was in his mid-twenties and had a pair of sunglasses tucked in his breast pocket similar to ones I carried. After turning on my various devices to make sure they were not a decoy, he began staring at my legs. 'Those jeans,' he said, pointing at the dark blue pair I was wearing. 'Is this the style American girls like, or do they prefer the faded kind with holes?' I laughed and explained that I am profoundly ill-informed on the fashion tastes of American girls. But my nervousness did not subside. My devices were still on, right in front of me, and I feared he might browse through them and discover the various Shiʿi prayer apps I had downloaded onto them. His mind, though, was elsewhere. 'Abercrombie or Aéropostale? Which brand is more popular in California right now?'

1 I worked at Amnesty International from 2006 to 2009 as the Advocacy Director for the Middle East and North Africa. From 2009 to 2011, I was a senior foreign policy aide to Congressman Keith Ellison, a Democrat from Minnesota. Ellison was the first Muslim elected to the United States House of Representatives.

he asked. I gave him an answer—I can't remember what I said—and then he let me off and into Saudi Arabia.

In this chapter, I shall explore how technology—and in particular the wide scale availability of affordable mobile phones and tablets—has allowed minority Muslim communities to bypass Saudi censorship rules and to experience the hajj in entirely new ways. I focus on Shiʿi Muslims because, as I argue in this chapter, the Shiʿi pilgrimage experience on the hajj is about, among other things, experiencing, negotiating, and pushing up against the Saudi government's attempt to monopolize definitions and parameters of religious expression.

But how does one's experience of the hajj change if you can block the Saudi state by plugging in your headphones and listening to a Shiʿi prayer or even a Shiʿi preacher of your own choosing? How does this alter, if at all, the minority Muslim's narrative of being an 'outsider' in Mecca, especially given that Shiʿis have long enjoyed a fraught relationship not just with the Saudi state but also with other pilgrims? And finally, how do these new technologies have the capacity to change the power relations between Shiʿi pilgrims and Saudi religious authorities in Mecca and what limits are still there on Shiʿi religious performativity through prayer and bodily postures?

This chapter seeks to address these questions and to examine how technology continues to re-shape not only the logistics of the hajj, but also the realms of religious possibility for Shiʿi Muslims.

2 Background and Approach

In conducting this research, I focused on a Toronto, Canada based hajj group that was founded in the early 1980s and caters mostly to the Khoja Shiʿi Ithna Asheri Muslim community.[2] Through interviews with its founders, as well as with pilgrims who have joined this group over the course of its history, coupled with my own experiences of visiting Mecca with this same group, I explore how Shiʿi pilgrims are now able to carry digital copies of Shiʿi supplication books—as well as audio files of Shiʿi prayers—that were once often confiscated upon entry by Saudi airport security when they were previously carried in their physical form.

2 Because of the sensitive nature of my interviews, and because the organizers of this group did not want to lose access to Saudi Arabia, they asked that I do not disclose the name of the group.

My interest in this subject developed, in part, out of my observations of media coverage on the use of technology on the hajj. In 2014, outlets like BuzzFeed, CNN and others published articles about how some Muslim clerics were outraged by the 'selfie craze' on the hajj that year.[3] These articles raise important questions, such as how technology is changing the physical and psychological landscape of the hajj, and how GPS devices might help reduce the occurrence of stampedes. But they also made me wonder if these reporters had ever spoken to Shiʿi Muslims on the hajj to assess whether their use of technology differed, if at all, from Sunni Muslims.

I should state, at the outset, that I admit the inherent problem in labeling something (or someone) as 'Shiʿi,' given the fluidity and intermixing of identities and texts within Islam. However, I use this term because it speaks to my own experience of visiting Mecca, as well as those I interviewed for this chapter, many of whom, like myself, were told by Saudi authorities that the things they carried, including their copies of the Qur'an, were 'Shiʿi' and not 'Muslim'.[4]

My first visit to Saudi Arabia in 1994 for the *ʿumra* testifies to this. It was seven years after the killing of mostly Iranian pilgrims in what is often called 'the Mecca massacre' and tensions were high between the Saudi and Iranian governments (Bangash 1998). Upon entering the country, our prayer books such as *Mafātīḥ al-jinān* were taken from us by a Saudi officer at the airport, as were our copies of the Qur'an.[5] We were also told in Mecca by both Sunni pilgrims and by Saudi religious police that we were praying 'incorrectly' for keeping our hands to the side during prayers, as opposed to folded across our bodies as many Sunnis do.

This echoed my own experience of growing up in the US. I was born and raised in Sacramento, California, and my parents are Khoja Shiʿi Ithna Asheri from Tanzania. There were fewer Muslims in the US back then and for most of my childhood, there was only one mosque near my home, which called itself a 'Muslim mosque'. However, this mosque was, for all practical purposes, a Sunni

---

3 Nashrulla, Tasneem. 2014. 'Hajj selfies.' *BuzzFeed*, October 1, 2014; see also Keen, Andrew. 2014. 'Selfies at the hajj: Is how tech allows narcissism to run riot?' *CNN*, October 30, 2014.

4 According to those I interviewed for this chapter, the definition of what is 'Muslim' keeps contracting, at least on the hajj, and the definition of what is 'Shi'a' keeps expanding. Elderly pilgrims, for example, told me that Muslims of all sects, at least those from South Asia, often recited Urdu songs in praise of the Prophet Muhammad in the 1960s and 1970s. Today that practice, they told, is not only less common among Sunnis, but many Sunnis now regard it as 'Shi'a,' a comment they also heard from Saudi religious police.

5 *Mafātīḥ al-jinān* is a Shi'a Ithna Asheri compilation of supplications compiled by ʿAbbās Qūmī (1877–1941).

mosque, as no Shiʿi programmes, prayers, or preachers were allowed there. I attended Sunday school at this mosque, and I was taught Islamic history there. However, the history I learned rarely, if ever, mentioned any of the figures loved and revered by Shiʿi Muslims, such as the sixth *Imām* in the line of succession after the Prophet Muhammad, Jaʿfar al-Ṣādiq.

And yet the history I learned was never presented as 'Sunni history'. It was presented as 'the history of Islam', the assumption being that anything else is non-normative. This confused me as a kid, to see the way Shiʿi identity was pushed off to the side, whereas in my house it was central. Despite this, I loved going to the mosque, if only because of the friendships I forged there, especially while playing basketball in the mosque parking lot.

But I realized early on that as a Shiʿi Muslim I had to hide, and to give up, a part of myself to be accepted inside that mosque. What I wanted from that space—and later in Mecca—was to be able to be my full self.

It was disappointing then, but not surprising, that my first experience of being in Mecca in 1994 was similar to what I encountered growing up. In fact, I had to leave behind my Shiʿi prayer books to be able to enter Mecca. So, when I returned in 1999 to Saudi Arabia—this time on my own for the hajj—I carried no Shiʿi books and no Qurʾan. The strategy paid off as I was able to enter the country without hassle. However, I longed for these Shiʿi prayers when I was sitting in front of the Kaʿba, reciting my prayers. It was in 2011, on my most recent hajj, that I was able to experience the pilgrimage the way I always wanted. I carried an MP3 player loaded with Shiʿi supplications and as a result, the hajj felt entirely different. When I entered the Prophet's Mosque in Medina, for example, I could listen to Shiʿi supplications like *Jawshan kabīr* that I had grown up reciting and that moved me on a deep, emotional level. Suddenly—thanks to technology—the hajj felt a little bit like my own. And it made me wonder: did other Shiʿi pilgrims feel this same way about technology? Or had technology impacted, or perhaps hindered, their pilgrimage in ways I had not accounted for or imagined?

In June 2019, I wrote a questionnaire and sent it to pilgrims who travelled to Mecca with a Toronto based group, which I shall call the Hajj Council of North America (HCNA). I have changed their name per the requests of the organizers of HCNA, who fear that the Saudi government might deny them visas if they speak openly about the hajj. In fact, part of the reason I picked HCNA was because I knew I could earn their trust. I have known the organizers for twenty years, having completed my first hajj with them in 1999. As a result, they were able to open up with me about issues they might not reveal with others because, as one organizer told me on condition of anonymity, 'the Saudis are finnicky and you never know who you can trust.'

The second reason I focused on HCNA is because of their history. The founders were both born and raised in Dar es Salaam, Tanzania and belong to the Khoja Shiʿi Ithna Asheri community, a group which traces their lineage back to India's western state of Gujarat. When members of this community first immigrated to Canada in the 1970s, they observed a trend among recent immigrant Muslim communities in Toronto to 'return back' to their home countries such as India or Tanzania to join a hajj group from there. The founders of HCNA wanted to cut out that step, which they regarded as unnecessary. It was, in a sense, a statement that they were making to themselves about their intention to make Canada—and not Tanzania—their home.[6]

But HCNA also did something else that changed the way many North American Khoja Shiʿi Ithna Asheri communities completed their pilgrimage: they conducted everything in English. At the time, it was a controversial decision. Urdu has long been, and for many it still is, the language of religious traditions like the *majlis*, a Shiʿi gathering in which a lecture is given about the family of the Prophet Muhammad, and the *marthiya*, an elegy recited in usually Arabic, Persian or Urdu about the family of the Prophet Muhammad. By picking English, not only were they displacing religious scholars who cannot speak English; they were, as one organizer told me, 'making a statement that they would be western facing.'

When I sent out my research questionnaire, I did not know what to expect or who would respond. The group continues to maintain an active email list, which is open only to those who have gone on hajj with them. I was floored by the number of responses I received, many of which pushed me to reevaluate not only my assumptions about technology, but also my very definition of technology itself. Most of the respondents were female and younger, between the ages of 20 and 40. Female respondents were more likely to be comfortable with me using their real names in this chapter, while male respondents overwhelmingly asked me to change their names. However, for the purpose of consistency and safety, all of the names below have been changed.[7]

---

6 The history of HCNA was narrated to me by Shakir, who co-led the group from 1983 to 2009.

7 I realize, of course, that those who fill out a questionnaire like the one I sent out might be disposed to a certain perspective on technology use at the hajj. For this reason, I sent several calls out for responses and also reached out, at random, to various people on the email list. I also did my best to ensure a diversity in terms of gender, education level, class, religiosity, and geographic location.

3 Organizers Perspectives

Today, HCNA brings about 300 pilgrims a year on the hajj, with a staff of about five and around twenty volunteers including chefs, drivers, medical staff, etc. I spoke to three of the core staff members, two males and one female. Mansoor has co-led this group for the past 19 years. During the hajj he co-led in 2018, the group brought 305 pilgrims. Of those, Mansoor told me, he estimates that around 90 % live either in Canada or the US, with the remaining pilgrims residing in Europe or parts of Africa and Asia. The bulk of the pilgrims, around 80 %, are from the Khoja Shiʿi Ithna Asheri community. Each year there are some Sunnis who join, many of whom are married to Shiʿis.

Mansoor emphasized that he does not turn anyone back who wants to complete the hajj. They have had pilgrims from the LGBTQ community, as well as pilgrims who were formerly incarcerated.[8] The group can do this, he told me, because the group skews young—around 60 % are 'probably under 40'. He was also insistent to point out how the costs of hajj have skyrocketed. As a point of reference, my first hajj in 1999 cost me around 3000 dollars, including a roundtrip airfare from San Francisco. In 2011, I paid 7000 dollars to travel with HCNA. In 2019, Mansoor said he would charge just over 10,000 dollars per pilgrim.[9] While anonymous donors each year fully fund about five to seven pilgrims who require financial assistance, Mansoor said the demographic of his group has shifted over the past decade, from middle class to 'solidly affluent.'

In some ways, technology has made the pilgrimage easier. Mansoor remembers a time, in the early 2000s, when he had to carry a suitcase full of Shiʿi supplication books in case other pilgrims had their copy confiscated at the airport. 'It was a hassle,' he told me. 'The weight of the books, the interrogation, the fear that would rise in my stomach on the flight to Jedda. It's one worry that has gone away.' In other ways, though, technology has created new problems, he explained:

> There was a time, in the 1970s and the 1980s, when [Ayatollah Ruhollah, ZJ] Khomeini was alive, when if you pull out a Shiʿi prayer book and a Saudi guard saw you, you will never know if he was going to beat you. Now, I tell new pilgrims: 'You are lucky.' They have no idea what you are

---

8 It is telling, perhaps, of his views on homosexuality that when I asked him if they would welcome LGBTQ members, he responded by telling me: 'Sure, and we have even brought former prisoners, too.'

9 At the time of my interview with him, he presumed that the 2020 hajj would go on. This was, of course, long before the COVID-19 pandemic.

> reading on your iPhones. The downside, of course, is that people stare at their phones too much.

Of the three organizers I spoke with, Mansoor, who is in his late 50s, was the most enthusiastic advocate of technology on the hajj. One reason, perhaps, is that he regularly uses technology in his medical practice and has seen how it has improved his professional life. But another reason is that technology has deepened his spiritual experience of the hajj. He recalled:

> When you are sitting in Medina, and you are listening to a beautiful Urdu poem about Imām Ḥusayn, there is nothing like it. It is who we are as Shiʿis. And now that I have these wireless headphones, it has become so easy.

Mansoor was effusive in his praise of technology but he also reminded me of some of its pitfalls. Topping his list were two gripes: crowded outlets and complaints from pilgrims about the lack of Wi-Fi access. In the past, fights within his hajj group were likely to be caused by sleeping arrangements; now they are often technology related.

> In Mecca, we stay in this, I don't know, 1970s or 1980s built hotel. It was not designed for modern life with all the things we carry. If I hear someone shouting in our hotel lobby, it's probably because they are arguing about another person hogging an [electrical, ZJ] outlet.

Another annoyance technology brings, he said, is increased distraction. Mansoor observed:

> It's weird, because I used to say, forget about your life back home. Focus on hajj. But then I remember that they need their devices to read their Shiʿi *duʿās*. Other times, when I am giving instructions on safety and people are on their phones, it can be dangerous if they are not listening, because there are serious safety issues on the hajj.

Other organizers from his hajj group told me that they view the issue of technology differently. Shakir is a recently retired from HCNA and is based in Toronto, where he runs a small business. He accompanied this group on their first hajj in 1983 and co-led it for 26 years. For him, the difference is not so much technology. It is in the Saudis themselves, who have, in his words, 'finally opened up'. He too, like Mansoor, remembers a time, which he also referred to as 'Khomeini's time', in which 'Saudis were outright hostile towards Shiʿis.' He acknowledged that some Shiʿi pilgrims—Iranian, Iraqi, or Syrian nationals, in particular—have it tougher than Khojas. A moment later, he seemed to change his mind and said, 'The Saudis see any Shiʿis and they think Iran.'[10]

Shakir continued to change his opinions during our interview, a sign, perhaps, about how conflicted he feels not only about the Saudis, but also in talking about this topic. For example, I asked him why there has been a shift in Saudi attitudes towards Shiʿis, but he quickly responded, saying 'I don't get into politics.' Moments later, he cited one example of how things are improving: on Thursday evenings in Medina, Shiʿis hold a mass gathering to recite Duʿā Kumayl, something he said was unheard of in the 1980s.[11] For him, there is no problem being a Shiʿi on the hajj. The issue is about Shiʿis gathering without Saudi approval.

He recalled one incident in which a large Khoja Shiʿi Ithna Asheri family from Toronto was sitting on the rooftop of the Ḥaram listening to a young family member reciting Qurʾan from an iPad. His recitation was so beautiful that a crowd formed around him. Soon after, Saudi guards came and made them disperse. For Shakir, it is not that the Saudis fear Shiʿi beliefs. It is that they fear Shiʿis will organize, something he said has often led to hilarious encounters. He elaborated:

> I was sitting with this Shiʿi *mawlānā* (religious scholar) and he and I were watching a Manchester United game streaming on my laptop outside our hotel. The guards came and told the *mawlānā*, he can't be preaching. I tried to explain that we are just talking about football, but they didn't care.

Shakir, who is in his early seventies, added that bringing Shiʿi books on tablets or mobile devices is a rather trivial, moot point. The biggest technology advance on the hajj, in his estimation, are things like the water-cooled marble, fans, and escalators—things that benefit all pilgrims, not just Shiʿis. For the most part, he believes, the experience of hajj is about the same as when he first went decades ago, despite the incremental changes he believes the Saudi government has made toward Shiʿis. He went on:

---

10 I asked him to clarify why Khojas, who are of South Asian descent, often do not face the same scrutiny. His answer: 'Simple. The Saudis are not at war with their home countries.'

11 For a photo of *Duʿāʾ Kumayl* being held in Medina, see this photo from 2005: http://sfbasic.org/site/islamic_life/hajj/hajj1426h/duaa_komeyl_in_medina.php, accessed July 21, 2021.

> Can I recite *Du'ā' kumayl* now a bit easier on my iPhone? Sure. But make no mistake: we are always reminded there that we are Shi'is. We feel it at Janna al-Baqī'.[12] We feel when we see the history they have demolished; we feel it when we have to be careful who we pray next to in the Ḥaram. That will never change.

For him, the very landscape of Mecca and Medina—and specifically how the Saudis have remade it—enforced in him his otherness, that his view of history, at least to the Saudis, was contrary to their understanding, which is to say, 'the norm'.

Zainab, one of several women co-organizers of this group, concurs. While mobile devices and tablets have made her less anxious about carrying Shi'i books, she told me that, 'If a guard is in a bad mood and doesn't like Shi'is, they can pick something about you—your *'aqīq* ring or *fayrūz* ring—and harass you.'[13]

She related to me an incident which illustrated both the advantages and disadvantages of using technology on the hajj. On a recent pilgrimage, she began listening to a lamentation of Imām Ḥusayn on her iPhone's headphones. But that led to problems she had never encountered before. 'As I was listening, I began to cry. Soon a small crowd of Sunni women gathered around me,' she said. 'They wanted to know what I was listening to. When I told them, they said such material is not Islamic. It was humiliating but ...' Her voice trailed off and she double checked to make sure I was not planning to use her real name. When I gave her my assurance that her name would in fact be changed, she continued. 'Technology has changed. Sunnis have not,' she said. Moments later, she added, 'But Sunnis are becoming more tolerant towards Shi'is, especially the younger generation.'

She also shared some of Mansoor's annoyances about technology. Chief among them is that she often finds that pilgrims have not really left their work

12 Janna al-Baqī' is the cemetery that houses the graves of several of the members of the family of the Prophet Muhammad, as well as his companions. Shi'i Muslims believe there are blessings in visiting these gravesites while some Sunnis believe it is heretical to do so.

13 The stones in her rings—*'aqīq*, which is made of carnelian, and *fayrūz* which is made of turquoise—are commonly worn by Shi'i men and women, usually on the right hand, as some Shi'is believe these stones carry special spiritual powers and were favoured and worn by members of the Prophet Muhammad's family. On the website Artefact, Fatima Batool has a good write-up about the Islamic significance of the *'aqīq* and *fayrūz* stones, especially as it relates to Shi'i Muslims. See here: https://www.artefactmagazine.com/2019/02/22/islamic-stones-spirituality/#:~:text=The%20ninth%20Imam%20for%20Shia,to%20a%20person%20while%20travelling, accessed July 21, 2021.

back home like they once did. 'The hajj doesn't feel the same,' said Zainab, who works in the medical industry. 'People are on conference calls, checking their emails. Hajj used to be about getting away.' Today, her biggest concern is not so much about being Shiʿi on the hajj, but about being a woman. In the future, she would like to see Saudis use technology to monitor when and how crowds get abusive, especially towards women. 'All the cameras are pointed at us,' she said. 'Why not use them to ensure women are not grabbed?'[14] With the Saudi government planning, to increase the number of pilgrims on the hajj each year, she fears what this will mean for women's safety. She rattled off a list of ways in which technology could be used to safeguard women. 'I am not worried about the future of hajj as a Shiʿi. I worry about being a woman, given how many people the Saudis say they want on hajj,' she said.

4 Participant Perspectives

Of the twenty or so pilgrims from this group who I spoke with, many were in their late 20s and early 30s. Because of rising costs of the hajj, as well as stricter Saudi rules about pilgrims who return for the hajj, the group has seen a drop in what Mansoor called 'serial *ḥājjīs*', pilgrims who perform hajj frequently. Among male pilgrims, one reoccurring theme that kept coming up is that they wanted the hajj to be harder. They lamented how technology had made the trip more convenient and more 'western'.[15] Azhar, a pharmacy student in his mid-twenties who now lives outside Chicago, was a bit confused by my interest in technology on the hajj. He cannot remember a time in which technology—and the use of devices in particular—was not a part of his religious practice. At the Shiʿi mosque that he attends, for example, all the prayers are projected onto a screen using PowerPoint. 'Why would technology not be used at the hajj?' he asked. For him, if he could change one thing about the hajj, it would be to 'cut off the internet and destroy all the hotels.' The problem with the Ḥaram, he said, 'is that it looks like an Apple store, with clean lines and no personality of its own.' Azhar had always heard stories, especially from his grandparents, about Mecca. Back then, according to what they told him, there were 'lamps, *minbar*s, Ottoman art, and an actual well for Zamzam.' In short, he thought and

---

14 According to a 2017 article, the Saudis installed 6000 security cameras to ensure the safety of pilgrims. See https://www.arabnews.com/node/1154856/saudi-arabia, accessed July 21, 2021.

15 In his 2012 *New Yorker* piece, Basharat Peer reported on the modernization of Mecca. See https://www.newyorker.com/magazine/2012/04/16/modern-mecca, accessed July 21, 2021.

wanted Mecca to look qualitatively different from 'back home.' He wanted it to look exotic and at times during our conversation, it sounded like he wanted Mecca to look like a scene from the Disney movie *Aladdin*.

This theme came up a lot, particularly among male respondents: that the construction boom in Mecca has stripped the city of its 'soul' as one respondent told me. Several of the respondents—like Azhar—had never left North America. They expected, and hoped, for Mecca to look more 'eastern'. One person even told me: 'Even the Arabs don't stay in tents there.' Azhar wants to go back to Saudi Arabia when the weather is hotter, so that he can experience more hardship. 'The hajj was too easy. It's not meant to be that way,' he said.

Others, particularly female respondents, said they saw new possibilities in the use of technology at the hajj. One said she felt safer knowing she could use GPS to find her husband if they were separated by crowds.[16] Another said that technology had given her space to articulate her grievances. She recalled visiting the Starbucks in Mecca, only to notice how small the 'family' section is where women are permitted to sit. After she returned to Toronto, she tweeted at Starbucks and they responded right away, saying they would look into the matter.

One previous participant with this group, an early 30s bank employee who lives in Florida, told me that having internet on hajj allowed her to educate her colleagues about Islam by posting trip updates during her pilgrimage. 'It's good for people to see what we do, because they have so many misperceptions and biases,' she said. For Masooma, a high school teacher in her mid-thirties who lives in Toronto, having technology at the hajj made her aware of her class privilege for the first time. On her last visit in 2015 with this group, she packed her iPad, per their recommendation. One evening in the Ḥaram, a crowd gathered around her as she was reading Qur'an from it. 'Some had never seen an iPad before and I think they were jealous,' Masooma said, who was born in Kenya. She started speaking to the other pilgrims and began to realize 'how inequitable the hajj can be.'

But by far the most interesting insight, at least in my estimation, came from a recent college graduate named Leila who lives in Toronto. For her, having technology on the hajj allowed her to push back on the group's resident Islamic scholars—all of whom were male on her hajj in 2018. Each year, the group hires a few religious scholars, or *'ulamā'*, usually individuals trained in Qum, Najaf, or Lucknow, who guide pilgrims during hajj. When Leila went, she found these

16 The BBC wrote about e-bracelets on the hajj in a 2016 article. See https://www.bbc.com/news/technology-36675180.ba, accessed July 21, 2021.

scholars to be 'condescending and totally boring.' During her hajj journey, she and a few young women found a Wi-Fi spot and downloaded the lectures of a female scholar they admire from Canada, who they listened to throughout the pilgrimage using headphones. What technology allowed them to do, she said, was 'to shut off male voices and to follow women.' Leila then used a phrase to describe technology that kept coming up throughout my interviews: 'It lets me do my own thing.'

5 Conclusion and Postscript

When I began conducting research for this chapter, I had, admittedly, a rather narrow definition of what technology is and how it is used by North American Khoja Shiʿi Ithna Asheri Muslims. But in conducting interviews, I observed that technology is creating a multiplicity of new ways of being on the hajj, not just in spaces like the Ḥaram, but within hajj groups themselves. I also learned that not only are the uses of technology varied, but also the very definition of what technology is. Younger pilgrims tended to look at personal devices such as mobile phones as being technology, whereas older pilgrims saw advances such as escalators and air-conditioners to be technological advancements.

Technology, I observed, often allows pilgrims a higher degree of agency: they can, for example, call their own taxi using the Uber app on their phone; they can listen to whatever preacher they want, in whatever language they prefer; they can find their way around Mecca using GPS. In the past, groups like HCNA had a monopoly on these services. You needed them, for example, to arrange your transportation. But now technology has shifted the power away from the group towards the individual. Technology has also displaced the role of the scholar. Previously, a group like HCNA would have its paid, approved Islamic guides that it brought along with them on the hajj. Today, if pilgrims are bored or frustrated by HCNA's religious scholars, they can seek their own religious guidance on their iPhone. But how then does this redefine the role and authority of HCNA?

Among pilgrims who travelled with HCNA, I saw a clear divide in the way men and women view technology on the hajj. Men told me that they did not want just to remember Imām Ḥusayn during the hajj; they wanted to be like Imām Ḥusayn. That is to say, they wanted hajj to be arduous, and fraught with persecution, as if Mecca were a modern-day Karbala, Iraq. In short, they wanted to be martyred, just as Imām Ḥusayn was. Women, for the most part, wanted the hajj to feel safer, more equitable and for there to be less 'masculinity both within the group and within the Ḥaram,' as Leila described it. When I asked Leila to elaborate, she said she wanted men to take up less space; both figuratively and literally. Women should be given more space in the hotel, Leila said. There should also be more acceptance within HCNA that women often experience things on hajj that men do not, such as groping, harassment, etc.

My research also made me eager to understand how technology is used among other religious minorities and among groups on the hajj such as queer Muslims. The interviews I conducted lead me to conclude that, if pilgrims are given a chance to express themselves, more stories will emerge that may complicate our understanding of who does, and does not, fit in on the hajj.

After I finished my interviews, several of the participants from HCNA continued to contact me, wanting to share their joys, and frustrations, of being on the hajj. To me it suggested that there is demand for these types of inquiries and for a more robust conversation about these topics. It also illustrates, perhaps, the ways in which HCNA has *not* allowed for these types of introspective conversations. When I asked an HCNA volunteer why that was, he told me:

> We aren't really having the tough conversations internally about how hajj is changing. I think we fear we will be replaced. People will not see a need any more for hajj organizers and we will go out of business.

A few months after conducting this research, I visited Saudi Arabia in December 2019. Advances in technology meant that I did not even have to leave the comfort of my home to apply for a visa. I uploaded my photo and obtained an 'e-visa' online. My airline ticket was also booked online, as was my hotel. Gone were the *ʿumra* brokers, the paper forms, the long queues at the Saudi embassy. Upon arrival in Jedda, I did not fear a security guard would search through my devices because they were too preoccupied looking at their own phones. When I left the Jedda airport and made my way to Mecca, I hailed a car, using the Uber app. I tried to talk to the driver about how things have changed in Saudi Arabia, but he was watching YouTube the entire way there—yes, while driving.

During my previous visit, in 2011 when I completed the hajj with HNCA, mobile technology was still relatively new. The iPhone had just been released a few years earlier, in 2007. Today the smartphone has taken over our lives and I have to say, it made my experience of visiting Mecca all the more meaningful. Technology made it easier for my wife and I to find each other after prayer; it made it possible for me to video chat with my parents in front of the Kaʿba; and it allowed me to put in my headphones and listen to whatever Shiʿi prayer I wanted. At its core, I believe, the pilgrimage to Mecca is about connecting with yourself and with those you love, and technology *enhanced* my ability to do this.

I should also add that the Saudis seemed to have softened their grip on pilgrims, such as breaking down barriers where men and women can eat. They have even started allowing Shiʿis to gather in small groups.[17] I had become so accustomed, during my prior visits, of tensing up while visiting Mecca because I am a Shiʿi. But no one seemed to care anymore, and it filled me with a sense of calm and hope that Mecca might be more becoming more inclusive.

It did not last long, though. The day before I left Mecca, a South Asian migrant worker began following me while I walked around the Kaʿba. When the crowds thinned, he pointed to his feet and began speaking with me in Hindi. His shoes were falling apart, and he could not afford a new pair. He worked long hours doing construction work and was in a lot of pain, he explained. Would I help him buy him new ones, something with more stability, more protection, he asked?

In conducting my research for this chapter, perhaps I viewed technology too narrowly, conceiving of it largely as the devices we keep in our pockets. But the things in our shoes that help us stand straight, that give us support, that protect our toes such as a steel cover—this can also be seen as a type of technology, a technology he did not have access to, a technology that could have made his life more bearable.

I have always wanted to feel like I could worship and be in Mecca the way I wanted to as a Shiʿi Muslim. Technology allowed me to do this, to bring in the prayers I wanted, and to hear the Shiʿi supplications that I cherish. Technology also allowed me to connect with my family and friends, and to have a fuller, and more meaningful, experience on the hajj. But meeting that South Asian worker, begging for money, reminded me that for many others, some technology—as well as ease of being—is still out of their reach in Mecca.

References

Bangash, Zafar. 1988. *The Makkah massacre and the future of the Haramain*. London: Open Press.

Sharma, Parvez. 2015. 'A sinner in Mecca.' Netflix, April 29, 2015.

17 My wife, I should add, was still routinely asked to fix her hijab, so in some ways, this progressive spirit only extends so far.

FIGURE 14.1 The author, wearing headphones, during his pilgrimage in 2019
PERSONAL PHOTOGRAPH AUTHOR

CHAPTER 15

Curating Post-hajj Experiences of North American Pilgrims: Information Practices as Community-Building Rituals

Nadia Caidi

1 Introduction

For the first time in over 40 years, the 2020 edition of the hajj pilgrimage (corresponding to year 1441 of the Muslim lunar calendar) provided a stark contrast to what the hajj usually looks like, with its crowded buses and sea of bodies circumambulating around the Kaʿba. The restrictions imposed on travel and mass gatherings by the Saudi Ministry of hajj were a result of the COVID-19 pandemic that ravaged the region and the world: instead of the 2 million people that usually converge each year in the Holy Cities, the hajj welcomed only about one thousand pilgrims. Only Saudi nationals or other nationals who resided in Saudi Arabia were allowed to attend the hajj and complete the rituals (Iftikhar 2020; Saudi Press Agency 2020).

As if to compensate for the absence of pilgrims physically partaking in the hajj rituals, social media was replete with images of this unusual hajj. On Twitter, the hashtags *#hajj*, *#hajj2020* and *#hajj1441* were trending with several thousands of people tuning in to catch a glimpse of the scenes of masked cleaners sanitizing the holy premises and the eerie pictures of an almost empty *ṭawāf* area near the Kaʿba. These images circulating on social media (as provided both by official sources as well as individual pilgrims) stood as the closest proxy for the collective experience of partaking in the rituals typical of that time of year. The scale of the pandemic was indeed amplified by the images of empty airports and the otherworldly visions of the Holy Cities; Muslims (and non-Muslims) the world over devoured the images as they bore witness to the extraordinary circumstances and let out a collective sigh of distress and empathy at the spellbinding images of loss and emptiness.

As Muslims witnessed the trending *#hajj1441* images on Twitter and other social media platforms, it was a shared imaginary about the hajj that was disrupted and laid bare. In this chapter, I examine the role of information activities and media practices in community-maintenance rituals. The premise is that pilgrims engage in a range of information practices (e.g., seeking, using and sharing information) as they prepare for their pilgrimage, complete it, and return home. Throughout the process, they engage with information gleaned from various sources, assess the credibility of said information, and partake in documenting and sharing narratives and images of their own. The meaning-making that pilgrims engage in both validates their own notion of what hajj ought to be (e.g., doing it the right way) as well as leads to new texts (stories, images, podcasts) that are circulated online and offline. These, in turn, shape the collective hajj imaginary and contribute to would-be pilgrims' aspirations and representations about completing hajj in the twenty-first century.

This chapter focuses specifically on an under-studied aspect of the pilgrimage: the post-hajj phase and the associated information practices that pilgrims engage in upon returning home. Among the questions raised by this phase of the pilgrimage are: What happens to pilgrims upon return from hajj? How do pilgrims make sense of their experience at the holy sites that make up the hajj? What are the information-related activities and media practices that pilgrims engage in upon return (and for what purposes)? How do pilgrims sustain their lived experience of completing the pilgrimage? This project brings an information science perspective to elucidate the informational and techno-spiritual practices of global pilgrims and their role in community-maintenance rituals. Pilgrims' engagement with media (in its multiple forms) is conceptualized in Ito's sense, where they become 'reactors, (re)makers and (re)distributors, engaging in shared culture and knowledge through discourse and social exchange as well as through acts of media reception' (Ito 2008, 3). Three concepts related to information activities—meaning-making, community-maintenance, and building religious capital—emerge out of my findings and the reviewed literature to elucidate how pilgrims make sense of their hajj experience upon return and negotiate their new status as Ḥājji or Ḥājja.

2 Method

This chapter is part of a broader project that examines the expressions of spiritual and religious identities of Muslim youth and is based on a subset of interviews with twelve young Muslims (aged 18–35) who completed hajj. The aim is to examine the everyday information practices of these hajj pilgrims with the hajj being framed as dynamic and constituted through the rich and nuanced interactions that produce pilgrims' social life (Feldman and Orlikowski 2011). Semi-structured interviews were used to collect detailed information with open-ended questions enabling participants to elaborate on their experiences of hajj. Participants were also asked about their everyday information practices and their perceptions about various media and how these contributed to shaping their pilgrimage experiences.

The twelve participants (P1–P12) in this study included five men and seven women, stemming from a range of locations with most being located in North America (N = 9), 2 in France, and one in Bangladesh. All the participants had completed hajj but two had also completed *ʿumra*, and one participant had performed a total of two hajj and two *ʿumra* pilgrimages. The participants were equally divided between two age groups: 25–29 (N = 6) and 30–35 (N = 5), were typically well-educated, and employed professionals (with the exception of one participant who was in the 18–24 age group and was a student living at home). Of the 12 participants, 9 were married, some with young families. While they all spoke English, the participants' fluency in several languages (Urdu, French, Arabic, Pashto, Bahasa, and Bengali, among others) speaks to their diverse backgrounds (South Asian (N = 7), North African (2), Middle Eastern (1), Indonesian (1), and Afghani (1)), thus reflecting the global nature of the *umma*.

The interviews were completed in 2018 and were designed to capture pilgrims' experiences of completing hajj (and associated information practices) before departure, during their time in Saudi Arabia, and upon their return from hajj. It must be noted that the media usage reflects the social media platforms prevalent at the time. I have examined elsewhere the routinized practices and various forms of learning in the accounts of the 12 hajj pilgrims interviewed (Caidi 2020; 2019). In this chapter, I focus on the practices associated with the post-hajj phase—after the pilgrim returns home.

3 Hajj in the Age of Information

In 2019, 2.48 million pilgrims performed hajj, 74% of whom came from outside Saudi Arabia (*General Authority of Statistics 2019*). Global mobility, along with affordable and convenient modes of travel are contributing to sociodemographic changes among religious travelers, including younger people completing the pilgrimage. Moreover, the prevalence and ubiquity of mobile devices and sharing platforms have reshaped the pilgrimage landscape in today's media and technology-intensive environment (Caidi and Karim 2022; Buitelaar 2020; 2015; van der Beek 2019; 2014; Caidi, Beazley and Marquez 2018; Flaskerud and Natvig 2018; Bianchi 2017; Campo 2016; Janmohamed 2016; Jenkins 2016; Hill-Smith 2009).

The twelve participants in this study both actively sought and passively encountered information about hajj through a variety of means: stories about hajj learned in childhood; advice from family members and trusted friends who already performed hajj; guidance from community religious leaders and licensed travel operators; and online browsing. Social information, in particular, pervades every aspect of hajj and relies on the development of trusted social relationships and on the collective imaginary in enabling a shared construct of the hajj. Along the way, new ways of knowing are established to support the pilgrim's understanding of hajj and the reintegration of the pilgrim into society upon their return.

These emergent social media practices add another layer of context to individuals' contemporary expressions of spiritual and religious identities. Pilgrims are increasingly plugged into wireless networks and can tweet, blog, and post photos of their experience as it unfolds (Caidi, Beazley and Marquez 2018; Ameli 2009; Lövheim 2004). While photography and video-recording without a licence is prohibited in certain holy sites during the hajj, it is harder to confiscate smartphones, because they are easier to conceal and are often needed by the pilgrims for other, essential purposes. As long as there are pilgrims, there will continue to be stories retold about their experiences. Online blogs and vlogs are only the most recent instantiation of a long tradition of recounting one's hajj journey and contributing one's story to the global hajj archive.

4 Curating Post-hajj Memories and Experiences

Pilgrims embark on hajj for a variety of reasons: a search for redemption, authenticity, or sheer curiosity. Most usually return transformed. When exploring pilgrimage rituals that involve (presumably) personal transformation and change, the experiences of return are equally important and have been documented, for example, in the tales of 'Camino Blues' (van der Beek 2019). Academic research about the return from hajj, however, remains limited despite the pilgrims in this study keenly pointing out that the post-hajj phase has great significance to them. Indeed, through its intensive spiritual and physical experience, rituals and invocations, the hajj exemplifies Schatzki's (1996) interpretation of embodied know-how: understandable by those who perform it (a form of experiential learning) and who espouse the same belief framework. The routinized practices and various forms of learning by the 12 hajj pilgrims interviewed have been reported elsewhere (Caidi 2020; 2019). Their hajj practices highlight what Reckwitz (2002, 250) defined as 'routinized way[s] in which bodies are moved, objects are handled, subjects are treated, things are described and the world is understood.' In this chapter, the focus is on what happens upon return from hajj and how pilgrims engage in curating their hajj-related memories and experiences (and for whom?). The findings from the post-hajj phase point to three important dimensions (and associated activities and practices): meaning-making, community-maintenance rituals, and building religious capital. These are discussed below.

4.1 *Information Activities as Meaning-Making Processes*

> You can easily assess people's spirituality from the stories about hajj they tell when they come back: someone who just did the rituals vs. someone who rediscovered themselves and their *īmān* (faith) from being there. (P1)

The insight offered by P1 in the quote above hints at the importance of stories as a window onto one's spiritual and material journey and points to the importance of information sharing as both a documentary and a performative practice. While the 12 pilgrims interviewed recounted diverse aspects of their return (from the feelings of rapture they experienced after reintegrating into the hectic pace and daily grind of everyday life to their strategies for coping with the return), they also reflected on the importance of narrating their experiences as a means of making sense of their journey. P6 states:

> It is like a dream for one month [while at hajj, NC], and then we wake up. For two weeks afterwards, I told and shared my story with everyone. So, I felt like I was still there reliving it. But when I came back, with the busy life, it is changed. During the hajj, the whole day, we just read the Qur'an and pray. There are no worries about anything. Like in a dream. I felt when I was leaving Mecca that something was taken from my heart [pause, NC]. When I am at home, I feel OK. But outside, it is very different and it is hard. So, I sit for a few moments, thinking about that journey; how I practiced there; how my life changed when I was there. (P6)

Like P6, P10 expresses a similar yearning for reconnecting with the state that they were in while at the hajj: 'I came back depressed. There, we were all surrounded by other Muslims. When I returned, I felt lost, nostalgic, depressed.' Several pilgrims reported practicing self-care to deal with restlessness and deep nostalgia. Many attempted to re-create this spiritual bubble by channeling the feelings and associated emotions that best described their state while at hajj. Interestingly, many of their strategies to deal with the return from hajj can be considered information-rich. I examine below the practice of documenting as a form of remembering and processing one's experiences.

Pilgrims' embodied experiences at the holy sites, which were often described in great detail, seem to have found an expressive release in the practice of documenting one's hajj. This practice took various forms such as journalling, painting, taking and organizing photographs, as well as sharing their journey through social media postings (e.g., selfies, blogs, vlogs and videos; also see Buitelaar and Al-Ajarma elsewhere in this volume).

These documentary practices were deemed helpful for the pilgrims to remember and reconnect with the state they were in while performing hajj; and the traces left behind constitute mementoes and reminders of their experiences. For P1, keeping a diary during hajj allowed her to make sense of her journey:

> I wanted to understand the spiritual dimensions of hajj: the true meaning of it, beyond the rituals. I kept a journal to remember. I highly recommend it. I made the decision to keep it private and it was a very valuable experience. I got this idea of a journal from a blog actually from a North American woman called 'Ten things you didn't expect about hajj.' It is actually very common to see people write their diaries at hajj. We saw people doing that all the time. It is the small things that you need to absorb while there. That's why you keep it. (…) I used to keep notes such as: 'Today I went to 'Arafa. This is how I felt.' Since I returned, I looked at the diary many times. Every few months, I would read one entry. I highly recommend this. (P1)

Several things stand out in P1's account: journalling for her is a very private activity, one that is meant to be the entry point into her psyche and her deepest feelings. The temporal element is also an important consideration. P1 accesses her diary 'every few months' and the document thus becomes not only an anchor that grounds her in her present condition *but also* a reminder of what she experienced while at the hajj. Lastly, P1's impetus to keep a diary was a result of her online browsing and reading behaviour (of another pilgrim's blog). In addition to journalling, other participants talked about documenting their journey through various means. P8 narrates a special moment that she has shared often with friends, the image and symbolism of which she has transposed into her artistic endeavours post-hajj:

> Before hajj, I didn't do any overly Islamic art form. I started to explore more after my first *'umra*. I started exploring Islam and art together. One

FIGURE 15.1 Intergenerational Hajj selfie (with consent from study participant)

of my favorite memories was being on the third floor of the mosque [in Mecca, NC] and looking at the birds making *du'ā'*. I was reminded of *sūra al-Fīl* [a chapter in the Qur'an, NC], and I remember thinking: 'Here I am here, 17, and my Prophet was here!' You feel connected. This is me. I am so far removed from him [the Prophet Muhammad, NC], but I am not. (P8)

P1 and P8's accounts illustrate the importance of reminiscing and sharing as a central part of meaning-making and community-building. Whether through Facebook groups, Instagram, YouTube or other social media platforms, my findings from the data highlight the importance of capturing, preserving, and sharing special moments and experiences with a range of publics (Kim, Caidi and Chah 2019; Thomson 2019; Forcier 2017). Sharing these hajj stories contributes both to the development of a personal identity and also signals membership within a broader community of practice. Ultimately, the artifacts created and curated (diaries, scrapbooks, selfies, videos, blogs, tweets, art pieces) are meaningful for those who produce them, and also allow Muslims to have agency in how they want to represent themselves and their relation to Islam, as is evident in the accounts below with their unapologetic tone about young Muslims' rapport with technology:

> We [he and the other pilgrims in his group, NC] didn't really talk about it [filming, videotaping, NC]. It was just something we did. We had the video camera and the camera and we used it. We saw people filming. Everyone had a cellphone to communicate with the outside. They even took selfies. I did it too. This was an important place and we wanted to document that. (P3)

> Now, with cell phones and smartphones, everyone takes pictures or videos. Even selfies. People take tons of selfies. We took one too. We posted the selfie on Facebook. To show friends and family, and also for fun. We were posing with the eye cam or with the site. (…) We are not paper people: we are all digital. We had everything on our phones. (P7)

> I had an iPhone. In it, I also had a Qur'an app and a hadith app. I downloaded these for facility and convenience. I also had a PDF reader because everything we had, like itinerary or forms, was in digital form. The map app was not working. We used the camera a lot: we took videos and pictures. We used Skype to communicate with our family back home. We also used WhatsApp for texting abroad without getting charged. On the Facebook app, I posted a few things while at hajj. Maybe 2–3 pictures. I posted the rest on Facebook when I returned, to share our experience with family and friends. Technology can be used for good or for bad. In our case, it was very good for us. We were able to store all in one place. It would have been too messy to go with paper, so we embraced the technology. (P8)

These examples show that mobile media pervade people's lives, extending their everyday practices from managing calendars to sustaining remote friendships and accessing local/global news. For pilgrims (and young pilgrims in particular), their identities are increasingly enacted and negotiated online, and social media platforms are fostering environments where individuals of all faiths are expressing their social and religious identities by capitalizing on the power of global networks (de Sousa and da Rosa 2020; Caidi, Beazley and Marquez 2018; Golan and Martini 2018; Echchaibi 2013; El-Nawawy and Khamis 2009; Eickelman and Anderson 2003). Some online blogs and YouTube videos recount personal hajj experiences and provide important information to pilgrims. Local authorities and regional tech-businesses have produced multiple apps that aim to cater to pilgrims' needs. While documenting one's hajj is deemed essential for the purpose of meaning-making and remembering, communities of practice also shape the information-related practices, which includes uploading and consuming content but also sharing technology-related tips. P8 recounts:

> We were provided with [a] mini-Qurʾan that we could transport in our purses, but it gave me headaches the small fonts. Instead, I had the Qurʾan app. It is great! You can bookmark it, make annotations. Qurʾan is not just a book; it is content that you can access anytime. It is very useful if you know how to use it. We taught my mom how to use the Qurʾan app on her phone but she would still not use it at hajj. She is not as literate with the technology. (P8)

P8's account is a good example of new media practices and related literacies developed by young pilgrims. The account however also hints at tensions and fault lines (the refusal of P8's mother to use the Qurʾan app, as to not alter the sanctity of the place or of her own experience). There were several occurrences in the data that displayed this tension between religious and information behaviours. Several participants have echoed P10's sentiment (below) toward selfie-taking, which she deems disruptive and unworthy of the holy sites:

> I am concerned that the Kaʿba will become like the Eiffel Tower. That is not why we go there. I understand that people want to document being in front of the Kaʿba, but I am worried. If it were once or twice, then OK, but I saw people taking pictures and selfies every single day. (P10)

Moreover, the reception of, and reactions toward, these digital artefacts as produced and shared by participants (given the technology available circa 2017) varied a fair bit. P3, who took videos and photographs to document and share his hajj, recalls an unexpected reaction:

> I was showing my cousin what I videotaped around the Kaʿba. He said: 'I thought this was a journey between you and God, why would you show me this? You are showing this on YouTube and to your family on the computer. Why?' I was angry inside at this comment. My thought was to bring a memory from when I did [hajj, NC]. To show the Kaʿba both for myself and to share. We are living in the age of technology, and we live with it. (P3)

When his cousin questioned his media practices (e.g., filming a video while at the Kaʿba and sharing it with others), P3 felt attacked. His anger stems from the collapsing of one's faith/spirituality with one's information practice. P8 provides another example of tensions arising post-hajj. In this case, P8 was coming to terms with a newfound interest in Sufism and was reluctant to share this widely (perhaps out of fear of conflict or negative judgment, given some perceptions about Sufism within Islam):

> The essence of the journey remains mysterious. Hajj is a blessing, but I also realized that I was interested in this broader humanity. [participant appears uncomfortable and hesitant for long seconds before resuming his train of thought, NC.] I am fascinated by Sufism. Lately, I have been reading about it. I have even considered going to the Festival of Sacred Music in Morocco. These are things that interest me now. (P8)

For P8, there seems to exist a meaningful link (whether conscious or not) between his pilgrimage journey, his continued spiritual learning, and the growth that ensued even if his path did not fit the standard narrative expected of a new *ḥājjī*. This quest for meaning post-hajj led P8 and several other participants to seek solace in consuming (even binge-watching at times) various media content. As the quotes below suggest, the purpose is to *remember* and even *reconnect* with a state they had experienced while at hajj:

> There is this one channel, al-Mubashir [a Saudi livestreaming channel of hajj, NC]. I put it on my computer and concentrate on that, and it makes me very energetic. It helped me a lot since I returned. I see the live transmission of hajj and it reminds me of my own experience there. (P6)

> I used the satellite dish to watch Saudi Arabia channels, especially scenes of Mecca, to remember. It was like a sanctuary. (P10)

As per the examples above, audiovisual media (along with live-streaming and YouTube videos) can act as a prompt and a refuge for pilgrims seeking to recall those ephemeral yet profound moments they experienced. Consuming video and other media as a means of reliving sensations has been documented elsewhere. Merchant (2011, 68), for example, reports how scuba diving students who were presented with video footage were able to recall 'physical responses to sounds and images' about their diving experiences. Several quotes from the participants in this study offer similar evidence of information activity associated with viscerally remembering pilgrimage, which suggests the important role such activities have on the post-hajj phase. Indeed, it seems that information activities such as seeking, consuming, and sharing content are not just cognitive practices, but are also associated with recalling emotions and sensations, as if one were present there once again. For participants, their engagement with media is an extension of their emotional and embodied experience at the hajj. By recreating this state, participants were able to reflect more deeply on their personal transformation, as exemplified by the quote below:

> What really changed me, in me, is that I really detached from the material aspects of life. I have already changed since I returned from hajj, because when you are surrounded by this [post-hajj, NC] environment, you need a tune-up. I see hajj as being like a gas station to allow you to fuel up a bit. There is this life and the life in the hereafter. One should enjoy life's pleasures but not forget to invest in the hereafter. If I don't have any gas left, I need to fill the tank again and put more fuel to replenish. Since I have been to hajj, it has become a therapy. I have spoken to friends of mine, and when they ask me about hajj, I always talk to them about these benefits. (P9)

P9's account illustrates a recasting that is typical of many participants' accounts. It is most evident when pilgrims draw comparisons, as they frequently do, between hajj and back home. The newly acquired insights and experiences position the pilgrims as valuable sources of information for others. In the next section, I examine how pilgrims' information practices allow them to not only reflect on their personal transformation post-hajj, but also to navigate and negotiate their social identity as a member of the broader *umma*.

4.2 *Information Activities as Community-Maintenance Rituals*

> When you are doing prayers with all these Muslims around you, millions are gathered. It is overwhelming and humbling. It is incredible how much this religion has spread over the world and touched so many people. It washes over you when you are there. (P4)

P4's account of this connected experience with other pilgrims during hajj is a recurring theme in the data and is well documented in pilgrimage scholarship. In the previous section, there was ample evidence of the personal identity work that the 12 pilgrims engaged in upon return from hajj, including how their information practices mediated that phase of their lives (remembering, reflecting, moving forward). Additionally, participants spoke about finding their place in their community and society upon return, especially given their newly acquired status as Ḥājji or Ḥājja. The process of developing a social identity associated with a religious or spiritual activity often unfolds in stages as participants prepare to enter the social world (the hajj), then become socialized into it, and finally participate and perform their identity both in and beyond the social world (Stebbins 2009, 626–627; Green and Jones 2005, 172). Information activities associated with the post-hajj phase include the communication of information and knowledge in the form of community-maintenance rituals, replete with such activities as 'exchange (or social exchange), interaction, dialogue and conversation' (Savolainen 2017, 48). I find several indications of such engagement in participants' accounts, and our data suggest that different modes of engagement are activated, most notably through the pilgrim's body, as well as through their knowledge-brokering role. The participants shared the myriad ways in which they tended to their bodies:

> Before I did the hajj, I used to sometimes miss the prayer times. I no longer do this. I used to be more flexible about avoiding something slightly sinful. Now I keep reminders to avoid. My wife noticed these changes, especially the waking up on time for all *fajr* (early morning) prayers. (P12)

> The status of Ḥājja is important in our community. So, one has to preserve that image, and the responsibilities that come with it: you cannot go dancing, can't go to mixed gender weddings. One hears of these remarks: 'She is a Ḥājja' It becomes problematic for youth, especially girls, because they start thinking that they are not ready to go to hajj because then they will no longer be able to do this or that. (…) So, I was a Ḥājja, yes. It was an

> even bigger deal in Morocco, when I went to visit. It mattered even more there. It was a prestigious status. But I did hajj for myself, and for Allah. Not to get a Ḥājja status. (P10)

In P12 and P10's accounts, the work on the body (and the mind) required to wake up for *fajr* prayers and for effecting change required of a Ḥājja is illustrative of Wacquant (2005)'s notion that the body is 'not only socially constructed … but socially constructing' (454). Within the social world of hajj, pilgrims exchange social information through various means including their grooming conventions (growing a beard for the men, wearing the hijab for women), manner of physical presentation (dressing more modestly), and engaging in—or refraining from—certain practices (such as dancing, eating non-halal, or shaking the hand of a member of the opposite sex). These types of activities socially construct and serve to demarcate status (Mackellar 2009; Kane and Zink 2004) within the social world of pilgrims. In other words, pilgrims' bodies become informational, and they establish their newly acquired social position in a given social context (Wacquant 2011; Lizardo and Strand 2010, 209; Goffman 2008; Howson and Inglis 2001; Bourdieu 1984).

The quote below by one of the female pilgrims (P4) illustrates both how status is acquired within the community and the risk involved in going against set norms and values:

> Prior to the trip, I was adamant about not wearing the hijab. I don't need it to be a Muslim and to believe. After a month of wearing a hijab there, I almost didn't want to take it off. I wore it after I got back for a while. I wore it on a regular basis for 4–5 months when at work or at my uncle's house. Then, about a month ago, I stopped wearing it. People asked me what happened, and whether I had lost my faith. No, it is just a piece of fabric on my head. I stopped wearing it because when you come back [from hajj, NC], it is all fresh. You want to be a better person, make Allah happy, etc. A few months went by and you realize it is a lot harder to wear because it is not just about the scarf, it is about how you carry yourself; how you speak to others; how you conduct yourself. I was struggling with that. It was too much. I was thinking I would be at peace, but I did not feel that peace. I struggled with it and it became too stressful. It was too much for me, and I wasn't happy. I would like to bring it [the hijab, NC] back someday. So, I try to embrace the meaning of the hijab without wearing it. But at least I made some other changes: now I only eat halal food, whereas before I used to love eating burgers at Wendy's. No more of that. (P4)

In P4's account, becoming a Ḥājja involved both performing particular embodied tasks, like refraining from certain reprehensible actions (such as eating non-halal meats) and acquiring the habitus or physical disposition of a Ḥājja, as in looking like one (in this case, sporting a hijab). It is expected that, over time, pilgrims develop specific literacies in their practice of their faith, notably when it comes to adhering to conventional or prevalent beliefs around morality or lifestyle. That is, pilgrims establish social position from the acquisition of certain capital that is endowed with status within their particular context (Leschziner and Green 2013; Wacquant 2004; Bourdieu and Wacquant 1992). By not complying with such rules, P4's spirituality and religious status are questioned ('People asked me what happened, and whether I had lost my faith'), and her religious capital appears to be depleted. I elaborate on this notion of religious capital below. Specifically, I seek to augment the notion of religious capital beyond ways of *being* (Finke and Dougherty 2002) to include ways of *knowing*, which refers to the extent to which the pilgrim is able to assess the credibility of the information accessed, to navigate complex information environments, and to become a trusted source of meaningful and relevant information for others. This form of knowledge-brokering is thus conceptualized as an important aspect of community-maintenance rituals and an essential dimension of religious capital for twenty-first-century pilgrims (Caidi 2020).

5 Information Activities as a Form of Capital Building

Depictions of hajj have existed for a very long time and remain relatively consistent in their representations of hajj-as-a-sacred place with its sanctity mostly untouched by capital, politics, and class divides (Cooke and Lawrence 2005). This is most evident in the retelling of stories about one's hajj, but also appears in the framing of online hajj narratives, such as through selfies—with their focus on the sacred sites and symbols and away from the rampant Meccan consumerism (Caidi, Beazley and Marquez 2018). Whether conscious or not, this longing for an otherworldly space is reproduced and disseminated by hajj pilgrims, thus lending legitimacy to the pilgrim and increasing their religious capital.

Scholars have long been discussing different types of capital such as body capital (for example, in sports (Wacquant 1995)) or emotional capital (see Reay 2004 in educational settings). For Bourdieu (1987), religious capital is the amount of knowledge and practice pertaining to religious culture one can bring to bear and the extent to which these determine one's hierarchical status in the religious field. Finke's (2003, 3) definition provides nuance: he refers to 'the degree of mastery of and attachment to a particular religious culture', which includes both the knowledge needed to participate fully, along with 'the strengthening of emotional ties' (see also Baker and Smith 2014; Finke and Dougherty 2002). As a multimodal sensory experience, hajj is hard to fully convey to non-pilgrims. P10 and other pilgrims in our study spoke about the importance of experiential, lived knowledge to fully comprehend this life-altering journey:

> The hajj, you do not prepare for it on the day of departure. You have to do a lot of that work of sifting through your life and your soul much earlier and decide on what you want to change and improve in your life. After we came back, we were thinking, my sister and I, of creating a website containing advice and tips about how to truly prepare for hajj. (P10)

P6 recalled the valuable role of information and stories gleaned from family, friends, and the broader *umma* (online) as they prepared for their hajj:

> I heard stories from people about how to manage things. Some had done it recently, but others did it maybe 4–5 years ago. These other pilgrims gave me information: they told me about the Maqām Ibrāhīm and al-Ḥajar al-Aswad (Black Stone). (P6)

Cooke and Lawrence (2005) point to the travel literature genre from the tenth to fifteenth centuries that emerged as a means of describing the hajj to those unable to otherwise perform it for themselves—an early form of a proxy (Sourdel and Sourdel-Thomine 2006). Social media provide an extension for this tradition in that they facilitate access to, and sharing of, hajj-related information as a means of perpetuating the collective imaginary about hajj (Caidi and Karim 2022). Whether face to face or through social media, participants capitalized on a range of channels and platforms to share their experiences with a broad set of publics, using stories, images, and metadata (captions or tags) to describe the mood of the moment, thus documenting the temporal, spatial, and spiritual experiences of pilgrims. Because social media artefacts are also designed for public consumption, they stand as evidence of the pilgrim's religious positioning and membership into the faith: the hajj pilgrim is in effect 'outed' as Muslim by the mere fact of posting such information. This was most evident in North American participants' accounts, who seemed more aware of privacy settings when sharing their pictures and videos online (perhaps as a result of being a Muslim in the West post 9/11).

Participants shared many accounts of how they became mentors and sources of information for friends and would-be pilgrims online and in their community:

> Some of my friends have wanted to talk to me. For something more personal and spiritual. My own, real account of my experiences there. Because we are similar, maybe they trust me. I know that the technical things, they can get elsewhere. So, I tell them: it is not easy. There is a reason Allah wipes away your sins: because it is not easy. As time goes by, we want instant gratification, and when things don't go the way we want, we get upset. So, I tell them: 'It is not a vacation, it is God's invitation. Not something that you can get your own invitation to. It is a big deal; it is an honor.' (P8)

What the participants engaged in is a tailoring of information to their specific audience. I noted several instances of this practice throughout the data. At times, the audience is live, as in the case of P8; at other times, though, the audience is imagined, as when pilgrims share blog entries, photos, and videos online. Either way, pilgrims become facilitators and intermediaries for others. This role of knowledge-broker (with its emphasis on the curation and filtering aspects) refers to the ability of a pilgrim to provide vetted and trusted information based on one's lived experiences. This form of capital is not only one that is derived from one's knowledge about the hajj, but also from one's ability and skills to navigate the information environment and provide usable and meaningful information on a needed basis. The value added by each specific pilgrims' account is their personal insights, the references to the various sources mentioned, and the willingness to both inform and inspire others. Some go even further, such as P5 who recounts how he became aware of his own bias (as a Western-born and raised Muslim) against what he perceived to be an overly materialistic and consumeristic Mecca. P5's account encapsulates his own meaning-making around his situated hajj experience.

> From a Western perspective, we are coming from a particular standing. We don't necessarily want to see our own reality and lifestyle replicated when we are going to do the hajj. Whereas, for people from other parts of the world, that pilgrim will have positive experience of the hajj also because of the tiled floors, the AC, the McDonald's, the tall hotels. For some of us, that is a negative thing. We don't want to see so much similarity with our daily environment. For others, it is not. I can imagine it being quite incredible for people coming from elsewhere, a poorer country, and

> for them this would be a positive thing, a part of the hajj experience. (P5)

When reflecting on their post-hajj experience, several female participants related the ways in which their religious capital was often linked to (or enabled by) their bodies (as in wearing a hijab, or behaving in expected ways). This mediation seemed important for effectively bridging into their knowledge-brokering roles. P1 recalls:

> I talked to many women and friends, and I encourage people to do hajj when they are young and healthy. Spiritually and physically, the hajj is very demanding. Better to do it when one is able and healthy. My wearing hijab triggered lots of interest and conversation. Women are not well informed about wearing or not hijab after hajj. Even I did not speak to people other than my parents and my husband's parents before hajj, because I didn't want any pressure: if you go to hajj, you will have to wear hijab, or do this or do that. Doing hajj is actually easy in North America. It is also less judgmental. At my age, in Pakistan, people would have said: 'Wear the hijab, no sleeveless outfits, etc.' Here, you can have access to resources and advice without being judged. Our imams are well educated, and have no qualms about being open and liberal about things. (P1)

> When I returned from hajj, people asked me about my hijab out of curiosity. I am comfortable with who I am. My clothes are also slightly more modest than before. Most of my friends have not gone yet to hajj. Many are not planning to go until they are married. I became their source for information about hajj preparation. Like me, people thought that hajj was only *ṭawāf*, then they saw me posting pictures, like when in Muzdalifa, they could see there are lots of things that you have to do in hajj. (P7)

> All the tour leaders are men. This did not make sense to me. I didn't like that. (...) Having men as tour leaders is also an issue when you have to ask about what is to be done when, for example, you have your periods [and what to do in terms of rituals when menstruating, NC]. There was one lady available for questions like that, so of course the information took longer to obtain because many wanted to speak with her or felt more comfortable approaching her than a man. (P7)

As these examples illustrate, participants' lived experiences make them ideally suited for disseminating insights and information within their circles. Their knowledge practices contribute to the shaping of the next generation of pilgrims in the same way that the experiences of those who came before them affected their expectations and associated information practices. Despite the limited size of the sample, it is evident that pilgrims' literacies and modes of engagement continue to incorporate, even after return from hajj, the communicative and social aspect of human information activities (Irvine-Smith 2017). Other potential pilgrims' learning is critically shaped by the imageries of hajj presented in narrative and practice by those who have returned from hajj.

6 Conclusion

In this chapter, I have examined different examples of pilgrims' information activities upon return from hajj, as the core activity of making sense of their journey. It is also clear that information practices are important not just for one's personal growth and identity-building but also for the construction of one's social identity. Too often, studies of information behaviour have paid attention to specific, short-term interactions rather than the evolving information environment over time and how this contributes to the (re)shaping of one's identity (see Guzik 2018; 2017). As my data suggest, upon return Ḥājjīs and Ḥājjas are tasked with developing both a personal and social identity through different modes of engagement: through their body, their actions, and their ability to curate and impart knowledge onto others. Becoming a pilgrim is thus constituted holistically within situated rituals and embodied practices that transcend both individual (cognitive, affective) and social processes (through shared imaginaries and a wide network of people and resources). I argue that trust and community bonds shape the flow of information thus reconstituting capital, and I invite a deeper reflection on how community membership through the status of Ḥājji or Ḥājja is a form of religious capital that requires evidence of particular ways of being and of knowing.

This chapter contributes to a growing interest in understanding the role of information practices for larger sociological processes that include interpretations of the meanings held by communities, and the ways in which information practices persist and build capital. These insights highlight the importance of studying how people engage in knowledge production and collective learning within communities. In analysing the embeddedness of information and communication technologies in the spiritual realms, this research reveals the social nature of these contexts and the various shared practices and routinized behaviours that pilgrims are ingrained in and that help constitute their existence in ways that are both social and intimate.

References

Ameli, Saied Reza. 2009. 'Virtual religion and duality of religious spaces.' *Asian journal of social science* 37 (2): 208–231.

Baker, Christopher, and Greg Smith. 2014. 'Spiritual, religious and social capital—Exploring their dimensions and their relationship with faith-based motivation and participation in UK civil society.' Accessed May 1, 2020. https://williamtemplefoundation.org.uk/wp-content/uploads/2014/03/Spiritual-Religious-Social-Capital-Baker-Smith.pdf.

Bianchi, Robert. 2017. 'Reimagining the hajj.' *Social sciences* 6 (2): art. 36. https://doi.org/10.3390/socsci6020036.

Bourdieu, Pierre. 1987. 'Legitimation and structured interests in Weber's sociology of religion.' In *Max Weber: Rationality and modernity*, edited by Scott Lasch and Sam Whimster, 119–135. London: Allen & Unwin.

Bourdieu, Pierre. 1984. *Distinction: A social critique of the judgement of taste*. Cambridge, MA: Harvard University Press.

Bourdieu, Pierre, and Loïc Wacquant. 1992. *An invitation to reflexive sociology*. Chicago: University Of Chicago Press.

Buitelaar, Marjo. 2020. 'Rearticulating the conventions of hajj storytelling: Second generation Moroccan-Dutch female pilgrims' multi-voiced narratives about the pilgrimage to Mecca.' *Religions* 11 (7): 373. https://doi.org/10.3390/rel11070373.

Buitelaar, Marjo. 2015. 'The hajj and the anthropological study of pilgrimage.' In *Hajj: Global interactions through pilgrimage*, edited by Luitgard Mols and Marjo Buitelaar, 9–25. Leiden: Sidestone Press.

Caidi, Nadia. 2020. '"I was not willing to risk my hajj": Information coping strategies of hajj pilgrims.' *Journeys: The international journal of travel and travel writing* 21 (1): 41–62.

Caidi, Nadia. 2019. 'Pilgrimage to the hajj: An information journey.' *The international journal of information, diversity & inclusion* 3 (1): 44–76.

Caidi, Nadia, and Mariam Karim. 2022. 'Mediated spaces of collective rituals: Sacred selfies at the hajj.' In *The Oxford Handbook of Religious Space*, edited by Jeanne Halgren Kilde, 227–243. Oxford: Oxford University Press.

Caidi, Nadia, Susan Beazley, and Laia Marquez Colomer. 2018. 'Holy selfies: Performing pilgrimage in the age of social media.' *The International journal of information, diversity & inclusion* 2 (1/2): 8–31.

Campo, Juan. 2016. 'Representations of a changing sacred landscape past and present.' In *The Hajj*, edited by Eric Tagliacozzo and Shawkat Toorawa, 269–288. Cambridge: Cambridge University Press.

Cooke, Miriam, and Bruce Lawrence. 2005. *Muslim networks from hajj to hip hop*. Chapel Hill: University of North Carolina Press.

de Sousa, Marco Túlio, and da Rosa, Ana Paula. 2020. 'The mediatization of Camino De Santiago: Between the pilgrimage narrative and media circulation of the narrative.' *Religions 11* (10): 1–19. https://doi.org/10.3390/rel11100480.

Echchaibi, Nabil. 2013. 'Muslimah media watch: Media activism and Muslim choreographies of social change.' *Journalism* 14 (7): 852–867.

Eickelman, Dale, and Jon Anderson. 2003. *New media in the Muslim world: The emerging public sphere*. Bloomington: Indiana University Press.

El-Nawawy, Mohamed, and Sahar Khamis. 2009. *Islam dot com: Contemporary Islamic discourses in cyberspace*. New York: Palgrave MacMillan.

Feldman, Martha, and Wanda Orlikowski. 2011. 'Theorizing practice and practicing theory.' *Organization science* 22 (5): 1240–1253.

Finke, Roger. 2003. Spiritual capital: Definitions, applications, and new frontiers. Accessed December 2, 2020. https://www.metanexus.net/archive/spiritualcapitalresearchprogram/pdf/finke.pdf.

Finke, Roger, and Kevin Dougherty. 2002. 'The effects of professional training: The social and religious capital acquired in seminaries.' *Journal for the scientific study of religion* 41 (1): 103–120.

Flaskerud, Ingvild, and Richard Natvig. 2018. *Muslim pilgrimage in Europe*. London: Routledge.

Forcier, Eric. 2017. 'Re(a)d wedding: A case study exploring the everyday information behaviours of the transmedia fan.' In *Proceedings of the association for information science and technology*, edited by Sanda Erdelez and Naresh Agarwal, 93–101. Hoboken, NJ: Wiley.

General Authority of Statistics, Kingdom of Saudi Arabia. 2019. 'Haj Statistics'. Accessed August 12, 2020. https://www.stats.gov.sa/en/28.

Goffman, Erving. 2008 [1963]. *Behavior in public places*. New York: Simon and Schuster.

Golan, Oren, and Michele Martini. 2018. 'Digital pilgrimage: Exploring Catholic monastic webcasts.' The Communication Review 21 (1): 24–45. https://doi.org/10.1080/10714421.2017.1416795.

Green, Christine, and Ian Jones. 2005. 'Serious leisure, social identity and sport tourism'. *Sport in society* 8 (2): 164–181. https://doi.org/10.1080/174304305001102010.

Guzik, Elysia. 2018. 'Information sharing as embodied practice in a context of conversion to Islam.' *Library trends* 66 (3): 351–370.

Guzik, Elysia. 2017. *'Informing identities: Religious conversion experiences of Muslims in the Toronto area.'* PhD diss., University of Toronto.

Hill-Smith, Connie. 2009. 'Cyberpilgrimage: A study of authenticity, presence and meaning in online pilgrimage experiences.' *The journal of religion and popular culture* 21 (2): 6–34. https://doi.org/10.3138/jrpc.21.2.006.

Howson, Alexandra, and David Inglis. 2001. 'The body in sociology: tensions inside and outside sociological thought.' *The sociological review* 39 (3): 297–317. https://doi.org/10.1111/1467-954X.00333.

Iftikhar, Arsalan. 2020. 'The covid hajj.' *The week*, July 28, 2020. https://theweek.com/articles/926902/covid-hajj.

Irvine-Smith, Sally. 2017. 'Information through the lens: Information research and the dynamics of practice.' *Information research* 22 (1): 1–16.

Ito, Mizuko. 2008. 'Introduction.' In *Networked publics*, edited by Kazys Vernelis, 1–14. Cambridge: MIT Press.

Janmohamed, Shelina. 2016. 'Young Muslims will be experiencing hajj in a very different way this year.' *The Independent*, September 9, 2016. http://www.independent.co.uk/voices/hajj-mecca-social-media-snapchat-youngmuslims-very-different-way-a7233426.html.

Jenkins, Kathleen. 2016. 'Family.' In *Handbook of religion and society*, edited by David Yamane, 219–239. Springer, Cham. https://doi.org/10.1007/978-3-319-31395-5_12.

Kane, Maurice, and Robyn *Zink. 2004*. 'Package adventure tourism: Markers in serious leisure careers.' *Leisure Studies* 23 (4): 329–345.

Kim, Alice, Nadia Caidi, and Niel Chah. 2019. '"Our Korea": Transcultural affinity as negotiated through YouTube encounters.' *Information research 24* (1): art. isic1828. Accessed Dec 2, 2020. http://InformationR.net/ir/24-1/isic2018/isic1828.html.

Leschziner, Vanina, and Adam Isaiah Green. 2013. 'Thinking about food and sex: Deliberate cognition in the routine practices of a field.' *Sociological theory* 31 (2): 116–144.

Lizardo, Omar, and Michael Strand. 2010. 'Skills, toolkits, contexts and institutions: Clarifying the relationship between different approaches to cognition in cultural sociology.' *Poetics* 38 (2): 205–228.

Lövheim, Mia. 2004. 'Young people, religious identity and the Internet.' In *Religion online: Finding faith on the Internet*, edited by Lorne Dawson and Douglas Cowan, 59–73. New York: Routledge.

Mackellar, Jo. 2009. 'An examination of serious participants at the Australian Wintersun Festival.' *Leisure studies* 28 (1): 85–104.

Merchant, Stephanie. 2011. 'The body and the senses: Visual methods, videography and the submarine sensorium.' *Body & society* 17 (1): 53–72. https://doi.org/10.1177/1357034X10394670.

Reay, Diane. 2004. 'Gendering Bourdieu's concepts of capitals? Emotional capital, women and social class.' *The sociological review* 52 (10): 57–74. https://doi.org/10.1111/j.1467-954X.2005.00524.x.

Reckwitz, Andreas. 2002. 'Toward a theory of social practices: A development in cultural theorizing.' *European journal of social theory* 5 (2): 243–263.

Saudi Press Agency. 2020. 'Ministry of hajj and *umrah*: hajj 1441H is decided to take place this year with limited number of pilgrims from all nationalities residing in Saudi Arabia.' Accessed online, June 22, 2020. https://www.spa.gov.sa/viewfullstory.php?lang=en&newsid=2100951.

Savolainen, Reijo. 2017. 'Information sharing and knowledge sharing as communicative activities.' *Information research* 22 (3). Accessed on December 3, 2020. http://www.informationr.net/ir/22-3/paper767.html.

Schatzki, Theodore. 1996. *Social practices: a Wittgensteinian approach to human activity and the social*. Cambridge: Cambridge University Press.

Sourdel, Dominique, and Janine Sourdel-Thomine. 2006. *Certificats de pèlerinage d'époque ayyoubide: Contribution à l'histoire de l'idéologie de l'Islam au temps des croisades*. Paris: Académie des inscriptions et belles-lettres.

Stebbins, Robert. 2009. 'Leisure and its relationship to library and information science: Bridging the gap.' *Library trends* 57 (4): 618–631.

Thomson, Leslie. 2019. '"Doing YouTube": Information creating in the context of serious beauty and lifestyle YouTube.' PhD diss., The University of North Carolina at Chapel Hill.

van der Beek, Suzanne. 2019. 'Post-Camino storytelling: Navigating transformation in a digital age.' In *Ritual in a digital society*, edited by Martin Hoondert and Suzanne van der Beek, 65–80. Groningen: Institute for Ritual and Liturgical Studies.

van der Beek, Suzanne. 2014. 'Pilgrim narratives in dialogue.' In *Pilgrim paths: Journeys of transformation*, edited by Mary Farrelly and Vivienne Keely, 45–53. Oxford: Inter-Disciplinary Press.

Wacquant, Luc. 2011. 'Habitus as topic and tool: Reflections on becoming a prizefighter.' *Qualitative research in psychology* 8 (1): 81–92. https://doi.org/10.1080/14780887.2010.544176.

Wacquant, Luc. 2005. 'Carnal connections: On embodiment, apprenticeship, and membership.' *Qualitative sociology* 28 (4): 445–474. https://doi.org/10.1007/s11133-005-8367-0.

Wacquant, Luc. 2004. *Body & soul: Notebooks of an apprentice boxer*. Oxford and New York: Oxford University Press.

Wacquant, Luc. 1995. 'Pugs at work: Bodily capital and bodily labour among professional boxers.' *Body & society* 1 (1): 65–93.

CHAPTER 16

Mediating Mecca: Moroccan and Moroccan-Dutch Pilgrims' Use of the Smartphone

Marjo Buitelaar and Kholoud Al-Ajarma

1 Introduction[1]

In conversations with pilgrims from Morocco and the Netherlands about their experiences of the pilgrimage to Mecca, more often than not, the authors of this chapter noted that those who were in the possession of a smartphone would reach for their phone to show pictures to accompany their stories. Initially they might do so to illustrate a particular object or location that they were telling about. Nearly always, scrolling through pictures of their hajj or *ʿumra* journey resulted in further recollections of the pilgrimage experience. Quite often, harking back to the photos they had taken whilst on pilgrimage would stir emotions in these narrators. Having a collection of pictures on their smartphones thus functioned both to evoke and revive memories about the pilgrimage for the narrators themselves and to support or even steer narrations about their pilgrimage experiences to others. It is fair to say that using the smartphone to mediate Mecca, either through photographs, WhatsApp messages, or posts on platforms like Facebook and Instagram, has become part of the repertoire of performing hajj itself (cf. Renne 2015).

In this chapter, we explore how pilgrims from Morocco and the Netherlands deploy the affordances of the smartphone to mediate the sacred atmosphere in Mecca and establish co-presence between themselves and their friends and relatives who stayed home.[2] As Birgit Bräuchler and John Postill argue, exactly because the fundamental quality of media as 'something in between', the meaning of a medium like the smartphone is always emergent and contingent on the micro-historical circumstances of its use, and can only be studied in the

1 We would like to thank Elisabetta Costa and Welmoed Wagenaar for their valuable feedback on a previous draft of this chapter and their encouragement to delve deeper into the field of digital anthropology.

2 Affordances are the enabling and constraining material possibilities of digital media. Affordances do not dictate participants' behaviour, but configure the environment in ways that shape participants' engagement (cf. Davis and Jurgenson 2014; boyd 2011, 39).

practices in which it is used (Bräuchler and Postill 2010, 23). Taking what Elisabetta Costa (2018) has called 'affordances-in-practice' as a starting point, in this chapter we sketch how our research participants engage with smartphones to connect the sacred time and space in Mecca with their everyday lives in Morocco and the Netherlands as they imagine, recollect, and narrate the pilgrimage to Mecca. We discuss such instances by asking how pilgrims' smartphone-related activities are to be understood against the background of the wider social configurations, contexts, and processes in which they are embedded in and, vice versa, what implications their use of a smartphone might have for their various forms of sociality and daily lifeworlds (cf. Bräuchler and Postill 2010, 16; Moores 2000, 56–57). Choosing a practice-related approach over a media-centred perspective, our focus is on the entanglements of pilgrims' use of digital media with other activities, objects, and feelings through which these media are used, experienced, and operate (cf. Pink et al. 2016a, 10). In this sense, rather than approaching pilgrimage-related uses of the smartphone as a category of practice in and of itself, we conceive of them as activities that are part of other practices, such as keeping in touch with one's dear ones, identity-construction, or ethical self-formation (cf. Costa and Menin 2016; Couldry 2012; Madianou and Miller 2011; 2004). In doing so, we explore how social change comes to the fore in the appropriation of the smartphone and how cultural-specific use of the smartphone may affect the performance and meanings of ritual.

The data sets we draw on were produced for our respective sub-projects within the larger research project 'Modern Articulations of the Pilgrimage to Mecca' that formed the point of departure for this collected volume. Al-Ajarma conducted ethnographic fieldwork in Morocco to study the socio-cultural embeddedness of the pilgrimage to Mecca in the everyday lives of Moroccans (cf. Al-Ajarma 2020). She also visited Mecca twice to conduct participant observation among pilgrims performing the *'umra*. Her data therefore consists predominantly of her personal observations in Moroccan public and private settings and informal conversations with people among whom she conducted participant observation in Mecca and Morocco. Buitelaar's project consisted of ethnographic interviews with Dutch pilgrims with Moroccan and Turkish backgrounds in the Netherlands concerning the meaning of the pilgrimage to them in relation to their various senses of identity and belonging.

We did not set out to study the use of the smartphone when we began our research projects. Rather, the topic emerged as an inductive code once we began to realize its significance for many of our research participants in their experiences of the pilgrimage to Mecca. While the smartphone and Internet access are relatively expensive in Morocco in comparison to the Netherlands, smartphone use has risen enormously over recent years; in 2011 only 12% of Moroccan citizens possessed a smartphone, whereas in 2020 75.5% of the population owned one, using it, amongst other things, to access the Internet and often as an alternative for a computer.[3] Considering that 84.5% of the Moroccan population is younger than 54 years old,[4] these figures appear to confirm our personal observations that it is mostly younger Moroccans and those in mid-adulthood who own a smartphone. Being illiterate considerably hampers the use of the smartphone for the elderly and (rural) lower classes.[5] Since Buitelaar's research project concentrated on the descendants of migrants who grew up in the Netherlands, nearly all interviews were with pilgrims between the age of 20 and 55, all of whom possessed a smartphone. Their parents who came to the Netherlands as economic migrants between the mid-1960s and 1970s originate predominantly from rural areas and most of them are illiterate or low literate. Not surprisingly, the hajj narrations of the ten pilgrims of this migrant generation who were interviewed contained only few references to the use of a telephone whilst on hajj. Indeed, as we shall see later, some older pilgrims prided themselves in having used a phone only rarely or not at all during the pilgrimage to Mecca. Buitelaar's impression that most pilgrims from the Netherlands over the age of 60 did not use a smartphone during the pilgrimage except maybe for taking photographs or making occasional phone calls home was confirmed by interviewees of younger generations, many of whom explicitly mentioned the use of the smartphone as a significant point of difference between their own hajj practices and those of pilgrims of their parents' generation.

Broadly speaking, there are two ways in which pilgrims use the smartphone during the pilgrimage in Mecca. We will first look into the activity of informing oneself about hajj locations and the appropriate rites and supplication prayers to perform at these locations, and then move on to discuss how pilgrims use their phone to communicate with fellow pilgrims and with relatives and friends at home.

---

3 https://www.moroccoworldnews.com/2019/07/278384/telecommunications-76-moroccans-smartphones/, accessed October 1, 2020.

4 https://www.indexmundi.com/morocco/demographics_profile.html, accessed October 1, 2020.

5 For an empirically rich and particularly insightful study on how the ways class, age and gender intersect in access to and the use of the smartphone, see Tenhunen (2018) who studied the use of the smartphone in poor rural India.

2 Information Applications

A simple search on an iPhone's or Android's application store shows tens of apps available to help pilgrims perform the pilgrimage rites. A 2016 survey showed that Google Play housed 246 hajj and *ʿumra* related apps in 24 different languages, of which 51.7% were in English. Most of these apps were downloaded between 10,000 and 50,000 times, while the live video supporting 'Watch Makkah Live HD' was downloaded over a million times (Khan and Shambour 2017, 40).

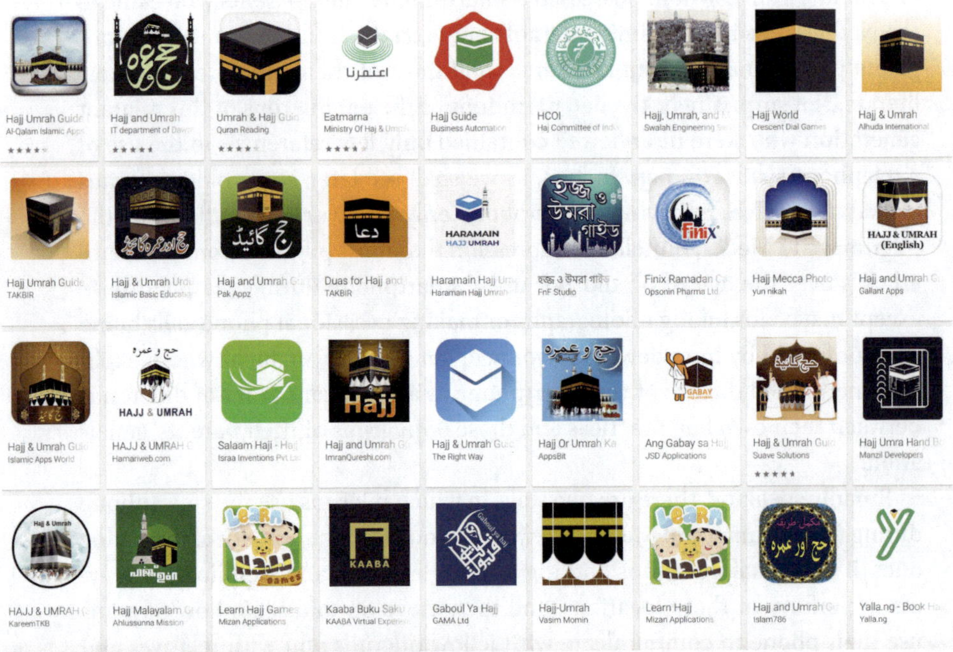

FIGURE 16.1 Screenshot of some Android Store results for 'hajj' search[6]

Such applications provide navigation services, information about the rites of hajj, and lists of suggested supplication prayers for the different steps of the pilgrimage. Many of these apps present themselves as hajj guides. In fact, Khan and Shambour found twelve apps with different publishers and services that went by the name of 'Hajj Guide' (ibid.). The version of an app by that name we looked at contained both text and images. It provided a general introduction to the hajj as well as information about the different rites it consists of.

6 See https://play.google.com/store/search?q=hajj&c=apps&hl=en, accessed 13 April 2022.

Pages from the app can be downloaded to be read offline later. The app is suitable as a manual to be studied before or during hajj, but it does not provide an actual virtual on-site guide. We also looked at 'Tawaf', an app that helps pilgrims who are circling the Kaʿba keep track of the number of rounds they have completed. Other apps, such as 'Hajj Salam' include tools that prompt pilgrims to read, repeat, or simply listen to the appropriate prayers at the right time and place, while some, such as 'Al Hajj' are more interactive and provide prospective pilgrims with a pre-hajj preparation checklist, a hajj map, and an emergency contact list in addition to relevant Qur'anic quotations and supplication prayers.

Our conversations with research participants reveal a differential evaluation by pilgrims with regard to the use of mobile information applications. A Moroccan-Dutch male pilgrim in his late thirties, for example, stated that he had been very happy to find all the information he felt he needed on his phone:

> It's an intense journey, that's for sure. But it is much more difficult and exhausting for older people than for us. They have to memorize supplication prayers or repeat them after the leader. And they have to stick to the group. So, they are dependent on the tour guide. (…) Whereas I, I was very mobile, literally: I had my phone and access to Internet, so I knew exactly where I was, I was in charge myself. I was with a group of guys and we discussed between ourselves what we'd do: Eat in the hotel or dine out? Take the bus or walk to the Grand Mosque? If we decided on a taxi, all I had to do was phone one, easy enough. So, we could go there and perform the prayers on our own. That was great: we knew exactly what supplication prayers to say.

As this interview excerpt indicates, the affordances of the smartphone allow pilgrims to be more 'in charge' themselves and personalize the hajj, allowing them to focus on their own, individual journey. Within the limits of the ritual programme, instead of having to rely entirely on tour guides, as older pilgrims who often have enjoyed no or little formal education tend to do, pilgrims in the possession of a smartphone are thus relatively free to shape the hajj experience according to their own wishes.

It would be a mistake, however, to interpret the changes in the hajj experience that result from using information applications exclusively in terms of the possibilities the smartphone offers. In keeping with Costa's argument about the relevance of studying how users in different socio-cultural contexts actively appropriate affordances, our point is rather that the particular use of hajj information applications is shaped by the desires and needs of pilgrims that rise from being informed by a specific constellation of cultural contexts and 'grand schemes': powerful yet never fully attainable ideals that operate as models for a good life (Schielke 2015, 13). Daniel Miller and Jolynna Sinanan address the role that digital technology can play in such aspirational models in what they call the 'theory of attainment' (Miller and Sinanan 2014, 12). According to the theory of attainment, the cultural use of technology derives for the most part from the desires of (potential) users rather than being a necessary consequence of the invention of that particular device. Miller and Sinanan argue that once people have gotten used to it, the same technology is likely to stimulate new aspirations (ibid.).

As Buitelaar and Kadrouch-Outmany argue elsewhere in this volume, particularly younger pilgrims from Western countries like the Netherlands have developed a desire for autonomy and self-reliance on the basis of their embeddedness in a highly individualistic socio-cultural environment. To a certain extent, this also goes for young urban professionals in Morocco who perform hajj. The specific information services the smartphone enables thus dovetail with the wishes of cosmopolitan urbanites to be 'in charge' themselves rather than having to depend on a hajj tour guide and to adapt to the group of pilgrims they travel with.[7] In this respect, these higher educated younger pilgrims differ significantly from their parents' generation. The latter mostly grew up in a group-oriented lifeworld and often feel more comfortable and safer operating in a group of pilgrims. Similar to what Farooq Haq and John Jackson have described for different generations of Pakistani pilgrims from Pakistan and Australia (Haq and Jackson 2009), older Moroccan and Moroccan-Dutch pilgrims tend to be content to rely on a group leader to guide them through the rituals and more readily accept his authority than younger pilgrims do.[8] In keeping with the critique formulated by Miller and others concerning an anxiety that is often expressed in popular discourse about hyper-individualism fostered by the smartphone, we argue that this particular use of the smartphone should not be interpreted as causing the desire for and a specific cultural style of individualism, but rather as reflecting it before further stimulating it (Miller et al. 2016, 181–192).

Our data indicates, for instance, that most pilgrims do not uncritically accept all the possibilities the smartphone offers. Reservations concerning the use of

7 According to Saudi hajj regulations, pilgrims cannot organize their own hajj journey, but have to book a package tour through Saudi recognized tour operators.

8 See the chapter by Buitelaar and Kadrouch-Outmany in this volume for more information about the experiences of a Dutch-based hajj travel agent concerning differences in the attitudes of older and younger pilgrims.

the device pertain mostly to the spiritual dimensions of their pilgrimage. For instance, most hajj applications focus on the bare facts about the correct performance of hajj rites rather than on their spiritual dimensions. Also, depending on one's smartphone rather than on others can have its drawbacks. While operating in a group can be a burden, it is exactly being part of a flow of millions of other pilgrims which contributes to the spiritual experience of the hajj and its power as a 'sensational form' (cf. Meyer 2016). Indeed, the hajj stories of most of our interlocutors contain narrations about enriching encounters with fellow pilgrims. As a 30-year-old female pilgrim from Morocco who performed the hajj with her 70-year-old father noted, following one's smartphone too much can deprive pilgrims from such experiences:

> During the hajj, we went out to perform the hajj rites by following other pilgrims. When we lost the way to the hotel, we asked other pilgrims. An Egyptian young man showed us the way and we had an enjoyable conversation ... This kind of conversation I cannot have with a mobile app.

A Dutch-Moroccan woman in her early forties similarly expressed ambivalence about her tendency to habitually grab her phone. In response to a question whether she had used her phone during the hajj rites, she stated: 'Sure, to do supplication prayers. But ... uhm, I was always in two minds: will I do that, or will I get my *tasbīḥ* (string of prayer beads) or Qur'an, you know?' She then explained that she sometimes deliberately suppressed the habit to use her phone and instead opted for reading out her printed copy of the Arabic Qur'an in sotto voce or saying supplication prayers by using her *tasbīḥ*.[9]

What makes this woman's story particularly interesting is that it points to the importance of the materiality of mediating devices to both affect and shape the content which they transmit, rather than merely acting as tools for transmission (Meyer 2011, 27–28). As Daniel Miller and Heather Horst argue in the introduction to their influential book *Digital Anthropology*, artefacts like the smartphone do far more than just express human intention. Miller and Horst point out that we become human 'through socializing within a material world of cultural artefacts that include the order, agency and relationships between things themselves and not just their relationships to persons' (Horst and Miller

9 Some Moroccan pilgrims that Al-Ajarma spoke to, reported a similar hesitance to use apps that provide 'recommended' supplication prayers, stating that they while they are all good, they do not come from one's heart, nor are they specific enough to convey what one wants to ask from God. For this reason, some people said that the simpler a prayer, the better it is.

2012a, 24). They therefore identify materiality as the 'bedrock for digital anthropology' (ibid.).

The fact that the female pilgrim quoted above pondered which device to choose for her worshipping acts illustrates that her affective relationship with each of the three options available to her is different. In the context of its dominant use in her daily lifeworld, the smartphone belongs to what Arjun Appadurai (1986, 34) would call a 'different regime of value' than the printed Qur'an copy and the *tasbīḥ*, the latter two being situated in a long tradition of Muslim worship, while the former is only recently emerging as a tool in worship in addition to serving numerous other purposes as well. As a result, these three alternative devices to mediate the sacred have different symbolic meanings for their owner, illustrating that it is not technical affordances as such that shape the use and meanings of the smartphone, but rather the relationship between mediating 'things' and the people who engage with them (Pink et al. 2016a, 62). The woman weighing her options to decide when and for which purposes to use her smartphone, her Qur'an copy, or her *tasbīḥ* points to what Ilana Gershon calls the 'media ideologies' that shape the ways people think about and use different media (Gershon 2010). Gershon argues that people's normative conceptions concerning one medium are always affected by those they have about other media. On the basis of media ideologies that circulate, an 'idiom of practice' is developed, including the development of shared understandings of how different media relate to each other and how they are used in socially appropriate ways (cf. Fernández-Ardèvol et al. 2020).

Such shared understandings do not go uncontested, however. Navigating multiple media ideologies to determine the appropriate use of a medium in a specific situation can be a complex process, as a further remark by the same Dutch female pilgrim about her devotional acts during the hajj illustrates. Concerning her reflections on whether to use her phone, Qur'an copy, or *tasbīḥ*, she elaborated by saying that she had sometimes deliberately chosen to read her printed Arabic Qur'an copy, for example when sitting down in the courtyard of the Grand Mosque of Mecca facing the Kaʿba in order to immerse herself in the sacred atmosphere. At other times, however, such as back in the hotel or in the tent camp in Minā, she preferred to read a translated version of the Qur'an from her smartphone:

> That's because I don't understand the Arabic. (…) So, I wanted to read it in translation as it is so terribly important for me understand the text. I have asked my *fqih* (Qur'an teacher) about this: I explained to him that not understanding the Arabic it does not give me the same feeling. He stated that while reading the Qur'an in Arabic gives you more *ḥasanāt* (religious credit), it is allowed to read a translation.

Various considerations thus came into play for the woman when choosing between a *tasbīḥ*, a printed copy of the Qur'an in Arabic, or a translation on a smartphone for engaging in devotional acts during the pilgrimage. For the purpose of experiencing the sacred ambience first and foremost, the sensory dimensions of the mediating device mattered most to her. Using a *tasbīḥ* is a highly tactile act that enables the user to take in the view while passing the beads of the *tasbīḥ* through one's fingers to underscore and keep track of the recitation of Arabic supplication prayers. Similarly, for Muslims the Arabic script of the Qur'an is a highly charged visualization of God's direct words that affects the reader in a very different way than a translation of the text in languages that are not directly associated with Islamic language use. In situations in which the woman wished to focus on the meaning of the sacred text rather than having the Arabic script speak directly to the visual and auditory senses by softly reciting it, the opportunity to read the text in Dutch determined her choice, but it is important to note that 'understanding' for her is not only a cognitive process, but also involves affect. The different considerations that informed her choice of device underscore the point made by several scholars in digital anthropology mentioned above concerning the relevance of media ideologies and contextual needs and desires that shape people's particular use of information applications. More specifically, the situational choices the female pilgrim in this example made for a particular device to access sacredness point to the significance of people's sensory perceptions of the wider environment when deciding which medium is most appropriate to use; like the Qur'an copy and the *tasbīḥ*, her engagement with her smartphone is experienced corporeally. Beyond a focus on its representational or symbolic status, this illustrates that smartphone use should be analysed as a sensory medium (cf. Waltorp 2020; Pink et al. 2016b). The case studies discussed so far all indicate that digital technologies and devices have become part of most of today's pilgrims' sensory embodied experience of the environment, while at the same time, these technologies allow the pilgrimage to be experienced in new ways (cf. Pink et al. 2016a, 23).

3 Communication Applications

Pilgrims use the smartphone most frequently for communication services like WhatsApp or Facebook. Often, WhatsApp group is created for pilgrims who travel together. In the Netherlands, many hajj tour operators organize a preparatory meeting for their customers and create a WhatsApp group in advance to provide the prospective pilgrims with tips for what to bring along on hajj as well as information about the state of affairs concerning visa, flight details, etc. During the hajj journey itself, the WhatsApp group is used to provide updates concerning daily programmes, departure times from hotels, meeting points after the performance of rites, etc.

Several Moroccan-Dutch female pilgrims pointed out in the interviews that being updated through the (gender-mixed) WhatsApp group can be particularly convenient for female pilgrims; as yet, hajj guides are almost invariably men and tend to address male pilgrims rather than female ones (also see Caidi elsewhere in this volume).[10] Especially in the tent camp in Minā, where pilgrims sleep in sex-segregated tents, it can be difficult for female pilgrims to find out what is being discussed and decided in the men's tents. At the same time, however, exactly because hajj guides are in closer contact with men, it often happens that once information is shared orally with male pilgrims, it is not communicated through WhatsApp, leaving women uninformed. 'As women, we're always at least one step behind', a female pilgrim in her early fifties complained.

As this critical remark indicates, the use of a WhatsApp group for pilgrims who travel with the same tour operator can have both positive and negative implications for different categories of pilgrims and for intragroup relationships. The impact on group dynamics extends beyond the pilgrimage journey itself: both in Morocco and in the Netherlands, long after the pilgrims return home, WhatsApp groups tend to be sustained as a platform to share photographs and organize reunions. Thus, a new format for the collective production of hajj stories has emerged.

While a WhatsApp group can be convenient for the communication between pilgrims and guides about the logistics of the hajj journey, far more important for individual pilgrims is their communication with family and friends at home. Without a doubt, the smartphone has an enormous impact on how the pilgrimage to Mecca is currently experienced, as well as on how it is narrated. Until a few decades ago, for most of their hajj journey, pilgrims were not able to communicate with those they left at home. Today, except during flights towards their destination, pilgrims are able to keep in touch with

10 In addition to the compulsory involvement of a *muṭawwif*, an officially appointed local hajj guide, pilgrims are also accompanied by hajj guide who travel with them from the Netherlands. These Dutch tour leaders may either be staff members of the travel agency or imams who accompany a group of pilgrims from their own mosque. Of late, some travel agencies have started to include female assistants to male hajj guides, but going by the accounts of our interlocutors, this is, as yet, rare.

their loved ones 24/7 should they wish to do so. Since 2015, there is even free Wi-Fi in the courtyard of the Grand Mosque in Mecca.[11]

In addition to factors like the reduced period of time that today's pilgrims are away from home in comparison to former times and the less hazardous nature of the journey thanks to modern air travel, the stories of our research participants indicate that the opportunity to remain in contact with friends and relatives at home had a considerable impact on their preparatory activities before departure, notably concerning settling disputes and taking leave of their family and friends. Before they embark on the journey to Mecca, pilgrims should settle their debts and ask forgiveness from people whom they might have wronged. Both in Morocco and in the Netherlands, until recently it was customary for pilgrims to visit or at least phone their family members, friends, and even neighbours and colleagues to apologize for any injustice or harm they may have caused in the past and to ask for forgiveness for their wrongdoings. While some pilgrims continue to make such a generalized round of *musāmaḥa* or forgiveness visits or phone calls, the majority of our research participants indicated that they had contacted only a few people.

Settling disputes requires forgiveness from both sides. While asking for forgiveness takes courage, being forgiving can be even more challenging, as several research participants pointed out. A female pilgrim in her mid-thirties related how only on the way to Schiphol Airport to fly to Saudi Arabia did she realize that it gnawed at her not to have reconciled with her sister-in-law. Already getting in touch with the sacred atmosphere now that her journey had started, she felt she was at last ready to forgive her husband's sister, so she phoned her from the car to ask for forgiveness. To her relief, her sister-in-law not only assured her that all was forgiven and forgotten, but in addition she pronounced the wish that the hajj of her brother and his wife would be accepted by God, and she asked for a supplication prayer to be said on her behalf near the Kaʿba.[12]

---

11 https://www.phoneworld.com.pk/free-Wi-Fi-facility-introduced-in-masjid-al-haram/, accessed October 9, 2020.

12 Since the hajj is so special and sacred that no one should wish to prevent a pilgrim from embarking on the journey with unsettled issues, the power of the ritualized act of seeking reconciliation as a preparatory step in going on hajj is considerable. While it would be impolite to refuse reconciliation, pronouncing forgiveness involves more than politesse. This can be illustrated by the story of one of Buitelaar's interlocutors who had an argument with her mother shortly before she was to go on hajj. While her mother forgave her daughter for speaking up her mind, the woman herself realized that although she might be forgiven, the tiff was related to longstanding issues with her mother that she had not yet managed to come to terms with. Realizing that not yet being ready to forgive her mother

The woman who shared this story clearly took the last-minute reconciliatory phone call with her sister-in-law quite seriously. Several research participants indicated, however, that being able to ask forgiveness through the smartphone can also render the practice devoid of meaning. A Moroccan-Dutch female pilgrim in her late forties, for example, was rather sceptical about messages she had received from some people who were preparing to go to Mecca:

> What you often see nowadays is that people send you a WhatsApp message with a more or less standard text stating something like 'Dear sister, should I have hurt you, please forgive me.' You know, that kind of standard text. That's not how I did it before I went on hajj. In my view, if there are issues between yourself and another person, you should discuss that person-to-person instead of sending a WhatsApp message to all people in your address list.
> [Interviewer]: How do you respond to such messages?
> I don't. Well, there was this one person whom I had not been able to say good bye to, so to her I wrote back: have a good hajj and *inshallah* (God willing) we'll meet upon your return. But otherwise … no.

While it might seem obvious to interpret the quick and less personal way to ask for forgiveness before going on hajj through WhatsApp in terms of the affordances of the device itself, the more interesting question is what circumstances might make pilgrims decide to acquit themselves of the recommended task thus. We suggest that two factors play a role: (1) shifting conceptions on sociality and (2) changes in conceptions on the hajj as a once-in-a-life time event. The types of wide (online) sociality that characterize the networks in which young Muslims in the Netherlands participate are of a different kind than the obligations inherent to the tight-knit sociality in the more traditional communities where older generations operate. The contacts in the networks of young Muslims tend to be looser, more flexible, and operate at least as much online as they do face-to-face (cf. Roeland et al. 2010).

Secondly, a central argument of this chapter is that while digital media obviously contributes to shifts in social dynamics, these dynamics cannot be reduced to the effect of digital media but relate to wider societal changes. The globalized context where events like going on hajj take place is characterized by a rapidly increasing scope and density of people's mobility. As a result, repres-

---

for injustice done to her in the past, she decided she was not ready to go on hajj and cancelled her trip.

entations of time and space as well as people's conceptions about the purposes and effects of mobility shift (Buitelaar, Stephan-Emmrich, and Thimm 2021, 7). Mobility no longer necessarily entails a clear-cut rupture or transition from one life stage or territory to another, but concerns a fluid and porous movement, a moving back and forth between here and there, and between past, present, and future (Mincke 2016, 16). In terms of people's expectations with regard to their life-trajectory, this means that rather than conceiving of one's life as going through a limited number of transitions between fairly stable time-space constellations, particularly among younger generations 'being on the move' seems to have become a mode of living and is accompanied with corresponding 'mobile socialities' (cf. Hill, Hartman, and Andersson 2021).

Such lifestyle developments have significant implications on people's travel practices, including hajj performance. Until a recently, most Muslims tended to conceive of the pilgrimage to Mecca as a once-in-a-lifetime event and a major rite of passage marking a radical change in one status and lifestyle. Our own observations and interviews as well as those of other scholars seem to suggest, however, that many younger pilgrims do not expect to perform the hajj just once, but anticipate making multiple pilgrimages to Mecca (cf. the contributions of Buitelaar and the one by Safar and Seurat in this volume; also see Saghi 2010). As a result, we would argue that the hajj tends to become a rite-de-passage 'light' resulting in a decreasing significance of asking everyone in one's network for forgiveness for past wrongdoings. In other words, there is not a one-directional causal relation between the decline of the custom of paying face-to-face *musāmaḥa* visits and the affordance to acquit oneself of the task more quickly through WhatsApp. The new trend of sending out messages to ask forgiveness by phone is at least as much a consequence of the diminishing significance of *musāmaḥa* rites as a factor that contributes to it.

The smartphone does appear to play a more constitutive role in the decline of another separation rite: having farewell parties. Sharing recollections from their childhood in Morocco, older pilgrims, particularly those who grew up in rural areas, told us about farewell parties that could last several days. In the weeks prior to departure, pilgrims would organize one or several *ṣadaqa* meals—charity meals for a wide circle of people. On the day of departure, music bands would accompany the pilgrims to the outskirts of the village, and villagers would walk along while clapping their hands and singing hajj songs. If one is lucky, modest versions of such processions can still be observed at Moroccan airports, but overall, processions and other communal acts when pilgrims take leave are much less common today than they were forty years ago. In the Netherlands, farewell parties for pilgrims are sometimes organized at mosques or community centres, but there too, their occurrence is diminishing.[13] While a new phenomenon among young Dutch Muslims is to organize a 'hajj shower' for close friends and relatives, most research participants stated to have only shared a farewell meal with close family members or not to have organized anything special to mark their departure at all. Some stated that to avoid all the 'hassle', they had kept their travel plans a secret until the last minute (cf. Buitelaar 2018, 37).

Besides hajj performance becoming more common in Morocco and even much more so among Muslims in the Netherlands,[14] several other factors may account for the decline in celebrations surrounding the departure of pilgrims. First of all, it fits in with a worldwide trend to 'purify' religious obligations as stipulated in authoritative texts from what have come to be considered local cultural 'accretions' (cf. Roy 2004). An older Moroccan-Dutch interlocutor in her late sixties, for example, stated:

> I remember that it [bidding farewell to pilgrims, MB] used to be a lot more fun than nowadays. (…) Now, the imams say that hajj is just like the *ṣalāt* and fasting: everything should be done without calling attention to it. Only your close family should be informed, but otherwise it's just like saying your prayers: just go, no one else should know about it.

This call for a certain privatization of religiosity points to the impact of reformist teachings according to which one's piety is an issue between oneself and God.[15] In particular, having conducted the pilgrimage should not enhance one's social status. What may also contribute to the decrease of collective farewell celebrations among younger pilgrims is the aforementioned shift for this category of Muslims in the Netherlands away from 'thick' social engagement with traditional communities and religious institutions to new, to more loosely and often online operating networked forms of sociality.

The mobile phone also plays an important role in the decline of farewell parties indirectly. For pilgrims with a smartphone (or pilgrims who travel with

13 For an interesting study analysing shifts in other rites of passage among Muslims in the Netherlands with migration backgrounds, see Dessing (2001).

14 Muslims in the Netherlands do not face the same competition for scarce hajj visa as those in Morocco; until the COVID-19 outbreak in 2020, any Dutch Muslim resident wishing to perform the pilgrimage could get a visa.

15 Also see Flaskerud (2018, 46), who refers to a Shiʿi imam in Oslo who similarly admonishes his audience not to boast about their hajj performance. See Scupin (1982) and Bowen (1992) for more examples of how modernist interpretations have affected local practices concerning the hajj among Thai Muslims and the feast of Sacrifice for Indonesian Muslims respectively.

someone who brings one), bidding farewell to one's loved ones implies a less radical break than in former times; most pilgrims expect to remain in contact with those back home throughout the journey through WhatsApp or Facebook. Our findings indicate that pilgrims' farewell stories are changing accordingly. While the sample of ten interviews with older Moroccan-Dutch pilgrims from the Netherlands is too small to make any statistically significant inferences, it is remarkable that all ten contained a version of a narration about anxiety and sadness about leaving one's loved ones behind—in some cases to the extent of nearly calling off the journey—only to discover that one could miraculously 'leave everything behind' once one had actually departed. A 70-year-old Moroccan-Dutch female pilgrim, for example, stated:

> At Schiphol airport already, my mind was already in Mecca. Once in Mecca, you could see people cry and phone their families, but I could think of nothing else than my *ʿibādāt*. Only after having concluded my religious duties I was able to think of other things again.

In an article on his study on British Pakistani pilgrims to Mecca, Seán McLoughlin quotes a female pilgrim, in this case a 26-years-old pilgrim, who uses almost exactly the same words as the woman above (McLoughlin 2009, 135).[16] The close resemblance between these stories on forgetting one's everyday life and other identifications than being Muslim suggests that they constitute a trope in conventional hajj storytelling, a recurring self-presentation as a committed pilgrim with a strong *niyya* (intention) and *īmān* (faith). Playing upon traditional conceptions of women as primary care takers to highlight the extraordinary impact of the hajj on them, older female pilgrims mentioned in particular how difficult it had been for them to leave their children behind, only to find that they had forgotten all about them once their hajj journey had begun. Indeed, several other older Moroccan-Dutch female pilgrims prided themselves in having been so absorbed by their hajj performance that they never once thought of home or felt the urge to talk to their children.[17] A woman in her early sixties, for example, stated:

16 The exact quote: '[Y]ou forget everything, your children, your families. I thought England was everything for me, my lifestyle was everything, but once I got there all I thought about was me as a Muslim.'

17 Our impression that 'forgetting about one's children' is a trope to express how taken in one is by the sacred atmosphere of the hajj is furthermore confirmed by the story of an older Moroccan-Dutch female pilgrim who has no children herself; recollecting her first sighting of the Kaʿba, she described the experience as being so overwhelming that 'it makes one forget one's children.'

> I never talked to anyone at home, no one. For an entire month, I never phoned anybody. My husband would come up to me and say: 'I've phoned the children.' So, I'd say: 'Did you now? How are they?' He'd reply: 'They're fine.' So, I'd say: 'Ok.' That's all! I never phoned anyone, nor did I carry a phone.

Compare the stories above to that of a 42-year-old female pilgrim from the Netherlands regarding the impact of the smartphone on what she called 'farewell pain' (*afscheidspijn* in Dutch):

> *Alḥamdullillah* (praise be to God) we've got WhatsApp. I did not have that farewell pain. You forget about your children, so to speak,[18] but they were in good hands, and I would get photos every day and speak to them daily. So, there was that permanent connection.

Similarly, in reply to a question concerning her use of a smartphone during the hajj, a Moroccan-Dutch female pilgrim in her late thirties exclaimed laughingly: 'Of course! We are the smartphone generation; I wouldn't know what it is like to go without.' Besides making being away from her children easier for herself, she indicated that talking to them every day was also an effective tool in teaching them about the beauty of the hajj: 'I'd go: "Look, this is what Mecca is like," you know, that kind of thing? It was great being able to share that.'

Nevertheless, like many of our interlocutors she also mentioned the 'danger' of being easily accessible through the phone:

> It's not just your kids, you know, there's also your friends, your parents, your sisters. They all want to be kept up-dated all the time, and that can be too much, it can distract you from what you came for. So, I had to make conscious choices when to be online and when not.

Quotations like these illustrate that the smartphone has become an integral part of the lifeworld of younger generations of pilgrims; they are 'digital natives' (Palfrey and Gasser 2008) for whom texting has become 'second nature' and who cannot imagine a world where they cannot be in constant touch

18 Note that the interjection 'so to speak' seems to confirm our impression that the topic of the 'pain of departure' and its disappearance the moment once on the way to Mecca is a recurring theme in conventional hajj story telling.

with others (cf. Wijers 2019; Miller and Sinanan 2014, 10). Several research participants from the Netherlands stated that although keeping in touch with home can be distracting, they felt that, most likely, not being able to keep in contact would have distracted them even more, because they would have been worrying how their children were doing. In their experience, the fact that they could speak to their kids any time that suited them had helped them to concentrate on their *ʿibādāt* or acts of worship while performing them.

From the above it can be concluded that although forgetting about one's dear ones at home and being fully drawn in by the hajj experience continues to be an important topic in the stories of pilgrims from the Netherlands, the plot line has clearly changed. In the narratives of older pilgrims, forgetting about home as such is foregrounded. The stories of younger generations indicate that for pilgrims whose daily lives are characterized by online sociality across different geographic locations the possibility of staying in touch with the people at home when not performing rites is a condition for being able to concentrate when engaged in devotional acts. The stories of older pilgrims point to a time-space conception according to which the hajj implies a radical break with one's ordinary lifeworld, while those of younger pilgrims tend to be based on a time-space conception in which the boundaries between home and Mecca are porous. These different temporalities and spatialities tie in with differences between the view of mostly older people concerning hajj performance as transformational and marking a new life-stage, versus a view that predominates among younger pilgrims about the hajj as a 'spiritual boost' or a step in a process of gradual ethical self-formation (cf. Buitelaar 2020, 7; also see Caidi in this volume).

4 Photography

As we mentioned in the opening section, both in Morocco and in the Netherlands practically all research participants who own a smartphone produced their phones to illustrate their stories with photos. Also, scrolling through their hajj album on their phone almost inevitably prompted more stories. Officially, photography is prohibited in the Grand Mosque in Mecca and in the mosque in Medina where the Prophet Muhammad is buried. In the past this rule was strictly applied; if one was lucky, guards might turn a blind eye, but one could equally well be summoned to remove the film from one's camera or risk having one's camera confiscated. With the introduction of the smartphone, it has become nearly impossible to prevent pilgrims from taking pictures. After having tolerated it for some years, in 2017, the Saudi government tried to enforce the ban on photography and filming once more.[19] Their efforts were in vain, however; no measure could stop the huge numbers of pilgrims from eagerly and openly documenting their pilgrimage.

Asked about their views on and use of photography during the pilgrimage, pilgrims from Morocco and the Netherlands gave similar answers, which varied between positive and negative stances. A 55-year-old male pilgrim from Morocco, for instance, saw no harm in taking pictures. To the contrary; he had made sure to document every step of his pilgrimage and share them with his family back home. He explained that the pilgrimage is journey of a lifetime that deserves to be shared. In the quotation below, note his efforts to include Muslims from other countries in his photographs, indicating that besides taking pictures of the sacred sites he also values documentation of the ideal of the *umma*, the global community of Muslims:

> I took many pictures at the Holy Places, preferably with people from different countries I met, and I made videos. (…) I did not share pictures live on social media but I did share some later when I returned to Morocco. (…) When I was in Mecca, I just shared them with my family over the WhatsApp. (…) A picture is easy and fast to take.

A 65-year-old female pilgrim from Morocco, to the contrary, took a more negative view:

> I was very annoyed by all of the people stopping to take selfies. I needed to move out of the way of people taking photos and stopping suddenly to pose … I myself don't need pictures to remind myself of the beauty of hajj.

Despite her critical stance regarding selfie-taking, the woman cherishes some pictures that others took of her in the Grand Mosque and at other sites around Mecca, and she happily shared them with her daughters over a family WhatsApp group. Many pilgrims we talked to took a similar ambivalent stance. An often-mentioned strategy to deal with this ambivalence concerns carefully planning when to take pictures and when not to. A Moroccan-Dutch female

19 Cf. https://egyptindependent.com/no-more-hajj-selfies-photography-banned-at-holy-mosques-in-mecca-medina/, accessed September 29, 2020; https://www.dailysabah.com/religion/2017/11/23/saudi-arabia-bans-photos-videos-at-islams-two-holiest-sites, accessed September 29, 2020.

pilgrim in her early forties narrated how she had handled the issue of taking pictures during the hajj rites as follows:

> I noticed that some people took pictures while doing the *ṭawāf*, can you imagine?! I felt like telling them: 'Are you here for a holiday or for your *ʿibādāt*?' But I must admit I was in two minds myself: I really wanted to take a picture of the Kaʿba too, it is so incredibly beautiful. (…) Knowing myself, I deliberately left my phone in the hotel when off to do my first *ʿumra*,[20] and went back to fetch it and take pictures afterwards.

Besides the pragmatic objection to being hampered in one's own hajj performance by pilgrims who stand still to take photos, in these last two interview excerpts objections of a more normative nature also come to the fore. The statement 'I don't need pictures to remind myself of the beauty of hajj' points to a view according to which it should suffice for a pious pilgrim to remember the sacred ambience of the hajj solely on the basis of one's *īmān* rather than requiring external aids like pictures. The rhetorical question 'Are you here for a holiday or for your *ʿibādāt*?' points to a connotation that connects taking pictures with holidaying, something that the narrator apparently considers inappropriate in relation to visiting Mecca (also see Caidi in this volume).[21] The remark illustrates that contrary to most anthropologists, who would argue from an outsider's perspective that pilgrimage cannot clearly be distinguished from tourism,[22] the majority of our interlocutors have ambivalent feelings about the more touristic dimensions of the pilgrimage. Many pilgrims stated that activities like buying souvenirs and taking pictures are a 'waste of time' and not in line with the correct *niyya* or intention of pilgrims, who should be oriented exclusively towards acquitting themselves of their religious obligation.

---

20 The *ʿumra* consists of doing the *ṭawaf*, the sevenfold circumambulation of the Kaʿba, drinking water from the well Zamzam, and performing the *saʿy*—the running between the hillocks of al-Ṣafā and al-Marwa. All three elements are carried within the premises of the Grand Mosque in Mecca. While performing the *ʿumra* is part of the hajj ritual, it can also be carried out on its own any other time of the year as a voluntary pilgrimage.

21 Discussing British-Pakistani pilgrims who are critical of the consumerist dimensions of the hajj journey, McLoughlin (2009, 139) quotes a pilgrim who criticizes the behaviour of some pilgrims as holidaying rather than doing their religious duty in nearly exactly the same words: 'Have they been on hajj or some holiday?'.

22 Cf. the statement by Victor and Edith Turner that 'a pilgrim is always half a tourist, and a tourist is always half a pilgrim' (Turner and Turner 1978, 20). Also see for example Di Giovine and Picard (2015, 33); Stausberg (2011); Olson and Timothy (2006).

Both quotations also indicate, however, that living up to the image of the ideal pilgrim is difficult to fully realize. Despite her view that one should not need pictures to remember the hajj, the female pilgrim from Morocco was obviously glad to have some pictures to help her to keep in touch with the sacred atmosphere once she had returned home. She was also happy to share them with others and show that she had fulfilled the religious obligation of hajj. That pilgrims can never be 'purely' pilgrims, but operate on the basis of a habitus that is inevitably informed by various cultural traditions and 'grand schemes' simultaneously, comes to the fore even more strongly in the remark 'Knowing myself, I deliberately left my phone in the hotel', stated by the Dutch-Moroccan pilgrim quoted above. This strategy illustrates the performative, situational, and dialogical nature of practical moral reasoning that is also addressed in the chapter by Buitelaar and Kadrouch-Outmany elsewhere in this volume. Acknowledging her habitual self, the pilgrim realized that should her smartphone have been within reach, she might not have been able to resist the tourist in her that would want take pictures regardless of her intentions as a pilgrim.

On a more general level, her remark illustrates the extent to which the use of smartphones has become such an integral part of the daily lives of most younger pilgrims that they need to take strong measures to avoid their habit of documenting their activities and/or directly communicate with others about them. Celebrating or at least respecting the extraordinariness of the pilgrimage and the sacred atmosphere in Mecca entices many pilgrims to distance themselves as much as possible from comportment that marks their ordinary lives in order to try and focus on their religious commitments. Others, however, are more inclined to accommodate their multiple desires, to 'take oneself as one is', and strive to be 'better version of oneself' rather than aiming at a radically transformed exclusively religious self.

This is, for instance, the stance of 'Brother Alkhattab', a self-trained Muslim preacher in his forties who is very popular among young Moroccan-Dutch Muslims. Each year, Alkhattab organizes several *'umra* tours for young Dutch Muslims.[23] In Buitelaar's interview with him, the preacher emphasized the importance of taking into account the different desires and habits of his clients as young modern citizens for whom the use of the smartphone is an important part of their everyday lives and social contacts. Concerning photography, he stated:

23 Cf. https://www.instagram.com/p/BtwG3_YFwMc/?hl=en, accessed October 26, 2020.

> There is this general sense of discomfort concerning photography: uncertainty regarding what is allowed, and what is *ḥarām* (forbidden). I think we should be realistic: we live in the age of social media. Forbidding it just won't work anymore. (…) My point has always been: live your life by steering the middle of the road. Don't denounce things as *ḥarām* too quickly, but don't take an 'anything goes' attitude either. Strike a reasonable balance instead! So, I tell my group when we get there: 'Listen, we're here for the *ʿumra* rites. So, focus on what you've come for. Enjoy that moment to make a good picture before we start, absolutely fine. But then, open up your heart and soul for the *ʿumra* and put your camera away. Take pictures again once you're done, but don't live stream your *ʿumra*.' (…) Some guys take pictures, others don't. My point is that they should respect each other's choices.[24]

The above quotation illustrates how in specific cultural contexts new normativities quickly emerge to accommodate the use of digital technology (cf. Horst and Miller 2012b, 107). The preacher creatively mixes and merges different moral registers to articulate his take on adapting the use of the smartphone to hajj morality.[25] The ambivalent stances of the female pilgrims concerning taking pictures during the hajj illustrate that this is not a smooth process; practical moral reasoning is situated (cf. Buitelaar and Kadrouch-Outmany elsewhere in this volume). Contradictory views do not only exist between people, but individuals can also experience tension between the different moral registers that inform their normative conceptions (cf. Ribak and Rosenthal 2015).

Note that Brother Alkhattab objects most strongly to sharing one's pilgrimage experience by live-streaming it. Some of our interlocutors apparently consider live-streaming so absurd that they mentioned the option as though it were a joke, but would not elaborate on it. Most probably, live-streaming occurs only rarely. Taking hajj-selfies and posting them on communication platforms like Twitter and Facebook, on the contrary, is very popular and much discussed, both by our interlocutors, and, more widely, among pilgrims in different

24 In Dutch: *'Laat een ander in zijn waarde'.*

25 Also see Costa, who demonstrates that the desires of the young Kurdish-Turkish women she studied for living both a pious and a romantic life can be fulfilled by new mediated practices made possible by social media. Costa argues that for the women concerned, the moral registers of piety and romance do not oppose but mutually shape each other (Costa 2016, 213).

countries: a critical piece about selfies in the *Arab News* during the hajj of 2014 sparked a public debate.[26] Following Twitter, which had announced 2014 the 'year of the selfie', 2014 was coined 'year of the hajj-selfie',[27] and the hashtag *#hajjselfie* went viral on Twitter (Caidi, Beazley, and Marquez 2018, 8). This hashtag, however, raised serious objections from conservative religious leaders, who denounced the self-centredness of taking images during the pilgrimage.[28] However, as Nadia Caid and her co-authors point out, many pilgrims—particularly younger ones—continue to post selfies from Mecca and share their pilgrimage experiences with others.[29]

This is also the case among our research participants. For example, a male pilgrim in his late fifties from Morocco who had been on *ʿumra* during the month of Ramadan in 2015 and again in 2017 shared with Al-Ajarma his postings of photos on his personal Facebook page. He showed her a photo of himself in front of the Grand Mosque of Mecca, along with the caption, 'From the Holy Sanctuary; May God never forbid anyone from such a visit *#umrah #Alhamdullillah*.'[30] He had shared other pictures with his sisters via WhatsApp. In addition, a friend of him had tagged him in a picture they had taken together near the Mosque of the Prophet Muhammad in Medina. After returning to Morocco, he carefully filtered the images he had taken in Mecca, and reposted some of them later. Before his second journey to Mecca in February 2017, he posted an image of his 2015 *ʿumra* with the caption, 'May God reward us another visit to the Holy Sanctuaries; and grant the same to all my brothers and sisters; You are the One who accepts our prayers.' Also, at the end of December 2017, he posted

26 Cf. https://www.arabnews.com/islam-perspective/news/637771, accessed October 20, 2020.

27 Cf. https://time.com/3462348/hajj-2014-the-year-of-the-selfie/, accessed October 20, 2020.

28 Cf. https://www.telegraph.co.uk/news/worldnews/middleeast/saudiarabia/11141770/Hajj-selfies-cause-controversy-among-conservative-Muslims.html, accessed October 26, 2020.

29 For a both quantitative and qualitative content analysis of selfies taken during the pilgrimage to Mecca that are posted on Facebook, see Caidi, Beazley, and Marquez (2018). The authors found that most selfies were taken near the Kaʿba; that pilgrims featuring in them are mostly under 60; and that 55% of the photographs were taken during *ʿumra*, versus 33% during hajj. A tentative explanation they offer for the latter is that pilgrims may feel more inhibited to take selfies during the hajj due to its sacred and formal nature. While, indeed, pilgrims may find it more difficult to take selfies whilst being absorbed in the huge crowds during performance of the hajj rites, another possible explanation might be that the number of young pilgrims performing the *ʿumra* is much larger than those going on hajj.

30 In Arabic '*Allah lā yaḥrumunā min dhāk al-maqām*' meaning 'May God never prevent us from going to that holy place'. It is often used by Moroccans when discussing the hajj.

a picture of his *ramaḍān ʿumra* earlier that year with the caption 'Memories of Ramadan 2017 in the Mosque of the Prophet.'

For this pilgrim, taking a picture in Mecca and then posting it on social media does not go against the spiritual nature of pilgrimage. Rather, like the preacher Alkhattab mentioned above, he views it as 'a sign of the times'. He added that out of respect for the sacredness of the Grand Mosques in Mecca and Medina, he had made sure not to 'overdo' the taking of pictures. Moreover, he objects to pilgrims who are so absorbed by taking selfies that they miss what he called 'the real experience'. A similar concern was expressed by a Moroccan-Dutch interviewee in his forties, who questioned the trend of sharing hajj-selfies by stating that 'documenting one's hajj might easily degenerate into experiencing it through documentation on Facebook.'

In an article on the 'emotional affordance' of smartphones, media studies scholar Christoph Bareither focuses on another dimension of the fine line between experience and documentation referred to above. Bareither points to the affordance of smartphones to closely connect simple documentation and the capacity to mobilize or communicate emotions (Bareither 2019, 15). Bareither's analysis of selfies made at holocaust memorial sites invites us to take the 'emotional affordance' of the smartphone seriously and to look at hajj selfies from another perspective than an often heard critique according to which they hinder the 'real experience' or smack of self-glorification. In line with Bareither's argument, we would argue that reposting pictures, for example to tune in with the passing of religious seasons as the Moroccan pilgrim discussed above did, allows pilgrims to keep alive the memories of their experiences in Mecca. As captions like 'I miss that place' and 'May God grant me another visit' indicate, these images are often imbued with nostalgia and function to fulfil the desire to reminisce about one's pilgrimage. Allowing pilgrims as time passes to continue to tap into the emotions the journey stirred in them, pictures can be used as a tool in an ongoing process of ethical-self fashioning or a source of consolation in difficult times.

Furthermore, another affordance of the smartphone is to enable 'co-presence' (cf. Madianou 2016; Baldassar 2008). Smartphones can be a very powerful tool for pilgrims to mediate the sacred atmosphere to those at home, as Buitelaar experienced when a friend sent her a picture from Mecca through WhatsApp showing her name in proximity of the Kaʿba with the caption 'You are here with us'. Besides being touched by the kindness of her friend to think about her whilst in Mecca, to her own surprise, even as a non-Muslim, it moved Buitelaar to see her own name in close proximity of the Kaʿba, which for is Muslims the most sacred location on earth and closely associated with

FIGURES 16.2–3 Pilgrims creating co-presence with relatives and friends at home by sending them photographs depicting their names in proximity of the Kaʿba
PHOTOGRAPH LEFT: TAKEN BY AL-AJARMA, PHOTOGRAPH RIGHT: SENT TO BUITELAAR BY A FRIEND

God's blessings. It gave her a sense of being in touch with the sacred, however one choses to define it.

Creating co-presence through taking these kind of pictures has become customary among pilgrims from all countries, as Al-Ajarma noted during her two *ʿumra* visits to Mecca. One of her interlocutors in Morocco showed her another variety of personalized messages; this woman cherished a series of very short video clips on her smartphone that her brother had sent her from Mecca. The clips showed pilgrims from countries like Indonesia, Sudan, Egypt, Palestine, and Jordan who greeted her in their own language or local Arabic dialect and expressed the wish that she might visit Mecca too. The videoclips of pilgrims directly addressing her had deeply touched her and stimulated her own longing for the Holy Places. She still often looks at the clips fondly and declares that she will never delete them.

The practice of creating co-presence in Meccan sacred space by sending those at home photographs or videoclips that feature their names resonates with Martin Zillinger's argument concerning the redefinition of people's conceptualizations of religious space that may result from media practices (Zillinger 2014). Zillinger describes how adepts of the ʿIsāwa and Ḥamadsha trance cults in Morocco integrate the use of the smartphone in their ritual practices to translate the evocation of *baraka*, God's blessings, across space and time to migrants living in Europe. Although they cannot be physically present, clients attend the event online from their European homes. Alternatively, one of the ritual practitioners sees to it that a smartphone showing the portrait of the absent client is put close to the sacrificial animal or held high in the air for all to see while somebody else films the event, the recording of which is sent to the client in Europe afterwards.

Zillinger makes two points that are relevant to our discussion here. First of all, he argues that his interlocutors do not assume that the *baraka* itself is being transmitted through the smartphone, but rather its evocation is mediated. Secondly, at least as much as the evocation of *baraka*, what is mediated with the aid of a camera is *qarāba*—literally 'closeness' in Moroccan-Arabic, referring to one's ties to family members and other 'close ones' (cf. Eickelman 1976, 95–105). In a similar vein, we would argue that creating co-presence in the sacred space of Mecca operates to confirm pilgrims' ties with their close ones at home and to stir emotions in their friends and relatives that remind them of God's closeness in their own lives.[31]

Once such images are shared, their informational and emotional power reaches pilgrims' broader social networks, enabling a wider circle of people to partake in imparting meaning to the pilgrimage experience (cf. Schwarz 2014). On the basis of the examples that people on the receiving end shared with us, we would argue that pilgrims' motivations to take and share pictures is not limited to concerns with self-promotion, as some critics are inclined to think, but can also include the wish to mediate the sacredness across time and space. How such digitized mediations are assessed by others often depends on whether their circulation is restricted to pilgrims' personal networks or also extends to public platforms (cf. Costa 2018). The materialization of personal

31 Pilgrims, and Muslims more generally vary in their views as to *baraka* itself can be mediated. Most people would agree that Zamzam water carries *baraka* or at least has beneficial attributes. Some of our interlocutors told us stories about (seeing others) rubbing a Qur'an copy, prayer beads or other objects they intended to give away as souvenirs, such as headscarves or prayer mats against the *kiswa*, the cloth covering the Kaʿba, so as to take home some of its *baraka* (cf. Enes in chapter 10 elsewhere in this volume). For others, the power of *baraka* is only transmitted through one's personal contact with God, even if the idea that an object has been at the sacred site can increase its emotional value. As for those at home 'being there' in the form of pilgrims showing your name on their phones or pieces of paper as they say supplication prayers for you should not be mistaken as vicarious hajj performance. While pilgrims who have fulfilled their religious duty to perform hajj are allowed to perform it again in the name of somebody else, views vary whether this can only be done for people who died before being able to carry out the ritual itself or also for living people who for other reasons are not able to perform the hajj.

hajj experiences in a broader digital environment exposes the personal memories of pilgrims to a large number of different publics.[32]

5 Conclusion

In this chapter we have explored how pilgrims from Morocco and the Netherlands appropriate the affordances of the smartphone to mediate the sacred atmosphere in Mecca. Our discussion of hajj-related uses of digital technology illustrates that such affordances only unfold and acquire meaning in the very practices in which they are enacted (cf. Bareither 2019, 18). Our findings demonstrate that the specific use of digital media is shaped by the embeddedness of pilgrims in a specific constellation of cultural contexts and power structures. At the same time, however, these media allow pilgrims to experience the hajj in new ways.

The main purposes for which the pilgrims we interviewed and observed use the smartphone concern information services, communication, documentation, and self-presentation. The dynamics between lifeworld, digital practice, and meaning-making came to the fore, for instance, in the ways that young pilgrims use the informational services the smartphone offers to gain more control over their own, personal journey. Although it is the affordance of the smartphone that makes this use possible, the very desire for oneself to be in charge points to the specific habitus these pilgrims have acquired by having grown up in an individualized, consumerist societal context.

Similarly, this generation of highly mobile 'digital natives' is habituated to continuous connectivity to the world beyond their specific location. Staying connected during the pilgrimage implies a less radical break from daily life than it did for previous generations. We would argue that using WhatsApp in preparatory activities like asking forgiveness and taking leave rather than doing so through face-to-face communication are both an effect of, and co-constitutive to, the modification of conceptions and ideologies about mobility. The diminishing relevance of separation rites characterizing the hajj journey is related to a shift from a representation of space and time in terms of bounded entities that one leaves behind as one moves from one place or phase to the next, towards a conception in which temporal and spatial boundaries are viewed as fluid and porous.

32 For a comparison of hajj representations posted on YouTube and public Facebook pages by pilgrims from Morocco and the Netherlands, see Al-Ajarma and Buitelaar (2021).

The porosity of boundaries between social orders and between locations that are considered sacred and the domains of everyday life is, of course, not new and has been addressed often in pilgrimage studies (cf. Coleman 2019, 5–7; Gershon 2019). The stories of our interlocutors demonstrate how the use of the smartphone increases this porosity and affects pilgrims' hajj experiences. In addition to the habit of smartphone users to stay connected, the tendency to minutely document moments and interactions in one's life contributes to a further blurring of these boundaries. This works in two ways: firstly, sharing photographs whilst on hajj with those who stayed at home allows mediation of the sacred atmosphere across space. Secondly, archiving photographs on their smartphone allows pilgrims to revive memories and evoke the emotions they experienced during the pilgrimage whenever and wherever they wish afterwards, thus enabling them to tap into the sacred atmosphere of Mecca across time and space.

Exactly because in the Muslim imagination Mecca is—or ideally should be—posited above the messiness of daily life, the stories of our interlocutors indicate that the increased visibility of the interpenetration of the quotidian and sacred space in Mecca due to the use of the smartphone creates ambivalent feelings in pilgrims. These feelings particularly concern the issue of what constitutes an appropriate balance between fully immersing oneself in the ritual on the one hand, and documenting it (as though one were a 'tourist') on the other. Most of our interlocutors have found an effective strategy for dealing with such ambivalence for themselves. Yet, photography, specifically taking selfies that are shared on social media, continues to be a contested practice.

Taken together, the various forms of digital mediation of the hajj discussed in this chapter demonstrate that media technologies and the materiality of digital devices are capable of having enormous symbolic significance. They are embedded in, but also shape the habits, expectations, experiences, and feelings of pilgrims. Digitized mediation of hajj experiences is an 'integrative practice' that combines personal memory, interpersonal bonding, and communal history production (Couldry 2012, 51). As such, they are an important new input in hajj practices as well as adding a new dimension to the socially evolved conventions of hajj-storytelling.

References

Al-Ajarma, Kholoud. 2020. 'Mecca in Morocco. Articulations of the Muslim pilgrimage (Hajj) in Moroccan everyday life.' Unpublished PhD thesis, University of Groningen.

Al-Ajarma, Kholoud, and Marjo Buitelaar. 2021. 'Representations of the hajj on social media. Challenging Moroccan and Dutch mainstream media frames.' *Journal of Muslims in Europe* 10, 2 (June): 146–147.

Appadurai, Arjun. 1986. *The social life of things: Commodities in cultural perspective.* Cambridge: Cambridge University Press.

Baldassar, Loretta. 2008. 'Missing kin and longing to be together: Emotions and the construction of co-presence in transnational relationships.' *Journal of intercultural studies* 29 (3): 247–266.

Bareither, Christoph. 2019. 'Doing emotion through digital media. An ethnographic perspective on media practices and emotional affordances.' *Ethnologia Europaea* 49 (1): 7–23.

Bowen, John. 1992. 'On scriptural essentialism and ritual variation: Muslim sacrifice in Sumatra and Morocco.' *American ethnologist* 19 (4): 656–671.

boyd, danah. 2011. 'Social network sites as networked publics: Affordances, dynamics, and implications.' In *A networked self: Identity, community, and culture on social network sites*, edited by Zizi Papacharissi, 39–58. London and New York: Routledge.

Bräuchler, Birgit, and John Postill. 2010. *Theorising media and practice.* New York and Oxford: Berghahn Books.

Buitelaar, Marjo. 2020. 'Rearticulating the conventions of hajj storytelling: Second generation Moroccan-Dutch female pilgrims' multi-voiced narratives about the pilgrimage to Mecca.' *Religions* 11 (7): 373. https://doi.org/10.3390/rel11070373.

Buitelaar, Marjo. 2018. 'Moved by Mecca. The meanings of the hajj for present-day Dutch Muslims.' In *Muslim pilgrimage in Europe*, edited by Ingvild Flaskerud and Richard Natvig, 29–42. London and New York: Routledge.

Buitelaar, Marjo, Manja Stephan-Emmrich, and Viola Thimm. 2021. 'Introduction. Muslim pilgrimage through the lens of women's new mobilities.' In *Muslim women's pilgrimage to Mecca and beyond. Reconfiguring gender, religion and mobility*, edited by Marjo Buitelaar, Manja Stephan-Emmrich, and Viola Thimm, 1–18. London and New York: Routledge.

Caidi, Nadia, Susan Beazley, and Laia Colomer Marquez. 2018. 'Holy selfies: Performing pilgrimage in the age of social media.' *The international journal of information, diversity & inclusion* 2 (1–2): 8–31.

Coleman, Simon. 2019. 'On the productivity of pilgrimage palimpsests: Traces and translocations in an expanding field.' *Journal of global catholicism* 3 (1): 2–10.

Costa, Elisabetta. 2018. 'Affordances-in-practice: An ethnographic critique of social media logic and context collapse.' *New media & society* 20 (10): 3641–3656.

Costa, Elisabetta. 2016. 'The morality of premarital romances. Social media, flirting and love in Southeast Turkey.' *Middle East journal of culture and communication* 9: 199–215.

Costa, Elisabetta, and Laura Menin. 2016. 'Introduction: Digital intimacies: Exploring digital media and intimate lives in the Middle East and North Africa.' *Middle East journal of culture and communication* 9: 137–145.

Couldry, Nick. 2012. *Media, society, world. Social theory and digital media practice*. Cambridge: Polity Press.

Couldry, Nick. 2004. 'Theorising media as practice.' *Social semiotics* 14 (2): 115–132.

Davis, Jenny, and Nathan Jurgenson. 2014. 'Context collapse: theorizing context collusions and collisions.' *Information, communication & society* 17 (4): 476–485.

Dessing, Nathal. 2001. *Rituals of birth, circumcision, marriage and death among Muslims in the Netherlands*. Leuven: Peeters.

Di Giovine, Michael, and David Picard. 2015. 'Introduction. Pilgrimage and seduction in the Abrahamic tradition.' In *The seductions of pilgrimage. Sacred journeys afar and astray in the Western religious tradition*, edited by Michael Di Giovine and David Picard, 3–51. New York and London: Routlegde.

Eickelman, Dale. 1976. *Moroccan Islam. Tradition and society in a pilgrimage center*. Austin and London: University of Texas Press.

Fernández-Ardèvol, Mireira, Francesca Belotti, Francesca Ieracitano, Simone Mulargia, Andrea Rosales, and Francesca Comunello. 2020. '"I do it my way": Idioms of practice and digital media ideologies of adolescents and older adults.' *New media & society* (September): 1–19. https://doi.org/10.1177/1461444820959298.

Flaskerud, Ingvild. 2018. 'Mediating pilgrimage. Pilgrimage remembered and desired in a Norwegian home community.' In *Muslim pilgrimage in Europe*, edited by Ingvild Flaskerud and Richard Natvig, 43–57. London and New York: Routledge.

Gershon, Ilana. 2019. 'Porous social orders.' *American ethnologist* 46 (4): 404–416.

Gershon, Ilana. 2010. 'Media ideologies: An introduction.' *Journal of linguistic anthropology* 20 (2): 283–293.

Haq, Farooq, and John Jackson. 2009. 'Spiritual journey to hajj: Australian and Pakistani experience and expectations.' *Journal of management, spirituality & religion* 6 (2): 141–156.

Hill, Annette, Maren Hartman, and Magnus Andersson, eds. 2021. *The Routledge handbook of mobile socialities*. London and New York: Routledge.

Horst, Heather, and Daniel Miller. 2012a. *Digital anthropology*. London and New York: Bloomsbury Publishing.

Horst, Heather, and Daniel Miller. 2012b. 'Normativity and materiality: A view from digital anthropology.' *Media international Australia* no. 145 (2): 103–111.

Khan, Esam Ali, and Mohd Khaled Yousef Shambour. 2017. 'An analytical study of mobile applications for Hajj and Umrah services.' *Applied computing and informatics*, 14 (1): 37–47.

Madianou, Mirca. 2016. Ambient co-presence: Transnational family practices in polymedia environments. *Global networks* 16 (2): 183–201.

Madianou, Mirca, and Daniel Miller. 2011. *Migration and new media: Transnational families and polymedia*. London: Routledge.

McLoughlin, Seán. 2009. 'Holy places, contested spaces: British Pakistani accounts of pilgrimage to Makkah and Madinah.' In *Muslims in Britain: Race, place and identities*, edited by Richard Hopkins and Richard Gale, 132–149. Edinburgh: Edinburgh University Press.

Meyer, Birgit. 2016. 'How to capture the 'wow': R.R. Marett's notion of awe and the study of religion.' *Journal of the royal anthropological institute (N.S.)* 22 (1): 7–26.

Meyer, Birgit. 2011. 'Mediation and immediacy: sensational forms, semiotic ideologies and the question of the medium.' *Social anthropology/Anthropologie sociale* 19 (1): 23–39.

Miller, Daniel, Elisabetta Costa, Nell Haynes, Tom McDonald, Razvan Nicolescu, Jolynna Sinanan, Juliano Spyer, Shriram Venkatraman, and Xinyuan Wang. 2016. *How the world changed social media*. London: UCL Press.

Miller, Daniel, and Jolynna Sinanan. 2014. *Webcam*. Cambridge: Polity Press.

Mincke, Christophe. 2016. 'From mobility to its ideology: When mobility becomes an imperative.' In *The mobilities paradigm: Discourses and ideologies*, edited by Marcel Endres, Katharina Manderscheid, and Christophe Mincke, 11–33. Abingdon and New York: Routledge.

Moores, Shaun. 2000. *Media and everyday life in modern society*. Edinburgh: Edinburgh University Press.

Olson, Daniel, and Dallen Timothy. 2006. 'Tourism and religious journeys.' In *Tourism, religion and spiritual journeys*, edited by Timothy Dallen and Daniel Olsen, 1–21. London and New York: Routledge.

Palfrey, John, and Urs Gasser. 2008. *Born digital: Understanding the first generation of digital natives*. New York: Basic Books.

Pink, Sarah, Heather Horst, John Postill, Larissa Hjorth, Tania Lewis, and Jo Tacchi. 2016a. *Digital ethnography. Principles and practice*. London: Sage.

Pink, Sarah, Jolynna Sinanan, Larissa Hjorth, and Heather Horst. 2016b. 'Tactile digital ethnography: Researching mobile media through the hand.' *Mobile media & communication* vol. 4 (2): 237–251.

Renne, Elisha. 2015. 'Photography, Hajj things, and spatial connections between Mecca and Northern Nigeria.' *Photography and culture* vol. 8 (3): 269–295.

Ribak, Rivka, and Michele Rosenthal. 2015. 'Smartphone resistance as media ambivalence.' *FirstMonday* 20 (11). http://dx.doi.org/10.5210/fm.v20i11.6307.

Roeland, Johan, Stef Aupers, Dick Houtman, Martijn de Koning, and Ineke Noomen. 2010. 'The quest for religious purity in New Age, Evangelicalism and Islam. Religious renditions of Dutch youth and the Luckmann legacy.' *Annual review of sociology of religion* vol. 1: 289–306. Leiden: Brill.

Roy, Oliver. 2004. *Globalized Islam. The search for a new Ummah*. New York: Columbia University Press.

Saghi, Omar. 2010. *Paris-La Mecque. Sociologie du pèlerinage*. Paris: Presses Universitaires de France.

Schielke, Samuli. 2015. *Egypt in the future tense: Hope, frustration, and ambivalence before and after 2011*. Bloomington and Indianapolis: Indiana University Press.

Schwarz, Ori. 2014. 'The past next door: Neighbourly relations with digital memory-artefacts.' *Memory studies* 7 (1): 7–21.

Scupin, Raymond. 1982. 'The social significance of the hajj for Thai Muslims.' *The Muslim world* 72 (1): 25–33.

Stausberg, Michael. 2011. *Religion and tourism: Crossroads, destinations and encounters*. New York and London: Routledge.

Tenhunen, Sirpa. 2018. *A village goes mobile: Telephony, mediation and social change in rural India*. Oxford: Oxford University Press.

Turner, Victor, and Edith Turner. 1978. *Image and pilgrimage in Christian culture: Anthropological perspectives*. New York: Columbia University Press.

Waltorp, Karen. 2020. *Why Muslim women and smartphones: Mirror images*. Abingdon: Taylor&Francis Group.

Wijers, Gijs. 2019. 'Jong en Nederlands in Mekka. Een onderzoek naar de betekenissen van de bedevaart voor jonge, Nederlandse moslimmannen.' Unpublished MA thesis, University of Amsterdam.

Zillinger, Martin. 2014. 'Media and the scaling of ritual spaces in Morocco.' *Social compass* vol. 61 (1): 39– 47.

EPILOGUE

Narrating Mecca: Between Sense and Presence

Simon Coleman

The hajj provides perhaps *the* iconic example of a major pilgrimage that appears—at first glance—to be strictly circumscribed in time and space. Non-Muslims are prohibited from participating in its annual rituals, and they are not the only ones kept at a distance. If in the past Muslims were often unable to reach Mecca owing to the perils of the journey, many nowadays possess the resources to travel but face barriers of national quotas and labyrinthine bureaucracies, even when global pandemics are not raging. In light of such restrictions, one of the virtues of this volume is its use of narrative to illuminate how the hajj as spiritual and social imaginary circulates across vast social and cultural fields: it diffuses through ontological, literary, and ritual worlds in ways that cannot be confined. As the hajj is invoked by pilgrims—past, present and prospective—its sacred spaces and ritual actions are anticipated, remembered, and remediated beyond the temporal and spatial limitations of any single ritual experience.[1]

While a focus on narrative extends our horizons on the hajj, it also encourages the rich interdisciplinarity that we see in this volume, creating dialogue between historical, textual, and ethnographic approaches. Contemporary pilgrims are prone to reflect on the past as they seek to orient themselves in relation to the lives and actions of others who have journeyed before them, whether family members or revered saints. Written or spoken, inscribed on parchment or tapped out on a computer, narratives relating to the hajj have their own literary integrity but must not be studied in isolation. They are deeply implicated within other practices that shift across scales of imagination, degrees of formality, and levels of publicity—perhaps educating a child in the pillars of the faith, sharing personally meaningful experiences with a friend, or articulating resistance against a religious regime.

If such narration must be analysed as an inherently socially entangled activity, many of the chapters of this volume uncover productive links between

1 For an excellent ethnography of Mecca mediated beyond the Hijaz see Al-Ajarma (2020). Compare also Flaskerud's (2018) account of how the hajj is invoked within a Norwegian mosque through sharing of stories and references in speeches.

DOI:10.1163/9789004513174_019

representation and presence, between pilgrimage (*re-*)*described* and pilgrimage (*re-*)*embodied* through the affordances entailed in reading, hearing, sharing, inscribing, and creating narrative. An obvious example is Marjo Buitelaar and Kholoud Al-Ajarma's chapter on contemporary ways of 'mediating Mecca'. These authors observe that when interlocutors from Morocco and the Netherlands talk about experiences of Mecca they often reach for their smartphone to illustrate their accounts. The photos displayed are likely to have an evidentiary as well as a visual dimension, indexing and invoking past proximity to the Holy Places. Indeed, the phone itself may mediate between 'there' and 'here,' 'then' and 'now,' given its use as a human prosthetic, one of the few physical objects liable to be transported and kept close to the body in both sacred space and everyday life. Buitelaar and Al-Ajarma state that—for younger people at least—'using the smartphone to mediate Mecca, either through photographs, WhatsApp messages or posts on platforms like Facebook and Instagram has become part of the repertoire of performing hajj itself.' In this sense taking a picture *is* pilgrimage: a default form of engagement for those generations used to approaching the world with fingers pressed to a screen.

Notice the complex mixture of temporalities and spatialities evident in Buitelaar and Al-Ajarma's case study. Taking a photo indicates faith in the future, imagining a time when that photo will be viewed again and found to be significant. By definition, it enables the pilgrim to re-narrate the memory of Mecca. But it may also permeate the experience of the present, not merely through action involved in taking photos but also as use of social media enables those beyond Mecca to be invited—in so-called 'real time'—to share vicariously in the individual pilgrim's experience of sacred space.[2] This combination of tenses, narrations, and mediations supports Nadia Caidi's argument in this volume that we must examine information behaviours beyond the confines of short-term interactions. The hajj as it is manifested both at and beyond Mecca—anticipated, enacted, recalled, diffused—prompts the accumulation and dissemination of different genres of knowledge across the lifetime of the pilgrim. Apparently very different types of narrative may form chains of storied association and intertextuality: logistical information about how to act appropriately at Mecca perhaps blends with a grandparent's fond recollections of having been there, and both will frame the hajj experience on the journey before leaving further traces in the pilgrim's recounted memories to others. And so the cycle goes on—not repeating itself, but combining and blurring numer-

2 For work on the taking of 'selfies' at Mecca see Caidi, Beazley and Marquez (2018).

ous narratives over generations, and adapting all the time to new technologies of both travel and communication.

I am obviously using narrative in a broad sense here. A dictionary definition I find useful refers to an 'account of connected events', which highlights the idea of occurrences being marked out as significant while also suggesting the agency of the narrator in establishing the connections between such occurrences.[3] This is one meaning of 'making sense': the encapsulation and arrangement of actions in order to orientate attention. Another productive definition refers to 'a way of presenting or understanding a situation or series of events that reflects and promotes a particular point of view or set of values.'[4] In this latter characterization the political and strategic dimensions of narration come even more to the fore, so that stories are not only interesting but also interested—expressive of a point of view in contrast to other potential understandings.

While narrations may shift between the informative and the normative, both forms direct and delimit understandings in significant ways. Thus the nineteenth- and twentieth-century travelogues described in this volume by Thomas Ecker and Ammeke Kateman move readily from description to prescription in suggesting how and what to experience on the journey. As Kateman notes, just as centuries of travelogues and other textual and visual forms of hajj representation had prepared authors for what to feel, so these travelogues reiterated and re-shaped the journey for future travelers. Again, one of the advantages of this volume's approach of bringing together historical and ethnographic accounts is that we can discern tropes that recur over the long as well as the short durée, even if their specific connotations may shift. Such tropes often revolve around forms of affect that apply particularly well to the task of journeying across Muslim landscapes of ritual effort and aspirational belonging. For instance both Yahya Nurgat, writing of tales based in the seventeenth century, and Kateman, referring to the twentieth, point to yearning as a common feature of narratives, and one that may increase as pilgrims come closer to holy places that they have heard about for so long. It is also notable that references to *ṣabr*, or patience, stretch across genres and generations, suggesting how the effortful qualities of pilgrimage may be lent meaning as well as disciplinary power through a Muslim lexicon of affect. In this vein, Al-Ajarma's chapter on ineffable experience emphasizes *ṣabr*'s highlighting of a pious refusal to be distracted by the discomforts of the journey. For Buitelaar and Khadija Kadrouch-

3 https://www.google.com/search?q=definition+of+narrative&rlz=1C1GCEB_enCA857CA857&oq=definition+of+narrative&aqs=chrome..69i57j0l9.3479j0j7&sourceid=chrome&ie=UTF-8, accessed 2 September 2021.

4 https://www.merriam-webster.com/dictionary/narrative, accessed 2 September 2021.

Outmany, such patience is a highly valued Islamic virtue yet it is also one that rouses ambivalence, given that debate exists as to whether it refers to 'a stance of passive endurance' or 'a virtuous disposition that must be actively cultivated.' Their chapter goes on to show how, in practice, pilgrims may shift attitudes in the course of the same pilgrimage, or as they return from the pilgrimage and recall their experiences several months later. Ethical and affective registers, like narratives, contain recurring features but should not be assumed to have a false coherence. They combine and recombine across social frames and temporal trajectories.

Admittedly, physically performing the pilgrimage in and around Mecca entails following certain established and shared plot lines, stories, sequences, as pilgrims collectively retrace the life of the Prophet and the origins of Islam. Such narratives may be concentrated in and around Mecca, but they spill out into wider, adjacent behaviours. In this volume, Jihan Safar and Leila Seurat refer to the ways package tours take visitors to the mount of Uḥud outside Medina to teach them of a battle between followers of the Prophet Muhammad and the ruling Quraysh: topography and history working together. However, many of the narratives discussed in this volume are not supplied to pilgrims for their official edification. Part of the fascination of the contributions lies in the fact that they focus on the creation of numerous tales—memoirs, diaries, commentaries on social media, even responses to anthropologists' questions—that raise highly nuanced questions concerning the voice, subjectivity, and perceived self-determination of narrators in relation both to the hajj and to broader questions of authority. This point is brought out strikingly in Piotr Bachtin's analysis of four Iranian accounts of the pilgrimage that were written in the last two decades or so of the nineteenth century by female members of the Qajar aristocracy. Bachtin calls the chapter 'Othering and being Othered,' and the women's accounts express forms of agency that are constantly faced by countervailing forces and influences. The women are aristocrats and literate but restrained by the expectations of their class and gender. Both the journey and their diaries provide them with unusual opportunities for frankness and freedom of expression (at least to other women); but, even as they are given opportunities to experiment with and redefine their subjectivity, their observations calibrate distinctions that focus on preserving status along already established lines—religious adherence, ethnicity, language, and so on.

The attitudes of the women described by Bachtin demonstrate the constant interplay between the idiosyncratic and the conventional that we see in many accounts of the hajj as authors wrestle with landscapes, stories, expectations, that are widely known or at least frequently narrated. Perhaps all human discourse might be said to be about accountability, but the hajj and other journeys to Mecca provide events where much is at stake—prompting the constant need for editing, highlighting, sequencing, and so on. Status is asserted or inscribed, disquieting incidences concealed or ignored, parallels with exemplarity asserted, connections made, and so on, depending on how public such stories are intended to be. In his contribution on an early twentieth-century narrative by a Moroccan shaykh, Richard van Leeuwen provides a fascinating observation on the standardization or otherwise of pilgrimage experience. He argues that positive representations tend to fall into conventional tropes: 'After all, acknowledging that one does not feel elated by the first view of the Ka'ba would really spoil the account and even throw doubt on the sincerity of the pilgrim's faith.' On the other hand, the expression of complaints does not have readily available templates, and thus may come closer to the personal voice of the pilgrim. We might be reminded here of Tolstoy's famous opening line of *Anna Karenina*: 'All happy families are alike; each unhappy family is unhappy in its own way.' There is a kind of conservativism in contentment.

Narratives are used to 'make sense' and 'provoke presence' both at and away from Mecca; they draw on common tropes but shift over time; and, in so doing, they reveal struggles between conventional and idiosyncratic perspectives and expressions. A number of chapters reveal what I think of as disarticulations expressed through narrative—significant gaps, discrepancies or incommensurabilities between modes of representation.[5] A fascinating example is presented by Miguel Ángel Vázquez in his analysis of a sixteenth-century poem whose 'traditional' Spanish poetic form is used to express a Muslim message. This counter-hegemonic work, written in Spanish of the sixteenth century but rendered with the Arabic alphabet, resonates with the writer's experience of living under religious persecution in Habsburg Spain.

If the poet described by Vázquez must engage in a degree of concealment of his religious sentiments, the active cultivation of a contrast between pilgrimage as visible/present on the one hand, and hidden/absent on the other, is discussed by Neda Saghaee and Van Leeuwen in their reflections on the hajj in Sufi literature. Pilgrimage in such accounts becomes a complex metaphor for varieties of movement, not all of them physical, and may even challenge the assumed virtue of gaining material proximity to holy places. In one perspective Saghee and Van Leeuwen discuss, 'whoever passes the stages of pilgrimage and is physically in Mecca but does not see God, is similar to a person who stays confined to his home without any spiritual improvement'. The moral of the story

5 For a more detailed discussion of the concept of articulation applied to pilgrimage see Coleman (2021).

is that material presence itself is not enough: true perception depends making oneself spiritually receptive to the divine.

Although it appears to be describing an utterly different set of circumstances, Vladimir Bobrovnikov's chapter on the Soviet writer Fazliddin Muhammadiev's account of the hajj also reveals multiple tensions between different framings of the journey. However, in this case the push is toward a teleology of the secular rather than of the sacred. Suspended between the ethical demands of Mecca and Moscow, Muhammadiev's novel combines distance and proximity, satire with serious and detailed account, even as the narrative—whose ontological status is already complicated by purporting to be fictional, yet informative—provides a politically loaded commentary on disjunctions between global Islam, Soviet ideology, and Western capitalism.

The most ethnographically detailed example of disarticulations between narrative frameworks is provided by Zahir Janmohamed's gripping account of the use of mobile phone and tablet technologies used by Shiʿi pilgrims to bypass Saudi censorship rules. Buitelaar, Caidi, and other contributors show how media technology helps to bridge distances between pilgrims and far-flung publics; in the case described by Janmohamed, however, such technology actively creates distance between the ritual surveillance put in place by the Saudis and the experiences of those who wish to frame the hajj in different ways. In Janmohamed's words:

> When I entered the Prophet's Mosque in Medina, for example, I could listen to Shi'a supplications like *Jawshan kabīr* that I had grown up reciting and that moved me on a deep, emotional level. Suddenly—thanks to technology—the hajj felt a little bit like my own.

We see how mediation itself need not interpose between pilgrim and sacred space: it can actually create a stronger sense of being present. Moreover, such narrative reframing links the pilgrim to childhood dispositions and memories. The hajj may not have physically moved, but it has shifted semiotically: it comes to feel 'entirely different'.

Janmohamed shows that such reframings are not only about theological differences. He records the comments of Leila, who joins other young women in finding a Wi-Fi spot where they can download the lectures of a Canadian female scholar. Leila thus shuts off male voices and, in her words, is enabled to 'do my own thing.' Her actions point to a significant double shift that we see across the chapters of this volume as whole: in crude terms, the obligations of authorship and the subjectivity associated with being a pilgrim are becoming looser, more individualized, more relativized by being framed in relation to wider religious, cultural, and social lexicons. No doubt pilgrims have always 'done their own thing,' but in many parts of the contemporary world they have access to many more ways to imagine, narrate, and compare their pathways. This is not a tendency that is complete or inevitable, and it should not be taken as signifying a denial of sociality in making the hajj. Buitelaar's chapter on 'coming of age in Mecca' focuses on the pilgrimage accounts of two young Muslims living in the Netherlands, and beautifully encapsulates the frequent dilemmas and constant decision-making of pilgrims who see going to Mecca not as a conclusion to a life trajectory, but rather as one way of preparing them for their adult lives, and indeed an experience that may be repeated. The hajj fits in complex ways into wider narratives of emergent lives that appear full of choice and thus retain much uncertainty—about how to relate to parents, whether to acknowledge or seek distance from familial homelands, what to make of a pilgrimage that appears to contain 'mandatory' elements.[6] Buitelaar also includes a quotation from Enes, a young Muslim man, that is both an illustration and a salutary lesson about assuming the importance of narrative for pilgrims. Enes talks of how in preparation to go to Mecca he watches a DVD, but otherwise takes his grandfather's advice 'not to seek too much information on the meanings of the hajj, but to just "let it happen."' He goes on:

> My grandfather is the only person in our family who has been on hajj. I was still a child at the time. Besides the ring he gave me upon his return, what I remember is what he'd say when someone asked him about the hajj: 'You cannot describe it, you can only feel it.' (…) When I told him that I was going on *'umra*, he said: 'Just go. You will see what I mean when I told you that it cannot described. Just feel it.' And so I decided to let myself be surprised.

This is a story that denies the importance of narrative in capturing what it is like to go to Mecca. Yet at the same time it is a framing device, a powerful use of words both despite and because of its rhetorical and paradoxical dismissal of the power of the verbal. To be sure, it suggests the need to be physically present at the holy sites; but it also illustrates the unconfinable capacity of the hajj to

6 These uncertainties relate closely to what Buitelaar in her introduction calls the tensions between 'limit-form' representations of space and time, constituted by bounded entities that are left behind as the person travels between places or phrases of life, and more 'flow-form' conceptions of movement, in which temporal and spatial boundaries are perceived to be fluid and porous.

become a consequential story that can be shared between Muslims, wherever they happen to be located.

References

Al-Ajarma, Kholoud. 2020. 'Mecca in Morocco. Articulations of the Muslim pilgrimage (Hajj) in Moroccan everyday life.' Unpublished PhD thesis, University of Groningen.

Caidi, Nadia, Susan Beazley, and Laia Marquez Colomer. 2018. 'Holy selfies: Performing pilgrimage in the age of social media.' *The International journal of information, diversity & inclusion*2 (1/2): 8–31.

Coleman, Simon. 2021. *Powers of pilgrimage: Religion in a world of motion*. New York: New York University Press.

Flaskerud, Ingvild. 2018. 'Mediating pilgrimage. Pilgrimage remembered and desired in a Norwegian home community.' In *Muslim pilgrimage in Europe*, edited by Ingvild Flaskerud and Richard Natvig, 43–57. London and New York: Routledge.

Glossary

ʿAbd al-ʿAzīz Āl Saʿūd (1876–1953) Founder of the kingdom of Saudi Arabia in 1932. After conquering power in the Najd region with his Wahhābī allies, he succeeded in defeating Sharīf Ḥusayn, ruler of the Hijaz on behalf of the Ottoman government, and in establishing an independent regime in 1924. His government inaugurated far-reaching changes in the hajj on the levels of infrastructure and organization, and established a strict religious supervision of its procedures. It resulted in the demolition of many historical sites in Mecca and Medina, in order to prevent ritual and devotional practices which were deemed irreconcilable with the concept of God's unity (*tawḥīd*).

ʿĀʾisha (d. 678) One of the wives of the Prophet Muhammad, who reached a prominent status among the believers.

ʿAlī (598–661) Nephew and adopted son of the Muhammad. He married the Prophet's daughter Fāṭima. After the Prophet's death, a faction of the leaders of the Quraysh tribe preferred ʿAlī as his successor instead of Abū Bakr. Later, the tensions led to an armed conflict between the two factions, which resulted in the split between Sunnism and Shiʿism, the main doctrinal currents in Islam.

ʿArafa The plain outside Mecca where during the hajj the main rite of the *wuqūf* takes place. Here the Jabal al-Raḥma (Mountain of Mercy) is situated where, according to a popular understanding of the Islamic tradition, Adam and Eve were reunited after their expulsion from paradise.

ʿashūrāʾ Day on which the martyrdom of ʿAlī's son Ḥusayn is commemorated by the Shiʿis, who was killed during the struggle of the ʿAlid faction for the Caliphate in 680 (10 *muḥarram*).

ʿaṣr Afternoon prayer.

ʿālim/ pl. ʿulamāʾ Religious scholar; jurist.

Abū Bakr al-Ṣiddīq (573–634) Successor of Muhammad as leader of the Muslim community; first caliph.

adab/ pl. ādāb A term indicating 'cultural refinement' or 'good manners'. It refers to a literary corpus which comprises the requirements and standards of cultural sophistication, but also indications for proper conduct and accepted procedures. The *adab al-ziyāra*, for instance, refers to the procedures for the visit to the Prophet's grave in Medina.

adhān The call for prayer, performed by a muezzin.

ajr Reward in the Hereafter for proper conduct on earth.

al-Azhar Most important mosque and religious university in Cairo, considered as authoritative throughout the Muslim world; founded in 971.

amīr al-ḥajj The commander of the hajj caravan. In present days, often used to designate hajj tour leaders.

amīr al-mu'minīn title of the Caliph; 'commander of the faithful'. Also: honorary title of the Moroccan king.

al-Baqīʿ-cemetery Cemetery in Media, where the graves of many family members and companions of the Prophet are located, as well as those of prominent scholars. Under the Saudi government, the monumental tombs were destroyed, to prevent them from becoming places of worship.

baraka Litt. 'blessing' or 'grace'; spiritual power contained in persons, places or objects, which can benefit the believers in diverse ways.

bidʿa Litt. 'innovation'; illegitimate practice or belief introduced by Muslims in contradiction to the Qur'an or the sharia.

Black Stone See above '*al-ḥajar al-aswad*'.

dhikr Sufi ritual commemorating God's name, consisting of various practices ranging from recitation and devotional singing, to ecstatic dancing.

dhū al-ḥijja Last month of the Muslim year, in which the hajj takes place.

duʿā Supplicatory prayers.

fajr Morning prayer.

farḍ Religious obligation, such as the hajj.

al-Fātiḥa The opening sura of the Qur'an, often recited as a short prayer.

al-Ghazālī, Abū Ḥāmid (d. 1111) One of the most prominent scholars in the Islamic tradition. His main work is the voluminous theological reference work *Iḥyā' ʿulūm al-dīn* ('Revival of the religious sciences'), which is also concerned with mystical philosophy.

Grand Mosque The mosque in Mecca which contains the Kaʿba, the 'House of God'.

Hadith The corpus of texts containing the Sunna, the acts and sayings of the Prophet.

Hājar The Muslim name of the Biblical Hagar.

al-ḥajar al-aswad The Black Stone, inserted in one of the corners of the Kaʿba. It is mostly believed to be recommended to kiss it during the *ṭawāf*, in emulation of the Prophet. It is considered to have descended from paradise and has many symbolic and religious connotations, according to the Islamic tradition.

ḥajj al-ifrād One of the types of hajj, in which, according to Islamic law, the hajj and *ʿumra* are separated by temporarily suspending the *iḥrām*; the others are *tamattuʿ* suspending the obligations of *iḥrām*, and *qirān*, an uninterrupted combination of *ʿumra* and hajj.

al-Ḥājj(i)/ al-Ḥājja honorific title for pilgrims during the hajj. In common parlance, it is bestowed on persons who have visited Mecca, as well as being used as a polite way to address older people, regardless whether they have conducted the pilgrimage or not.

Ḥamza Uncle of the Prophet Muhammad who was martyred at

the battle of Uḥud, near Medina. His grave at Uḥud was an important site for pilgrims in previous times before it was demolished by the Wahhābīs.

ḥarām 'Forbidden', according to Islamic law.

Ḥaram The sacred precinct around Mecca and Medina.

Ḥaramayn The two Holy Places, Mecca and Medina.

Hijaz The region in the Arabian Peninsula in which Mecca, Medina, Jedda and Ta'if are situated.

Hijra The 'migration' of the Prophet from Mecca to Medina, in 622. It marks the beginning of the Muslim era.

Ḥirā' The cave near Mecca where the Prophet Muhammad received his first revelations.

Ḥusayn ibn 'Alī Son of 'Alī and grandson of the Prophet Muhammad, who died in the wars of succession between the 'Alids and the Umayyads in 680. He is considered a martyr by the Shiʿis. And his mausoleum in Karbala is the most important pilgrimage site for them.

Ḥusayn (1853–1931) Sharīf of the Hijaz under the Ottoman government from 1908 until 1924, when he was expelled by 'Abd al-ʿAzīz ibn Saʿūd. During World War I, he concluded a treaty with the British to become king of a Middle Eastern kingdom, and unleashed the 'Arab Revolt' in 1916. However, after the war the British withdrew their support and refused to fulfil their promises, enabling the Sauds to gain the upper hand in Arabia.

'ibāda/ 'ibādāt The obligatory acts of veneration, which are the five 'pillars' of Islam, the *shahada*, the *ṣalāt*, the fasting in the month *ramaḍān*, the *zakat*, and the *ḥajj*.

Ibn 'Abd al-Wahhāb, Muḥammad (1703–1792) Arabian religious scholar and reformer, who concluded a pact in 1740 with the Saud family to establish a religiously inspired regime in Arabia, resulting in the first Saudi-Wahhābī revolt. After the coalition was defeated in the 1820s, it remained dormant until the end of the 19th century, when it was restored by 'Abd al-'Azīz ibn Saʿūd, who succeeded in conquering Najd, the Hijaz and finally the whole Arabian Peninsula in the 1920s. In the kingdom of Saudi Arabia, the Wahhābī doctrines are strictly adhered to. They are marked by a strict definition of God's unity (*tawḥīd*); an intolerant view of Sufism and spiritual practices, which they consider *bid'a* (illegitimate innovation); and ritual practices on historical and religious sites, such as tombs of pious saints and historical figures, which they destroyed as much as possible. Their intolerant vision of the faith has greatly influenced the practice of the hajj, and is often criticized by more tolerant Muslims.

Ibrāhīm The Muslim name of the Prophet Abraham.

'īd al-aḍḥā The Feast of Immolation, on the tenth day of the last month of the Islamic calendar *dhū al-ḥijja*, which concludes the rites of the hajj. Every pilgrim should sacrifice an animal, or take upon themselves a compensation.

al-ifāḍa Part of the hajj rites; the return from ʿArafa to Muzdalifa after the *wuqūf*.

iḥrām Ritual state during the performance of the hajj. It is adopted at one of the prescribed places (*mīqāt*), and includes the 'intention' to perform the hajj, the donning of the ritual dress (two unstitched white cloths for men), and accepting a number of prohibitions, such as the killing of animals, the clipping of nails, shaving, sexual acts, etc. After the hajj rites it is ended before the ritual 'haircut' and sacrifice.

ijāza Certificate issued by a scholar to another, proving the latter's proficiency in a specific text or religious 'curriculum'. Also a certificate proving the fulfilment of the obligation of the hajj, or the initiation into a Sufi brotherhood.

Imam; imam Honorific title indicating several honorary qualities: imam: leader of prayer; *imām*: title for a prominent legal scholar; Imām: religious leader in the lineage of ʿAlī, venerated by Shiʿis.

īmān faith, belief.

ʿishāʾ Evening prayer.

Ismāʿīl The Biblical Ismael; the son of Ibrāhīm and Hājar, who was sent to the desert with his mother to the Arabian desert, where they discovered the Zamzam well. In the Muslim tradition it was Ismāʿīl who was almost sacrificed by his father.

jamra The term used for the 'pillars' representing the devil, which are 'stoned' during the *ramy*. The term is also used as a synonym of *ramy*.

Janna al-Baqīʿ See al-Baqīʿ—cemetery.

Jedda The port town of the Hijaz, where pilgrimage ships arrive and depart, and where from the 1830s the European nations had their consulates to serve and supervise the pilgrims from their respective colonies.

Kaʿba The 'House of God' symbolizing God's bond with the believers. It is situated in the Grand Mosque in Mecca and indicates the direction of prayer for Muslims all over the world. According to the tradition, it was built by Ibrāhīm beneath God's throne. but desecrated by being used as a site of pilgrimage by pre-Islamic Arabs, and restored to its former sanctity by the Prophet Muhammad. It is the site for one of the main rites of the hajj, the *ṭawāf*, or the sevenfold circumambulation of the cuboid building.

karāma Miraculous act performed by a pious shaykh, in contrast to miracles performed by prophets (*muʿjiza*).

Khadīja (d. 619) First wife of the Prophet, and first convert to Islam. Her house and grave were traditionally important places visited by pilgrims, until the Wahhābīs demolished them.

kiswa The black covering of the Kaʿba, with gold-embroidered Qur'anic verses and sayings by the Prophet Muhammad. From the thirteenth century until 1926 it was manufactured in Cairo and sent as a gift to Mecca, with the ceremonial palanquin, or *maḥmal*, as a token of the bond between Egypt and the Hijaz, a practice which was ended by the Wahhābīs, who considered the ceremonies related to the *maḥmal* as *bid ʿa*. The cover is replaced every year.

Madīna al-Munawwara One of the names of Medina: 'the Illuminated City'.

maḥmal The ceremonial palanquin that in previous times was sent annually with the pilgrimage caravans from Egypt and Syria, containing gifts, subsidies, and the *kiswa* for the Kaʿba, from Egypt, and the covering of the Prophet's tomb, from Syria. The *maḥmal*s were usually escorted by musical bands and received with much pomp, until the Wahhābīs ended these practices in 1926.

maḥram A man who is legally forbidden to marry a woman for reasons of consanguinity, and who therefore can serve as male escort for female pilgrims. Women are obliged to be accompanied by a *maḥram* when they go on hajj.

Makka al-Mukarrama Litterally 'Exalted Mecca', one of the names of Mecca.

Mālik ibn Anas (711–795) Prominent scholar, particularly honoured by North African pilgrims, who used to visit his grave in al-Baqīʿ—cemetery in Medina.

Mamluk Sultanate Dynasty of sultans in Egypt (1250–1517), who attached great importance to the organization of the hajj caravans and connected traditions, and who attempted to impose their authority on the Hijaz.

manāsik al-ḥajj The 'rites of the hajj', according to the legal prescriptions, which are modelled after the example of the Prophet's pilgrimage. The term also refers to compendia of hajj rules, often inserted in hajj travelogues.

Maqām Ibrāhīm The place in the Great Mosque in Mecca, where according to the tradition, Ibrāhīm stood when he built the Kaʿba.

al-Marwa Hill outside the great Mosque, which, together with al-Ṣafā, is the site where the *saʿy* is performed, the running between al-Ṣafā and al-Marwa seven times, as part of the hajj.

Masjid al-Ḥaram The Holy Mosque in Mecca.

Minā Village between Mecca and ʿArafa, where pilgrims usually camp.

mīqāt Term indicating the places where it is legally prescribed to take on the *iḥrām* before entering the sacred precinct and performing the hajj. The place depends on the direction from which the pilgrim arrives.

muṭawwif Guide accompanying pilgrims during the hajj rites and helping them with practicalities, formalities, lodging, transport, etc.

Muzdalifa One of the halting places between Mecca and ʿArafa, where pilgrims spend the night in the open and collect pebbles to perform the stoning rite the following day.

nahḍa Term indicating the process of cultural and political reform from the 1850s onwards, during which the process of 'modernization' of the Arab/ Muslim world was debated, as a response to the expansion of the European nations and their economic and military hegemony.

Najd Region in the Arabian Peninsula bordering on the Hijaz, where the Saud family and the Wahhābīs built their power base.

niyya The 'intention' to perform a certain ritual, required to render it legally valid. It is pronounced when taking on the *iḥrām*.

Rābigh Town on the western coast of Arabia, where usually the *iḥrām* is adopted (although officially the *mīqāt* is a few miles away).

ramy Part of the hajj ritual: the throwing of stones to three pillars near Muzdalifa (*jamarāt*) symbolizing the devil. The number and size of the stones are prescribed; the *ramy* is performed in two turns, after the *wuqūf* and after the ending of the hajj. Also called *jamra*.

al-rawḍa Part of the Prophet's Mosque, next to the Prophet's tomb.

riḥla Litt. 'journey'; term referring to the genre of travel literature.

ṣabr Litt. 'patience'; term to indicate a preferred mental state of perseverance and patience during the hajj, to endure the many hardships it involves.

al-Ṣafā One of the two small hills outside the Great Mosque in Mecca, from where the *saʿy* is performed, the running between al-Ṣafā and al-Marwa seven times, as part of the hajj.

Saʿūdi family See ʿAbd al-ʿAzīz Āl Saʿūd; Muḥammad ibn ʿAbd al-Wahhāb.

saʿy The running between al-Ṣafā and al-Marwa seven times. It symbolizes the search for water of Hājar, when she was exiled to Arabia, but it is also meant to exhibit the prowess and strength of the Muslims *vis-à-vis* their enemies.

al-Shādhilī, Abū al-Ḥasan (1196–1258) Moroccan scholar and Sufi; founder of the Shādhiliyya, one of the most important Sufi brotherhoods in Islam.

shahāda Confession of the Muslim faith; one of the Five Pillars.

sharīf Honorary title of families claiming descendance from the Prophet.

Sharīf Title of ruling dynasty of the Hijaz, under the various Sultanates of Egypt and Istanbul.

shirk Litt. 'polytheism'; term indicating the violation of the doctrine of God's unity (*tawḥīd*). The term is used by the Wahhābīs to denounce practices which according to them contradict orthodoxy.

Sufism Muslim spirituality, including both mystical thought and spiritual practices, usually related to various brotherhoods. Practices of Sufis such as the visiting of graves of pious saints, asking their intercession before God, are particularly abhorred by the Wahhābīs. Because of this, tensions occurred between pilgrims from North Africa and Central Asia on the one hand, and the Wahhābīs on the other hand, concerning conventional practices during the hajj.

talbiya The formula 'Here I am, to serve you'/ '*Labbayka*', pronounced by pilgrims while entering Arabia.

ṭarīqa Sufi order.

ṭawāf Part of the hajj and *ʿumra* rites: the circumambulation of the Kaʿba seven times, in anti-clockwise direction. It symbolizes the approach to the House of God, as a guest, and is performed partly running and partly walking.

al-Ṭūr Compound for the quarantine of pilgrims entering or exiting Arabia in the direction of Egypt, on the eastern coast of the Sinai peninsula, from the end of the nineteenth century until 1940.

Uḥud See Hamza.

ʿUmar ibn Khaṭṭāb (585–644) Second caliph (634–644).

umma Term indicating the worldwide Muslim community.

ʿumra Non-obligatory pilgrimage to Mecca, also called 'lesser pilgrimage'. In contrast to the hajj, it can be performed throughout the year. It consists of the *iḥrām*, the *ṭawāf*, the drinking of Zamzam water, and the *saʿy*, concluded by a partial or complete cutting of the hair. It is also part of the hajj, if it is combined with the *wuqūf* on the prescribed day.

Wahhābī/ Wahhābism See Muḥammad ʿAbd al-Wahhāb.

wuqūf The main component of the hajj ritual, the standing as a congregation in the plain of ʿArafa, on 9 *dhū al-ḥijja*, to listen to the sermon from the Jabal al-Raḥma, after the example of the final sermon of the Prophet. It is often associated with the Last Judgement, when the believers gather to be judged.

Zamzam The well situated in the Grand Mosque in Mecca. According to the tradition it was discovered by Hājar and her son Ismāʿīl, when they were exiled to the desert by Ibrāhīm, enabling the foundation of Mecca as a settlement in the desert. Many miraculous properties are ascribed to its water, such as healing properties, *baraka*, preventing hunger and thirst. Often pilgrims not only drink from it, but also drench themselves with it and soak their burial shrouds with it.

zāwiya Sufi lodge or convent, often connected with the grave of a pious saint.

ziyāra Litt. 'visit'; more specifically a visit to the grave of a pious saint, or a visit to the tomb of Muhammad in Medina. The latter 'visit' is carefully described in conventions and practices. It is not part of the hajj and is discouraged by the Wahhābīs.

ẓuhr Midday prayer.

Index

Page numbers in **bold** refer to illustrations.

Although it is not customary, two interviewees are nevertheless included in the index, namely Asmae and Enes. As their interviews take up a complete chapter this seemed helpful to the user.

in Morocco *see* Morocco
motivation for *see* motivation
of Mudejars 76–78, 82–83, 86–88
see also 'Coplas del peregrino de Puey Monçón'
as once in a lifetime event *see* as conclusion of life's trajectory (above)
as physical journey 216
preparations for 383, 385, 401–402
as religious obligation 2–3, 46–47, 263, 303, 311, 318, 404, 405
as repetitive event 98n12, 267, 299, 363, 403
rites of *see under* rituals
ṣabr (patience) in *see under ṣabr*
safety/unsafety during *see* safety/unsafety
as sensational form 21, 32, 115, 278, 279, 397
spiritual vs. material aspects of 92–93
status change after *see* Ḥājjis/Ḥājjas
in Sufism *see* Sufism
supervising of *see* supervising of hajj/*ʿumra*
touristic elements of 409
types of 47–48
of Wahhābism *see* Wahhābism/Wahhābīs
by women *see* female pilgrims
hajj/*ʿumra* accounts
in general 1, 51–53, 56–57, 204, 422
and *adab* 54
audiences of *see* audiences
from different traditions 25–26, 57–59
digital technology *see* digital technology
from Egypt 66
European culture in 151–152
European/Europeanized women in 150–151
as hajj guides *see* hajj guides (printed)
illustration in 65–66
inserted references in 51–52, 53–54
and interactions *see* interactions
from Iran *see* Iran
in journal form 53
language use in 5
modern corpus of 64–66
and modernity 60–61, 226
narrators of 15–16
negative experiences in *see* negative experiences
from Netherlands *see* Netherlands
overlap between pre-modern and modern 45
and photography *see* photographs
poetry in 54
see also 'Coplas del peregrino de Puey Monçón'
political issues/political activism in 18, 54–55, 61–62, 64
and printing technologies 65, 183
religious framework in 16–17, 50–51, 61, 64
from Russia 229
ṣabr (patience) in *see under ṣabr*
from Soviet Union *see* Soviet Union
from Spain *see* Spain
standardization of 330, 345, 426
travel/travelling in *see* travel/travelling
by women *see under* female pilgrims
written vs oral transmission 45
hajj/*ʿumra* experiences
in general 26–27
class-specific 27
emotions in *see* emotions
empowering effect of 271
everyday life and *see* everyday life
and gender *see* gender
idealization of 16–17, 57, 87, 204–205, 288, 330
ineffability of 277–278, 295
modernization of 2
moral lessons taken from 10–11, 32–33, 263, 265, 272, 350
pre-determined by expectations 186, 293, 294–295
reliving/reconnecting 373–374, 378–379, 391
as sensational *see* sensational forms
sensory *see* sensory experiences
sharing via social media 374, 376, 377–378, 383–384, 412–413, 416, 423
sight in 280–284, 399
see also first sightings
smell in 287–288

Printed in the United States
by Baker & Taylor Publisher Services